The Study of Africa

Disciplinary and Interdisciplinary Encounters

Edited by
Paul Tiyambe Zeleza

CODESRIA

Council fo⋯ University of Edinburgh ⋯earch in Africa

© Council for the Development of Social Science Research in Africa, 2006
Avenue Cheikh Anta Diop Angle Canal IV, BP 3304 Dakar, 18524 Senegal.
http:\\www.codesria.org

ISBN: 2-86978-197-0 ISBN-13: 978-2-86978-197-9

Typeset by Hadijatou Sy

Cover designed by Ibrahima Fofana based on the Adinkra symbol of knowledge, lifelong education and quest for knowledge.

Printed by Lightning Source

Distributed in Africa by CODESRIA

Distributed elsewhere by
African Books Collective, Oxford, UK
www.africanbookscollective.com

The Council for the Development of Social Science Research in Africa (CODESRIA) is an independent organisation whose principal objectives are facilitating research, promoting research-based publishing and creating multiple forums geared towards the exchange of views and information among African researchers. It challenges the fragmentation of research through the creation of thematic research networks that cut across linguistic and regional boundaries.

CODESRIA publishes a quarterly journal, *Africa Development,* the longest standing Africa-based social science journal; *Afrika Zamani,* a journal of history; the *African Sociological Review; African Journal of International Affairs* (AJIA); *Africa Review of Books; Identity, Culture and Politics: An Afro-Asian Dialogue* and the *Journal of Higher Education in Africa.* It copublishes the *Africa Media Review.* Research results and other activities of the institution are disseminated through 'Working Papers', 'Monograph Series', 'CODESRIA Book Series', and the *CODESRIA Bulletin.*

CODESRIA would like to express its gratitude to the Swedish International Development Cooperation Agency (SIDA/SAREC), the InternationalDevelopment Research Centre (IDRC), Ford Foundation, MacArthur Foundation, Carnegie Corporation, the Norwegian Ministry of Foreign Affairs, the Danish Agency for International Development (DANIDA), the French Ministry of Cooperation, the United Nations Development Programme (UNDP), the Netherlands Ministry of Foreign Affairs, Rockefeller Foundation, FINIDA, NORAD, CIDA, IIEP/ADEA, OECD, IFS, OXFAM, UN/UNICEF and the Government of Senegal for supporting its research, training and publication programmes.

Table of Contents

Acknowledgement v

Notes on Contributors vi

Introduction: The Disciplining of Africa 1
Paul Tiyambe Zeleza

Part I: The Disciplines and African Studies

1. Anthropology and the Race of/for Africa 39
    Jemima Pierre

2. Africana Sociology: A Critical Journey from Pluralism
    to Postcolonialism 62
    Zine Magubane

3. Ethnography on an Awkward Scale: Postcolonial Anthropology
    and the Violence of Abstraction 75
    Jean and John Comaroff

4. Third Generation African Literatures and Contemporary Theorising... 105
    Pius Adesanmi

5. An Argument for Ethno-Language Studies in Africa 117
    Sinfree Makoni and Ulrike Meinhof

6. African Historiography and the Crisis of Institutions 135
    Esperanza Brizuel-Garcia

7. Writing and Teaching National History in Africa in the Era
    of Global History 168
    Toyin Falola

8. Rethinking Africanist Political Science 187
    Abdul Raufu Mustapha

9. Economics and African Studies 203
    Emmanuel Nnadozie

10. Trajectories of Modern African Geography 233
    Ezekiel Kalipeni, Joseph Oppong and Benjamin Ofori-Amoah

11. Psychology for a Contemporary Africa 274
    Kopano Ratele

Part II: Interdisciplinary Studies and African Studies

12. Feminist Studies in the African Contexts: The Challenge
    of Transformative Teaching in African Universities 297
    Amina Mama

13. Conceptualising Gender in African Studies 313
    Oyeronke Oyewumi

14. Studies of the African Visual Arts and the Politics of Exclusion 321
    Nkiru Nzegwu

15. The Study of African Religions: A Sketch of the Past and Prospects
    for the Future 338
    Elias Bongmba

16. Framing an African-centred Discourse on Global Health:
    Centralising Identity and Culture in Theorising Health Behaviour 375
    Collins Airhihenbuwa

17. Rethinking Communication Research and Development in Africa 393
    Francis B. Nyamnjoh

18. African Cultural Studies and Contemporary African Philosophy 417
    Lewis R. Gordon

19. Useless Provocation, or Meaningful Challenge?
    The 'Posts' vs. African Studies 443
    Kwaku Korang

Index 467

Acknowledgement

This book grew out of a seminar I run while I served as Director at the Center for African Studies at the University of Illinois at Urbana-Champaign, 'Curricular Development Seminar in African Studies', in Fall 2002 for faculty and graduate students enrolled in the course on 'The Development of African Studies'. I would like to acknowledge the generous funding from the National Endowment for the Humanities (NEH) Grant ED-22151-01, which enabled me to bring more than twenty scholars from the US, Europe, Asia, and Africa. Many of the contributors to the seminar are included in this collection. I would also like to thank others who are not but came to the seminar: David Wiley, Ato Quayson, Charles Piot, Munene Macharia, Khabele Matlosa, Mahmood Mamdani, Linda Hunter, Keletso Atkins, Cheryl Johnson-Odim and Yassine Fall. I am indebted to Jamie McGowan, the Center's Assistant Director, and Sue Swisher, the Administrative Aide, for their hard work in the preparation of the grant proposal and the organization of the seminar, as well as Shana Wills, then an MA student in the Center who assisted with driving the guests to and from the airport. Several faculty opened their homes for the evening seminars and I would like to express my deepest thanks to all of them: Kathy Perkins, Kwaku Korang, Alma Gottlieb, Tom Bassett, Jan Nederveen-Pieterse, Sundiata Cha-Jua, Gale Summerfield, Adlai Murdoch, and Charles Stewart for their generosity. In this regard, I would also like to thank Cassandra Rachel Veney who kindly helped me host several of the seminars at our home. For this volume I would like to acknowledge Jean Comarroff, another participant in the seminar, for the permission to reprint the paper she co-authored with John Comaroff, 'Ethnography on an Awkward Scale: Postcolonial Anthropology and the Violence of Abstraction', *Ethnography* 4, 2 (2003): 147-179; Nkiru Nzegwu for her slightly revised introduction to *Issues in Contemporary African Art* (1999), and Oyeronke Oyewumi for her essay in *Jenda: A Journal of Culture and African Women Studies* 2, 1 (2002), both of which are included in this volume.

Notes on Contributors

Pius Adesanmi is Associate Professor of English and Postcolonial Studies and Director, Project on New African Literatures (PONAL), Carleton University, Ottawa. He has written extensively on African and Black diasporic literatures and cultures in English and French. He is a two-time fellow of the French Institute of South Africa (IFAS). His writings have appeared in *Social Text*, *Comparative Literature*, *Arena Journal*, *Research in African Literatures*, *English in Africa*, and as chapters in numerous books. He is also a poet; his poetry collection, *The Wayfarer and Other Poems*, won the Association of Nigerian Authors Poetry Prize in 2001.

Collins O. Airhihenbuwa is Professor, Department of Biobehavioral Health, Pennsylvania State University. He is internationally known for his research on culture and health behaviour. Among his numerous publications are *Health and Culture: Beyond the Western Paradigm* (1995), *UNAIDS Communications Framework for HIV/AIDS: A New Direction* (1999), and *Healing Our Differences: The Crisis of Global Health and the Politics of Identity* (forthcoming).

Elias K. Bongmba is Associate Professor of Religious Studies at Rice University in Houston, Texas, where he teaches African Religions. He is the author of *African Witchcraft and Otherness: A Philosophical and Theological Critique of Intersubjective Relations* (2001) and *The Dialectics of Transformation in Africa* (2006). He has published essays on the African Renaissance, theology and power in Africa, religion and literature. His forthcoming essays include 'African Theology and the Question of Rationality', 'Evans-Pritchard and the Theoretical Demise of the Concept of Magic in Africa', and 'Beyond the Bible in Healing: HIV/AIDS and New Challenges for the Church in Africa'. He is currently completing a book on HIV/AIDS titled *Facing a Pandemic: Theological Obligations at a Time of Illness*.

Esperanza Brizuela-Garcia was born in Mexico City, Mexico. She received her undergraduate degree in History from the Universidad Nacional Autonoma de Mexico, an MA in Area Studies (Africa) and a Ph.D. in History from the School of Oriental and African Studies, University of London. Her research interests include historiography, philosophy of history and the intellectual history of Africa. She is currently Assistant Professor in African History at Montclair State University, New Jersey, and a post-doctoral fellow at the Center for African Studies, University of Illinois, Champaign-Urbana. She is the author of 'The history of Africanization and the Africanization of History', in *History in Africa* (2006).

Jean Comaroff is Bernard E. and Ellen C. Sunny Distinguished Service Professor of Anthropology at the University of Chicago. **John L. Comaroff** is Harold H. Swift Distinguished Service Professor of Anthropology at the University of Chicago and senior research fellow at the American Bar Foundation. Both are also honorary professors at the University of Cape Town, and members of the Chicago Center for Contemporary Theory. Their joint publications include *Of Revelation and Revolution*, vol. 1 (1991) and vol. 2 (1997), and such edited collections as *Modernity and its Malcontents* (1993), *Civil Society and the Political Imagination in Africa* (1999) and *Millennial Capitalism and the Culture of Neoliberalism* (2002).

Toyin Falola is a Distinguished Teaching Professor and the Frances Higginbothom Nalle Centennial Professor in History at the University of Texas at Austin. A Fellow of the Nigerian Academy of Letters, he is the author of numerous books, including *Violence in Nigeria: The Crisis of Religious Politics and Secular Ideologies* (1998), *Nationalism and African Intellectuals* (2002), and his award-winning memoir, *A Mouth Sweeter Than Salt* (2004). He is the co-editor of the *Journal of African Economic History*, Series Editor of University of Rochester Studies in African History and the Diaspora, Greenwood Press series on Culture and Customs of Africa, and the Africa World Press series on Classic Authors and Texts on Africa. He has received various teaching and book awards. For his distinguished contribution to the study of Africa he was presented with a set of *Festschrift* edited by Adebayo Oyebade, *The Transformation of Nigeria: Essays in Honor of Toyin Falola* and *The Foundations of Nigeria: Essays in Honor of Toyin Falola.*

Lewis R. Gordon is a Laura H. Carnell Professor of Philosophy and Religion and Director of the Institute for the Study of Race and Social Thought and the Center for Afro-Jewish Studies at Temple University. He is also an Ongoing Visiting Professor of Philosophy and Government at the University of the West Indies at Mona, Jamaica, and President of the Caribbean Philosophical Association. He is the author of several influential books, including the award-winning *Her Majesty's Other Children: Sketches of Racism from a Neocolonial Age* (1997), *Existentia Africana: Understanding Africana Existential Thought* (2000), and his latest book entitled *Disciplinary Decadence: Living Thought in Trying Times* (2006). He is also, with Jane Anna Gordon, co-editor of *Not Only the Master's Tools: African-American Studies in Theory and Practice* (2005), and *A Companion to African-American Studies* (2006).

Ezekiel Kalipeni is an Associate Professor of Geography and African Studies at the University of Illinois at Urbana-Champaign. Some of the books he has published include *Population Growth and Environmental Degradation in Southern Africa* (1994); *Issues and Perspectives on Health Care in Contemporary Sub-Saharan Africa* (1997); *AIDS, Health Care Systems and Culture in Sub-Saharan Africa: Rethinking and Re-Appraisal* (1999); *Sacred Spaces and Public Quarrels: African Economic and Cultural Landscapes* (1999); and *HIV/AIDS in Africa: Beyond Epidemiology* (2004). He has published numerous articles in scholarly journals such as the *Geographical Review*, *Social Science and Medicine*, *Population and Environment*, *Journal of Southern African Studies*, *Africa Today*, and *Population Research and Policy Review*.

Kwaku Larbi Korang holds a joint appointment in the Department of African American and African Studies and the Department of Comparative Studies at the Ohio State University, Columbus, Ohio. He is the author of *Writing Ghana, Imagining Africa: Nation and African Modernity* (2004), as well as recent essays in *Diacritics, Antipodes,* and *Research in African*

Literatures (of which he is now an associate editor). He is currently completing a book on late-modernity and African cultural criticism.

Zine Magubane is Associate Professor of Sociology, Boston College. She previously taught at the University of Illinois at Urbana-Champaign. She is the author of numerous book chapters and journal articles in such journals as *Africa Today*, *Gender and Society*, *Men and Masculinities*, *South Atlantic Quarterly*, *Cultural Studies and Critical Methodologies*, and *Journal of Men's Studies*, as well as the following books, *Bringing the Empire Home: Race, Class, and Gender in Britain and Colonial South Africa* (2004); *Postmodernism, Postcoloniality, and African Studies* (2005), and *Hear Our Voices: Black South African Women in the Academy* (2005).

Sinfree Makoni is Associate Professor in Linguistics and Applied Language Studies and African and African-American Studies at Pennsylvania State University. His recent publications include 'Disinventing and (re) Constituting Languages. Critical Enquiry in Language Studies' (2005), 'The Modern Mission: The Language effects of Christianity', *Journal of Language, Identity and Education* (2005), 'Western Perspectives on applied Linguistics in sub-Saharan Africa' (2004), 'Introducing Applied Linguistics in Africa' (2003), and a co-edited collection *Black Linguistics, Language, Society, and Politics in Africa and the Americas* (2004).

Amina Mama is Professor and Chair in Gender Studies at the African Gender Institute, University of Cape Town, South Africa. She has also held positions in the Netherlands (The Institute of Social Studies), Britain (University of Bradford and the University of London), and visiting appointments at St. Antony's College, Oxford University and at Wellesley College. She sits on the Board of Directors of the United Nations Institute for Research on Social Development, the Global Fund for Women, and the Scientific Committee of the Council for the Development of Social Science Research in Africa. She has authored and edited a number of books, including *Beyond the Masks: Race, Gender and Subjectivity* (1995), *Engendering African Social Sciences* (1997), and *The Hidden Struggle: Statutory and Voluntary Sector Responses to Violence against Black Women in the Home* (1996).

Ulrike Meinhof is Professor of German and Cultural Studies at the University of Southampton, the United Kingdom. Her areas of specialisation are discourse analysis and migration studies. Recent publications include *The Language of Belonging* (2005), *Living with Borders: Identity Discourses on East-West Borders in Europe. Border Region 1* (2002), and 'Bordering European identities', Special Issue, *Journal of Ethnic and Migration Studies* 29 (5).

Abdul Raufu Mustapha is a University Lecturer in African Politics at Queen Elizabeth House and Kirk-Greene Fellow at St. Antony's College, Oxford. He is also the Senior Researcher (West Africa) for the Centre for Research on Inequality, Human Security and Ethnicity, and a member of the Scientific Committee of the Council for the Development of Social Science Research in Africa. His publications include 'Ethnicity and Democratization in Nigeria' (2002), 'Coping With Diversity: The Nigerian State in Historical Perspective' (2002), 'Civil Rights and Pro-democracy Groups in and Outside Nigeria' (2001), 'Transformation of Minority Identities in Post-Colonial Nigeria' (2000) and 'The Politics of

Economic Reforms: Implications for Institutions and Poverty in the Rural African Setting' (2000).

Emmanuel Nnadozie is a Senior Economist at the United Nations Economic Commission for Africa (ECA) and previously Professor of Economics at Truman State University. His most publications include 'Transfer Dependence and Regional Disparities in Nigerian Federalism' (2005), 'Africa at the Crossroads of Globalization' (2004), 'Does Trade Cause Growth in Nigeria?' (2004), 'Post-Colonial African Achievement in Health' (2003), 'African Indigenous Private Entrepreneurship: The Determinants of Resurgence and Growth of Igbo Entrepreneurship during the Post-Biafra Period' (2002), and 'Undergraduate Research Internships and Graduate School Success' (2001), and several books, including *African Economic Development* (2003), *Historical Dictionary of Mozambique* (2003).

Francis B. Nyamnjoh is Associate Professor and Head of Publications and Dissemination with the Council for the Development of Social Science Research in Africa. His most recent books include *Negotiating an Anglophone Identity* (2003), *Rights and the Politics of Recognition in Africa* (2004), *Africa's Media, Democracy and the Politics of Belonging* (2005) and *Insiders and Outsiders: Citizenship and Xenophobia in Contemporary Southern Africa* (2006). He has also published three novels, *Mind Searching* (1991), *The Disillusioned African* (1995), and *A Nose for Money* (2006), and a play, *The Convert* (2003). Additionally, he served as vice-president of the African Council for Communication Education (ACCE) from 1996-2003.

Nkiru Nzegwu is Professor of Africana Studies and Philosophy, Interpretation and Culture at Binghamton University, New York, and the founder of Africa Resource Center, Inc., an online educational portal. She is the author of numerous book chapters and journal articles. Her book publications include *Family Matters: Feminist Concepts in African Philosophy of Culture* (2006), and edited anthologies, *Contemporary Textures: Multidimensionality in Nigerian Art* (1999) and *Issues in Contemporary African Art* (1998).

Benjamin Ofori-Amoah is Professor of Geography and Chair of the Department of Geography at Western Michigan University. His most recent books include: *Beyond the Metropolis: Urban Geography as if Small Cities Mattered* (forthcoming), and *Addressing Misconceptions about Africa's Economic Development: Seeing Beyond the Veil* (1998). His articles have appeared in such journals as *The Wisconsin Geographer*, *Review of Human Factor Studies*, *Environment and Planning A*, *Geoforum*, *The Canadian Geographer*, *Industry and Development*, and *Appropriate Technology*. He is currently the principal investigator of a large project titled 'Building Capacity to Use Geographic Information Systems for Local Government Planning in Uganda', funded by a grant from the Rockefeller Foundation.

Joseph R. Oppong is an Associate Professor of Geography at the University of North Texas. He has published extensively on health care issues and the AIDS epidemic in Africa. His most recent books include *Africa, South of the Sahara* (2006) *AIDS, Health Care Systems and Culture in sub-Saharan Africa: Rethinking and Re-Appraisal* (1999); *Ghana* (2003); *Kenya* (2004); *HIV/AIDS in Africa: Beyond Epidemiology* (2004); and *HIV/AIDS, Gender, Agency and Empowerment*. Some of his recent work has appeared in journals such as *Socio-Economic*

Planning Sciences, Social Science & Medicine, Applied Geographic Studies, Africa Today, The Professional Geographer, International Journal of Health Geographics and *African and Asian Studies.*

Oyeronke Oyewumi is Associate Professor at State University of New York, Stony Brook. She is the author of several books including *The Invention of Women: Making an African Sense of Western Gender Discourses* (1997), which won the 1998 Distinguished Book Award of the American Sociological Association and was a finalist for the 1998 Herskovits Prize of the African Studies Association, *African Women and Feminism: Reflecting on the Politics of Sisterhood* (2003), and *African Gender Studies: Conceptual Issues/Theoretical Questions* (2005), and has published numerous book chapters and articles in such journals as *Signs: Journal of Women in Culture and Society* and *History in Africa.* She is the recipient of a number of research fellowships, including three Rockefeller Fellowships, a Presidential fellowship, and a Ford Foundation grant.

Jemima Pierre is Assistant Professor in the Department of Anthropology and the Center for African and African American Studies at the University of Texas at Austin. She previously held a joint appointment in African American Studies and Anthropology at the University of Illinois at Chicago. Her research ethnographically explores processes of racialisation in Africa and the African diaspora by comparing and contrasting ideologies and practices of 'race' in urban Ghana and for postcolonial African immigrants in urban US. She is currently completing a book tentatively entitled, 'Historical Legacies and Contemporary Tranformations: Mapping Racialization in Urban Ghana'.

Kopano Ratele is Professor of Psychology at the University of the Western Cape. He teaches halftime in the Department of Psychology and the other half in Women & Gender Studies. His current areas of research are in intergroup and interpersonal relations, critical studies of men and masculinities, discursive psychology, sexualities, and methodology. His recent work includes 'Postcolonial African methods and interpretation', 'Proper Sex, Bodies, Culture and Objectification' (2005), 'Studying Men in Africa Critically' (2005), and 'The interior life of Mtutu: Psychological fact and fiction' (*South African Journal of Psychology*). He is the editor of *Intergroup relations in post-apartheid South Africa* (2006) and *Social Psychology: Identity & Relationships* (2003).

Paul Tiyambe Zeleza is Professor and Head, Department of African American Studies at the University of Illinois at Chicago. He has published scores of essays and has authored or edited more than a dozen books, including most recently *Rethinking Africas Globalization* (2003), the *Routledge Encyclopedia of Twentieth Century African History*, *Leisure in Urban Africa* (2003), *Science and Technology in Africa* (2003) and *African Universities in the Twentieth Century* (2 volumes) (2004). He is the winner of the 1994 Noma Award for his book *A Modern Economic History of Africa* (1993) and the 1998 Special Commendation of the Noma Award for *Manufacturing African Studies and Crises* (1997). He has also published works of fiction.

Introduction

The Disciplining of Africa

Paul Tiyambe Zeleza

Today, African studies is a vast international enterprise. Half a century ago, there were few institutions of higher education, whether in Africa itself or abroad, that took the study of Africa seriously. Despite all the noises we hear about the crisis of African universities in general or African studies in particular, there can be little doubt that thousands of people all over the world in multitudes of institutions earn their living teaching, researching, writing, or even celebrating and condemning Africa, in a way that would have been unimaginable at the end of the Second World War when Africa was still under colonial rule. And countless books, journals, reviews, and reference works are published on Africa in dozens of languages across virtually all the fields of academic inquiry. It is practically impossible now for any one individual, however prodigious, to read all that is produced in any discipline or area of specialisation in African studies as may have been the case forty or even thirty years ago.

Yet, the periodic temptation to take intellectual stock of African studies, indeed of any academic field, is always great. The production of disciplinary histories serves to commemorate the founders, socialise newcomers, and establish boundaries and guideposts for the future. I have been particularly susceptible to such temptations partly for institutional reasons—for eight years I headed the Center for African Studies at the University of Illinois, one of the largest in the United States, and I was paid to keep track of where the field was going; for intellectual reasons—I have always been fascinated by intellectual history, both the history of ideas and the history of knowledge producing institutions; and for personal reasons—as an African scholar based in the global North who has been intimately engaged with academic networks and institutions on both sides of the Atlantic I have to navigate and constantly negotiate diverse transnational scholarly communities of which I have to make sense to avoid tripping badly.

The idea for this book grew out of a graduate seminar that I used to run at the University of Illinois on 'The Development of African Studies', which examined the intellectual, institutional, and ideological dynamics in the construction of Africanist knowledges in different disciplinary, interdisciplinary, and international contexts. The seminar received a boost when the Center received a 'focus' grant from the US National Endowment for the Humanities, augmented by funds from the Ford Foundation and the US Department of Education Title VI programme, which enabled me to bring scholars from around the world for intensive and stimulating discussions highlighting new developments and the theoretical, methodological, and pedagogical challenges in African studies within their respective fields and locations. Many of the contributors to the collection participated; others were contacted afterwards to provide much needed input on areas not covered in the original seminar series.

Since the 1970s there have been several English-language assessments of African studies. But many of them are narrowly focussed in their disciplinary and regional coverage. One of the earliest is Christopher Fyfe's *African Studies since 1945* (1976), which looked at the development of African studies in several western countries, but is now quite dated. Almost twenty years later *Africa and the Disciplines* (Bates, Mudimbe and O'Barr 1993) was published to great anticipation but limited acclaim. Not only were the essays quite uneven in quality, more importantly, the book was constrained, if not compromised, by its rather utilitarian objective: the authors saw it as a manifesto to defend African studies and convince cash-strapped university administrators to support the field on the grounds that 'the study of Africa has shaped—and will shape—major fields of knowledge' (Bates et al., 1993: xi). 'Research in Africa', they enthused, 'has shaped the disciplines and thereby shaped our convictions as to what may be universally true' (Bates et al., 1993: xiv). Armed with this mantra, each author attempted to establish the impact of Africanist research on his or her specific discipline (seven in all). The content and contexts—intellectual and ideological—of Africa's apparent disciplinary contributions were largely unproblematised.[1] Unlike Fyfe's book, the collection primarily focused on African studies in the US academy, as did Martin and West's (1999) *Out of One, Many Africas: Reconstructing the Study and Meaning of Africa*, which offered a more vigorous critique of the politics and paradigms of African studies.[2]

Notwithstanding the size and global tentacles of the American academic system and its African studies establishment, it is always important to remember that there are other academic worlds out there with their own scholarly traditions and trajectories. This book was motivated, in part, by the need to capture and demonstrate the diverse and complex configurations of African studies in different world regions, in addition to encompassing and examining African studies on a much wider disciplinary and interdisciplinary canvas than has been attempted thus far. But even such a lengthy collection cannot claim comprehensiveness. Readers will notice the absence of the natural sciences, or even some social science and humanities disciplines and several of their favourite interdisciplinary fields. Even if not encyclopaedic, the collection is sufficiently broad and the contributions have adequate depth to provide perhaps the most wide-ranging portrait of African studies in the world today.

In discussing African studies, or any field for that matter, it is important to note that the economies and cultures of knowledge production are an integral part of complex and sometimes contradictory, but always changing, institutional, intellectual and ideological processes and practices that occur, simultaneously, at national and transnational, or local and global levels. This is simply to point out that African studies—the production of African/ist knowledges—has concrete and conceptual, material and moral, political and discursive contexts, which create the variations that are so evident across the world and across disciplines. The rest of this introduction is divided into three parts. First, I try to situate African studies in the ever-changing contexts of disciplinary and interdisciplinary knowledge production, dissemination, and consumption. Then brief summaries are provided in the second and third sections respectively of the disciplinary and interdisciplinary encounters of African studies.

The Changing Disciplinary and Interdisciplinary Architecture of Knowledge

African studies is interdisciplinary in the sense that Africa is studied in multiple disciplines and sometimes through paradigms that transcend specific disciplines. In other words, the study of Africa is encountered in both the disciplines and interdisciplines. This duality—the interdisciplinarity of African studies as a collective field and the persistence, indeed the continued predominance, of disciplinary constructions of Africanist knowledges—reflects the very duality, or rather complexity, of the modern scholarly enterprise. The contemporary academy in much of the world is typically divided into disciplinary and interdisciplinary fields. But the institutional and intellectual boundaries between the two are neither always clear nor uniform across universities, let alone across countries. In fact, the origins, definitions, and trajectories of disciplinarity and interdisciplinarity are often confused and contested. Interdisciplinarity is seen either as an unwelcome interloper or the saviour of the disciplines.[3] Many scholars these days in the natural sciences and the human sciences swear by interdisciplinarity.[4] Even the august professions, such as law, have not escaped the seductions of interdisciplinarity.[5] A whole range of professional and hybrid fields from women studies to environmental studies to area studies to cultural studies wear their interdisciplinarity as a badge of honour.[6] And guides abound on designing interdisciplinary programmes and courses in universities and schools and organising interdisciplinary teams outside academe in a variety of sectors from industry, commerce, technology, and communications to public services.[7]

Yet, the meaning of interdisciplinarity is not always clear.[8] To its detractors interdisciplinarity is seen as a threat to disciplinary boundaries, hierarchies, and rigour, while its proponents value it as a creative space between disciplines where new questions are asked, new approaches developed, new understandings advanced, and new fields and disciplines emerge. The debate between Thomas Benson (1998: 103-

8) and William Newell (1998a: 109-22) captures the two positions with poignant, if schematic, clarity. Benson offers five arguments against interdisciplinary studies: first, that its objectives and modalities are poorly defined and conceptualised insofar as borrowing among disciplines is normal; second, its pedagogical benefits are doubtful for students lacking strong disciplinary foundations; third, it offers students fragmentary exposure to bits and pieces of various disciplines and impedes their development of disciplinary competence; fourth, interdisciplinary studies program-mes are typically shallow in substituting intellectual rigour for topical excitement; and fifth, the costs of these programmes are too high.

For Newell the interdisciplinarian connects disciplinary insights to address ques-tions that transcend disciplinary boundaries and enhance the problem-solving capacities of scholarship. On the curricular benefits, he believes it is desirable for students to learn both the disciplines and interdisciplines because the two, if properly sequenced, are complementary and illuminate each other; interdisciplinarity promotes higher order thinking and more intellectual maturity than the disciplines. As for competence, more careers and employers require specialised backgrounds that are interdisciplinary. The charge that interdisciplinary studies tend to be topical and trendy seems to be a case of sour grapes by faculty who find themselves in fields of little interest or applicability to the world we live in for there is nothing inherently wrong with addressing the relevant issues of the day. Finally, the relatively high costs of team-teaching can be curtailed through creative methods of team-curriculum development and peer curriculum reviews.

All too often, these debates are tied to intellectual territoriality and struggles for resources. Claims of pedagogical, paradigmatic, or political superiority made for the disciplines or interdisciplines need to be taken with caution. Nevertheless, a case can be made that interdisciplinarity reflects the chaos, messiness, and indivisibility of real life better than the compartmentalised disciplines do. While advances in knowledge occur in the traditional disciplines, they are even more likely in the intersections, the liminal spaces between the disciplines, in the interdisciplinary fields that often emerge out of disciplinary interpenetration and struggles to overcome gaps and silences in the disciplines. Disciplinarity and interdisciplinarity also tend to display different predispositions: disciplinarians are more prone to academic ethnocentricity while interdisciplinarians are more inclined to openness. Disciplinary ethnocentricism is rooted in the very foundational logic and imperatives of the disciplines and reproduced through the sociological and cognitive dynamics of disciplinary development, institutionalisation, and socialisation (Bechtel 1998). If interdisciplinarians do not share analytical interests, methods, or problems, they share a predisposition to the possibilities inherent in various disciplines and of interdisciplinary collaboration or integration (Gunn 1998).

It tends to be assumed that, for better or for worse, interdisciplinarity is a recent phenomenon. In reality, the two have existed in dialectical tension and the dynamics of their interaction have changed ever since the emergence of the modern research university in the nineteenth century that laid the architecture of contemporary knowledge production and consumption (McKeon 1994). In fact, the disciplines emerged out of 'metadisciplines'—the natural sciences from the breakup of natural philosophy, and later the social sciences from moral philosophy, a process that was facilitated by the formation of scientific societies. As for the 'humanities', this is 'a twentieth century term of convenience for those disciplines excluded from the natural and social sciences. While modern philosophy was defined by what was removed from it in the creation of the sciences, the other modern humanities emerged first in the form of classical philology, which produced history, modern languages, and even art history as descendants' (Shumway and Messer-Davidow 1991: 204). This academic division of labour spread from Europe to several parts of the world on the back of European imperialism. The pecking order among the three disciplinary configurations parallels this history and reflects the scientific fixation of modern society in which the natural sciences enjoy the most prestige, followed by the social sciences, and at the bottom are the humanities, and within each there is internal jostling for supremacy and shifts in relative status. The unequal disciplinary claims of the cognitive authority of science have translated into the uneven allocation of resources and reputations.

Notwithstanding the passions with which the gatekeepers often guard their disciplinary boundaries, duly fortified with internal legitimating histories, it is evident that both disciplinarity and interdisciplinarity are not static phenomena, but changing epistemic constructions that evolve as part of the continuous transformations in the nature and function of the academy, which in turn, reflect the changing dynamics in the wider society and the wider world. It has been suggested that if 'disciplinarity and the research university emerged in conjunction with the social and economic transformation at the turn of the twentieth century, then it is plausible to imagine that current social and economic transformations may also have corresponding changes in higher education. Moreover, the current crisis in graduate education—it affects virtually all academic disciplines—and recent changes in the way higher education is funded suggest that such a restructuring is already underway' (Shumway 1997: 7). If that is indeed the case, David Shumway (1997: 8, 9) suggests, 'it would be symmetrical to name the next knowledge system "postdisciplinary"', not interdisciplinary—a nebulous, utopian space between disciplinary confines that remains 'firmly rooted in the disciplinary university'.

It is remarkable how new most of the disciplines and interdisciplines are. Many acquired their distinctive institutional and intellectual identities in the course of the twentieth century, a process that was driven as much by administrative as by academic imperatives to divide knowledge production and pedagogy into manageable units, to departmentalise and discipline scholars and students into specific branches of knowledge, each with its own epistemic cultures and communities, foundational projects and commitments, and mechanisms of authorising new knowledge. The disciplines erected guild boundaries, with varying degrees of permeability, around their objects and methods of inquiry, and developed specialised discourses and theories, training and credentialing systems, discursive practices, publishing protocols, professional networks, regulatory mechanisms, and autonomous departments. Clearly, the modern disciplines are historically and rhetorically constituted social practices, 'regulated and regulating elements in a larger disciplinary regime' of modern society (Shumway and Messer-Davidow 1991: 211), integral to the institutional exercise of power and control as Michel Foucault (1972; 1978) noted. Interdisciplines came to be distinguished by their lack of departmentalisation, to refer to intellectual activities between disciplines, to various forms of disciplinary transgressions, intersections, borrowings, and collaborations.

Various metaphors have been used to capture the divide between disciplinary and interdisciplinary formations. Geographical metaphors about 'boundaries' are particularly popular. Disciplines are seen as 'territories', 'fields' or 'turf' that aspiring interdisciplinarians seek to 'cross', 'explore' or even 'annex' and 'colonise'. Territorial images turn the disciplines into immobile structures, so some prefer the more ebullient metaphor of 'river', 'current', or 'flow'. As one ardent supporter of interdisciplinarity writes: 'Perceiving disciplines as rivers, one acknowledges the narrow origins from which academic groupings spring and the influence of surroundings or contexts on the flow itself; moreover, the metaphor draws disciples' attentions to the decisions of their thinking and the potentially oceanic outcomes of the discipline's decisions and research agendas' (Lyon 1992: 682). In this view, it is possible to break out of the 'local knowledge' of the disciplines, disciplinary frames need not control interdisciplinary conversations, which is offered as a riposte to those who believe disciplinary reflexes cannot be tamed.

Others prefer the metaphor of language, that interdisciplinarity entails learning the language of another discipline, which transforms one's relations to one's own discipline. In other words, 'the division of the intellectual realm into disciplines is analogous to the division of humanity into different language groups. Just as languages are distinguished more by grammar and syntax than by vocabulary, so disciplines are distinguished more by theoretical and methodological points of view than by the "facts" they contain' (Bauer 1990: 112). This is an argument for caution, that interdisciplinary work is akin to multilingualism and multiculturalism and requires acknowledgement of differences of values, epistemologies, ideologies, habits, teaching styles, meanings of scholarship, methods of argumentation, and notions of 'truth'. In short, interdisciplinarity is possible, even desirable, but as an act of translation and transculturation.

There are even those who prefer the metaphor of marriage. To quote Giles Gunn (1998: 253): 'The process of disciplinary revisionism usually begins with a period of courtship between two distinct and often diverse disciplines that suddenly discover spheres of mutual interest and complementary resources, then proceeds to a kind of marriage based on the belief that there are significant areas of compatibility between their respective methods and intellectual focus, and culminates in the pro-duction of offspring who share the parental genes and some of their dispositional features but possess a character of their own'. In this sense, interdisciplinarity emerges out of cooperative exchanges between disciplines that require alterations in the very questions and issues framing the inter-disciplinary inquiry and interaction, which result in the production of new fields between and across disciplines.

Whatever metaphor is used, disciplinarity and interdisciplinarity are mutually constitutive: the latter entails, indeed requires, the existence of the former. As one ardent supporter of disciplinarity colourfully puts it: 'You cannot cross boundaries if you don't know where they are' (Hunt 1994: 1). Interdisciplinarity will not conti- nue to mean anything, she insists, in the case of the hunmanities if they 'dissolve into an undifferentiated pool of cultural studies ... Disciplinary practice, with all its connotations of rigorous training, supervision of conduct, and potential for cen- sure, forms the basis for learning between disciplines as well as within them' (Hunt 1994: 2). For much of the twentieth century and even today, disciplinarity has enjoyed the upper institutional hand, with interdisciplinarity left to claim intellectual innovativeness or greater practical utility.

The metaphorical diversity of defining the disciplinary-interdisciplinary inter- face is in itself indicative of the difficulties of conceptualising and capturing the differences between the two. The distinctions can be drawn on multiple levels in terms of the organisation, objectives, and outcomes of the two branches of knowledge. In organisational terms, there is the institutional dimension—the admi- nistrative and bureaucratic location of academic units on campuses; an intellectual dimension—the epistemological foundations of academic fields in their conceptual, theoretical, and methodological orientations; and an ideological dimension—the political pressures and social imperatives of knowledge production. In terms of objectives, the teaching, research and public service functions of the academy frame disciplinarity and interdisciplinarity in different ways. And so do the outcomes of knowledge production with regard to its audiences and patterns of knowledge dissemination and consumption.

In many cases what distinguishes the disciplines and interdisciplines is adminis- trative conventions and convenience rooted in historical precedence in which, at any one moment, the two represent older and newer branches of knowledge that enjoy varying degrees of institutionalisation. Many contemporary disciplines are unstable, porous entities which house increasingly fractious or distant subunits and specialties that overlap with those in other disciplines. 'Because most research work tends to occur within identifiable areas that are subsidiary to an entire discipline', notes Julie Klein (1998: 278), 'broad disciplinary labels confer a false unity on a discipline. The notion of disciplinary unity is triply false: minimizing or denying differences that exist across the plurality of specialties grouped loosely under a single disciplinary label, undervaluing connections across specialties of separate dis- ciplines, and discounting the frequency and impact of cross-disciplinary influences'. This permeability—the blurring, cracking and crossing of disciplinary boundaries as Klein calls it—afflicts the 'hard' natural sciences such as physics as much as the 'soft' humanities like history, both of which have spawned so many specialties that it is best to think of them as federated disciplines or superdisciplines or interdisciplines (Klein 1998: 286-90; Kockelmans 1998: 72-75).[9] For such disciplines intradisciplinarity can face the same challenges as interdisciplinarity.

Clearly, disciplines are not static, inflexible, unambiguous, and firmly demarcated bodies of scholarship. They have always exchanged information, techniques, methodologies, and theories. Presently, as is evident in this collection, many traditional disciplines have become increasingly interdisciplinary, while many interdisciplinary fields have become disciplinary, and exhortations regarding the benefits of intellectual conversations between disciplines and of departmentalisation for interdisciplines are quite common.[10] For example, in the American academy the age-old discipline of anthropology is often divided into three barely compatible subfields—that sometimes degenerate into warring factions—of cultural or social anthropology, physical or biological anthropology, and archaeology, while women studies programmes born out of feminist militancy and resistance to the androcentric conformities of institutionalisation have increasingly become disciplined by the disciplines or through departmentalisation.

One indication of the shifting terrain is the terminological migration of the word studies previously restricted to the interdisciplines—as in women studies, area studies, cultural studies, and postcolonial studies—to some of the traditional disciplines as in English studies, literary studies, historical studies, and religious studies (Garber 2001).[11] If this is correct, then interdisciplinarity can, in one sense, be seen as a contingent phenomenon referring to the spaces and constructs of intellectual conversation between disciplines prior to the full institutionalisation through the bureaucratic processes of departmentalisation and compartmentalisation. Interdisciplinary study, then, 'is not a simple supplement but is complementary to and corrective of the' existing disciplines (Klein and Newell 1998: 3). It serves as a forum where disciplinary boundaries, which constitute artificial barriers to the transaction of knowledge claims, are renegotiated.

What leads to interdisciplinarity?[12] Various social and cognitive motivations are obviously involved. Scholars cross disciplinary lines in response to the rise and fall of specialties and the perceived opportunities, both real and symbolic, of academic migration (Bechtel 1998: 403-408). The emergence of interdisciplinary studies is related to the very permeability of disciplines noted above, which in turn, is rooted in the epistemological structures and relations among disciplines and shifts in what they consider intrinsic and extrinsic, as well as 'the pull of powerful or fashionable new tools, methods, concepts, and theories; the pull of problem solving over strictly disciplinary focus; [and] the complexifying of disciplinary research' (Klein 1998: 275). The impulses of what Marjorie Garber (2001) has called 'disciplinary envy', the wish by disciplines or scholars within disciplines to model themselves on, borrow from, or appropriate the terms and vocabulary of more esteemed disciplines and their authorities in the perennial struggles for resources and reputational capital in the academy, which have intensified as public fiscal support for the universities has declined, certainly play a role.[13] Also fuelling the drive to interdisciplinarity is the explosion of knowledge and the growing conviction by many scholars, and sometimes by university administrators interested in closing small departments, that the nineteenth-century intellectual division of knowledge is increasingly becoming obsolete; each discipline is incapable, by itself, of explaining the complex and interconnected social, ecological, and physical phenomena and processes that characterise our increasingly globalised world.

What constitutes interdisciplinary studies? Like disciplinarity, interdisciplinarity entails a series of different activities, has varied programmatic, paradigmatic and pedagogical dimensions, and means different things as an attribute of the work, the scholar, and the audience. It is important to unpack interdisciplinarity in its various incarnations. In the narrow sense 'it refers to efforts geared towards the constitution of a new discipline whose field of study lies between two other disciplines already in existence ... In these cases interdisciplinarity is often distinguished from other nondisciplinary approaches to research and education through the use of such expressions as *multidisciplinarity, pluridisciplinarity, crossdisciplinarity, transdisciplinarity*, etc.' (Kochelmans 1998: 68; italics original). Multidisciplinarity involves studying or engaging multiple disciplines that are not connected; pluridisciplinarity entails competence in a specific discipline and thorough knowledge of other disciplines; crossdisciplinarity usually involves projects in which people of different disciplines work to solve a common problem but do not seek to develop a common outlook; transdiciplinarity seeks to develop an overarching theoretical or conceptual framework that transcends the fragmented nature of the existing knowledge. There is a hierarchy in levels of complexity or desirability. According to one typology, at the bottom is intradisciplinarity, followed by, in ascending order, crossdisciplinarity, multidisciplinarity, interdisciplinarity, and transdisciplinarity (Stember 1998: 340-1).

According to Jeffrey Wasserstrom (2006: B5), five types of interdisciplinary activities can be identified: first, what he calls *exploratory* interdisciplinarity that involves borrowing ideas and methods from other disciplines; second, *team-based* interdisciplinarity in which scholars from different disciplines collaborate to solve a problem or understand a phenomenon; third, *paradigmatic* interdisciplinarity that arises out of synthetic theories that operate across disciplines, such as Marxism, feminism, and postmodernism; fourth, *cross-over* interdisciplinarity in which new fields are constituted from overlapping areas of separate disciplines, such as social psychology, biochemistry, biotechnology, and psycholinguistics; and fifth *free-range* interdisciplinarity that refers to people with eclectic interests whose disciplinary homes are hard to fathom. Needless to say, in practice and for many people, these categories overlap. According to the definitional schema in the previous paragraph, the first set resembles *multidisciplinarity*, the second *crossdisciplinarity*, the third aspires towards *transdisciplinarity*, the fourth constitutes *interdisciplinarity* in the narrow sense, and the fifth evokes *pluridisciplinarity*.

Further complicating the definition of interdisciplinarity is the question of its practitioners as individuals or groups and its practice in terms of teaching or research.

The demands and implications of interdisciplinarity vary depending on 'whether individuals are attempting to be interdisciplinary or multidisciplinary or whether a team of people is working collaboratively to produce the integrated knowledge. The challenge of integrating or combining disciplines is different for individuals and groups' (Friedman 1998: 310). Also, the connotations of interdisciplinarity for teaching and students may not be the same for research and faculty. There can be interdisciplinary *teaching* without the faculty themselves engaging in interdisciplinary *research* and *scholarship*, which actually tends to be the case in many so-called interdisciplinary programmes in the social sciences and humanities in the United States.[14] The question of interdisciplinary teaching is obviously a critical one but lies beyond the scope of this introduction.[15]

It is worth remembering that no student's education is ever strictly disciplinary and research specialisation for faculty members comes towards the end of their own education—often at the doctoral level—and is not characteristic of their entire educational history. In this sense, the debate about interdisciplinarity is more about the research interests and positioning of faculty than about realities or the nature of undergraduate education, which is inherently multidisciplinary or interdisciplinary. General education is in fact designed to guard against disciplinary myopia, although general education programmes are often not interdisciplinary (Hursh et al., 1998; Newell 1998b, 1998c; Gaff 1998). Thus, 'the problems at stake are largely pragmatic or organizational, not theoretical' (Klein and Newell 1998: 5). Often the struggle is over the distribution of resources between existing disciplinary departments and upstart interdisciplines that is then translated into questions of autonomous disciplinary departmental status—the basic organisational structure of the modern university— for the interdisciplines and the development of interdisciplinary majors, minors, and concentrations. For Newell (1998c: 224), insofar as the disciplines and interdisciplines develop different and complementary forms of critical thinking, 'students would be best served by a balanced curriculum of disciplinary and interdisciplinary courses'.

Interdisciplinary activities are articulated in a wide range of social and institutional arrangements from independent programmes, centres, institutes, and think tanks, to the establishment of inter-departmental programmes or committees, or interdisciplinary colleges or faculty location in colleges rather than departments to promote wider intellectual affiliation and dilute disciplinary loyalties. There are also the problem-focussed research projects, interinstitutional consortia and networks, and shared facilities and databases. All these activities are, and need to be, supported by their own apparatus of publications, conferences, and associations (Shumway and Messer-Davidow 1991: 213-4; Klein and Newell 1998: 6-8; Bechtel 1998: 409-414). Usually the battles for or against interdisciplinarity are about the visibility and legitimacy of multidisciplinary teaching and learning and of crossdisciplinary research collaboration and communication. In short, how to promote and validate interdisciplinary modes of education and research, to devise the best ways of studying 'disciplines' and doing 'science', to assess and evaluate, resource and reward novel forms of interdisciplinary work.

In producing interdisciplinary work, a scholar seeks to reach an audience both inside and outside one's own discipline, but the practice of interdisciplinarity varies for a scholar performing as a writer and as a reader. As writers, scholars inclined to interdiscplinarity happily pick bits and pieces from other disciplines to enrich their work framed by a disciplinary unconscious despite protestations to the contrary, while as readers they tend to be critical, even dismissive, of works that borrow from their disciplines, faulting them for misunderstandings and simplifications (Wissoker 2000). In the first instance disciplinary borrowing—intellectual tourism really—is praised, while in the second it is pilloried. This simply underscores the fact that it is more difficult for an individual to produce interdisciplinary work that pleases audiences in different disciplines than for the work by several scholars undertaken collaboratively and involving serious and sustained interdiscussive conversations (Hutcheon and Hutcheon 2001).

This is particularly a problem in the more individualistic human sciences than it is in the more collaborative natural sciences. While all disciplines are collective in nature, in some disciplinary work tends to be more isolated (Schleifer 1997). The ethic of individuality so valorised in the humanities—the ideal of solitary research, individual authorship, and the lonely genius—militate against collective academic life. This has become a matter of grave concern to those anxious about the declining public support and academic standing of the humanities as their cultural capital has dwindled considerably. At least in the case of the American academy the humanities appear to have renounced their responsibility to society as they have become more self-referential and indulge in turgid theoretical writings and in overheated but petty debates of limited public interest (Byrne 2005a; 2005b). Some seek salvation in interdisciplinarity, or what Walter Mignolo (2000) calls spaces of transdisciplinarity incorporating the natural and social sciences and the professional schools where conversations and interactions take place among them without domination from any one person or discipline. In this brave new transnational and postnational world the humanities would provide translation and transculturation. Others simply urge the humanities, in the words of Cathy Davidson (1999), 'to borrow the collaborative aspects of lab culture', which would require new humanities structures, including abandoning the use of 'the single-author monograph as the benchmark for excellence, and to confront what new kinds of collaboration mean for tenure review, accreditation, and more' (Davidson and Goldberg 2004).[16]

Interdisciplinary programmes have grown faster than the establishment of new procedures to handle interdisciplinary scholars in terms of tenure and promotion regulations, for example. Many academic institutions often do not take into account the relatively higher costs of research networking and start-up times that also tend to be longer for interdisciplinary than for disciplinary scholars, and the demands of teaching for more than one unit (Pfirman et al., 2005; Gidjunis 2004). In the contexts of curricula based on choice rather than requirements, interdisciplinary offerings often compound the challenges of course sequencing. As one writer puts it referring to the United States: 'The supermarket model of course acquisition has had the intended effect of allowing students to create their own shopping lists, but the unintended effect of allowing bad intellectual nutrition and binge academic eating' (Davis 2005). All this only underscores the difficulties of constructing and maintaining truly productive interdisciplinary spaces in the academy for scholars, students, researchers, writers, and readers.

Interdisciplinarity is often presented as an effective means to halt the drive towards ever-narrower specialisation and knowledge fragmentation, a powerful mechanism to integrate or synthesise disciplinary knowledges. Yet, interdisciplianrity itself often breeds and represents new kinds of specialisation, which incorporate and intersect with the specialisations spawned by the disciplines. The problem with 'pluralist forms of interdisciplinarity', as Steve Fuller (1998: 129-30) calls it, that is, the mutation of interdisciplinary studies '*without replacing some already existing fields* ... is that they reinforce the differences between disciplines by altering the *products* of research, while leaving intact research *procedures*' (italics original). For interdisciplinarity to realise its full potential it needs to transcend this fallacy of eclecticism and embrace methodological innovations and theoretical insights that transcend the disciplines drawn upon. One critic notes that despite the establishment of numerous interdisciplinary degree pro-grammes, centres and institutes, the academic cultures of the what C.P. Snow called 'the two cultures'—the sciences and humanities—'are less mutually interpenetrating now than in Snow's day, perhaps because the institutionalisation of bridge builders serves, ironically, to marginalise them, and keep them out of the main academic thoroughfares ... It seems that higher education—like politics—is more polarized than ever' (Barash 2005).

The Disciplinary Encounters of African Studies

In their encounters with Africa, the disciplines have travelled a considerable distance from their unadulterated Eurocentric origins, but many traces remain which continue to envelope Africa in the analytical shadows of difference and even derision. Eurocentricism is rooted in the very origins of the Enlightenment project and its unyielding hierarchical geographies of knowledge in which ethnology was for 'savage' static societies and sociology for 'civilised' historical ones, certitudes that were articulated with unshakeable conviction by the architects of anthropology and sociology, whose foundational philosophical basis was provided by Hegel and Durkheim. Hegel's dismissal of Africa's historicity and diminution of its humanity left a lasting pall on the study of Africa: the Eurocentric construction of African exceptionalism, Africa as always less than, as lack, as Europe's alterity, its permanently inferior 'Other'. Durkheim's historical sociology and functionalism naturalised binary comparisons between Europe and Africa and sealed the latter in unchanging ethnographic enclosures.

Jemima Pierre traces the origins and trajectory of anthropology and argues forcefully that race has always structured the anthropological project, even if 'racial difference' in the early days of the discipline was subsequently repackaged as 'cultu-ral difference'. She revisits and rereads several canonical texts in Africanist anthropology and shows the lingering reproductions of racial difference in several key recent texts. She believes, as Archie Mafeje (1998) does, that while it is possible to deconstruct colonial anthropology, it is doubtful whether anthropology can be deracialised as the study of the 'other', escape its racial, racialising and racist past. As is well known, colonial anthropology disregarded colonialism as a constitutive force for both the colonised and colonising societies, integral to the emergence of both modern Africa and modern Europe. In the anticolonial wrath of decolonisation anthropology faced banishment, charged with colonial complicity, of exonerating colonialism from the cultural, cartographic, and cognitive violence it wrought on Africa.

In the meantime, sociology gained curriculum space in African universities. Africanist sociology came armed with a succession of theoretical approaches, from what Magubane calls the pluralist model, Marxist theory, the nationalist perspectives, and the postcolonial paradigm. Each viewed African societies from its own particular set of conceptual and methodological lenses, emphasising certain features and dynamics, from the 'acculturation' and 'modernisation' theses of the pluralists, to the materialist and class concerns of the Marxists, to the nationalists' celebration of Africans as agentic subjects and their vigorous condemnations of the social disruptions of colonialism and its neocolonial legacies, to the posts' (postcolonialism and postmodernism) fascination with the construction and contingency of identities and ideologies, practices and psychologies, discourses and desires.

From the 1970s, anthropology sought to reconstitute itself through the prism of the 'posts', to recast its conceptual categories, analytical concerns, transnational horizons, historical affiliations, reflexive ambitions, and narrative aspirations. The Comaroffs caution against fetishising method for its own sake, and call for a critical, committed anthropology that transcends the neat antimonies between the local and the global, field and context, ethnography and metanarrative, method and theory, for a discipline that integrates the contested processes of globalisation in the production of localities, interrogates the ideological construct of modernity and similar powerful tropes, and incorporates findings from other disciplines. They proceed to demonstrate the analytical possibilities of this approach by examining the development and dialectics of a specific phenomenon, what they call the occult economy in the 'new' postcolonial South Africa.

Much has indeed changed in Africanist anthropology: small-scale communities have lost their splendid sovereignties and seclusions as the singularity of places, traditions, customs, or cultures has become increasingly subsumed in socioeconomic and political geographies of multiple scales and coordinates, as the connectedness between the past and the present is acknowledged, and as 'metropolitan' metanarratives no longer enjoy authority among the 'natives' who can speak for themselves. Yet, the ethnographic method remains supreme and those with sharp intellectual noses can still smell the odour of the 'racing' and 'othering' of Africa.

If postcolonial theory rescued anthropology from the doldrums among the social sciences, it catapulted literature into the queen of the humanities, and generally transformed the study of Africa previously dominated by liberal and radical approaches rooted in idealistic and materialist conceptions of history and society. While anthropology had found itself in a theoretical and curricula impasse in the 1960s and 1970s, especially in Africa, its primary research field, African literature began to flourish, buoyed by the explosion in creative writing and the insatiable appetite for Africa's own textual imagination in the rapidly expanding schools and universities across the continent and abroad where postcolonial theory provided a much needed badge of entry into academic respectability and legitimacy.

At the height of empire anthropology was of course not the only discipline that sought to establish epistemic control over Africa, to subject it to the self-legitimating teleologies and myths of imperialism. Literature was another. The textual conquest of Africa was reflected not only in the vast corpus of European representational literature from fiction to travel writing, but also in the emergence of the languages of colonial domination as the pre-eminent languages of African literary imagination and production, and of western models of criticism and institutional inscription for the dissemination, legitimation, and canonisation of African literature. In the 1930s and 1940s protest came from the aggrieved poetry and philosophy of negritude, and in the 1950s and 1960s the assured writings of decolonisation inspired by the aesthetics of cultural nationalism and nativist criticism. For the generation of writers born after 1960, their creative and critical flowering came in the 1980s and 1990s, the era of pervasive crisis for the postcolony and the triumph of postcolonial theory both of which marked and mediated their work.

The versions of postcolonial theory dominant in literature departments in the Euro-American academy tend to privilege the identity politics of diasporic location, alienation and deracination. The African writers, whose works are ensconced in the generous niches of multicultural syllabi, argues Pius Adesanmi, are either based in the West or their themes are set in the West. Missing from their work or its interpretation is any serious and sustained engagement with the politics, problems, paradoxes, pleasures, and possibilities of the postcolonies that animated previous generations of writers. That, ultimately, is the boon and bane of postcolonial criticism: it has opened doors to African literature in the Euro-American academy more than was possible a generation ago but the literature being canonised is increasingly decentred and filtered through the formulaic focus on transnational and migrant subjectivities and textualities.

Literary criticism drew some of its conceptual tools from the linguistic turn in the humanities. Yet, in African studies linguistics has largely remained in relative disciplinary isolation. Language debates have of course periodically broken out among writers and literary scholars,[17] but few have been informed by theoretical discourses among linguists. There is much to be gained from conversations between linguists and other students of African cultures and societies. The chapter by Sinfree Makoni and Ulrike Meinhof interrogating the construction of African languages illustrates this quite well. They focus on the language question in Africa, whose framing, they argue, reflects a theory of literacy rather than of language. To some, Africa's 'language problem' is the existence of too many languages; to others this constitutes cultural wealth. But both models—the monolingual and multilingual approaches—are flip sides of the same coin, resting on a misleading understanding of the social construction of African languages.

African languages, like other human artefacts, are social inventions, products of social processes and historical interventions. In this context, colonial literacy had a profound impact on the creation of African languages as texts with specific meanings and boundaries, as markers of social identity, rather than merely as conduits of communication or media of instruction. While nationalism played a crucial role in bringing about the notion of separate languages in Europe, in Africa this was facilitated by the Christian colonial project of literacy. This challenges the simplistic tendency to see 'indigenous' languages as authentic, as unproblematic repositories of African culture, for many of Africa's contemporary languages were invented by colonialism as discrete systems in which some language varieties were separated (such as Xhosa and Zulu) and others integrated (such as Yoruba). The census ideology of language, inventories aggregated by missionaries and linguists, which emerged in the colonial period persisted in the postcolonial era as governments and applied linguists continued the enumerative modalities of demarcating discrete languages and conflating ethnicity with language proficiency instead of regarding language as a multilayered chain of communication and social interaction. Makoni and Meinhof contend there is a need to deconstruct the study of African languages as it has been defined by Euro-American professional linguists from monolingual traditions who more often than not do not speak these languages, or western educated Africans who have largely accepted Eurocentric conceptual categories.

Similar deconstructive impulses have been raging in contemporary African philosophy. From the 1960s and 1970s, African philosophers were preoccupied with dismantling the hegemony of European thought and defending the historicity of African thought, in affirming African humanity long denied by the European geopolitical self and the metaphysics of white normativity. Like other scholars, they have been confronted by two challenges: first, that of translation—articulating the tenets of African culture and ideas in western academic terms; and second, that of formulation—framing their own theories, interpretations, and criticisms. This explains their preoccupation with philosophical anthropology—the retrieval and reconstruction of the distilled thought of specific African societies and sages, and the place accorded the concept of invention as agency and discourse in their writings and debates, which examine the ways of knowing 'Africa', how representations and meanings of African phenomena including ideas, institutions, ethics, and practices are constituted—invented and reinvented—by contingent systems of knowledge, processes of resistance and adaptation to those systems, and acts of self-fashioning. It is from the philosophical challenge of contemporary African philosophy, Lewis Gordon argues in his chapter on African philosophy and cultural studies, that the African social sciences and humanities will draw the insights and intellectual resources to advance their own disciplines and interdisciplinarity in African studies in general.

Clearly, African and Africanist scholars have been preoccupied with the need to decolonise African studies. The possibility of disciplinary conceit aside—I am a historian—it would generally be agreed that historians waged the earliest and most successful struggles against Eurocentric hegemony. Esperanza Brizuela-Garcia offers an intriguing comparative analysis of the development of African history at six universities in Africa, Britain, and the United States between the 1950s and 1990s, which shows the complex interplay of intellectual, institutional and ideological dynamics at national and international levels during what she calls the formative years, the golden era, and the decades of crisis. It is a fascinating story. The formative years were characterised by staffing and curricular challenges, but also the excitement of building a new interdisciplinary field, all underpinned by the rise and eventual triumph of African nationalism. During the golden era the discipline matured as new universities were founded across Africa, vibrant historiographical schools emerged in Dar es Salaam, Ibadan and elsewhere, African studies programmes grew in the United States and Britain, the range of African history courses expanded, and undergraduate and graduate student enrolments increased. The development of Africanist history, culminating in the Cambridge History and UNESCO General History of Africa, each in eight thick volumes, was a spectacular achievement, one of the most impressive historiographical successes of the twentieth century as Jan Vansina (1993) has attested.

No sooner had African history become consolidated than its institutional standing began eroding due to budgetary constraints tied to the collapse of the welfare state in the global North and the developmental state in the global South and the rise of neo-liberalism. African countries and universities were hit especially hard. The institutional changes were tied to new ideological and intellectual currents. History and historians fared less well as the nationalist fervour of the 1950s and 1960s gave way to the developmental preoccupations of the 1970s and the deflationary structural adjustment prescriptions of the 1980s and 1990s. In the meantime, the nationalist narrative of African historiography collapsed in the face of new radical approaches influenced by dependency, Marxist, and feminist theories, and later by cultural studies and postcolonial studies. The effect of all this was that African historiography became fragmented. More important, perhaps, is the sad fact that African universities lost their lead in the production of African historical knowledge and became increasingly subordinated to Northern institutions to their detriment and to the development of the entire discipline. Also, research focus shifted from the longue durée of African history to contemporary history—the twentieth century (the colonial and postcolonial eras).

Toyin Falola's chapter takes the story from where Brinzuela-Garcia leaves off, and examines the interface between national history and global history in the contemporary era. He celebrates the heroic efforts of Africa's early nationalist historians who besides creating distinct national histories, helped recast Africa's place in the world, investing it with civilisational presence, dignity, and pride. He argues that contemporary African historians face a dual challenge: first, to deepen and broaden national history without glossing over internal differences and social inequalities or turning it into an instrument of state repression and an ideology of national chauvinism; second, to insert Africa centrally into the unfolding tapestry of global connections and change. The Atlantic slave trade, for example, remade Africa as much as it remade Euro-America, and was critical to the construction of the modern world, warts and all. Falola concludes with an exhaustive list of specific themes and topics that national historians need to continue paying close attention to, namely, the development and dynamics of colonialism, decolonisation and nationalism, and the postcolonial state and society. Despite the considerable achievements of the historiographical revolution pioneered by the nationalist historians and their followers variously influenced by Marxist, feminist, ecological, and postcolonial perspectives, African history has yet to rid itself entirely of the epistemic erasures, omissions, fabrications, stereotypes and silences of imperialist historiography. The struggle to liberate African history will have to continue resting on a double intellectual manoeuvre: provincialising Europe that has monopolised universality and universalising Africa beyond its Eurocentric provincialisation (Zeleza 2005). This requires not only continued vigilance against Eurocentric conceptions of history and categories of analysis, but also vigorous reconstructions of history that re-centre African history by deepening and globalising it in its temporal and spatial scope. After all, Africa is the cradle of humanity, the continent where humans have lived the longest.

History as a discipline may have been in the vanguard of the struggles for intellectual decolonisation, but it was political science and economics that claimed pride of place in postcolonial Africa's great political and policy debates. Political scientists sought not only to understand African politics but also to redirect it in particular desirable directions. The will-to-knowledge and the will-to-power were locked in a fateful paradigmatic and prescriptive embrace that has always characterised Africanist political science. The discipline wrestled with two fundamental questions: how to construct coherent political communities in the territorial contraptions inherited from colonialism—nation-building—and how to build institutions and technologies for effective governance over the newly forged political communities—state-building. There was no shortage of prescriptions, nor a check on their mutability, although the references and recommendations were always predicated on an imaginary of political modernity incarnated elsewhere, either in the capitalist West for those enamoured by Euro-American liberal democracy, or the communist East for those enchanted by Soviet socialist democracy. Much of the discourse was guided by the evolutionary tenets of modernisation theory, in which Africa was placed at the bottom of the developmental ladder. By the 1980s, the postcolonial state had fallen from grace, seemingly unable to deliver the material promises and moral possibilities of independence. Euro-America was drifting to the right and its patience with Third World demands for new international orders had run out. It was in this ideological and intellectual context that political scientists, especially in Euro-America, began to recast African politics and states as crisis-ridden. It was as if there was a reputational lottery to see who could coin the most gratuitous epithets for the postcolonial leviathan.

Underpinning this new political sociology for Africa, as Dickson Eyoh (1996) has called it, was a new project of social engineering for Africa: political and economic liberalisation under the ascendant ideology of neo-liberalism.

Abdul Raufu Mustapha traces the development of Africanist political science from its origins to the present. The field was born in the throes of decolonisation and the Cold War, during which two main competing theoretical and thematic concerns emerged: some focused on the dynamics of African nationalism and the imperatives of modernisation, others were inspired by Marxist and dependency perspectives and preferred more radical analyses of African political economies. Since the 1980s, which constitute the main focus of the chapter, the shifts in Africanist political science have been reflected primarily in changing notions of the state as the organisation of public power, the market as an organising principle of society, and civil society as the expression of the popular will. Mustapha outlines the mutating characterisations of the state, from depictions of the African state as an instrument for the ruinous rent-seeking behaviours of the elites influenced by rational choice theory to culturalist views of the state in which it is argued African political systems are derived from a specific cultural logic marked by the lack of differentiation of the political realm from other spheres of society and the informalisation of politics. This cultural logic of political behaviour accounts for the corruption, criminality, and conflicts that apparently typify Africa.

Mustapha offers a vigorous critique of the technocratic and culturalist analyses of the state for their simplifications, pathologisation and racist stereotyping of Africa's astonishingly diverse cultures, societies and histories. Also questioned are the highly ideological conceptions of the market and civil society and how the two have been deployed in political science discourse in Africa, in which one is seen as the panacea for development and the other for democratisation. In both cases the accent is more on ideal imagined markets and civil societies rather than real existing ones. It is quite evident that conceptions and misconceptions of the state, market, and civil society and the nexus between them have profoundly influenced policymaking and exacted a high price for African development and democracy. The policies inspired by Africanist political science have led not only to intellectual obfuscation, but bolstered neo-liberalism that has contributed to Africa's economic marginalisation and de-industrialisation. Africa can do without the reckless policy prescriptions manufactured and peddled from Euro-American Africanist foes, often pretending to be friends of Africa, some of who even call for Africa's recolonisation through 'international trusteeship'. Africa needs, Mustapha concludes, a service delivery and transformative state; in short, a developmental state. The chapter offers a compelling example of the power of ideas, including misguided ones, and the need for African scholars to deconstruct received orthodoxies and for African policy makers to pay heed to them.

For a long time political science has suffered from the disciplinary envy of economics, while economics itself was becoming more mathematical in its relentless drive to become more like physics. In the process the study of real economies became increasingly secondary to academic economics enthralled by abstract theories and modelling techniques. Theoretical developments in economics have obviously affected the relationship between Africa and the discipline, which has not been a close or happy one. This is the subject of Emmanuel Nnadozie's comprehensive chapter which begins by making the ironic observation that Africa, the world's least developed continent, has been peripheral to a discipline whose preoccupation is economic growth, distribution and human welfare. Also, despite the developmental obsession of African studies, economics has largely been marginalised in African studies as an academic field. Thus neither African economic experiences nor Africanist scholarship have played much of a role in the development of mainstream economics, except perhaps for the stepchild of the discipline—development economics—and its unwelcome orphan—dependency theory, both of which have largely disappeared from economics departments (Mkandawire 2006). Africa's epistemic invisibility is palpable in the major branches of economics from the classical theory of the eighteenth century that launched the discipline, the Marxist political economy of the mid-nineteenth century that nearly subverted it, the neo-classical revolution at the turn of the twentieth century that set the broad contours of mainstream economics in Euro-America, and the assorted schools that appeared in the course of the twentieth century.

From the vast corpus of economic thought, three approaches to development can be discerned—neoclassical, Marxian, and structuralist—each of which presents its own growth models rooted in specific intellectual and ideological traditions. In the mid-twentieth century as the Cold War crystallised and the winds of decolonisation gathered momentum, the problems of developing countries began to attract some attention. But the proposed linear stages of growth, as well as the models of the structuralists, were derived from the stylised facts of Euro-American economic experiences that had little relevance to Africa. Marxist economics won adherents in revolutionary states seeking to substitute underdeveloped capitalism with doctrinaire socialism, but many of the experiments were eventually aborted in the great meltdown of actually existing socialism in the late 1980s and early 1990s. Particularly attractive in intellectual circles and the circuits of Third World solidarity and international summitry was dependency theory, which emphasised external constraints to development and saw salvation in the vague ideology of self-reliance or rhetorical agitation for a new international economic order. This tendency, too, perished in the convulsions of the 1980s, presaged by the resurgence of the uncompromising tenets of neoclassicism, of market fundamentalism.

The costly failures of neo-liberalism have punctured its inflated certitudes and encouraged the flowering of new Africa-specific research and concession to the complexity and multiplicity of factors behind Africa's underdevelopment, which is welcome. But there is a danger that unless backed by truly interdisciplinary modes of analysis, economists who are poorly trained to understand historical, political, cultural, and geographical factors may continue devising perilous policies based on simplistic variables. Indeed, Africa's tragedy has never been the lack of prescriptions, but the overabundance of naïve, ideologically driven prescriptions based on ignorance and prejudice masquerading as research and knowledge. The litany of economic policy prescriptions over the last half-century is a long one indeed: from trickle-down, human needs, and industrialisation through import substitution, to structural adjustment programmes and sustainable development.

The disciplines examined above have dominated African studies either in terms of research or policy discourse or both. But there are other social science and humanities disciplines whose engagement with Africa has grown to the mutual advantage or anxiety of the disciplines concerned and the interdiscipline of African studies. Two of these disciplines represented in this volume are geography and psychology. Kalipeni, Oppong and Ofori-Amoah provide an exhaustive and highly informative overview of geographic research on Africa over the last forty years with particular emphasis on the period since the 1990s, which reveals the existence of a vast and vibrant discipline that straddles the social and natural sciences and ought to be better represented in African studies. The range of studies reviewed fall into the three main sub-disciplines of geography, namely, human geography, physical geography now commonly known as earth systems science or global change studies, and geographic information systems. There are considerable theoretical and methodological overlaps among the three subdisciplines, and a general drift towards interdisciplinary approaches seen as essential to explaining Africa's rapidly changing and complex geographies.

Human geography is by far the most dominant in Africanist geography. Before the 1990s the field was characterised by neo-Malthusian analyses bemoaning the disastrous combination of rapid population growth, environmental degradation, and economic decline. More recent work paints a more complex picture of the dynamic interactions between population, resources, and the environment that challenge many previous analyses. It is informed by a wide range of theoretical perspectives, including those developed by geographers themselves such as the Boserupian, political ecology, or liberation ecology approaches, and others derived from other fields such as political economy, feminist, dependency, modernisation, neo-liberal, postmodernist and postcolonial perspectives. Africanist geographers have also made significant contributions to the literature on development by underscoring the spatial modalities of the development process. Particularly impressive has been the recent work on urban and regional development and the geography of disease and health care, in which old Eurocentric ideas and interpretations about African settlement patterns and disease ecologies have been reformulated or replaced. Much of the Africanist work in earth systems science or global change has focussed on climate change, while GIS and remote sensing have increasingly come to be used as tools for studying environmental change on the continent. It is quite clear that the contributions of geography to African studies are critical and need to be better known in the field.

Psychology is even less well integrated into the mainstream of African studies. Yet, as Kopano Ratele shows in his extensive and instructive chapter, its importance as the discipline that has shaped popular conceptions of human cognitive endowments and cultural behaviours cannot be denied. Epistemologically, psychology embodies most poignantly the problem of universality, how truth-claims are constructed, given the enduring desire among psychologists, notwithstanding all the deconstructive rage, to discover universal laws with regard to the essence and nature of human beings. It is a discipline that has had great difficulty in shedding its Eurocentric blinders, in seeing that its cherished ideas and abstractions have been moulded out of the particular psychological lives of white people in Euro-America. No less contentious is the scope of the discipline. Ratele bemoans the tendency to confine psychology to an increasingly ossified and narrow range of issues that ignore topics of greater efficacy, certainly for Africa, concerning social, economic, cultural, and political structures.

But important changes are taking place. Ratele notes that while quantitative analyses may still rule the conceptual and methodological roost of the discipline, qualitative research is now more widely accepted, and the ideas of 'race' and sex as social constructs are well known, thanks to the seminal interventions of the 'posts'. The challenge African critics face is how to unpack psychology's foundational theses, its fictions of disinterested impartiality, its craving for scientific objectivity, the progressivist narratives of its development with its cast of great men, its problematic idea of the individual, and its limited thematic and topical horizons, while simultaneously avoiding the countervailing danger of proclaiming African exceptionalisms and exoticisms; in short, how to re/build a more inclusive discipline, an organic and ethical psychology. He maintains that if African/ist psychology is to make significant contributions to Africa and the discipline it must be grounded in African realities, in the continent's economic and existential conditions, its socio-political and interpersonal psychic relations.

The Interdisciplinary Challenges

As can be seen above, the disciplinary configurations in studies of Africa exhibit enormous variations based on each discipline's methodologies, concepts, theories, and discourses, as well as its political interests and public engagements. The interdisciplinary dimensions of African studies are no less varied and complex. Interdisciplinarity in African studies is motivated by many of the same forces examined in the first part of this introduction. But the field of African studies has also been shaped by more specific imperatives spawned by powerful ideological, intellectual, and institutional forces. To begin with, as is evident from the previous section, African and Africanist scholarship has been marked by strong deconstructive impulses, an abiding desire to commit epistemic patricide against the foundational figures and figurations of the Eurocentric disciplines. As I argued elsewhere, the insurgency of African studies, together with the other so-called area studies in the academies of the global North, have been critical to the decomposition of the western epistemological order, the paradigmatic disorder that has been so evident over the past few decades, which is often attributed, incorrectly in my view, to the belated rise of the 'posts' (Zeleza 1997: 494-510). The deconstruction of the dominant western meta-narratives, of Eurocentric certainties and disciplinary conceits, has done much to open space for interdisciplinarity.

The interdisciplinary inclinations of African studies can also be attributed to intellectual necessity, the need to construct an African 'library', a body of knowledge that can fully encompass, engage, and examine African phenomena. When this drive began in earnest in the post war era the existing disciplinary methodologies and theories were found seriously wanting. There is hardly a discipline again as shown in the previous section that was not forced to reformulate its concepts and methods in the endeavour to excavate and elevate Africa from the onerous weight of Eurocentric epistemology. This is quite evident in history, the discipline I know best. Africanist historians were more open to the use of multiple sources including archaeology, documentary evidence, oral tradition, historical linguistics and data from the natural sciences in their reconstruction of the histories of African societies, some of which lacked the kinds of written sources prized in European historiography. As Joseph Miller (1999) has observed, some of their methods, questions, and perspectives are useful and illuminating for, indeed they have been incorporated in Euro-American historiography and in several interdisciplinary fields such as women's studies that prize deconstruction, reflexivity, and oral narratives.

This openness, not to say eclecticism, is particularly evident in my own specialty, economic history. Anthony Hopkins (1985: 41), one of the doyens of African economic history, has argued that Africanist economic historians have a generous definition of economic history, one which embraces anthropology and political history as well as economics, which can be attributed to 'the youthfulness of the subject, the fortunate failure of any one school of thought to impose its dominance, and the diversity of evidence...' Consequently, the field has been 'dominated by no single national or methodological tradition', a heterogeneity that permits 'a wide range of scholarly standards' and 'guarantees an openness to new ideas and acts as a protection against the dominance of a single orthodoxy' (Hopkins 1980: 154). This has made economic historians of Africa, Patrick Manning (1989: 53) claims, 'much more interdisciplinary than other economic historians'. What is interesting is that economic historians of other regions and older historiographical traditions appear to be moving in the Africanist direction. Readings on European economic history suggest growing interest in reconnecting economic and social history, indeed, in integrating economic, social, and political history (Daunton 1985; Coats 1985; Feldman 1986; Zeleza 2002, 2005).

No less important are the institutional contexts in which African studies have developed. Outside Africa, the field has developed in area studies programmes. Also, Africanists isolated in their various disciplines have found solace in interdisciplinary conversations and collaborations with each other. Within Africa itself, powerful political, social, and economic forces have shaped the growth of scholarly communities and traditions prone to interdisciplinarity. From the beginning the postcolonial university was under strong pressures to help advance—consciously, constructively and creatively—what Thandika Mkandawire (1997: 2005) calls the historic and humanistic tasks of African nationalism: decolonisation, development, nation-building, democracy, and regional integration. This meant that 'ivory' or 'brick' tower scholasticism was deeply distrusted. The instrumentalist orientation of African scholarship and knowledge production facilitated the embrace of problem-solving interdisciplinarity.

The widely reported crisis that afflicted African universities from the 1980s reinforced this trend, as desperate academics sought pecuniary support, and occasionally political refuge, in consultancies for donor agencies, which often required interdisciplinary skills, or at the very least the skills to mediate scholarly research and policy prescription. The drift towards the privatisation of universities from the 1990s, as reflected in the explosion of private universities and the privatisation of programmes in public universities, spawned in part by dwindling fiscal support for public education, provided an added spur for departments and programmes to sell themselves to a rapidly expanding and increasingly diverse clientele of students consisting of young people seeking professional skills and professionals seeking career enhancement (Zeleza and Olukoshi 2004). Departments in the less marketable fields, especially in the humanities, found themselves reconfiguring their identities and adding on potentially lucrative courses or even inventing new disciplinary labels.

Women's and gender studies have been in the forefront of the interdisciplinary studies movement. In the African context, according to Amina Mama, the rapid growth of the field can be attributed to the expansion of African universities and a radical intellectual culture that valorises social responsibility and is critical of western disciplinary knowledge that has translated into a preference for interdisciplinary approaches. Also, these programmes are products of the vibrant research networks outside the academy that proliferated in response to the crisis of the universities. Further, the uptake of feminism within the development industry has also helped provide instrumentalist legitimacy to African gender studies. Above all, they are linked to activist feminist movements. Feminist scholarship and activism were initiated outside the universities and was clearly not a western import, although western overdetermination of African feminist research in terms of both the quantity of publications and theoretical interests articulated persists. Mama traces the growth of these programmes from the late 1970s to the present and outlines the results of a survey indicating the number of universities offering courses in gender studies, the institutional structure of gender programmes, levels of teaching, the intellectual content, and the establishment of several collaborative continental research and publishing projects. Thus, the scope of African gender studies has been wide, ranging from the provision of technical services to concern with the broader epistemological concerns of transformative feminism. Despite the advances made these programmes suffer from inadequate resources and their impact on the wider intellectual environment in the patriarchal academic institutions remains limited.

Outside the continent African gender studies do not enjoy institutional autonomy; they are lodged in women studies programmes and in disciplinary courses. This, together with their location outside Africa, makes for relatively weak connections between theory, activism, and policy-making that is the hallmark of feminist scholarship on the continent. In this context debates and contestations over theory and representation assume a particular salience. Many African feminists in the academies of the global North have relentlessly challenged the epistemological hegemony of western feminism, a struggle that has taken many forms including critiquing the very foundational categories of western feminist scholarship such as 'gender', 'woman' and the 'body'. They urge that these categories must be subjected to critical analysis and there is a need to privilege the categories and interpretations of African societies. Perhaps the most famous interventions are those made by Ifi Amadiume (1987) and Oyeronke Oyewumi (1997).

In her chapter in this book Oyewumi argues that the dominant analytic categories in feminist studies refer to social constructs that are not universal, but distilled from Euro-American experiences, and are especially rooted in the nuclear family as an institutional and spatial configuration and occlude other fundamental organising principles that might or might not intersect with gender in African and other societies. The patriarchal nuclear family is a gendered institution and a space par excellence in which woman is reduced to wife and the inflections or social intersections of race and class are either absent, muted, or invisible. But it remains alien in much of Africa notwithstanding the corrosive influences of colonial and neo-colonial forces. As an example, Oyewumi examines what she calls the non-gendered traditional Yoruba family, whose fundamental organising principle is seniority based rather than gender based; the former unlike the latter is fluid and dynamic. She is emphatic that the theoretical challenge of African gender studies involves the need to transcend Euro-American feminist constructs with their binaries, and to develop analytical categories derived from and illuminated by African experiences and epistemology.

Studies of the African visual arts in the Euro-American academy, now conducted in several disciplines including art history, were conceived and nurtured within the exoticizing gaze of anthropology, which left a lasting mark. Nkiru Nzegwu argues that critical interpretations of African art have remained largely trapped in the binary opposition of traditionality and modernity. Placed in an ethnological closet, African art is seen as lying outside the modern, notwithstanding its very centrality to modernism. In this exclusionary logic, critical preference is given to 'traditional' not 'modern' African art, in which the former is mystified as authentic and the latter dismissed as imitative. The only concession to contemporary African art is to the so-called 'popular art' of low-grade commercial signs. The notion of authenticity serves to police the Eurocentric evaluative criteria of African art and protect its commodification, reproduces the racialised dichotomies between Africa and Europe and reinforces simplistic negative images that freeze African creativity in a pristine past, in an unchanging same. Hence the propensity to present African art and artists in hermetically sealed ethnic bubbles.

For Nzegwu the conceptual emancipation of modernity from the clutches of Europe's narcissism is imperative insofar as there are multiple modernities including Africa's own modernity that has its own historical and contemporary forms and spirit. It is also crucial to develop critical art theory that is culturally and historically grounded in African realities and experiences and that foregrounds contemporary African art. She uses 'contemporary' as a technical term like the 'modern' in 'modern European art', as an act of conceptual naming and self-definition. Contemporary African art adumbrates an assortment of styles and presents visual arguments with Europe and ongoing commentary, representation, and interrogation of transformations within Africa.

Religious studies have become an increasingly important disciplinary and interdisciplinary branch of Africanist scholarship. In his chapter Elias Bongmba offers a comprehensive overview of the studies that have been conducted on the three dominant African religions: the so-called indigenous or traditional religions, Christianity, and Islam. For each he explores the different phases and shifting analytical trends. Writing on the indigenous religions has come a long way from the days when they were dismissed and condemned by self-righteous European missionaries and other colonial ideologues. European anthropologists dominated the first phase in the serious study of these religions. The second phase was characterised by the engagement of African scholars trained in theology, philosophy, anthropology, and history who sought to elevate the status of the indigenous religions. This was followed by what Bongmba calls the global phase when the racial divisions in the field became less salient, the numbers of scholars increased, and diverse theoretical perspectives were developed, including the 'culture area' and the critical dialogical pluralism approaches.

Studies of Christianity have also undergone changes from the days when Christianity was considered a Western religion. Now, the African roots and contributions to the theological and institutional development of early Christianity are widely recognised. The study of modern Christianity has been dominated by five successive themes: the linkages between African Christianity and the Western imperial project; social scientific studies on the social and cultural dynamics and impact of Christian conversion; African agency; the emergence of interdisciplinary research on various aspects of Christianity; and work on the growth and development of Christianity in specific regions and countries in which issues of church-state relations, theological movements, and gender and feminist analyses have received a lot of attention. Particularly rich has been research on Christian reform movements, which began in the late nineteenth century and have introduced important theological, ecclesiological, and liturgical innovations.

No less remarkable is the rich literature that has grown on the development of Islam across Africa from north to south, west to east. The literature has examined the differentiated patterns and the profound impact—religious, cultural, social, demographic, economic, and political—that the expansion of Islam had and continues to have in various parts of the continent. Bongmba mentions the research work on the role of the Islamic brotherhoods and orders, the efforts to recover Africa's Islamic scholarship and contributions, the studies on Islamic theology and law, social activism, and politics and social reform among African Muslims. He ends the chapter with a set of research topics, which he argues are central to advancing the study of African religions and understanding the vibrant religious imagination of what he terms the post-neocolonial state and society. They include: religious conceptualisation of the spirit; religion and the state, violence, gender, felt needs, and the occult including witchcraft.

A crucial area of interdisciplinary research but one that tends to be left out of the mainstream of African studies circles dominated by the social science and humanities discipline is the field of public health, whose conceptual apparatus is constructed out of quite familiar social science theories and perspectives. Health and medical data occupy a central position in how communities are defined and are of obvious concern to academics, governments, and the public within and across countries as the case of the HIV/AIDS pandemic has amply demonstrated. In his chapter Collins Airhihenbuwa begins by noting that as is the case in much of the field of African studies, theories of health interventions are part of a racialised discourse that construct the African herself as a problem from whom no solutions can be expected. The deficit framework of this hegemonic gaze stigmatises the African identity itself before any stigmatisation from disease. Theories of public health are derived from the same paradigm and language of western universality notwithstanding calls to public health professionals to examine the root causes of health problems rather than focusing on the behaviour outcomes at the individual level.

Airhihenbuwa traces the traditions from which public health and health behaviour in Africa grew, specifically the mental health research conducted by pioneers like Professor Adeoye Lambo, traditional healing systems, and the environmental sanitation movement in the US and Europe. The latter came to emphasise the individual action component of environmental sanitation rather than community oriented action, an approach that has dominated public health research in Africa, which has tended to focus on a series of attitudinal and behaviour change models predicated on the individual. Airhihenbuwa argues for models that incorporate questions of cultural identity and belonging. Analysis and theorisation of social cultural infrastructures—the non-physical values that shape the moral and ethical codes by which relationships and expectations in health behaviour are defined, measured, and rewarded—should be more central in African public health research. The chapter outlines an intriguing model that he developed in 1989 and has been refining ever since.

Francis Nyamnjoh introduces us to the field of African communication and development studies, which has witnessed spectacular growth in recent years given the ubiquitous role the media plays: it serves as a vehicle for the transmission of ideas, images, and information; it is a communicative space for public discourse and of the discursive public; it is also an arena of sign-communication and sign-communities; and it constitutes a process for performing social identities and identifying social performances. Needless to say, media forms can fruitfully be differentiated between mass communication media, interpersonal media, and 'small' media. Much of the research and study of African communications systems has focused on the intersections between the media and development, and more recently the media and democratisation. Development as a process of sustainable socioeconomic change, of material societal transformation, has long been a preoccupation of African states, societies, and scholars. The development project has been articulated principally through modernisation theory and its latest incarnation neo-liberalism, and dependency theory and its ideological ally Marxism. Nyamnjoh examines the troubled encounter between communications research and the modernisation paradigm. Except for a brief interlude when socialism held sway in African radical circles, modernisation theory, duly recycled for the post-Cold War era of so-called globalisation, currently dominates development discourse. It has lost none of its Eurocentricism in its equation of modernisation with westernisation, the orientation of its research questions and methods, and the prescriptive thrust of its analyses.

Thus, according to Nyamnjoh, the crass developmentalism of modernisation theory, which provided an alibi for internal repression by African states and exploitation by foreign interests, is back with a vengeance talking at, talking on, talking past and talking to, but not talking with the African masses who are the ostensible beneficiaries of its benevolent interventions. Communications research in African studies betrays these paradigmatic impulses: it is western-centred, tends to neglect the structural constraints for both African communication and development imposed by the international system, and blames African cultures, societies, and states for their backwardness, poverty, and misguided policies, for the underdevelopment of their economies and communication systems. Salvation does not lie, Nyamnjoh contends, in importing ever more elaborate theories from the global North, but in developing alternative communications research that is democratic, participatory, and decentralised, whose questions address the issues of greatest interest to local communities, and whose methods include rather than exclude them, and whose findings reinforce progressive change, not inhibit it.[18]

These five interdisciplinary fields often exist in specific academic programmes. Other interdisciplinary formations tend to be theoretical paradigms and orientations that cut across various disciplines. One of the most influential of these is cultural studies, which emerged in the mid-1960s at the University of Birmingham where a group of neo-Marxist scholars established an interdisciplinary programme to study culture (Hall 1990; Gilroy 2002). Much of their work and subsequent work in the field focused on the popular cultures of working class communities as well as the popular cultures of the rapidly growing marginalised migrant and minority populations. A field with continuously shifting theoretical and methodological interests and frameworks, cultural studies has had close, complex, and critical relations with a series of the more traditional disciplines and other interdisciplinary areas.

But what has not fundamentally changed is the preoccupation with popular cultural activities in Euro-American cities. In other words, Africa was peripheral both in the making and mapping of cultural studies, that is, in the conceptual development of the field and as a site of research. This is the subject of the chapter by Lewis Gordon, which interrogates the place of Africa in cultural studies. Gordon notes that Africa began to enter cultural studies in the 1980s and 1990s through the auspices of postcolonial studies and diaspora studies, and the work of exiled South African literary scholars scattered in a handful of American and British universities. A far more important development than the emerging engagement between Africa and cultural studies, in his view, were the revolutionary developments taking place in contemporary African philosophy, discussed above in this introduction, whose import for African studies, he believes, is likely to be more profound.

Far more influential in African studies has been the related field of postcolonial studies already alluded to in reference to several disciplines. While the influence of postcolonial studies has been most marked among literary scholars, few disciplines in the humanities and social sciences have escaped the insistent breeze of ideas from the 'posts'. The nearly ubiquitous epistemic presence that the 'posts' had achieved by the 1990s provoked intense reaction in African studies. The rejectionists were suspicious of the globalist ambitions of 'post' theorising and cultural critique, and its deflationary discourse of Africa that seemed to glibly dismiss African difference and world-significance by trying to absorb it into the West's self-indulgent modernity with what Kwaku Korang calls its monocentricism, monolingualism, monologism, and monovision. On the other hand, the accommodationists with their cosmopolitan internationalism have sought to Africanise the 'posts', to find an African habitation for it, based on the conviction that Africa is inescapably immersed in the West's material and cultural economy and assimilated into its cognitive and discursive hegemony, thanks to the imperial-colonial intervention.

Korang carefully navigates between the two positions. Through careful and close reading of two scholars, Dennis Ekpo and Kwame Anthony Appiah, he seeks to demonstrate the contexts in which it may be useful or not useful to align 'Africa' with the 'posts'. Korang endorses Appiah's moderate postcolonial perspective over Ekpo's aggressive postmodernist advocacy. The latter offers a trenchant critique of what he regards as the misguided modernist foundations of nationalist/Afrocentric thought, which has reached a performative impasse, from which it can only be liberated by (Western) postmodernism. In contrast, in Appiah's more nuanced posture, the 'posts' ought to facilitate both Africa's interrogation of the world and its interrogation by the world, to translate African difference for the world, not the difference of exceptionalism of the nationalists, but the difference of the same, that Africa is an integral part of modern, transnational culture, that Africa and the West have mutually constituted each other. Appiah (1992, 2004) seeks to rehabilitate an ethical universal, a modernist humanism that is negotiated between world cultures that are contaminated and inscribed with each other. The power of the 'posts' lies in the extent to which they are able to promote such a project, to bring together the Africa-for-the-world and the Africa-for-itself. To achieve this requires that the accommodationist position, Korang insists, be vigilantly self-aware, protected by the armour of a healthy rejectionism.

Conclusion

Clearly, African studies is a complex field in its disciplinary and interdisciplinary configurations. The methodological and theoretical variations among the disciplines and interdisciplines are quite obvious. But there are some overriding similarities in terms of the contexts in which the disciplines and interdisciplines engage Africa, the broad political and social forces that have influenced the construction of African/ist knowledges in the academy. There can be little doubt that the historical development of African studies, or the studies of Africa, was a direct product of the rise of African nationalism and decolonisation, which led to the establishment of new African nation-states and universities. These transformations provided the institutional, intellectual and ideological bases for the emergence of ever larger African scholarly communities and engendered the pressures and need for the production of knowledges about, for, and on Africa that were more relevant to Africa's historic and humanistic conditions and challenges, problems and possibilities, anxieties and aspirations. Another comparable feature among the disciplines and interdisciplines engaged in African studies has been the struggle for intellectual decolonisation and deconstruction. The impulses to strip Eurocentric epistemology that has dominated the construction and organisation of knowledge in the colonial and postcolonial world are evident among all the disciplines and interdisciplines.

Both African and Africanist scholars have been preoccupied, with varying degrees of energy and efficacy, with the need to renegotiate the epistemic terms of knowledge production, to rid the disciplines and interdisciplines of the civilisational and cognitive conceits of Europe and Eurocentricism. Obviously some disciplines have been more successful than others, the humanities such as history and literature perhaps more than the social sciences such as economics and political science, and among the interdisciplines women studies more so than cultural studies. In so far as knowledge production is fundamentally a social practice conditioned by the always changing configurations and circuits of complex and sometimes contradictory political, economic, and cultural dynamics, there can be little doubt that the current disciplinary and interdisciplinary constitution of African studies, whether on the continent or abroad, will change. The challenge for committed African and Africanist scholars is to ensure that we continue to struggle for the production, organisation, dissemination, and consumption of knowledges that enhance, rather than undermine, Africa's possibilities.

Notes

1. For my review of this book see Zeleza (1997: Chapter 22).
2. Another important US study is Guyer (1996).
3. According to Horn (1986: 428) the term 'interdisciplinarity' was first used in a sociological article published in 1937.
4. See the sections on the social sciences, humanities and the arts, and the natural sciences in Newell (1998: 299-444).

5. 'In the beginning', writes Kathleen Sullivan (2002: 1217), 'there was law. Then came law-and. Law and society, law and economics, law and history, law and literature, law and philosophy, law and finance, statistics, game theory, psychology, anthropology, linguistics, critical theory, cultural studies, political theory, political science, organizational behavior, to name a few'. This is a cause for celebration, not lament, for increased interdisciplinarity in legal knowledge improves the teaching of law and the production of better lawyers.

6. See the sections on some of these fields in Newell (1998: 447-526).

7. For a good guide on organising interdisciplinary teaching and learning see Klein and Doty (1994).

8. This is quite evident in the literature. For a sample, see the short idiosyncratic responses by forty-two scholars who responded to a call from the Journal of the Modern Language Association, *PMLA* 111, 2 (1996): 271-282, for comments on the impact of interdisciplinarity in literary studies.

9. The term 'blurring' is derived from the influential essay by Clifford Geertz (1998), 'Blurred Genres: Refiguring Social Thought', in which he noted the explosion of genre mixing in the social sciences and the turn from physical analogies to symbolic ones, including the analogies of game, drama, and text.

10. See, for example, the interesting case made for Rhetoric to learn from History by Elizabeth Ervin (1993) and for the departmentalisation of women studies made by Judith Allen and Sally Kitch (1998).

11. Literary studies expanded their intellectual horizons by incorporating findings and appropriating texts from philosophy, anthropology, linguistics, psychology, and history some of which have been abandoned in their original disciplines, which gave the field pre-eminence among the humanities in the 1980s and 1990s (Guillory 1994; Gallagher 1997; and Zeleza 2003: 260-4). As for my own discipline, history, the interdisciplinary turn in professional historical studies, argues Horn and Ritter (1986: 427) can be attributed to 'their gradual tendency to become increasingly comprehensive in scope and more experimental and eclectic in conception and method'. This comprehensiveness refers to both temporal and spatial coverage, and methodological eclecticism to the fact that historians routinely make use of results, theories, and analyses from other disciplines depending on their thematic focus.

12. The corollary of this is what prevents interdisciplinarity. The obstacles can be epistemological, institutional, psychosociological, and cultural. See Kochelmans (1998: 86). Stanley Fish believes that arguments for interdisciplinarity are basically political, not epistemological. Epistemologically, 'being interdisciplinary is more than hard to do: it is impossible to do' (Fish 1998: 244).

13. She quotes a humorous ode to the disciplines: 'Speaking of ranking the various disciplines—/Politicians think they are Economists./Economists think they are Social Scientists./Social Scientists think they are Social Psychologists./Psychologists think they are Biologists./Biologists think they are Organic Chemists./Organic Chemists think they are Physical Chemists./Physical Chemists think they are Physicists./Physicists think they are Mathematicians./Mathematicians think they are God./God ... ummm ... so happens God is an Astronomer'.

14. The import of this can lead to diametrically opposed conclusions as seen in the debate over interdisciplinary research in women studies. For example, Allen and Kitch (1998: 281) believe this can be overcome by establishing doctoral programmes in women studies that will train a new cohort of faculty, who will carry forward the mission 'to develop integrative, synthesizing, erudite, boundary-crossing, comparative, and interrogative problem-focused scholarship'. In their view, women's studies scholarship is multidisciplinary rather than interdisciplinary as reflected in the nature of the dominant journals in the field and the tendency towards

specialisation and 'disciplinary drift' in which gender is added or women's studies reverts back to disciplinary frameworks, trends that are reinforced by structural barriers rooted in conflicting mandates for women studies and lack of institutional legitimation, which departmentalisation and graduate programmes would help overcome. On the other hand, Susan Friedman (1998: 312) opposes doctoral programmes in women studies on the grounds that there is a contradiction 'inherent in training graduate students to do something that the faculty themselves do not and may not even want to do'. She believes disciplinary grounding remains essential for strong interdisciplinarity, and that women studies suffers from having too many methodologies to offer coherent doctoral programmes. There are also pragmatic reasons concerning the limited employment prospects of graduates of such programmes and budgetary considerations.

15. The process of designing interdisciplinary courses involves assembling an interdisciplinary team, selecting a topic, identifying the appropriate disciplines, developing the subtext or analytical framework, structuring the course, selecting readings, designing assignments, and preparing the syllabus. Interdisciplinary teaching requires several crucial forms of support, effective advising and assessment, as well as substantial support from interdisciplinary leaders including administrators, advisors, faculty members, and students. See the following instructive texts representing thinking about interdisciplinary pedagogy from the perspective of the late 1970s, early 1990s and early 2000s: Mayville (1978), Newell (1994), and Haynes (2002).

16. Davidson and Goldberg's 'Manifesto for the Humanities in a Technological Age' is a heartfelt, if desperate, plea for the continued relevance of the humanities, which they argue are even more necessary than ever to understand the value, meaning and significance of the rapid and vast developments in science and technology and the challenging times in which we live. Only the humanities can make sense of these complex transformations because they are the repositories of historical scholarship, a relational view of society, and creativity. They serve as conscience and memory of intellectual and social life and the academy itself, have been the principal and principled site of diversity and diversification, privilege communication and critical policy making, and they promote linguistic and intercultural literacy.

17. For Ngugi wa Thiong'o (1986, 1993, 2005) it has been a permanent preoccupation.

18. Nyamnjoh gives a fuller treatment of these issues in his book (Nyamnjoh 2005).

References

Allen, J. A. and S. L. Kitch, 1998, 'Disciplined by Disciplines? The Need for an Interdisciplinary Research Mission in Women's Studies', *Feminist Studies* 24 (2): 275-299.

Amadiume, I., 1987, *Male Daughters, Female Husbands*, London: Zed.

Appiah, K.A., 1992, *In My Father's House. Africa in the Philosophy of Culture*, New York: Oxford University Press.

Appiah, K.A., 2004, *Cosmopolitanism: Ethics in a World of Strangers*, Princeton, NJ: Princeton University Press.

Barash, D. P., 2005, 'C.P. Snow: Bridging the Two-Cultures Divide', *The Chronicle of Higher Education. The Chronicle Review* November 25: B10.

Bates, R. H., V. Y. Mudimbe, J. O'Barr, eds., 1993, *Africa and the Disciplines. The Contributions of Africa to the Social Sciences and Humanities*, Chicago and London: University of Chicago Press.

Bauer, H. H., 1990, 'Barriers against Interdisciplinarity: Implications for Studies of Science, Technology, and Society (STS)', *Science, Technology, & Human Values* 15 (1): 105-119.

Bechtel, W., 1998, 'The Nature of Scientific Integration', in W. H. Newell, ed., *Interdisciplinarity: Essays from the Literature*, New York: College Entrance Examination Board, 399-426.

Benson, T. C., 1998, 'Five Arguments against Interdisciplinary Studies', in W. H. Newell, ed., *Interdisciplinarity: Essays from the Literature*, New York: College Entrance Examination Board, 103-108.

Blyden, Edward Wilmot, 1887, *Christianity, Islam and the Negro Race*, Edinburgh: Edinburgh University Press.

Byrne, R., 2005a, 'Humanities Scholars Debate Whether Anyone Is Listening to Them', *The Chronicle of Higher Education. The Chronicle Review* May 20: A 15.

Byrne, R., 2005b, 'Scholars Mull Their Separation from the Mainstream', *The Chronicle of Higher Education. The Chronicle Review* January 7: A31.

Coats, A. W., 1985, 'What is Economic History?', *History Today*, February: 41-43.

Daunton, M. J., 1985, 'What is Economic History?', *History Today*, February: 28-30.

Davidson, C. N., 1999, 'What if Scholars in the Humanities Worked Together, in a Lab?', *The Chronicle of Higher Education*, May 28: B4.

Davidson, C. N. and D .T. Goldberg, 2004, 'A Manifesto for the Humanities in a Technological Age', *The Chronicle of Higher Education. The Chronicle Review* February 13: B7.

Davis, L. J., 2005, 'The Perils of Academic Ignorance', *The Chronicle of Higher Education. The Chronicle Review* May 20: B13.

Dedieu, J.-P., 2002, 'US Exit, African Voices and Francophone Loyalty', *African Issues* 30 (1): 66-9.

Ervin, E., 1993, 'Interdisciplinarity or "An Elaborate Edifice Built on Sand"? Rethinking Rhetoric's Place', *Rhetoric Review* 12 (1): 84-105.

Eyoh, D., 1996, 'From Economic Crisis to Political Liberalization: Pitfalls of the New Political Sociology for Africa', *African Studies Review* 39 (3): 43-80.

Feldman, G. D., 1986, 'German Economic History', *Central European History*, 19: 174-185.

Fish, S., 1998, 'Being Interdisciplinary Is So Very Hard to Do', in W. H. Newell, ed., *Interdisciplinarity: Essays from the Literature*, New York: College Entrance Examination Board, 239-249.

Foucault, M., 1972, *The Archaeology of Knowledge*, Trans. by A. M. Sheridan Smith, New York: Pantheon.

Foucault, M., 1978, *Discipline and Punish: The Birth of Prison*, Trans. by Alan Sheridan, New York: Pantheon.

Friedman, S. S., 1998, '(Inter)Disciplinarity and the Question of the Women's Studies Ph.D', *Feminist Studies* 24 (2): 301-325.

Fuller, S., 1998, 'The Position: Interdisciplinarity as Interpenetration', in W. H. Newell, ed., *Interdisciplinarity: Essays from the Literature*, New York: College Entrance Examination Board, 123-149.

Fyfe, C., ed., 1976, *African Studies since 1945*, London: Longman.

Gaff, J. G., 1998, 'Avoiding the Potholes: Strategies for Reforming General Education', in W. H. Newell, ed., *Interdisciplinarity: Essays from the Literature*, New York: College Entrance Examination Board, 153-170.

Gallagher, C., 1997, 'The History of Literary Criticism', *Daedalus* 126 (1): 133-153.

Garber, M., 2001, 'Coveting Your Neighbor's Discipline', *The Chronicle of Higher Education. The Chronicle Review* January 12: B7.

Geertz, C., 1998 [1980], 'Blurred Genres: The Refiguration of Social Thought', in W. H. Newell, ed., *Interdisciplinarity: Essays from the Literature*, New York: College Entrance Examination Board, 225-237.

Gidjunis, J., 2004, 'Interdisciplinary Research Urged', *The Chronicle of Higher Education. The Chronicle Review* December 3: A25.

Gilroy, P., 2002, 'Cultural Studies and the Crisis in Britain's Universities', *The Chronicle of Higher Education. The Chronicle Review* July 26: B20.

Guillory, J., 1994, *Cultural Capital: The Problem of Literary Canon Formation*, Chicago: University of Chicago Press.

Gunn, G., 1998, 'Interdisciplinary Studies', in W. H. Newell, ed., *Interdisciplinarity: Essays from the Literature*, New York: College Entrance Examination Board, 251-271.

Guyer, J. I. with the assistance of A. M. Virmani and A. Kemp, 1996, *African Studies in the United States: A Perspective*, Atlanta, Ga.: African Studies Association Press.

Hall, S., 1990, 'The Emergence of Cultural Studies and the Crisis of the Humanities', *October* 53 (Summer): 11-23.

Haynes, C., ed., 2002, *Innovations in Interdisciplinary Teaching*, Westport, CT: Oryx Press.

Hopkins, A. G., 1985, 'What is Economic History?', *History Today* 35 (February): 41-2.

Hopkins, A. G., 1980, 'Africa's Age of Improvement', *History in Africa* 7:141-160.

Horn, T. C .R. and H. Ritter, 1986, 'Interdisciplinary History: A Historiographical Review', *The History Teacher* 19 (3): 427-448.

Hountondji, P., 1997, 'Introduction: Recentering Africa', in P. Hountondji, ed., 1-39, *Endogenous Knowledge: Research Trails*, Dakar: CODESRIA Book Series.

Hunt, L., 1994, 'The Virtues of Interdisciplinarity', *Eighteenth-Century Studies* 28 (1): 1-7.

Hursh, B., P. Haas, and M. Moore, 1998, 'An Interdisciplinary Model to Implement General Education', in W. H. Newell, ed., *Interdisciplinarity: Essays from the Literature*, New York: College Entrance Examination Board, 35-49.

Hutcheon, L. and M. Hutcheon, 2001, 'A Convergence of Marriage: Collaboration and Interdisciplinarity', *PMLA* 116 (5): 1364-1376.

Klein, J., 1998, 'Blurring , Cracking, and Crossing: Permeation and the Fracturing of Discipline', in W. H. Newell, ed., *Interdisciplinarity: Essays from the Literature*, New York: College Entrance Examination Board, 273-295.

Klein, J. T. and W. G. Doty, 1994, *Interdisciplinary Studies Today*, San Francisco: Jossey-Bass Publishers.

Klein, J. T. and W. H. Newell, 1998, 'Advancing Interdisciplinary Studies', in W. H. Newell, ed., *Interdisciplinarity: Essays from the Literature*, New York: College Entrance Examination Board, 3-22.

Kockelmans, J. J., 1998, 'Why Interdisciplinarity', in W. H. Newell, ed., *Interdisciplinarity: Essays from the Literature*, New York: College Entrance Examination Board, 67-96.

Lima, M., 2006 (forthcoming), *Let the Drums Sound: The Teaching of African History*.

Lyon, A., 1992, 'Interdisciplinarity: Giving up Territory', *College English* 54 (6): 681-693.

Mafeje, A., 1998a, Anthropology in Post-Independence Africa: End of an Era and the Problem of Self-Redefinition, *African Sociological Review* 2 (1): 1-43.

Mafeje, A., 1998b, 'Conversations and Confrontations with My Reviewers', *African Sociological Review* 2 (2): 95-107.

Manning, P., 1989, 'The Prospects for African Economic History: Is Today Included in the Long Run?', *African Studies Review* 32: 49-62.

Martin, W. G. and M. O. West, eds., 1999, *Out of One, Many Africas: Reconstructing the Study and Meaning of Africa*, Urbana and Chicago: University of Illinois Press.

Mayville, W. V., 1978, *Interdisciplinarity: The Mutable Paradigm*, Washington, D.C.: American Association for Higher Education.

Mazrui, A. A., 1986, *The Africans: A Triple Heritage*, Boston: Little, Brown.

McKeon, M., 1994, 'The Origins of Interdisciplinary Studies', *Eighteenth-Century Studies* 28 (1): 17-28.

Mignolo, W. D., 2000, 'The Role of the Humanities in the Corporate University', *PMLA* 115 (5): 1238-1245.

Miller, J. C., 1999, 'Presidential Address: History and Africa/Africa and History', *The American Historical Review* 104 (1): 1-32.

Mkandawire, T., 1997, 'Globalization and Africa's Unfinished Agenda', *Macalaster International* 7: 71-107.

Mkandawire, T., 2005, 'African intellectuals and nationalism', in T. Mkandawire, ed., *African Intellectuals: Rethinking Politics, Language, Gender and Development*, Dakar and London: CODESRIA and Zed Books.

Mkandawire, T., 2005, 'Maladjusted African Economies and Globalization', *Africa Development* 30 (1 & 2): 1-33.

Mkandawire, T., 2006, 'The Spread of Economic Doctrines in Postcolonial Africa', Ms.

Newell, W. H., 1994, 'Designing Interdisciplinary Courses', in Klein, J. T. and W. G. Doty, eds., *Interdisciplinary Studies Today*, San Francisco: Jossey-Bass Publishers, 35-51.

Newell, W. H., 1998a, 'The Case for Interdisciplinary Studies: Response to Professor Benson's Five Arguments', in W. H. Newell, ed., *Interdisciplinarity: Essays from the Literature*, New York: College Entrance Examination Board, 109-122.

Newell, W. H., 1998b, 'Interdisciplinary Curriculum Development', in W. H. Newell, ed., *Interdisciplinarity: Essays from the Literature*, New York: College Entrance Examination Board, 51-96.

Newell, W. H., 1998c, 'Academic Disciplines and Undergraduate Interdisciplinary Education: Lessons From the School of Interdisciplinary Studies at Miami University, Ohio', in W. H. Newell, ed., *Interdisciplinarity: Essays from the Literature*, New York: College Entrance Examination Board, 213-224.

Ngugi wa Thiong'o, 1993, *Moving the Centre: The Struggle for Cultural Freedoms*, London: James Currey.

Ngugi wa Thiong'o, 1986, *Decolonizing the Mind: The Politics of Language in African Literature*, London: James Currey.

Ngugi wa Thiong'o, 2006, 'Europhone or African Memory: The Challenge of the Pan-Africanist Intellectual in the Era of Globalization', in T. Mkandawire, ed., *African Intellectuals: Rethinking Politics, Language, Gender and Development*, Dakar and London: CODESRIA and Zed Books, 155-164.

Njubi, Nesbitt, F., 2002, 'African Intellectuals in the Belly of the Beast: Migration, Identity, and the Politics of Exile', *African Issues* 30 (1): 70-75.

Nkrumah, Kwame, 1964, *Consciencism: Philosophy and Ideology for Decolonization*, New York: Monthly Review Press.

Nyamnjoh, F. B., 2005, *Africa's Media, Democracy and the Politics of Belonging*, London: Zed Books.

Oyewumi, O., 1997, *The Invention of Women: Making African Sense of Western Gender Discourses*, Minneapolis: University of Minnesota.

Priman, S. L., J. P. Collins, S. Lowes and A. F. Michaels, 2005, 'Collaborative Efforts: Promoting Interdisciplinary Scholars', *The Chronicle of Higher Education. The Chronicle Review* February 11: B15.

Rodney, W., 1982, *How Europe Underdeveloped Africa*, Washington, DC: Howard University Press.

Schleifer, R., 1997, 'Disciplinarity and Collaboration in the Sciences and Humanities', *College English* 59 (4): 438-452.

Shumway, D., 1999, 'Disciplinarity, Corporatization, and the Crisis: A Dystopian Narrative', *The Journal of the Midwest Modern Language Association* 32 (2/3): 2-18.

Shumway, D. R. and E. Messer-Davidow, 1991, 'Disciplinarity: An Introduction', *Poetics Today* 12 (2): 201-225.

Stember, M., 1998, 'Advancing the Social Sciences Through the Interdisciplinary Enterprise', in W. H. Newell, ed., *Interdisciplinarity: Essays from the Literature*, New York: College Entrance Examination Board, 337-350.

Sullivan, K. M., 2002, 'Forward: Interdisciplinarity', *Migration Law Review* 100 (6): 1217-1226.

Vansina, J., 1993, 'UNESCO and African Historiography', *History in Africa* 20: 337-352.

Wasserstrom, J. N., 2006, 'Expanding the I-Word', *The Chronicle of Higher Education. The Chronicle Review* January 20: B5.

Wissoker, K., 2000, 'Negotiating a Passage Between Disciplinary Borders', *The Chronicle of Higher Education. The Chronicle Review* April 14: B4.

Zeleza, P. T., 1997, *Manufacturing African Studies and Crises*, Dakar: CODESRIA.

Zeleza, P. T., 2002, 'The Challenges of Writing African Economic History', in George Bond and Nigel Gibson, eds., *Issues in African Studies*, Boulder, Co.: Westview Press, 59-84.

Zeleza, P. T., 2003, *Rethinking Africa's Globalization, Volume 1: The Intellectual Challenges*, Trenton, NJ: Africa World Press.

Zeleza, P. T., 2004, 'The African Academic Diaspora in the United States and Africa: The Challenges of Productive Engagement', *Comparative Studies of South Asia, Africa, and the Middle East* 24 (1): 265-278.

Zeleza, P. T., 2005a, 'Rewriting the African Diaspora: Beyond the Black Atlantic', *African Affairs* 104 (1): 35-68.

Zeleza, P. T., 2005b, 'Banishing the Silences: Towards the Globalization of African History', Paper presented at the 11th General Assembly of the Council for Development of Social Science Research in Africa (CODESRIA), Maputo, Mozambique, 6–10 December.

Zeleza, P. T., 2005c, 'History, Economic', in Maryanne Cline Horowitz, ed., *New Dictionary of the History of Ideas*, Volume 3, New York: Charles Scribner & Sons, 1002-1005.

Zeleza, P. T. and A. Olukoshi, eds., 2004, *African Universities in the Twenty-First Century*, 2 vols., Dakar: CODESRIA.

I

The Disciplines and African Studies

Chapter 1

Anthropology and the Race of/for Africa[1]

Jemima Pierre

How do embedded assumptions of racial (not racist) language work in the literary enterprise that hopes and sometimes claims to be 'humanistic'? When, in a race-conscious culture, is that lofty goal approximated?—Toni Morrison (1992)

... while liberal Euro-American anthropologists and their kith and kin in the ex-colonies can consciously deconstruct colonial anthropology, it is doubtful if they can deracialize the original idea of anthropology as the study of the 'other'.—Archie Mafeje (1998b)

I expect a great artist ... who is interested in Africa, not to make life difficult for us. Why do this? Why make our lives more difficult?—Chinua Achebe (2003).[2]

The three statements above reflect a set of ongoing and intense critiques of representations and conceptualisations of Africa, Africans, and people of African descent in literary and ethnographic texts. Toni Morrison and Chinua Achebe, in particular, have produced two well-known texts exposing the signs, strategies, and codes used in European and US literary imaginings and representations of the African Other (Achebe 1988; Morrison 1992). In all major texts in the US literary canon, Morrison argues, there is an 'Africanist' presence that is crucial to the construction of 'Americanness'. This trope of 'Africanism' is specific and acute, and represents the 'denotative and connotative blackness that African peoples have come to signify, as well as the entire range of views, assumptions, readings, and misreadings that accompany Eurocentric learning about these people' (1992:6-7). Achebe describes Joseph Conrad's *Heart of Darkness* as a work that celebrates the 'dehumanization of Africa and Africans' and wonders whether such a novel, 'which depersonalizes a portion of the human race, can be called a great work of art' (1988: 12). Significantly, both authors point to the violence of language that, according to Morrison, 'can powerfully evoke and enforce hidden signs of racial superiority, cultural hegemony, and dismissive "othering" of people' (1992: x). Archie Mafeje, an African anthropologist, is also well known for his unrelenting challenge of the Western 'Africanist' enterprise and has been engaged in a decades-long project of advocating the 'complete deconstruction of anthropology as a discipline' (1998a). For Mafeje, the question is whether anthropology, a discipline 'founded on "alterity"' and particularly known for its intimate relationship to trope the African Other, 'can escape being racist' (1998: 2). Taken together, the epigraphs above reflect the general concern with the seemingly intractable nature of African exceptionalism and the relationship of that exceptionalism to 'racialized knowledge production' (Goldberg 1993).[3] It is no wonder, then, that the critiques work to challenge the very foundations of knowledge making about Africa.

Yet, unlike those of Morrison and Achebe, Mafeje's concerns, which echo a number of other African anthropologists (Magubane 1971; Mamdani 1990; Rigby 1996), have not managed to elicit much thoughtful and sustained engagement. Rather, the general US/Western Africanist response seem to conjure up an unsettling image: picture a glass room with a group of people (the critiqued) inside confidently and intently engaged in its own conversation while it notices the frantic gestures, but does not hear the protests of the group (the critics) stranded outside. I suggest that there is another aspect to the story that is also significant, but that I will address at a later date. What does it mean to think that the tone of the critiques—simultaneously angry, urgent, and often distressing—has everything to do with the fact that the scholars are Africans (or people of African descent)?[4] Taking this and other issues surrounding this important subject as a point of departure, I attempt, in this essay, to enter into the fray, so to speak. I want to show that the critique levelled at anthropology by African scholars in particular—that the discipline's 'Africa' contin-ues to serve as a foil to Europe—remains salient. Although my strong inclination, in this discussion, is to echo the sentiments of Mafeje and his colleagues by challenging *in toto* Western knowledge production and the epistemological pitfalls of Africanist anthropology, I will restrict myself to a more modest aim.

This essay argues that anthropology's often unwitting construction of African exceptionalism can be better understood through an examination of the discipline's relationship to the concept of race and the processes of racialisation through which it was constructed and practised. My argument is partly informed by another set of critiques that has emerged in the past decade: anthropology's general reluctance to address race as a category of analysis that refers to a set of socio-historical proc-esses distinct from—though interdependent with—the categories of 'culture' or 'ethnicity,' and the discipline's penchant for engaging 'cultural difference' while re-maining unable to account for persistent (global) racial inequality (Harrison 1995, 1999, 2002; Shanklin 1998, 2000). The very foundations of the anthropological project are, after all, based on conceptualisations of race that encompass both late nineteenth century notions of 'primitive differentness' and twentieth century anti-racist cultural relativism (Stocking 1993; see also Baker 1998; Harrison 1995). My analysis will extend the theoretical and practical reach of this legacy to explore how race structures the current anthropological project itself, fundamentally shaping the discipline's epistemology and methodology. Consequently, I will show that processes of racialisation continue to underpin ethnographic practice and are manifest in two ways: (i) the deployment of an ambiguous notion of 'culture' that continues to have racial underpinnings; and (ii) the often unsuspecting role of Africanist anthropology in naturalising African cultural difference. In other words, the seeming acceptance of cultural difference as given without the acknowledgement of the subtleties of race implied in this difference, authorise ethnographic practice that reinforces Africa's (global) marking as the site of racial otherness.

In what follows, I begin with a discussion of the theoretical shift in anthropology from a focus on concepts of 'racial' differences to one of 'cultural' differences. Exploring this shift is important because it exposes the contemporary commonsense slippage among the terms; or, more specifically, it affirms the embeddedness of race in prevailing anthropological 'cultural' conceptions. The bulk of the chapter will examine the relationship between Africanist ethnographies and the construction of African cultural exceptionalism. I will use a few texts to demonstrate the ways in which notions of race and racialised difference are articulated in discussions and representations of cultural difference. My goal here is not to provide a comprehensive review of all Africanist ethnographic texts, nor is it to broadly condemn and dismiss all these texts as engaging in this racialising process. Rather, my randomly selected texts serve to show how, even in the most minute and unintentional ways, some Africanist ethnography continue to Other in very systematic ways. I am particularly interested in how the terms of anthropological engagement with Africa work to become some of the most powerful sites of racialisation. These terms, I argue, consist not only of various categorisations of African societies and peoples, but also the way we conceive and construct our research on such communities and, more importantly, the language we use to describe African phenomena. I end the essay by contextualising this discussion outside of the narrow confines of academic (anthropological/Africanist) discourse and critique. With notions of African racial and cultural difference so deeply enshrined in Western institutions, and in light of global relations of race and power, our work can be implicated in the continued socio-political and economic marginalisation of African peoples; it can indeed serve to 'make [African] lives more difficult' (Achebe 2003).

The Race-ing of Difference: A Partial Trajectory

> In the nineteenth century, anthropologists used an explicit racist ideology to make colored people into different human beings than white people. Later, when scientific racism became less popular, anthropologists achieved almost the same result with the concepts of culture and cultural relativism (Willis Jr. 1972).

Much is known about anthropology's role in the development of a global discourse of racialised understandings of human diversity. Nevertheless, despite the discipline's 'central place in the construction and reconstruction of race as both an intellectual device and a social reality', anthropologists have hardly systematically dealt with the concept in the past few decades (Harrison 1995: 47, 1999; see also Baker 1998,

Shanklin 1994, 1999; Visweswaran 1998). The reasons stem from various movements both within the discipline and in the wider global context. Specifically, the concept of race fell out of favour with anthropologists, among others, in the middle of the twentieth century as its ethnocentric and deterministic (biological) qualities became untenable. Although it is not the object of this essay to recount the entire history of the idea of race,[5] it is important to demonstrate how closely associated anthropology's early professionalisation was with the racial classification of human difference (Baker 1998; Haller 1971; Hannaford 1996; Hudson 1996; Malik 1996; Stocking 1968, 1993; Smedley 1993). This biography has two significant features. First, the racialised understandings of human difference that emerged in the eighteenth century 'took shape under the social and intellectual forces of the time—an expanding imperial order, a new science, and the creation of a new, secular myth of human origin and human nature' (Hudson 1996: 259). Second, by the turn of the nineteenth century, the classic pattern of racial thinking was the idea of race as an 'integrated physical, linguistic, and cultural totality' (Stocking 1993:15). Indeed, the key constructs of 'culture' and 'evolution'—imbued with 'biomoral assumptions'—set the terms of early anthropological inquiry about the natural history of human variation (Harrison 1995:50). Ideas about race, then, have not only always meant more than just physical difference, but have also operated along with what was described as 'culture'. Between 1860 and 1900, in fact, it was these two classificatory devices—race and culture—that were used to describe all differences between human beings. Whereas race was a well-developed concept in the natural sciences (anthropology's predecessor), culture was not. Yet, as analytical constructs, the two were variously and interchangeably used to cover all explanations of human difference (Shanklin 1994:32-33).

The development of the concept of race coincides with European expansion and the attendant rise of racial capitalism (Robinson 1983) and colonialism. Anthropology's integral and dubious relationship to this history has been firmly established and consistently critiqued (Asad 1973; Gough 1968; Mafeje 1976; Magubane 1971; Stauder 1993). The subjection of whole populations to invalid forms of hierarchical classification based on presumed biological difference demanded 'scientific' justification, justification that anthropology, as the emergent 'science of races' and unique among humanist and scientific fields, could provide. Africa's particular history within both European exploitation and anthropology is instructive. Well before the formal doctrine of 'race', Africans were quickly losing their local and diverse identities by the homogenising impulse of the slave trade: Africans became 'racialised' (i.e., they became 'African' and 'Black') through a uniform system of debasement (Hudson 1996). As the racialising techniques took hold and 'racial science' flourished with anthropology at the helm, the meaning of the concept of race itself was to be riddled with contradictions. George Stocking has shown us, for example, that several historically distinguishable traditions of racial thought in anthropology—ethnological, Lamarckian, polygenist, and evolutionist—all converged to form an integrated idea of race that began to emerge in the eighteenth century and that persists to the twenty-first (1993:6). By the onset of formal colonialism on the

African continent, race became the term extraordinaire used to interpret perceived social and biological differences among subjected populations. Mental capacity, social organisation, behaviour, and aesthetics all were understood to operate within an innate, biological realm of race—a realm that ranked white-skinned Europeans at the top of civilisation and black-skinned Africans as the epitome of the most extreme variant of racial alterity (Harrison 1995: 51). While most historians of the race concept have stressed its relation to European political thought, race was, to a much greater extent, 'the expression of attitudes towards dark-skinned, and especially black-skinned peoples' (Stocking 1982[1968]: 36).[6]

Both monogenists and polygenists, regardless of their conceptual differences, assumed the natural superiority of whites and the inherent inferiority of blacks, the opposing poles of the global racial hierarchy (Harrison 1995:51; Curtin 1964). The scientific endeavour to prove this as well as the political reality of racial slavery and, later, racial colonialism, allowed the continued ranking of human differences. Notions of 'nation' and 'culture' were used alongside the concept of race to promote European superiority. Hudson argues that the terms 'nation' and 'race' often implied one another—in terms of their biological meanings—until the turbulent theoretical debates about the nature of race brought about a distinction between the two. Enlightenment scholars came to define 'nation' as a heritage of social customs and beliefs (often identified with a printed heritage) and race specifically denoted visible differences in physiology (Hudson 1996). The term 'nation' became reserved solely for Europeans. Since late-eighteenth century travel writers and historians also dismissed 'national' variations among Africans as insignificant, the general feeling was that the uncivilised did not merit the honorific title of 'nation' (Hudson 1996: 257). The term 'tribe', was thus taken from its originally specialised meaning in the Bible and reconfigured in ethnographic terms to replace 'nation' in descriptions of so-called 'savage' peoples (1996:258; see also Amselle 1990:7). Over the period of a century:

> ... 'race' gradually mutated from its original sense of a people or single nation, linked by origin, to its later sense of a biological subdivision of the human species. 'Nation' began to be used as a subdivision of 'race' or, even more commonly, as a term denominating a cultural or political group of a certain sophistication (Hudson 1996:258).

There was, moreover, the correlation between the hierarchisation of races and the hierarchisation of territories. In other words, the racialisation of people from 'Africa' into 'Black' and 'tribal' had everything to do with the link between identity and place. Race, then, was not just about cultural/behavioural and mental difference; it was also about geographic and time distance/difference. The racialised 'tribe' was only natural in particular locations, isolated in its particular spatiotemporal context. In this evolutionary fresco, various human groups all were on a path that traversed geographical, spatial, and temporal terrain, a 'racial itinerary' of sorts: from social organisation founded on 'peoples', 'clans', and 'tribes' (i.e. savagery, barbarism) to those founded on territory, the state, and the 'nation' (i.e. civilisation) (Amselle 1990:9).

As it provided the necessary data—such as meticulous studies of brain size, among other things—anthropology rapidly became institutionalised as the discipline supporting biological human variation and white supremacy. By the end of the nineteenth century, within the context of a 'Darwinian milieu', a racio-cultural hierarchy had been scientifically established where:

> ... civilized men, the highest product of social evolution, were large-brained white men, and only large-brained white men, the highest products of organic evolution, were civilized. The assumption of white superiority was certainly not original with Victorian evolutionists; yet the interrelation of the theories of cultural and organic evolution, with their implicit hierarchy of race, gave it a new rationale (Stocking 1982 [1968]: 122).

This evolutionary picture—where savagery, dark skin, and a small brain represented an integrated view of 'primitive' and 'uncivilised' behaviour and social organisation—represented the full spectrum of the racialised nature of the science of human variation. Franz Boas's intervention, then, came at a crucial time. His critique of evolutionism was specifically a rejection of its racial determinism. In fact, it is exactly the interrelated patterns of race, culture, and evolution that defined Boas's significance.

Boas's crusade against racial determinism effected a 'radical break with the assumptions of racist categorization and ranking' (Sanjek 1994: 5). The Boasian[7] impact was in 'reorienting anthropological thinking and in establishing culture, not race, as the key object of anthropological study' (Malik 1996:151). This intervention was important given that, in the early 1900s, the belief in polygenesis, racial colonialism throughout Africa and Asia, racial segregation in the US, and the eugenics movement, all worked to propagate the idea that race accounted for differences in the mental and social capabilities of human beings.[8] The Boasian influence worked in two specific ways: first, by orchestrating a shift in racial theory that distinguished race from culture and language, and also by positing that racial hierarchies were scientifically untenable (Baker 1998: 100; see also Degler 1991; Malik 1996; Stocking 1968; 1992); and second, by the ceaseless public articulation of the concept of 'culture' in the early 1900s by Boas's intellectual descendants and their sympathisers.

In response to biological determinism, Boasians stressed the insignificance of racial (i.e., 'biological') difference, and posited 'culture' as more important for understanding human societies. Culture was 'learned behaviour, socially transmitted and cumulative over time', and was the paramount determinant of human behaviour instead of race (Amselle 1990:19). In addition, whereas nineteenth century anthropology produced comparative, historical work with a central project of delineating the stages of human development, early twentieth century Boasian scholars denied that some social structures were superior to others and sought to demonstrate instead how particular (cultural) groups were constituted (Risjord 2000). They rejected assumptions about racial achievement and posited alternative cultural ones. Culture came to define what was perceived as racial human difference.

The effort to move away from perceived racist judgments about the status of different groups necessitated both a near-exclusive focus on 'cultural' factors influencing human difference, and active and public distancing from 'racial' conceptualisations. Yet, the move against racial determinism did not completely distance many of the Boasians (and their counterparts in Europe) from a belief in the idea of biological racial difference (Amselle 1990; Stocking 1968; Visweswaran 1998). Indeed, the shift from racial to cultural explanations of difference was not necessarily a case of substantiated theories being unambiguously disproved and overturned by new conclusive evidence. Rather, 'it was the case that culture and history could account for human differences as well, if not better, than race and biology ... the shift from "race" to "culture" was largely painless and fuelled by ideological commitment rather than scientific knowledge' (Malik 1996: 159). Cultural theories were perceived as more egalitarian at a time of pronounced global racial injustice. Hence, historical and political imperatives determined that certain segments of social sciences choose between racial determinism and the vague sociobiological explanations that attempted to contradict it: in effect, to choose between race and culture. In anthropology culture provided a 'functionally equivalent substitute for the older idea of "race temperament"' (Stocking 1968: 265). It used non-biological terms to explain all the same phenomena. Most importantly, this all happened quite simply and naturally. For the Boasians:

> All that was necessary to make the adjustment ... was the *substitution of a word*. For 'race' read 'culture' or 'civilisation', for 'racial heredity' read 'cultural heritage', and the change had taken place. From ... 'racial instincts' to an ambiguous 'centuries of racial experience' to a purely cultural 'centuries of tradition' was a fairly easy transition... (Stocking 1982[1968]: 265-6; my emphasis).

The shift from race to culture, therefore, was nothing more than *a shift in terms* (Amselle 1990; Malik 1996; Stocking 1968; Visweswaran 1998). And, despite their liberal politics, Boasians did not relinquish the value of the scientific study of race, and they avoided clarifying, against the racial determinist position, whether all races were actually equal. A.L. Krober, a Boas student, even revealed that he was 'agnostic' about such issues. What he stressed, however, was that, in light of contemporary racial politics of the time, racial equality (real or not) was *a necessary assumption* for cultural anthropology (Stocking 1982[1968]: 268; see also Malik 1996: 160-161).

In fact, the culture concept was never specifically defined; instead, it was what Michel-Rolph Trouillot calls an 'anti-concept' (2003). Culture was 'everything race was not, and race was seen to be what culture was not: given, unchangeable, biology' (Visweswaran 1998: 72). Paradoxically, it was the cultural anthropologists (primarily Boasians) who most strongly *affirmed* the existence of race in order to clearly distinguish it from culture. Intellectual imperatives (influenced as such by political expedience) dictated that Boasians assumed race to be strictly biological while culture was not. More importantly, culture was not hierarchical and 'cultures' not amenable to ranking; and each culture was deserved recognition in its own right. With this we saw the rise of 'cultural relativism', anthropology's main theoretical contribution to the social sciences. Each 'culture' had it own internal dynamics and patterns of being; each resulted from a relation of internal forces, and as such, each had its own, self-evident boundary.

As cultural relativism, enhanced by notions of bounded cultural groups, en-gulfed anthropology on both sides of the Atlantic,[9] studies of human societies (and difference) became increasingly specialised and fixated on delineating the internal workings of specific cultural groupings. Ethnographic studies treated communities as cultural isolates as the goal was to emphasise the 'wholeness' of distinct cultures (Trouillot 2003).[10] Against earlier histories of evolutionary progress, the move to focus on the relative character of individual societies was laudable. At the same time, it led to the 'erection of rigid cultural barriers enclosing each group in its singularity' (Amselle 1990:20). The result was a distinct and ironic cultural determin-ism that recalled—or reverted back to—the biological determinism of the earlier evolutionary period. To continually stress a community's singular practices and so-cial formations is also to calcify its 'differences' and, in the context of ethnographic fieldwork research, to justify its territorial (as well as temporal) confinement. Cul-ture became a 'thing' and, as such, it shifted from a descriptive conceptual tool to an explanatory concept. The more it explained, the more reified it became:

> For Columbus as for Montaigne, savages were those who had no state, no religion, no clothes, and no shame—*because they had nature*. For ... anthropology, primitives became those who had no complexity, no class, and no history that really mattered—*because they had culture*. Better still, each group had a single such culture whose bounda-ries were thought to be self-evident (Trouillot 2003:102, my emphasis).

The sociocultural anthropology uses of 'culture' thus ironically reconciled the Boasian agenda with the taxonomic schemes of earlier times. Conceptions of difference based on ideas of culture became racialised; in effect, culture became race. But were ideas about cultural difference not always really about racial difference?

The ultimate confluence of mid-twentieth century understandings of the culture concept and late-nineteenth century 'race' concept is not surprising and has every-thing to do with the relationship between the intellectual and political contexts within which early twentieth century anthropologists operated. First, the shift from a focus on race to one on culture was an *intellectual* response to *a political* situation (Trouillot 2003). As such, the deployment of 'culture' as a marker of human difference merely masked common 'racial' understandings of human difference. Not only did this *theoretical* move within anthropology not expunge the baggage of racial conceptualisation, worse yet, it did not challenge the continued *political* practices of racism—colonial exploitation, Jim Crow racism, apartheid. Second, by relegating race to the realm of 'biology' anthropology failed to interrogate both its continued global significance and how race actually works to create meaning and structure inequality. This interrogation would at least have been able to determine how actual 'racial knowledge production' (Goldberg 1993) worked to reinforce the established representations and hierarchies from the nineteenth century deployment of the racial concept. Third, because the trajectory of culture is 'that of a concept distancing itself from the context of its practice' (Trouillot 2003), it necessarily cannot erase anthropology's racial, racialising, and racist past.

Thus, even as race has dropped off the agenda of most cultural anthropologists, it is clear that the culture concept continues to operate much like race. In fact, along with 'ethnicity'—another concept used by anthropologists to solidify their move away from race and toward culture—culture often is a replacement for race/racial difference. Kamala Visweswaran (1998:76) describes the logic of this interchange:

> ... culture came to be seen as interchangeable with ethnic group, and ethnic group or culture came to substitute race ... But as the dominant view of race is a biological one, when this substitution of terms is effected, culture and ethnicity are themselves essentialized or biologized.

In the meantime, much anthropological research continues without missing a beat. But the discipline's 'fetichization of culture' (Trouillot 2001)—without acknowledging culture's own underlying racial logic—in both theory and practice affirms as *a priori* and natural cultural difference and renders the treatment of African phenomena as always already exceptional and (not so implicitly) *racially* distinct. The race-ing of Africans occurred as a result of anthropology's establishment as the 'science of races'. The effects of such racialisation on both research and theory on and about the continent (as well as its consequences for the racial structuring of African peoples and communities in today's global socioeconomic and political hierarchies) rarely enter the discussion. And changing the *terms* of the discussion does not eradicate its racial subtext or the real and detrimental effects of racialisation. This is clear when we review anthropology's engagement with Africa and African peoples.

Ethnography and African Cultural Exceptionalism

> The construction of identity in the twentieth century cannot be extricated from the overt and implicit constructions of race that emerge from Africa's metaphoric and troubled space (Kanneh 1998: 192).

Indeed the legacy—and burden—of anthropology in Africa is its historical construction of African Otherness that has served to mark the continent in ways that are unparalleled elsewhere (Hickey and Wylie 1993). Contemporary critiques of ethnographic constructions of its objects notwithstanding, Africa continues to exist within a particular context of an anthropologically specific kind of 'difference'. The unrelenting attack from scholars both within and beyond the anthropological and 'Africanist' enterprise speaks to this. In *The Invention of Africa* (1988), V.Y. Mudimbe argues that Africa is invented through 'gnosis', the imperial trope of authentic alterity. He demonstrates how anthropology contributes greatly to the 'invention of primitive Africa' with its continued 'search for primitiveness'. Mudimbe further assails the 'epistemological determinism' within the discipline that testifies—even to this day—to its general 'ethnocentrism'. Similarly, Ebere Onwudiwe (2001: 217) asserts that the minds of western anthropologists are 'still filled with malicious notions of Africa and Africans', notions of the continent that are unintelligible—and untranslatable—outside of an explicitly, racially, 'Black' African context. As an instrument of colonialism, Onwudiwe argues, anthropology cannot be objective 'in the application of descriptive terms to Africa'. 'The adopted Western vernacular for an alien Africa', he continues, at worst perpetuates 'the idea that African identities and conflicts are in some way more "primitive" than those in other parts of the world' (Ibid.).

The strength of these critiques lies in both their frequency and consistency. They are certainly not new. Africanist anthropologists in particular, perhaps because of the obvious dubious history of their discipline, have often acknowledged, and at times addressed, the critiques–however marginally (Moore 1998; Guyer 1999; Apter 1999). Archie Mafeje (1997), in his most recent articulation of the same critique, castigated the anthropological study of Africa as linked to racism and imperialism. Jane Guyer (2004: 510) calls for these issues to be 'brought into new philosophical and macrohistorical/comparative perspective'. Andrew Apter (1999), feeling compelled to respond to Mafeje and Mudimbe, explains (or admits?) that, though anthropology's 'imperial subtexts' cannot be negated, they must be acknowledged.

But what makes these critiques so palpable? What makes them so raw? What makes them contemporary? I want to engage these questions through a critical re-reading of both 'classic' and contemporary Africanist anthropological texts. My aim here is simple: it is an attempt to affirm these critiques by demonstrating the continued importance of race in anthropological engagement with African communities.

The three 'classics' that are particularly relevant for this discussion are: *The Nuer* by E.E. Evans-Pritchard (1940); *The Forest People* by Colin Turnbull (1961); and *Nisa* by Marjorie Shostak (1981). These ethnographic studies have been lauded for their specific theoretical innovation and methodological contribution to anthropology. Evans-Pritchard is the first trained anthropologist to conduct fieldwork in Africa and his work on the 'Nuer' is lauded for providing a paradigmatic model of 'segmentary lineage' systems. Colin Turnbull's *The Forest People* is recognised for popularising anthropological accounts and for presenting a study of the harmonious life of the so-called 'Mbiti Pygmies' with their environment (the 'forest'). Shostak's *Nisa* is known as a 'proto-feminist' text and one of the first ethnographic monographs about Africa that focussed primarily on women and uses their voices. All three texts are considered to be not only 'timeless classics', but also texts that, at least in the case of Evans-Pritchard and Turnbull, challenge 'evolutionism'. Furthermore, they continue to be favoured texts for contemporary introductory courses in anthropology. That these Africanist texts remain so extremely popular despite years of varying sets of critiques is remarkable. More remarkable, I suggest, is the benign nature of such critiques and the silences they continue to foster. *The Nuer*, for example, has been critiqued on every aspect from its rhetorical style (especially questions about its ethnographic 'authority') to its theoretical models (particularly Evans-Pritchard's characterisation of 'Nuer' society as egalitarian and patrilineal). Turnbull's idyllic image of the Mbiti has often been described as crossing the boundary between ethnography and fiction. In the context of revisionist studies of both populations of the Kalahari Desert as well as those against cultural determinism, *Nisa* has received particular scrutiny for its presentation of !Kung life as bounded and ideal. Yet, little attention is given to the racial subtext of the representation of Africans in these 'classics'.

Despite their entrenchment within anthropological teaching and production of theory, I want to demonstrate how all three texts use a particular set of techniques that work to racialise and pathologise the African communities under study, even when there is no explicit use of race as an explanation of cultural difference. I argue that the three texts Other (through racialisation) Africans in three specific ways: (i) by locating the community under study within 'nature' and, often, in symbiotic relation to animals and inanimate objects; (ii) through what I call moments of 'differentiating distancing', where, at a specific point in the text, the author explicitly distinguishes her/himself as the extreme cultural (racial?) opposite of those under study; and (iii) by both generalised and explicit racial distinctions of the ethnographer and subjects.

Within both *The Nuer* and *The Forest People*, respectively, we find two arresting passages:

> ... [The] symbiotic relationship [between 'Nuer' and cattle] is one of close physical contact ... No high barriers of culture divide men from beast in their common home, but the stark nakedness of Nuer amid their cattle and the intimacy of their contact with them present a classic picture of savagery (Evans-Pritchard 1969 [1940]: 40).

> ... they reappeared, announcing their presence with low whistles that sounded like the call of a night bird. They were in two pairs, each pair carrying between them, over their shoulders, a long slender object. Even at that moment I wondered if they would veer off into the complete blackness of the forest ... (Turnbull 1961: 75).

In these descriptions, it is difficult to distinguish between the people being studied and their environments. The 'Nuer' are one with their cattle; the two species are caught up in a relationship so close that it is difficult to separate out humans from animals. Relatedly, the Mbiti 'pygmies' are one with the forest—particularly the 'blackness' of the forest—and are so connected to it that they can potentially fade into it. In these descriptions we find a direct link to late-nineteenth century images of the dark-skinned savage as well as attendant racialist assumptions about Africans' relationship to nature, their biomoral characteristics, and their primitiveness. The sentiments reflected in the above passages are not unique moments in the texts. In fact, Evans-Pritchard's photographic representations of the 'Nuer' have a similarly disturbing effect. They depict what he calls the 'crudity' and 'savagery' of the 'Nuer' life as well as the close physical contact between 'man and beast' (Evans-Pritchard 1969 [1940]: 40). And Turnbull's account is replete with similar descriptions of Mbuti oneness with the forest.

Turnbull's *The Forest People* also racialises its subjects by employing the technique of 'differentiating distancing'. Despite the author's utopian and liberal claims of universal humanity and empathy toward the Mbiti, there is a moment in the text where he nevertheless openly acknowledges his extreme distance from them. Amazingly, Shostak has an identical moment. Here is Turnbull describing the hunt and capture of a sindula:

> The youngster ... had speared it with his first thrust, pinning the animal to the ground through the fleshy part of the stomach. But the animal was still very much alive, fighting for freedom ... Maipe put another spear into its neck, but it still writhed and fought. Not until a third spear pierced its heart did he give up the struggle.
>
> *It was at times like this that I found myself furthest removed from the Pygmies* (1961:101, my emphasis).

Compare Shostak's moment:

> [Nisa] planted the stick, with the skewered insect at the top, upright in the ground and tapped it gently with her fingers. The insect's wings burst into motion ... then it stopped. Nisa tapped the stick again ...
>
> I watched horrified ... what Nisa was doing was different. It seemed like inexcusable torture...
>
> My gaze was drawn once again toward Nisa. Her head and the upper parts of her body had begun to move rhythmically ... as the insect held itself erect, Nisa's body also became erect; when the insect circled, drooped, and strained, Nisa's body did the same...the incident ... reminded me of *the cultural gulf between Nisa and me* ...
>
> *The differences in our backgrounds, though I sometimes tried to deny them, would always be there* (1981: 312-322, my emphasis).

This process of differentiation reinforces African racial distinction through a double strategy. First, both scenes depict the person's intimate relationship to the animal s/ he is in the process of killing. Nisa's body, for example, is in harmony with the insect; when it moves, she moves, as well, her 'face and torso echoed the insect's plight' (Shostak 1981: 321). Second, and probably most revealing, is the author's explicit and unapologetic personal distancing from her or his interlocutors. At each of the moments described above, African humanity is questioned, both in its proximity to the animals, and in its distance from the *human* (European) anthropologist.

The racio-cultural differentiation between European/Western anthropologist and her or his African subject in all three texts is the third racialising technique. Done particularly through the juxtaposition of 'Europeans' or 'Westerners' and the (tribal?) group under study, each text engages in this differentiation. For example, in *The Nuer*, Evans-Pritchard (1969 [1940]: 51) makes direct contrasts between 'Nuer' and 'Europeans', and between 'all white men' and the 'Nuer': 'From a European's point of view, Nuerland has not favourable qualities ... It is throughout hard on man and beast'. Turnbull takes it a step further and differentiates through ongoing and brute physical descriptions of various members of the group under study.[11] Furthermore he takes liberties of using racial identifiers in his description of subjects. Thus, he describes Ekianga, a member of the community, as 'hairy, broad-chested, and powerful almost to the point of ugliness' (Turnbull 1961: 35). Or, there is 'Cephu's handsome nephew ... a very light-skinned youth who had two children lighter than he'; and 'Masisi's children had finer features, with longer faces and straight noses, and they were slimmer and less stocky' (33).

How is it possible for contemporary anthropologists to read, teach, and theorise about these texts so exhaustively and never mention, much less provide a satisfactory treatment of, these racialising tendencies and techniques? My aim in reviewing these 'classic' texts is not only to provide specific detail on the racialising techniques of Africanist ethnographies, but also to demonstrate that we cannot relegate them to discussions of late-nineteenth century evolutionism. Nor should we relegate this discussion only to issues of negative and problematic representations of ethnographic subjects. It is also not enough to justify them by rendering such representations to the 'context' of the time. (*Nisa*, for example, was written in 1981—*after* the first of the postcolonial critiques.) Rather, these texts should show us that even theoretical innovation marked by the idealism of political liberalism continues to be mapped unto the racial palimpsest of nineteenth century evolutionism.

In his response to critics (who condemned his call for an end to anthropology), Mafeje (1998) argues that his critique of European constructions of African 'alterity' goes beyond the challenge to Eurocentrism. He states that he should have been more forceful in his argument that, 'while liberal Euro-American anthropologists and their kith and kin in the ex-colonies can consciously deconstruct colonial anthropology, it is doubtful if they can *deracialize* the original idea of anthropology as the study of "other"', (my emphasis). This point is important in helping to contextualise the nature of the critiques levelled at Africanist anthropology, particularly by African scholars. Even as the discipline diligently works to change the theoretical and methodological orientation of work dealing with African communities, there are codes, symbols, signs, words, and concepts that continue to dictate the terms of engagement. They reflect the *political* reality of Africa's entrenched historical position in the global racial order. In 'Anthropology in Post-Independence Africa', Mafeje (1998) reviewed the more recent 'anti-colonial' texts that aimed at a liberal deconstruction of anthropology, but still found them wanting in ideas for a radical transformation of anthropological practice. Apter (1999), in a review article entitled, 'Africa, Empire, and Anthropologists', engaged the African scholars' critiques of anthropology by acknowledging the discipline's 'imperial subtexts' while providing evidence of the contemporary 'dialogical' production of ethnographic texts, especially those from the 'anthropology of colonial spectacle'. He demands that African scholars recognise how 'imperial centers and colonial peripheries developed in reciprocal determination' (Apter 1999: 592), and ends by stating that Africanists

should not forget the imperial subtexts. But is not forgetting enough? Better yet, what does 'not forgetting' entail?

There is another response to Mafeje's type of critique. It is to challenge static representations of African phenomenon by taking, as a point of departure, the 'co-evalness' of Africa with the rest of the world, and treating sociocultural practices as unexceptional. Thus, in some anthropological studies, the phenomenon under discussion and the analysis of the phenomenon is said to not depend upon context as much as process, 'less our locus than our focus' (Comaroffs 1992 as quoted in Mafeje 1998). For example, in the introduction to their edited text, *Modernity and Its Malcontents: Ritual and Power in Postcolonial Africa*, John and Jean Comaroff (1993: xxviii) explain why their focus on ritual is not intended to further exoticise Africa:

> ... let us remind ourselves of contemporary forms of Western witchcraft, witchcraft that addresses the contradictions of advanced capitalist societies. A clutch of images in the recent popular culture of North America are especially revealing in this respect: the 'Fatal Attraction' of the corporate harridan who would use sexual and professional wiles to destroy home, husband, and family; the dangerous market woman of Wall Street, a trader in the vortex of voodoo economics...; the standardized nightmare of child abuse, embodied in the callous babyminder, whose 'Hand ... Rocks the Cradle'...

If we put aside, for a moment, the issue we might have with the comparison of movie plots with the 'real' situations of ritual and witchcraft practices that the essays in the book analyse, and if we also put aside the extremely exoticised and racialised subtext of the terms, 'voodoo economics' and 'market woman', we are still able to ask if a book with a title of 'Modernity and Its Malcontents', and with the subjects of 'ritual' and 'witchcraft' could really be about Europe or North America. Do the stories about ritual, witchcraft, and the malcontents of modernity work (especially as anthropological texts) if they are not in Africa? Or, more importantly, if they are not in rural Africa? And if the stories were not to be about (rural) Africa, would they elicit the same response, the same acceptance? These questions, though seemingly simple, are extremely important for this discussion. In making the comparisons between witchcraft in African societies and images that *may* (or may not) be associated with witchcraft in North America, the Comaroffs make a pre-emptive (and defensive?) move against the potential well-known (well-worn?) critiques of exoticisation. Why else would this comparison be needed if 'witchcraft', 'ritual', and 'Africa' did not already invoke a complex set of images? A set of images that has everything to do with the very processes of racialisation—including racialised notions of difference in anthropological writings—that enable the invocation of such images in the first place? My point here is not to say that the analyses in the text—on their own—are necessarily problematic. Rather it is demonstrate that, regardless of intentions or theoretical programme, anthropology's racialising effect on Africa remains salient. Because deep within the heart of Africanist anthropology is its association with race, the Comaroffs do not—and cannot—forget its 'imperial subtexts' (Apter 1999).

Indeed, they acknowledge that Africa's 'modern' witches are part of the economic and cultural processes of globalisation and that they 'embody all the contradictions of the experience of modernity itself'. At the same time, however, particular ideas about 'witchcraft', 'ritual'—as well as other 'savage slot' (Trouillot 1991) topics—emerge and exist in the metaphoric and racialised spaces of Africa.

What has Africanist anthropology done to address this issue? And are all research projects in and about African phenomena always already 'indexed ultimately to race' (Guyer 2004)? I briefly turn here to Apter's own efforts at complicating the research, theory, and analysis of African phenomena. In 'The Pan-African Nation: Oil-Money and the Spectacle of Culture in Nigeria', (a 1996 article that prefigures his 2005 monograph with a similar title), Apter provides a historical ethnographic examination of the 1977 'Second World Black and African Festival of Arts and Culture' (Festac '77) hosted by the then-military regime of Lieutenant-General Olusegun Obasanjo. Placing Nigeria's 'oil-wealth' at the centre of his analysis, Apter explores the ways the state used newly found riches to forge a new nation through the commodification of culture and the construction of expansive notions of 'blackness'. We then see how Nigeria's current post-colonial predicament of crises—on all levels—are directly related to the ways the 'money-magic' of the state's oil-wealth worked to bind culture to politics and ultimately informed governance failures. Apter (1996: 444) wants to know how Festac's 'utopian dream' turned into such a 'dystopian nightmare'. Festac '77, according to him, proved to be a 'grand illusion' since the modern Nigeria envisioned by the state did not materialise. As a result, today's Nigeria is not in good shape:

> What was once a monument to a booming oil-economy is now crumbling and cracking at the seams, like the *morally* and economically *bankrupt* nation-state so thoroughly plundered by its ruling military clique ... Oil, once the demi-god of national rebirth, now stands for national pollution and decay ... After years of rapacious looting of oil revenues, today Nigeria is a mess (Apter 1996: 443, my emphasis).

As a result, corruption (a new form of 'money-magic') abounds and acts a contagion, even migrating from the structures of the state to individuals as foreign businesses and 'businessmen' continue to be victimised by unscrupulous Nigerians.

This is certainly not a 'traditional' ethnographic representation of Africa and Africans—there are no thick descriptions of ritualistic practices, of witchcraft (modern or not); no detailed esoteric discussions of 'gift-exchange' economies; no analysis of lineage segments. It is a study, not necessarily of a people, but of a state and its structures (of politics and culture). Nevertheless, both Apter's *tone* and analytical bent reflect a 'culturalising of corruption of sorts that seem to work to make Nigeria (Africa?) exceptional and to make us forget the universality of corrupt state practices' (Amselle 2003). The content (and veracity) of the analysis aside, there is no denying that the way the essay attributes this type of abuse of power—one that, like a disease, later seeps through state façade into the general population—to a specific geographic and cultural entity does a particular kind of work outside the intellectual frame of an anthropological/ethnographic study of money, culture, and politics. Given that in the late-twentieth century specialists in African politics 'focused on corruption … as a fundamental cultural characteristic of the African continent', it should cause little surprise when some wonder if 'corruption' (linked, of course, to state and governance failures) is not the 'new racial stereotype' for Africans (De Figuereido 2005). What is fascinating about the study is the presentation of the Nigerian predicament as particularly insular. There is no discussion that explores the economic and political structures in the movement between colonial and post-colonial moments. Instead, from Festac '77 onwards, the Nigerian state acted like a 'vampire state' (Akpan 2005) that deploys culture (even mimicking colonial cultural practices) to feed on the blood of its own people.

My point here is not to argue that the subjects of state decay, corruption, commodity fetishism are not permissible topics of study for contemporary Africanists. Indeed, as some have argued in varying contexts, these things are happening in post-colonial Africa and are practical problems that need attention.[13] There seems to be, nevertheless, a way in which scholarly excitement over particular topics—and the *terms* of engagement with them as well as the lively debates among Africanists—'masks the deeper question of Western representations of Africa as a continent of absolute horror, a theatre of primordial savagery only temporarily interrupted by European colonization' (Amselle 2003). The inherently racialised nature of such representations of Africans make the 'excessive *anthropologizing*' (Akpan 2005) of their cultural (racial?) practices even more significant.

Then, of course, there are specific ways this 'anthropologising' is made even more potent. Here I want to focus on an aspect of the anthropological terms of engaging Africans. Toni Morrison once lamented that, as a black writer, she has struggled with the deployment of language that works to both evoke hidden signs of racial superiority and to 'other' people in dismissive ways (1992: x). She recognises the 'embedded assumptions' of language and its often-singular power in constructing and calcifying hierarchies. Africanist anthropology is no stranger to this kind of linguistic and conceptual 'othering'. Terms such as 'tribe', 'primitive', 'savage', 'pre-modern', and concepts such as 'ritual', 'witchcraft' all continue to have explicit racial coding. And then there are the thick and lively descriptions of 'animalistic' and 'predatory' practices—be they in the form of the failed state, or 'soul-eating' witches. Coupled with the examples above, Alan Barnard's recent review of Africanist texts, where he contrasts Joy Hendry's (2001: 163) relativist comparison of English and Amba (Uganda) witchcraft, is instructive:

> Witches, in an Amba view, exhibit an inversion of physical and moral qualities of human beings. They hang upside down, eat human flesh, quench their thirst with salt, go about naked, and … shake their victims from their own villages and share them with witches in other villages …

> It is difficult to say whether current witchcraft practices in England are related to any kind of crisis or social change, or, indeed, whether they have ever really abated in the intervening years. It is certainly true, however, that magic and witchcraft continue to

intrigue members of the wider society, and practising witches are found among the most apparently staid and middle-class professions.

Notice the animal-like, predatory description of the Amba witches and the non-specific, generalized language used to talk about the English witches.[14]

We see in these differentiating descriptions of similar phenomena how knowledge 'lays about in linguistic images and forms of cultural practice' (Morrison 1992: 49); how within particular uses of language, we can find embedded specific themes, fears, and forms of consciousness (Morrison 1992: 50); we find the racial logic of language.

Ultimately, what this discussion suggests is that, at the very least, the racial inflections that undergird researching, theorising, and writing about Africa remain under-analysed. What seems most stark in our current anthropological enterprise is 'the desire to understand better other cultures so as to preserve more effectively the differences' (Malik 1996: 150). Yet, in a thoroughly racialised world (Winant 2001), the failure to acknowledge the hierarchies that Africanist anthropology (specifically) structure, is both an 'act of enforcing racelessness', in our work and 'itself a racial act' (Morrison 1992: 46).

(Africanist) Ethnography: Race, Power, and the Politics of Otherness

Relativism is the bad faith of the conqueror, who has become secure enough to become a tourist (Stanley Diamond, quoted in Scott 1992).

The construction of African Otherness is not reducible only to a politics of representation. More significant is what Trouillot refers to as the 'referential value of ethnographies in the wider field within which anthropology operates and upon whose existence it is premised' (1991). Gupta and Ferguson (1997b: 46), in a similar vein, argue that cultural distinctiveness has already been produced within a field of power relations and thus, is part and parcel of the global system of domination. The Africanist ethnographic project, along with its constructions of African cultural and racial difference, operates within this field of power.

That Africa has become a 'totalized vision of otherness' is given (Kanneh 1998: 39). That this Otherness has been conferred in terms of race is also evident, but this fact needs explicit—and particular—articulation. David Goldberg (1993: 150) correctly asserts that

Racial knowledge consists ... in the making of difference ... An epistemology so basically driven by difference will 'naturally' find racialized thinking comfortable; it will uncritically (come to) assume racial knowledge as given ... Naming the other, for all intents and purposes, is the Other [and] the Other is just what racialized social science knows ... Production of social knowledge about the racialized Other, then, establishes a library or archive of information, a set of guiding ideas and principles about Otherness: a mind, characteristic behavior or habits.

There seems to be an overall reluctance within Africanist anthropology to systematically addresses race and processes of racialisation—both as constituted and articulated through ethnographic practice and representation. The very practices of anthropology are deployed in real contexts and, as such, racialisation occurs in many sites, on many levels: in the field, in the relationship between the anthropologists and the subject of study; in ethnographic texts (particularly in the *language* of these texts); in the dynamics of anthropology departments.

Although the main context of anthropological practice is academia, the 'ultimate context of its relevance is the world outside' (Trouillot 2001: 22). Thus, this current discussion must be understood as part of a universal struggle against imperialism and racism (Mafeje 1976). Mafeje astutely suggests that we need not single out anthropology and treat it in isolation from 'bourgeois' social sciences that were also implicated in the imperialist project.[15] Thus, the problem of Africanist anthropology is more universal than specifically colonial, more general than exceptional. Anthropology's inadequate handling of race in its past and current constructions of Africa, then, reflects a broader social science problem of reinforcing African racial difference and therefore perpetuating racial inequality. In this case, tracing anthropology's role in the late-nineteenth and early twentieth centuries' deployment of racist and imperialist ideology, and demonstrating its continuation at this current moment, is an important first step in addressing such inequalities.

Anthropology has its beginnings in the proliferation of racial thinking and the support of racial science. In later developments, a theoretical shift in concepts led the discipline from a focus on racial differences to cultural differences. The deployment of 'culture', however, was an 'intellectual maneuver against the background of a social, political, and intellectual context' (Trouillot 2001: 4-5) of race and racism. In this rush away from race, the strategy to disconnect race from culture (and its precepts) did not address persistent racism. Thus, while the focus on culture helped to diminish the theoretical relevance of race within academia (at least in some circles),[16] it did not effectively challenge racism in the public or political field. In effect, race and racism are constantly reproduced, perhaps because the general conditions of their production have remained virtually unchanged. By not acknowledging the strength and power of past and present racial inequality, how such inequality structures the lives of the racially marked, and how the continued essentialisation of culture in current anthropological research and practice contributes to the persistent (racial) marking of some groups, the discipline, however inadvertently, reinforces this inequality. Africa's historic and contemporary marginalisation within the global racial capitalist system is not by accident. Full appreciation of this history will open up a space for us to better understand the ways that our work is located in a 'field of power relations' that inform, in concrete ways, notions of (Western) intellectual, social, and political superiority, global notions of social justice, IMF/World Bank policies, and even refugee resettlement schemes—in a world of turmoil and unequal distribution of resources.

I have argued that Africanist anthropologists, even those that recognise the discipline's racial 'imperial subtext', have tended not to fully engage the topics of race and racism. This is because, I believe, they 'do not recognize that racism is one of the fundamental constituent elements of the rise of capitalism, bourgeois culture, and alienated science, and is still necessary for their reproduction [today]' (Rigby 1996: 3). To do so would be to: (i) relinquish the ideological and epistemological belief in, and practice of, constructing African exceptionalism; (ii) accept responsibility for the construction and maintenance of this exceptionalism; and (iii) consciously and actively construct decolonised counter-narratives that challenge rather than affirm global structures of race and power.

Notes

1. I thank Paul Tiyambe Zeleza for the opportunity to revive this essay, Harvey Neptune for asking the difficult questions, and Toussaint Pierre-Vargas for his comforting patience.

2. Quoted in Phillips 2003.

3. Here David T. Goldberg refers to the production of social knowledge about racialised others. Inversely, however, the construction of these racial others is integral to the development of social science.

4. See Armory (1997) for a discussion on what she terms the 'racial division of labour' in African Studies.

5. As this is necessarily a partial history, I will not be making specific distinctions between various national traditions of the development of anthropology. I am fully aware, however, that anthropology developed differently in Britain, France, and the US and a full account of the discipline must be sensitive to these differences. Nevertheless, I must stress that in view of the eighteenth and nineteenth century theories and classifications of human difference, the various strands should not be too sharply contrasted. As Peter Pels (2000: 25) has recently reminded us, all early anthropology traditions subscribed to the idea that race was a natural difference and that difference implied a natural hierarchy.

6. In fact, Stocking continues, 'Negroes' were the last to benefit from the concept of the 'noble savage' which had been used at least a century earlier in discussions of AmerIndians.

7. Although Boas is known as the father of 'American' anthropology, not only was there cross-fertilisation (especially between the US and England) across the Atlantic, but also Boas himself was very much influenced by the German anthropological tradition (Amselle 1990). Furthermore, after the Second World War, the 'British' and 'American' traditions were merged and often called, simply, 'socio-cultural' anthropology.

8. Faye Harrison (1992) as well as Lee Baker (1998) have pointed to the parallel development of W. E. B. Du Bois's crusade against the biological determinism of race and culture. Du Bois and Boas were in contact. Furthermore, although my focus on this history is necessarily about the theoretical developments within anthropology, I want to stress that I am also well aware of the various other intellectual denunciations of scientific racism and the racial inferiority of blacks, particularly those of African scholars.

9. Specifically, the French tradition focussed on culture as a 'total social fact', and the British tradition as 'Social Structure' (Amselle 1990).

10. This was both within the US as well as in French 'structuralism' and British 'functionalism'.

11. Here is an example: 'Most Pygmies have unmistakable features ... Their legs are short in proportion to their bodies; they are powerful, muscular, and usually splay-backed; their heads are round and the eyes are set wide apart; they have flat noses almost as broad as their mouths are long ... Another characteristic is the alert expression of the face, direct and unafraid, as keen as the body, with is always already to move with speed and agility at a moment's notice' (Turnbull 1961: 32).

12. Apter is explicit about this. He distinguishes between 'Africanist anthropology' and 'African anthropologists' which, though perhaps benign, works to reinforce the long-standing racial division of intellectual labour existing in the study of Africa.

13. John and Jean Comaroff make this point most specifically in a recent article, 'Occult Economies and the Violence of Abstraction: Notes from the South African Postcolony' (1998). In addressing what they see as the general reluctance to acknowledge the pervasive nature of the 'practice of mystical arts' in postcolonial Africa, they state: 'The fact is ... there is a lot of witchcraft about just now. And 'natives' do speak about it; for many, it is an ontological given in this age of rapidly shifting realities' (284).

14. There is also the difference between 'English' as a national identity, and 'Amba' as an ethnic (or tribal?) identity.

15. Peter Rigby echoes this sentiment with 'Anthropology was a "child of imperialism"; but it was not the only child of imperialism' (1996: 48).

16. A number of under-recognised ethnographies, mainly by US scholars of African descent, dealt with race and race relations during over the course of these periods (see, for example, Hurston 1990 [1938], 1990 [1935]; Powdermaker 1939; Davis 1941; Herskovits 1941; Robeson 1940; Cayton and Drake 1945; Gregory 1998; Jackson 1999; Twine 1998; Gordon 1998).

References

Achebe, C., 1988, *Hopes and Impediments: Selected Essays 1965-1987*, Oxford: Heinemann.

Akpan, W., 2005, (Review), *The Pan-African Nation: Oil and the Spectacle of Culture in Nigeria*, by Andrew Apter, *African Sociological Review* 8 (2): 185-188.

Amory, D., 1997, 'African Studies as American Institution', in A. Gupta and J. Ferguson, eds., *Anthropological Locations: Boundaries and Grounds of a Field Science*, Berkeley: UCLA Press.

Amselle, J.-L., 2003, 'Africa: A Theme(s) Park', *Anthropoetics 9* (1).

Amselle, J.-L., 1998, *Mestizo Logics: Anthropology of Identity in Africa and Elsewhere*, Trans. by Claudia Royal, Stanford University Press.

Apter, A., 1997, 'Africa, Empire, and Anthropology: A Philological Exploration of Anthropology's Heart of Darkness', *Annual Review of Anthropology* 28: 577-598.

Asad, T., ed., 1973, *Anthropology and the Colonial Encounter*, Atlantic Highlands, New Jersey: Humanities Press.

Baker, L. D., 1998, *From Savage to Negro: Anthropology and the Construction of Race*, Berkeley: UCLA Press.

Barnard, A., 2001, 'Africa and the Anthropologist', *Africa* 71 (1): 162-170.

Blyden, E., 1862, *Liberia's Offering*, New York: John Gray.

Cayton, H. and St. Clair Drake, 1945, *Black Metropolis: A Study of Negro Life in a Northern City*, New York: Harcourt, Brace and Co.

Comaroff, J. and J. Comaroff, 1998, 'Occult Economies and the Violence of Abstraction: Notes from the South African Postcolony', *American Ethnologist* 26 (2): 279-303.

Comaroff, J. and J. Comaroff, 1993, *Modernity and its Malcontents: Ritual and Power in Postcolonial Africa*, Chicago: University of Chicago Press.

Comaroff, J. and J. Comaroff, 1992, 'Of Totenism and Ethnicity', in Comaroff and Comaroff, *Ethnography and the Historical Imagination*, Boulder, CO: Westview Press.

Curtin, P., 1964, *The Image of Africa: British Ideas and Actions*, Madison, WI: University of Wisconsin Press.

Davis, A., et al., 1941, *Deep South*, Chicago: University of Chicago Press.

de Figueiredo, A., 2005, 'Is Corruption a New Racial Stereotype?', *New African*, July.

Degler, C., 1991, *In Search of Human Nature*, New York: Oxford University Press.

Drake, St. Clair, 1982, 'Diaspora Studies and Pan-Africanism', in Joseph Harris, ed., *Global Dimensions of the African Diaspora*, Washington, DC: Howard University Press.

Drake, St. Clair, 1975, 'The Black Diaspora in Pan-African Perspective', *The Black Scholar*, September: 2-13.

DuBois, W. E. B., (1971 [1897]), 'The Conservation of Races', in J. Lester, ed., *The Seventh Son*, Vol. I., New York: Random House.

DuBois, W. E. B., (1970 [1956]), *The Negro*, London and New York: Oxford University Press.

DuBois, W. E. B., 1939, *Black Folk Then and Now*, New York: Henry Holt and Company.

Evans-Pritchard, E. E., 1940, *The Nuer: A Description of the Modes of Livelihood and Political Institutions of a Nilotic People*, New York: Oxford University Press.

Goldberg, D. T., 1993, *Racist Culture: Philosophy and the Politics of Meaning*, Oxford: Blackwell.

Gough, K., 1968, 'New Proposals for Anthropologists', *Current Anthropology* 9 (5): 403-435.

Gregory, S., 1996, Black Corona: Race and the Politics of Place in an Urban Community, Princeton, NJ: Princeton University Press.

Gupta, A. and J. Ferguson, eds., 1997a, *Anthropological Locations: Boundaries and Grounds of a Field Science*, Berkeley: University of California Press.

Gupta, A. and J. Ferguson, 1997b, *Culture, Power, Place: Explorations in Critical Anthropology*, Durham, N.C.: Duke University Press.

Guyer, J., 2004, 'Anthropology in Area Studies', *Annual Review of Anthropology* 33: 499-523.

Guyer, J., 1999, 'Anthropology: The Study of Social and Cultural Originality', *African Sociological Review* 3 (2): 30-53.

Haller, J. S., Jr, 1971, 'Race and the Concept of Progress in Nineteenth Century American Ethnology', *American Anthropologist 73* (3): 710-724.

Hannaford, I., 1996, *Race: The History of an Idea*, Baltimore: The John Hopkins University Press.

Harrison, F. V., 2002, 'Global Apartheid, Foreign Policy, and Human Rights', *Souls: A Critical Journal of Black Politics, Culture, and Society 4* (3): 48-68.

Harrison, F. V., 1999, 'Introduction: Expanding the Discourse on "Race"', *American Anthropologist 100* (3): 609-631.

Harrison, F. V., 1995, 'The Persistent Power of "Race" in the Cultural and Political Economy of Racism', *Annual Review of Anthropology* 24: 47-74.

Harrison, F. V., 1992, 'The DuBoisan Legacy in Anthropology', *Critique of Anthropology* 12 (3): 239-260.

Hendry, J., 1999, *An Introduction to Cultural and Social Anthropology: Other People's Worlds*, London: Macmillan.

Herskovitz, M., 1943, 'The Negro in Bahia, Brazil: A Problem in Method', *American Sociological Review* 8 (4): 394-404.

Herskovits, M., 1941, *The Myth of the Negro Past*, Boston, MA: Beacon Press.

Hickey, D. and K.C. Wylie, 1993, *An Enchanting Darkness: The American Vision of Africa in the Twentieth Century*, East Lansing, Michigan: Michigan State University Press.

Hooker, J. R., 1963, 'The Anthropologists' Frontier: The Last Phase of African Exploitation', *The Journal of Modern African Studies* 1 (4): 455-459.

Hutchinson, S., 1996, Nuer Dilemmas: *Coping with Money, War, and the State*, Berkeley: University of California Press.

Hudson, N., 1996, 'From "Nation" to "Race": The Origin of Racial Classification in Eighteenth-Century Thought', *Eighteenth-Century Studies* 29 (3): 247-264.

Hurston, Z.N., 1990 [1938], *Tell My Horse*, New York: Harper.

Hurston, Z.N., 1990 [1935], *Mules and Men*, New York: Harper.

Jenkins, R., 1986, 'Social Anthropological Models of Inter-Ethnic Relations', in J. Rex and D. Mason, eds., *Theories of Race and Ethnic Relations*, Cambridge: Cambridge University Press.

Jenkins, D., 1975, *Black Zion*, London: Wildwood House.

Kanneh, K., 1998, *African Identities: Race, Nation and Culture in Ethnography, Pan-Africanism and Black Literatures*, London: Routledge.

Mafeje, A., 1998a, 'Anthropology in Post-Independence Africa: End of an Era and the Problem of Self-Redefinition', *African Sociological Review* 2 (1): 1-43.

Mafeje, A., 1998b, 'Conversations and Confrontations with My Reviewers', *African Sociological Review* 2 (2): 95-107.

Mafeje, A., 1976, 'The Problem of Anthropology in Historical Perspective: An Inquiry into the Growth of the Social Sciences', *Canadian Journal of African Studies* 10 (2): 307-333.

Magubane, B., 1971, 'A Critical Look at Indices Used in the Study of Social Change in Colonial Africa', *Current Anthropology* 12 (4-5): 419-445.

Malik, K., 1996, *The Meaning of Race: Race, History and Culture in Western Society*, New York: New York University Press.

Mamdani, M., 1990, 'A Glimpse at African Studies, Made in USA', *CODESRIA Bulletin* 2: 7-11.

Martin, W.G. and M.O. West, eds., 1999, *Out of One, Many Africas: Reconstructing the Study and Meaning of Africa*, Urbana and Chicago: University of Illinois Press.

Moore, S.F., 1998, 'Archie Mafeje's Prescription for the Academic Future', *African Sociological Review* 2 (1): 50-56.

Morrison, T., 1992, *Playing in the Dark: Whiteness and the Literary Imagination*, Cambridge: Harvard University Press.

Mudimbe, V. Y., 1988, *The Invention of Africa: Gnosis, Philosophy, and the Order of Knowledge*, Bloomington: Indiana University Press.

Omi, M. and H. Winant, 1994, *Racial Formation in the United States: From the 1960s to the 1990s*, New York: Routledge.

Omi, M. and H. Winant, 1986, *Racial Formation in the United States: From the 1960s to the 1980s*, New York: Routledge.

Onwudiwe, E., 2001, 'A Critique of Recent Writings on Ethnicity and Nationalism', *Research in African Literatures* 32 (3): 213-228.

Pels, P., 2000, 'Occult Truths: Race, Conjecture, and Theosophy in Victorian Anthropology', in R. Handler, ed., *Excluded Ancestors, Inventible Traditions: Essays toward a More Inclusive History of Anthropology*, Madison: The University of Wisconsin Press.

Phillips, C., 2003, 'Out of Africa', *The Guardian Unlimited*. February 24.

Powdermaker, H., 1939, *After Freedom: A Cultural Study in the Deep South*, New York: Viking Press.

Rigby, P., 1996, *African Images: Racism and the End of Anthropology*, Oxford: Berg.

Risjord, M., 2000, 'The Politics of Explanation and the Origins of Ethnography', *Perspectives on Science* 8 (1): 29-52.

Robinson, C., 1983, *Black Marxism: The Making of the Black Radical Tradition*, London: Zed Books.

Sanjek, R., 1994, 'The Enduring Inequalities of Race', in Steven Gregory and Roger Sanjek, eds., *Race*, New Brunswick, NJ: Rutgers University Press.

Scott, D., 1992, 'Criticism and Culture: Theory and Post-Colonial Claims on Anthropological Disciplinarity', *Critique of Anthropology* 12 (4): 371-394.

Shanklin, E., 2000, 'Representations of Race and Racism in American Anthropology', *Current Anthropology* 41 (1): 99-103.

Shanklin, E., 1998, 'The Profession of the Color Blind: Sociocultural Anthropology and Racism in the 21st Century', *American Anthropologist* 100 (3): 669-679.

Shanklin, E., 1994, *Anthropology and Race*, Belmont, CA: Wadsworth Publishing Company.

Shostak, M., 2000, *Nisa: The Life and Words of a !Kung Woman*, Cambridge, MA: Harvard Univ. Press.

Smedley, A., 1993, *Race in North America: Origin and Evolution of a Worldview*, Boulder, CO: Westview.

Stauder, J., [Kath Levine], 1993, 'The "Relevance" of Anthropology to Colonialism and Imperialism', in S. Harding, ed., *The Racial Economy of Science: Toward a Democratic Future*, Bloomington: Indiana University Press.

Stocking, G. W., Jr, 1993, 'The Turn-of-the-Century Concept of Race', *Modernism/Modernity* 1 (1): 4-16.

Stocking, G. W., Jr, 1992, *The Ethnographer's Magic and Other Essays in the History of Anthropology*, Madison, WI: University of Wisconsin Press.

Stocking, G. W., Jr, 1982 [1968], *Race, Culture, and Evolution: Essays in the History of Anthropology*, Chicago: University of Chicago Press.

Trouillot, M.-R., 2003, *Global Transformations: Anthropology and the Modern World*, New York: Palgrave Macmillan.

Trouillot, M.-R., 1991, 'Anthropology and the Savage Slot: The Poetics and Politics of Otherness', in Richard Fox, ed., *Recapturing Anthropology: Working in the Present*, Santa Fe, New Mexico: School of American Research Press.

Visweswaran, K., 1998, 'Race and the Culture of Anthropology', *American Anthropologist* 100 (1): 70-83.

Willis, W. S., Jr, 1972, 'Skeletons in the Anthropological Closet', in Dell Hymes, ed., *Reinventing Anthropology*, New York: Pantheon Books.

Winant, H., 2002, *The World is A Ghetto: Race and Democracy Since WWII*, New York: Basic Books.

Chapter 2

Africana Sociology: A Critical Journey from Pluralism to Postcolonialism

Zine Magubane

Anyone who wishes to study the most terrible manifestations of human nature will find them in Africa. The earliest reports concerning the continent tell us precisely the same, and it has no history in the true sense of the word. We shall therefore leave Africa at this point, and it need not be mentioned again. For it is an unhistorical continent, with no movement or development of its own ... What we understand as Africa proper is that unhistorical and undeveloped land ... which had to be mentioned before we cross the threshold of world history itself (Hegel 1975 [1822]: 142).

[E]thnology studies only barbaric and savage societies; sociology is interested, at least as much, in civilized societies. Ethnography can only be linked to the present, for one can only describe what one has seen; sociology also takes into account the past ... [T]oday it may be that there is rather more to be gained by examining the great civilized societies of the West of the present day (Durkheim 1982 [1907]: 209).

In his *Lectures on the Philosophy of World History* Hegel argued that, from a philosophical perspective, non-European peoples—Native Americans, Africans, and Asians—were less human than Europeans because they were not fully cognizant of themselves as conscious, historical beings; nor had they contributed in any meaningful way to the historical development of the world. Thus history, as a disciplinary practice, could effectively proceed as if the inhabitants of these benighted areas of the world did not exist. Durkheim can be seen as engaged in a similar project of delineating a 'geographical basis' for the practice of sociology. He also distinguished the 'unsociological and undeveloped' parts of the world where, presumably, barbarism rules from those parts of the world where individuals were aware of themselves as conscious, sociological agents. In the above excerpt from an article entitled 'Debate on the relationship between ethnology and sociology', like Hegel, Durkheim left no doubt as to which societies and peoples are the proper objects of historical sociological consciousness and inquiry. The dividing line between ethnography and sociology, according to Durkheim, lies primarily in the latter's ability to 'take into account the past'.

It is in the classics that we can locate the roots of how and why macro-sociology, although methodologically comparative, was thoroughly Eurocentric when it came to the construction of theory. When we consider the methodological blueprints and models historical sociologists inherited from the classics we see that methodologies are not neutral sets of techniques. Rather, they are profoundly influenced and inflected by a set of assumptions about society, history, and the purpose of scholarship.

Theoretical Underpinnings of Classical Sociology

Durkheim's theories assumed a contrastive difference between so-called primitive and modern societies. Indeed, it was Durkheim who first postulated that comparative sociology was sociology itself and that if sociology was to advance from being purely descriptive and become a science it had to embrace the comparative method (Durkheim 1982 [1907]). In Durkheim's work, however, the primitive exists not as a spectre of what the West is not, but rather as a purified and simplified example of what the West once was. In his own words:

> [T]he so-called lower societies have a very special interest for the sociologist: all the social forms which are observable as distinct and organized in more complex societies are to be found there in a state of inter-penetration which highlights better their unity. Moreover, the functioning of more advanced societies can only be understood when we are informed about the organization of the less developed societies (1982 [1907]: 209).

Durkheim's theories about the transition from societies based on mechanical solidarity to those based on organic solidarity (in other words the transition from pre-industrial to industrial society) were also premised on the idea that so-called primitive societies lay totally outside the influence of and were completely untouched by the economic machinations of European states in the form of imperialism and colonialism. Durkheim's texts are marked by a curious elision whereby he must repeatedly deny any knowledge of precisely those colonial practices that make his work possible. In *The Elementary Forms of the Religious Life*, for example, Durkheim repeatedly points to Australian aboriginal and Native American religious practices as examples of primitive religions in their purest forms, utterly untouched by any Western influence. However, much of the extant ethnological information available about so-called primitive religious practices existed precisely because of the fact that their practitioners were continually being dragooned into one colonial imbroglio after another. Indeed, being that he was a 'classic example of the armchair theorist', Durkheim relied extensively on the writings of district commissioners, colonial agents, missionaries, and other colonial officialdom (Fenton 1980: 163). The fact that Durkheim's ethnographic sketches of 'untouched' societies were based on information made available to him by colonial relationships opened him up to rather severe criticism from his contemporaries. For example, H. van Gennep, who reviewed *The Elementary Forms of the Religious Life* shortly after it was published, 'scoffed at the abundance of references to documents provided by sundry informants, police agents, unspecified colonialists, obtuse missionaries, etc.' (quoted in Lukes 1973:525).

The idea that the West has remained sociologically 'untouched' by the presence of Africans, Asians, and Native Americans is not only erroneous, but also theoretically limiting. For example, ignoring the existence of colonialism allowed Durkheim to construct a theory of the transition from pre-industrial to industrial societies which focused exclusively on internal factors such as the growing complexity of the division of labour and increased societal volume and density, and to posit that cultural differences between peoples ultimately explained their different rates and paths of development. As Fenton (1980: 169) correctly observed, Durkheim's functionalism, which insisted on viewing societies as functioning wholes, was premised on the idea that so-called primitive societies were 'integral units with an internal coherence and meaning system, rather than [parts] of a historically developing system of colonial relationships'.

Impact of Classical Sociology on Contemporary Africanist Scholarship

Functionalism, or its related theories of structural-functionalism and systems theory, has been one of the most influential of all social science theories, not only in political science and sociology, but in anthropology. A number of scholars in African studies, particularly those based in the West, carried forth the traditions of historical sociology launched by Durkheim in the form of studies that relied on paired comparisons of social formations. Such comparisons were made in the interest of either developing an explanation for a well-defined outcome or pattern in history or making contrasts among cases in order to highlight features particular to each.

When the sociologist Max Weber (1949: 72) argued that there was 'no absolutely "objective" scientific analysis of culture [or] "social phenomena" independent of special and "one-sided" viewpoints according to which—expressly or tacitly, consciously or unconsciously—they are selected, analyzed, and organized for expository purposes', he could easily have been describing the theoretical and methodological battles over the interpretation of colonial society that have plagued Africanist scholarship over the twentieth century. The very notions of what constituted colonial society and what units of analysis were given the most attention in its analysis were strongly influenced by the theoretical assumptions that underwrote particular schools of thought as well as the methods of analysis that were associated with them.

It is possible to identify four broad categories within which most theoretical analyses of African society fell: pluralist, Marxist, nationalist, and post-colonial. There are, thus, four associated methods of analysis: structural functionalism, class analysis, psychoanalytic analysis and class analysis, and textual/postmodernist approaches. Although each of these schools of thought sought to understand the interaction between the economic system imposed by colonial rule, the interaction between different ethnic and racial communities, the impact on gender relations, and the transformations that occurred in the cultural realm, each differs as to the emphasis or importance placed on these various social factors as well as the correct method whereby they should be analysed.

Structural Functionalist Approaches in African Studies

Starting from the earliest decades of the twentieth century, there emerged a considerable body of literature dealing with problems of what was then called 'acculturation' or 'culture contact' and social change in African society. The first people to produce a coherent body of writing on this topic were evangelical missionaries and colonial administrators with scholarly leanings whose access to indigenous and settler communities allowed them to conduct the first 'field studies' of colonial communities. Anthropology, which emerged as a serious discipline with a defined corpus of scholarship between the World Wars, took its methodological cue from these initial studies. 'In political terms, the anthropologists of this period were essentially secular missionaries' (Wallerstein 1986: 5). Social anthropology and sociology, closely related disciplines, centred on analysing the ways in which the colonial situation forced various communities into contact, and the changes that occurred from it. The most well-known exponents of this analytical approach, which has been termed pluralism, are writers like Mayer (1961) and Kuper (1965) on Southern Africa, and Mitchell (1960) on Central Africa. The Pluralist School was underwritten by the assumption that colonial societies were 'plural societies' characterised by different ethnic groups and races living in close proximity, occasionally coming into conflict, and influencing one another through the diffusion of culture. Because pluralists were interested in the dynamics which structured interactions between different ethnic and racial groups in colonial society, their preferred method of analysis was participant observation and systematic recording.

Pluralist analyses were frequently used to understand family forms in colonial societies, which were taken as a reliable index of whether 'tribalism' or 'tribal values' were able to withstand the experience of acculturation that was the concomitant of living in colonial society. The work of Miner (1953), for example, focused on family structures among the Arab, Tuareg, and Songhai in Timbuktu. Miner argued that Arab people were able to maintain the integrity of their extended family forms, even in the face of immense culture contact and strong pressures towards acculturation. Miner's work catalogued helping patterns, socialising patterns, friendship networks, and support activities amongst the three populations and concluded that acculturation had impacted family forms, but nevertheless, extended family ties retained their traditional importance.

Likewise, modernisation theorists, who also leaned heavily on structural functionalism, argued that a linear process existed whereby developing countries progressively become industrialised; the reasons for the underdevelopment of countries were seen within the different societies in internal factors. For example, some scholars blamed governmental incompetence and corruption for Africa's failure to develop (Decalo 1988; Diamond 1995; Hess 1970; Potholm 1972). Still others pointed to the lack of sufficient capital investment on the part of African states and governments (Ghosh 1984; Ikiara 1989; Ware 1981).

Although all of these studies proceeded from the assumption that 'the Europeans are in a position of social superiority and the Africans aspire to the civilization which is the particular characteristic and perquisite of the socially superior group' (Mitchell 1961: 13), their analyses did not extend to the specifics of European life, religion, and culture in Africa. Nor did they consider the fact that European cultures could undergo their own processes of 'acculturation' or 'Africanisation'. In fact, the colonial situation fell completely outside their analyses. The failure of pluralist analyses to account for the ways in which colonialism, as a global system of economic relations, imposed an urban order on conquered indigenous societies and, further, that this order fundamentally altered patterns of social organisation, family structure, and culture, was the major impetus behind the critique of pluralism, structural functionalism, and empiricist approaches launched by Marxist social scientists.

Marxist Approaches in Africana Sociology

The conservatism of traditional Africanist sociology had as its antidote, however, a fiercely critical Africana sociological practice, which borrowed heavily from Marxism. Marxist Africanist sociologists sharply disagreed with the tenets, methodological practices, and theoretical assumptions of pluralism, structural functionalism, and modernisation theories. Their desire to offer a vision of world history that would ultimately lead to the emancipation of African peoples led them to adopt a highly critical posture towards the favoured analytical theories of both classical and contemporary sociology. Thus, a major methodological challenge to the classics came in the form of their critique of the notion that comparisons were the best analytical device for highlighting the particular features of historical cases and, from there, developing coherent explanations for patterns in history.

Bernard Magubane, a South African sociologist, used the principles of Marxism to attack the indices used by the pluralists for studying colonial society and social change. In particular he singled out the work of Clyde Mitchell on Northern Rhodesia, whose analyses he charged with having mystified real social relations because they failed to account for the fact that the trajectory of British colonialism in Central and Southern Africa was of the industrial-extractive type, whereby the advanced sector (mining camps and towns) was more organically connected to the metropole than to the rural hinterland. He charged pluralist scholarship with having 'a general reluctance to analyze African societies in the context of the colonial situation or as extensions of capitalist societies. This results in a tendency to regard any crisis as having been generated by forces wholly independent of capitalist characteristics' (Magubane [1969] 2000: 30).

Magubane also criticised the manner in which pluralist scholars explained the social changes that were taking place amongst Africans in colonial societies as being simply the result of 'acculturation' or 'culture contact', with no analysis of how social patterns evolved in response to the economic exigencies of colonialism. 'The acquisition of "European" goods was not, therefore, in any sense "imitative" or indicative of status, but a necessary consequence of being absorbed in a milieu dominated by factory-made goods' (Magubane [1971] 2000: 72). Further, he stressed seeing Africans' desires to acquire material goods as being indicative not of a hapless desire to be European but, rather, as an index of their desire to confront and transform the situations that they faced as a result of being reduced to non-persons in the colonial society:

> In reality of course education and occupation, as well as a taste for conventional clothing and food, are instrumental in the struggle for power. The African cannot dispel the feeling of inferiority engendered by the system until he is able to meet and deal with the 'superior' classes on their own terms as regards education in the broadest sense—and that includes styles of dress and diet (Magubane [1971] 2000: 73).

The framework for the idea that colonial society in Africa could only be understood by seeing Africa as part of the capitalist world system was articulated most clearly by Immanuel Wallerstein (1986). Wallerstein questioned the utility of comparing individual capitalist nation-states, noting that the logic of such comparisons is inapplicable to the global capitalist economy, which is composed of partial and variously integrated nation-states. As Ragin and Chirot (1984: 286) explained, focusing on a single social system has important methodological implications: 'Because the capitalist world economy is defined as a single social system, its mechanisms cannot be discovered by comparing it to "other" capitalist world economies. If only one case exists, there is no choice but to establish its nature by knowing its history'. Wallerstein's influence can be seen in the work of a number of scholars. Leroy Vail and Landeg White's (1980) work on capitalism and colonialism in Mozambique analysed how the Portuguese government attempted to control the region by means of neo-mercantilist policies which forced the Quelimane district to furnish Portugal with regulated quantities of produce. The work of Vail and White also demonstrated that the leisure activities of workers, particularly popular protest and work songs, which took up colonial themes, were not examples of 'acculturation' but, rather, indexed the African population's resistance to alien rule.

Nicola Swainson's (1980) work on the development of corporate capitalism in Kenya identified the driving force behind the entry of foreign firms into Kenya as the search for raw materials and the competition between industrial powers. Likewise, Tabitha Kanogo's (1987) work on squatters in Kenya analysed the development of various institutions, such as voluntary self-help educational programmes (*harambee*), which enabled African people to 'turn the White Highlands into a place in which they could feel "at home"' (74). She demonstrated that the development and transformation of indigenous cultural forms were closely connected to the fact that 'squatters had to cope with their positions as workers in a colonial situation'. Thus she saw workers' efforts to transfer wholesale cultural and political institutions such as elders' councils (*ciama*), circumcision (*irua*), and marriage ceremonies not as evidence for the persistence of 'tribalism' or the failure of 'acculturation', but rather as dynamic responses to the colonial situation which changed in order to 'meet the growing challenges from the settler economy' (Kanogo 1987: 74).

Patrick Manning's work on the expansion of European and Muslim culture in francophone Africa also demonstrates that changes in African religious practices were closely related to the changes introduced by the spread of global capitalism. Thus, he analysed Christian conversions, not as examples of 'Westernisation' but, rather, as dynamic responses to a changing world. In answer to the question 'why, then, should Africans have found any advantage in Christianity or Islam?', he suggested that conversion came about because Africans 'were now in a world-wide political system, that of colonies and their European mother countries, so their beliefs should extend to a world-wide frame of reference. In this sense, conversions to Islam and Christianity may not have been renunciations of the old religions, but translation of the old religions into new terms' (Manning 1988: 102).

Nationalist Approaches in Africana Sociology

This emphasis on exploring Africans as agentic subjects, and colonial society as a site marked by ethnic, racial, and class conflicts which structured and gave meaning to large scale concepts like 'the West' and 'Africa' was most strongly articulated by the inventors of Négritude, which was both a philosophy of history and a mode of anti-colonial resistance. This school of thought also sought to extend the idea of colonial society beyond a focus on individual societies, instead seeing colonised people the world over as sharing similar experiences and a similar consciousness. For scholars like Senghor, the experience of colonialism was a racial experience, which created what he called a 'collective personality' of the black people (Senghor [1970] 1994: 28).

Like Marxist and World System analyses, Négritude also focused on the fact that European colonialism systematically underdeveloped the colonised world. Like pluralist scholars, they also concerned themselves with assessing the impact of European cultures and values, imposed during colonialism, on African societies. Négritude, however, completely reversed the hierarchy of values that underwrote pluralist scholarship. Aimé Césaire, for example, opened his *Discourse on Colonialism* with a damning indictment of the West: 'Europe is morally, spiritually indefensible' (Césaire [1955] 1972: 9). He then went on to dispute the idea that Europe brought anything resembling civilisation to its colonies:

> I ask the following question: has colonization really *placed civilizations in contact?* Or, if you prefer, of all the ways of establishing contact, was it the best? I answer no. And I say between *colonization* and *civilization* there is an infinite distance; that out of all the colonial expeditions that have been undertaken, out of all the colonial states that have been drawn up, out of all the memoranda that have been dispatched by all the ministries, there could not come a single human value (Césaire [1955] 1972: 12; my emphasis).

Unlike the pluralists, Négritude scholars placed equal emphasis on exposing the changes wrought by colonialism on the societies and cultures of the coloniser and of the colonised. Thus, Césaire argued that the most profound alteration that took place within colonial society was that which impacted the coloniser, who steadily brutalised and de-humanised himself by his refusal to acknowledge and accept the humanity of his fellow African. 'First we must study how colonization works to *decivilize* the colonizer, to *brutalize* him in the true sense of the word, to degrade him, to awaken him to buried instincts, to covetousness, violence, race-hatred, and moral relativism ...' (Césaire [1955] 1972:13; my emphasis). Thus, in recovering their voices and stories it was possible to mount a historiographical revolution of sorts.

Critiques of European colonialism, such as those articulated by scholars working in the Négritude tradition, operated, in effect, as challenges to this idea of Europe as a kind of ideal and unchanging abstraction, which possessed a set of indisputable and readily identifiable positive traits. Négritude, originally a literary and ideological movement of French-speaking black intellectuals, reflects an important and comprehensive reaction to the colonial situation. This movement, which influenced Africans as well as blacks around the world, specifically rejects the political, social, and moral domination of the West. The term, which has been used in a general sense to describe the black world in opposition to the West, assumes the total consciousness of belonging to the black race.

Aimé Césaire, the founder of the Négritude movement, questioned the objectivity of concepts such as rationality and civilisation, arguing that they were based upon an ontological and epistemological distinction being made between 'the West' and 'the Rest' that was by no means objective. Césaire maintained that the barbarism of the Third World and the civilisation of Europe were discursive effects produced when Africa, Asia, and Latin America were looked at through the categories of modern European social science. Hence, he railed against the conceptual categories developed by bourgeois European intellectuals, which he saw as national myths which provided 'the appearance of historical narrative to what was in actuality part fact and part class-serving rationales' (Robinson 1983: 267). As Césaire (1972 [1955]: 57) put it: 'One of the values invented by the bourgeoisie in former times and launched throughout the world was man—and we have seen what has become of that. The other was the nation. It is a fact: the nation is a bourgeois phenomenon.' Thus, in his *Discourse on Colonialism*, Césaire argued that there was no such thing as 'Western civilisation'. As he put it, 'at the present time the barbarism of Western Europe has reached an incredibly high level, being only surpassed—far surpassed, it is true—by the barbarism of the United States' (Césaire 1972 [1955]: 26). According to Césaire, Europe, rather than being an exemplar of rationality, had actually 'undermined civilization, destroyed countries, ruined nationalities, and extirpated root of diversity' (59).

Postcolonial Studies and African Studies

The themes first explored by Césaire have been taken up and refined by scholars who identify themselves with postcolonial studies, which 'operates within the discipline as a kind of insurgency with respect to conventional academic forms of history' (Young 1990: 160). Postcolonial studies began with the goal of establishing a new critique of both colonialist and nationalist perspectives in the historiography of colonised countries. Postcolonial scholarship, in the words of Catherine Hall (1996: 70), seeks to demonstrate that 'the political and institutional histories of "the centre" and its outer circles [are] more mutually constituted than we used to think'. Recognising that political ideas, ideals, and strategies cannot be confined to national or geographic boundaries, sociologists working within this tradition, in addition to comparing the experiences of different nations, also are interested in identifying, exploring, and explaining varying instances of dialogue across different nations.

The 'post' in postcolonial is taken not to mean 'past' but rather to capture the idea of engaging with, moving through, and moving beyond coloniality (Appiah 1992). Postcolonial scholarship borrows a number of its analytical models from Marxist scholarship and its themes from the work done by Négritude scholars. In particular, they eschew a narrow focus on individual colonial societies in favour of looking at how colonialism worked as a system of both economic relations and discourse, which produced a set of ideological constructions that are currently termed 'Africa' (Mudimbe 1994). Thus, they seek to understand the ways in which colonial societies were shaped both by a system of economic relations and a system of cultural and symbolic representations that impacted Africans and Europeans profoundly, albeit in different ways. While acknowledging the importance of class relations in structuring the relationship between the coloniser and the colonised, they also seek to use other analytical methods in concert with class analysis—including deconstruction, symbolic interactionism, literary criticism, discourse analysis, and psychoanalysis. In their analyses, colonial society emerges not as a space of 'acculturation' or even a space of economic or racial 'exploitation', but rather as a space of cultural negotiation or 'hybridity'. Thus, Robert Young (1995: 24) argues that 'hybridization as creolization involves fusion, the creation of a new form, which can then be set against the old form, of which it is partly made up'.

Postcolonial analysis has been particularly influential on scholars from South Africa. Anne McClintock (1995) has examined the connections between anti-racist, anti-imperialist, and feminist politics in Britain and colonial South Africa. Jean and John Comaroff (1992) have looked at the ways in which empire shaped the making of the British working and middle classes, while scholars David Theo Goldberg (2002) and Zine Magubane (2004) have examined the transnational circulation of racist ideologies and practices.

Postcolonial scholarship has put forth a significant challenge to traditional thinking in macro-sociology. As was mentioned above, comparative-historical sociologists have been strongly committed to identifying independent units for use in comparative assessments. For the most part nation-states, which were seen as geographically bounded and independent wholes, have been the preferred cases. However, sociologists whose work is informed by post-colonialism, such as Paul Gilroy (1993), have focused on diaspora populations and transnational communities. In so doing their work draws upon a long tradition of scholars and activists who defined themselves as part of a larger international black community and thus sought to 'devise a theoretical framework or conception of history that treat[ed] the African diaspora as a whole' (Kelley 1996: 103).

Viewing societies as transnational, rather than national, phenomena has important methodological implications. Although it is possible to envision a study that compares the origins and historical trajectories of different diaspora populations by juxtaposing aspects of a small number of cases, most diaspora scholars eschew such an approach in favour of one that seeks to understand the culturally-embedded intentions of individual and group actors with the idea that parallel situations exist in different geographical areas. Thus, scholarship on the African diaspora, for example, seeks to explore the specific situations of black people in different geographical areas while remaining cognizant of the 'black world' as a totality. Methodologically this has meant that the act of drawing historical comparisons has been supplanted by a search for historical parallels and a more thorough exploration of what Stuart Hall termed processes of 'transculturation' or 'cultural translation'. According to Hall (1996: 247), post-colonialism is a method of analysis that 'obliges us to re-read the very binary form in which the colonial encounter has for so long itself been represented. It obliges us to re-read the binaries as forms of transculturation, of cultural translation, destined to trouble the here/there cultural boundaries forever'.

Thus, when postcolonial scholars consider the ways in which African modes of dress or 'self-fashioning' changed with the advent of colonialism, they focus on the ways in which the struggles over how African bodies were to be clothed and represented 'were a crucial site in the battle of wills and deeds, the dialectic of means and ends, that shaped the encounter between Europeans and Africans. And transformed both in the process' (Comaroff and Comaroff 1997: 222). Similarly, religion, particularly the conversion to Christianity, is also seen as further evidence of how Africans, although 'encompassed by the European capitalist system', sought to 'seize its symbols, to question their authority and integrity, and to reconstruct them in their own image' (Comaroff and Comaroff 1991: xii). Postcolonial scholarship on Arab nationalism in the Middle East and North Africa has also shown how nationalists 'invested colonially created territorial units with their own meanings of community or nation by drawing upon myths of Arab origin or the Islamic golden age of the Caliphates, even though some early Arab nationalists were Christian' (Loomba 1998: 197).

Because postcolonial scholarship was originally the province of literary critics, it is overwhelmingly concerned with questions of language and its impact on identity formation. Taking their cue from Fanon (1967: 31), who argued that 'to speak means to assume a culture', postcolonial scholars have analysed the role that the coloniser's metropolitan language played in the process of erasing cultural memory. Postcolonial scholars have also sought to engage how language works to simultaneously buttress and challenge the will to power. Thus, Chinua Achebe argues that African fiction, even when written in English, transforms so as to reflect a uniquely African sensibility. He argues that 'I feel that the English language will be able to carry the weight of my African experience. But it will have to be a new English, still in full communion with its ancestral home but altered to suit its new African surroundings' (Achebe [1975] 1994: 434).

Gender and sexuality, and their relationship to the production of race, together with the ways in which they were transformed by colonial rule, have also been at the forefront of postcolonial scholarship. Unlike pluralists, who sought to examine how Westernisation altered sexual and family relationships or Marxists, who sought to analyse how the migrant labour system transformed African family forms and gender relationships, postcolonial scholars instead focus on the symbolic importance of sexual and racial alterity in the representation of the colonised as 'Other'. Thus, they analyse the policing of sexual and racial boundaries of sexuality in colonial society as a critical component of the project to demarcate 'Self' and 'Other' both within individual colonial societies, as well as in the empire as a whole, with female bodies marking the 'boundaries' of empire (McClintock 1995).

Conclusion

As was shown above, an important trend has emerged in Africana sociology whereby scholars are less wedded to a vision of society as an essentially closed system and, instead, have become open to the idea that societies are constituted by relations of exchange and are marked by a significant degree of interpenetration. Since macro-sociologists can no longer treat societies as independent units, they have had to search for alternative methodologies. The comparative method, whereby contrasts are made among cases in order to either highlight features particular to discrete historical contexts or to establish causal regularities, has been shown to be inadequate in those instances where cases cannot be viewed as essentially independent. Thus scholars have opened themselves up to alternative methods, many of which owe a strong debt to post-modernism and post-structuralism. Discursive analysis, Foucauldian 'archaeological' approaches, and deconstruction have all emerged as alternate research strategies in Africana sociology.

The effort to rid sociology of its Eurocentrism has introduced significant tensions into scholarship—different questions must be asked, different sources of evidence must be drawn upon, and different analytical methods must be developed. These tensions have, on the whole, been productive, rather than disabling. Current moves to understand what Said (1979: 4) called our 'overlapping territories and intertwined histories' have had a profound impact on the practice of historical sociology—mostly for the better. Theda Skocpol (1984: 356) concluded *Vision and Method in Historical Sociology* with the observation that 'the stream of historical sociology has deepened into a river and spread out into eddies running through all parts of the sociological enterprise'. One might make the same observation about studies of Africa—they too have deepened into a river and spread out into eddies running though all parts of traditional sociology.

References

Achebe, C., 1994 [1975], 'The African Writer and the English Language', in P. Williams and L. Chrisman, eds., *Colonial Discourse/Postcolonial Theory*, New York: Columbia University Press, 428-434.

Appiah, K.A., 1992, *In My Father's House: Africa in the Philosophy of Culture*, London: Oxford.

Césaire, A., 1972 [1955], *Discourse on Colonialism*, New York: Monthly Review Press.

Comaroff, J. and J. Comaroff, 1991, *Of Revelation and Revolution* Vol I. Chicago: University of Chicago Press.

Comaroff, J. and J. Comaroff, 1992, *Ethnography and the Historical Imagination*, Boulder: Westview.

Comaroff, J. and J. Comaroff, 1997, *Of Revelation and Revolution* Vol. II, Chicago: University of Chicago Press.

Decalo, S., 1988, *The Psychosis of Power: African Personal Dictatorships*, Boulder: Westview.

Diamond, L., 1995, 'Nigeria: the Uncivic Society and the Descent into Praetorianism', in L. Diamond, J.J. Linz, and S.M. Lipset, eds., *Politics in Developing Countries: Comparing Experiences with Democracy*, Second Edition. Boulder: Lynne Rienner Publishers, 417-472.

Durkheim, E., 1982 [1907], *The Rules of Sociological Method*, New York: The Free Press.

Durkheim, E., 1965 [1915], *The Elementary Forms of the Religious Life*, New York: The Free Press.

Fanon, F., 1967, *Black Skin, White Masks*, New York: Grove.

Fenton, S. C., 1980, 'Race, Class, and Politics in the Work of Emile Durkheim', in UNESCO, ed., *Sociological Theories: Race and Colonialism*, Paris: UNESCO, 143-181.

Ghosh, P.K., ed., 1984, *Developing Africa: A Modernization Perspective*, Westport: Greenwood Press.

Gilroy, P., 1993, *The Black Atlantic: Modernity and Double Consciousness*, Cambridge: Harvard University Press.

Goldberg, D. T., 2002, *The Racial State*, London: Basil Blackwell.

Hall, C., 1996, 'Histories, Empires, and the Post-Colonial Moment', in I. Chambers and L. Curti, eds., *The Post-Colonial Question: Common Skies, Divided Horizons*, New York: Routledge, 65-77.

Hall, S., 1996, 'When was the Post-Colonial: Thinking at the Limit', in I. Chambers and L. Curti, eds., *The Post-Colonial Question: Common Skies, Divided Horizons*, New York: Routledge, 242-60.

Hegel, G.W. F., 1975 [1822], *Lectures on the Philosophy of World History*, trans. H.B. Nisbet, New York: Oxford.

Hess, R.L., 1970, *Ethiopia: The Modernization of Autocracy*, Ithaca: Cornell.

Ikiara, G., 1989, *The Role of Culture in the Development Process: The Case of Kenya*, Nairobi.

Kanogo, T., 1987, *Squatters and the Roots of Mau Mau*, London: James Currey.

Kelley, R., 1996, 'The World the Diaspora Made: C.L.R. James and the Politics of History', in G. Farred, ed., *Rethinking C.L.R. James*, Cambridge: Blackwell, 103-130.

Kuper, L., 1965, 'Sociology: Some Aspects of Urban Plural Societies', in R. A. Lystad, ed., *The African World: A Survey of Social Research*, New York: Praeger.

Loomba, A., 1998, *Colonialism/Postcolonialism*, London: Routledge.

Lukes, S., 1973, *Emile Durkheim: His Life and Work*, London: Allen Lane.

Magubane, B., 2000, *African Sociology: Towards a Critical Perspective*, Trenton: Africa World Press.

Magubane, Z., 2004, *Bringing the Empire Home: Race, Class, and Gender in Britain and Colonial South Africa*, Chicago: University of Chicago Press.

Manning, P., 1988, *Francophone Sub-Saharan Africa, 1880-1985*, Cambridge: Cambridge University Press.

Mayer, P., 1961, *Townsmen or Tribesmen*, Cape Town: Oxford.

McClintock, A., 1995, *Imperial Leather: Race, Gender, and Sexuality in the Colonial Context*, London: Routledge.

Miner, H., 1953, *The Primitive City of Timbuctoo*, Philadelphia: American Philosophical Society.

Mitchell, C., 1961, *Tribalism and the Plural Society*, Oxford: Oxford University Press.

Mudimbe, V. Y., 1994, *The Idea of Africa*, Bloomington: Indiana University Press.

Potholm, C. P., 1972, *Swaziland: The Dynamics of Political Modernization*, Berkeley: University of California Press.

Ragin, C. and D. Chirot, 1984, 'The World System of Immanuel Wallerstein: Sociology and Politics as History', in T. Skocpol, ed., *Vision and Method in Historical Sociology*, Cambridge: Cambridge University Press.

Said, E., 1979, *Orientalism*, New York: Vintage.

Skocpol, T., ed., 1984, *Vision and Method in Historical Sociology*, Cambridge: Cambridge University Press.

Senghor, L. S., 1994 [1970], 'Negritude: a Humanism of the Twentieth Century', in Patrick Williams and Laura Chrisman, eds., *Colonial Discourse/Postcolonial Theory: A Reader*, New York: Columbia University Press, 27-35.

Swainson, N., 1980, *The Development of Corporate Capitalism in Kenya, 1918-1977*, Berkeley: University of California Press.

Vail, L. and L. White, 1980, *Capitalism and Colonialism in Mozambique*, Minneapolis: University of Minnesota Press.

Wallerstein, I., 1986, *Africa and the Modern World*, Trenton: Africa World Press.

Ware, H., 1981, *Women, Education, and Modernization of the Family in West Africa*, Perth: Australian National University Press.

Weber, M., 1949, *The Methodology of the Social Sciences*, New York: Free Press.

Young, R., 1990, *White Mythologies: Writing History and the West*, London: Routledge.

Chapter 3

Ethnography on an Awkward Scale: Postcolonial Anthropology and the Violence of Abstraction[1]

Jean and John Comaroff

... talking to the natives is evidently a dangerous experiment.
—Violetta Lee [1890] (1998:407).

More than thirty years ago we met a madman in Mafeking, now the hyphenated capital of the North West Province in the 'new' South Africa.[2] Or, to be more precise, we met a prophet in polythene robes who had been incarcerated in a mental asylum by the apartheid state. We spoke of him in a scholarly essay (Comaroff and Comaroff 1987): outside of his extravagantly coloured costume, what had marked his presence on the local scene before his 'admission' to hospital was a fondness for standing, hour after hour, as a silent witness near the local railway depot. It was from here that generations of black men were transported nightly to the cities of *Makgoweng*, the Place of Whites, to toil in its mines and factories. It was from here, too, that the capillaries of racial capitalism, South Africa-style, became visible to anybody who cared to gaze upon the twilight movement of migrating males across a cloven landscape. Anybody troubled enough. Or mad enough.

Three decades on, after the demise of the *ancien régime*, we passed the very spot, in Station Road, where the mute madman used to linger. He had died, anonymously, some years before. It was early afternoon on a Saturday, a sparkling winter day in July. As we crossed the street on our way to the local police station we noticed a small knot of men-in-blue nearby. They had surrounded a decidedly strange figure: an adult male, nude except for a pair of threadbare boxers, covered in white paste. Emaciated, his eyes showed no animation whatsoever. With a measure of gentleness not usually associated with the law here, he was taken to the Mafikeng Community Service Centre; police stations are now 'community service centres,' just as the old

South African Police *Force* has become the South African Police *Services*—where he was fed and allowed to wander around unhindered. Which he did, every now and again climbing on a chair or a desk, every now and again curling up in foetal repose. All the while, like the madman of earlier vintage, he uttered not a word. We asked the officers on desk duty who, or what, the figure was.

'A zombie,' we were told.

'What is to become of him,' we asked.

'We hope that his people, maybe a maternal uncle (*malome*), will come for him,' said one officer.

'How did he come to be wandering in Station Road?'

'Who knows? Perhaps his owner lost him or let him go by mistake.'

As we have noted (Comaroff and Comaroff 1999c; cf. Ralushai et al. 1996: 5), there are a fair number of living-dead about these days. Termed *dithotsela* or *dipoko* (sing. *sepoko*, from the Afrikaans *spook*, 'ghost'), they are thought to be the creatures of witches who, by nefarious means, have sucked away their human essence and turned them into brute labour power; this to make them toil away at night in the fields. Indeed, the (then) acting Vice Chancellor of the local University of the North West, himself a scholar of the white Afrikaans occult, casually promised to introduce us to one about whom he had long known.

He did not have to. We encountered many more in the course of our own research.[3] Some of them appeared in circumstances much less benign, much more violent and troubled than those that brought the frail phantom to the attention of the Mafikeng police. One such circumstance ended in the murder of a well-known personage in the province, 'Ten-Ten' Motlhabane Makolomakwa. Sometime middle-level state employee, owner of a local football team, successful farmer, and the chairman of the tribal council of Matlonyane village, he was set alight by five youths who insisted that he had killed their fathers and turned them into spectral field hands.[4] Another, in 1995, involved striking workers at a coffee plantation in nearby Mpumalanga Province: they refused to work for three supervisors whom they accused of killing employees and turning them into zombies for their private enrichment.[5] A third case—immortalised in a play, *Ipizombi*, well-known in local cultural circles and beyond—was sparked by a taxi accident in Kokstad in which twelve schoolboys were killed. Much discussed all over South Africa at the time, it involved the murder of two elderly 'witches' who were said to have stolen the corpses and conjured them into living-dead.[6]

Cases like this are often reported in matter-of-fact terms by the national media (cf. Fordred 1998) and—along with Hollywood horror movies, local *telenovelas* of witch killings, and other iterations of spectral death-and-dread—are widely consumed. Significantly, they are sometimes invoked, either before the fact or in the act, by those who perpetrate occult-related violence in the South African countryside. On occasion they have also become the stuff of cyber-talk, not least among southern Africans abroad, whose anxious internet exchanges, intermittently filtered through EuroAmerican urban legends, have flowed back onto local soil, there to be fabricated into new kinds of fact. Thus it is that reality and its representations become confounded in one another, at once both cause and effect, each inseparably a part of the phenomenology of everyday life in the postcolony. Thus do imported and domestic spirits infuse each other; all being signs of both the local and the translocal, here and elsewhere, now and then, the concrete and the virtual. Thus it is that the national population of living-dead is thought, in some parts of South Africa, to have been joined by transnational zombies, entering the country from Mozambique and other places (see n. 3), just as they did in earlier times (Harries 1994). Thus it is, too, that home-grown phantoms bear more than passing, if culturally inflected, resemblance to images originating in Haitian Voodoo, to the celluloid freaks that haunt such films as *Night of the Living Dead* (George Romero 1968) or *The Serpent and the Rainbow* (Wes Craven 1988), and to ghouls that rise to the rhythms of various popular musics.

These spectres, in turn, evoke others: most obviously, a trade in human beings and body parts at once local and transnational, real and imagined, legitimate and illicit, more or less coerced. It is a trade, as we all now know, that stretches from the import and export of sex-workers, domestic workers, and mail order brides (these often being hard to tell apart); through the sale and adoption of babies (also difficult to distinguish, the latter often being an ethicised, affectively-acceptable euphemism for the former); to transactions in blood, genes, eyes, hearts, kidneys, and the like, transactions in which the medical may run into the magical (Ehrenreich and Hochschild 2003; Scheper-Hughes and Wacquant 2002). Some of this trade, when it entails fully sentient persons, evokes the horrors of slavery; where less than whole persons are involved, it extends the logic of commodity exchange to ever more divisible components of *homo sapiens*. Almost everywhere it is regarded, by those whose populations are being harvested, as a new form of *Empire* erected under the increasingly contested sign of global free trade and its highly inequitable flows of wealth; a curious footnote, this, to Hardt and Negri (2000).[7] Elsewhere, we argue that these phenomena are all interrelated features of an 'occult economy,' itself spawned by a brand of neoliberal capitalism that attributes to the free market an ineluctably salvific, redemptive, even messianic quality. By 'occult economy' (Comaroff and Comaroff 1999a) we intend a set of practises involving the (again, real or imagined) resort to magical means for material ends; or, more expansively, the conjuring of wealth by inherently mysterious techniques. Of course, what counts as 'magic' varies, although it is always set apart from habitual, more transparent forms of production. This arcane economy has other, well-known manifestations: among them, an alleged rise in many parts of the world of witchcraft and satanism (J. Comaroff 1997; Geschiere 1977; La Fontaine 1997), of 'fee for service' faiths (Weller 2000; Comaroff and Comaroff 2002; cf. Kramer 1999), of enchanted financial practises that, like pyramid schemes and lotteries, promise fabulous wealth without work.

All this enchantment, tellingly, is making itself felt at just the moment when the global triumph of modernity was supposed to put an end, once and for all, to such putatively premodern things. The iron cage, so feared by Max Weber, turns out to have been a cage of ironies. To be sure, if ever there was a figure that typified the magical production of wealth without work, of the occult grounding of neoliberal capitalism *tout court*, it is the zombie: all surplus value, no costly, irrational, troublesome human needs. This kaleidoscopic figure, the ultimate embodiment of flexible, 'non-standard,' asocial labour, comes to us in a range of ethnographic, historical, and literary accounts that point both to subtle differences and to non-coincidental similarities. Zombies appear, simultaneously, as antemodern and postmodern, simultaneously supralocal, translocal, and local, simultaneously planetary and, refracted through the shards of vernacular cultural practises, profoundly parochial. Which is why the living-dead now regularly cross international borders; why, say, a South African doctor of Indian origins could claim to have been turned into a ghostly automaton by a Nigerian satanist.[8] And why zombification, the stuff of much urban legend across the world right now, has become an allegorical touchstone for describing the ostensible alienation, loss of individuality, and corporate mastery of an epoch, as yet in its infancy, already being described as Post-Human (Halberstam 1995; Fukuyama 2002). As it did, albeit in somewhat different guise, with the rise of Fordism and the mode of human abstraction (dis)embodied in its production lines[9]— and, before that, on the plantations and in the mines of far-flung colonies.

Our concerns here, we stress, are *not* theoretical or conceptual.[10] We came across zombies, recall, through an *empirical* conjuncture: it was by force of historical fact, rather than by way of abstract analytical interest, that we found ourselves compelled to make sense of them *in situ*. Consequently, what detains us here is much more immediate, much more modest, much more, well, methodological. By what ethnographic means does one capture the commodification of human beings in part or in whole, the occult economy of which it is part, the material and moral conditions that animate such an economy, the new religious and social movements it spawns, the modes of producing wealth which it privileges, and so on? Inherently awkward of scale, none of these phenomena are easily captured by the ethnographer's lens. Should each of them nonetheless be interrogated purely in their own particularity, their own locality? Or should we try to recognise where, in the particularity of the local, lurk social forces of larger scale, forces whose sociology demands attention if we are to make sense of the worlds we study without parochialising and, worse yet, exoticising them. Geertz (1973), for whom ethnography defined the generic *practice* of anthropology, once remarked famously that we do not study villages, that we study *in* villages. The point was well-taken. But how—given that the objects of our gaze commonly elude, embrace, attenuate, transcend, transform, consume, and construct the local—do we arrive at a praxis for an age that seems ... post-anthropological? Of an age in which we are called upon not to study *in* places at all, indeed not to trust 'anthropological locations' (Gupta and Ferguson 1997), but rather to study the *production* of place (Appadurai 1996)? If we are not sure where or what 'the field' is, or how to circumscribe the things in which we interest ourselves, wherein lie the ways and means by which we are to make the knowledges with which we vex ourselves?

Of course, the question of Method, in the upper case, is not new. It has been with us throughout the life of the discipline, if in different forms and formulations. Nor, right now, are we alone in this. Postcolonial historians, for example, seem to be anguishing a lot these days about the death of history. Not *The End of History* as proclaimed a decade ago, somewhat infamously, by Francis Fukuyama (1992), but an altogether new kind of death: death by diffusion into memory, biography, testimony, heritage tourism, and other expressions of history-as-lived rather than history-as-learned (Minkley, Rassool and Witz n.d.; cf. J. Comaroff 2005). In times past we anthropologists plagued ourselves over the epistemic, ethical, and political dimensions of what we do: over whether ours was not an endemically colonising enterprise—a pre-emptive seizure of authority, of voice, of the right to represent and, incidentally, to profit—or, worse yet, an activity founded, voyeuristically, on the violation of 'the' other. Now, like those postcolonial historians, we worry whether our subject matter is ours at all or whether it has forever dispersed itself beyond our privileged dominion. Once we were told that we would be out of business just as soon as our natives were no longer authentically native (a.k.a. primitive, colonised). Today we are undermined by the fact that those very 'natives' have seized the terms of our trade, terms in which we once described *them*, terms that seem not to work very well any more as analytic constructs, terms that, now essentialised and commodified by 'others' one and all, return to haunt us. Add to this two other considerations, themselves intimately connected: first, the aforementioned fact that almost everything which falls within the discursive purview of contemporary anthropology exists, in the phenomenal world, on a scale that does not yield easily to received anthropological theories or methods; and second, that our 'subjects' no longer inhabit social contexts for which we have a persuasive lexicon, not least because abstract nouns like society, community, culture, and class have all been called into question in this ever more neoliberal age (cf. Stoller 1997: 82), this age of the scare quote-around-everything, this age of ironic, iconic detachment. What, in the upshot, are we left with? A very stark question: Has ethnography become an impossibility? Have we finally reached its end?

Ethnography and its Global Distractions

> ... what actually happened, the facts of the case, who said what ... all that is incidental. The real truth is behind all that. The real truth may be swimming in a completely different direction ... And that's what you have to get to ... Forget the appearances.
> —Neil McCarthy, *The Great Outdoors*.[11]

Not surprisingly, in light of this Big Question, there has been a fair bit of debate, over the past few years, about the fate of ethnography in the age of globalisation. We have addressed the matter ourselves, most pointedly in our Max Gluckman Memorial Lecture of 1998 (Comaroff and Comaroff 1999a). Its title, 'Occult

Economies and the Violence of Abstraction,' sought to invoke the stark dislocations wrought on the everyday lives of ordinary citizens in the northerly provinces of South Africa by material forces of ever more planetary scale, dislocations about which many of them spoke with both anxiety and passion. We also meant to underscore the challenge involved in grasping, ethnographically, the processes by which those world-historical forces were being made meaningful and tractable by the human beings in question: how they laboured to condense and personalise values and relations in conditions which *they* presumed to be labile, difficult to understand, inherently mysterious in their effects. Among our objectives, in sum, was an effort to reflect on the interplay of theory and method in the treatment of an anthropological location of changing proportions. Although of pressing concern at the moment, this is a problem as old as the discipline itself. Our essay, after all, was written to commemorate a scholar who tried long ago to subject the broad sweep of the colonial encounter to the ethnographic gaze.

In the post-Marxist age, the strongest suit of anthropology, in the eyes of most of its practitioners, remains its 'ability to get inside and understand small-scale communities, to comprehend local loyalties and systems of knowledge' (Graeber 2002: 1222). Our disciplinary concerns may alter, our genres may blur, our theories may come and go, but ethnography remains 'the anthropologist's muse' (Lewis 1973), the source of solace to which we turn in the face of epistemic or political doubt. An extended spell of 'participant-observation' is still the irreducible minimum of professional credentials required in the discipline, Sherry Ortner (1997: 61) notes. This in spite of the ambiguity that attaches to each of the two terms, not to mention the oxymoron built into their hyphenation. This in spite, also, of the fact illustrated by Ortner's own account of studying the 'postcommunity'—that contemporary anthropological practice deviates, as it probably always has done, from the foundational fiction of fieldwork: the conceit, now long criticised (cf. Gupta and Ferguson 1997), that it is possible to access 'the totality of relations' of a 'society,' or the essential workings of 'a culture,' in any one place.[12]

And yet the axiom that lies behind this fiction, that *any* knowledge derived at first-hand by proximity to natives has an *a priori* privilege, continues to shape the analytical vision of the discipline. 'Ethnography', says George Marcus (1994: 44), 'functions well and creatively without a sense that it needs a positive theoretical paradigm—that is, conventional social theory—to guide it. Instead, it breeds off the critique of its own rhetoric'. As a result, anthropology has, for the most part, remained unrelentingly positivist in spirit. Much of its shared wisdom consists in generalisations about the particular that are also particularisations of the general; empirical aggregates, in short, not abstract propositions or explanatory schemata. The role of this species of knowledge, like its politics (Graeber 2002), has been to show that, even in the act of accommodating to ineluctable macrocosmic forces, different peoples do things differently, be it because of their distinctive cultures, their social situations, or their will to resist (cf. Marcus 1994). The epistemic consequences that follow are plain enough: a committed realism, and a form of relativism that sits uneasily with 'general' theory grounded in history, philosophy, political economy, or whatever. True, there have always been counter tendencies: those who have espoused evolutionary, Marxist, feminist, sociobiological, or psychoanalytic approaches, for instance, have been more partial to higher-order abstraction, generalisation, explanation. But this minority has tended to be the exception that proves the rule.

The epistemic foundations of anthropology's empiricism received somewhat less scrutiny than they might have done during the 'reflexive moment' of the 1980s. But in practice, ethnography was already undergoing a metamorphosis. The discipline was coming face to face with the consequences of what had begun to make itself felt in the 1960s: that 'local' systems—or, to be more precise, the signs and practices observable within any given social world, however it was constituted—could no longer be studied, or accounted for, with reference to conventional geographies; that the fiction of sovereign cultures, however deftly described or ethnographically authenticated, could no longer be sustained; that established modes of representation were no longer sufficient unto the political and ethical demands of 'writing culture' (Clifford and Marcus 1986). Yet, in the absence of 'an explicit paradigm for experimentation' (Marcus 1994: 46), the methodological revolution one might have expected to flow from these shifts of perspective—themselves sharpened with every passing year by the complex, uneven effects of processes of planetary integration—has not been forthcoming. *Per contra*, notwithstanding some creative efforts to author new kinds of anthropology, the reaction in many quarters, in Europe as well as in North America, has been conservative. There has been a tendency to batten down the hatches in fervid defence of the particular, the local, and the parochial against the onslaught of 'the global' (for example, Sahlins 1999; Kapferer 2000; 2001; Englund 1996; Rutherford 1999), the latter, in anthropology-talk, having become a generalised, under-motivated sign of the changing universe in which we live and work.

Why? One consequence of globalisation for the human sciences, argues Appadurai (1997: 115), has been to instil an anxiety that the 'space of intimacy in social life' will be lost; the very space of intimacy that has always been the ethnographer's stock-in-trade. Whether or not this is a sufficient explanation for the anthropological *angst* of the present moment, it certainly *is* the case that our latest 'crisis of representation' has been transposed into a methodological key—as if the survival of the discipline depended entirely on preserving its established modes of producing knowledge. Note how, in some quarters, ethnography is being depicted as an endangered species. Englund and Leach (2000: 238), for instance, appear to believe that 'it' is engaged in a mortal struggle with 'generalising perspectives' whose powerful, if unnamed, proponents have allegedly decreed that 'localised fieldwork has had its day'. For Englund and Leach, the enemy is the 'meta-narrative of modernity', a somewhat ill-defined construct which, despite their protestations to the contrary, seems suspiciously like a synonym for 'Theory' in the upper case.[13] And for an ensemble of 'familiar sociological abstractions', among them commodification, space-time compression, individualisation, disenchantment. This 'metropolitan' meta-narrative, they argue, 'undermine(s) ... what is unique in the ethnographic method—its reflexivity, which gives subjects authority in determining the context of their beliefs and practices' (Englund and Leach 2000: 225). The apprehensiveness about the future of fieldwork palpable here seems to stem, above all, from a crisis of identity, from sacred boundaries breached, and, concomitantly, from the desire to preserve a unique scholarly patrimony from the encroachment of an ever more generic social science. It cannot have gone unnoticed, in this regard, that *other* disciplines have lately laid claim to ethnographic methods. Thus Englund and Leach (2000: 238) insist that '[t]he uniqueness of the ethnographic method is at stake in the current fascination with multiple modernities ... Sociocultural anthropology merges into cultural studies and cultural sociology, and ethnographic analyses become illustrations consumed by metropolitan theorists'. How unlike an earlier, brilliantly iconoclastic Leach (1961), who encouraged anthropologists to move, by 'inspired guesswork', beyond hide-bound empiricism.

There are serious political issues at stake in arguments like this. In the effort to privilege 'the local', however worthy it may be, we risk slighting or misrecognising the global forces that—increasingly, if with varying degrees of visibility—are besetting 'little guys' (Graeber 2002: 1223) all over map. Many of those among whom we work, apparently unlike Englund and Leach's 'natives',[14] are *very* anxious about the effect of those forces, which, *they* tell us, are putting their social and material survival at risk. In the *faux* egalitarianism of these neoliberal times, it is easy to become mired in trivial arguments over whether 'meta-narratives of modernity', or 'Theory', removes from 'others' the capacity to represent themselves or to determine their own futures. All this while the masters of the market, and powerful political pragmatists, fashion new modes of extraction, abstraction, and explanation. We would do well to ponder, in this respect, why it is that so many 'native' intellectuals have been distrustful of even the most sensitive, ostensibly other-centred knowledge produced by our discipline, why they believe that this knowledge is *intrinsically* inimical to their own authority and interests (cf. Banaji 1970; Magubane 1971, Asad 1973). Mafeje (1998: 67; cf. Sharp 1998), for one, holds that ethnography, to be true to itself, needs to be liberated entirely from anthropology, thus to become—without even the most reflexive of ethnographers—a source 'of social texts authored [solely] by the people themselves'. The logical end point of reducing our practice to the elicitation of narratives of local experience is not a unique anthropology at all. Nor is it a politics of positive engagement. Quite the opposite. In a postcolonial age in which 'natives' everywhere speak for themselves, it is, simply, redundancy. The alternative, patently, is to argue for a theoretically and politically principled social science.

For our own part, we continue to have confidence in ethnography and the forms of insight—both reflective and reflexive, both imaginative and empirical—to which it gives access. There is a proviso, however: that, instead of fetishising method, instead of romancing the idea that it might itself yield up naked truths, we face up to the epistemic challenge of what it takes to 'commit social science' in the postcolonial world: in a world in which 'globalisation' is an increasingly contested, troubling reality, in which 'modernity' is an increasingly contested, troubling ideological formation (Knauft 1997). Those anthropologists who have chosen to take on this challenge have tended *not* to decry 'localised' ethnography, but to insist on its unique value in plumbing the nature and effects of large-scale social, economic, and political processes (for instance, Appadurai 1997; 1996; Geschiere 1997; Meyer 1999; Weiss 1996). Their work points to the fact that our modes of producing knowledge demand critical review even 'redesign' (Marcus 1994: 46)—in the face of history; especially the history of a time such as this, when popular discourses across the planet posit that the world is undergoing changes of major proportions. This perception, after all, does not exist only in the imagination of anthropologists afflicted with 'the meta-narrative of modernity'. What is more, we need to concede that our craft is not, and never has been, analytically self-sufficient. Part of a shifting division of labour within the human sciences, it is engaged in dialogue with other ways of making sense of the present in both its macro- and microcosmic dimensions (Stoller 1997; Sharp 1998). This is all to the good, since it is only by broadening our frames of reference that we may address some of the awkward questions that have come to confront us about our methodology: can we be sure, for example, that 'the particular' we seek to study, or the cultural worlds we presume to exist, may actually be *empirically* bounded? Is 'the local' not the constantly refashioned *product* of forces well beyond itself (Appadurai 1996; also 1997)? Does it not exist only as part of a socio-political geography of multiple scales and coordinates (Ortner 1997)? Is it not true that the singularity of places, just like the singularity of 'traditions', 'customs', and 'cultures', is being fashioned ever more in response to the market? Surely, neat antinomies between the local and the global, between field and context, between ethnography and metanarrative, beg the very questions that we should be asking.

These questions have also been at the core of a friendly exchange we have had with Sally Falk Moore (1999) over the susceptibility of large-scale analytic claims to ethnographic proof. Her critique of our Gluckman Lecture hinges on a methodological point: the unverifiability of its central thesis, namely, that the rapid expansion of an occult economy in postcolonial South Africa has been a by-product of the material *and* experiential impact on rural populations of the cumulative effects of a globalising capitalism—specifically, of the processes of abstraction and alienation built into it. The 'imaginative sociology' by means of which we arrive at this thesis may be illuminating, concedes Moore. But it does not offer sufficient evidence either to substantiate or to falsify a claim of cause-and-effect. Moreover, by ascribing the growth of a local occult economy to world-historical forces, we 'turn general context into particular explanation' (1999: 306). We also *confuse* the general and the particular. How so? At times, she suggests, we deny that resort to the magical, and to its associated forms of violence, is unique to South Africa; at other times we imply that there is something special about its deployment here.

Allow us to recall what the disagreement is about. Our objectives in the Gluckman lecture were twofold. One was to make sense of some highly visible, much discussed, old-yet-new practices in postcolonial South Africa. Taken together, these practices, themselves rooted in variously defined 'localities', appeared to constitute a discernible phenomenon: an occult *economy*. As we have implied, this term describes an empirically-grounded abstraction, an abstraction derived from, but not reducible to, the narrated experience and social activities of a large number of diversely positioned human beings. In short, it is an analytic concept based in the concrete. Located between the global and the local, subsuming them in a four-dimensional geography,[15] that concept is mobilised to arrive at 'thick', moving portraits of peoples' lives and labours; also *to elucidate the motivation, the meaning, and the consequences* of their actions. It is a tool that enables the dialectic of deduction and induction on which, in our view, all principled social science ought to be founded.

The other objective of our analysis of 'occult economies' was to explain why that enchanted economy should manifest itself so palpably now, when conventional wisdom would have us expect otherwise; why it calls forth received cultural practices, yet transmutes them into virulently altered forms; why, while clearly a domestic product, it bears close resemblance to similar economies in other places, most of all in post-totalitarian contexts, where neoliberal reform has suddenly and simultaneously liberated and disempowered, enriched and impoverished. These parallels are striking and yet hard to pin down. They bear witness to the play of large forces (i) that, although volatile and only partly visible, are not random; (ii) whose existence may be inferred only through their effects; (iii) whose workings vary across the axes of the planetary map, making them impossible to grasp at only one site; (iv) which, because they have not yet fully run their course, elude proof by ordinary means. The problem that we set ourselves, then, was to account for the workings of a metamorphosing capitalism that is *both* global in its reach and localised in its protean manifestations. Built into that problem is an effort to engage at once with the general and the particular, with variance and similarity, with continuity and rupture. Far from being a confusion yielded by our method, it is a necessary requirement thereof. Respectful of the empirical without being empiricist, we seek to open up new angles on a world-historical process of awkward, shifting scale.

At issue here, then, are alternative ideologies-of-method, alternative epistemes. The differences that flow from them, not least over what it takes to prove an argument or to verify a theory, are substantial. Which is why we stand accused, in this exchange, of not having provided enough evidentiary support for claims about some very general transformations in the South African economy and society; even more, about their location in the broad sweep of the history of capital. Even if we agreed that we ought to render as 'provable propositions' our analysis of these transformations—or of the ways in which they are locally inhabited, experienced, narrated, acted upon—we find it hard to see *how* to do so without resorting to reduction *ad absurdum*. But we do *not* believe that this is what we should be doing; indeed, we resist the positivist reflex that would encourage us to do so. After all, if they were held to the demands of empiricist validation, or subjected to the blinding lights of Western science, some of the most enduring insights of modernist social thought would not pass muster. We have in mind, *inter alia*, Marx's analysis of the commodity, Weber's elective affinity between Protestantism and the rise of capitalism, and Durkheim's theory of the elementary forms of religious life.

Marx, Weber, and Durkheim, of course, all argued against both ungrounded historical conjecture and theory deduced purely from philosophical first principles; although each of them indulged in these things on occasion. More to the point here, each sought to take the measure of the difficult relation between the *experience* of social phenomena and the forces and facts, the rhymes and reasons that lay behind it. Each exercised a fertile sociological imagination, seeking, in the Great Outdoors of their changing worlds, to 'forget the appearances', the better to discern the 'real truths' swimming behind them (McCarthy, cited above). Each knew that social action, like the fabrication of social meaning, is not pursued by human beings just as they please; that its determinations have to be explained; that the job of the social scientist is to construe the *processes* by which realities are realised, objects objectified, classes of persons and things classified, and so forth. All of which returns us to the dialectics of deduction and induction—to the co-production of fact and sociological imagining—implicated in 'doing ethnography'.

It also returns us to a very basic question: Precisely what kinds of methodological operations are entailed in 'doing ethnography' as we envision it? That question is not, we suggest, best answered in the abstract. Just as method is always profoundly theoretical in its provenance, so its substance ought always to be practice-based and context-sensitive.

Confronting the Great Outdoors

Our time: 1989, near the end of apartheid.

Our place: the North West Province of South Africa where, long ago, we did doctoral research.

We returned to the Mafikeng District after an enforced absence of some twenty years; our research, in the interim, had crossed over into Botswana and into the colonial past. Driving in from across the veld, we crested the foothill to the south of the Tshidi-Roong capital to behold a strikingly discordant landscape. The contours of the old Tswana town—weathered red-clay walls, desiccated thatch roofs, giant boulders, cattle-trodden trails, spry camelthorns—had been dwarfed by a skyline of altogether different scale. The precocious, postmodern outlines of a new city, its architecture a bold pastiche of various international styles of the 1970s and 1980s, proclaimed an assertive, upstart governmentality. History and Hubris, both capitalised, had consummated a brazen, quick and dirty *affaire* on this arid terrain: on it, one of apartheid's most elaborate ethnic 'homelands,' had been put in place. The illegitimate insta-polity of Bophutatswana, and the simulacra of its bastard sovereignty, had been erected on land long owned and inhabited by the Tshidi, subjecting them and scores of other Tswana chiefdoms across the northwest to the violent authority of a puppet-state empowered by the material, military, and ideological might of the apartheid regime.

What met our astonished gaze, in sum, was the enactment, in concrete, of that regime's version of indirect rule: the tight, closely-policed integration of local polities, under their 'traditional' rulers, into an ostensibly independent ethno-nation. Herein lay the completion of the process, endemic to colonialism, by which those polities— now designated 'tribal authorities'—were relegated to the peripheries of a nation-state predicated on difference. The running together of humble adobe and soaring plate glass made visible another juxtaposition: the affirmation, on one hand, of a sense of Tshidi cultural particularity, and, on the other, its encompassment within a wider, multi-ethnic state that was itself a maelstrom of powerful economic, social, and moral currents. It hardly seemed accidental that the independent-minded Tshidi chief, Kebalepile, had died in Mafikeng in the early 1970s, allegedly as a result of witchcraft at the hands of the recently-installed president of Bophuthatswana, Lucas Mangope.[16] Mangope, a subaltern sovereign if there ever was one, was seen by the citizenry of Mafikeng as the new colonising cuckoo in their nest. By blaming him for the occult killing of their traditional leader, Tshidi sought to name the spirit of a spiritless age, the *Zeitgeist* of late-colonial history.

This magical murder, refracted through the local moral imaginary, might have opened a new chapter in the unfolding confrontation between the late Tshidi world and the wider universe that embraced it. But the history of which it was part went back a long way. As we have noted before (Comaroff and Comaroff 1991; 1997), *setswana*, the more-or-less open, more-or-less labile ensemble of signs and practises taken locally to constitute vernacular 'culture'—the term is used as freely by black South Africans these days as it is by others was itself the offspring of a protracted colonial encounter. Mafikeng bore all the scars of that encounter, of earlier struggles, of earlier conjunctures. In the mid-1800s, for example, it was at the nub of a frontier along which white settlers and African chiefdoms fought over land, labour, and sovereignty; along which, too, evangelists fought for souls and civilisation. Later, at the turn of the twentieth century, during the South African War, it became an imperial battleground on which heroes and villains of all races vied for national gains and personal glory. More recently, it has been branded as a commodity, a heritage site on the newly-wrought tourist map of the postcolony. And for all this time it has lain at the crossroads of an intricate web of exchange relations: relations among the various Tswana polities of the region, relations between them and diverse 'strangers', relations that fan out, today, across the globe. The embarrassment of historical traces we found here stubbornly resists the foreshortened lens of the ethnographic here-and-now.

Consequently, in order to account for the social archaeology of the place, and for the ebullient memories of its people, we were forced from the first to historicise our methods; this, in the early 1970s, at a time when there was a great deal of antipathy within anthropology toward history. We had no alternative *but* to develop an ethnography of the archives to discern the processes by which the past and the present had constructed each other; an ethnography that, among other things, entailed scouring the records—images, inventories, accounts, material shards, documents, linguistic residues, even silences and absences—for the constellation of ordinary practices, the passions and interests, that produced and reproduced this site as an empirical fact, a named-and-known locale (Comaroff and Comaroff 1992). Often this meant trawling texts for what they were *not*, putting into conversation pieces of paper that, in the cold storage of the archives, languish as solitary objects. It also necessitated our transposing inert verbs and nouns into depictions of living things, of vibrant ritual activities, of expressions of collective affect, effort, effect.

If the ethnography of the archives proved anything, it was that Mafikeng, 'Place of Stones,' had, from the start, been situated between a rock and a hard place. The town was established by the ruling Tshidi chief, in the 1850s, with two ends in mind: to ward off the seizure of his land by white settlers and to quarantine the rise of Christianity, along with its Eurocentric forms of civility. In time, and for complicated historical reasons, Mafikeng would become the capital of the chiefdom. It was here that Tshidi asserted their autonomy as fully as they could from the colonial state, the settler economy, and the British missions; here that they fashioned an ethnically-marked localism referred to, explicitly, as *setswana*, 'Tswana ways and means'—that quietly fused into itself the cultural practices of various others. For their part, the Protestant converts, original residents of the place, were also to make common cause with a national black petite bourgeoisie anxious to proclaim its modernity.

We hardly need insist here that, to be read ethnographically, these economies of signs and practices have to be situated in the intimacy of the local contexts that gave them life. At the same time, they require to be inserted into the translocal processes of which they were part *ab initio*: processes—commodification, colonisation, proletarianisation, and the like—composed of a plethora of acts, facts, and utterances whose very description demands that we frame them in the terms of one or other Theory of History. The emerging substance of Tshidi religious, legal, literary culture, their styles of costume and senses of self, all deployed images and materials at once fresh and familiar, autochthonous and imported. Each, in its own idiom, replayed, and sought to redress, the mutually-constitutive antinomies of the colonial world: in marking the contrast between magic and faith, custom and reason, folk dress and fashion, the living forms of *setswana* recycled and remade the contrast between the culturally particular and the universal, between ethnic subjects and modern persons. Between Africa and Europe.[17]

For much of its modern existence, anthropology has been trapped inside this set of antinomies. Its ethnographic habitat has, conventionally if not always, been the first term of each: the particular, ethnic subjects, Africa. Conventionally, too, these terms have been taken to signify analytic domains that may be treated as self-sufficient unto themselves. And, for heuristic purposes at least, as hermetically, hermeneutically closed. This was certainly the orientation that framed our first fieldwork among '*the* Tshidi-Rolong' of Mafikeng in the late 1960s, when the proclivities of a British structural-functionalist training seemed perfectly reflected in the ethnology of African 'tribes' invoked by high apartheid. Yet our field-site—chosen because it gave us an alternative venue across the Bostwana border if we were expelled by a regime hostile to research on the 'wrong' side of the colour bar—proved stubbornly intractable to this perspective. Whether in respect of political or religious life, of kinship relations or healing rites, there simply were no 'customary' practices that did not bear the imprint of long-standing engagement with various elsewheres, with (often coercive) embodied social and material forces beyond themselves. The production of the local here was always also entailed in the effort to fabricate some measure of existential coherence and closure against the cross-currents of history, a history of overrule and economic expropriation, of colonial evangelism, of apartheid, of the ravages of deliberately exploitative labour markets. Of prophets and profiteers, madmen and migrants.

For all their discordant hyper-modernity, then, the built-forms of the *bantustan* were but an increment in a drawn-out dialogue between the local and the translocal, here and elsewhere—these tropes being understood *not* as antonyms but as imaginative axes on maps of shifting scale. As it turned out, for all its concrete confidence, this edifice of apartheid was in its death-throes. The long colonial history that had spawned it was coming to an abrupt end, swept away by the changes that marked the close of the Cold War and the realignment of the old international order. So, too, was the national economy that underpinned the *ancien régime*, its industrial infrastructure and its sovereign autonomy recalibrated by the cumulative effects of neoliberal capitalism. By the time we next visited Mafikeng, two years after South Africa's first free democratic elections, its civic structures had been inhabited by functionaries of a new provincial government. The old white town, once set off from its black counterpart by the railway-line, and by equally caste-iron cultural and legal barriers, had been significantly integrated.

Other auguries also suggested that Mafikeng had entered a new era—or, rather, that the proportionate relationship between rupture and continuity had, for the moment, tilted somewhat toward the former; history, in our view is *never* all one or the other, *always* a complex analytic equation-to-be-resolved. Unfamiliar forces, emanating less from the old international order than from the global economy, were making themselves felt as never before. Some of them promised the infusion of cargo that black South Africans had expected with their liberation: an army of NGOs, of 'universal' neo-protestant churches, of distance-learning corporations, of internet services had opened up around town. Almost immediately, locals tried to capture the bounty promised by these technicians of twenty-first century 'development'. Not only did satellite dishes mushroom across the veld. One mud-brick building, nestling beneath a thorn tree on an otherwise barren stretch of land, sported a rough, hand-painted sign: 'We teach in English, in step with the global age'.

At the same time, less sanguine signs gave Tswana cause for anxiety. Many pointed out—to us, in letters to newspapers, on local TV—that the old migrant labour system had collapsed and that this collapse, along with a severe recession, had made jobs extremely scarce, especially for young black males. An unusual number of people appeared to be dying in accidents, to be committing suicide, to be victimised by brutal crime, to be ill, to be depressed. Public facilities and welfare services were receding by the month. There was a growing population of 'black people' on the streets, immigrants from elsewhere in Africa who were drawing much suspicious and scandalised talk: having eluded state regulation, it was said, they were plying their wares noisily on once pristine sidewalks, thus usurping the trade of South African merchants. Not only that: they had brought drugs and AIDS with them, and had taken the few available jobs on the surrounding farms. And yet, despite all this pessimism, notwithstanding all this apocalyptic talk, in the midst of this economy of genuine hardship, some locals seemed, mysteriously, to be prospering. As we note elsewhere (Comaroff and Comaroff 1999a), it is this that has fed the raw underside of the occult economy: the killing of alleged witches and zombie conjurers.

Zombie-conjurers. This brings us back full circle to where we began. To the strangely dissociated man in the police station, to the youths who killed because they believed their fathers to have been turned into phantom labourers, to popular representations of the violent abstraction entailed in witchcraft. Recall what we said at the outset: that the zombie is a figure metonymic of the playing out of world-historical forces in the northerly reaches of South Africa right now; also of the domestication of a form of neoliberal capitalism thought to enable the production of wealth without work. Recall, too, the question that followed: how are we to make sense *methodologically* of this figure, of those forces, of their determinations, of the unfolding connections between them? That the question demands a sociological imagination at once local and translocal, empirical and analytic, was brought into sharp relief for us in a context part pedagogic, part ethnographic. During a history class at the University of the North West, a graduate student broke suddenly across the discussion: 'Do Americans believe in *diphoko*, in magical medicines?' he asked. 'Is it like here? Is there also trouble with zombies in America?'

By what methodological means, then, *did* we actually address the question of the living-dead in the late Tswana world?

Discursive Flows and the Dialectics of Discovery

[Writing a novel is] *like playing chess in three dimensions.*—David Lodge (1999: 52).

So, too, is doing ethnography. Four dimensions, actually, if one includes the terrain of the virtual: the electronic commons that has interpellated itself—as a medium of translocal communication, as a vehicle for the flow of money and other kinds of capital, as a mechanism of the market, as an instrument for the establishment of public spheres of different scales—into even quite remote social worlds.

Unlike chess, however, ethnography-as-practice has, in the first instance, to construct its own field of play, its heuristic landscape. Strategically, it has always seemed logical to us to locate the centre of that field around one or more focal points to which the anthropological senses are drawn because they are the crucibles in which contemporary vernacular concerns—whatever they may be, whatever their phenomenal scale—are construed, enacted, played out, socially contextualised. Given that our anthropology seeks to be empirically-grounded without being empiricist, our objects of research have invariably been defined with reference to the prevailing preoccupations of the times and places in which we have worked, whether they be the politics of chieftainship or ecstatic religious movements, agrarian development and its undersides, the colonial encounter, occult economies, or, most recently, crime, policing, and the metaphysics of disorder. In the dialectic of the concept and the concrete, it is the latter that sets methodology in motion, serving as the *fons et origo* of the operations by which we set out to apprehend the existential processes of everyday life. Our ethnography, in other words, takes off *not* from theory or from a meta-narrative, but from the situated effects of seeing and listening. Of course, the *way* in which we see, *what* we pay attention to, and *how*, is not empirically ordained; that, ineluctably, depends on a prior conceptual scaffolding, which, once the dialectic of discovery is set in motion, is open to reconstruction.

In the late 1990s, the zombie, and the enchanted economy of which it was part, provided just such a focal point at which the preoccupations of the period had taken tangible shape. How did we know this? It came at us, insistently, from a number of diverse sources, some of them already alluded to: in such episodes as the encounter with the almost-naked man on Station Road, in what followed at the police station, and in the sheer ordinariness of the whole thing to the men in blue; in the murder of alleged corpse-conjurer, Motlhabane Makolomakwa, in its avidly-consumed press coverage, in its courtroom arguments, and in the conversations to which it gave rise, many of them about the 'epidemic' of occult violence afflicting the northerly provinces; in 'mob' attacks, committed by local youths in the name of their communities, against those suspected of practicing the arcane arts; in personal stories of the sort told to us by the scion of a ruling dynasty—a man with a first-class graduate degree in development studies, an excellent job in government, and a large following as a DJ in a large city nearby—who had lost a beloved sibling, snatched away secretly by a witch for whom he worked until rescued many months later; in a remarkable incident in which police tried to save a young boy from the persistent attacks of a vicious *tikoloshe*, a translocal witch familiar,[18] first by calling in the local television channel in the hope that its cameras might immobilise the creature and then by eliciting the help of several technicians of the sacred; in the reactions of the state to outbreaks of witchcraft killings, which included tough law enforcement, high level conferences on the topic, and the appointment of a commission of enquiry; in discussions on the internet, in national and regional TV dramas, documentaries, news broadcasts, and talk shows, in local genres of cultural production; and, most of all, in our everyday exchanges in homes and schools, stores and shebeens, taxi ranks and churches across the length and breadth of the Mafikeng district.

This was not all, not by any means. But it gives a sense of the way in which a flow of narratives, incidents, activities, dramas, material exchanges, conversations, and representations embedded in the 'natural' discourse of different and complementary public spheres may come to organise the ethnographic gaze—and, thereby, to set method in motion. Discursive flows, although having focal centres, are inherently open, flexible in scope, and shifting in both their content and their constituents. Determining what, exactly, falls within the purview of any such flow is itself a product in part of paying careful attention, in part of inspired guesswork, in part of theoretical and philosophical predilection; making sense of its substance depends on what, previously, we have spoken of as an 'imaginative sociology'. We use 'imaginative' here in two senses. It refers to (i) doing ethnography by plumbing—through whatever resources of the *analytic imagination* are available to us within the political and ethical imperatives of our practice—the phenomenal worlds in which we situate ourselves; this by (ii) seeking to grasp the manner in which those worlds are *indigenously imagined* and inhabited by people variously positioned within them. Note all the plurals. They point to an anthropological cliché, albeit an important one: that most of the signs and practices with which we concern ourselves are either contested or, if not, are the object of a polyphony of perceptions, valuations, means and ends.

To the extent that doing ethnography necessitates, in the first instance, tapping into focal discursive flows—and, lest we be misunderstood, we reiterate that this includes not 'just' talk or texts but *practices* as well, not 'just' the meaningful but also the material—it demands three critical methodological operations. Each is a condition of the others' productivity.

The first is the pursuit, in respect of any given discursive flow, of points of articulation among the various spheres in which it manifests itself; this by tracing the co-presence of persons, texts, images, or arguments (and especially arguments of images) across them. Thus, for example, the imaginative sociology we were able to construct surrounding the figure of the zombie—and that was to sediment into our ethnographically-rooted abstraction, the 'occult economy'—took shape when we began to hear similar words and see similar pictures over and over: when, among many other things, the accused youths in the Makolomakwa murder trial claimed that the deceased had 'killed their fathers and put them to work'; when stories about zombification kept returning to the 'fact' that the witches in question, invariably sexual 'perverts', had 'turned people into tools', thereby preventing ordinary citizens from earning a living or starting a family; when an old woman, said to have amassed 'mysterious' wealth, was told, as she was set on fire by the 'boys' of her village, that they had no income because of her; when so much local opinion, from the most intellectual to the most humble, blamed the living-dead for the absence of employment, for denying young black males the opportunity to graduate to adulthood, for the despoliation of community. This is not to say that all representations of, or explanations for, the postcolonial (re-) appearance of zombies are the same. Nor that they are ascribed the same social salience by everyone. However, where there *is* argument about the matter—be it in courts of law or over quarts of beer, on soccer fields or in the maize fields, around backyard fires or among fired workers, in university classrooms, church meetings, or the electronic media—it usually turns back to the connection of witchcraft to the dearth of work and the impossibility of securing the future; the last being what we, in theory-speak, might refer to as a crisis of social reproduction. This, in short, is the animating vernacular around which the discursive flow is organised. It turns out to be crucial in the dialectic of the concept and the concrete, of theory and ethnography.

The first methodological operation, then, is to *map the substance of the phenomenal landscape* on which any discursive flow is grounded, thus to identify its animating vernaculars and to chart the object world in which it interpolates itself. The second is to follow the traces of that discursive flow, of its various signs and images, tracking the migration of the latter from their densest intersections to wherever else they may lead.

Let us give a couple of instances from the situation with which we were concerned here. One is the allusion to the sexual perversion of witches, a submerged theme in many zombie narratives. At face value, this allusion seems, in itself, to have little to do with the workings of the occult economy or the figure of the zombie, more with the figuration of the witch as 'standardised nightmare' (Wilson 1951), the epitome of anti-sociality and immorality. But in pursuing the allusion, in posing questions about it, in seeing where else it turned up, we found ourselves drawn into a meaning-maze that took in AIDS, the sexualisation of death, bad blood, compromised masculinity, and drought—and culminated, by fusing all of these things, in the clear and present threat to the future of communities everywhere attendant on the fact that young men cannot find work or make families. As sexual pervert, the witch, in short, embodies social destruction, fertility abused, social reproduction violated.

The other instance also arose out of a recurrent theme in zombie narratives: What precisely is the reach of the occult economy? What is the reach of the modern witch? Is corpse-conjuring, or the arcane fabrication of wealth without work, purely a parochial matter? Or does it somehow extend beyond? One night, the local TV channel held a phone-in talk show in which the special guests were a pair of young 'reformed' satanists, each with his spiritual advisor. Asked about the difference between witchcraft and satanism, one answered, in a fluent mix of Setswana and English: 'Satanism is high-octane witchcraft. It is more international' (Comaroff and Comaroff 1999a). This comment called forth a flood of responses from the virtual community constructed by the programme. The station switchboard was overrun. Audiences across the province were fascinated. Satanists were said, by and large, to be youthful, male, and black, just the social category most under threat of joblessness, most likely to dabble in nefarious new technologies. Witches, by contrast, were held to be motivated, more often, by local conflicts, framed in long-standing idioms of kinship and community; although they, too, appear to be widening their horizons and their range of techniques. As the 'high octane' petrochemical image suggests, what 'satanic' youth bring to the occult economy is a capacity to 'ride the tiger'— actually, in these parts, a leopard—'of time-space compression' (Harvey 1990: 351): to move across vast distances instantly, thus to accumulate riches, without visible effort, by means unknowable to ordinary persons. The symbolic references in this are too dense to unravel here: they extend from the 'fast' wealth being produced in the postcolony by control over the transportation of people, signs, and things to the changing salience of borders and transnational elsewheres in neoliberal South Africa. Above all, however, what became plain, listening both to the participants in the show and to those with whom we watched it, was the fact that the occult economy is understood to link the most local of concerns, activities, and relations—understood in the most local of terms—to inscrutable forces arising out of an equally inscrutable world beyond, a world ever more 'global'. This last, we stress again, is not our gloss. Recall that sign on the mud-brick school, the one that promised an education 'in step with the global age'.

In short, the second methodological operation involves *mapping the extensions of the phenomenal landscape*, the four-dimensional geography (see no.15) with reference to which any discursive flow constitutes itself. Self-evidently, this, like mapping its substance, demands more than 'multi-sited' ethnography. It demands an ethnography that, once orientated to particular sites and grounded issues, is pursued on multiple dimensions and scales: an ethnography as attentive, say, to processes occurring in virtual space as to those visible in 'real' places-under-production; to the transnational mass-mediation of images as to ritual mediations between human beings and their ancestors; to the workings of state bureaucracies or international courts as to the politics of 'traditional' chieftainship and customary moots; to the flow of commodities across the planet as to marriage payments between lineages; and so on and on. Often it turns out that there are intimate, if invisible, connections across dimensions and scales: just as planetary commodity flows may, these days, determine bride wealth in an African village, so bride wealth in an African village may have an impact on the planetary flow of labour, cash, and goods; similarly, just as the purview of local chiefs and their 'traditional' courts may be decided by global human rights jurisprudence, global human rights jurisprudence is being challenged by demands for the recognition of 'traditional' cultural imperatives.

The third methodological operation is to trace the passage of a discursive flow over time; this to establish what, precisely, is new about it and what is not, what are the relative proportions of rupture and continuity to which it speaks, what is unique and what is merely a local instance of a wider phenomenon. How? By means of a counterpoint: by (i) eliciting a *local* genealogy of cultural precursors and (ii) running it up against a *comparative* archaeology of similar signs and practices to ascertain where else, and in what circumstances, parallel discourses might be found. In respect of the zombies of the North West Province, and the occult economy of which they are part, local genealogies make it clear that they have *not* been around for much more than a decade; regarded thus, they signal a rupture. But there did exist a foreshadowing: *sefifi*, observed by missionaries in the nineteenth century (Comaroff and Comaroff 1991: 143), a condition—in which 'manhood is dead, though the body still lives' (Brown 1926: 137)—brought about by the eclipse of a person by another, more powerful than s/he. This condition, it seems, provided a semantic frame within which the zombie has been accommodated. As to a comparative archaeology, there is evidence of at least two broadly parallel historical situations in Africa—in Mozambique and Cameroon earlier this century—in which living-dead have appeared (Comaroff and Comaroff 1999c). In both instances, their presence was intimately tied to radical changes in colonial labour conditions, to the disruption of received connections between persons, production, and place, to the precariousness of wage employment, and to the alienation attendant on new forms of work. Put all this together and the point becomes clear: once historicised and interpellated into its local cultural context, the discursive flow surrounding the figure of the zombie has most immediately to do with labour history, with a burgeoning fear of the eclipse and commodification of people and social relations, with a sense of lost control over the means of producing value, with threats to the survival of local worlds under the impact of enigmatic forces from outside, with the unmooring of horizons and expectations occasioned by shifts in the workings of capital.

Conclusion

This brings us back, one last time, to the dialectic of induction and deduction, of theory and ethnography, of the concept and the concrete.

When we resumed our work in post-apartheid South Africa in the 1990s, as we have said, we had no idea that we would run into a fully fledged occult economy; or, to be more precise, into the phenomena captured in this ethnographically-grounded abstraction. Nor could we have known how that economy had become a public preoccupation. The appearance of a new breed of witches and zombies, and the anxieties they heralded, might have been interpreted purely as an expression of parochial conflicts and relations gone bad. What is more, in the hands of a cultural anthropologist with only the pristine horizons of the particular in view, a case could no doubt have been made for the idea that the living-dead of the present are a transformation of the *sefifi* of old; that the mystical evil of the here-and-now is an extension of 'traditional' notions of witchcraft and sorcery. However, once we had traced out the discursive flow in which zombification is caught up—made manifest, methodologically, by charting the landscape on which it had taken shape, rendered decipherable by recourse to local genealogies and comparative archaeologies, mediated by our own conceptual categories and commitments—it became obvious that this kind of explanation would have been woefully incomplete. For one thing, it would have left unaccountable thè fact that similar phenomena have appeared in very different cultural contexts at roughly the same time and in response to the same broader historical conditions. For another, it would also have paid scant respect to the real-world concerns of Tswana living in the North West: to *their* arguments about the impossibility of social reproduction, about arcane means of producing wealth, about new forms of labour, commodification, and alienation, about witchcraft, satanism and globalisation.

In seeking to take account of those arguments and their social motivation, and to grasp the phenomenology of the lived, material world out of which they arose, we brought to bear an explicit theoretical orientation; it is one about which we had written a fair amount over the previous decade, one which contained within it a particular understanding of the contemporary history of capital. That orientation primed our early readings—and misreadings—of the 'new' South Africa. But it did not take long for its insufficiencies to make themselves plain. Apart from all else, our take on the workings of modern industrial capitalism and its colonial extensions did not prepare us for the postcolony, for its postmodern zombies and unemployment-related witch killings, for its 'crisis' of masculinity and generation, for the complex absent-presence of the state. It was, in other words, the *incompleteness* of our theoretical scaffolding—incomplete, that is, in the face of the concrete world which we were encountering—that set the dialectic in motion anew, altering our conceptual repertoire just as that repertoire was being mobilised to make sense of the unexpected landscape on which we found ourselves.

Ethnography is like much else in the social sciences; indeed, more so than anthropologists often acknowledge. It is a multi-dimensional exercise, a co-production of social fact and sociological imagining, a delicate engagement of the inductive with the deductive, of the real with the virtual, of the already-known with the surprising, of verbs with nouns, processes with products, of the phenomenological with the political. Robert Foster (2002: 247) has recently remarked, as we have ourselves (Comaroff and Comaroff 1999a), that the key problem of doing ethnography 'is ultimately a question of scale'. For him, that question boils down to the avoidance of 'dissolving local particularities in the uniform sameness of global conditions without treating the radical distinctiveness of the local as if it stood against or apart from the global'. For us, the challenge goes yet further. It is to establish an anthropology-for-the-present on an ethnographic base that dissolves the *a priori* breach between theory and method: an anthropology, of multiple dimensions, that seeks to explain the manner in which the local and the translocal construct each other, producing at once difference and sameness, conjuncture and disjuncture. An anthropology that takes, as its mandate, the need to make sense of the intersecting destinies of human lives, wherever they may happen to be lived out.

Notes

1.   We should like to thank Loic Wacquant for his creative, insightful editing of the original text of this essay. An earlier version was presented at *Ethnografeast*, a conference on 'Ethnography for the New Century: Practice, Predicament, Promise,' sponsored by this journal and held on 12-14 September 2002 at the University of California, Berkeley. Our opening ethnographic vignette is from fieldwork conducted in 1999-2000; the study, provisionally entitled *Policing the Postcolony: Crime, Cultural Justice, and the Metaphysics of Disorder in South Africa*, was funded by the American Bar Association.

2.   In the apartheid years, Mafeking was divided: the 'white' town was separated by a railway line from *Mafikeng*, 'The Place of Stones,' the Tshidi-Rolong capital. When the ethnic 'homeland' of Bophuthatswana was created in the 1970s, its centre, Mmabatho, was built alongside Mafikeng/Mafeking. The conurbation is referred to these days, rather awkwardly, as Mafikeng-Mmabatho. The old Mafeking, as exclusive white enclave and as a spelling for the place, has disappeared.

3. Since we first wrote about zombies in the North West Province (1999c), we have been regaled with stories, from scholars and non-scholars alike, of their presence elsewhere in South Africa. Recently, for example, Ilana van Wyk (University of Pretoria)—who is conducting research in northern KwaZulu-Natal—told us that, according to local people, a large number are crossing the border from Mozambique. These spectral figures, who are said 'not to speak', appear strikingly similar to those that we encountered on the other side of the country.

4. The youths were sentenced to 20 years each for the murder by the Supreme Court of Bophutatswana. For accounts of the case, see 'Bizarre Zombie Claim in Court', Nat Molomo, *The Mail*, 31 March 1995; 'Petrol Murder Denial', *The Mail*, 2 June 1995, p. 2; 'Five Men Jailed for 100 Years', *The Mail*, 22 September 1995, p. 23. We are grateful to the primary (eye)witness in the case, Thaisi Medupe, the Registrar of the High Court in Mmabatho, Reggie Mpame, the headman of Matlonyane, Abraham Maeco, and several associates of the victim for retelling the events in question.

5. This case was reported in the South African media; see for example, 'Spirits Strike at Labour Relations,' *Mail & Guardian*, 27 September 1995.

6. The play, by Brett Bailey, featured at the Standard Bank National Arts Festival in July 1996; it was later televised. A TV documentary series, *Issues of Faith*, also dealt with the topic on 12 July 1998 on SABC 2; for one of many newspaper accounts, see 'Disturbing Insight into Kokstad Zombie Killings', Ntokozo Gwamanda, *Sowetan*, 15 July 1998, p.17.

7. Even where the trade occurs entirely within a national economy, it is often seen as a means by which the new rich, stereotypically portrayed as global in their operations and orientations, extract the essence of the poor and/or the racially marked for their own nefarious ends. This is so in South Africa, where there is an active market in body parts for medicines—and a lively local discourse about it. So much so, that prices for hearts, eyes, and other organs have been quoted in the media (Comaroff and Comaroff 1999a) and, recently, in fiction (for example, Williams 2002: 46).

8. 'I Was Turned into a Zombie', Mzilikazi Wa Afrika, *Sunday Times* [Extra], 11 July 1999, p.1.

9. Thus, for example, a significant number of films featuring zombies were made in the 1930s and 1940s. So were several in which zombification on the production line was a central motif, even if the figure of the zombie itself was absent; perhaps the most celebrated was Charlie Chaplin's *Modern Times* (1936).

10. We address some of the theoretical and conceptual issues raised by the figure of the zombie, and by occult economies, in a series of loosely interrelated essays (see for example, 1999a; 1999c; 2000; 2002).

11. The *Great Outdoors* premiered at the Standard Bank National Arts Festival on 30 June 2000. We thank Neil McCarthy, who made the unpublished script available to us.

12. This conceit was already called into question in the 1930s in, among other things, the works of Isaac Schapera (see Comaroff and Comaroff 1988), in Monica (Wilson) Hunter's *Reaction to Conquest* (1936), in Godfrey Wilson's *Economics of Detribalisation* (1942), and in the writings of the Manchester School in Central Africa.

13. As Sangren (2000: 244) notes, Englund and Leach claim that they are not against meta-narratives in general, only *this* meta-narrative. However, their claim seems empty in light of (i) their silence on their own theoretical orientations and (ii) the promiscuity with which they represent anthropological writings on modernity, many of which—including our own—treat the term *not* as a theoretical construct at all but as a problem for anthropological theory. In this and other respects, the critiques of the essay by Gupta (2000) and by Meyer (2000), under the *Current Anthropology* format, are instructive.

14. In their discussion of colonialism in Papua, for example, Englund and Leach (2000: 233) eschew accounts that dwell upon exploitation and violence; this because local narratives do not stress these things. In this, they confuse native *experience* and its *narration*, the importance of which few would deny, with an adequate *analysis* of the workings of colonial overrule.

15. The fourth dimension—the conventional three, of course, being length, breadth, and depth— is located in the virtual reaches of cyberspace, in which the constitutive connections between the local and the global are constantly remapped.

16. Strictly speaking, Mangope was not yet President of Bophuthatswana. He was Chief Minister of the Tswana Territorial Authority (TTA), a position to which he acceded when the TTA was created, in 1969, as the first step in the establishment of the 'independent' ethno-nation. Bophuthatswana only came formally into being a couple of years later. In Tshidi historical consciousness, however, the brief existence of the TTA has been obliterated: local knowledge has it that Bophuthatswana was founded, under President Mangope, at the end of the 1960s.

17. Elsewhere (Comaroff and Comaroff 1997: 25) we have explained *why* these antimonies tend to be reproduced over the long-run, despite the fact that the sociology of the worlds to which they refer constantly vitiate easy dualisms. We have also taken care to make the point that, however insistently they may be invoked in vernacular discourse such oppositions can never be deployed as viable analytic or conceptual terms.

18. The *tikoloshe*—a small, hairy figure with exaggerated sexual organs—has long been associated with the Nguni-speaking peoples of the east coast of South Africa; until recently, it was not part of the cultural landscape of the North West or the Sotho-speaking regions. But, in this age of translocality, it, like many things 'traditional,' has migrated and is now found across much of the subcontinent.

References

Appadurai, A., 1996, *Modernity at Large: The Cultural Dimensions of Globalization*, Minneapolis: University of Minnesota Press.

Appadurai, A., 1997, 'Discussion: Fieldwork in the Era of Globalization', in S. Bamford and J. Robbins, eds., *Fieldwork in the Era of Globalisation*, Special issue of *Anthropology and Humanism* 22 (1), 115-8.

Asad, T., ed., 1973, *Anthropology and the Colonial Encounter*, London: Athlone Press.

Bamford, S. and J. Robbins, 1997, 'Introduction', in S. Bamford and J. Robbins, eds., *Fieldwork in the Era of Globalisation*, Special issue of *Anthropology and Humanism* 22 (1), 3-5.

Banaji, J., 1970, 'The Crisis of British Anthropology', *New Left Review* 64:71-85.

Brown, J.T., 1926, *Among the Bantu Nomads: A Record of Forty Years Spent among the Bechuana*, London: Seeley Service.

Clifford, J. and G. E. Marcus, eds., 1986, *Writing Culture: The Poetics and Politics of Ethnography*, Berkeley: University of California Press.

Comaroff, J., 1997, 'Consuming Passions: Nightmares of the Global Village', in E. Badone, ed., 'Body and Self in a Post-colonial World', Special issue of *Culture*, 17 (1-2): 7-19.

Comaroff, J., 2005, 'The End of History, Again? Pursuing the Past in the Postcolony', in S. Kaul, A. Loomba, M. Bunzl, A. Burton, and J. Esty, eds., *Postcolonial Studies and Beyond*, Durham: Duke University Press.

Comaroff, J. and J.L. Comaroff, 1988, 'On the Founding Fathers, Fieldwork, and Functionalism: A Conversation with Isaac Schapera', *American Ethnologist* 15 (3): 554-65.

Comaroff, J. and J.L. Comaroff, 1991, *Of Revelation and Revolution, Volume I, Christianity, Colonialism, and Consciousness in South Africa*, Chicago: University of Chicago Press.

Comaroff, J. and J.L. Comaroff, 1999a, 'Occult Economies and the Violence of Abstraction: Notes from the South African Postcolony', *American Ethnologist* 26 (3): 279-301.

Comaroff, J. and J.L. Comaroff, 1999b, 'Second Thoughts: A Response to Sally Falk Moore', *American Ethnologist* 26 (3): 307-309.

Comaroff, J. and J.L. Comaroff, 1999c, 'Alien-nation: Zombies, Immigrants, and Millennial Capitalism', *CODESRIA Bulletin* 3/4: 17-28, Reprinted in B.K. Axel, ed., *Historical Anthropology and its Futures*, Raleigh: Duke University Press, 2002.

Comaroff, J. and J.L. Comaroff, 2000, 'Millennial Capitalism: First Thoughts on a Second Coming', in J. Comaroff and J. L. Comaroff, eds., *Millennial Capitalism and the Culture of Neoliberalism*, Durham and London: Duke University Press.

Comaroff, J. and J.L. Comaroff, 2002, 'Second Comings: Neoprotestant Ethics and Millennial Capitalism in South Africa, and Elsewhere', in P. Gifford, ed., with D. Archard, T.A. Hart, and N. Rapport, *2000 Years and Beyond: Faith, Identity and the Common Era*, London: Routledge.

Comaroff, J. and J.L. Comaroff, (n.d.), 'Criminal Obsessions: Imagining Order in Post-apartheid South Africa', ms.

Comaroff, J.L. and J. Comaroff, 1987, 'The Madman and the Migrant: Work and Labor in the Historical Consciousness of a South African People', *American Ethnologist* 14 (2): 191-209.

Comaroff, J.L. and J. Comaroff, 1992, *Ethnography and the Historical Imagination*, Boulder: Westview Press.

Comaroff, J.L. and J. Comaroff, 1997, *Of Revelation and Revolution*, Volume II, *The Dialectics of Modernity on a South African Frontier*, Chicago: University of Chicago Press.

Ehrenreich, B. and A. R. Hochschild, eds., 2003, *Global Woman: Nannies, Maids, and Sex Workers in the New Economy*, New York: Metropolitan Books.

Englund, H., 1996, 'Witchcraft, Modernity and the Person: The Morality of Accumulation in Central Malawi', *Critique of Anthropology* 16 (3): 257-279.

Englund, H. and J. Leach, 2000, 'Ethnography and the Meta-narratives of Modernity', *Current Anthropology* 41 (2): 225-48.

Fordred, L., 1998, *Narrative, Conflict and Change: Journalism in the New South Africa*, unpublished Ph.D. dissertation, University of Cape Town.

Foster, R. J., 2002, 'Bargains with Modernity in Papua New Guinea and Elsewhere', *Anthropological Theory* 2 (2): 233-51.

Fukuyama, F., 1992, *The End of History and the Last Man*, New York: Free Press.

Fukuyama, F., 2002, *Our Posthuman Future: Consequences of the Biotechnology Revolution*, New York: Farrar, Straus and Giroux.

Geertz, C., 1973, *The Interpretation of Cultures: Selected Essays*, New York: Basic Books.

Geschiere, P., 1997, *The Modernity of Witchcraft: Politics and the Occult in Postcolonial Africa*, Charlottesville: University of Virginia Press.

Graeber, D., 2002, 'The anthropology of globalization (with notes on Neomedievalism, and the end of the Chinese model of the nation-State)', *American Anthropologist* 104 (4): 1222-1227.

Gupta, A., 2000, 'Comment on Harri Englund and James Leach, "Ethnography and the Meta-Narratives of Modernity"', *Current Anthropology* 41 (2): 240-1.

Gupta, A. and J. Ferguson, 1997, 'Discipline and practice: "the field" as site, method, and location in anthropology', in A. Gupta and J. Ferguson, eds., *Anthropological Locations: Boundaries and Grounds of a Field Science.* Berkeley: University of California Press.

Halberstam, J. and I. Livingston, eds., 1995, *Posthuman Bodies*, Bloomington, IN: Indiana University Press.

Hardt, M. and A. Negri, 2000, *Empire*, Cambridge, MA: Harvard University Press.

Harries, P., 1994, *Work, Culture, and Identity: Migrant Laborers in Mozambique and South Africa, c.1860-1910*, Portsmouth, N.H.: Heinemann.

Hunter, M., 1936, *Reaction to Conquest: Effects of Contact with Europeans on the Pondo of South Africa*, London: Oxford University Press.

Kapferer, B., 2000, 'Star wars: About Anthropology, Culture and Globalisation', *Australian Journal of Anthropology* 11 (2): 174-198.

Kapferer, B., 2001, 'Sorcery and the Shapes of Globalisation: Disjunctions and Continuities—the Case of Sri Lanka', *Journal of the Finnish Anthropological Society* 26 (1): 4-28.

Knauft, B., 1997, 'Theoretical Currents in Late Modern Anthropology: Toward a Conversation', *Cultural Dynamics* 9 (3): 277-300.

Kramer, E., 1999, *Possessing Faith: Commodification, Religious Subjectivity, and Community in a Brazilian Neo-Pentecostal Church*, Unpublished Ph.D. Dissertation, University of Chicago.

La Fontaine, J. S., 1997, *Speak of the Devil: Allegations of Satanic Child Abuse in Contemporary England*, Cambridge: Cambridge University Press.

Leach, E. R., 1961, *Rethinking Anthropology*, London: Athlone Press.

Lee, V., 1890 [1998], 'A Lasting Love', in I. Calvino, ed., *Fantastic Tales: Visionary and Everyday*, New York: Vintage International.

Lewis, I. M., 1973, *The Anthropologist's Muse*, Welwyn Garden City, Hertfordshire: Broadwater Press.

Lodge, David, 1999, *Home Truths: A Novella*, London: Penguin.

Mafeje, A., 1998, 'Anthropology and Independent Africans: Suicide or End of an Era?' *African Sociological Review* 2 (1): 1-43.

Magubane, B., 1971, 'A Critical Look at Indices Used in the Study of Social Change in Africa', *Current Anthropology* 12 (October-December): 419-431.

Marcus, G., 1994, 'After the Critique of Anthropology: Faith, Hope, and Charity, but the Greatest of these is Charity', in R. Borofsky, ed., *Assessing Cultural Anthropology*, New York: McGraw-Hill.

Meyer, B., 1999, *Translating the Devil: Religion and Modernity among the Ewe in Ghana*, Edinburgh: Edinburgh University Press.

Meyer, B., 2000, 'Comment on Harri Englund and James Leach, "Ethnography and the Meta-Narratives of Modernity"', *Current Anthropology* 41 (2): 241-2.

Minkley, G.,C. Rassool and L. Witz, (n.d.), 'Thresholds, Gateways and Spectacles: Journeying through South African Hidden Pasts and Histories in the Last Decade of the Twentieth Century', ms.

Moore, S.F., 1999, 'Reflections on the Comaroff lecture', *American Ethnologist* 26 (3): 304-6.

Ortner, S.B., 1997, 'Fieldwork in the Postcommunity', in S. Bamford and J. Robbins, eds., *Fieldwork in the Era of Globalisation*, Special Issue of *Anthropology and Humanism* 22 (1): 61-80.

Peel, J. D. Y., 1995, 'For who Hath Despised the Day of Small Things? Missionary Narratives and Historical Anthropology', *Comparative Studies in Society and History* 37 (3): 581-607.

Ralushai, N. V., M. G. Masingi, D. M. M. Madiba et al., 1996, *Report of the Commission of Inquiry into Witchcraft Violence and Ritual Murders in the Northern Province of the Republic of South Africa* (To: His Excellency the Honourable Member of the Executive Council for Safety and Security, Northern Province), No publisher given.

Rutherford, B., 1999, 'To Find an African Witch: Anthropology, Modernity and Witch-Finding in North-West Zimbabwe', *Critique of Anthropology* 19 (1): 89-109.

Sahlins, M. D., 1999, 'What is Anthropological Enlightenment? Some Lessons of the Twentieth Century', *Annual Reviews of Anthropology* 28 (1): i-xxiii.

Sangren, P. S., 2000, 'Comment on Harri Englund and James Leach, "Ethnography and the Meta-narratives of Modernity"', *Current Anthropology* 41 (2): 243-4.

Scheper-Hughes, N. and L. Wacquant, eds., 2002, *Commodifying Bodies*, London: Sage Publications.

Sharp, J., 1998, 'Who Speaks for Whom? a Response to Archie Mafeje's "Anthropology and Independent Africans: Suicide or End of an Era"', *African Sociological Review* 2 (1): 66-73.

Stoller, P., 1997, 'Globalizing Method: The Problems of Doing Ethnography in Transnational Spaces', *Anthropology and Humanism* 22 (1): 8-94.

Weiss, B., 1996, *The Making and Unmaking of the Haya Lived World*, Durham: Duke University Press.

Weller, R.P., 2000, 'Living at the Edge: Religion, Capitalism, and the End of the Nation-State in Taiwan', in J. and J. L. Comaroff, eds., *Millennial Capitalism and the Culture of Neoliberalism*, Special Edition of *Public Culture* 12 (2): 477-98.

Wilson, G., 1942, *An Essay on the Economics of Detribalisation in Northern Rhodesia*, Rhodes-Livingstone Papers, 5-6, Livingstone: Rhodes-Livingstone Institute.

Chapter 4

Third Generation African Literatures and Contemporary Theorising

Pius Adesanmi

These are weighty statements indeed. And very reassuring too, especially in this post-structural, post-modern, post-colonial, post-Marxist, post-humanist era in which everything, every value, seems to have been deconstructed out of humanising relevance, with old social and epistemological staples such as meaning, knowledge, history, truth, beauty, even morality and justice destabilised by theoretical undecidabilities. Attention has shifted from literature as a transitive medium of social and cultural exchange to literature as an arrogant, self-sufficient, autolectic text, a dehydrated, disembodied thing rendered thoroughly incomprehensible by turgid, impenetrable theorising.—Niyi Osundare, 'The World Around Oe' (1995: 5).

It is no longer news that modern African literature was born into a broader field of cultural production in which energies were geared mainly towards coming to terms with the identity crises occasioned by the trauma of Africa's contact with the West. The self-legitimising myths of imperialism, powered by the Enlightenment and the teleological dynamics of a modernity authored by Europe, did not emerge only to enhance the economic instrumentalisation of colonial Africa as Walter Rodney has so brilliantly argued in his classic *How Europe Underdeveloped Africa* (1972), nor were they aimed solely at a political and cultural subjugation of Africa as texts like Frantz Fanon's *The Wretched of the Earth* (1963) and Chinweizu's *The West and the Rest of Us* (1975) have established beyond doubt. Allied to these goals was the significant need for those myths to bring the African subject within the hegemonic determinations of Western knowledge systems, a precondition for establishing epistemic control, monopolising the tropes of representation, and constructing a pliant, psychologically-damaged, inferiorised subject of Empire. This epistemic violence aimed not only to disarticulate the existing knowledge structures and belief systems which inhered in Africa's antecedent oral and scribal traditions but also, and perhaps most importantly, to replace it with its own textual monolith: the vast body of representational literature produced by throngs of European traders, explorers, missionaries, travel writers, 'discoverers', and colonial officers which, in turn, fed other texts in an interweaving temporal continuum to produce an Africa and Africans of European imagination along lines now made famous by Edward Said's seminal *Orientalism* (1978).

If the Africa of European textual imagination was an 'Africa that never was', to borrow the memorable title of Alta Jablow's and Dorothy Hammond's *The Africa that Never Was* (1970), that fertile imagination produced seismic consequences that *were* and still *are*: the Historyless Africa of Hegel and Trevor-Roper on the one hand, and the tarzanised Africa of Sir Rider Haggard on the other hand. These creations were all real, concrete consequences of the textual conquest of Africa. Given this scenario, modern African literatures, written in the languages of colonial domination, emerged in the first half of the twentieth century not as an isolated process but in tandem with other cultural and political topoi of Africa's will to subjecthood. Each of the three levels of decolonisation—political, ideological/economic, and cultural—occasioned an inter-related set of dynamics in the public sphere. For instance, the imperative of political decolonisation occasioned the rise of nationalist movements, pan-Africanist consciousness, and armed struggle in some cases. The need for ideological/economic decolonisation accounted in part for Africa's presence in Bandung and the continent's subsequent subscription to the ethos of the non-aligned movement. Finally, cultural decolonisation impelled the birth of a committed literature that could challenge the representational tropes of the colonial library and unsettle the dubious hegemony of the texts of modernity.

From the Négritude poetry of the 1930s-1940s to the cultural and political nationalism of the novelists that succeeded it in the 1950s-1970s in Anglophone and Francophone Africa, modern African literature was imbricated in a series of contradictions and dilemmas contingent on the very condition that gave birth to it: imperialist Euromodernity. Although the poetry of L.S. Senghor, David Diop, Birago Diop, Bernard Dadié; and the novels of Chinua Achebe, Ayi Kwei Armah, Ngugi wa Thiong'o Mongo Beti, Ferdinand Oyono, and Sembene Ousmane achieved the aim of wresting the representational modalities of the African space and subject from the orientalist paradigms of the colonial library, a fresh set of challenges arose to undermine the ontological autonomy of African writing. First was the unresolvable paradox of writing those texts in the very European languages that were the vehicles of colonial oppression and humiliation. Second was the question of the hermeneutic models that would constitute an enabling critical tradition and, lastly, were problems relating to the institutional structures through which the literature and its criticism could be canonised within the broader context of world literatures.

Of these three dilemmas, the last two have proven to be the most atavistic. It is true that the language debate, inaugurated by Obi Wali in his polemical essay 'The Dead End of African Literature?' (1963) and sustained through nearly three decades by the relentless campaign of Ngugi wa Thiong'o for a return to African language writing, has remained pertinent in current theoretical discussions of African literature largely because of renewed critical investment in the Prospero-Caliban equation, with its emphasis on the slave's seizure of the Master's language and its deployment as an instrument of resistance. It would however be incongruous today to question the legitimacy of texts written in the erstwhile imperial languages, what with the successful domestication of those languages by writers such as Chinua Achebe, Ahmadou Kourouma, Flora Nwapa, Efua Sutherland, Zulu Sofola, Niyi Osundare, Femi Osofisan, Ola Rotimi, and Gabriel Okara.

The development of viable critical models, the institutional inscription of African literature, and the methods and modalities of its entry into global circuitries of dissemination and legitimation, especially in the contemporary context of transnationalism and globalisation, in which the asymmetries of power between the North and the South have become even more acute, constitute the sites in which African literature continues to be subject to extraneous determinations and imperialist preferments. The ground for this situation was prepared at the birth of modern African literature, the first set of critics having been Westerners trained in Euromodernist strategies of critical and aesthetic perception and who, consequently, could only approach the new African texts with critical tools developed for Western texts. In Francophone Africa, the foundational critical paradigm for Négritude poetry was established by Jean-Paul Sartre whose famous essay, 'Orphée noir', served as introduction to Senghor's *Anthologie de la nouvelle poésie nègre et malgache d'expression française* (1948). French critics such as Lilyan Kesteloot, Jacques Chevrier, and Bernard Magnier also played a foundational role in the establishment of cirtical paradigms for Francophone African literatures. In Anglophone Africa, critics such as Ulli Beier, Janheiz Jahn, Adrian Roscoe, Charles Larson, and Bernth Lindfors were central to the development of a critical tradition for African literature.

The net consequence of this foundational Western critical intervention in African literary discourse was the pervasive deployment of the parameter of universalism as the sole determiner of which work was deemed successful or not. Needless to say, universalism, in the understanding of Western critics, was a synonym for westernness. This parameter became so pervasive in the evaluation of African works that a frustrated Achebe called for it to be banned.[1] Achebe was not alone in sensing that exclusive foreign determination of the hermeneutics of African literature and its structures of production was an indication of recolonisation. Other African writers and critics also deplored the situation throughout the 1960s-70s, notably John Pepper Clark whose assertions in 'The Legacy of Caliban' (1970) remains the most evocative of such concerns:

> For a variety of reasons the European sector has been more articulate and of overwhelming influence upon African writers. Jealously, it holds fast to its claim of being the original owner and therefore the natural custodian of the European language the African is using in his works. These in turn belong to the tradition of literate literature which again goes back to Europe. The very machinery for publication and distribution of African works is to be found chiefly in the capital cities of Europe. Then, of course, there is the old economic supremacy ... Finally, there are the agents

of this ubiquitous complex operating right in the midst of the African sector, and ironically the scouts and promoters of new talents are often to be found among their ranks. *The net effect is the imposition of their standards upon African writing* (emphasis added).

The stage was thus set in the 1960s-1970s for a series of continuous confrontations between an emergent African critical establishment and an active Euro-Africanist establishment over critical standards, modalities of institutionalisation and canonisation of African literatures. These confrontations played into the already existent scenario in other disciplinary and cultural aspects of African knowledge production in which strategies roughly defined as traditional were pitched against an overwhelming aura of modernity. In literature, the challenge was to fashion traditional or vernacular critical traditions to curtail the inevitable misrepresentations of African texts resulting from an unbridled deployment of Western hermeneutic standards.

The move towards evolving African critical paradigms was beset by a number of obvious pitfalls. The producers of the texts in question—first and second generation writers of the first half of the twentieth century—were in the main hybrid products of Africa's oral lores and the Western academic/literary tradition. The texts they produced necessarily bore the stamp of this dual heritage. African novelists owed as much to the narrative patterns and the linguistic resources of oral tradition as they owed to the textual strategies of Western European novelists, especially the nineteenth century fictions of France, England, and Russia. Poets like Senghor and Christopher Okigbo exploited traditional resources and the riches of French and English poetry with considerable brio. The ontological hybridity of the African literary text thus posed enormous challenges to the critic desirous of developing pure or traditional critical standards for texts that were neither strictly pure nor traditional. Added to this was the academic pedigree of the African critics themselves, mostly groomed in Western Universities or their fledgling appendages in Ibadan, Nsukka, Legon, Fourah Bay, and Makerere.

Trained in Western literary traditions, these critics were themselves complicit in the deployment of the same foreign critical standards and theoretical models they challenged. Sunday Anozie for instance laboured to apply structuralist models to African poetics.[2] Thus, in English and French departments African literature was filtered to students through the prism of Western critical traditions ranging from Marxism to the neo-Marxist permutations of the Frankfurt school; from structuralism to post-structuralism; from the sociological strategies of Lucien Goldmann to the *engagé* existentialism of Sartre. Even today, the young and engaging Nigerian critic, Obi Iwuanyanwu (Obiwu), displays traces of this serious problem as he proposes abstruse and forced Lacanian readings of Achebe's oeuvre.[3] This critical problem, along with the pervasive influence of Western literary fashions on African writers, was the situation that eventuated in the highly polemical call for a second decolonisation by Chinweizu and his co-authors of *Toward the Decolonization of African Literature* (1980).

I have undertaken this cursory review of the evolution of first and second generation African writing and its criticism to underscore the fact that African literature has always existed within the scopic regime of Western interpretive practices and institutions. This inevitable Western alterity has in turn created a situation where any hermeneutic model fashioned for African texts must, of necessity, be transnational and translational in the sense in which Homi Bhabha theorises the two concepts in 'The Postcolonial and the Postmodern' (1993). More on Bhabha later in the conclusion. Suffice it to assert at this juncture that my aim in what follows is to trace the contours of the emerging politics around the translationality of postcolonial theory, one of the most formidable discursive models to have arisen in Western academe after the publication of Chinweizu's book. My interest is not so much in undertaking yet another inquiry into the disciplinary and theoretical claims of postcolonial theory and the various political praxes it enacts in the public spheres of the West and the Global South as it is in teasing out the continuities between the new politics of alterity and the old forms that I have analysed. Just as theories like Marxism, structuralism, and poststructuralism were transnationalised, translated, and contested as (un)viable critical paradigms for African literature, so is postcolonial theory now undergoing the same process in discussions of African literature.

But something else comes into the scenario to make it far more dramatic and theoretically challenging: the African literary alterity that post-1990 postcolonial theory is interpellated to engage comprises an entirely new set of writers whose thematics and contexts of production are not identical with those of the first two generations of African writers. The explosion of postcolonial theory—consequent upon the publication of Said's *Orientalism* in 1978 and, later, Bill Ashcroft's, Gareth Griffiths's, and Helen Tiffin's *The Empire Writes Back* in 1988—coincided with the emergence all over Africa of a new set of writers whose corpus has now come under the critical rubric of third generation African writing.

Born mostly after 1960, the signal date of African independence from colonial rule, these writers have also been referred to as the postcolonial generation. The Zimbabweans Tsitsi Dangarembga and Yvonne Vera; the Ghanaian Amma Darko; the Ugandan Moses Isegawa; and the Nigerians Sefi Atta, Biyi Bandele, Ike Oguine, Okey Ndibe, Helon Habila, Akin Adesokan, Chris Abani, Promise Okekwe, Unoma Azuah, and Chimamanda Adichie are the most prominent novelists in the new generation. Notable Francophone novelists in the same generation include Calixthe Beyala, Abdourahman Waberi, Bessora, Patrice Nganang, Daniel Biyaoula, Kossi Effoui, Sami Tchak, Alain Mabanckou, and Fatou Diome. Poetry in the generation is, arguably, an exclusive Nigerian phenomenon with poets like Uche Nduka, Afam Akeh, Victoria Sylvia Kankara, Chiedu Ezeanah, Nduka Otiono, Ogaga Ifowodo, Toyin Adewale, Lola Shoneyin, Olu Oguibe, Remi Raji, and Amatoritsero Ede being the leading versifiers.

The arrival of these new writers on the scene, their increasing visibility on the international map—Beyala, Mabanckou, Waberi, Vera, Adichie, Habila, and Abani have all won international literary prizes—throws up the immediate challenge of determining the extent to which their works interpellate a postcolonial reading as well as their imbrication in the globalist dynamics of postcoloniality. In much of what is now commonly referred to as the Global South, the postcolonial condition has been marked largely by the failure of the state and the consequent defoliation of the dreams of political independence. The delegitimation of the Third World state has occurred in the context of seismic political, economic, and cultural realignments where the gains of the information age and the dynamics of globalisation have occasioned the massive flow of ideas, people, and cultures across increasingly porous geo-political borders. Arjun Appadurai has proposed five useful dimensions of current global cultural flow in his essay 'Disjuncture and difference in the global cultural economy' (1990).

As the postcolony atrophied and the soporific rhetoric of one, indivisible nation-ness with which it fashioned the subject in various African nation-states (this was especially true of Francophone West Africa and its one-party states) were unsettled by localised pressures of identity competing for relevance within the validating mechanisms of the new transnationalist order, the resulting centripetal direction of global cultural processes towards the Euro-American metropole imposed what Cornel West (1993) has termed 'a new politics of difference' (p.257) on those sites. The postcolonial atrophy of the erstwhile colonised margin now translates to a concentration of plural alterities in the centre: displacement, deracination, exile, alienation, and diaspora have become the discursive categories with which the modalities of being of the Third World subject in Western *loci* are engaged.

These conditions also constitute the informing postcolonial theoretical framework with which works by new immigrant writers from the Third World are approached. My purpose here is to examine the extent to which the dominant versions of postcolonial theory currently in use in First World academe could shape not only the interpretation of third generation African texts but, more important, could determine the modalities of transnational institutionalisation and canonisation of those works. My analysis will focus mainly on Nigeria's third generation writing because the Nigerians constitute the largest group of third generation writers in Africa and developments within the said generation are often reflective of—but not always coterminous with—trends elsewhere in the continent. I will proceed by examining the short history of African literature's troublesome romance with postcolonial criticism before zeroing in on the possible implications for third generation writing.

What's in a Name? African Literature and the Academy

Recent critical texts such as Olakunle George's *Relocating Agency* (2003), Kwaku Korang's *Writing Ghana, Writing Modernity* (2003) and Gaurav Desai's *Subject to Colonialism* (2001) would seem to indicate that African(ist) critics have now overcome the initial aporia which greeted attempts to deploy postcolonial theory in African literary and cultural criticism. Yet a close reading of these and other new critical texts will underscore the fact that there is hardly any African critic who deploys the concepts and idioms of postcolonial theory without entering caveats and qualifications that are indicative of their awareness of the dangers of embracing wholesale yet another Western theoretical construct at this crucial stage in the evolution of African literatures. The epigraph taken from Osundare is fairly indicative of African(ist) scepticism towards postcolonial theory. Although the question of the deceptive temporality of postcoloniality, which seemingly projects the time of the Other into an after-colonialism, is the most frequently cited reason for its suspected unworkability in an Africanist context, where the effects of colonialism are still very real in the present, I suggest that a deeper problem exists because of postcolonial theory's inevitable articulation as an onomastic performance.

A crisis of naming marks all ex-centric literatures, especially those that emerged mainly as dissident reactions to the othering and subalternisation of non-Western peoples by Europe. The well-known historical conditions that produced the 'fighting'[4] element in the literatures we now refer to as African, Caribbean, African-American, 'Native American', 'First Nations', and 'Aboriginal' also guaranteed from the onset that those textual processes would evolve within ontological pressures played out in the field of naming. First there was the need to name such literary formations as an indication of their separateness, distinctiveness, difference, and independence from an appropriative Euro-American discursive mechanism.[5] This move is based on suspicions that the West is always seeking to classify, codify, and compartmentalise[6] othered entities as a precondition for dominating and subsuming them within its own cognitive régime, where they either disappear or become discursive and institutional exotica. Such imperialist régimes of appropriation through (mis)naming were responsible for the old *faux pas* of treating the emerging literatures of Africa as curious, insignificant branches of metropolitan European literatures. This taxonomic imperative undergirds the politics of the Chinweizu and his co-authors in *Toward the Decolonization of African Literature* (1980). Their strategy consists not only in naming the literatures of Africa but also in naming the critical and evaluative parameters by which they may be approached.

Ensconced within institutional and discursive structures that cocoon them in the prison-house of otherness, non-Western literatures, even when they are named by 'autochthonous insiders' as aggressive as the Chinweizu troika, are in a seeming no-win situation. In the nature of things, such autochthonous naming manoeuvres can only be authorised and processed for consumption by the dominant, validating, and appropriating structures they are meant to resist, in this case the Euro-American academy. Needless to say that appropriation, othering, or outright occlusion can occur at any point during this process. Jean-Paul Sartre's (1948) categorisation of Négritude as 'racisme antiracisme'[7], Fredric Jameson's (1986) classification of all Third World literatures as "national allegories"[8] are two of the most famous instances of naming the Other that have been appropriated by an Academy on whose validating mechanisms they now depend for their continued relevance, reproduction, and circulation.

When minoritised literatures are (mis)named in the volatile context of the Euro-American Academy, the resultant labels seem to predestine them for appropriation or for politically correct showcasing as diversity exotica. If the fear of this scenario institutes the opposite manoeuvre of not naming them at all, they risk the certainty of oblivion in a context that already denies them coevality, to use Johannes Fabian's apt expression in *Time and the Other* (1983). This is what I call the catch-22 condition of non-Western minoritised literatures in their Euro-American host sites: be named and risk perishing, be not-named and risk perishing still!

This onomastic crisis has a particularly strong resonance for modern African literatures. The situation is such that those whose genius and raped history produce the literatures in question have always had to operate on the defensive. The defensive position from which people who have suffered centuries of physical and epistemic violence are forced to operate is ensconced in structures of feeling that are manifested in the form of an extreme sensitivity to acts of naming. For naming is the originary act, the first step in the world-historical processes that crystallised in the subjugation of non-Western peoples.

Naming precedes and begets (mis)representation which, in turn, is deployed as justification for all the forms of violence that have been masquerading for five centuries as a *mission civilisatrice*.[9] In the introduction to their edited book *Blackness in Latin America and the Caribbean* (1998) Arlene Torres and Norman Whitten assert that the political process of naming the other is deeply imbricated in what they call 'structures of domination'.[10] According to the two scholars, language, operating as simile (as in the sentence: 's/he sure doesn't look like a Negro') or metaphor (as in the statement: 'she is black') are clear examples of the ways in which naming maintains structures of domination.

The philosopher V. Y. Mudimbe operates essentially within this perception of naming as a politically determined act integral to the construction of structures of domination. The titles of his two most influential books, *The Invention of Africa* (1988) and *The Idea of Africa* (1994) exemplify this position. The keywords, 'invention' and 'idea', presuppose an onomastic move on the part of those whose self-imposed burden it was to 'discover' that space. Invention, in Mudimbe's deployment of the term, is a synonym for the Africa that Europe created and named through the fertile racist imagination of some of her best minds: Immanuel Kant, G. W. F. Hegel, Lucien Lévy-Bruhl, Albert Schweitzer, and Hugh Trevor Roper. Significantly, the first chapter of *The Idea of Africa* contains a subsection entitled 'naming and metaphorizing' in which Mudimbe, like Whitten and Torres, examines the consequences of being named by the conquering Other. Mudimbe (1988: 29) writes:

> Such is the context which metaphorizes the names of Africa. To concern myself with only the discourse produced ... which endlessly repeats itself in the books of the 'colonial library', the context—or more exactly its will to truth fissures ancient words—constructs stereotypes, allocates remarkable adjectives to Africans and other 'primitives,' and finally establishes its civilizing mission. It is thus the late eighteenth—and early nineteenth—century conjunction of anthropology and colonial projects that

hones the concepts and actualizes, in the image of the colonized, all negative metaphors worked out by five centuries of European explorations of the world.

It is clear from this picture that Europe's unenviable legacy of misnaming its others—
at least from the perspective of the named—accounts for the huge anxieties, and
sometimes outright hostility, that often greet attempts at deploying postcolonial theory,
with all its complexities, consistencies and contradictions, as a hermeneutic grid for
modern African literatures and discourses. It is hard to imagine any theory that does
not function at a fundamental level as an act of naming. Literary theory must
necessarily name its object of knowledge, that entity it claims to be the theory of,
before it can move on to function as exegesis.

One must equally bear it in mind that theory, especially in its postcolonial version, performs more than the political function of naming and generating knowledges
on literature. As Gail Gilliland puts it in her book, *Being a Minor Writer* (1994), theory
has become the god on whose authority the literary critic and the Academy centre
some texts and decentre others, determine which writer and literature are canonical
and which ones become marginal institutional curios. The idea of theory as a form
of naming informs some of Osundare's most virulent critiques of postcolonial
theory, which he considers to be fundamentally inapplicable to the African condition. In 'How Postcolonial is Postcolonial Discourse?', a subsection of his well-known
essay, 'African literature and the Crisis of Poststructuralist Theorizing', [11] Osundare
(2003: 41) expresses concerns about the politics of naming that are worth quoting in
some detail:

> The world is shaped—and frequently determined—by the words we use for ex-
> pressing it. In naming the world we also name ourselves, evoking a recognizable,
> tangible construct of that panoply of realities which constitute what we call the
> human experience. Names serve as the door to the house of experience, a guide to
> hidden meanings in the shadowy nooks of time and place. Names tell stories,
> liberate or imprison; they may also serve as self-fulfilling prophecies. Names com-
> mit; which is why the Yoruba say that it is only mad people who do not mind what
> names they are called, or who refuse to see the difference between the names they
> choose to bear and the ones the world prefers to call them by. The negative 'politics
> of representation' so famous in contemporary literary discourse is very much the
> product of misapprehension as it is of mis-naming and mis-verbalization.

It is obvious that Osundare's position bears considerable thematic affinity with Achebe's
well-known reservations on the practice of naming Africans and their cultural products
in the series of essays collected in such volumes as *Morning Yet on Creation Day*
(1975) and *Hopes and Impediments* (1988). In *Home and Exile* (2000), his most recent
volume of essays, Achebe returns to the effects of these processes of naming by
arguing that they create an imbalance of stories between the North and the South.

Postcolonial Theory and Third Generation African Writing: The Problematique

Despite its claims to an undeniable leftist pedigree; despite its self-perception as an instrument for the agency of all those subalternised on the basis of race, ethnicity, gender, and creed—'a broad anti-imperialist emancipatory project' (as Linda Hutcheon (1995: 8) puts it—postcolonial theory is a form of naming that comes to African literature enmeshed in the complex politics that is now traditionally summed up in the Foucauldian power/knowledge equation. This equation stages knowledge as a non-neutral, hierarchising phenomenon: the knower, by virtue of knowing, is invested with power and this occludes every possibility of neutrality. Knowledge ontologises the knower as the dominant/hegemonic entity in a hierarchical relationship with the known. The object of knowledge is consequently the subalternised recipient of the master's gaze. Viewed from this perspective, the source and location of certain forms of knowledge become instrumental to their perception as forms of dominance. Thinkers like Anthony Appiah, Arif Dirlik, and Ella Shohat have sufficiently established the fact that the most popular version of postcolonial criticism is a certain diasporic, internationalist strand that inhabits the seminar rooms of the Euro-American Academy. It articulates its scribal essence in books published essentially by Euro-American presses and, above all, in journals mostly edited by that self-defined, post-Cartesian subject of History: the Western white male. [12]

This locational pedigree is a major albatross of postcolonial criticisms in the context of theoretical approaches to the African literary process and accounts largely for the manifest unease in some African critical circuits. Hutcheon (1995: 9) captures the situation when she acknowledges the existence of concerns that postcolonial theory 'represents yet another of the First World academy's covert colonizing strategies of domination over the cultural production of the Third World'. The politics of location has therefore begun to play itself out in how third generation African texts are read, institutionalised, and canonised from the perspective of the postcolonial. The point must be borne in mind that a significant proportion of third generation African writers are now located in Euro-America. Virtually every known producer of Francophone African fiction in the generation is based in Paris. Nigeria accounts for the highest rate of third generation exile in Anglophone Africa. These writers have now filled the ranks of cultural workers who, in the words of West (1993: 257) are:

> Marginalized First World agents who shun degraded self-representations, articulating instead their sense of the flow of history in the light of the contemporary terrors, anxieties and fears of highly commercialized North Atlantic capitalist cultures (with their escalating xenophobias against people of colour, Jews, women, gays, lesbians, and the elderly).

One major consequence of postcolonial theory's obsession with the identity politics of diasporic location is that alienation and deracination have become quasi-inescapable preconditions for the institutional validation of the works of Africa's new writers. In the case of first generation writers like Soyinka, Achebe, Ekwensi, and Ngugi, and second generation writers like Ofeimun, Osundare, Osofisan, and Iyayi, Western theories like Marxism and social realism had operated as true 'travelling theories', to borrow Said's felicitous expression, making their way to the continent to meet the creative writer and his/her texts, engaging them *in situ*.

In other words, the African writer of the first and the second generations did not have to leave the continent in order for his/her works to be institutionally validated in local and international circuits of interpretation and legitimation, as the case of Amos Tutuola and John Pepper Clark clearly demonstrates. Apart from the presence of Western and African critics in the pioneer universities of the continent as previously noted, there also existed a welter of respectable journals such as *Black Orpheus* and *Transition* that were able to make critical elaborations on African writing available to a global audience even while based in Africa.

Postcolonial theory's privileging of migrant subjecthood and textualities has ensured that the situation is markedly different for Africa's third generation writers. This situation is especially true of Nigeria. Virtually all the successful novelists in the new generation are, for instance, based in the West, their works gradually joining the ranks of those diasporic, migrant textualities that are the prized features of Western diversity/multicultural syllabi. Even when the story is set in Africa, as is the case in novels like Adichie's *Purple Hibiscus* (2003), Habila's *Waiting for an Angel* (2002), Abani's *Graceland* (2004), Nwosu's *Invisible Chapters* (2002), and Ndibe's *Arrows of Rain* (2000), a certain deontology of postcolonial critical reception still predisposes them to being received as the diasporic texts of migrant cultural agents, the continental setting being construed as a sort of glance back, a return narrative or a peep into the postcolony by a cultural agent who has escaped its ravages.

Like the novelists, Africa's new poets have also been compelled to relocate to the West to discover their postcoloniality: Uche Nduka, Afam Akeh, Ogaga Ifowodo, Unoma Azuah, Angela Nwosu, and Amatoritsero Ede are some of Nigeria's most visible third generation poets, all now located in the West. The forced postcolonial dislocation of these writers is further compounded by the fact that there now exist practically no scholarly literary journals of repute publishing from the continent: *Research in African Literatures, African Literature Today*, and *Transition* are all based in the United States. South Africa-based journals like *English in Africa* and *AlterNation* are widely circulated in the West but are largely unknown in sub-Saharan and northern Africa. We therefore have a situation in which institutional validation of an African text is now predicated, to a considerable extent, on the diasporic credentials of its author, a direct consequence of the multicultural identity frenzy that postcolonial discourse has unleashed on Western academe.

The centrality of the politics of location to any serious apprehension of third generation Nigerian writing from the perspective of critical postcolonialism is further underscored by the controversy surrounding the modalities for awarding the 'Nigerian Prize for Literature', instituted recently by the Nigerian Liquefied Natural

Gas Company. The monetary reward that comes with the prize—US$ 20,000—easily makes it Africa's most prestigious literary prize at the moment.

With regard to content and thematic preferments, one important question that postcolonial theory would have to address, if it is to become an enduring paradigm for apprehending Africa's new writing, is the generalised absence of the most important temporal markers of postcolonial textualities from the work of the new writers: Empire and colonialism. No matter how disparate and complex positions on the meaning and scope of postcolonial criticism have become, Empire and colonialism remain the overarching temporal events around which value, meaning, self-fashioning, and agency revolve.

The postcolonial leitmotif of writing back, striking back, resisting, or deconstructing are all positions deployed within the framework of the inescapable referentiality of Empire, colonialism, and their effects in the present, manifest in the interweaving articulations of nation, ethnicity, gender, religion, race, class, and geospatial location. This constant revaluation, probing, and unsettling of the after effects of Empire constitutes the 'centre' of the postcolonial creative text, from Achebe to Salman Rushdie, and from Derek Walcott to Assia Djebar. It is equally by continuously semiotising the power relations and the localised, dissident praxes of the subaltern characters of these 'centred' postcolonial fictions that thinkers like Said, Bhabha, Spivak, Anthony Appiah, Ato Quayson, and Simon Gikandi have been able to carve an institutional space for othered third world texts in Western academe.

The departure—sometimes radical, sometimes insidious—of third generation African writers from centred and centrist narratives in which the drama of contact with the West and conscription into its modernist teleology is played out in the context of the multiple, often overlapping binaries it wills into existence (centre/margin, coloniser/colonised, European self/African Other), is reason enough for partakers in postcolonial discursivity to begin to interrogate the possibilities that postcolonial theory holds for the new writing, especially in its dominant Western sites of articulation. Such an inquiry is made more imperative by the fact that the texts that postcolonial theory still largely filters into syllabi and seminars in Western institutions are those that lend themselves easily into the thematic staging of the aforementioned stereotypical binaries, their gradual deconstruction within the oppositional economy of the text, and the subsequent emergence of liminal, blurred, interstitial spaces or borderlands where subjecthood and agency are validated through quotidian negotiations and contingent performances.

The critic Harry Garuba is the only one to my knowledge who has explored the impact of the shift from centred paradigms in third generation Nigerian poetry. In his essay 'The Extreme Lightness of Being: Discursive Refigurations in New Nigerian Poetry', Garuba (2005) explores the lack of a central, organising temporal event in the work of some of the most representative figures of current Nigerian poetry. Garuba observes correctly that whereas poets of the first and second generation like Okigbo, Soyinka, Ofeimun, and Osundare had mined oral resources such as myths and rituals and deployed them in the service of centralising narratives like the cultural nationalism and the utopias of a post-imperial, coherent nation-ness in the 1960s, such altruistic engagements do not constitute the thematic fulcrum of third generation works like Akeh's *Stolen Moments* (1988), Nduka's *If Only the Night* (2002), Ifowodo's *Madiba* (2004), and Shoneyin's *So All the Time I Was Sitting on an Egg* (1998).

What needs to be added to cogent analyses such as Garuba's is how these decentredness, and the subsequent absence from the new texts of the staples of institutional and canonical postcoloniality, especially in Western academe, could impact on their legitimation in those contexts. What, for instance, could be the possible conditions for institutionalising and canonising a novel like Toni Kan's *Ballad of Rage* (2004) in the West, a work that self-consciously shuns the identity dilemmas of postcolonial discourse? Kan's novel is a deliberately austere narrative which dispenses with those investments in a Balzacian luxuriance of geo-spatial description, reference to the fault lines of Empire, the dysfunctionality of the postcolony, often at the root of what transnational fluxes and migrations, and the inevitable politics of fractal, transcultural subjectivity. Rather, Kan weaves a tripodal love plot around three characters: the doctor, the wife, and the lover. On the surface, the narrative seems simple enough. A middle aged doctor marries a voluptuous young woman who enters into an extra-marital affair with the lover, a young aspiring musician closer to her age. The doctor discovers the affair, strangles his wife, and goes to jail for murder, awaiting execution.

Beyond this plot, however, Kan displays extraordinary talent in the psychological exploration of his characters. This dimension transforms a deceptively simple story into a discursive probing of universal human emotions and conditions that is reminiscent of Dostoyesvsky, Kafka, and Coetzee. Although the inevitable intrusions of local colour suggest that the story is set somewhere in postcolonial Nigeria, the narrative self-consciously avoids naming a geographical setting and is thus able to live up to its universal dimensions as a human tragedy.

Conclusion: What Prospects for Institutionalisation and Canonisation?

The obvious lessons to be drawn from the largely unanchored narrative in *Ballad of Rage* and, indeed, from the growing body of third generation Nigerian poetry, is that postcolonial criticism, as currently practised in Euro-American academe, must expand its brief beyond the formulaic focus on transnational identity politics and the reconfigured idioms of global asymmetries in order to be able to canonise and grapple effectively with new and divergent African texts that continually aspire beyond such entrapments. Two passages from Bhabha's (1993:190) previously cited essay will suffice to underscore the seemingly immutable preferences of contemporary postcolonial criticism:

> Postcolonial criticism bears witness to the unequal and uneven forces of cultural representation involved in the contest for political and social authority within the

modern world order. Postcolonial perspectives emerge from the colonial testimony of Third World countries and the discourses of 'minorities' within the geopolitical divisions of East and West, North and South. They intervene in those ideological discourses of modernity that attempt to give a hegemonic 'normality' to the uneven development and the differential, often disadvantaged, histories of nations, races, communities, peoples. They formulate their critical revisions around issues of cultural difference, social authority and political discrimination in order to reveal the antagonistic and ambivalent moments within the rationalizations of modernity.

On the institutional nomenclature of this dominant version of postcolonial critique, Bhabha (1993:194) avers that:

> The enunciative position of contemporary cultural studies is both complex and problematic. It attempts to institutionalize a range of transgressive discourses whose strategies are elaborated around non-equivalent sites of representation where a history of discrimination and misrepresentation is common among, say, women, blacks, homosexuals and Third World migrants. However, the 'signs' that construct such histories and identities—gender, race, homophobia, post war diaspora, refugees, the international division of labour, and so on—not only differ in content but often produce incompatible systems of signification and engage distinct forms of social subjectivity.

As Garuba has pointed out in respect of new Nigerian poetry—and as I have further demonstrated with Kan's *Ballad of Rage*—a significant number of third generation African texts simply do not privilege Bhabha's 'signs' of 'histories' and 'identities' as the centre of their narrative universe. Far from claiming that these topoi do not exist in the new writing, the intention here is to signal the ways in which they are being transcended and, therefore, interpellate novel strategies of postcolonial semiotising. Alongside texts like, say, Jhumpa Lahiri's *The Namesake* (2004) and Darko's *Beyond the Horizon* (1995), which privilege hybridity and the identity impasse of Third World migrants in the West and, therefore, always secure automatic entry into postcolonial theory syllabi, we must devise means of introducing texts like Kan's *Ballad of Rage* (2004) and Akeh's *Stolen Moments* (1988) if only to show that Akeh's masterful evocations of the rain, heat, and harmattan of Ibadan are also worthy subjects of scholarly inquiry.

Notes

1. See his volume of essays, *Morning Yet on Creation Day* (1975).
2. See his *Structural Models and African Poetics* (1981).
3. See Obiwu's (2005) essay, 'Achebe's Poetic Drive'.
4. I am making an obvious reference to Frantz Fanon's idea of 'fighting literature' in *The Wretched of the Earth*.
5. For a fuller discussion of the compulsive pre-occupation with—and sensitivity to—naming on the part of the dispossessed subject, see Ann DuCille's (1994) analysis of the increasingly popular practice of adopting and revaluating African, especially Ghanaian names by African-

Americans in her essay, 'Postcolonialism and Afrocentricity: Discourse and Dat Course'. With regard to the specific case of African literature, the famous African writers conference held in Kampala, Uganda, in June 1962, signalled what has become African writers' engagement with the anxieties of naming. Tagged 'A Conference of African Writers of English Expression' and attended by the likes of Wole Soyinka, Chinua Achebe and Christopher Okigbo, the conferees sought to define 'African literature'. A significant outcome of the conference was Obi Wali's highly polemical *Transition* essay 'The dead end of African literature?' (1963), an attempt to name African literature by excluding texts written in European languages. The language debate has remained one of the most atavistic themes of African literary criticism.

6. See Wole Soyinka's *Myth, Literature and the African World*, for a discussion of the West's compulsion to classification and compartmentalistion.

7. See his essay, '*Orphée noir*', which serves as introduction to Léopold Sédar Senghor's (1948) *Anthologie de la nouvelle poésie nègre et malgache de langue francaise*.

8. See his essay 'Third World literatures in the era of multinational capitalism'.

9. Naming was Christopher Columbus's first act of dominance and mastery in the new world. The island on which he established his first colony he named Hispaniola. The Arawakan-speaking Taino people he 'discovered' along with their lands he named Indians. The deleterious historical consequences of these political acts of (mis)naming bear no repeating here.

10. Norman E. Whitten, JR., & Arlene Torres (1998). 'To forge the future in the fires of the past: an interpretive essay on domination, resistance, and liberation'.

11. Except otherwise stated, all references are to the version of this essay that appeared in Osundare's (2003) recent book, *Thread in the Loom: Essays on African Literature and Culture*.

12. I address the question of the location of postcolonial theory and its links with diasporicity in my essay, 'Africa, India, and the postcolonial: notes toward a praxis of infliction' (Adesanmi 2004).

References

Abani, C., 2004, *Graceland*, New York: Farrar, Straus, and Giroux.

Achebe, C., 1975, *Morning Yet on Creation Day*, New York: Anchor Books.

Achebe, C., 1988, *Hopes and Impediments*, New York: Anchor Books.

Achebe, C., 2000, *Home and Exile*, Oxford: Oxford University Press.

Adesanmi, P., 2004, 'Africa, India, and the Postcolonial: Notes towards a Praxis of Infliction', *Arena Journal* 21: 173-196.

Adichie, C., 2003, *Purple Hibiscus*, Chapel Hill, NC: Algonquin Books of Chapel Hill.

Akeh, A., 1988, *Stolen Moments*, Lagos: Update Publications.

Appadurai, A., 1990, 'Disjuncture and Difference in the Global Cultural Economy', *Public Culture* 2 (2): 1-24.

Bhabha, H., 1993 [1975], 'The Postcolonial and the Postmodern: The Question of Agency', in S. During ed., *The Cultural Studies Reader*, pp. 189-208, London: Routledge.

Chinweizu, 1975, *The West and the Rest of Us*, New York: Random House.

Chinweizu et al., 1980, *Toward the Decolonization of African Literature*, Enugu: Fourth Dimension.

Clark, J. P., 1970, *The Example of Shakespeare*, Evanston: Northwestern University Press.

Davies, C. B., 1994, *Black Women, Writing, and Identity: Migrations of the Subject*, London and New York: Routledge.

Darko, A., 1995, *Beyond the Horizon*, Oxford: Heinemann.

Desai, G., 2001, *Subject to Colonialism: African Self-Fashioning and the Colonial Library*, Durham: Duke University Press.

DuCille, A., 1995, 'Postcolonialism and Afrocentricity: Discourse and Dat Course', in W. Sollors and M. Diedrich, eds., *The Black Columbiad: Defining Moments in African American Literature and Culture*, Cambridge: Harvard University Press, 28-41.

Fabian, J., 1983, *Time and the Other*, New York: Columbia University Press.

Fanon, F., 1963, *The Wretched of the Earth*, New York: Grove Press.

George, O., 2003, *Relocating Agency: Modernity and African Letters*, Albany: SUNY Press.

Gilliland, G., 1994, *Being a Minor Writer*, Iowa City: University of Iowa Press.

Habila, H., 2002, *Waiting for an Angel*, London : Hamish Hamilton.

Hutcheon, L., 1995, 'Colonialism and the Postcolonial Condition: Complexities Abounding', *PMLA* 110 (1): 7-16.

Ifowodo, O., 2004, *Madiba*, Trenton, NJ: Africa World Press.

Nengi-Ilagha, B., 2002, *Condolences*, Lagos: Treasure Books.

Jameson, F., 1986, 'Third World Literatures in the Era of Multinational Capitalism', *Social Text* 15: 65-88.

Kan, T., 2004, *Ballad of Rage*, Lagos: Hybun Publications.

Korang, K., 2003, *Writing Ghana, Imagining Africa: Nation and Modernity*, Rochester: The University of Rochester Press.

Lahiri, J., 2004, *The Namesake*, New York: Mariner Books.

Mudimbe, Y. V., 1988, *The Invention of Africa*, Bloomington: Indiana University Press.

Mudimbe, Y. V., 1994, *The Idea of Africa*, Bloomington: Indiana University Press.

Ngugi wa Thiong'o, 1986, *Decolonising the Mind*, London: James Currey.

Ndibe, O., 2000, *Arrows of Rain*, Oxford: Heinemann.

Nduka, U., 2002, *If Only the Night*, Amsterdam: Sojourner Press.

Nwosu, M., 2002, *Invisible Chapters*, Nigeria: Hybun Books.

Obiwu, 2005, 'Achebe's Poetic Drive', *Sentinel Poetry Quarterly* 5: 23-48.

Osundare, N., 2003, *Thread in the Loom: Essays on African Literature and Culture*, Trenton, NJ: Africa World Press.

Osundare, N., 1995, 'The World Around Oe', *Glendora Review* 1 (2): 5-8.

Rodney, W., 1972, *How Europe Underdeveloped Africa*, Washington: Howard University Press.

Said, E., 1978, *Orientalism*, New York: Pantheon.

Senghor, L. S., 1948, *Anthologie de la nouvelle poésie nègre et malgache de langue francaise*, Paris: Presses Universitaires de France.

Shoneyin, L., 1998, *So All the Time I was Sitting on an Egg*, Ibadan: Ovalonion House.

Soyinka, W., 1976, *Myth, Literature, and the African World*, Cambridge: Cambridge University Press.

Wali, O., 1963, 'The Dead End of African Literature?', *Transition* 10: 13-15.

West, C., 1993, 'The New Cultural Politics of Difference', in S. During, ed., *The Cultural Studies Reader*, London: Routledge, 256-267.

Whitten, N. and A. Torres, eds., 1998, *Blackness in Latin America and the Caribbean: Social Dynamics and Cultural Transformations*, Bloomington: Indiana University Press.

Chapter 5

An Argument for Ethno-Language Studies in Africa

Sinfree Makoni and Ulrike Meinhof

'Africa's language problem, like its problem of "tribalism", is imagined at the extreme as a condition of plenty, its fate is to suffer from oversupply, in short, Africa seems to be marked by death or glut, but never a just or appropriate measure'. We focus on the so-called 'language problem' which—it is claimed—arises out of Africa's complex multilingualism underwritten by 'oligolinguistic' tendencies in language planning (Fardon and Furniss 1994:1; Blommaert 1999:179). We analyse the assumptions made about 'language' in Africa which encourage this perspective. Given the breadth and diversity of Africa this is an enormous task which we consider necessary, since any analysis either of a geographical region or individual nation/ states is sociolinguistically untenable (Adegbija 1996; Samarin 1996:389).

Language use in Africa is best analysed in terms of transitional and transnational networks—something analogous to 'imagined communities' or the 'narration of the nation', and on the basis of a (pre) literate and literate continuum (Anderson 1991; Hall 1997). Such a continuum enables us to examine the ways in which 'languages' are constructed and the role of literacy in shaping the assumptions made about them. We are restating the argument that linguistic theory in Africa is more a theory of literacy than of language. Until recently, the 'language problem' was conceptualised as the existence of too many languages in Africa. In terms of language planning the solution proposed to 'overcome' the over-supply of 'languages' was to advocate the use of a single 'European' language as a national language, because African policies were predicated upon a one nation = one language policy (Bambgose 2000).

The rhetoric of multilingualism construes the existence of many languages not as a problem but as an asset, a 'resource' (Bloch 2002: 24), a notion which may be regarded as somewhat insensitive by impoverished multilinguals. To such persons it is of little comfort to be told that multilingualism constitutes a form of cultural wealth. If we are to convince lay people about the validity of our arguments it is important to formulate alternative ways of speaking about the issues we address.

But how different are the monolingual models and the multilingual approaches from each other in their assumptions about 'language'? Both conceive of 'language' in a similar way. From both perspectives multilingualism is a variant of monolingualism if one is referring to 'different' languages which are expressions of inter-translatable languages, such as, for example, Xhosa/Zulu, Ndebele/Zulu. Plural monolingualism is of reduced value.

In this article we illustrate how languages are socially constructed and the consequences of these constructions for our own understandings of language. However, we resist the temptation of assigning victory to particular perspectives about language, but instead hold the different views about language in mind without 'suppressing' any, because, as Nagel (1986:2) states: 'there is no view from Nowhere'.

We examine the assumptions about 'language' made in Africa in the contexts of colonialism and post-independent (class-apartheid) Africa, and how they may match or at times distort prevailing language practices. The issue is important both linguistically and ethically. 'All solutions to language problems have knock-on effects to the conditions of people's lives', so ethical issues inevitably emerge (Brumfit 2004). Linguistic descriptions in that sense constitute a form of social intervention. Misrepresentation of these realities can have harmful effects, even if the descriptions are well intentioned (Grace 1981). Hence, development of a 'standard' in African languages that was too different from any variety actually spoken, or of a standard that was oversimplified inhibited the development of literacy, rendering it more difficult than necessary (Irvine 2001:169). Such disabling repercussions for literacy and creative writing are the material consequences arising from some assumptions about language.

Ways in which African languages are socially constructed have relevance beyond the African continent. They have implications for the ontological status of African American Vernaculars (AAV) in so far as it is claimed that AAV has an African language base (McWhorter 1998). If the exact nature of African languages is debatable, it is difficult to see how scholars working on AAV can determine the nature of African languages at least four centuries ago. We are suggesting that purely linguistic criteria are inadequate for determining the African language base of AAV.

Processes in the Social Construction of Language

But what do we mean by saying that African languages are social constructions? We mean that a language is an invention, a construction just like other categories such as 'time.' Speaking of time as a construction does not dispute the geophysical fact that the earth rotates on an axis, but it means that the signification of time has a social and variable base. In a similar vein what is socially constructed in languages is 'a language', and not a natural category 'Language'. A capacity for language is natural in humans, but 'languages' are a product of social and historical interventions.

There are three processes underpinning the social construction of languages: iconisation, fractal recursivity and erasure (Irvine and Gal 2000). 'Iconization imputes to a linguistic feature or system the inherent nature of the social group indexed by it. A linguistic feature is iconic if it is treated as if it portrays the group's essence' (Irvine & Gal 2000:38). For example, clicks have an iconic status with speakers of Nguni languages even though clicks are Khoisan in origin. Fractal recursivity is the projection of an opposition, salient at some level of relationship, onto another level. When such oppositions are reproduced within a single person, they do not concern contrasting identities so much as oppositions between activities or roles associated with prototypical social persons. In any case, the oppositions do not define fixed or stable social groups. Rather, they provide actors with the discursive or cultural resources to claim and thus attempt to create shifting 'communities', identities, selves, and roles, at different levels of contrast within a cultural field' (Irvine and Gal 2000:38). By adopting clicks Nguni speakers 'create lexical substitutions that were absent in everyday speech'. The substitutions of clicks for everyday words produced an avoidance register, *Hlonipha* (Irvine & Gal 2000). Erasure explains away facts that are inconsistent with the ideological scheme. In addition to the three processes we include a literacy narrowly defined as production and reception of 'written texts'. Texts such as marriage certificates and labour passes were significant in so far as they had an impact on how Africans constructed the ontological status of African languages. It was the 'reduction' of these speech forms to writing and their use in literacy and instruction which led to the 'emergence' of African languages—not only in Africa but in other parts of the world as well (Samarin 1996: 390).

Literacy had an impact not only on the emergence of these languages, but also on the social meanings which Africans had of their 'own' languages and other languages, notably English and French. When we argue that the colonial encounter facilitated the 'emergence' or the 'springing up' of languages in Africa, we are not saying that prior to colonialism and literacy there was no speech in Africa or that there was any less 'talk' before colonialism, but that the 'shredding' of these speech forms into languages and some of our current ways of thinking about language in Africa are a product of literacy and colonialism. We can see this, for example, in the connection between Christianity, literacy, and language, including English. Schools that taught English also taught literacy and Christianity, so 'perforce' engagement with one led to an engagement with the other, an engagement reinforced by the dual status of teachers as preachers (Summers 2002).

If applied linguistics is to address 'real' world issues then we have to examine our assumptions, because most of the concepts were neither conceived with African contexts in mind nor aimed at addressing African 'language' problems. Adjusting our categories to suit the problem is necessary because practical problems require the use of categories appropriate to their solution. For example, it is frequently repeated that additive bilingualism is cognitively, socially, and linguistically beneficial (Webb & Kembo-Sure 1999). The bilingualism which the analysts usually have in mind includes a European language and an African language, and rarely African languages only, even though the latter form is more widespread than the former.

Our focus here is not whether or not bilingualism does indeed have such effects but on how the construction of language in (additive) bilingualism falls into the trap of 'objectivising' languages as 'if (they) were akin to having access to clean water, fuel, or food so that accessing them would produce cognitive and material benefits' (Pennycook 2004: 149; see also Makoni & Meinhof 2004). The objectivisation of language encourages policy makers to think in terms of who has languages, of how many people can be persuaded to use them, or of how people can be given these languages.

Efforts to determine the nature of language problems in Africa are complicated by the fact that 'language' as an object is different depending on how we look at it. Furthermore the assumptions to describe language are typically couched in conceptual metaphors. Hence if we are to avoid being held captive by 'our own semiotics' and categories (Halliday and Brumfit, personal communication) an analysis of these metaphors is necessary.

Language in Applied Linguistics and the Lay Public in Africa

In applied linguistics 'language' raises different expectations for linguists, who construct language in terms of rule-governed generative systems, as against psychologists, preoccupied with the use symbols for the realisation of meaning, or sociologists, concerned with the ideological implications of structures of shared meanings (Brumfit 2001). In applied linguistics we must not only take into account the assumptions about 'language' made by different sub-disciplines, but we must also understand how the discourses about language are understood by language users, reflecting the complications that arise as applied linguists serve the 'lay' public. Lay people do not necessarily have categories corresponding to those of applied linguists, and even if they did the meanings for the same categories would be different. For example, Bamanankan, a language in the Republic of Mali, has no lexical distinction between 'language' and 'dialect'. The Shona in Zimbabwe do not define themselves in terms of the language they speak but in terms of the geographical space which they occupy (*vana vevhu*)—children of the soil. For the Shona, the notion of language— if it exists at all—is subordinate to geography (Dwyer 2002). 'The vocabulary of the dictionary in Africa is synonymous with the vocabulary of the language—a vocabulary which no speaker can actually "know" independently of the printed record' (Liddicoat 2000: 425). It becomes an objectified and authoritative 'thing' whose supreme authorities are the 'book' and the expert, held in reverence even amongst those who can neither read nor write. Language becomes a text whose meanings cannot be negotiated and adapted to context. Lists of words are far more common than grammars in Africa, reflecting an orientation towards understanding 'language' as the use of words rather than speech.

... And Then There Were Languages: The Emergence of Languages in Africa and Applied Linguistics in Africa

In a review of languages in sub-Saharan Africa, Samarin writes: 'The map of Africa we would start with would be white, or gray, or black—whatever best iconized a "clean slate". A continent without languages. Yes, a continent without languages. Of course, Africans used language in a linguistic sense to communicate with each other ... ' (Samarin 1996: 390). Samarin is suggesting that prior to colonisation and the introduction of Christian evangelism and literacy, the notion of 'language' as a marker of social identity did not exist. Although their speech forms shared common linguistic structures they did not constitute common languages because there was no shared identity. Shared identities based on language only emerged with the introduction of colonisation and Christianity. Is Africa unique in this regard? Heryanto 1995; 2005), with his mind on Indonesia, writes:

> Once the success of the European project of invention was established, other em-
> pires sought to emulate it: The newly acquired meanings of Bahasa were derived
> from one or more modern European languages. At least in the two most widely
> spoken and influential languages in Indonesia (Malay and Javanese) there was no
> word for 'language', and no need for expressing its idea until the latter part of the
> past century.

Indeed, Heryanto argues that Bahasa Indonesia was introduced into 'language-free communities'.

In speaking of 'language-free communities' the point is not that these contexts involved any less language use, but rather that we need to view this through a different lens (Makoni & Pennycook 2005). Prior to nationalism, Germany and Italy could be described as 'language-free-communities'. Even though nationalism played a role in the emergence of 'languages' in Europe, in Africa literacy rather than nationalism played a more crucial role in bringing about the notion of separate languages. Languages (and not language) and the meta-languages emerged literally as part of the Christian colonial project. The project of socially constructing languages is ongoing, continuing under the guise of the Summer Institute of Linguistics. Within a Christian framework language proficiency is understood as the ability to translate from one language to another, rather than as verbal communication (Fabian 1986).

At a philosophical level an analysis of the language categories is germane if applied linguistics is construed as a subject within African studies. African scholarship is thus subjected to a double critique. In the contexts of 'tribalism', African scholarship has been criticised for discarding concepts because they have fallen out of favour in Euro-American centres. On the other hand, it has been criticised for not rejecting inappropriate European models such as nation state in language planning (Fardon and Furniss; Lucko and Wolf 2003).

Although we question the validity of some of the western assumptions about the African language situation which form the basis of some of our thinking, we urge caution in the use of 'local knowledge' as an alternative foundation for African applied linguistics in postcolonial Africa (Geertz 1983). How valid is 'local knowl-edge' as an alternative basis for framing ethno-applied linguistics in postcolonial Africa? There is a tradition of critiquing western theories of colonial and postcolonial Africa best exemplified in philosophy, religion and history texts (Hountondji 1977, 1995; Towa 1979; Mudimbe 1998). The critiques of rationality have succeeded insofar as they have weakened the 'rational' hold which the West exerts epistemologically over postcolonial Africa's knowledge production (Bates, Mudimbe, & O'Barr 1994). At another level, they had limited success because they replicated the mind set which they were challenging.

If we are dealing with the real world issues in which language is implicated, it is necessary to re-examine the descriptions of Africa so as to explore whether it is possible for applied linguistics to formulate conceptualisations about language out-side Eurocentric frameworks. When Mudimbe posed the same question with a fo-cus on history, his answer was a qualified yes. In this paper we raise the same ques-tion for applied linguistics. There are a number of recurring assumptions about Africa's linguistic situation which we now review.

Assumption 1: The Primary Function of Language Is to Convey Factual Information

Imagining language via the 'conduit metaphor' assumes that its primary function is to convey factual information. The conduit metaphor has a strong hold over our thinking about language as is apparent from some language planning discourses in Africa embedded within the nation state paradigm. For example, arguments have been advanced about the validity of using 'indigenous' languages as the medium of instruction (Bamgbose 1976, 1984; Rubagumya 1990; Fafunwa et al. 1989; Webb 1999). The concept of a 'medium' is widely used in academic literature on applied linguistics in Africa as can be seen from recent publications. For example in a book entitled *New Language Bearings in Africa: A Fresh Quest* (2004), Muthwii & Kioko (eds) have a chapter entitled 'Challenges of using English as medium of instruction in the multilingual contexts: a view from Ugandan Classrooms'. This notion of language as a medium is not restricted to Africa. Such widespread use in current writing on Africa shows that contrary to what Brumfit (personal communication) argues, 'the "medium" is not a "dead" metaphor'. In this section we are arguing that the construct of medium of instruction—however misleading it might be—still has currency. The continued use of the metaphor has consequences for our conceptions about language. Rather than debating whether 'indigenous' languages can be a panacea to Africa's complex educational problems, our paper will comment on the metaphors underlying the notion of indigeneity and critically examine the notion of 'medium of instruction'. The focus on the medium metaphor is not to deny the existence of other more humanistic conceptualisations of language, particularly those shaped by the thinking of Paolo Freire. The issue is that the humanistic conceptualisations of language may be widespread in creative literature but are rare in discussions about language planning.

The Relevance of Indigenous Languages as Christian Languages to Applied Linguistics in Africa

It is easy to construe 'indigenous' languages as authentic. Hence unproblematic repositories of African cultures which contribute towards the formation of a nation state—a view influenced by Anderson (1991) *Imagined Communities*—unfortunately regard 'languages as essentially unproblematic' (Joseph 2004). The interest in the 'invention' of national heritages foregrounds the social dimension of custom and ethnicity and leads us to question the naturalness implied in terms such as 'indigenous' languages (Spear 2003:4) There is an increasing number of studies focussing on how 'indigenous' languages such as Tswana, chiShona, and Tsonga were socially and linguistically constructed (MacGonagle 2003; Cook 2002) Our understanding of the social construction of 'indigenous' languages is analogous to Blommaert's (1999: 104) 'discovery attitude' or what Said (1985:156-7) calls 'being there', which arises from the simple fact of having been present in Africa, the Middle East, and South East Asia. Irrespective of length of stay or nature of association, having been there is deemed adequate to claim 'knowledge' of the native languages and cultures.

The fact that 'indigenous' languages were socially constructed is relevant to applied linguistics in Africa. The argument is not that we should dispense with the concept of separate languages but rather that we need to be aware of what lies behind it. Since languages are socially constructed they need to be deconstructed from time to time, with the goal of making the reconstructed languages as comprehensive as possible so that the standard approximates to the student's usage. Like Shirley Brice Heath (1998) in the US, we suggest that the language of schooling should change so that it corresponds with that of upbringing. However, such a correspondence can only be approximate, so some students will still be left out. The alternative would be to build sociolinguistic awareness into the curriculum so as to get across the idea of differential functional appropriateness of various usages. The argument for such a procedure is not entirely unlike one which promotes a standard language for institutional use in general, but gives full recognition to variant forms in other domains. The other alternative is to experiment with using language teaching materials based on authentic texts from different varieties. If such an educational strategy were pursued, African language speakers would be relieved of extreme pressure to make their language approximate a standard (Makoni & Meinhof 2004).

The orthography for such a language can be constructed in a way which allows maximum variation within it. African languages do not necessarily have to be standardised to be teachable.

If the teaching of indigenous languages is to be effective, it will be necessary to minimise the disjuncture not only between the 'medium of instruction' and home language practices but more importantly to reduce the differences between pedagogy as practised in schools and pedagogy as understood in 'traditional' African societies. Traditional African educational thought and practice is characterised not only by its concern with the 'good person', however defined, but by its interweaving of social, economic, political, cultural, and educational threads into a common tapestry. There is extensive literature on African educational practices rarely tapped by those who write on indigenous languages in Africa (Cheikh Anta Diop 1962; Fafunwa et al., 1989; Abdou Moumouni 1968).

This is not to say that there is no research into educational practices in African societies, but rather that such research constitutes research into western education in non-western contexts. Western education research in non-western contexts subjects non-western educational practices to a treatment analogous to 'Orientalism' by framing it as socialisation.

The 'indigenous' languages have changed under the impact of Christianity because old words assumed new meanings, following the tendency within Christianity to use existing words to describe Christian concepts, rather than opt for neologisms. It also influenced the 'indigenous' concepts of time when it introduced 'salvation', which was future-oriented. Prior to the onset of Christianity, indigenous conceptions of time referred to the past and present and not the future. Christianity, by using old words to convey new meanings, pre-empted its own message in the African context.

But how 'authentic' are these indigenous languages? (Fardon & Furniss 1992: 26) suggests that intellectuals' and politicians' accounts of authenticity are unconvincing to rural people since they feel that proponents of such a view are living in a comparatively splendid, but inauthentic, style, appropriating the signs of authenticity from the villages they have left . Furthermore what elite African intellectuals define as authentic is inauthentic to the rural poor. It is thus important to situate authenticity within wider African discourses. Unfortunately, the discourses of authenticity to which those of indigeneity are aligned were appropriated by Mobuto Sese Seko, the ex-Zairean dictator, as *authenticité* in the 1970s, and recently by Robert Mugabe in his historiography of 'Patriotic History' (Crossman 2004: 22; Ranger 2004).

Assumption 2: Languages Exist Ontologically Outside the Communicative Event

The assumption that language/s exist ontologically outside and prior to a communicative event reinforces a structuralist view of language. Harris (1981; 1990) in his critique of modern linguistics refers to this as a segregationalist orientation, as opposed to an 'integrationist' perspective, which examines the complex interdependence between forms of communication and 'the multitude of environmental factors' (Muhlhausler 1996:8) The structuralist tradition in African linguistics reflects strong beliefs about how languages were thought to be spoken and not how they were or are actually spoken. Within this structuralist/segregationalist perspective 'grammar' is a pre-requisite of speech, not as Hopper (1987) might say a by-product of communication. Previous discourses are today's language; today's discourse is tomorrow's language. A perspective of grammar as existing ontologically prior to a communicational event has implications for language use in the real world within postcolonial Africa, since once established the grammatical rules were portrayed as operating autonomously of their creators. Their person-made origins were occluded and they were conceived as givens operating according to the laws of science (Harries 1987: 43). 'Because of pressures for "objectivity" in linguistic science, the personal, or socially situated character of authors and speakers disappeared—or was made to disappear—at both the speaker and the linguist end, in pursuit of a science of a language' (Irvine 2001). Within an African context, the constructed knowledge was to be subsequently presented as natural knowledge, and the natural knowledge transformed into an official description of the language in question. The notion that grammar exists prior to communicative events also has further sociolinguistic implications in an African context in that it encourages a more normative approach to language description. This redefines what constitutes language expertise as the capacity to write grammatical rules of so-called languages. Since most of the linguistic analysts in Africa are either European or American professional linguists who more often than not have learnt African languages as second languages, or western-educated Africans, native speakers are displaced as legitimate experts of their 'own' languages, influenced by a descriptive appropriation: a process which reveals the 'essentially defensive nature of codifications and formulations in the fields of language study and language policy' (Fabian 1986: 136).

Assumption 3: Languages Are Made up of Discrete Units and Dual Linguacism

Another problematic assumption about language reinforced by census ideology is that language is made up of discrete systems (Makoni & Pennycook 2005). Some of the language assumptions in census ideology are problematic. That we cannot say with any confidence how many languages there are in Africa and indeed in the world at large suggests that African languages (indeed language) do not divide neatly into individual entities. Yet this is precisely how they are represented in censuses when used by governments to articulate categories, gather data and to put them to work. We are also focusing on censuses because in addition to the language provisions in constitutions they are amongst the most powerful ways in which 'official' views about the construction of 'language' in Africa and other categories such as ethnicity and race can be gleaned.

There is also no clear answer to the question to which language the utterances belong. For example, it's not clear whether the following utterances are in Shona or English or both. The examples are taken from the section on obituaries and memorials in the *Herald* and *Sunday Mail*, national newspapers in Zimbabwe.

1   Baba *(Father)* it's been 6 long years. *Tave nherera* (we are now orphans). Rest in peace. *Vana venyu* (your children).

2   I long for the time we spent together. The lord gives, the Lord will take away, *Rudo rwangu haruperi rwakakura samakomo* (My love is endless it's a as big as a

mountain), *rwadzama samadziva* (as deep as a river),*rugosimba kunge rufu* (is as strong as death). Till we meet again. (October 1999)

The problem of determining which language the writing is in extends into the area of fiction as well. Some African novelists provide an excellent example of the problem of determining the language from a fictional writing perspective. Determining to which language an utterance belongs to is not a problem peculiar to less well-known languages but is also experienced with 'major' languages such as English. For example, when the 15-part series of the Story of English was televised, many of the dialects were subtitled, because they were not mutually intelligible. Nearer home, speakers of what linguists call pidgins insist that what they are speaking is English. So are their utterances in English or Pidgin? Perhaps the problem is the assumption that all utterances are necessarily in a 'language'.

Our critique of languages as discrete entities should not be construed to mean that we are simple repeating the familiar observation about the existence of geographical continua between German and Dutch on the border between the Netherlands and Germany, or are arguing for a simple chain model in which each individual is located with a particular social and geographical location. We are making a different argument.

African languages, like European languages, represented varieties which are not spoken by anybody, but for different reasons. In the standardisation of European languages the representation was based on the continuum, while in Africa they were combinations of speech forms aggregated by the missionaries and linguists. In some cases this entailed combining the speech forms of different 'ethnic' groups (Harries 1992)—that is to say compiling an 'inventory' of speech forms as Harries describes it. The language now called 'Tsonga'—which means in Zulu 'the language of the conquered'—is an example of such a compilation.

Census ideology forms the basis of one of the enumerative modalities which arose in the colonial period, and has continued in postcolonial Africa. The unitary language is 'not something given (dan) but is always in essence posited (zadan)—and at every moment of its life it is opposed to the realities of heteroglossia' (Bakhtin 1934 [1981]: 270. The enumerative modality is based on the assumption that the languages could be separated from other forms of behaviour and enumerated in terms of the number of speakers for each language. The problematic nature of censuses in dealing with real world issues can be illustrated using South Africa as a case study.

In nineteenth and twentieth century South Africa censuses were held at ten year intervals and at five year intervals since 1991. Both the 1980 and 1991 censuses were based on questionnaires in English and Afrikaans only and included ethnic/ race and language questions. For selecting race (or population group as it was referred to) the respondent had four options: 'White/Coloured/Asian/Black'. The 'language' question asked the respondent to indicate whether they could communicate, read, and/or write any of the following languages: 'English/Black Language/Other'.

Two additional questions were posed:

> 'State which language each person most often speaks at home and if more than one language is usually spoken at home, state the other language which is spoken.' The 1996 census, unlike earlier censuses, was available in eleven languages and also added more ethnicity options: African/Black, Coloured, Indian/Asian, and White.

The censuses had some flaws because only the first home language was included, so no data were available for languages other than the first home language spoken at home. Dialects such as Pretoria Sotho, and languages of recent African immigrants Yoruba and Swahili were excluded. We adopt a different perspective from that of Broeder et al. We analyse how censuses shed light on government views of language, race, and ethnicity. Censuses thus offer 'categories that have the effect of making up people, or engendering the existence of groups of people and languages.

If censuses nominated people and languages into existence it means censuses do not only describe prevailing realities but create realities useable for 'governmentality', 'erasing' other competing realities. For example, it is difficult to infer from the censuses the extent to which people may communicate by using different languages, i.e. a Zulu speaker interacting in Zulu with a Tswana speaker responding in Tswana. Dual linguacism is thus elided by a government view of sociolinguistics.

Jeater and Hove (undated) describes how evangelists in contemporary Zimbabwe use isiZulu when speaking to Ndau speakers, and indeed described isiZulu as the 'own tongue' of the Ndau speakers. The definition of isiZulu as the own tongue of Ndau speakers is important in so far as it marks a radical departure of what constitutes a mother tongue, namely to include the language which one 'hears' and not necessarily what one is able to speak. Dual linguacism is not restricted either to historical or contemporary Africa (see Dwyer 2002 for examples of dual linguacism in Europe).

It is possible that the categories used by ordinary speakers do not correspond to official ones. For example, in the 1981 South African census African languages nominated into existence were simply referred to as 'Black' Languages. In the 1996 census the racial categorisation had been dropped and replaced with 'first mother tongue' moving away from an overtly race-based category towards a more linguistic one. The 'official' accounts of language which can be gleaned from censuses are different from those used by other public bodies, such as the media. For example, the most popular radio channel in South Africa was the one which produced English programmes, followed by a channel simply called 'multilingual'.

The multilingual channel contrasted with other channels which broadcast in Setswana, Sepedi, Sesotho, and Xitsonga. Multilingualism is construed within the South African Broadcasting Corporation (SABC) as a language, a 'lingua franca' (Fardon and Furniss 1994:4). To us the official categories are interesting because of what they tell us about the government beliefs about language.

The general tendency in both the SABC and the official censuses is to treat 'languages' as if they were discrete entities, and independent social actors. This may produce unintended effects in which rights are attached to languages, and not people, and where languages are treated as 'killer' languages (Mufwene 2004). The census ideology, with its emphasis on languages as discrete units, exaggerates the linguistic heterogeneity of the African sociolinguistic situation because 'varieties of the same language(s) are given different labels and described as full blown languages in their own right' (Djite 1988:1).

The exaggerated complexity makes language planning more difficult than it should be. It creates an image of an African sociolinguistic situation made up of numerous discrete units and artificial boundaries which do not correspond to social and functional realities, particularly of speakers who have verbal repertoires made up of fragments from many 'languages' and do not focus exclusively on genetic classifications.

What we need to do is to move beyond a perception of Africa as made up of linguistic 'things' to a description of the social and linguistic experiences of the language users. Such a view of language is possible if our thinking about language and African languages is predicated upon the whole language experience of the person, including the ability to translate from one language to another.

The metaphor which aptly describes what we have in mind here is that of 'language' as a multilayered chain which offers an individual a set of options to be used in the immediate environment and a 'steadily diminishing set of options to be employed in more distant interactions, albeit a set that is always liable to be reconnected more densely to a new environment by rapid learning, or the development of new languages' (Fardon & Furniss 1994: 4). The use of highly symbolic speech in the poor housing estates in France are an excellent example of fine layering in 'language' in which the focus is not on language per se but on communicational activities

Assumption Four: Languages Have Names

Literacy and politics played a key role in the naming of African languages. Naming was initiated by non-Africans literate in European languages and Arabic when they wanted to know to whom they were talking. This resulted in some cases in over-differentiation: for example Kanre (or Pana or Tali) in the Central African Republic were named as separate languages. The converse also occurred when speech forms were compiled and fused into the same language. The emergence of Tsonga is an excellent example (Harries 1987). The names given to African languages were not new, but had completely different meanings. For example, the terms KoreKore and Zezuru were nicknames for highlanders and northerners which were subsequently used as linguistic and ethnic labels (Chimhundu 1992).

The naming contributed to a conflation of ethnicity and language proficiency: a Zulu speaker spoke Zulu, a Yoruba spoke Yoruba (Rampton 1995; Blommaert 1992). To us what is even more important than the political nature of the naming is that it was founded on a categorisation of 'language' predicated upon a botanical or animal world perception about language (Blommaert 1999:176).

Naming was also relevant to applied linguistics since research into language attitudes was predicated on naming practices. Prior to the naming of the speech forms as languages it was not feasible to have language attitudes, hence the argument that language 'attitudes were brought to Africa' (Samarin 1992:390). The study of language attitudes in Africa began with the emergence of 'languages' as a phenomenon that could be identified with certain groups (Samarin 1992: 390).

If western representations of African realities are open to question, the fundamental question then becomes about using 'local' knowledge as a foundational discipline. Is it possible to conceptualise African applied linguistics outside Anglo-American frameworks? It is to this question that we now turn.

From Local Knowledge to Ethno-Applied Linguistics

'Local knowledge' is made up of beliefs and 'vernacular' discourses not legitimated by any institution (Geertz 1983; Canagarajah 2002:243). Because 'local' is endogenous practice and not a body of knowledge, we avoid developing essentialised, romantic, and gendered views of knowledge (Makoni & Meinhof 2004). It is site specific, and pluralistic. Such an orientation to knowledge enables us to understand some of the problems with which linguists are confronted in Africa and indeed in other parts of the world such as Papua New Guinea, namely, how to come to terms with the problem arising when linguists are claiming that the speech forms constitute different languages, while the speakers suggests that they belong to the 'same' language (Romaine 1992). For example, in Côte d'Ivoire Djite (1988) suggests that speakers of Guere and Wobe regard the two languages as the same language while linguists define them as different languages. The Guere/Wobe issue demonstrates that the external perspective of the linguists may not necessarily coincide with the inside perspective of the speakers. Resolving the problem is complicated because 'language' on the one hand differs from the quests for knowledge in other areas in that the object of study 'language' is not given in advance. On the other hand 'linguists risk only developing a partial understanding of a linguistic situation if we dismiss popular perceptions outright because they contradict scientific data or we cannot easily access them' (Joseph 2004:160).

We therefore need to take into account the 'lay' person's 'stories' about what they speak, their beliefs about what they think they speak, how they think they should talk, and not necessarily restrict ourselves to how they speak (Cook 2002). Ignoring the perceptions of the users may produce negative results when applied linguists intervene, a problem which is however not unique to postcolonial Africa.

Historically, there has always been a 'struggle' to determine which type of knowledge about African languages should be accepted. The trend to discount certain types of knowledge arose from sustained contact with speakers of African languages in the nineteenth century and developed when African linguistics as practiced in the metropolitan centres sought to become 'objective'. In its quest for objectivity the 'language accounts of missionaries who were now participating in the academy in the metropole were discarded as unsystematic and "biased"—the metropole was not to be ruled from the periphery' (Irvine 2001: 87).

If in the metropole the debate was between missionaries and European linguists, in contemporary Africa the debate revolves around the role and status of what has unfortunately been disparagingly called 'folk' linguistics. The notion of 'local' applied linguistics situates 'folk' linguistics within an anthropological approach to language. Incorporating a lay person's views is problematic because the views have to be ferreted out, and even when that is done it will still be necessary to demonstrate that an applied linguistics programme can be based on the local ideas.

Conclusion

In this article we have focused on 'language'. Our main interest has been to deconstruct the assumptions held about language with a special focus on Africa. Our argument is that those who view language from the perspective of governments and nation-state understand language differently from those who by adopting local level perspectives try and capture the user's experiences of those languages. Descriptions of language useable by governments may seem insensitive, if not coercive to local level language practices, while detailed local level descriptions of language practises may seem impractical from a nation state-government perspective. The interest in 'language' is important in an ethno-applied linguistics which analyses the ways in which language is understood. An analysis of these ways is necessary because the descriptions have an impact on language users.

An examination of perceptions about language is also necessary if any social intervention is to achieve desired results. Because there are multiple and at times conflicting ways in which language is constructed, any intervention has to take into account the multiple ways in which these communities comprehend 'language'. Such an approach requires more rather than less 'mediation' from applied linguistics. Therefore in a sense although the construct of ethno-applied linguistics is new, the notion of applied linguistics which underpins—'mediation'—is not. It is a return to an earlier and more conventional view of applied linguistics as 'mediation'. There is however one major distinction between the mediation of applied linguistics in earlier eras (Corder 1973; Brumfit 2001, 2004) and 'mediation' as understood in ethno-applied linguistics. Mediation entails much more than interfacing between different disciplines. Applied linguists can only mediate when it interprets the different constructs of 'language', for which the applied linguist has to use her own taxonomy. That taxonomy subsequently shapes other points of view, introducing 'other values' and other ways of understanding 'language'. Mediation therefore also brings to the discussion perspectives of language other than those of applied linguists. The first obstacles to 'mediation' are applied linguists themselves. This is inevitable, since as Nagel (1986: 6) argues, 'But since we are who we are, we can't get outside of ourselves completely. Whatever we do, we remain subparts of the world with limited access to the real nature of the rest of it and of ourselves. There is no way of telling how much of reality lies beyond the reach of present or future objectivity or any other conceivable form of human understanding'.

References

Adegbija, E., 1994, *Language Attitudes in Sub-Saharan Africa*, Clevedon: Multilingual Matters.

Anderson, B., 1991, *Imagined Communities: Reflections on the Origin and Spread of Nationalism*, London: Verso.

Bernstein, B., 1971, *Class, Codes and Control, Vol. 1. Theoretical Studies Toward a Sociology of Education*, London: Routledge.

Anderson, B., 1991, *Imagined Communities: Reflections on the Origin and Spread of Nationalism*, London: Verso.

Bakhtin, M., 1934 [1981], *Dialogic Imagination*, ed., M. Hoilquist, Austin TX: University of Texas Press.

Bamgbose, A., 2000, 'Language Planning in West Africa', *International Journal of the Sociology of Language* 14, 1, 101-17.

Bates, R., Mudimbe, V.Y, O'Barr, J., eds., *Africa and the Disciplines: The Contributions of Africa to the Social Sciences and Humanities*, Chicago: University of Chicago Press.

Bloch, C., 2002, 'Nurturing Biliteracy through Interactive Writing', Reports on Mother-tongue Education', Project for the Study of Alternative Education in South Africa, Occasional Paper No. 8: 23-31.

Blommaert, J., 1999, 'Reconstructing the Sociolinguistic Image of Africa: Grassroots Writing in Shaba (Congo)', *TEXT* 19 (2): 175-200.

Bokamba, E., 2002, *African Language Program Development and Administration*, Madison, Wisconsin: NARLC Press.

Breckenbridge C. and P. van der Veer, eds., 1993, *Orientalism and the Postcolonial Predicament: Perspectives from South Asia*, Philadelphia: University of Pennyslvania Press.

Broeder, P. et.al., 'Multilingualism in South Africa with a focus on KwaZulu-Natal and Metropolitan Durban'. In http://www.uct.ac.za/depts./praesa/occPapers7pdf.

Brokensha, D., D. Warren and O. Werner, 1980, *Indigenous Knowledge Systems and Development*, Lanham, Maryland: University Press of America.

Brumfit, C., 2001, *Individual Freedom in Language Teaching*, Oxford: Oxford University Press.

Brumfit, C., 2004a, 'Applied Linguistics in 2004: Unity in Diversity', *AILA Review* 17 (1): 133-6.

Brumfit, C., 2004b, 'Colloquium: Applied Linguistics and Real World Problems', American Association of Applied Linguistics, Portland, Oregon.

Canagarajah, A. S., 2002, 'Celebrating Local Knowledge on Language and Education', *Journal of Language, Identity, and Education* 1 (4): 243-261.

Chimhundu, H., 1992, 'Early Missionaries and the Ethnolinguistic Factor During the Invention of Tribalism in Zimbabwe', *Journal of African History* 33, 87-109.

Chiwome, E. and J. Thondhlana, 1992, 'Sociolinguistics and Education: A Survey Concerning Attitudes on the Teaching of Shona through the Media of Shona', in R. Herbert. ed., *Language and Society in Africa: The Theory and Practice of Sociolinguistics*, Johannesburg: Witwatersrand University Press, 247-63.

Cook, S., 2002, 'Urban Language in Rural Setting, the Case of Phokeng in South Africa', in G. Gmlech and W. Zenner, eds., *Urban Life Readings in the Anthropology of the City*, Prospect Heights: Il: Waveland Press, 106-13.

Corder, S. P., 1973, *Introducing Applied Linguistics*, Harmondsworth: Penguin.

Crossman, P., 1999, *Endogenisation and African Universities. Initiatives and Issues in the Quest for Plurality in the Human Sciences*, Belgian Administration for Development Corporation.

Crossman, P. and R. Devisch, 2001, 'Endogenous Knowledge: An Anthropological Perspective', in C. Odora-Hoppers, ed., *Towards a Philosophy of Articulation: IKS and its Integration of Knowledge Systems*, Cape Town: New Africa Education Publisher, 96-125.

Diop, C. A., 1962, *The Cultural Unity of Negro Africa*, Paris: Presence Africaine.

Djite, P., 1988, 'Correcting Errors in Language Classification: Monolingual Nuclei and Multilingual Satellites', *Language Problems and Language Planning* 12 (1):1-11.

Dwyer, D., 2002, *The Language Dialect Problem*, http//www.msu.edu/:course/426.

Ela, J-M., 1998, *Innovations Sociales et Renaissance de l' Afrique noire*, Paris: Harmattan.

Fabian, J., 1986, *Language and Colonial Power: The appropriation of Swahili in the Former Belgian Congo, 1880-1938*, Berkeley and Los Angeles: University of California Press.

Fafunwa, B. A., I. McValualey, J. and J. A Sokoya, 1989, *Education in the Mother Tongue the Primary Education Research Project (1970-1978)*, Ibadan: University Press, Ltd.

Fardon, R and G. Furniss, 1994, 'Introduction: Frontiers and Boundaries: African Languages as Political Environments', in Fardon, R. and G. Furniss, eds., *African Languages, Development and the State*, London: Routledge, 1-29.

Geertz, C., 1983, *Local Knowledge: Further Essays in Interpretive Anthropology*, New York: Basic Books.

Grace, G.W (1981) *An Essay on Language*, Columbia SC: Hornbeam Press

Hall, S., 1997, 'The Local and the Global: Globalization and Ethnicity', in A. D. King, ed., *Culture, Globalization and the World System*, Minneapolis: University of Minneapolis Press, 19-40.

Harris, R., 1981, *The Language Myth*, London: Duckworth.

Harris, R., 1990, 'On Redefining Linguistics', in H. Davis and T. Taylor, eds., *Redefining Linguistics*, London: Routledge, 18-52.

Harries, R., 1987, 'The Roots of Ethnicity: Discourse and the Politics of Language Construction in South Africa', *African Affairs*, 87 (346) 125-52.

Heath, S. B., 1998, 'Working through Language', in S. Hoyles and C. T. Adger, eds., *KidsTalk Strategic Language in Later Childhood Years*, New York: Oxford University Press, 217-240.

Heryanto, A., 1995, *Language of Development and the Development of Language: the case of Indonesia*, Pacific Linguistic Series, D-86, Canberra: Department of Linguistics, Australian National University.

Hopper, P., 1998, 'Emergent Grammar', in M. Tomasello, ed., *The New psychology of Language: Cognitive and Functional Approaches to Language Study*, London: Lawrence Erlbaum Associates.

Hountondji, P., 1995, 'Producing Knowledge in Africa Today', *African Studies Review* 38 (3): 1-10.

Hountondji, P., 1977, *Sur la 'philosophie africaine': critique de l'ethnophilosophie*. Paris: Maspero

Irvine, J. and S. Gal, 2000, 'Language Ideology and Linguistic Differentiation', in Kroskrity, P.V. (org.) *Regimes of Language: Ideologies, Politics and Identities*. Santa Fe: New Mexico: School of American Research Press, 33, 27-44

Irvine, J., 1993, 'Mastering African Languages: The Politics of Linguistics in 19th Century Senegal', *Social Analysis*, 33, 27-44.

Irvine, J., 2001, 'Genres of Conquest: From Literature to Science in Colonial African Linguistics', in K. Knoblauch and H. Kotholf, eds., *Verbal Arts Across Cultures: the Aesthetics and Proto-aesthetics of Communication*, Tubingen Gunter Verlag, 63-89.

Jeater, D and C.Hove (in press) 'And the God was Made Word: Exploring the Limitations of Translation and Power' (manuscript undated).

Joseph, J., 2004, *Language and Identity: National, Ethnic, and Religious*, Palgrave: Macmillan.

Kashoki, M., 2003, 'Language Policy Formulation in Multilingual Southern Africa', *Journal of Multilingual and Multicultural Development*, 24 (3): 184-194.

Kroskrity, V. Paul, ed., *Regimes of Language: Ideologies, Politics and Identities*, Santa Fe, New Mexico: School of American Research Press, 35-85.

Liddicoat, A.J., 2000, 'The Ecological Impact of a Dictionary', *Current Issues in Language Planning* 1,3:424-430.

Lucko, P., L. Peter and Hans-Gerg Wolf, eds., 2003, *Studies in African Varieties of English*, Frankfurt: Peter Lang.

Makoni, S. and U. Meinhof, 2004, 'Western Perspectives in Applied Linguistics in Africa', *AILA Review* 17: 77-104.

Makoni, S. and A. Pennycook, 2005, 'Disinventing and Reconstituting Languages', *Critical Inquiry in Language Studies, an International Journal*, 2 (3):137-156.

Masolo D., 1994, *African Philosophy in Search of Identity*, Bloomington, Indiana: Indiana University Press.

McWhorter, J., 1998, *The Word on the Street: Fact and Fable about American English*, New York: Plenum Press.

MacGonagle, E., 2002, *A Mixed Pot: History and Identity in the Ndau Region of Mozambique*, PhD Thesis, Michigan State University.

Moumouni, A., 1968, *Education in Africa*, New York: Praeger.

Mufwene, S., 2004, 'Multilingualism in Linguistic History: Creolization and Indigenization', in T. Bhatia and W. Ritchie, eds., *The Handbook of Bilingualism*, Malden: Blackwell.

Mudimbe, V.Y., 1988, *The Invention of Africa: Gnosis, Philosophy and the Order of Knowledge*, London: James Currey.

Muhlhausler, P., 1996, *Linguistic Ecology: Language change and linguistic Imperialism in the Pacific Region*, London: Routledge.

Muthwii, Margaret Jepkirui and Angelina Nduku Kioko (eds) *New Language Bearings in Africa: A Fresh Quest.*Clevedon: Multilingual Matters.

Nagel, T., 1986, *The View from Nowhere*, New York: Oxford University Press.

Pennycook, A., 2004, 'Language Policy and the Ecological Turn', *Language Policy*, 3:213-239.

Rampton, B., 1995, *Crossing: Language and Ethnicity Among Adolescents*, London: Longman.

Romaine, S., 1992, *Language, Education and Development*, Oxford: Oxford University Press.

Ranger, T., 2004, 'Nationalistic Historiography, Patriotic History and the History of the Nation: The Struggle Over the Past in Zimbabwe', *Journal of Southern African Studies* 30 (2):15-24.

Samarin, W., 1996, 'Review of Adebija Efuroshina, Language Attitudes in Sub-Saharan Africa: A Sociolinguistic Overview', *Anthropological Linguistics* 38 (2):389-395.

Rubagumya, C., ed., 1990, *Language in Education in Africa: a Tanzanian perspective*, Clevedon: Multilingual Matters.

Said, E., 1985, 'An Ideology of Difference', *Critical Enquiry* 12 (1):38-58.

Scollon, S., 1977, 'Language, Idiolect and Speech Community: Three Views of the Language at Fort Chipewyan, Alberta', *Department of Linguistics, University of Hawaii: Working Papers in Linguistics* 9 (3): 65-76.

Spear, T., 2003, Neo-traditionalism and the Limits of Invention in British Colonial Africa. *Journal of African History*, 44:3-27

Spivak G., 1987, *In other Worlds: Essays in Cultural Politics*, London. Routledge.

Wallerstein, I., 1999, 'The Social Sciences in the Twenty-first Century', in UNESCO, *World Social Science Report*, Paris: UNESCO.

Summers, C., 2002, *Colonial Lessons: Africans' Education in Southern Rhodesia, 1918-1940*, Portsmouth: James Currey.

Towa, M., 1979, *L'idée d'une Philosophe africaine*, Yaoundé: CLE.

Webb, V. and Kemobo-Sure, eds., 1999, *African Voices: An Introduction to the Languages and Linguistics of Africa*, Cape Town: Oxford University Press.

Chapter 6

African Historiography and the Crisis of Institutions

Esperanza Brizuela-Garcia

During the 1950s and 1960s an important tradition of historical writing about Africa emerged in the Anglophone world.[1] Africanist historiography, as it is often referred to, asserted the viability and significance of African history, arguing that the past of African peoples could be studied by using methods different to those traditionally used by historians. It also emphasised the value of African history for the social and political development of African communities that were going through the process of decolonisation. By the end of the 1960s Africanist historiography had been successfully introduced in numerous academic institutions in Africa, Great Britain and the United States where, in less than twenty years, African history became a recognised area of historical research.

This paper will examine the experiences of six universities during the 1950s and 1960s, the golden years of African historiography. It will also present a brief overview of the trends that have signalled a decline in the importance of African history in these institutional settings during the 1970s, 1980s and 1990s. The institutions that will be studied are the University of Ghana, the University of Dar es Salaam, the University of Cape Town, the School of Oriental and African Studies, Northwestern University and the University of Wisconsin-Madison. The story of these institutions highlights the role of academic centres in the development of Africanist historiography. Most importantly, it underscores the importance of African universities in the relatively rapid and successful development of the field during the 1950s and 1960s, and raises the question of whether the often called crisis in African history is not, to a large extent, a function of the gradual decline of African institutions and their inability to participate more actively in the production of African history.

Formative Years

The University College of the Gold Coast was inaugurated in 1948. It was one of several institutions created by the British government in their attempt to increase and improve the provision of higher education in the colonies (Nwauwa 1997). During the 1940s the British colonial administration took important steps to introduce higher education in its dependencies. In 1943 it appointed the Asquith and Elliot Commissions that were charged with investigating the conditions of higher education in Africa. Two years later the commissions recommended that three institutions already established in Tropical Africa should become university colleges. These were Khartoum in the Sudan, Makerere in Uganda, and Achimota in the Gold Coast. In addition to these a new institution was to be created in Ibadan, Nigeria.

The University College of the Gold Coast (also referred as Legon) started its life as a college of the University of London following a scheme of special relationships created to insure the quality of education and a successful transition to full university status (Maxwell 1980). This meant that most of the decisions related to staffing and curricula had to be approved by the University of London. However, there was a strong emphasis on the importance of adapting the degrees offered by the University of London to the needs and circumstances of the local population (Colonial Office 1945). Thus, the main goal of the new institutions was to preserve the standards required by the University of London while creating a university adequately connected to the communities it was meant to serve.

Under these circumstances, the main challenge of the history department was to build up an intellectual and educational infrastructure that could support the development of African historiography and the teaching of African history. The first issue that had to be addressed was staffing; recruitment for historians willing to develop the new field began almost immediately and it progressed relatively smoothly thanks to the terms and conditions that were offered to new hires. These were appealing to young scholars that were facing a shortage of jobs in Great Britain.[2] Such was the case of John Fage who joined the History Department in 1949 (Fage 1995, 2002). Neither Fage nor his colleagues at Legon had received training in African history since the field did not exist at the time. It was their job to define what was to be taught to young undergraduate students reading for history at the new university college.

The revision of the curriculum was the most significant challenge for historians at Legon. In 1949, the College was getting ready to introduce the London History Honours degree. This, however, had to be modified to adapt to the needs of students in the Gold Coast. As it stood, the syllabus was aimed at giving students a good grounding in English and European history. Members of the London History Board (which was in charge of determining what was taught as part of History degrees at the University of London) argued that the study of European history provided students with a good model for the study of History in general and would, in the long run, enhance their ability to develop a critical understanding of Africa's past. At this point in time, they added, the field of African history was not mature enough to offer solid teaching materials to undergraduate students.[3] Thus, the revision of the curriculum required constant and careful negotiations with the London History Board that was keen to insure that the quality of education was not being compromised in the process of introducing a new syllabus.

This meant that during the early years, the History Honours programme was focused on European and English history. In 1955 students were, for the first time, allowed to take two courses in African history (instead of one course in European history and one on the European Penetration of Africa). However, only half of the candidates were able to do so because students were required to know French as their second language, at a time when it is likely that English was already a second, if not a third, language for a good number of them.[4] As the decade progressed more courses with African content were gradually introduced culminating in 1959 with the opening of a course on Ancient Ghana. It was also in this year that candidates of the honours programme were able to use African languages as their required second language.[5]

The need to revise the curriculum encouraged faculty to become involved in research projects focused on the history of the Gold Coast and West Africa in general. J.R. Lander, started a project recording the state histories in Ashanti; and D.S. Coombs became interested in Dutch West Africa.[6] Fage embarked in the recording of Mamprussi and Dagomba drum histories and other projects on the early history of West Africa. These efforts allowed him to publish two textbooks: *An Introduction to the History of West Africa* (1955) and *An Atlas of African History* (1958).

Despite the intense work done in the department, the tight grip of the History Board would continue to carefully regulate the introduction of African history in the college. For example, in 1953 the department proposed the creation of the Gold Coast History Series. The purpose of this venture was to publish collections of documents that could be used by students as well as other unpublished materials. It would also allow for the reprinting of classic works that had become rare and difficult to get. Unfortunately, the Academic Board rejected the proposal arguing that it was too early to embark on an editorial project.[7]

In South Africa, the University of Cape Town (UCT), one of a handful of institutions of higher education that already existed in this country, showed little interest in the teaching of African history. Their focus was on the history of South Africa, mostly on the history of Europeans in South Africa, and European history. The creation of The School of African Life and Languages in 1921(Levy 1971) had virtually no impact on the introduction of African history at UCT. In many ways the School exemplified the state of African studies in South Africa; it had little support from the government, its work was marginal to the educational activities of the University and, moreover, it understood African studies as 'Bantu' studies, focussing mainly on the study of colonial administration, linguistics and anthropology (Mamdani 1996).

The History department did not show great interest in the teaching and study of African history as it was being developed in other African institutions. There were both structural and political reasons for this. In 1951, the department was very small, with only four full-time members and it was facing a serious shortage of staff. Between 1930 and 1950 the number of students had gone from 140 to 288 while the number of teachers had remained the same.[8] On the political front the Nationalist Party rose to power in 1948, officially starting the era of apartheid. These circumstances made it very difficult for members of the department to introduce a new area of study, particularly one such as African history.

The work being done at the new university colleges, however, did not go unnoticed at UCT. Leonard Thompson, a young lecturer in the History department, was positively impressed by it. In 1953 he had spent time doing research in the Institute of Commonwealth Studies and, in 1960, he attended the Leverhulme History Conference at the University College of Rhodesia and Nyasaland. In these trips he had come to appreciate the intellectual energy of the new field and the importance of introducing it in UCT.[9] Following these ideas, Thompson tried to argue for changes in the study of Africa at UCT. Together with Monica Wilson and H.M. Robertson he prepared a memorandum entitled 'Expansion in the Study of Africa' that was presented to the University Council in April 1960.[10] The memorandum set down a number of proposals to expand the range of African Studies offered at UCT. African History was among the new areas that were to be offered. The document suggested that funds might be obtained from an application to the Ford Foundation, and indicated the desire for the University to adopt a long time commitment to the expansion of African Studies. Finally, the memorandum requested that students accepted into the new courses be selected on the basis of merit and not race.[11] The Senate accepted most of the recommendations set out in this document. In reality, however, little was done to implement them. A year after the memorandum was submitted Thompson resigned from UCT and took a position at the University of California in Los Angeles.

In Great Britain, the School of Oriental and African Studies (SOAS) took the lead in introducing the study of African history. The involvement of SOAS in this process was guided by the need to develop the field in the new African university colleges. As part of the University of London, the School was charged with overseeing and coordinating the teaching of African history at the new colleges. Thus, at SOAS itself, there was no immediate need to introduce a syllabus or an undergraduate teaching programme, but rather to develop research and expertise that could be used to collaborate with the newly created colleges. The fulfilment of this mission was facilitated by an increased interest in the study of non-Western peoples at the end of the Second World War.

SOAS first opened its doors on 1917.[12] Until the 1950s, its function was to train colonial servants and military personnel. However, during the post-war period, it underwent significant changes stimulated by the ongoing policies of decolonisation and the creation of a Commonwealth. In 1946, the Scarborough Report stated the recommendations of a committee that had investigated the state of educational facilities for the study of Oriental, Slavonic, Eastern European and African studies (Foreign Office 1947). The report acknowledged the need to build 'an academic tradition comparable in quality and continuity with those of the major humanities and sciences'. It recommended the creation of new university departments and the strengthening of existing ones. Most importantly, this was to be done even when undergraduate demand would likely be small (Foreign Office 1947). The Scarborough recommendations launched a period of expansion and redefinition of the School's educational role.[13] By 1956 the number of students attending SOAS from the government and the military had decreased, while there was an increase in the amount of students reading for first and higher degrees.[14]

The then Chair of the History department, Cyril Philips, influenced by a recent trip to East Africa, took the initiative to introduce an African field taking advantage of the resources made available by the recommendations of the Scarborough report (Philips 1995). The History Board accepted his proposal and, in the 1947-48 session the department was able to introduce a special subject in the field of Tropical African History (Philips 1995). Philips then needed to fill two positions in African History. The first was taken by John Fage in the History Department at Legon. The second went to a young Cambridge graduate, Roland Oliver.

During his first year at SOAS Oliver's job was greatly helped by the fact that he had no teaching responsibilities, nor the immediate need to develop an African history curriculum. Furthermore, being at SOAS, he had at his disposal valuable human and intellectual resources that were very important in defining the interdisciplinary nature of African history. From his contacts with Lawrence Hollingsworth, Malcolm Guthrie and Diccon Huntingford, Oliver was introduced to current linguistic and ethnographic scholarship on Africa. He was also able to attend a seminar on the history of tropical dependencies chaired by Keith Hancock, from the Institute of Commonwealth Studies, that allowed for constructive discussions with other historians (Oliver 1997). These connections and the gradual growth of the Africa section in the department, allowed Oliver to institute the African history seminar, which became a major forum of discussion for historians and other scholars interested in the African past. This was arguably the first step in defining one of the main roles of SOAS at this time as a place of debate and articulation of new ideas about African history.

This role was confirmed years later when Oliver and his colleagues embarked on the organisation of two international conferences on African History and Archaeology that took place at SOAS in 1953 and 1957. These conferences allowed for scholars of diverse backgrounds and nationalities to discuss the notion of African history. The agreements reached regarding the centrality of African agency, the role of interdisciplinary practice, the value of oral traditions and the importance of supporting teaching and research in African colleges have remained central to the project of African history up to the present (Hamilton 1955).

In contrast with the progress made in organising and supporting the efforts of scholars interested in Africa, the training of new graduates at SOAS was limited by ideological and financial constraints. Even though historians at SOAS were convinced of the importance of African oral sources for the writing of a new African history, the immaturity of the field and the lack of financial resources forced students to focus on research topics that could be studied from European documentary sources. Nevertheless, graduate students did benefit from the debates that were taking place around them, the impressive SOAS library, and the rich archival holdings available in London. Attitudes towards more innovative research gradually changed to the point that, at the end of the decade, SOAS welcomed Allan Ogot, its first East African student and the first one to work primarily on oral sources (Oliver 1997).

It is important to emphasise that the significant role of SOAS in the development of African history during this period was closely connected to the development of African colleges. Many of the historians of Africa that SOAS employed during the 1950s and 1960s had previously worked at African colleges, and many of the students that went to SOAS for graduate training in African history were also graduates of African colleges and most of them went back as teachers to those colleges after the completion of their degrees.

The introduction of African history at the North American universities of Northwestern and Wisconsin took place in the context of the expansion of Area Studies in general and African studies in particular. This was possible due to a changing intellectual climate prompted by multiple factors such as the development of the Cold War, the growth of the higher education system and the eruption of the Civil Rights movement. Private foundations were the first to offer financial support for the creation of programmes of African Studies in American universities. In 1952 the Ford Foundation sponsored a conference aimed at exploring 'the conditions existing in Africa, the present and proposed programmes of governmental and non-governmental agencies there, and the needs and opportunities for further activities by private American voluntary agencies'.[15] Later, in 1958 the Foundation commissioned a report to assess the importance of Africanist research in the formulation of foreign policy. In both instances the conclusions stated that the growing importance of African affairs required increased and careful attention from American scholars and, that it was necessary to support the creation and development of programmes that could increase the available expertise on African issues.[16]

The United States government also started to offer financial support through the Title VI of the National Defense Education Act of 1958. During the next ten years this would provide substantial financial backing to American institutions for the development of African studies in general and the study of African languages in particular.[17] The importance of government assistance was highlighted in a 1959 report to the United States Senate aimed at examining American Foreign Policy on Africa. This document stated that private organisations could no longer support the educational and research activities needed to inform foreign policy. The report then continued to recommend the increase of economic support by the government for research and education on African studies (Interdisciplinary Committee on African Studies and Herskovits 1959).

In 1948 Herskovits obtained a grant from the Carnegie Corporation for the creation of a Program of African Studies (PAS). It is important to mention that Herskovits's first application to Carnegie requested support for a programme in African and African American studies. However, the Corporation emphasised that the money granted should be devoted to the study of Africa only (Guyer 1998).[18]

Herskovits considered African history an important component of the programme, but he experienced difficulties introducing the new field.[19] At the time, the History department at Northwestern was rather small and there was little opportunity for expansion.[20] Franklin D. Scott, a historian of Scandinavia, was appointed as the department's representative to the interdepartmental committee of the PAS, and was charged with introducing an African element to his courses on the Expansion of Europe.[21] Furthermore, it was difficult to recruit a specialist on African history at a time when the demand for such individuals was greater than the speed at which they were being trained.[22]

Given these difficulties, Herskovits tried to promote the study of African History through an interdepartmental faculty seminar.[23] Towards the end of the 1950s two courses in African History were introduced: The History of West Africa and Seminar in African History. This provision, however, was not permanent. Kenneth Dike, who was visiting lecturer during the 1957-58 academic year, taught the courses. From this year on, the department relied on visiting lecturers to offer courses on African History.

In Wisconsin, African history was introduced directly in the history department by the initiative of Philip Curtin who was hired in 1956. Curtin was brought to Wisconsin to substitute Professor Knaplund, a specialist on Imperial history. Ironically, the department was not interested in Curtin's expertise on Africa, but in his ability to teach both Latin American and Imperial History.[24] Curtin, however, had been influenced by the efforts to teach and write African history in African colleges and at SOAS and, shortly after his arrival, he proposed a course called 'History of Africa. European Penetration of Africa South of the Sahara and the inter-action of European and African Cultures'.[25] He also suggested that John Fage be invited as Professor of Commonwealth History and took advantage of his visit to offer the first seminar in African History in Wisconsin.[26] Curtin's crowning achievement of this decade was the creation of the Program in Comparative Tropical History (PCTH) in 1959 with the financial support of the Carnegie Foundation.[27] This was an important first step towards the introduction of African History in Wisconsin.

At the time, Curtin faced opposition and criticism from other members of the history department.[28] However, his efforts were aided by the significant increase in the demand for higher education that characterised the 1960s. In 1957 the department had 21 members of staff, and it was planning to add to this number due to a projected growth in the number of students.[29] Curtin also had the support of important members of the administration such as Professor Fred Harrington, a member of the History Department, and also the Vice-President of the University. He backed Curtin's initiatives and encouraged him to contact the Ford and Carnegie Foundations in search of their financial aid.[30]

The Golden Era

The process of institutionalisation of African history during the 1950s was, for the most part, inspired and influenced by the efforts to develop the field of African history in African university colleges. The experiences of institutions like SOAS, Northwestern and Wisconsin, although enabled by local developments, were connected in multiple ways to the work of African institutions. During the 1960s, these connections were reinforced, while British and American institutions continued to search for ways of asserting the role of African history in their academic and educational endeavours.

The success of African nationalism during the 1960s consolidated the place of African history in African institutions and allowed them to adopt an even more important role in the development of African historiography. The aims of nationalist politics came to be shared by many historians of Africa who created a constructive marriage between history and nationalism (Boahen 1975; Denoon and Kuper 1970). This reinforced the position of African history in African universities.

The University College of the Gold Coast became the University of Ghana in 1961 after severing its links to the University of London. Soon after independence the new government heavily criticised the university and called for its reform (Agbodeka 1998). These calls for change accelerated the pace of recruitment and curricular revision. The Africanisation of faculty and staff was an important element of the university reform. Although there were instances of conflict and tensions between expatriates and natives, the environment in the history department remained one of cooperation and constructive debate.[31] By 1960 the history department at Legon had already recruited two Ghanaian lecturers, A.A. Boahen and I. Tufuoh. Both had Honours degrees from Legon and had done postgraduate work at SOAS and Oxford respectively. The arrival of Boahen and Tufuoh signalled the beginning of a period of healthy growth and expansion. During the 1960s the department lost most of its original staff. By 1969 just one of the original members of the faculty remained and the number of lecturers had gone up to twelve from which nine were Africans.[32]

Between 1963 and 1970 the general structure and content of the History Honours syllabus was constantly revised and modified.[33] The increase in staff made it possible to finally shift the general orientation of the syllabus from European to African history.[34] By 1967 the syllabus covered the whole of the African continent. It included a paper in the archaeology of Africa, only two papers in the history of Europe, papers on Modern Russia, Latin America and India and the possibility to follow a two-subject combined course that allowed students to combine history with Economics, Political Science or Sociology.[35] In 1963-64 it became possible for students in the University of Ghana to pursue MA and PhD courses. Particularly important was the MA in African Studies offered in the Institute of African Studies.

The Institute of African Studies (IAS) was an important component in the development of African history during this decade. It was established in 1961 as a centre for research and teaching within the University of Ghana. The first director was Thomas L. Hodgkin and it consisted of four sections: Modern African States, African Music and Related Arts, African Historical Studies, and African Languages. Nkrumah saw the creation of the Institute as a useful political platform. He charged the IAS with the responsibility of promoting Pan-African ideas and the elimination of colonial influences. He also made sure that the IAS received substantial economic support to undertake its projects.[36] This allowed a very healthy growth of the institute. Within three years of its creation almost all its sections were adequately established.

The IAS housed important research projects in African history such as the Arabic Manuscripts Project and the Asante Court Records Project.[37] It also offered an MA in African Studies that included an impressive component in African history. Students could take courses in Eastern Africa, Northern Africa, the Western Sudan, Central and Southern Africa, Historical Geography, West Africa, the Caribbean, and the Americas. In addition to this, students also had the option to take African historical linguistics, from the Linguistics studies offerings, courses on social change, political evolution and economic development. This variety of courses and the quality of teachers and researchers in the IAS made of this MA course one of the most complete in this decade, something that attracted students from beyond Ghana. In 1968-69 UNESCO designated the IAS as a regional centre for research in the forest zone of West Africa.[38]

The visibility and importance of the University of Ghana for the study of African history during the 1960s were only rivalled by the University of Ibadan where an important group of historians, led by Professor Ajayi, were also making enormous progress in the development of African history (Ajayi 1995). Legon and Ibadan were among the leading universities that became well-known academic destinations for students and scholars interested in African history. The success of these institutions is intimately linked to their approach to African history, which was strongly focussed on the collection and interpretation of African sources, either oral or written in Arabic language. There was a strong commitment to documenting and asserting the role of Africans as the primary agents of their own history. This was seen as an important contribution to the process of nation-building and it was often used as a historical justification and explanation of the success and promising future of African nationalism.

Also during the 1960s, the history department at the University of Dar es Salaam became well known for its contributions to the teaching and writing of African history.[39] In 1963 the University of East Africa was inaugurated and the University College of Dar es Salaam became part of it, together with the University College of Makerere in Uganda, and the University College of Nairobi in Kenya. In 1964 the Faculty of Arts and Social Sciences started its activities and within it the new history department.

In a short period of time, the department made significant progress. Between 1964 and 1967 the department was adequately staffed with a group of young historians who had taken the offer to research and teach African history (Ranger 1995). Among them were J. McCracken, J. Iliffe, E. Alpers, J. Lonsdale, W. Rodney, J. Sutton, A.J. Temu, I. Kimambo, A. Roberts, G. Gwassa and T. Ranger. The challenges faced by these men were, in many ways, similar to those faced by Fage ten years before. However, they were able to take advantage of the significant achievements made by their predecessors. This, and the fact that the department was new, with no colonial baggage, and was set in an institution that took pride in its radical intellectual climate, allowed for a high level of innovation and success (Kimambo 1993). After just three years it was able to incorporate three Tanzanian historians, I. Kimambo, A. Temu and G. Gwassa, the three of them specialised in East African history. In 1967 they were also able to introduce a remarkable syllabus with numerous pedagogical innovations, oriented to the study of the African continent and open to the comparative study of world history.[40]

Historians at Dar es Salaam were focussed on investigating what Ranger later called 'African initiative' (Ranger 1969). Their focus was on political histories; they were primarily interested on the activities of Africans in the formation and running of states and in their dealings with the colonial governments. In 1967, after the Arusha Declaration was proclaimed, Tanzania started a new era as a socialist nation. This would effect important changes in the approach of historians at Dar es Salaam and a sharp critique of the nationalist history of the 1960s. Despite this, the impressive achievements of the 1960s are testament to the importance of African nationalism and the favourable intellectual climate that Dar es Salaam offered for the discussion and development of ideas about the study of the African past (Kimambo 1993).

The importance of nationalism in the consolidation of African historiography is underscored by the case of UCT in South Africa. The rise of apartheid inhibited the free discussion of ideas, particularly those that were seen as subversive to the dominant regime. African history, with its strong connections to African nationalism and African liberation, was certainly not welcome at South African institutions. Under these conditions, the introduction and development of the new field of African history were negatively affected (Bozzoli and Delius 1990).

Eric Axelson took over the running of the department during the 1960s. At UCT, Axelson excelled as an administrator and eventually became Dean of the Faculty of Arts. The department continued to be understaffed and the possibilities for expansion under these circumstances were limited. However, Axelson proposed the introduction of a course in African History to replace the teaching of Constitu-tional Law. The proposal was approved in October 1963 and the course was sched-uled to appear in 1964. In 1969 he was making plans to increase the teaching of African history from one to two courses and to provide funds for more doctoral research. A year later the economic history department also presented proposals to introduce a course on African Economic History.[41]

The introduction of these courses, however, did not have an immediate impact on the production of history at UCT. Research in the department continued to be focussed on South African history and mostly fell under what has been called the 'liberal' approach (Saunders 1988). Liberal historians were mainly concerned with political history and paid little attention to the activities of the African population. Axelson's own work was still focussed on the activities of Europeans in Africa. Although he was clearly interested in the new ideas on African history and this led him to propose the production a new survey work to replace the *Cambridge History of South Africa*. In 1962 he contacted J. S. Marais at Wits University and proposed him to act as co-editor. However, later that year Axelson was informed by Oxford University Press and by Marais that Thompson had already secured support from Clarendon Press to publish a two-volume history of South Africa. This cancelled Axelson's project (Saunders 1988).

Axelson's failure to get this project off the ground epitomises the marginal role of South African institutions in the introduction of the new approaches to African history. Despite this, the impact of the new historiography had an important out-come. Young South African historians influenced by the new ideas decided to leave South Africa to pursue new areas of research. Some of these students, such as Shula Marks and Antony Atmore, went to London, to the School of Oriental and African Studies. From there, they embarked on studies of African resistance and colonial rule, and later encouraged the emergence of the new radical school that challenged traditional liberal approaches (Bozzoli and Delius 1990).

After African colleges became independent universities, SOAS was forced to redefine the role of African history in its educational and academic activities. The growth of SOAS during the 1950s had not been accompanied by an increase in undergraduate enrolment. Successfully justifying the teaching of African history to British undergraduates was the final step in the consolidation of African history in the United Kingdom.[42] In the 1960s governmental support for the development and expansion of African and Asian studies remained strong, fuelled by the publication of the Hayter and Robbins Reports.[43] These documents recommended the increase of teaching of African and Asian studies at the undergraduate and MA levels. SOAS had already taken steps to introduce courses at the Masters level and it was time now to move to the undergraduate curriculum (Philips 1967).

Towards the end of the 1950s, Oliver and his colleagues were planning the introduction of a BA honours programme with special reference to the history of Africa. They had to contend with some remaining scepticism about the relevance of

African studies for British students. But in the end, the Board approved the department's proposal. Oliver and his colleagues then got down to the details. At that stage the history department had three specialists on African history: Oliver, Douglas Jones and John Fage. The smooth running of the degree, however, would require at least another two positions. Oliver managed to secure a fourth position for Richard Gray. But by the time Gray joined the department he ended up replacing Fage who moved to chair the recently created Centre of West African Studies at Birmingham. The staffing situation in the department continued to improve with the additions of Shula Marks, Anthony Atmore, Humphrey Fisher, David Birmingham, and Richard Rathbone. By the end of the decade, the department had eight specialists in African history (Oliver 1997).

Postgraduate research continued to flourish at SOAS. Between 1958 and 1968 the history department took eighteen African students, nine Americans, eight British, three Canadians and one Guyanan. From these, all but one of the African students returned to university appointments in their own countries. Twelve of the non-African students also took positions in Africa and eight of the nine Americans students returned to the United States (Oliver 1995). With this output of professional historians, SOAS, by the end of the 1960s, was certainly the main centre of research and training in African history. Researchers at SOAS adopted a similar approach to historians in African institutions in that they focussed on political history and advocated the investigation of African agency. However, their links to African nationalism were not as clearly defined as those of historians based in Africa. Much of the work done at SOAS was also an attempt to re-interpret European sources, such as government and missionary documentation, in the search of African experiences and testimonies.

American universities, as their British counterparts, needed to define the relevance of the study of Africa if they were to ensure the long-term survival of the field. This was successfully achieved during the 1960s due to the success of African nationalism. However, the eruption of the Civil Rights movement and the consolidation of the field of African American studies (Meier and Rudwick 1986) marked the beginning of important trends in the development of African history in the United States. In 1969, during the African Studies Association (ASA) Annual Meeting at Montreal, members of the African Heritage Studies Association (AHSA) confronted the leadership of the ASA for what they called the 'ideological' foundations of the association that, in their view, failed to adopt a pan-African approach to African studies and were tacitly in support of colonialist and neo-colonialist views about Africa. They also argued that African peoples were under-represented in the decision-making bodies of the organisation and that specific measures were to be taken to remedy this lacking. Finally, they advocated that the ASA became more actively involved in cases where the rights of African peoples were being violated (ASA 1969). The confrontation had a history and it sparked heated intellectual and institutional debates. The ASA introduced changes in its organisation and searched for better representation of African and African-American scholars. However, after months of negotiations the AHSA severed its links from the ASA (ASA 1969; Clarke 1976; Cowan 1970; Clarke 1969). What surfaced at Montreal was caused by a fundamental intellectual and institutional split between the fields of African and African-American studies. The development of African studies in the United States would be marked by the tension between the two fields and attempts to find common ground between them. This has affected the institutional role and standing of African history in the American context.

During the 1960s, there were other important trends in the development of African history in American institutions. First, within the general expansion of African studies, the discipline of history registered a significant growth. It went from being 12.7 per cent in 1960 to 19.6 percent in 1970[44] (Curtin 1971). However, the expansion of the 1960s required more than the American system had been able to produce. In this context, there was a need to attract European scholars to fill the positions opened by the large expansion of African studies. This was particularly common in the field of history, where, according to Curtin's estimates, more than 80 percent of the professorships in African history were held by staff recruited overseas (Curtin 1971).

The PAS at Northwestern continued to grow during the 1960s. Support from the Ford Foundation was renewed in 1961 for a ten-year period.[45] This new grant allowed the Program to expand and reinforce its staff and courses. In 1964 Gwendolen Carter became the new director and the Department of Linguistics was established. The latter enhanced the PAS position and it allowed it to become Language and Area Centre of the Office of Education in 1965. This appointment made PAS eligible to additional economic support from the Office of Education. Although much of these funds were aimed at language training, other areas benefited from it. History students, for example, who needed to learn an African language for their research, made good use of this funding.

Carter worked tirelessly to improve the Program. During her tenure course offerings and staffing improved greatly.[46] Student demand was also on the rise. The number of graduate students enrolled in the Program went from 35 in 1964-65 to 130 in 1968-69. The number of undergraduates taking courses related to Africa also increased.[47] The number of PhDs awarded by PAS up to 1969 was 88. The disciplinary breakdown of this number however, will show that not all areas were developing at the same speed. From the 88 degrees awarded 38 were in Anthropology, 14 in Political Science and 11 in History.[48] Nine of the eleven degrees in History were granted between 1962 and 1970.[49]

The growing demand from history students made it more pressing to secure the services of a full time historian, something that was very difficult at the time.[50] Much of the responsibility of finding a historian seems to have fallen on Carter who kept a constant search for potential candidates. In 1963 Robert Hess joined the department as the first full-time historian of Africa. He was soon replaced by John

Rowe who arrived in 1965. Rowe did postgraduate work at Wisconsin and was part of a small group of young American historians who were available at the time.[51] Rowe's appointment certainly helped but there was still a need for more staff and, arguably, at least one senior professor. Carter corresponded with several potential candidates of the likes of Terence Ranger and Michael Crowder. Finally, in 1966, Northwestern recruited Ivor Wilks who had conducted extensive research on Asante as a member of the Institute of Extra-Mural Studies at the University of Ghana and then became a leading historian at the Institute of African Studies. The volatile political situation in Ghana forced him to leave and, for a while, he contemplated employment in England. However, he felt that Northwestern offered better opportunities to send students to the field and to continue his own research activities.[52]

Despite the staffing problems the Program managed to modestly expand and strengthen its course offerings in history. At the beginning of the decade the Program only offered one course and one seminar in African history that were generally in charge of visiting professors. In 1965 a new Survey course was added and in 1967 an Independent Study option was also included. By the end of the decade more specialised offerings were set in place. The course in History of Africa was divided in three parts, each one focussed in East, West and South and Central Africa (Rowe 1970). The work of graduate students very much followed the trends seen in Africa in that it emphasised the study of African agency, political history, and the extensive use of African sources. The availability of funding for language study, the interdisciplinary setting of African studies and the late arrival of an Africanist historian allowed students at Northwestern to conduct more research on African oral materials and forced them to fully explore the use of other disciplines.[53]

Rising student demand also encouraged the History department at Wisconsin to recruit a second historian of Africa. Curtin was able to secure a second appointment with the support of Vice-President, Fred Harrington. In 1960 Jan Vansina joined the University with a joint appointment in the History and Anthropology departments.[54]

By the mid-sixties The Program of Comparative Tropical History was flourishing. It had a staff of six and seventy-four graduate students of which thirty-three had Africa as their main concentration.[55] At this stage, the main challenges faced by the programme were to maintain healthy levels of funding after the termination of the initial Carnegie grant, and the recruitment of staff. The first problem was solved through the increasing support for students' research from the National Defense Education Act (later Title VI). This support was possible thanks to the creation of the African Studies Program and the establishment of the Department of African Languages and Literature in 1963-64.

Towards the end of the 1950s Curtin got in touch with other scholars in the university who were interested in African studies: Frederick Simoons in Geography, David Ames in Anthropology and Aristide Zolberg in Political Science. These informal contacts were later formalised with the creation of the Program of African Studies in September of 1961.[56] By this time there was little opportunity for Wisconsin to obtain funding from the Ford Foundation or other sources. Initially, the Program was sustained from the University regular operating funds. In 1961 the Program received some extra help from a grant made by the Ford Foundation This money was mainly used to support the recruiting of staff, to improve library holdings, and to support fieldwork by graduate students.[57] Between 1961 and 1964 there was a significant growth in the number of staff and students. In 1961 there were four members of staff involved and twenty-five graduate students. In 1964 the staff increased to fourteen and the number of students was fifty.[58] In 1965 the Program was designated African Languages and Area Studies Center.

This expansion, however, was not evenly distributed among the different departments. In 1963 the history department had twenty-five students that accounted for more than half of the total number of graduate students enrolled in the Program.[59] But even a large department like Madison was struggling with the growing demand. In the academic year of 1968-69 the Program reported that: 'Pressure on graduate admissions continues to be strong, particularly in the field of History where only about 15 or 20 percent of those applying for graduate work can be admitted'.[60] It was soon clear that provisions needed to be made to secure more staff, particularly when Vansina was not sure about staying in Wisconsin.[61] This was the beginning of a search similar to that carried out in Northwestern. Among the candidates that were considered were John Rowe, Robert Rotberg, G.B. Martin, Martin Legassick, Ralph Austen, Leonard Thompson, and Steve Feierman, who was finally hired.

The hiring of Feierman allowed Vansina to take the final step in the consolidation of African history in Wisconsin. In 1965 he promoted the creation of an African history programme, independent from Comparative Tropical History or African Studies. This initiative was successful and would be the next chapter in what became a long and successful tradition in training historians of Africa. The Wisconsin school, as came to be known combined the interests and expertise of its two founding members, Vansina and Curtin. While Curtin encouraged comparative approaches to the study of Africa, Vansina emphasised the importance of oral sources, anthropological and ethnographic research, and the appreciation of Africa's unique cultural structures.

Decades of Crisis

The word crisis has been often used to describe the state of Africanist historiography during the past three decades. There is little agreement, however, on what constitutes this crisis or whether it even exists (Zeleza 1997; Ranger 1976). Nonetheless, the institutional standing of African history has suffered significantly and, if one is to talk about a crisis, one needs to start by examining this decline. African institutions have endured more than their American and British counterparts (Ake 1994; Tadesse 1999). But this has had a domino effect on the way in which Africa is studied in Britain and the USA. Not only has the enterprise become widely disconnected from its main object of study, Africa and its peoples, but there has also been discontent, disagreements and competing views on how and for whom African history should be written and taught. In the following paragraphs I will describe some of the general trends of institutional decline as they can be observed in the six institutions we have been following.

The deterioration of historical studies in African universities took place in the midst of widespread scepticism about the value of professional academic history for the economic and social development of African societies. This was accompanied by the gradual erosion of the social, economic and political conditions in many African countries. Historians faced shrinking departmental budgets, dependence on external funding, and increasing teaching loads that severely undermined their ability to conduct research.[62] During the 1980s and 1990s financial institutions such as the World Bank and the IMF imposed stringent economic policies on African institutions demanding 'budgetary discipline and academic relevance from universities'. There was a strong emphasis on the production of skilled personnel which was bad news for the humanities in general. As Mamdani pointed out, it was 'a return to the developmental logic of the independent state, but without vision or ambition' (Mamdani 1994: 3).

Legon and Dar es Salaam experienced severed disruptions between the late 1960s and the 1990s. At Legon, there were serious student demonstrations and strikes by university workers. The University was forced to close in a number of occasions. These were usually accompanied by shortages of water, electricity and fuel that worsened working conditions at this institution (Agbodeka 1998).

Although student numbers taking history classes did not decrease significantly, students reading for an Honours degree in History did become fewer and fewer.[63] This meant that less students were willing to continue to graduate school to become professional historians. Furthermore, these were difficult times for teachers at the university. Many left the department and moved to other universities either in Africa or the United States, while the teaching loads of those who stayed increased significantly. The department went from 14 to five members, making research virtually impossible.[64]

The adverse economic situation affected the effectiveness of university libraries. It became more difficult to keep abreast with international publications. African libraries could not afford books and journals. In a rapidly changing field like African History, this dealt a serious blow to local research. Publishing locally became more difficult and publishing in international journals became harder because editors argued that African authors' concerns were too local for wider audiences.[65] The high costs of publishing locally and the obstacles for publishing abroad made it almost impossible for younger generations of historians to significantly advance their careers, delivering a serious blow to the growth of the field in many parts of Africa.

These conditions had a disastrous effect on the ambitious teaching programme and the diversification of research at Legon. The department could not sustain the variety and quality of courses that had been offered, and it was difficult to introduce new subjects.[66] The political history of the different groups that constituted Ghana remained the main area of research. The department remained strongly committed to the notion of nation-building that had been so important in the development of African History in the previous decade (Boahen 1975).

Conditions at Dar es Salaam were also gradually deteriorating but the History department retained its reputation for vital and valuable debates due to the sharp critique of nationalist historiography. Nonetheless, research outputs did decline. In 1970 the University of East Africa was dissolved and the independent University of Dar es Salaam was inaugurated. This brought heated debates about the role of the university in a socialist Tanzania that were followed by structural changes throughout the university. The guiding principle behind these transformations was the need to contribute to the man-power needs of the country.[67] In addition, financial stringency had a crippling effect on the University of Dar es Salaam. The money allocated for education in the national budget went from fourteen percent in 1970/71 to four percent in 1989/1990 (Itandala 1996). Funding for higher education suffered even more with the introduction of economic reforms by the World Bank and IMF under the programme of structural adjustment after 1986.

Under these circumstances historians at Dar es Salaam were forced to re-think their role and they concluded that their 'study of African History should help workers to understand the historical forces which have shaped the problems Africans now face'.[68] The need to justify the study of history in the context of a socialist Tanzania coincided with the broader popularity of Marxist approaches to the study of history in general and the increasing appeal of development studies. These factors were important in the emergence of what has been called the second Dar School of historiography, which presented a strong criticism of the nationalist history of the 1960s (Temu and Swai 1981; Slater 1985).

The criticism formulated by the New Dar School, however, focussed heavily on philosophical debates about history. Unfortunately, its historiographical output was relatively poor. The most influential publication from this period was Rodney's *How Europe Underdeveloped Africa*. The emphasis on the discussion of theory was explained by Kimambo as the result of the difficult political circumstances at the time that made it safer for faculty members to engage on theoretical discussions rather than to produce historical research. But as Kimambo (1993: 15) continued to say, 'From the historians' point of view, the two decades of debating theory did mean lost opportunity [sic] to produce historical knowledge for almost a whole generation'.

The new perspectives also had an impact on the teaching programme at Dar es Salaam Economic history and philosophy of history became important areas, and a strong emphasis was given to the introduction of what was termed a 'scientific' approach to history.[69] Nevertheless, the department experienced sharp declines in the numbers of students, particularly those reading for graduate degrees. In 1994 the department reported that there were no history majors that year.[70]

The debates that characterised the New Dar School were possible due to the fact that the exodus of historians experienced by the Legon history department did not affect Tanzania at the same level. Even when the university was beginning to experience difficulties attracting and retaining staff, these did not affect the history department until the 1980s.[71]

Budgetary cuts eventually had negative effects on both research and teaching. External examiners repeatedly reported that students in the department lacked the necessary materials to become familiar with new historiographical approaches and had the tendency to repeat what they had heard in class.[72] There had been interest in introducing new courses and perspectives but this has been hampered by the lack of staff and bibliographic resources.[73] Historians at Dar es Salaam often discussed the establishment of agreements with foreign universities to ameliorate these problems.[74] On the other hand, they were also concerned by the difficulty of dealing with external donors, which had proven to be a challenging experience after the opening of a new Archaeology unit in 1985-86 with the support of the Ford Foundation and Brown University.[75] This example shows the new kind of relationship that began to develop between African and Western institutions and how, in many cases, these were far from being the collaborative ventures that existed during the 1950s and 1960s.

The past three decades have witnessed dramatic changes in the field of South African history. The Radical School emerged during the 1970s, mainly through the work of South African historians working outside South Africa, but eventually went back home where it flourished at the University of the Witwatersrand. From there it influenced the transformation of historical studies throughout South Africa and became an important intellectual force within Africanist historiography (Marks 1985; Bonner 1997). Much of the vitality of the Radical tradition was aimed at making South Africa an integral part of African history, an endeavour that proved quite difficult at UCT.

During the 1970s and 1980s, the history department at UCT unsuccessfully pursued a better integration between African and South African history. The African history course introduced by Axelson was having great success among students and there were plans to introduce a second course. However, this did not include a proposal to integrate the teaching of African history as part of the First or Honours degrees.[76] The new chairman, Colin de B. Webb, introduced some changes that allowed for students who had taken the course in African history to use it towards a history major. However, it still was not a required course.[77]

The most important source of change during this period was the arrival of Robin Hallet who took over the teaching of African history in 1972 and who is credited for introducing new ideas among members of the department. He took the study of African History at UCT closer to what was being taught in African, American and European universities, and increased the awareness among historians about what was happening in other parts of the continent.[78] Hallett encouraged young historians to explore new approaches to the study of the South African past. He started working on social and urban history, and other members of the department and research students followed in his footsteps.[79] Despite this, it is fair to say that the strictures of the apartheid educational system and a widely sustained view on South African particularism made it difficult for African History to flourish at UCT.

The limited changes experienced by the History department had an effect on the general standing of African studies at the University. As a result of the efforts of various members of staff and faculty, the languishing School of African Studies was replaced by the Centre of African Studies in 1976.[80] In contrast with the old School of African Studies, the new Centre was founded on a broad conception of African studies. In other words, African studies would not only be understood as the African population of South Africa but as its constitution said: 'the word "African" should be understood to include all inhabitants of the African continent'.[81]

The decline of apartheid during the mid-1980s and its collapse in the 1990s presented South African universities with two fundamental challenges: the need to reduce costs and, a drive to Africanise 'historically white' institutions. The budget cuts that were imposed on universities during the mid-1980s forced UCT to explore ways of reducing spending by re-structuring its administrative framework and its academic programmes. This revision encouraged changes in the History syllabus that finally managed to introduce African history as an integral part of the major and not just as an added bonus.[82] Despite this, the department did not hire a historian that specialised in the tropical history of Africa, and this would put a question mark on their commitment to its integration in the department.

The difficult financial situation also forced the closure of the Economic History department that had housed historians that were heavily influenced by the radical historiography emanating from Wits. These historians were incorporated in the History department and their presence created significant tension in the department.[83]

In 1993 changes started to accelerate. The Faculty of Arts went into a process of self-review that proved to be quite difficult for the History department.[84] The final result was the proposal of a BA in Historical Studies in 1998 that involved the departments of History, Archaeology, Classics, Art History, Religious Studies, Classics, Hebrew and Jewish Studies. It encouraged links with the Social Sciences and Education and emphasised the role of historical disciplines as areas that enhanced the development of analytical and critical skills.[85]

In the midst of administrative and academic reforms, the History Department found itself in the middle of another debate. This time it was directly related to its attitudes towards African History. During the 1990s there was a proposal to introduce a core course called 'Introduction to Africa'. Mahmood Mamdani, then chairman of the Centre for African Studies, was called to collaborate in the design of the course. Mamdani had joined UCT in 1996 and since then had been vocal about the changes that needed to be brought about in the area of African Studies. When the proposal for the new course was first presented, Mamdani found serious problems in the way it portrayed Africa's experience. Mamdani's most important criticism was the lack of a 'historical sociology'. He thought the course, particularly the first part, did not promote an analytical understanding of the processes that affected the development of African societies and thus obscured the relationship between these and the processes experienced in South Africa. Moreover, he said, 'the absence reflects a key weakness of the History Department at UCT. The department has made choices over the past decade so that it has no one with a research focus on equatorial [sic] Africa' (Mamdani 1998: 6).

Mamdani's criticism was not well-taken by members of the department who felt it disregarded the very real limitations that apartheid had imposed for the integration of African history.[86] Justified or not, Mamdani's critique forced a serious examination of UCT's attempts to integrate South Africa within African history.

In 1998 the University deemed that the department was an area 'under stress' and submitted it to an external review:

> The present Department of History absorbed, with some difficulty, a group of senior Economic historians some time ago; attempts to fill the endowed King George V Chair of History have failed; the most recently appointed head of department asked to be allowed to stand down long before his term was completed; there is some controversy as to how African History should be approached in the post-1994 context, both by the Department of History and the Centre of African Studies ...[87]

The final report praised the work of the department in terms of its innovative teaching, the research records of its members and its leadership in the formulation of the new Historical Studies Programme. There were, however, some areas that needed to be addressed. Some problems that came to the attention of the committee were the lack of leadership, a poor sense of community among members, and the gender and racial profile of the staff, among others. On the crucial issue of the teaching programme the Committee said:

> ... the Committee is concerned that the temporal and geographic span of teaching and research in the Department is fairly limited even though the quality is not in question. Although the Committee realises that the lack of direct research expertise in a particular area does not preclude teaching in that area, it is noticeable - if understandable - that nearly all the research expertise in the department is focused on Southern Africa, and most of that on South Africa, and even the Cape. While this has built an enviable depth, the Committee shares concerns which were expressed that the department does not have a wider research and teaching expertise - notably relating to the African continent.[88]

In a climate of financial stringency these challenges produced great anxiety among historians at UCT. However, this was mixed with a sense of liberation and excitement at the opportunity to explore common grounds and bring South Africa back into African history.

The 1970s marked the beginning of tough economic times for SOAS. The two fundamental roles of SOAS were undermined by this decline. Its ability to serve as a centre for discussion was diminished by the increasing isolation of African institutions and its role as a major destination for training was affected by increased tuition fees and the reduction of financial aid for overseas students.

During the 1970s the crisis mainly affected expansion at the undergraduate level. Graduate training maintained its vitality and productivity. Oliver (1997) remembers this period as one of the most productive in the training of doctoral candidates. Approximately 46 degrees were granted between 1970/71 and 1979/80.[89] Unfortunately, the signs of a serious slow-down in the growth of the field were becoming clear, and there were increasing concerns that historians of Africa would have greater difficulties in securing academic positions (Oliver 1997). On the upside of things, students at SOAS were able to expand their areas of research. There was an increase in research on pre-colonial times and a significant amount of work on South African history by historians who were contributing to the new radical history. In this regard, the 1970s had a bright side in the history of SOAS.

Unfortunately, things became worse during the Thatcher era, which was deemed to be disastrous for African studies (McCracken 1993). Between 1977 and 1982 the proportion of the Social Science Research Council's budget devoted to African Studies decreased from 2.3 to 0.8 percent. This was translated into significant cuts on travel grants and libraries' funding. Important centres of research in African studies, such as Edinburgh and Birmingham, faced closure. At a time when many Africanist historians were reaching retirement age, there were no funds available to replace them. The only two chairs designated to African History, those held by Roland Oliver and John Fage, remained vacant after their retirement. When John Hargreaves retired early from Aberdeen and Paul Hair from Liverpool, they were not replaced by historians of Africa. All this was bad news for younger generations who became more disillusioned with the prospects of finding employment in academia (McCracken 1993).

During the academic year of 1980-81 SOAS experienced significant budgetary cuts. First, there was a reduction in the amount of money given to universities aimed at preventing overseas student from benefiting from British subsidies. This was a significant blow to the school. Historically it had been an important centre for the training of overseas graduate students. In addition to this, the government reduced the recurrent grant for universities by £30 million in 1980. This was the first of a number of cuts aimed to reducing the income of universities.[90]

The history department went through a period of transition with older faculty retiring and being replaced by a younger generation. This introduced new research approaches such as gender, population, agriculture, urban and environmental history, identity formation, slavery, among others. Unfortunately, these younger scholars faced tougher working conditions. They had heavier teaching loads, stagnant salaries and an ever increasing cost of living in the London metropolitan area. This made recruitment and retention of faculty difficult for SOAS.[91]

The training of graduate students continued to be an important part of SOAS' contribution to the field, although the number of doctoral degrees was smaller than in earlier years.[92] There were roughly fifty doctoral degrees granted between 1980 and 1996, compared to forty-six degrees granted between 1970 and 1980.[93] The most significant trend, however, was the marked emphasis on colonial and postcolonial history, while earlier periods became less popular among students.

The declining importance of Africa for national security and the end of the period of expansion in higher education during the 1970s presented important challenges to the development of African studies in the United States. The tensions that surfaced at Montreal had a sobering and long-lasting effect on the credibility of African studies and have continued to influence the work of historians in American institutions (Martin and West 1999; Curtin 1995).

The 1970s caught PAS in the middle of financial difficulties. The grants that had supported the running and growth of the Program were reaching their end and Northwestern University seemed unable or unwilling to commit to fund the activities of PAS at the same level that they had existed. Carter's correspondence is full of pleas to the University for a stronger commitment and warnings about lost opportunities.[94] Despite the financial concerns, the PAS retained a healthy level of popularity among students. The total enrolment did not grow dramatically, but neither did it fall. In the early seventies, the History Department reported approximately thirty PhD candidates working on African History, something that made history the most popular discipline in the Program.[95] This improvement was reflected in the staffing situation. Throughout the 1970s and 1980s other historians joined the department: I. Sundiata, Carl Petry, J. Hunwick, and Sterling Stuckey who eventually became chairman of the African-American department.

The additions to the staff allowed for the introduction of more courses and research perspectives. Particularly important was the introduction of African Studies courses at the undergraduate level. This was a clear move towards making the field more popular and to broaden its social appeal. Particularly, it was said: 'It is anticipated that the new programme will have a specific appeal to black undergraduates concerned to explore objectively their own heritage, as well as to a wide cross-section of the undergraduate community increasingly concerned with third world studies...'[96] Some courses from African-American studies were incorporated in the Program such as Literature in African-American History and culture. Other additions reflect some of the changes in the field. For example, more attention was given to South African History. Debates on historical materialism and other social science theory approaches were incorporated in the teaching programme, but had a limited influence on the research output of the faculty.[97]

In 1998 the PAS celebrated the fiftieth anniversary of its foundation. By then, it had incorporated young and promising historians, its Africana library continued to be internationally recognised, and continued to attract good numbers of students. However, it had been unable to retain its status as a Title VI centre. To commemorate its anniversary, the Program created an exhibition called *Living Tradition in Africa & the Americas. The Legacy of Melville J. and Frances S. Herskovits.*[98] One can hardly escape the irony of this celebration. One should remember that the intentions of the founder, Herskovits, were precisely to link the study of Africa to that of African-Americans.

By recovering the original motivations of its founder, the Program made a powerful and persuasive argument for its contemporary relevance and survival.

At Wisconsin, the problems were less acute but still significant. Curtin recognised that history in general and African history in particular were being forced to justify their relevance to American audiences. Student numbers started to decline and this resulted in a reduced budget.[99] Curtin tried to face these challenges by transforming the PCTH into a Program on Comparative World History. But this was not enough to secure more funding for it.[100] In 1975 Curtin left for Johns Hopkins University, a loss deeply regretted at Wisconsin.

The ASP and the Program of African History managed to remain competitive, but they were forced to make significant adjustments. In 1972 the director of the Program, David Wiley, informed the African Studies Committee of some changes in the NDEA funding. At that point there were 101 Language and Area centres, but the expectation was that there would only be 40-45 for 1972-73. This was considered to be a 'crucial period' in the funding of the Program. The Office of Education had established new priorities and more emphasis was to be given to interdisciplinary research (understood as problem-oriented research), and to the relationship between language problems and area studies.[101] The next year (1973-74), the ASP was one of only four programmes to be designated a NDEA Language and Area Center by the Office of Education.[102] As the decade progressed, demands by funding agencies became more specific. In 1976, for example Wiley informed the committee that: 'This year a new regulation requires an explicit 15 percent of budget to be spent on outreach activities'.[103]

Wisconsin was able to introduce some innovation in their approach to African History. One important step was the introduction of the Program in African Economic History, which was again an initiative of Curtin and Marvin Miracle.[104] Another important innovation was the incorporation of staff members from the African-American Studies department that had been recently created. During the 1970s, Richard Ralston and Tom Schick joined the staff of the ASP as members of the African-American Studies department.[105] Many of these changes reveal the attempt by the ASP to please the funding bodies by encouraging research and outreach work that was more visibly relevant to a wider population. Towards the end of the decade, the Program registered a shift from the initial domination of historical studies to 'the professional and language and linguistic skills'.[106] In spite of the difficulties the number of historians of Africa involved to the ASP increased. Curtin's departure coincided with the return of Vansina. He was joined by Steve Feierman, William Brown, Byron D. Cannon, Joseph Corry, Robert L. Koehl, and Norman L. Cigar.

In Vansina' (1994: 184) words 'The major intellectual innovation in the program following 1975 was the growing importance given to the formal teaching of social science theory'. Feierman was a strong supporter of this idea. He wanted to introduce young students to the classics of social theory thought, since he sensed this was becoming a major trend in the study of history in general.[107] As the 1970s passed new approaches became popular, and Wisconsin, as other history departments diversified its approaches and perspectives.

However, there is a trend that is worth mentioning. Wisconsin had traditionally been a centre of great importance in the study of pre-colonial history. As the 1970s progressed, Vansina remained convinced that historians should concentrate on this area. However, Feierman realised that many things were happening in the study of more recent periods of history. He thought it would be unfortunate if Wisconsin students were not exposed to such new ideas. Thus, he moved his research towards the nineteenth and twentieth centuries to complement their history program.[108] This trend was quite characteristic of the 1970s, when research into the pre-colonial past started to decrease. This was the result of a number of causes. This kind of research demanded excellent language skills and extended periods of fieldwork. Given the increasing cuts in the funding of programmes, it became more difficult to achieve these conditions. In addition, the unstable political and economic circumstances in Africa were also a serious deterrent. All these added to the increased interest in the study of colonialism and underdevelopment, and contributed to the gradual neglect of the study of the pre-colonial period.

Despite the efforts to adapt to the needs and concerns of potential students, the number of students who enrolled to do graduate work on African History started to decrease. This was undoubtedly a consequence of the cuts in the financial support provided to students and of the increasing difficulties in securing a job. On the other hand, undergraduate enrolments increased. This again switched the emphasis from graduate training to undergraduate teaching.

The African Studies Program at Wisconsin was able to retain its Title VI Center status. But it still faced financial constraints. The need for change was soon evident to Vansina, who became its chair in 1986. He found the Program in a difficult financial situation. Funding was decreasing and private foundations were also considering cutting their support to African studies. It became clear that 'African studies programs needed to change in order to survive'.(Vansina 1994: 224). The main concern of the foundations was to make research in the social sciences and humanities more relevant to contemporary issues in Africa. In the end, the radical cuts were avoided. But it was clear to everyone involved that financial support could no longer be taken for granted.

The history department also had to contend with accusations of racism and debates about the hiring of African or African American candidates. An African scholar who had been in charge of outreach unsuccessfully applied for a position in the department and sued the University for racial discrimination (Vansina 1994). The case was finally settled by mutual agreement. In another instance, the department was considering hiring a well-regarded African scholar. However, a member of the department claimed mixed emotions about the appointment: 'Africans are equated with African-Americans as Blacks, but when Black students say they want Black professors, they want someone who, like themselves, is a product of the

African-American historical experience. Black students, while welcoming Africans, want African-Americans hired'.[109]

Conclusion

There is no doubt that the 1950s and 1960s were the golden years in the development of African historiography. The level of innovation, debate, and collaboration between historians and institutions was remarkable and allowed for great strides in the definition of a new field of study and the creation of a new historiographical tradition. The decade of the 1970s witnessed the gradual decline of African institutions that found themselves in the midst of political and economic crises. Even though American and British institutions have also experienced difficulties, it is the decline in African universities that has raised questions about the intellectual legitimacy and social relevance of the enterprise.

It is difficult to talk about a crisis since Africanist historiography has made enormous progress during the past fifty years. However, calls for the 'Africanisation' of knowledge reveal deep anxieties in a field that has retained much of its intellectual vibrancy and commitment to innovation, but has also become largely disconnected from African institutions and thus, African societies (Falola and Jennings 2002; Brizuela-Garcia 2006). Although it is encouraging and enriching that African history is taught and researched in many corners of the world, the future of the field cannot and should not rely on what foreign institutions consider to be relevant at any particular time. The future of African historiography will never be as secure and healthy as it was when African colleges were active participants in its production.

Notes

1. It is important to emphasise that the tradition of historical writing that this paper will examine represents one of many approaches to African historical writing. There are important bodies of historical literature in other languages such as French, Portuguese and Russian. Particularly important is the long and important historiographical tradition of African-American historians who have been engaged in the study of Africa. This is best exemplified by, although certainly not limited to, the work of W. E. B. Du Bois. This tradition had a marginal presence in American institutions before the 1970s. However, it had a place in the historically black colleges such as Howard, where some courses on African history were offered. More recently, we have seen the emergence of Afro-centric approaches that have produced yet another tradition of historical writing about Africa in the English language. All of these have, to some extent, influenced the historiographical tradition that this paper studies, but their evolution is not examined here.

2. In several interviews historians mentioned that they had decided to join the new university colleges because they were offered good salaries and allowances, while jobs in the UK were scarce. See Brizuela-Garcia 2001.

3. Draft Syllabuses in History. University College of the Gold Coast. *Academic Board Meetings.* 1949-1950. University of Ghana, Balme Library (UGBL).

4. University College of the Gold Coast. *Annual Report* 1954-55. p.10.

5. University College of the Gold Coast. *Regulations.* 1955. p.59.

6.   University College of the Gold Coast. *Annual Report.* 1952-53. pp.13-14. University College of the Gold Coast. *Annual Report.* 1954-55. pp. 9-10.

7.   Proposal for Gold Coast Historical Series. University College of the Gold Coast. *Academic Board Meetings.* 1952-53.UGBL. Publications Board Meeting. 15May 1953. University College of the Gold Coast. *Academic Board Meetings.* 1952-53.UGBL.

8.   H. J. Mandelbrote. 'Memorandum on Consolidation and development of the History Department'. April, 1951. Minute 12 April 1951. *Minutes of the Board of the Faculty of Arts.* University of Cape Town (UCT).

9.   L. M. Thompson. 'Report on special leave granted to attend the Leverhulme History Conference at the University College of Rhodesia and Nyasaland, 5th to 15th of September, 1960'. 27 September 1960. *Minutes of the Board of the Faculty of Arts.* UCT.

10. Minute 5 April 1960. *Council Minutes.* UCT.

11. Memorandum, 'Expansion in the Study of Africa'. Minute 5 April 1960. *Council Minutes.* UCT.

12. The School adopted this name in 1938 when its charter was amended.

13. 'Director's Review by Cyril Philips. SOAS. *Report of the Governing Body, Statement of Accounts, and Departmental Reports.* 1957/1958. pp.76-77.

14. Between 1942 and 1948 only eight percent of students were enrolled in Higher or First degrees. In contrast, in the period between 1948 and 1956 students pursuing First and Higher degrees increased to 28 percent. SOAS. *Report of the Governing Body, Statement of Accounts, and Departmental Reports.* 1942/43- 1956/57.

15. Carl B. Spaeth (Director of Division of Overseas Activities, Ford Foundation) to M. J. Herskovits. 29 July 1952. *Melville Herskovits Papers.* Northwestern University Archives (NUA).

16. Ford Foundation Conference in Africa. 'Findings and recommendations'. Evanston, Illinois, 18-23 August 1952. *Melville Herskovits Papers.* NUA. pp.6-7. Report of the Committee on African Studies. Prepared for the Ford Foundation. August, 1958. *Program of African Studies Records.* NUA. p.17.

17. Title VI funding for National Resource Centers was first introduced through the National Defense Education Act of 1958. In 1980 this funding became part of the National Education Act that incorporated elements of its predecessor. This funding has been very important in supporting language learning and fieldwork, two crucial elements in the development of African History.

18. M. J. Herskovits to Franklin B. Snyder. 27 October 1947. And J. W. Gardner to M. J. Herskovits. 22 December 1947. *Melville Herskovits Papers.* NUA.

19. Report of the Committee on African Studies. Prepared for the Ford Foundation. August, 1958. *Program of African Studies Records.* p.10. NUA.

20. F. D. Scott. 'Some reminiscences of the Northwestern History Department in the years 1935-1942'. *Franklin D. Scott Papers.* NUA.

21. Northwestern University. *Announcement of Courses in the Graduate School.* 1953-54. p.130-31; 'Franklin D. Scott. Inventory'. *Franklin D. Scott Papers.* NUA.

22. M. J. Herskovits to Mary Albertson (History Department, Swarthmore College). 19 March 1956. *Melville Herskovits Papers.* NUA.

23. M. J. Herskovits to Dr. H. R. Rudin (Department of History, University of Yale). 13 January 1949. *Melville Herskovits Papers.* NUA.

24. Oral History Project. Transcript of Interview with Philip D. Curtin. University of Wisconsin, 8/5/1975. p.1. University of Wisconsin-Madison Archives (UWMA).

25. Minute 15 October 1956. *History Department. Minutes of the Executive Committee.* UWMA.

26. Oral History Project. Transcript of Interview with Philip D. Curtin. 8/5/1975, p. 3. UWMA. Interview with P. Curtin. 13 November 1999.

27. Minute 5 October 1959. *History Department Departmental Meetings Minutes.* UWMA.

28. Oral History Project. Transcript from Interview with Philip Curtin. 8/5/1975. p.19. UWMA.

29. Department of History. 'Report of the Committee on the Future of the Department'. Minute 14 January 1958. *Department of History. Departmental Meetings Minutes.* UWMA.

30. Interview with P. Curtin. 13 November 1999. Oral History Project. Transcript of Interview with Philip D. Curtin. University of Wisconsin, 8/5/1975. p. 9. UWMA.

31. Interview with A. Boahen. 28 April 1999. Airport Residential Area, Accra.

32. University of Ghana. *Annual Report.* 1968-69. pp. 107-108.

33. 'Structure of degree courses and related matters'. [n.d] *Academic Board Meetings.* 1964-65. UGBL.

34. 'Amendments to syllabus in history'. [n.d.] *Academic Board Meetings.* 1963-64. UGBL.

35. Agenda, 29 June 1967. *Academic Board Meetings.* 1966-67. UGBL.

36. Interview with I. Wilks. 12 October 1999.

37. Interview with I. Wilks. October 12, 1999.

38. University of Ghana. *Annual Report.* 1968-69. p.148.

39. Although Makerere had a history department before Dar es Salaam, it was less well known and its advances were more modest. See Ingham (1995).

40. University of Dar es Salaam. *Report [of a] conference on the role of the University College Dar es Salaam in a Socialist Tanzania. March 11-13, 1967.* pp. 95-96. Unpublished manuscript. University of Dar es Salaam Africana Library.

41. E. Axelson to the Dean of the Faculty of Arts. 17 September 1964. Minute 6 October 1964; E. Axelson to the Dean of the Faculty of Arts. 1 October 1964. Minute 29 September 1964; 'Economic history revision of syllabuses and introduction of a course in African Economic history'. Minute 28 July 1970; Axelson, E. 'Proposed abandonment by the department of history of the teaching of Constitutional Law'. 8 March 1963. Minute 12 March 1963; Minute 8 October 1963; Axelson, E. 'Five Year Plan. History'. Minute 7 October 1969. *Minutes of the Board of the Faculty of Arts.* UCT.

42. 'Director's Review' by Cyril Philips in SOAS *Report of the Governing Body, Statement of Accounts, and Departmental Reports.* 1957-58. pp. 74-75.

43. The Hayter Report was instrumental in the creation of other centres for the study of Asia and Africa such as those at Hull, Leeds and Sheffield for Asian studies and the Centre of West African Studies at Birmingham. Two years later, the Robbins Report went one step further when it recommended the introduction of undergraduate and Master courses related to Africa and Asia.

44. Curtin's estimates were based in the number of Fellows of the African Studies Association in 1958 and a sample of grant recipients in the Program of Ford Foreign Area Fellowships up to 1958.

45. Payson S. Wild (Vice-President and Dean of Faculties, NU) to Melville Fox (Ford Foundation). 17 May 1960. *Melville Herskovits Papers.* NUA. And Melvin Fox to Payson S. Wild. 27 December 1960. *Melville Herskovits Papers.* NUA.

46. 'Report to the Ford Foundation 1969-1970 for the Program of African Studies and the National Unity Grant'. *Program of African Studies Records.* NUA.

47. NU. 'Application for Faculty Research/Study fellows'. September, 1969. *Program of African Studies Records.* NUA.

48. 'Annual Report for the Program of African Studies, 1971-1972'. Appendix A. *Program of African Studies Records.* NUA. This figure included a small number of degrees in anthropology that had been awarded before the creation of the PAS.

49. 'Report to the Ford Foundation 1969-1970 for the Program of African Studies and the National Unity Grant.' *Program of African Studies Records.* NUA.

50. Program of African Studies. 'Report 1961-1962'. September, 1962. *Program of African Studies Records.* NUA.

51. Interview with J. Rowe. 14 October 1999.

52. Interview with I. Wilks. 12 October 1999.

53. Interview with S. Feierman. 13 November 1999.

54. 'Report of the Committee on the future of the department'. Special Departmental Meeting Minute 14 January 1968. History Department. *Departmental Meetings Minutes.* UWMA. Philip Curtin to Executive Committee. 22 October 1962. Department of History. *Departmental Meetings Minutes.* UWMA. Minute 20 January 1966. History Department. *Minutes of the Executive Committee.* UWMA. Oral History Project. Transcript of Interview with Philip D. Curtin. 8/5/1975.p.19. UWMA.

55. PCTH. 'Annual Report for 1965'. *Office of International Studies. Area and International Studies Program Records.* UWMA.

56. Oral History Project. Transcript of Interview with Philip D. Curtin. 8/5/1975. p.4. UWMA. 'Annual Report for the Academic Year 1963-64'. Title VI Documents. *African Studies Program Records.* UWM.

57. Simoons, F. 'A plan of operation for the continuation of Language and Area Center for Africa at the University of Wisconsin for 1966-67'. Title VI Documents. *African Studies Program Records.* UWM.

58. 'Annual Report for the Academic Year 1963-64'. Title VI Documents. *African Studies Program Records.* UWM.

59. 'Annual Report for the Academic Year 1963-64'. Title VI Documents. *African Studies Program Records.* UWM.

60. 'A proposal to the Department of Health, Education and Welfare. USA Office of Education. Language and Area Centers Section for renewal of NDEA African Language and Area Center' 1968-69'. Title VI Documents. *African Studies Program Records.* UWM.

61. Minute 24 September 1964. History Department. *Minutes of the Executive Committee.* UWMA.

62. Association of African Universities. Workshop on the teaching of African History in African Universities. University of Lagos 21-24 September 1977. Report of the Commission of Research, training and exchange of information. p. 9.

63. Numbers compiled from the University of Ghana. *Annual Report.* 1964/65-1974/75.

64. Interview with A. Perbi. 27 April 1999. Interview with R. Addo-Fenning. 22 April 1999.

65. Interview with R. Addo-Fenning. 22 April 1999.

66. Interview with R. Addo-Fenning. 22 April 1999.

67. Kimambo, I. & A. G. Ishumi. 'Twenty years of the Faculty of Arts and Social Sciences: a critical review'. Seminar paper. History Department, University of Dar es Salaam. [n.d.]

68. 'Editorial'. *Tanzania Zamani.* 16, 1975. p.1.

69. University of Dar es Salaam. *Calendar.* 1980-81. p.149.

70. Minute 11 November 1994. *Departmental Meeting Minutes.* UDS.

71. University of Dar es Salaam. *Calendar.* 1970/71/72. p. 73.

72. Minute 11 April 1989. *Departmental Meeting Minutes.* UDS. History Department. External Examiner's Report. 1982-1983. p.1. UDS.

73. Interview with A. Tambila. 4 March 1999.

74. These discussions included links with Bergen University, University of Helsinki, University of Natal and the University of Florida.

75. Minute. 7 June 1995. *Departmental Meeting Minutes.* UDS.

76. A .M. Davey to Dean. 25 June 1973. Dean's Circular, 12 July 1973. *Transactions of the Board of the Faculty of Arts.* UCT.

77. C. de B. Webb to Dean, 2 May 1978. Agenda 9 May 1978. *Transactions of the Board of the Faculty of Arts.* UCT. Webb, C. de B. 'Syllabus revision and consequential prospectus amendments'. 13 June 1980. Dean's Circular 9 September 1980. *Transactions of the Board of the Faculty of Arts.* UCT.

78. Interview with H. Phillips. 11 December 1998. Interview with P. Harries. 20 January 1999. Interview with A. Davie and E.van Heynigen. 4 December 1998.

79. Interview with A. Davie and E. van Heynigen. 4 December 1998. Interview with H. Phillips. 11 December 1998.

80. Memorandum from Prof. N. J. van der Merwe to Dean. 18 October 1974. Agenda for 29 October 1974. *Transactions of the Board of the Faculty of Arts.* UCT.

81. Board of African Studies. 'Constitution and terms of reference'. Minute 10 September 1975. *Transactions of the Board of the Faculty of Arts.* UCT.

82. 'Annual Report to Senate for the period January to December 1986'. *Transactions of the Board of the Faculty of Arts.* UCT. Memorandum, B. Le Cordeur to Dean. 20 April 1983. Agenda. 26 April 1983. *Transactions of the Board of the Faculty of Arts.* UCT.

83. Minute 6 August 1991. *Transactions of the Board of the Faculty of Arts.* UCT. Strategic Planning Committee. 'Planning Review of Historical Studies at UCT. Appendix I. Recommendations from the Strategic Planning Committee'. Principal's Circular. 28 October 1998. I need to thank Prof. Nigel Worden for facilitating the provision of copies of this and other documents that had not yet been made available in the archives.

84. 'Interim Report from the Convenor of the Historical Studies Task Group'. Agenda August 1995. *Transactions of the Board of the Faculty of Arts.* 1995. 'Report of the Historical Studies Working Group'. Dean's Circular. 13 September 1995. *Transactions of the Board of the Faculty of Arts.* 1995. Dean's Circular. 8 November 1995. *Transactions of the Board of the Faculty of Arts.* 1995.

85. Agenda, 29 July 1997. *Transactions of the Board of the Faculty of Arts.* 1997. 'Proposal for a Historical Studies Programme to be introduced in 1999'.

86. Interview with Ann Mager. 21 January 1999.

87. Strategic Planning Committee. 'Planning Review of Historical Studies at UCT. Appendix I. Recommendations from the Strategic Planning Committee'. *Principal's Circular.* 28 October 1998.

88. Planning Review of Historical Studies. 'Recommendations from the Strategic Planning Committee. Review of Historical Studies'. *Principal's Circular.* 28 October 1998. p.4.

89. This is a calculation based on the information on degrees granted in the SOAS. *Report of the Governing Body, Statement of Accounts and Departmental Reports.* 1970/71-1979/80.

90. SOAS. *Report of the Governing Body, Statement of Accounts and Departmental Reports.* 1980-81. p.23.

91. SOAS. *Annual Register.* Part II. 1989-1990-1991. p.46.

92. SOAS. *Annual Register.* Part III. 1994-1995.

93. This is according to the degrees registered in the *Annual Report and Annual Register* of those years.

94. Gwendolen Carter to Dean Payson Wild. 5 May 1972; Minute of meeting between the Messrs. Wild, Noble, Hatter, Williams and Miss Carter. 19 October 1970; Payson S. Wild to Gwendolen Carter. 1 October 1971; Gwendolen Carter to Walter S. Owen. 20 April 1972; Walter S. Owen to Gwendolen Carter. 8 May 1972; Gwnedolen Carter to David Mintzer. 12 April 1974. *Program of African Studies Records.* NUA.

95. 'Annual Report for the Program of African Studies, 1972-73'. *Program of African Studies Records.* NUA.

96. 'B25 Africa and interdisciplinary survey. Interim Report'. 10 December 1971. *Program of African Studies Records.* NUA.

97. Interview with J. Rowe. 14 October 1999.

98. Mary and Leigh Block Museum of Art. Northwestern University. *Living Tradition in Africa & the Americas. The Legacy of Melville J. and Frances S. Herskovits.* 2 April - 9 August 1998.

99. E. David Cronon (Dean) to I. Kutler. 24 February 1976. *E. David Cronon. Correspondence.* UWMA.

100. Janet Berls (National Endowment for the Humanities) to Philip D. Curtin. 28 September 1973. *Philip D. Curtin General Files.* UWMA.

101. Minute 12 September 1972. African Studies Program Committee Minutes. *African Studies Program Records.* UWM.

102. The other three were UCLA, Northwestern and Indiana. Minute 2 October 1973. African Studies Program Committee Minutes. *African Studies Program Records.* UWM.

103. 'African Studies Program Announcements'. 3 February 1976. *African Studies Program Records.* UWM.

104. 'Performance Report for the year 1974-1975'. Title VI Documents. *African Studies Program Records.* UWM.

105. 'Performance Report for the years 1974-75 and 1975-76'. Title VI Documents. *African Studies Program Records.* UWM.

106. 'A Proposal to the Department of Health, Education and Welfare. US Office of Education. Language and Area Center Section. For Application for NDEA Title VI Support for the University of Wisconsin-Madison African Language and Area Center. 1981-1982'. Title VI Document. *African Studies Program Records.* UWM.

107. Interview with S. Feierman. 13 November 1999.

108. Interview with S. Feierman. 13 November 1999.

109. Minute 17 February 1989. History Department. *Minutes of the Executive Committee.* UWMA.

References

ASA, 1969, *African Studies Newsletter*, African Studies Association.

Agbodeka, F., 1998, *A History of the University of Ghana. Half a Century of Higher Education (1948-1998)*, Accra: Woeli Publishing Services for the University of Ghana.

Ajayi, J. F. A., 1995, 'African History at Ibadan', in *The Emergence of African History at British Universities: an Autobiographical Approach*, edited by A. H. M. Kirk-Greene. Oxford: WorldView Publications.

Ake, C., 1994, 'Academic Freedom and Material Base', in *Academic Freedom in Africa*, edited by M. Mamdani and M. Diouf, Dakar: CODESRIA.

Boahen, A. A., 1975, *Clio and Nation-Building in Africa: Inaugural Lecture Delivered at the University of Ghana, Legon, on Thursday, 28th November, 1974*, Accra: Ghana Universities Press.

Bonner, P., 1997, 'The University of the Witwatersrand History Workshop, a retrospect', in *Problematising History and Agency: From Nationalism to Subalternity*, University of Cape Town, Centre of African Studies.

Bozzoli, B. and P. Delius, 1990, 'Radical History and Southern African Society', *Radical History Review* 46/47:13-45.

Brizuela-Garcia, E., 2001, *Decolonising African History. Crisis and Transitions in African Historiography 1950-1990*, PhD Dissertation, History, School of Oriental and African Studies. University of London, London.

Brizuela-Garcia, E., 2006, 'The history of Africanization and the Africanization of History', *History in Africa*, (forthcoming).

Clarke, J. H., 1969, 'Confrontation in Montreal', Report presented by John Henrick Clark, President, African Heritage Studies Association. *African Studies Newsletter* II (6&7): 5-11.

Clarke, J. H., 1976, 'The African Heritage Studies Association (AHSA): Some Notes on the Conflict with the African Studies Association (ASA) and the Fight to Reclaim African History', *Issue: A Journal of Opinion* 6 (2/3): 5-11.

Colonial Office, Great Britain, 1945, *Report of the Commission on Higher Education in the Colonies*, London: Great Britain, Colonial Office.

Cowan, L. G., 1970, 'President's Report', *African Studies Review* 13 (3): 343-352.

Curtin, P. D., 1971, 'African Studies: A Personal Assessment', *African Studies Review* 14 (3): 357-368.

Curtin, P. D., 1995, 'Ghettoizing African history', *Chronicle of Higher Education* 41 (25): A44.

Denoon, D. and A. Kuper, 1970, 'Nationalist Historians in Search of a Nation: The "New Historiography" in Dar es Salaam', *African Affairs* 69 (277): 329-349.

Fage, J. D., 1995, 'Legon and Birmingham', in *The emergence of African History at British Universities: an Autobiographical Approach*, edited by A.H.M. Kirk-Greene. Oxford: WorldView Publications.

Fage, J. D., 2002, *To Africa and back. Memoirs of John Fage*, Birmingham: Centre of West African Studies, University of Birmingham.

Falola, T. and C. Jennings, 2002, *Africanizing Knowledge: African Studies Across the Disciplines*, New Brunswick, N.J.: Transaction Publishers.

Foreign Office, Great Britain, 1947, *Report of the Interdepartmental Commission of Enquiry on Oriental, Slavonic, East European and African Studies*, London: Great Britain, Foreign Office.

Guyer, J. I., 1998, 'Perspectives on the beginnings', *PAS News and Events*, 2&4.

Hamilton, R. A., ed., 1955, *History and Archaeology in Africa: Report of a Conference held in July 1953 at the School of Oriental and African Studies*, London: School of Oriental and African Studies, University of London.

Ingham, K., 1995, 'Makerere and after', in A. H. M. Kirk-Greene, ed., *The Emergence of African History at British Universities: an Autobiographical Approach*, Oxford: World View Publications.

Interdisciplinary Committee on African Studies, 1959, *United States Foreign Policy: Africa. A Study Prepared at the Request of the Committee on Foreign Relations, United States Senate by Programme of African Studies, Northwestern University*, United States, Congress. Senate. Committee on Foreign Relations. United States foreign policy. Study, no. 4, Washington: US Government Printing Office.

Itandala, A.B., 1996, 'Impact of one-party and multi-party politics on higher education in mainland Tanzania', *Tanzania Zamani* 1 (4): 10-26.

Kimambo, I. N., 1993, *Three Decades of Production of Historical Knowledge at Dar es Salaam*, Dar es Salaam: Dar es Salaam University Press.

Levy, L., 1971, 'The School of African Studies, UCT. Summary of the history of the School', collated from E. A. Walker, *The History of the South African College of Cape Town*, W. Ritchie, *The History of the South African College*, and other school records.

Mamdani, M., 1994, 'Introduction: The Quest for Academic Freedom', in M. Mamdani and M. Diouf, eds., *Academic Freedom in Africa*, Dakar: CODESRIA.

Mamdani, M., 1996, 'Centre of African Studies: Some Preliminary Thoughts', Seminar Paper, University of Cape Town, Centre of African Studies.

Mamdani, M., 1998, 'Is African Studies to be turned into the new home for Bantu education at UCT?', Seminar paper, University of Cape Town, Centre of African Studies.

Marks, S., 1985, 'The historiography of South Africa: Recent Developments', in B. Jewsiewicki and D.S. Newbury, eds., *African Historiographies: What History for which Africa?*, Beverly Hills; London: Sage Publications.

Martin, W.G., and M. O. West, 1999, 'Introduction: the rival Africas and paradigms of Africanists and Africans at home and abroad', in W. G. Martin and M. O. West, eds., *Out of One, Many Africas: Reconstructing the Study and Meaning of Africa*, Urbana: University of Illinois Press.

Maxwell, I.C.M., 1980, *Universities in Partnership: The Inter-University Council and the Growth of Higher Education in Developing Countries 1946-70*, Edinburgh: Scottish Academic.

McCracken, J., 1993, 'African History in British Universities: Past, Present and Future', *African Affairs* 92 (367): 239-253.

Meier, A. and E.M. Rudwick, 1986, *Black History and the Historical Profession, 1915-80, Blacks in the New World*, Urbana: University of Illinois Press.

Nwauwa, A.O., 1997, *Imperialism, Academe, and Nationalism: Britain and University Education for Africans, 1860-1960*, London: Frank Cass.

Oliver, R., 1995, 'African history: SOAS and beyond', in *The Emergence of African History at British Universities: An Autobiographical Approach*, edited by A.H.M. Kirk-Greene. Oxford: WorldView Publications.

Oliver, R., 1997, *In the Realms of Gold: Pioneering in African History*, London: Frank Cass.

Philips, C.H., 1967, *The School of Oriental & African Studies, University of London, 1917-1967: An Introduction*, London: University School of Oriental & African Studies.

Philips, C. H., 1995, *Beyond the Ivory Tower: The Autobiography of Sir Cyril Philips*, London: Radcliffe.

Ranger, T. O., 1969, *The Recovery of African Initiative in Tanzanian History. Inaugural Lecture Series, The University College, Dar es Salaam,* no. 2, Dar es Salaam: University College.

Ranger, T. O., 1976, 'Towards a Usable Past', in C. Fyfe, ed., *African Studies Since 1945*, Edinburgh: Centre of African Studies, University of Edinburgh.

Ranger, T. O., 1995, 'Concluding Remarks', in A. H. M. Kirk-Greene, ed., *The Emergence of African History at British Universities: An Autobiographical Approach*, Oxford: WorldView Publications.

Rowe, J. A., 1970, 'Major Themes in African History', in J. N. Paden and E. W. Soja, eds., *The African Experience, Vol. 1*, Evanston: Northwestern University Press.

Saunders, Christopher, 1988, *The Making of the South African Past: Major Historians on Race and Class*, Cape Town: David Philip.

Slater, H., 1985, 'Dar es Salaam and the post-nationalist historiography of Africa', in B. Jewsiewicki and D. S. Newbury, eds., *African Historiographies: What History for which Africa?*, Beverly Hills; London: Sage Publications.

Tadesse, Z., 1999, 'From Euphoria to Gloom? Navigating the murky waters of African academic institutions', in W. G. Martin and M. O. West, eds., *Out of One, many Africas: Reconstructing the Study and Meaning of Africa*, Urbana: University of Illinois Press.

Temu, A.J., and B. Swai, 1981, *Historians and Africanist History—A Critique: Post-Colonial Historiography Examined, Africa Series*, London: Zed.

Vansina, J., 1994, *Living with Africa*, Madison: University of Wisconsin Press.

Zeleza, P.T., 1997, *Manufacturing African Studies and Crises*, Dakar: CODESRIA.

Chapter 7

Writing and Teaching National History in Africa in an Era of Global History[1]

Toyin Falola

Their ambiguities notwithstanding, nation-states[2] are still alive and they remain, for political leaders, the media, and many analysts, the framework to understand political and economic realities. While the very notion of 'nation-state' may be controversial, even contested,[3] it remains the most common political mechanism to organize people into boundaries and governments, and history writing and teaching are partly formulated around it. For the powerful countries, the agenda of 'global history' is actually to retain their dominance, to build prestige around their location as the centres of the world, and to construct patriotism in such a way that their citizens see the advantages of birth and membership in a nation, such that migrants can be attacked and expelled when necessary. It is the weak nations that are being asked to adjust, to subordinate their national histories to the threatening agenda of a global world and a global history. While strong powers protect their economic and political interests and prevent migrants from entering, weak nations are being accused of reactionary and chauvinistic tendencies, fundamentalism, and excessive traditionalism.[4]

Global history is no more than a transitional narrative to globalisation. Strong advocates of global history and globalisation see the process of expanding capitalism, postmodernism, and post-industrialism as inevitable. Global civilisation, it is argued, will tear down the nation-state, reordering the nature of social institutions, production, and accumulation (see Ohmae 1990; Davis 1998; Sivanandan 1998; Harris 1998). Almost without any apology, one scholar gives us this 'preface' to the new orientation of global history:

> The 1990s is one of the great watershed decades in economic history. The postwar division of the world economy into the First, Second, and Third Worlds has ended. Not only has communism collapsed, but other ideologies of state-led development that were prevalent in the Third World for decades have fallen into disrepute. If the

> United States and the other industrial countries act with wisdom, they have a chance to consolidate a global capitalist world system, with profound benefits for both the rich and the poor countries (Sachs 1995: 50).

Global history may be triumphantly presented to weak nations as the end of national history, that is, the nation as the object of study. Global history, as a narrative of Western power and its expansion, provincialises history, turning the national history of one great power into the metanarrative of global history. National histories of Africa represent one of the powerful counters to the attempt to provincialise history. The very first task of writing and teaching national history in Africa is to understand the agenda of global history, the problems represented by the forces and pressures of globalisation, and the wisdom to understand that when the United States and other industrial countries 'act with wisdom,' it is not going to benefit rich and poor countries alike. World history has never seen such an ideology—intellectual, economic, or political—that benefits the rich and poor at the same time. African intellectuals are part of a 'globalised world,' as consumers of products and ideas. Their frameworks and universities benefit from national and global resources and ideas. The kind of connections we make, the preferences and choices we establish between national and global history may compel us to answer some of the many questions posed to us by Arjun Appadurai (2001) regarding our activism and pedagogy. In the quest to defend global history at the expense of the national, do we become agents of imperialism, the propagandists of capitalism? We cannot regard global history as an alternative to national history, only as a pressure. And as a pressure on national history, we have to understand the ideologies and agenda of global history and globalisation in order to meaningfully pursue the interests and concerns of national history. In withstanding the pressure, the aim is not to reject theories, ideas, and epistemologies that may facilitate our understanding of African issues irrespective of where they come from.

Nationalism is not dead either. Indeed, so-called internationalism has not undermined the power of so-called nationalism or even fundamentalism. The agenda imposed by a superpower is no more important than the one demanded by weak nation-states in the international arena. Global history, if its motive is to create a centre for the world, will only awaken nationalism that will make national history writing and research important to the so-called periphery. Africa had previously witnessed the attempt to impose a global (European-centred) history on its people, as part of the colonial project of imposing Western civilisation on so-called primitive people. The 'colonial library' that emerged ultimately failed, not because its creators were no longer alive to keep it going but because African nationalism was powerful enough to create alternative histories. Indeed, nationalism and the defence of national history and its identity have given me this conclusion to present: the study of the nationalist movements as well as the writings by nationalist leaders, in their non-elitist forms, remain the essential (and one can argue, timeless) aspects of African history. Whether it is Jomo Kenyatta and his culturalist-oriented writings, or Amilcar Cabral and the socialist orientation, or Kwame Nkrumah the Pan-Africanist, or Nelson Mandela and the anti-apartheid intellectuals, or a crowd of North African nationalists drawing on Islam (for example, Anwar Sadat of Egypt), all the issues they raised define what Africans will continue to live and struggle with in today's global era. Simply put, the core of the issues revolves around Africa's engagement with its indigenous past, with Western/Christian traditions, and with Arab/Islamic ones; in sum, with modernity (Langley 1979; Asante and Abarry 1996; Falola 2001). Global history is ultimately linked to globalisation; national history will respond by creating identities and nationalism to protect local interests and prevent the erasure of multiple (even different) voices.

If a valuable lesson is to be learned from the writings of these political pioneers, as well as intellectual leaders such as Wilmot Blyden, Anta Diop, and K.O. Dike, it is that there is no need to apologize for writing about national history in a particular way or manner. The goal of national history, as these pioneers saw it, was not to produce works to be consumed by outsiders or to seek global acceptability, but to see the nation and its people as the 'context' of study, and to give agency to Africans who had been denied a history. Procedures and universalist rules of writings were not necessarily questioned or ignored, but they wanted to write and teach in a way that history was connected with the concerns of the nation. Indeed, they accepted the notion of difference: that African history could be different in many ways from other histories or from how historians in other places defined and wrote African history. The pioneers faced the problems of 'global history' and imperialism, just as we face them today. They wanted to create the 'nation,' but we also face today the crisis of the nation-state in a global world. Africans have to cope with the crisis of the nation-state, the burden of inherited Western legacies, the turmoil of globalisation. We are not as far removed from the pioneers as we would like to think. Like the pioneers, we cannot relegate national history to the backwaters, and ask African students to know more about the United States than Africa. Some kinds of global history have a tendency to belittle African national histories, to undermine the significance of national identities, and even to pretend that other forms of identity within a nation constitute an obstacle to the spread of Western values. National history, when it becomes a mere appendage of global history defined in an imperialistic manner, becomes a tool to consolidate Western hegemony and imperialism.

History, like all forms of knowledge, is obviously not neutral. African historians are being asked to make hard choices, to balance the defence of Africa (and their countries) with those of global forces and history. If they defend Africa to an extreme, they become 'nativists' who lack a sense of proportion; if they extol global history to an extreme, they become 'xenophobic' (see Mkandawire 1997; Cvetkovich and Kellner 1997). Ideological options may be inevitable, but a starting point is to invest national history with its own dignity, and to deal with its contradictions without turning knowledge into an instrument of state repression.

The Past in the Present

Before anyone can complain about my having to run to the past to seek answers to the issues of the present, let me quickly say that Africa is not new to this global experience, to the vigorous attempts to erase the experiences of so-called local identities, sweeping the dust of the ethnic under the carpet of the national, and the national itself under the table of the universal. What was the slave trade if not a global trade, with Africa as part of the triangle in an evil commerce? Africans were exchanged for goods, notably objects of leisure and violence. We have a major topic already defined for us. Global history cannot marginalise the place of the trans-Atlantic slave trade and the African diaspora, which have to be studied on their own right and in comparisons with other diasporas, forced or voluntary. Compared to other diasporas and global migrations, for instance of Europeans to the New World, the trans-Atlantic slave trade still remains the least studied, not to mention our weak knowledge of the Indian diaspora to Africa, the Caribbean, and Southeast Asia.

Globalisation is not new. The slave trade is but one of many of its manifestations. And as the trans-Atlantic slave trade shows, globalisation is not limited to the traffic in goods, but also in ideas. The idea of racism circulated more widely in the Western world, with Africans regarded and treated as the most inferior of all races. The ideas have taken firm root, and national history in the era of global history must confront it. Modern globalisation tends to disguise the idea of race in the notion of cultural inferiority, marketing so-called universalist cultures and values as superior to indigenous ones. The world might have changed since the nineteenth century, but the perceptions of Africa remain.

'We believe that the Negro people as a race,' wrote Du Bois in 1897 as the first article of the racial creed that he proposed in *The Conservation of Races,* 'have a contribution to make to civilization and humanity which no other race can make.' This was a confident statement made against the background of racism in the late nineteenth century. But over a hundred years later, even if the tone and tenor have changed, Africans are being challenged to justify their humanity and existence. History cannot survive without responding to the challenge. Du Bois and others pioneered an approach which academic scholars popularised after the Second World War: nationalist historiographies. The idea then, one which should not be abandoned even now, is to interpret the achievements of the past. Without this approach, knowledge about the great kingdoms, the vibrant political institutions, and the enduring economies would never have been known. If the 'colonial library' wanted to suppress the knowledge about Zimbabwe, nationalist historiography rescued it.

Nationalist historiography links Africa's present to its past, the past existing in the memory of the present, as the present lays the foundation for the future. National history, in the conception of nationalist historiography, becomes a sort of 'political charter' linking history with the nation, the nation with nationalism. We cannot forget that the 'nationalist historians' were themselves the creation of nationalist movements. In defining themselves and their careers, national history was paramount:

they would decolonise history and decolonise the minds of their students. If politicians were afraid of history, for fear that it could promote the politics of ethnicity, nationalist historians wanted to use history in the service of nationalism, according pride to their people, demonstrating their rich heritage, showing that they once had capable leaders who managed complex societies, and that their people had the skills and talents to create better postcolonial nations. While the nationalist historians were elite who lived in two worlds—the modernising/Western and the indigenous/local—they were not always able to resolve the tensions of the culture divide. However, what they clearly understood was the need to build strong national histories, even if the components of change would be Western, as in the creation of schools, hospitals, factories, or even of their own jobs with the privileges enjoyed by colonial officers. In the words of Professor J. F. Ade Ajayi, one of the pioneers:

> When foreign learning began to be grounded on oral culture, it became enriched, energized and creative. That was the secret of Ibadan's innovations not only in African Studies, History, Psychiatry, etc. but in the ethos of the whole university as an institution of higher education. It was also the secret of the literary success of such giants as Soyinka and Achebe, brought up on European literature but decided to be creative and tell Africa's story in their own way, even in the medium of English (cited in Falola 2000: 401; see also Falola 2002; forthcoming).

This 'secret' should become open enough to guide the mission of national history in the age of global history: traditions, localism, communities, ruralism, indigenous knowledge should inform what we do against the background of external ideas and 'universal' methodologies and approaches. For example, even to those who regard nationalist historiography as elitist or obsolete, the stress on 'oral culture' remains valid.

The writing and research on national history reflects the conflicted minds of the intellectuals: should they stress aspects of globalisation and modernisation? Should they defend the ethnic origins and the aspirations of their local constituencies? As elites, have they become removed from the reality on the ground, using the privileges of Western education to distance themselves from the masses? National history, like the nation itself, was in the process of formation. Colonially created countries are artificial, and history writing and teaching is trying to 'homogenise' disparate identities. National consciousness is in the process of formation, and the tensions are captured in various writings. Even then, the promotion of national consciousness, supported by nationalist historiography, has not stopped the rise of ethnic fundamentalism and struggles leading to wars in many countries. In the case of Nigeria, many defenders of the nation in the 1950s supported secession in the 1960s. And in spite of the commitment of many to the idea of Nigerian national history, none of the pioneers was able to write a definitive single-volume history of the country.

'Whose history?' and 'whose nation?' become two of the questions that have complicated nationalist historiographies as they address national history with an excessive focus on kings, queens, merchants and states. Both will continue to face us even today, as we factor into national history the forces of class, ethnicity and culture. As professors struggle for power within and outside the universities, they, like the politicians, give politics a primacy that may fragment the very nation they seek to protect. National and 'tribal' histories can become the handmaidens of politics for an elite in search of wealth and power. What nationalist history in Africa has carried too far is not the kind of nationalism that produced racism or ethnocentrism in the West. Indeed, one could argue that most African countries have yet to even generate consensus on national histories that could build the platform for patriotism or racism. It is also clear that they have yet to succeed in using history to create national pride. As my students at the University of Ife in Nigeria asked me: 'Why should we care about the Oyo empire if our future is bleak?' On the contrary, nationalist historiography is propelled by nationalism rather than the documentation and theorisation of nationalism as an ideology. And when independence was attained, as the case of Nigeria shows, many scholars abandoned national history (and its advocacy) in preference for 'ethnic histories.' Many also drew from various perspectives of the day (modernisation, dependency, and Marxism) to offer various devastating critiques of the state. The extreme critique of the nation, rather than its defence, became a passion. A critic is not the enemy of the nation or of national history, even if political dictators think otherwise.

The Imperatives of Development

In the search for relevance, history writing and teaching are gradually being forced to demonstrate their 'practicalness'. Without showing how it is connected to development, history becomes criticised as one of the most irrelevant disciplines in the humanities. Even students ask their teachers what they are supposed to do with the degrees and the relevance of the topics they teach them. Globalisation and global history cannot but make the demand for relevance more aggressive, more salient. African countries are now being forced to deal with globalisation, not necessarily on their own terms. Elements of imperialism are at work, without gun boat diplomacy or the use of Gatling and Maxim guns. The relations among states are more intense, the scope more broad. Markets and popular cultures spread rapidly, threatening and displacing traditional, aristocratic and Islamic cultures.

As values spread, mainly from the West to Africa, in ways reminiscent of the colonial era, many people begin to talk of the end of the boundaries of nations. Globalisation is in part about the interactions of nations and the changes that come with them (see Griffin and Khan 1992). History writing and teaching must pay attention to its impact on Africa, and confront its negative aspects just as cultural nationalists did in the first half of the twentieth century. If globalisation intends to narrow the distance between nations, we are at a loss in understanding what roles Africa is allowed to take and how these are different from the exploitative colonial arrangement. No one is denying that Africa needs all the gains of modernity, but historians must measure the cost. For instance, what is the impact of migration and the brain drain on the overall development of the continent? Is African labour not being exploited? It is clear that the use of labour is not always positive to Africa's needs (see Mittelman 1995).

Globalisation, like imperialism, supports a development ideology. The orthodoxy which emerged from colonialism is that of 'free enterprise'; that of globalisation is the same. The thread is exploitative capitalism. This is a subject for us. When Africa's contact deepened with the West during the colonial phase, so too did the economy become organised around exportable items. Globalisation has enhanced communication flows, and information technologies have become so widespread that one can now use a cell phone from a remote village in Nigeria to speak with someone in New York. Physical boundaries are not disappearing, but the distances in space appear to shrink with the use of the telephone, fax, and computers. In its public face, globalisation sells itself as capitalism; in its hidden face, it may be nothing more than imperialism. One of our goals should be to evaluate the impact of developmental ideologies on national history. Neoliberalism calls on African countries to see the 'market' as the centre of economy, by privatising and transferring land from thousands of peasants to a handful of investors. Historians will be the first to show the failure of centralised state economies, of previous agendas of socialism and economic nationalism. But we also have data to expose the limitations of neoliberalism, the dangers of reducing peasants to economic agents with little political franchise. Capitalism wants to empower the market by expropriating the principal agents of production, and, at the same time, hopes that there will be peace and order in the land.

The ideology and orthodoxy of development will inevitably force us to pose serious questions on the impact of the West on Africa, similar to the inconclusive debates on the agency of colonialism in Africa. Just as the colonial officers regarded colonialism as the positive agency of change, advocates of globalisation use similar words to paint a rosy picture for Africa if it embeds itself in a global world. How far more should it be embedded, having been incorporated into the world economy since the fifteenth century? To the International Monetary Fund and the World Bank, Africa should seek greater incorporation. The failed Structural Adjustment Programmes are nothing but part of this incorporationist ideology, with the World Bank (1996) arguing that the end results will bring massive upliftment to the majority of the African population. Many of the gains of a globalised world have been mentioned, in part to keep attracting Africa to it: greater flows of goods and ideas, an integrated financial world, and better trade. The World Trade Organisation, in spite of many wide-scale demonstrations against it, continues to sell the idea of a unified world, even in the face of rising poverty in Africa.

Although not always in the Marxist tradition of the 1950s and 1960s, scholars of the radical persuasion see little but misery in globalisation, as they argue that Africa will see woes, inequities, domination, marginalisation, and underdevelopment (See Zeltzer 2000; Comaroff and Comaroff 2000; Ghai 1992; Mittelman 1994; Roy 1997; for a more radical critique of globalisation see Ake 1995; Amin 1997).

Global history, presented in the image of Structural Adjustment Programmes becomes in part a discussion of the expansion of economic liberalisation and privatisation, in ways similar to the expansion of the West in the late nineteenth century. The metaphors and imageries of Western expansion sound familiar: in the nineteenth century, it was against the background of a so-called Dark Continent; in the post-SAP era, of a repressive, backward continent. If the idea of 'progress' dominated discourse in the colonial era, for post-SAP Africa the themes revolve around democracy, human rights, and human dignity. To be sure, all these topics are important, but one of the tasks of national history is to deconstruct them, domesticating terminologies and applying them within specific contexts and historical milieu.

Neoliberalism is powerful, more so as it is being sponsored by external powerful forces in Africa in a way that is not just reshaping the economy but also intellectual ideologies. A number of practical issues also enter the academy to shape historical knowledge. As the number and power of non-governmental organisations to express opposition have grown so too have contemporary national histories sought to include topics on civil society. We are being forced to evaluate the role of Africa and its component states in a global system.

Africa lacks the power to curb the excesses of capitalism and its so-called 'economic liberty' that may affect the continent in a less than compassionate manner. Those who live by the market may die by the market. The responsibility of historians may be to explore the ways to prevent Africa from dying with the market as defined and imposed by globalization and imperialist domination. Many of our predecessors have devoted time and energy to seeking answers that we can continue to learn from and improve upon. The globalising tendencies of colonialism generated dissent; so too is contemporary globalisation creating its own critics all over the world (see for instance Cerny 1997). While some see the global trends as novel and distinct, there are those who regard it as a phase that will soon pass (compare and contrast the work of Held, notably Held 1995; Held and Hazel 1992; Held et al., 1999). Global history can capture the contradictions and dysfunctionality in the world system, talking about consensus and contests. The elements of fad and fashion in global history should not blind us into seeing the reality that faces Africa.

Specifics and Suggestions[5]

Some have denied the possibility of national history in an era of globalisation and global history. Some others think that writing about national history in the era of globalisation should be characterized as a paradox. To acknowledge the existence of globalisation, as some believe, is to grow beyond the boundaries and limitations of national history into a trans-national approach (see Featherstone 1990; Bhabha 1990; Dirlik et al. 2000). Nationalist frameworks are regarded as either weak or untenable in the face of 'transnational formation,' to use the phrase by Paul Gilroy (1993: ix). My own response is to pose just one question: where will the African voice be located? We have seen how a number of so-called global histories erase African voices. National histories may not be able to escape from the context of globalisation, as nations deal with the impact of received ideas. To cite some cultural studies as examples, David Coplan's (1985) study on South African music, Cole (2001) on concert party, and Savishinsky (1994) on reggae in West Africa outline how ideas from other parts of the world travel to Africa to popularise musical genres and shape popular cultures. Even in the spread of ideas, we see globalisation at work, but we also see local creativity, intelligent adaptations, and great talents that all validate the power of national history.

I am aware that not all national histories can be clearly defined. Even if it could be defined, national history can generate a consensus only for a limited time in history, as in the case of Africa during the years of decolonisation. Without hegemonic elites in power, it is always difficult to construct a consensus. The lack of a consensus does not mean that there is no national history, only that it is a contested one. I am also aware that generalisations that apply to all African countries may carry some risks, as countries do differ of course from one another. Nigeria and South Africa are not the same, even if they have to deal with a number of common problems such as the eradication of poverty and bridging the gap between the poor and the rich. Yoruba ethnicity and identity are not necessarily the same as those of the Zulu, and the consequences they produce may also differ. The differences underscore the importance of national history, providing historians with the opportunity to consider contexts and specific histories as they relate to various localities and countries.

The dangers of global history to Africa are clear to see. Implicit in the idea is that of a unified world, or what some call a unipolar world. Global history has been presented as the rise of Western civilisation, and now as the hegemony of the United States. Africa becomes the distant province in the construction of the centre of a unipolar world. National histories cannot see their nations and peoples as mere provincial elements and second-class citizens. Rather, Africa has to be the very centre of history while others, in spite of their dominance, are put at the margins. When Europeans tried this in the colonial era, consigning Africa to the irrelevant margins of history, African nationalist historians put Africa at the centre, exploring the power of resistance and nationalism. As we follow in the impressive footpaths of the pioneers, our own challenge is to use the challenges offered by economic development and political instability to combat the perils of global history. The current unipolar world should be treated in the same way that nationalist politicians and historians treated the colonial world order: to be resisted for its imperialistic combativeness. Global history, in its orthodoxy of liberalisation, may not be totally different from the totalitarian ideologies of colonialism. It is the very orthodoxy of liberalisation that may produce insurgent scholars who see the need to defend the nation and its history.

We must not only insist on the insertion of African voices, but we must empower national history such that historians are able to contribute to the gargantuan project of nation building. I have indicated the relative timelessness of the writings of independence leaders such as Leopold Senghor, Amilcar Cabral, Nelson Mandela,

Kwame Nkrumah and others, as well as those leaders involved in the non-aligned movement. Practical and intellectual efforts to find paths between capitalism and communism continue to have resonances with the current era in dealing with Africa's 'triple heritage': indigenous, Arab/Muslim, European/Christian. These political and intellectual leaders saw in national history an agency of liberation, of decolonisation: history became an 'ideology' to remake the nation.

While one sleeps, global economy and culture are at work. Not only do we have to analyse how globalisation works, but also its outcome on states and societies in Africa. During the nineteenth century and for most of the colonial era, African scholars and the educated elite wondered about the impact of the European encounter on African cultures. Today, we have to address issues around culture and capitalism, the extent to which they impact on national histories. The fear is that a unified culture will marginalise Africa, rather than empower it, turning its citizens into consumers of imported items. Imported goods and ideas will merge to give supremacy to capitalism and a political order defined largely in Western terms. African cultures that fail to succumb become condemned as obstacles in the way of constructing a grand narrative of global history.

We cannot escape the challenges posed by nation building. Responses to global history constitute part of this challenge, as well as the established interests in understanding sources of national division, ethnicity, political instability and other problems. Our predecessors wanted to use history to build pride because their peoples and institutions were condemned by Europeans. They deconstructed the colonial library. The present mission is to engage the postcolonial situations and empower the nations with the knowledge to transform them. Our predecessors wanted to demonstrate that they could overcome the limitations of the artificial nations created for them by colonial powers (they wrote on precolonial groups and nations to show relations and contacts); we have to show that we can work with and overcome the limitations imposed by globalisation as we use the understanding of the present to write about the past. Our predecessors, imbued with nationalism, sought an end to colonial domination; we have to extend their agenda into the task of completing the quest for autonomy, decolonisation, and development. As our predecessors sought to empower national history, they did so with a recognition of the crucial role of continentalism; we have to continue with the goal in locating national history within regional and continental histories, seeking the means to forge collective development, regional unity, and the strengthening of Africa in world politics.

Either to benefit from the products and processes of globalisation or to resist the fragmentation of their societies and cultures, national history will still be dominated by resistance. People and organisations will pressure their countries and governments to do more for them, as they seek access to modern goods and travel abroad for opportunities. We have to understand resistance and violence as they shape contemporary realities and define the notions of power and democracy. The pressure for democracy may actually promote religious and ethnic fundamentalism, as political actors use religion and ethnicity to organise to gain power or to resist local and global powers. Human rights, freedom, and democracy will all be linked in resistance and violence. The activities of non-governmental organisations continue to multiply and to affect new areas dealing with the environment, prison reforms, changes to land tenure systems, and demands for the rights of children and women. NGOs may be responding to global politics, but as they do, the pressure on the nations is greater than on external powers. Research and teaching national history have to deal with the frontiers of resistance and violence, symbolised by the activities of NGOs, youth movements, paramilitary and ethnic organisations, and religious fundamentalism.

African intellectuals, as researchers and teachers, are not always objective actors in the analysis of national and global histories. Their colleagues elsewhere have been implicated in the rise of totalitarian regimes, fascism, genocide, apartheid, and Eurocentricism, to mention some obvious ones. A good number of Western intellectuals are part of the marketing of imperialism and capitalism, disguised as global history, to Africa. If globalisation worships the market, African scholars may have to turn to the gods of nationalism and development to write on national history.

As scholars pursue research on national history, they are bound to confront other forms of pressure: local histories, especially where locality is also the basis of forming political units; and ethnic histories, significant in almost all plural societies. Universities are sometimes the creation of ethnic forces, with scholars championing the causes of particular ethnic groups, even using scholarship to promote ethnic interests in ways that may undermine the national. There are also the demands of regional histories, as each country is also part of a region that may seek to unite and benefit from greater interactions. And the pursuit of pan-African aspirations also has to be factored into the presentation of national history. What all these competing forces suggest is that national history is an ongoing dynamic construction with competing agendas and pressures. A unified structure is not always easy to accomplish, as the work of Benedict Anderson (1991) suggests. National history should not be interpreted as the history of the political class and the state it manages. The nation-state remains a powerful political idea, leaving us with little choice other than to analyse the role of the state. Since we are aware of the divisions in society, national history has to include the discussions of various loyalties and identities within a nation, the means to forge inter-group relations, the understanding of conflicts, relationships between tiers of government, and the kinds of state that may work for Africa.

If I were to be pinned down to be more specific, to offer a sort of a 'syllabus' for classroom use, I would provide the following as a list. We have to keep decolonising African historiography, to turn to indigenous creativity and ideas, to empower the marginalised voices, to shed light on the tremendous energy and success represented by popular cultures, market women, craft workers, and local cultivators, among others. Oral history should not be abandoned in the face of global history.

Students and researchers must contribute to our understanding of a variety of topics: migration flows within Africa and nation-states; regional conflicts; ethnic and religious divisions; inter- and intra-national relations within Africa; development and modernisation; processes of democratisation and participatory practices; neoliberal reforms; cultural transformations; market and economic networks; the Cold War and its aftermath; ecological history and sustainable development; and mass communication. All these topics can be framed as 'national history.' National history—rather than global history—can be the centre of the curriculum, with the goal of understanding a country's experience within a regional and continental framework and with other courses to compare and contrast experiences in a global world. National history does not mean that African or regional histories are ignored, or that global experiences are abandoned. Neither should national history ignore broad historical concepts and theories to understand big issues and transnational ideas, lest it become merely descriptive. National history must understand global forces. When students are exposed to global history, the terms may be explicit: to increase their knowledge of global events and their implications on their countries and the continent; to foster global consciousness but without losing freedom and autonomy; and to understand relationships between and among peoples.[6]

In connecting national history to 'global history,' we have to study the relative power of each country (and the continent) in relation to other continents, in particular the degree of autonomy they enjoy with regard to political and economic decisions. The point about autonomy is important if one of the transformations caused by globalisation is to marginalise weak states. Issues around economic development are still the primary concerns in Africa. Thus, we have to remain interested in national financial institutions and the extent to which pressures are mounted on them by multinational companies, the World Trade Organisation, the World Bank, and the IMF. Furthermore, it is crucial to understand the impact of the spread of transnational production and the use of African labour. International politics and national politics remain connected and important. We cannot fail to understand the role of global financial houses, the extent to which agencies of globalisation (such as the WTO) also serve as the agencies of imperialism. New information technologies stand to benefit Africa, and the potential to build archives, using resources drawn from various sources and countries, as well as the possibility to broaden knowledge and scholarship are all important. New technologies will assist us to access and present data in more creative ways, but Africa cannot just be on the receiving end of knowledge production. Ideas have to circulate in a global world, such that all countries can benefit. Historians must contribute to the study of wealth transfer. Goods and services now travel faster, thanks to improved communication and information networks. We should teach and research international flows of goods and services, not just to accumulate knowledge but to prepare the minds of students for greater understanding of international political economy. The various topics and issues connect national history to regional and continental histories, as well as to global history without losing focus, without pushing national history to an insignificant margin.

Still on specificity, and to address the concerns of those who demand chronologies while not ignoring themes, the topics above (as well as others) can be divided into three broad areas:

1. *Colonialism* in the context of state/society relations; social relations and class formation; Western education, world religions and elite formation; exploitation and political economy; formation of ethnicities; social change and social stratification; formal politics; formal economy and gender relations; etc. Contrasts are to be provided with precolonial formations in order to question the motives of the colonisers regarding change, race, civilisation, and the constitution of knowledge. One agenda is to see the values of old that are recoverable in the pursuit of nation building and identity. Old kingdoms cannot be recreated, but the values of kingship may be relevant to the understanding of contemporary cultures of participatory government, rule of law, and accountability. Colonial rule established the foundation of contemporary Africa: the origins of the boundaries of modern countries; the sources of ethnicity and wars; the origins of autocratic power; the source of economic dependence on external power and the creation of mono-crop economies; the establishment of police and armies as instruments of coercion and state autocracy; and the creation of a civil service that is prone to corruption.

2. *Decolonisation and Nationalism.* The emergence of the neocolonial state; modern state formation/structures of society; communal identities, ethnicity, and class formation; gender and generation. As the groundwork for the end of colonial rule was being laid, so too was that of inter-ethnic rivalries, contests over boundaries, neocolonial exploitation, and new forms of nationalism and identities that overwhelm the colonially created nation-states. Inheriting colonial territories became much easier than building on them; the sovereignty that came with independence is weak; the state itself is plastic. Decolonisation was often achieved at the expense of cross-border ties, and the relationships between people forged on the basis of pan-Africanism gradually weakened. The dismantling of the colonial state presented national history with a host of new challenges: Where is the nationalism to sustain the new nation? What nationalism does the new nation embody? Who embodies the 'nationality' of the nation that has no 'father', 'hero', mobilisational ideology, or popular political party? How should we characterise the postcolonial state? Who has the legitimacy and credibility to govern and what are the sources? Which elite (Islamic, traditional, Western educated) should control power and who should be defined as 'national'? The renaming of the colonial state as postcolonial says very little in terms of development and stability.

3. *The Postcolonial State and Society:*

(a) State disintegration and collapse—the process whereby states can no longer provide services and security. How can similar situations be prevented elsewhere? Why are some states stable and others not? Answers involve both the study of specific cases in detail, and comparative works of various countries (for example, Sudan vs Liberia, Congo vs Malawi, Ghana vs Gambia). Trends, patterns and warning signs of problems even in stable countries need to be studied/monitored. For instance, what is the future of Algeria and Nigeria against the background of their past history and present politics? To what extent can the political model of South Africa ensure stability and economic justice? Ethnic groups keep consolidating their identities in many countries, but it is clear that each ethnic group cannot constitute a political entity with the sovereignty of a 'country'. Similarly, there are inter-ethnic rivalries that create their own problems, usually less studied. Historians have to keep understanding the relationship between ethnicity and nationality and to join in the debates on the creation of a workable political nationality. Can Africa create a 'civic identity' in place of the ethnic?

(b) Statism and neo-patrimonialism, and how they affect the rule of law, accountability, autocracy, prebendalism and economic management. The nature of the patron-client system in a country is necessary to understand the behaviour and activities of members of the political class and warlords. Ethnic conflicts and democracy, although contradictory, remain two ongoing phenomena. Statism has imposed two limits on the growth of the nation: the political system is constricted, as those in power use violence to curb opposition; and no mechanism is in place to placate political losers, or find avenues to incorporate them into power.

(c) The crisis of the modern African state, in terms of the institutions of governance, leadership, popular cultures, and economic management. Why is the state, a project of development, either failed or not done well? Where citizens regard the state as 'irrelevant,' how do they organise access to schools, jobs, hospitals and other services? How can loyalty to a government be created? Citizens continue to seek the better management of state, especially as many lack jobs or opportunities for improvement. The resources available to sustain a system of political patronage continue to diminish, creating problems for those in power. If many countries are not free of external controls and are plagued by ethnic crises, to what extent are they 'sovereign' and 'independent'?

(d) The crisis of economic production. Cases of economic stagnation are many, and rural areas and poor farmers have been devastated by failed policies and lack of development. Income inequality is a serious problem, and the gap between the rich and poor keeps widening. We have to sustain attention on economic history. As countries seek to maximise economic opportunities and develop technologies, governments and leading state officers may see a limited need for history. Indeed, some African governments see the teaching and writing of national history (or any history for that matter) as useless because they relate education strictly to jobs and development. History students, too, are caught in the trap, asking what their contributions to economic production are. Thus, as we expose the crises of economic production, we also have to create a role for national history in the production of knowledge and skills.

(e) The rise of neoliberalism. We have to teach and research its various challenges to each country in particular and Africa in general. Students are bound to pose questions relating to its opportunities and threat. If degrees are supposed to be relevant according to some kind of market value, History students may seek the appreciation of their university diplomas along the narrow lines defined by neoliberalism. With the dominance of Western science and technology, popular culture and the market, young African students will continue to demand relevance. To what extent is capitalism working, and to whose interest? By and large, capitalism has promoted the development of a parasitic cabal, closing the door to genuine investors who lack access to state power.

(f) The African state and the international system: a history of foreign relations; analysis of specific issues such as the African states and the Cold War; pan-Africanism and the politics of African Unity; etc. As the world changes, and as the forces of globalisation become stronger, Africa and its various countries are forced to adjust. But many cases of adjustments are not all that new—national history has had to deal before with the marginal position of African countries in the world economy and politics. Historians have to capture the relations between countries. Without disparaging knowledge from other lands, we can engage in global history 'from below', focussing on the suppressed history of resistance from sailors, slaves, market women, etc., and other forms of resistance that took place in the context of global traffic and therefore involved numerous cultural and political collaborations and borrowing. I cannot deny the possibilities of 'global history from below' (see Linebaugh and Rediker 2000).

(g) The African state and international political economy. The role still assigned to Africa is to produce raw materials for Western countries, an economic structure created by colonialism. Competitive advantages based on technology and the production and dissemination of knowledge exclude Africa. Even the advantages derivable from agriculture continue to be weakened with Africa's inability to control prices and quantities of supply, to stop Western countries from offering protection and subsidies to their farmers, and offering food and textiles cheaper than those obtained from Africa. Such products as rice and used clothes dumped on Africa can undermine local production.

(h) The African state and the international system in the global era: post-contain-ment and the rise of globalism; multilateralism, bilateralism; national security; conflict resolution; democratisation; democracy and finance capital; democracy and development; the limits of democracy; etc. Globalisation is about the im-position of power and hegemonic order on various countries, the integration of African countries into world economies and power in ways that weaken them. Historians have to seek the ways to present national history in 'a world made up of fragments, of floating signs, of open texts, of flexible economies and ever moving meanings' (Mbembe 1998: 5).

(i) The marginality of African states in the global era. Marginality does not mean that nations are not drawn into a global world, only that they lack power as members and that integration does not bring wealth but poverty. What gains accrue to these countries, and how can they minimise the flow of wealth to developed nations? What does the spread of 'global cultures' mean to various religious and ethnic identities?

(j) Migration and Diaspora as aspects of the impact of globalisation. Do African migrants play any crucial role as intermediaries for various neoliberal schemes? This is certainly true for migrants such as Indians in the United States. Is there any relation between the challenges of African national histories and diaspora studies that has been dominated by non-African scholars?

(k) New global themes in the twenty-first century: internal and global economic exploitation; demography: the resilience of African societies against the back-ground of chaotic economies and politics; creativity and popular culture, in spite of political and economic constraints; migration and identities; cultural alienation and cultural choices; class formation; gender relations; ethnicities; religious fundamentalism; environment and ecology; science and technology; pandemics; communication and information; regionalism and cross-border economy and politics; etc. Historians have to remain interested in social move-ments, religious and ethnic identities, resistance and nationalism, as these are the places to see how the people and their leaders respond to the challenges of development, power, initiatives for local autonomy, and responses to globalisation and the messages from global history. The politics of survival (as a nation and people, and against state authoritarianism and the grip of global capitalism) will be the summary of teaching and writing about national history in Africa in the age of global history.

Notes

1. This essay was made possible by the kind invitation of the Department of History, University of Cape Town, South Africa. I cannot thank enough the coordination efforts of Professor Howard Phillips in arranging the trip, and facilitating other arrangements. The topic was

suggested by the Department. I received generous comments from Dr Joel Tishken of Columbus State University, Georgia, USA.

2. Nationalism, nationality, ethnicity, and other ambiguous terms have complicated the definition of the 'nation state'. In the context of this essay, nation-state refers to a sovereign 'state' with a government presiding over a 'country' with boundaries recognised by other countries and international law. National history refers to studies on the 'nation state' and its component elements as in, for example, the history of South Africa, the history of the United States, or the history of Germany.

3. Phil White, 'The Future of the "Nation State"', unpublished paper. Cited with permission. White advocates the abandonment of 'nation state' as a term on the basis of three reasons: 'First, its assumption that each of the world's sovereign governments includes peoples of only one ethnic group does not accord with the reality that ethnic mixes exist in nearly all of them. Second, if widely implemented the idea would surely exacerbate international animosities. Third, by creating an enormous number of new governments focused on ethnic concerns it would worsen the already critical difficulty of securing international cooperation to address a host of world problems.' He uses 'nation state' interchangeably with ethnicity and nationality, and calls for a nameless alternative, the 'creation of civic or political/territorial nationalities in which the government seeks to serve the interests of ALL people in its territory without regard to ethnicity'.

4. To be sure, not all the teachers and texts of 'world history' preserve the Western narrative, an approach which treats global history as Western civilisation 'plus' a few other places, with Africa dismissed in a few pages.

5. I have, more or less, treated writing and teaching history as facing similar challenges, although I have made some comments about the attitudes of students and provide a long section on the syllabus. Another distinction that can be made is the evolving role or possibilities for history at an undergraduate survey level versus at the graduate research level.

6. Space does not permit an elaboration of the various perspectives and texts on 'World History'. There are those who use World History as an academic tool to project Western dominance. One common example of the preservation of Western narrative is the texts on Western Civilisations, with a few pages devoted to the conquest of Africa. See, for instance, Robin W. Winks et al., (1995a; 1995b). Alternatives ideas and approaches exist, with some focussing on themes and comparative ideas, drawing case studies from different parts of the world. On this approach, see, for instance, Jerry H. Bentley and Herbert F. Zeigler (1999).

References

Ake, C., 1995, 'The New World Order: A View from Africa', in H. Hans-Henrick and G. Sørenson, eds., *Whose World Order: Uneven Globalisation and the End of the Cold War*, Boulder, CO: Westview, 19-42.

Amin, S., 1997, *Capitalism in the Age of Globalisation*, London: Zed.

Anderson, B., 1991, *Imagined Communities: Reflections on the Origins and Spread of Nationalism*, New York: Verso.

Appadurai, A., 2001, 'Grassroots Globalization and the Research Imagination', in A. Appadurai, ed., *Globalization*, Durham: Duke University Press, 1-21.

Asante, M. K. and A. S. Abarry, eds., 1996, *African Intellectual Heritage: A Book of Sources*, Philadelphia: Temple University Press.

Bentley, J. H. and H. F. Zeigler, 1999, *Traditions and Encounters: A Global Perspectives on the Past*, Boston: McGraw Hill.

Bhabha, H., ed., 1990, *Nation and Narration*, London and New York: Routledge.

Cerny, P., 1997, 'Paradoxes of the Competition State: The Dynamics of Political Globalization', *Government and Opposition* 32 (1): 251-274.

Cole, C. M., 2001, *Ghana's Concert Party Theatre,*. Bloomington, IN: Indiana University Press.

Comaroff, J. and Comaroff, J.L., 2000, 'Millennial Capitalism: First Thoughts on a Second Coming', *Public Culture* 12 (2): 91-343.

Coplan, D., 1985, *In Township Tonight!: South Africa's Black City Music and Theatre*, London: Longman.

Cvetkovich, A. and D. Kellner, eds., 1997, *Articulating the Global and the Local*, Boulder, CO.: Westview.

Davis, J., 1998, 'Rethinking Globalization', *Race and Class* 40 (2/3): 37-48.

Dirlik, A., V. Bahl, and P. Gran, eds., 2000, *History after the Three Worlds: Post-Eurocentric Historiographies*, Lanham, MD: Rowman & Littlefield.

Falola, T., ed., 2000, *Tradition and Change in Africa: The Essays of J. F. Ade Ajayi*, Trenton, NJ: Africa World Press.

Falola, T., 2001, *Nationalism and African Intellectuals*, Rochester, NY: Rochester University Press.

Falola, T., ed., 2002, *The Challenges of History and Leadership in Africa: The Essays of Bethwell Allan Ogot*, Trenton, NJ: Africa World Press.

Falola, T., ed., Forthcoming, *Africa in the Twentieth Century: The Adu Boahen Reader*, Trenton, NJ: Africa World Press.

Featherstone, M., ed., 1990, *Global Culture: Nationalism, Globalisation, and Modernity*, London: Sage Publications.

Ghai, D., 1992, 'Structural Adjustment, Global Integration and Social Democracy', Geneva: UNRISD Discussion Paper.

Gilroy, P., 1993, *The Black Atlantic: Modernity and Double Consciousness*, Cambridge: Harvard University Press.

Griffin, K. and Khan K., 1992, *Globalization in the Developing World: An Essay on the International Dimension of Development in the Post-Cold War Era*, Geneva: UNRISD.

Harris, J., 1998, 'Globalization and the Technological Transformation of Capitalism', *Race and Class* 40 (2/3): 21-35.

Held, D., 1995, *Democracy and the Global Order: From the Modern State to Cosmopolitan Governance*, Cambridge: Polity.

Held, D. and J. Hazel, 1992, *Dispelling the Myth of Globalization: The Case for Regionalism*, New York: Praeger.

Held, D., A. McGrew, D. Goldblatt, and J. Perraton, eds., 1999, *Global Transformations: Politics, Economics and Culture*, Cambridge: Polity.

Langley, J. A., 1979, *Ideologies of Liberation in Black Africa, 1856-1970: Documents on Modern Political Thought from Colonial Times to the Present*, London: Rex Collins.

Linebaugh, P. and M. Rediker, 2000, *The Many-Headed Hydra: The Hidden History of the Revolutionary Atlantic*, Boston: Beacon Press.

Mbembe, A., 1998, 'Editorial', *CODESRIA Bulletin* 3&4: 5.

Mittelman, J., 1994, 'The Globalization Challenge: Surviving at the Margins', *Third World Quarterly* 15 (3): 427-43.

Mittleman, J., 1995, 'Rethinking the International Division of Labour in the Context of Globalization', *Third World Quarterly* 16 (2): 273-96.

Mkandawire, T., 1997, 'Globalization and Africa's Unfinished Agenda', *Macalaster International* 7: 71-107.

Ohmae, K., 1990, *The Borderless World: Power and Strategy in the Interlinked Economy*, New York: Harper Business.

Roy, A., 1997, 'Imperialist Globalization and Labor', *Revolutionary Democracy*, 3, 2, September, Available at: http://revolutionarydemocracy.org/rdv3n2/index.htm

Sachs, J. D., 1995, 'Consolidating Capitalism', *Foreign Affairs* 98 (Spring): 50-64.

Savishinksy, N. J., 1994, 'Rastafari in the Promised Land: The Spread of a Jamaican Socioreligious Movement Among the Youth of West Africa', *African Studies Review* 37 (3): 19-50.

Sivanandan, A., 1998, 'Globalism and the Left', *Race and Class* 40 (2/3): 5-19.

Winks, R.W.C. Brinton, J. B. Christopher and R. L. Wolffe, 1995a, *A History of Western Civilizations, Vol. 1, Prehistory to 1715*, Ninth Edition, New York: Prentice Hall.

Winks, R. W., C. Brinton, J. B. Christopher, and R. L. Wolffe, 1995b, *A History of Western Civilizations, Vol. 2, 1614 to the Present*. Ninth Edition, New York: Prentice Hall.

World Bank, 1996, *Global Economic Prospects and Developing Countries*, Washington DC: World Bank.

Zeltzer, S., 2000, 'Global Victory in Seattle: Workers, Students, Activists Defeat World Trade Organization', *Revolutionary Democracy*, 6, 1, April available at http://www.revolutionarydemocracy.org/rdv6n1/

Chapter 8

Rethinking Africanist Political Science

Abdul Raufu Mustapha

The rising tempo of African nationalism after 1945 and the increasing prospect of independence gave rise to the study of African political systems. Political science, sometimes referred to as 'Government', now joined anthropology, languages, history and geography as a sphere of intellectual specialisation. The literature spawned by this new field of study reflected the post-World War milieu in which it was created. Firstly, it was centrally concerned with nationalism and the building of new nations in postcolonial Africa. Secondly, it was marked by the dominant western modernisation paradigm and the logic of Cold War confrontation (Rostow 1960). Within the dualist logic of the 'transition' from tradition to modernity, African societies and economies were characterised as pre-modern; the search was then for the social agents, and the constitutional and institutional models to power and the transition to modern statehood. The African state and African elites were seen as crucial agencies in this modernist transformation. Studies by Coleman (1958), Almond and Coleman (1960), Sklar (1963), Organski (1965), and Apter (1967) explored the themes of nationalism and national integration, the 'politics of modernisation' and the 'stages of political development' that were characteristic of this founding school of Africanist political science, with its implicit biases towards a western epistemological and ideological world view. Some African contributors to this genre of political science were Claude Ake (1967) and Billy Dudley (1968). Despite its ideological blinkers and Cold War prejudices, this school of thought contributed immensely to our empirical knowledge of African nationalism. It also developed some important conceptual tools for the analysis of African political parties and constitutions.

But the notion of Africa as pre-modern, and without reference to the pernicious impact of slavery and colonialism, was soon to face resistance from an emergent crop of African political scientists, eager to throw off the 'tyranny' of the western modernisation paradigm. This shift was also a product of the specific context of its days: the rise of an indigenous African intelligentsia; the anti-colonial struggles in

Asia and Southern Africa; the rise of the Dependency School in Latin America; and the emergence of the non-aligned movement and the influence of countries like Cuba. The University of Dar es Salaam became the cradle of a neo-Marxist African variant of the Dependency School which counted amongst its fold people like Walter Rodney, Anthony Rweyemamu, Claude Ake, Nathan Shamuyarira, Dan Nabudere, Yash Tandon, Mahmood Mamdani, Okwudiba Nnoli, Emmanuel Hansen and Nzongola Ntalaja. Following in the tradition of Fanon (1963), this stellar pan-African collective went on to produce some of the classics of Africanist political science of the 1970s: Rodney (1972), Rweyemamu (1973), Shivji (1976), Mamdani (1976), and Ake (1978). Other African and non-African streams of the same school of thought were Samir Amin (1972, 1973), Senghaas-Knobloch (1975) and Williams (1976). As with the modernisation school, there were also important variations within this dependency school. While some veered towards excessive structuralism and populism, others tried to balance both internal and external dynamics in their explanation of the trajectory of the African state. What they often shared in common was an implicit critique of the African postcolonial elite as 'petty bourgeois' and the state as 'neocolonial'. The African state was losing its modernist shine, and had started its journey from being the 'cornerstone' of African development to a 'millstone' around the neck of African society (Mkandawire 2001: 293).

However, Africanist political science in the 1970s should not be reduced to the often acrimonious conflict between the modernisation and dependency schools. There were a number of significant contributions which may be better understood if viewed outside of this binary framework. There was, for instance, the groundbreaking *Exit, Voice and Loyalty* (1970) which Hirschman wrote based on his observations of the Nigerian Railways. There was also the far-reaching critique of the basic assumptions of the modernisation school in Melson and Wolpe's *Nigeria: Modernisation and the Politics of Communalism* (1971). This book was a path-breaker in what has come to be the dominant constructivist view of African ethnicity. Finally, Billy Dudley's *Instability and Political Order* (1973), was one of the earliest applications of rational choice theory to the study of African politics.

State-Market-Civil Society Nexus in Post-1980 Africa

Since the 1980s, there have been major shifts in the organisation of political and economic life in African societies; these trends have been preceded, or closely followed, by equally fundamental shifts in intellectual representations of the dynamics of African societies. At play here, of course, are the interactions between power and knowledge; between the desire to shape Africa's future along particular paths and the deployment of explanations of her past and present. Of equal importance is the fact that the 'African crisis' which heralded these shifts has continued, if not intensified, despite decades of intense socioeconomic engineering. Central to our current intellectual understanding of the African situation—and the socio-political projects at work on the continent— are the changing notions of the state as the organisation of public power; of the market as an organising principle of society; and of civil society as the expression of the popular will. The continuing problems of African societies can partly be traced to the intellectual crises concerning our understanding of the nexus between these three dominant conceptual pillars in contemporary Africa. It is important to highlight the ways in which these three crucial concepts have been individually and collectively articulated in the project of African transformation since the late 1970s. Secondly, I suggest ways in which we may begin to address some of the problems implicit in our current (mis)understanding of these concepts and their implications for Africa's future trajectory.

The State

Regardless of the assertion by Chabal and Daloz (2005) that the concept of 'state' is inappropriate to the analysis of African political life, the state has always held a special place in the African political imagination. When Nkrumah exhorted Ghanaians to 'Seek ye first the political Kingdom', he was expressing a widespread belief in colonial Africa that the state was an instrument of social liberation. The state was an important object of African nationalist agitation, be it Afrikaner nationalist agitation against British imperialism, or the later brands of African nationalisms that accompanied 'the winds of change' from the late 1950s. Nationalism was importantly about capturing the reins of control of the state, often under the leadership of the indigenous middle classes of colonial society (Breuilly 1993). In keeping with prevalent global trends, and the special conditions of the African milieu, the state was seen as an instrument of socioeconomic transformation and progress.

But the connections between the state and the nation were very complicated right from the start. Nationalists inherited an instrument of colonial and racist oppression which had actively sought to divide the colonised. Postcolonial African societies therefore faced the dual tasks of state (trans)formation and nation-building. The state was seen as the instrument of this great transformation. However, as the late Abdullahi Smith (1987) rightly pointed out, this arduous task of state-building was often undertaken without recourse to Africa's own historical experience of state building. The nuanced experience of statecraft in precolonial Africa was completely ignored by the postcolonial elites (Mustapha 1999). Instead, as scholars like Mamdani (2005) have emphasised, the colonial inheritance was often appropriated without much effort at recasting its fundamental principles. Equally problematic was the totalising vision of nation-building which unfolded in much of postcolonial Africa; a vision whose central logic was the forceful incorporation of every social force into the party-state, or their delegitimation and demobilisation. By the time of the crises of the late 1970s, the African state was increasingly seen as a major cause of, and not the solution for, Africa's development problems (Bates 1981).

From the early 1980s, we begin to see fundamental shifts in the conceptualisation of the state, particularly with respect to its developmentalist role. At independence, the formal structures of government are said to have been formed by a combination of the colonial heritage and the high-minded aspirations of the nationalist movement. But these were 'institutional shells' since most states lacked the ability to structure political interests beyond a narrow urban segment (Levy 2004). Consequently, the mode of governance rapidly shifted from formal systems of checks and balances to a de facto system of personal rule, characterised as an all-embracing 'neopatrimonialism' with its associated institutional decay. The decline in bureaucratic rule was said to be matched by a declining capacity for economic management; the basic functions of clarification, monitoring, and enforcement of formal rules were replaced by informal, opaque, and capricious rules set by the personal ruler (Levy 2004). African nationalism and its primary vehicle, the state, became objects of attack by neoliberal ideologues like Elliot Berg (Mkandawire 2005) who decried the stranglehold of the state over the economy. The solution, as they saw it, lay in 'rolling back' the state.

The 'first generation' of neo-liberal reforms were therefore principally concerned with reducing the scope of the state; rolling back the state through the imposition of conditionalities. The market—both real and imaginary—became the dominant motor of African economic life. The fiscal crisis of the African state in the late 1970s might have rightly necessitated a drastic reduction in state expenditure and the reduction and streamlining of state functions. However, as Mkandawire (1999) has pointed out, the cognitive prism through which the reform of the state was carried out at the behest of the Bretton Woods Institutions (BWIs) was ideologically loaded. The objective was to create a 'minimalist' state, leading to the drastic erosion of state capacity. To the extent that some state institutions were not 'rolled back', the major concern was about enhancing administrative capacity at minimal cost and this usually took the shape of downsizing and reforming the civil service. As Janice Aron pointed out (cited in Mkandawire 1999: 37):

> The state in Africa has come full circle to the small government of pre-colonial days; but with the additional ... effects from past shocks of a seriously depleted current institutional capacity, deterioration in the current quality and scope of social services and infrastructure provision, coupled with a fiscal position highly vulnerable to changes in foreign aid.

With the aim of building administrative capacity in this 'minimalist state', over 70 civil service reform projects were implemented in Africa between 1987 and 1997. But these reforms were a colossal failure; of those completed by 1997, only 29 percent were rated by the World Bank as satisfactory (Levy 2004: 9). By 1997 therefore, it was becoming clear that everything would not magically fall into place once you diminished the role of the state and set up the appropriate market signals. A regulatory state of sorts was now seen as essential and attention turned from engineering the administrative capacity of a minimalist state to fostering institutional accountability. The 'good policies' of restrictive macroeconomic management, liberalisation of international trade and investment, privatisation, and deregulation were now to be matched by 'good institutions': democracy, a 'good' bureaucracy, an independent judiciary, strongly protected property rights, and transparent financial institutions and corporate governance (Chang 2005).

The 'second generation' of reforms therefore sought to intervene within the African state in ways which could not be readily achieved through previous conditionalities. Increasingly, both the BWIs and bilateral donors extended their agendas to all areas of national policy and de-concentrated their presence by reaching to all parts of the country, creating multiple donor-government dialogue arenas through which they penetrated many national institutions and influenced policy formulation and implementation (Whitfield 2005; Harrison 2004). 'Building State Capacity' (Levy & Kpundeh 2004) replaced rolling back the state. But this was a particular conception of the state, as a technocratic tool for the efficient operation of the market; a regulatory state, not a developmentalist state (Mkandawire 1999).

A 2004 World Bank review of building state capacity (Levy and Kpundeh 2004) has however pointed out serious deficiencies in the BWIs' experience since 1997. In their own contribution to the debate, Ribot and Oyono (2005), for example, point out that instead of getting governance closer to the people, increasing participation, promoting efficiency and responsiveness, equity and better resource management and cultivating pluralism, World Bank decentralisation programmes have often led to new forms of colonial 'indirect rule'. In some instances, power is transferred downwards but the actors receiving it are not representatives of the local community nor are they accountable downwards. The result is de-concentration and not decentralisation. In other instances, local level representatives are elected, but are given no effective powers, turning them into a mere 'advisory group'. Only in few cases do we have the essential ingredients of the transfer of discretionary powers, taxation powers and democratic authority combined. In some countries, unelected chiefly powers are being reconstituted in the name of decentralisation. While these changes reflect 'a new geography of state authority', they fall far short of the promises of decentralisation. Similarly, despite democratisation and reform programmes aimed at strengthening parliamentary functions, Barkan, Adamolekun and Zhou (2004) report that the politics of patronage continue to dominate parliamentary behaviour in all instances. As a result of these observed inadequacies, a 'paradigm shift' in building state capacity is being advocated within the World Bank:

> ... from a narrow focus on organisational and public management approaches to a broader perspective that incorporates both the institutional rules of the game within which public organisations operate *and the political dynamics* (Levy 2004:26, emphasis added).

In the 1980s and 1990s therefore, we see the elaboration of different conceptions of the African state. Bates (1981), from a rational choice point of view, emphasises a conception of the state as an instrument of self-interested and ruinous economic elites. While the BWIs initially bought into this view leading to the 'rolling back' agenda, they have however shifted towards a view of the state as an institutional structure of incentives, capable of being moulded to support market efficiency.

Increasingly, as the review by Levy and Kpundeh indicates, the technocratic, managerial approach towards building state capacity is now to be infused with greater political considerations. Significantly, as Mkandawire (2005) has pointed out, the failure of the 'good policies' to produce the desired results did not lead to a re-think of the deflationary strategy of the BWIs. Instead, there has been the increasing recourse to 'nebulous, eclectic and ... political' (Mkandawire 2005:164) reforms around 'good institutions' and 'good governance'.

The Cultural 'State'

To these shifting conceptions of the African state, with their explicit policy ramifications through the BWIs, must be added the culturalist conception of the state associated with the works of scholars like Jean-François Bayart (1999), Stephen Ellis (2003), and Chabal and Daloz (2005), which concentrate on the cultural repertoire through which power is acquired and exercised. Chabal and Daloz (2005) make the most wide-ranging claims, arguing that culture is not merely an additional dimension of politics but one of the 'key fundamentals of social life, the matrix within which that which we understand as political action takes place' (Chabal and Daloz 2005: 21). They agree with Geertz that culture provides 'the structures of meaning through which men give shape to their experiences...' (Chabal and Daloz 2005: 25); that there is an intimate relationship between cultural values and political behaviour.

Germans, for example, are said to have a predilection for clearly defined norms, preferably in written form, overseen by officials, while the Chinese are said to prefer the gradual and slow building up of informal relations of trust. While the Germans are uncomfortable with fluid and ambiguous situations, the Chinese thrive on them, leading to different business practices and ethical orientations. In their comparison of the cultural logics of Sweden, France and Nigeria, they point out that in Sweden jay-walking never occurs; in France, pedestrians battle with drivers who seldom give way; and in Nigeria, pedestrians and drivers refuse to give way leading to chaos and traffic snarl-ups (Chabal and Daloz 2005: 245). These formal and informal aspects of social behaviour also impinge on the understanding of the state (Chabal and Daloz 2005: 240-1), shaping local notions of civic duty, state responsibility, people's expectations, political legitimacy and accountability, notions of political representation, and social regulation.

Because of these cultural logics, the three countries have developed completely different understandings of the state, of representation, and of legitimacy. The Swedish state embodies social harmony and collective welfare, and legitimacy depends on subservience to the rules by the rulers. In Sweden, political representatives try to be as ordinary as possible because of deeply embedded values of equality and distaste for flamboyant display. French political representatives, on the other hand, have a schizophrenic orientation towards flamboyant display due to the conflicting heritages from Versailles and from the Revolution. The same ambiguity is extended to cultural orientations to the state; on the one hand French politicians pay homage to their strong Republican institutions, but find ways to cheat the system when it suits them.

In Nigeria, Chabal and Daloz argue, the concept of the state 'does not make sense' because it lacks all the attributes associated with the state in its original European conceptualisation. While the state in Europe is an impersonal system based on treating every individual as an 'abstract' citizen with equal rights and obligations regardless of identity, in African countries like Nigeria, the political community is defined less by defined geographical boundaries than by a collective consciousness connected to ancestral filiations, customs and religious beliefs. There is no room within this conception for notions of equality. The institutionalisation of political life becomes extremely difficult because of the lack of differentiation of the political realm from other aspects of society such as religion and kinship systems. Political activity is governed largely through informal channels.

In Africa, therefore, acceptable political behaviour is governed by these informal principles transmitted through oral tradition. Political actors draw on these shared cultural repertoires to build their power and assert their legitimacy. In Africa, they argue, politics is highly personalised around 'Big Men' who construct vertical unequal patron-client relationships as a political strategy, increasing the lack of institutionalisation of political life:

> Our research on Africa has revealed that local politicians are exceptionally loath to accept the authority of State institutions over their personal conduct. Within a particularistic political order accountability rests essentially on the rulers' ability to meet the demands of the communities and factions that support them. It is thus essential to demonstrate one's own pre-eminence over the realm of the formal (Chabal and Daloz 2005: 243).

Representation within the political system is therefore particularistic, and legitimacy is tied to patrimonial redistribution. Representative legitimacy is rooted in the display of external power, marked by flamboyance, conspicuous consumption, and being associated with glamorous females. Since the state has no conception of the 'abstract' equal citizen, people put themselves under the protection of these powerful men in order to further or defend their interests. Informal socio-political relations which appear disorderly from the outside are actually instrumentally useful within patrimonial, clientelistic politics. African bureaucracies have 'as many unwritten rules as there are employees', and personal relations determine bureaucratic outcomes (Chabal and Daloz 2005: 242).

Of course, this nebulous conceptualisation of the cultural logic of Nigeria and its political ramifications can be challenged on a number of important grounds. In the first place, while detailed historical and institutional analyses of Sweden and France are undertaken to isolate their dominant cultural logics and their implications, there is no comparable analysis in the Nigerian or African case. Instead all we have are passing references to two works of fiction: Achebe's *A Man of the People* and Aluko's *A State of Our Own*, as if fiction necessarily reflects reality or the totality of reality. Academic scholarship, which ought to be taken seriously—as in the Swedish and French cases—is either entirely ignored, or dismissed without consideration as deductive and mistaken. Secondly, Africa is the most culturally diverse continent while Nigeria is certainly one of the world's most culturally and linguistically complex countries. Indeed, Nigeria's painful problems of state and nation-building can be said to derive partly from the acrimonious co-existence of multiple cultural logics and the conflicting claims they bring to bear on the state. One would expect wise analysis to address these cultural realities and complexities. Culture does affect politics, but unfortunately, the two authors have failed to make a convincing case for Africa, shorn of prejudice, preconception, and sensationalism.

The most important aspects of the culturalist perspective on the African state, however, are their implications. Olivier de Sardan (1999), for example, writes of the cultural embeddedness of corruption in Africa, citing cultures of gift-giving, solidarity, predatory authority and redistributive accumulation. Janet Roitman (2004) writes of the common 'ethic of illegality' through which criminality is embedded in the institutional histories of northern Cameroon. William Reno (2000) argues that 'dysfunctional' state systems in Africa are built on personalised and informal 'shadow states', violent commerce, use of state office for personal profit, and the undermining of international norms of economic behaviour. In these so-called culturalist analyses, what we see is Africa pathologised. Another implication of these studies is their attitude towards African sovereignty. The implicit position of Chabal and Daloz is that there are no states in Africa; the concept is applied to Africa because leaders need a fig leaf for credibility in the international system. Reno (2000: 437) denounces 'the façade of formal sovereignty'. These views provide the intellectual justification for calls for the re-colonisation of Africa through 'international trusteeships' (Ellis 2005). We are now familiar with the all-powerful World Bank or IMF staff arrogantly swaggering through African capitals; it remains to be seen whether some of these culturalist 'experts' will one day turn up in Africa as colonial pro-consuls!

It is worth noting that there are indeed alternative explanations for the features of African life, such as patron-client politics and reliance on extra-economic means for appropriating resources, which these culturalists attribute to Africa's 'cultural logic'. Mushtaq Khan's (2006) examination of patron-client politics and extra-economic appropriation in countries like Nigeria (and most other developing countries!), suggests that economic characteristics in these countries 'make patron-client politics both rational for redistributive coalitions and effective as strategies for achieving goals of powerful constituencies within these coalitions'. Furthermore, Khan demonstrates why 'these political features of developing countries are intimately connected to the underdevelopment of economies, the limited scope of viable capitalist economies in developing societies, and the inevitable social transformations that these societies are experiencing'.

What is important for our analysis is that both rolling back the state and the building of state capacity by the BWIs have so far failed to transform the state into an effective organising principle responsive to the needs of African societies. And we cannot be sanguine about the potential policy implications of the culturalist representation of the African state. In our rethinking of the state, we must therefore not only address the malfunction of the post-independence nationalist state, but also the implications of the technocratic market-driven state and the implications of the culturalist perspective.

The Market

The ideological offensive against the state was matched by the uncritical promotion of the market as the all-embracing solution to Africa's problems. While some of the excesses of statist developmentalism in postcolonial Africa were truly deplorable, the root and branch promotion of market liberalisation was carried through without regard to local realities, leading to disastrous economic and social consequences (Mkandawire 2005). At issue here are a number of problems. Firstly, the conception of the market was more ideological than real; as scholars like Altvater (1993) have stressed, pure markets have never existed in history. They have always been politically regulated. Polanyi (1957) was quite emphatic on this point in *The Great Transformation*. The very nature of the market system calls forth a measure of state intervention:

> There was nothing natural about laissez-faire; free markets could never have come into being merely by allowing things to take their course ... laissez-faire itself was enforced by the state ... The road to the free market was opened and kept open by an enormous increase in continuous, centrally organized and controlled interventionism (Polanyi 1957: 139-40).

Looking at the relationship between the state, economy, and society up to the Second World War, Polanyi argued that counter movements for social protection invariably accompanied every movement towards free markets and economic liberalism. The state does play an active role even in market societies.

Yet in their internal and external trade regimes, in their financial markets, and in their social services, African states were forced to depend excessively on markets over which they had little or no control. These policies were advocated for Africa even when they were not consistent with early European and American economic history (Chang 2005). In many instances, particularly in rural areas, malfunctioning state institutions were replaced with fragmented or poorly regulated markets, since profit-maximising business concerns had no incentive or inclination to reaching out to them due to weak demand. Instead of the promise of the market, many rural areas were simply left to their own devices. The informal sector was now expected to step in where formal state activities had ceased (Grey-Johnson 1992). Health, education and other vital services like water provision were subjected to the market mechanism of 'cost recovery' or simply informalised, as was labour:

The 1980s have witnessed a process of informalization of the labour markets in Africa. Labour market informalization has taken two different forms. First, the production structure has been informalized in the sense that an increasing proportion of economic activity is taking place outside the formal sector. At present, formal wage employment represents merely 11 percent of the regional labour force. The second type of informalization concerns the conditions of employment in the formal sector. Modern sector labour standards have gradually been informalized. Money wages have declined in some countries while real wages have been flexible downwards in most countries, both in absolute and relative terms. The high wage levels that prevailed until the early 1970s have been replaced by near-starvation wages in the 1980s, especially in the public sector (JASPA/ECA/OAU cited in Grey-Johnson 1992: 77-8).

Much ideological obfuscation surrounded the characterisation of the burgeoning informal sector. The World Bank described it as the 'most competitive' sector of African economies. Others referred to it as 'the real economy' of African countries, promoting 'participation' and growth; the very justification of their laissez-faire predilections. But as Grey-Johnson (1992: 78) pointed out, these attempts to 'naturalise' informalisation could not hide the fact that it was policy-induced, and not a 'natural' phenomenon. The ideological predisposition towards a minimalist state and laissez-faire economics also meant that the increasing hordes of informal sector operators did not often get the sort of state support that would have improved their productivity. African countries were thereby leaving their

> ... growth prospects in the hands of semi-literate slum dwellers who produce for a market of the poor, with levels of productivity so low that they can have little impact on the livelihood of the community. The informal sector can be used to sustain poverty and as a means of coping with deprivation. It can be left to producing poor quality goods and sub-standard social services. The informal sector can be used to frustrate Africa's objectives of industrialization, middle- and high-level manpower development, and the modernisation of agriculture and the eradication of poverty (Grey-Johnson 1992: 80).

Critics like Mkandawire (1999) argue that this is precisely what has been happening in most African countries. More generally, Mkandawire (2005) argues that economic transformation through market liberalisation has led Africa to a dead-end. It is ironic that despite the fact that Africa is the most structurally adjusted continent in the world, it also has the worst performing economies and the greatest poverty. Growth rates since the 1980s are not higher than in the 1960s and 1970s. After decades of (mal)adjustment, Africa's non-oil exports have declined, and there has been no discernible change in the levels of savings and investments. The imaginary foreign investors that were expected to follow in the wake of market and financial liberalisation have largely failed to turn up, except in some enclaves like mining and telecommunications. And even in telecommunications, much of the investment is intra-African. There has been no discernible increase in Africa's non-oil trade; instead there is a process of de-industrialisation. Mkandawire (2005) argues that the sea-change in economic policy has not been matched by promised results; the structural adjustment policies of integrating Africa into the global economy have completely side-stepped Africa's developmental needs. Structural adjustment has not led to structural change; instead we have a perverse transformation which is driving Africa back to the type of colonial economies from which nationalist regimes struggled to escape (Mkandawire 2005:171). Increased exposure to the international system and heightened dependence have gone hand-in-hand with economic marginalisation.

We must therefore rethink the role of the market in Africa's external and internal economic relations. In particular, we must pay attention to the failure to achieve sustained growth and investment, the deepening of dependency, and the social dislocations caused by the ideological nature of the current conception of the market.

Civil Society

The increased role of civil society is another important element in contemporary Africa. In many respects, the resurgence of civil society is a welcome tonic in many African societies, long dominated by the party-state or military dictatorships of the earlier period (Monga 1996). Yet, problems abound in the way this concept has been translated into African economic and political life. As in the case of the market, civil society has been ideologically constructed in an erroneous manner as the panacea for African democratisation (Diamond 1994); a view rightly condemned by Kasfir and his fellow contributors (1998). What is often ignored is Africa's real existing civil society (Gibbon 2001; Gwarzo 2003). Mamdani (2005: 268) refers to this phenomenon of civil society as 'idealised prescription' as opposed to civil society as 'historical construct'. The result has been the ignoring of important aspects of African civil society or their delegitimation as 'uncivil society' (Diamond 2001).

These misconceptions are taking place when often weak African civil society organisations have to deal in a world dominated by International Non-Governmental Organisations (INGOs) often of Euro-American provenance. These INGOs have expanded in an 'associational revolution' which has seen their numbers increase from 6,000 in 1990 to 25,000 in 2002, constituting them allegedly into the 'second superpower' (Choudhary 2004).

These developments have a bearing on the type of democratic struggles these civil society organisations engage in (Mamdani 2000). Often urban-based, and led by suave university educated middle class youth, Africa's prescribed civil society often has no understanding of the history of political and economic struggles in rural Africa, and consequently has little to say about these struggles outside of some form of service delivery. Similarly, as Ribot and Oyono (2005) have argued, the proliferation of NGOs and other non-state actors in local service delivery has the tendency to fragment powers that should rightly belong to elected local institutions. These NGOs are erroneously being promoted as a replacement for the state in vital areas of service delivery (Barnard and Terreblanche 2001).

Furthermore, the monochromic conception of civil society *against* the state, dominant in the conception of African civil societies, can only lead to a cul-de-sac which does credit to neither the state nor to these civil societies themselves, and is likely to be harmful to the interests of the constituencies that the civil societies seek to serve. Equally problematic is the increasing absorption of African civil society organisations into market institutional mechanisms and their subordination to the INGOs, sometimes in a global patron-client relationship (Naidoo and Heinrich 2000).

A Problematic Nexus

What sort of nexus currently exists between these three discrete concepts in contemporary Africa? In order to answer this question logically, I start from the source of the problem: the economy. Mushtaq Khan (2004) has pointed out that in previous periods, economic failure would have been addressed through policies of economic reform with the objective of making markets more competitive and rent free. Rent-seeking creates rents and destabilises property rights, threatening economic growth. However, in Africa, a nexus was established by the BWIs between seeking to reform the market and simultaneously carrying out political and institutional change. The absence of democracy and weak bureaucracies were seen as promoting rent-seeking as *intentional*—not structurally driven—behaviour. Downsizing the state, promoting democracy, decentralisation and encouraging civil society were all seen as ways of changing the structures of incentive and limiting the state's ability to create arbitrary rents. Other measures include improving the efficiency and motivation of the civil service and the judiciary, and the implementation of anti-corruption measures. The ultimate aim is the creation of what Khan calls a service delivery state (Khan 2004: 171, 2006). But as the studies in Levy and Kpundeh (2004) have shown, this has so far been a forlorn hope; democracy on its own is not enough to consolidate productive classes in society whilst simultaneously undermining unproductive ones (Khan 2004: 168). There is no historical evidence to suggest that these sort of reforms are pre-conditions for growth (Khan 2004:190).

Mkandawire (1999:43) also points out another important nexus in contemporary Africa. Neoliberalism argues for the market, but cannot seem to deal with 'really existing capitalism' on the continent. There has been no attempt at building positive coalitions between the state and capitalists to promote growth, because in the context of the prevailing ideological blinkers, such relations must necessarily be collusive and rent orientated. The state is therefore distanced from local capitalists, with the pride of place going to technocrats from the BWIs; this is the service delivery state per excellence.

And as far as civil society organisations are concerned, there is no uniform orientation towards either the state or the market. The pluralism of civil societies is reflected in the pluralism of orientations: some are pro-state, or see themselves as partners with the state, while others see their role as anti-state. The same ambiguity characterises the orientation towards the market (Choudhary 2004).

Rethinking the Nexus

My fundamental argument is that there is a disjuncture between the current developmental needs of African societies and the ways these three important concepts of state, markets and civil society are conceived and related to each other. Our experience since the late 1970s suggests that these misconceptions have become a fetter on African development.

The first point to be made, following economists like Mkandawire and Khan, is that we need a new type of state that is consistent with Africa's needs; not a minimalist state or a service delivery state, but a transformative or developmentalist state. The state has always had a role in promoting growth, and it is inconceivable that Africa will be the sole exception to this rule. Indeed, as Khan (2004: 165) has argued, it is not an either-or question; historically, success in service delivery has depended on the state's success in pushing through rapid social transformation in the direction of growth. By privileging the service delivery state over the transformative state in Africa, the BWIs have effectively put the cart before the horse:

> Without strategies to enhance this role of the state, sustained progress on service delivery is also unlikely. Many of the consensus policies on reforming institutions to improve service delivery are based on a partial reading of theory and evidence. They are at best unlikely to work, and at worst could further undermine the state's institutional and political capacity for ensuring a dynamic transformation (Khan 2004: 165).

Not only is the idea of the market without any state intervention a fiction, the idea of a service delivery state without social transformation is equally without foundation in the long run. The appropriate capacities for the service delivery state—protection of stable property rights, low expropriation risk, low corruption, undistorted markets that have low levels of rent and democratic accountability and civil society participation—do not address the social transformation needs of Africa (Khan 2004: 166-7). By contrast, historical evidence suggests states which have succeeded in promoting growth have actively participated in the transformation of their economies and societies by helping to nurture a new capitalist class, creating the conditions for their access to technology and entrepreneurial capacity, negotiating adequate protection for their products in the international market, and intervening in property rights so as to create and manage growth enhancing rents (Khan 2004; Chang 2005; Samatar 2005). To assume that the market can carry out these tasks on its own, 'is a theoretical leap of faith that the historical evidence does not justify' (Khan 2004: 190).

Secondly, we need to rethink the good governance agenda. The state capacities identified in the current agenda are ideologically derived from liberal-democratic concerns and have no bearing on the state capacities needed for social transformation. Less corruption and deeper democracy are not the causes of growth, but the outcomes of successful economic development. The social distribution of power between social classes is one key to achieving a transformation state. Within this transformative state context, civil society and the business community should be actively involved in coalitions or 'action networks' (Ng and Ng 2002) based on consensus-seeking and the building of trust. This is the way to scale-up local civil society initiatives whilst protecting them from capture by more powerful local and international interests. The task before Africanist political science is to bring social transformation back on the agenda in Africa.

References

Ake, C., 1967, *A Theory of Political Integration*, Homewood, IL: Dorsey Press.

Ake, C., 1978, *Revolutionary Pressures in Africa*, London: Zed Press.

Almond, G., and J. Coleman, eds., 1960, *The Politics of Developing Areas*, Princeton, NJ: Princeton University Press.

Altvater, E., 1993, *The Future of the Market*, London: Verso.

Apter, D., 1967, *The Politics of Modernisation*, Chicago: University of Chicago Press.

Barnard, D. and Y. Terreblanche, 2001, *PRODDER: The South African Development Directory*, Pretoria: HSRC.

Bates, R. H., 1981, *Markets and States in Tropical Africa: the political basis of agricultural policies*, Berkeley: University of California Press.

Bayart, J-F., S. Ellis and B. Hibou, 1999, *The Criminalization of the State in Africa*, Oxford: James Currey.

Breuilly, J., 1993, *Nationalism and the State*, Chicago: University of Chicago Press.

Chabal P. and J-P. Daloz, 2005, *Culture Troubles: Politics and the Interpretation of Meaning*, London: Hurst & Company.

Chang Ha-Joon, 2005, *Kicking Away the Ladder: Development Strategy in historical Perspective*, London: Anthem Press.

Choudhary, K., 2004, 'Global Civil Society, Globalization and Nation-State', Paper presented at the ISTR Conference 2004, Toronto, Canada.

Coleman, J., 1958, *Nigeria: Background to Nationalism*, Berkeley: University of California Press.

Diamond, L., 1994, 'Rethinking Civil Society: Towards Democratic Consolidation', *Journal of Democracy* 5 (3): 4-17.

Diamond, L., 2001., 'Civic Communities and Predatory Societies', Paper delivered to the conference on 'Culture Matters: A Forum for Business, Education and Training Professionals', Intercultural Management Institute, American University, Washington, May 10.

Dudley, B., 1968, *Parties and Politics in Northern Nigeria*, London: Frank Cass.

Dudley, B., 1973, *Instability and Political Order: Politics and Crisis in Nigeria*, Ibadan: Ibadan University Press.

Ellis, S., 2003, 'Violence and history: a response to Thandika Mkandawire', *Journal of Modern African Studies* 41 (3): 457-75.

Ellis S., 2005, 'How to Rebuild Africa', *Foreign Affairs* 84 (5): 135-48.

Fanon, F., 1963, *The Wretched of the Earth*, Grove Press, New York.

Gibbon, P., 2001, 'Civil Society, Locality and Globalization in Rural Tanzania: A Forty-Year Perspective', *Development & Change* 32 (5): 819-44.

Grey-Johnson, C., 1992, 'The African Informal Sector at the Crossroads: Emerging Policy Options', *Africa Development* XVII (1): 65-91.

Gwarzo, T. H., 2003, 'Activities of Islamic Civic Associations in the Northwest of Nigeria: with particular reference to Kano State', *Afrika Spectrum* 38 (3): 289-318.

Harrison, G., 2004, *The World Bank and Africa; The Construction of Governance States*, London: Routledge.

Hirschman, A.O., 1970, *Exit, Voice and Loyalty: Responses to Decline in Firms, Organisations and States*, Cambridge, Mass: Harvard University Press.

Kasfir, N., ed., 1998, *Civil Society and Democracy in Africa*, London: Frank Cass.

Levy, B. and S. Kpundeh, 2004, *Building State Capacity in Africa: New Approaches, Emerging Lessons*, Washington, DC: World Bank Institute.

Levy, B., 2004, 'Governance and Economic Development in Africa: Meeting the Challenge of Capacity Building', in B. Levy and S. Kpundeh, eds., *Building State Capacity in Africa: New Approaches, Emerging Lessons*, World Bank Institute, Washington.

Mamdani, M., 1976, *Politics and Class Formation in Uganda*, New York: Monthly Review Press.

Mandani, M., 2000, 'The Politics of Peasant Communities and Urban Civil Society: Reflections on an African Dilemma', in Deborah Bryceson et al., *Disappearing Peasantries?* London: Intermediate Technology Publishers.

Mamdani, M., 2005, 'Identity and National Governance', in B. Wisner, C. Toulmin and R. Chitiga, eds., *Towards a New Map of Africa*, London: Earthscan.

Melson, R. and H. Wolpe, eds., 1971, *Nigeria: Modernisation and the Politics of Communalism*, East Lansing: Michigan State University Press.

Mkandawire, T., 1999, 'Developmental States and Small Enterprises', in Kenneth King and Simon McGrath, eds., *Enterprise in Africa: Between Poverty and Growth*, London: Intermediate Technology Publications.

Mkandawire, T., 2001, 'Thinking About Developmental States in Africa', *Cambridge Journal of Economics* 25 (3): 289-314.

Mkandawire, T., 2005, 'The Global Economic Context', in B. Wisner, C. Toulmin and R. Chitiga, eds., *Towards a New Map of Africa*, London: Earthscan.

Monga, C., 1996, *The Anthropology of Anger: Civil Society and Democracy in Africa*, Boulder, CO: Lynne Rienner.

Mushtaq, K., 2004, 'State Failure in Developing Countries and Institutional Reform Strategies', *Annual World Bank Conference on Development Economics-Europe 2003*, Paris: World Bank, 165-96.

Mushtaq, K., 2006, 'Markets, States and Democracy: Patron-Client Networks and the Case for Democracy in Developing Countries', in Julio Faundez, ed., *On the State of Democracy*, London: Routledge.

Mustapha, A. R., 1999, 'Back to the Future? Multi-Ethnicity and the State in Africa', in L. Basta and J. Ibrahim, eds., *Federalism and Decentralisation in Africa: The Multicultural Challenge*, Fribourg: Institut du Federalisme.

Naidoo, K and V. F. Heinrich, 2000, 'Global Civil Society and the Challenge of the New Millennium: Implications for Civil Society in Africa', CIVICUS, Johannesburg.

Ng, Catherine W. and G. H. Ng, Evelyn, 2002, 'State, Market and Civil Society in Hong Kong: A Study of Multi media Advertising on Busca', *Asian Journal of Public Administration* 24 (2): 287-303.

Olivier de Sardan, J. P., 1999, 'A Moral Economy of Corruption in Africa?' *Journal of Modern African Studies* 37 (1): 25-52.

Organski, A. F. K., 1965, *The Stages of Political Development*, New York: Knopf.

Polanyi, K., 1957, *The Great Transformation*, Boston: Beacon Press.

Reno, W., 2000, 'Clandestine Economies, Violence and States in Africa', *Journal of International Affairs* 53 (2): 433-59.

Ribot, J. C. and P. R. Oyono, 2005, 'The Politics of Decentralization', in B. Wisner, C. Toulmin and R. Chitiga, eds., *Towards a New Map of Africa*, London: Earthscan.

Rodney, W., 1972, *How Europe Underdeveloped Africa*, Dar es Salaam: Tanzania Publishing House.

Roitman, J., 2004, *Fiscal Disobedience*, Princeton, NJ: Princeton University Press.

Rostow, W. W., 1960, *Stages of Economic Growth: A Non-Communist Manifesto*, Cambridge: Cambridge University Press.

Rweyemamu, J., 1973, *Underdevelopment and Industrialization in Tanzania: a Study of Perverse Capitalist Development*, Nairobi: Oxford University Press.

Samatar A. I., 2005, 'National Institutions for Development: The Case of Botswana', in B. Wisner, C. Toulmin and R. Chitiga, eds., *Towards a New Map of Africa*, London: Earthscan.

Samir, A., 1972, 'Underdevelopment and Dependence in Black Africa—Origins and Contemporary Forms', *Journal of Modern African Studies* 10 (4): 503-24.

Samir, A., 1973, *Neocolonialism in West Africa*, London: Penguin.

Senghaas-Knobloch, E., 1975, 'The Internationalization of Capital and the Process of Underdevelopment: The Case of Black Africa', *Journal of Peace Research*, 12 (4): 275-92.

Shivji, I., 1976, *Class Struggles in Tanzania*, London: Heinemann.

Sklar, R., 1963, *Nigerian Political Parties: Power in an Emergent African Nation*, Princeton, NJ: Princeton University Press.

Smith, A., 1987, *A Little New Light: Selected Historical Writings of Abdullahi Smith*, Zaria: The Abdullahi Smith Centre for Historical Research.

Whitfield, L., 2005, 'Trustees of Development from Conditionality to Governance: Poverty Reduction Strategy Papers in Ghana', *Journal of Modern African Studies* 43 (4): 641-64.

Williams, G., ed., 1976, *Nigeria: Economy and Society*, London: Rex Collings.

Chapter 9

Economics and African Studies

Emmanuel Nnadozie

Arguably, economic development (or lack thereof) constitutes the most significant challenge facing Africa. One would therefore expect Africa, which presents the most daunting economic challenge in modern history, to occupy centre stage in the field of economics. Amazingly, economics, whose central preoccupation is income, growth, distribution, and human welfare, throughout time has either ignored Africa altogether or given it only peripheral attention. Indeed, economics and African studies might as well be perfect strangers—with an unusual relationship that gradually emerged into a tortuous cohabitation of mutual tolerance and convenience rather than a natural marriage, integration, and consequential blending. Several stylised facts illustrate the reciprocal neglect and curious cohabitation that have come to characterise the relationship between economics and African studies. First, a look at the development of economic theory as it has been presented reveals a Eurocentric history in which Africa does not exist. African studies programmes have reciprocated by ignoring, until recently, economics in their curriculum and methodology. Second, there has been a lack of institutional, organisational, and intellectual focus and support for Africa in economics.

African studies involves a multidimensional and multidisciplinary study of Africa, African peoples, African societies, and Africa's issues and problems. As a social science that focuses on human behaviour, efficiency, and utility maximisation, economics has a central role to play in African studies. After all, Africa's principal problem is lack of economic development. The question then is to what extent has the field of economics played a central role in African studies, and does economics constitute a key element of the African studies curriculum or does it provide theoretical and methodological tools used in Africa studies? We need to answer these questions to effectively discuss economics and African studies. Accordingly, this chapter focuses on answering these two key questions. First, we examine, mostly in the North American context, the relationship between economics and African studies, major theories and methodologies of economics, how economics and African studies have dealt with each other, how economics is viewed in and treated by African studies, and the prospects for a greater role of economics in African studies.

The starting point of economics and African studies, in particular, is the economics of developing countries—commonly referred to as the economics of development, or economic development. Because Africa is the least developed continent in the world, the importance of economics in the study of Africa cannot be overstated. When one considers that development is indicated by measurements of the quality of life and overall human welfare, it is clear that economics is central to African studies. By many measures of human welfare, Africa has not performed well and continues to lag behind the rest of the world. Yet until recently, the relationship between economics and African studies has been marked more by parallelism than convergence or integration—and both sides have failed to embed economics within African studies. There is little emphasis on economics in African studies and the economics discipline treats Africa not as a special case but as part of growth and development economics. As a result, the economics-African studies nexus has never satisfactorily materialised. Not only is the economic approach in and of itself germane to African studies, economics can be used as a tool in the analysis of political, social, and institutional issues. That is, economics can constitute a centrepiece or method of analysing issues and problems. Therefore, it is important to make economics a central focus of African studies programmes. Africa's repeated economic failures and persistent underdevelopment pose a serious challenge to the economic discipline and should not be treated lightly. African studies programmes ought to have a strong economics component in order to be able to examine and address these challenges. Fortunately, some action is being taken to address the neglect of Africa within the economics discipline and economics in African studies by way of Africa-specific and Africa-focused research centres, organisations, and journals. However, more needs to be done to bridge the gap and solidify the union.

It is important to move from the hands-off approach to a hands-on approach on the question of Africa in economics. A concerted and more integrative rapprochement between economics and African studies will generate a veritable focus on Africa, which will enable us to shed more light on the uniqueness of the African continent, its development difficulties and their global implications, and establish Africa-specific remedies necessary to bring about development in the African continent.

Theoretical Developments

In general, Africa has been under-studied in the field of economics and when it has been studied at all, it has been done either within the context of growth and development economics or within comparative and historical studies of economic conditions. Gerald K. Helleiner's (1988: 222) comments at a symposium on the

'State of Development Economics' held at Yale University's Economic Growth Center in 1986 sum up the neglect of Africa in economics:

> African countries do not figure prominently in the general papers on development presented at the Symposium. There were no Africans on the program; nor, indeed, were there any in attendance. Africa is on the periphery of Raúl Prebisch's periphery. Data limitations have left this continent substantially outside systematic cross-country investigations, such as those of Chenery and friends. Yet if poverty is the reason for our concern with development, surely we must devote more attention to the parts of the world where developmental progress has been most limited.

The study of economic development (of which Africa is part) has been driven by theories of economic development, which have developed along the lines of the classical ideas, Marxist idea, or a combination of both. Furthermore, some approaches have focussed on the internal causes of development or underdevelopment, while others have focussed on external causes. Growth has been used as proxy for development and, in some cases, has been treated as synonymous with development. Chenery and Srinivasan (1988) identify three approaches to development: neoclassical, Marxist, and structuralist. A taxonomy of theories and models to inform the teaching of and research on development exists—neoclassical growth models, Marxist, demand-driven models, balanced growth models, unbalanced growth models, structuralist models—each trying to explain development from a separate intellectual and cultural setting; each considering certain variables and relationships more important than others.[1]

It warrants noting that there still does not exist what could be considered a general theory of African economic development. The underlying assumption is that economic development in poor regions (of which Africa is part) will parallel the early stages of development in the rich countries. The belief that resource development and technological development can be transferred to the developing countries from the more advanced countries, allowing them to skip certain stages of development, is also widely accepted. The experience of the newly industrialised countries (NICS) has been used to demonstrate that this is possible.

Classical Thinking

Pioneers of modern economics, which is largely Eurocentric, such as William Petty, Gregory King, Francois Quesnay, Antoine Lavoisier, Joseph Louis Lagrange, and even Adam Smith, explored the concept of development (Sen 1988:10). Yet, it was Schumpeter's (1934) *Theory of Economic Development* that played the principal role in setting the stage for development economics as we know it today. Economic theory has come a long way since classicism originated in the eighteenth century.

Classical economic theory is founded on two maxims. First, it presupposes that each individual maximises his or her preference function under some constraints, where preferences and constraints are considered as given. Second, it presupposes the existence of interdependencies—expressed in the markets—between the actions of all individuals. Under the assumption of perfect and pure competition, these two features will determine resource allocation and income distribution. That is, they will regulate demand and supply, allocation of production and the optimisation of social organisation. The question then is do these postulates enable us to understand the functioning of an African economy? Is it necessary to modify them to take into account some peculiarities?

Led by Adam Smith and David Ricardo, with the support of Jean Batiste Say and Robert Malthus, the classical writers believed in Smith's invisible hand, self-interest, and a self-regulating economic system, as well as in the development of monetary institutions, capital accumulation based on surplus production, and free trade. They also believed in the division of labour, the law of diminishing returns, and the ability of the economy to self-adjust in a laissez-faire system devoid of government intervention. The circular flow of the classical model indicates that wages may deviate, but will eventually return to their natural rate of subsistence. If, according to the classical model, wages increase, food production will also increase, leading to population growth.

For the classical belief of diminishing returns, Ricardo uses Robert Malthus's population doctrine to argue that as more labour is applied to land of less fertility, the total returns fall. He believed that to offset the diminishing returns, there should be an increase in accumulation of capital per person. Some of the Ricardian classical theory is relevant today for Africa even though Ricardo wrote about England and Europe. For example, the law of diminishing returns applies to many areas in Africa. Ricardo's concern with land scarcity as it applies to cultivable land is today a problem for some African countries. Beyond that, one would be hard-pressed to find relevance in the classical school of thought for Africa.

Marxism

Because of the problems inherent in the classical paradigm—the underestimation of the impact of technology, the iron law of wages, and the neglect of history—Karl Marx advanced his historical materialism and a dynamic system in which there is flow: from primitive society-to-feudalism-to-capitalism-to-socialism-and-to-communism. This transition, in Marx's view, would result from changes in the ruling and the oppressed classes and their relationship with each other. He then envisaged conflict between forces of production, the organisation of production, relations of production, and societal thinking and ideology. What Marx did was provide the dynamic movement in the materialist movement.

Marx predicted capitalist cycles that, in his view, would ultimately lead to the collapse of capitalism. According to him, these cycles would be characterised by a reserve army of the unemployed, a falling rate of profits, business crises, increasing concentration of industry into a few hands, and mounting misery and alienation of the proletariat. The economic collapse of the socialist and communist countries that adopted Marxism or versions of it has shown its limitations. In addition, neither did the socialist revolution take place in advanced capitalist countries nor did workers overthrow capitalism when they became a majority of the labour force. Marx was writing fundamentally about capitalism, which had little or no correlation with Africa.

We now discuss some of the classical and Marxist antecedents to show major theoretical and methodological developments in the field of economics and demonstrate how these developments have affected the view of Africa.

The Stages of Growth Approach

The three models that exemplify the linear stages school of thought are Rostow, Harrod-Domar, and Gerschenkron. Their central idea is that countries pass through stages and arrive at a 'take-off' stage by following certain rules. They believe that internal constraints, mainly the lack of savings and capital stock (the necessary conditions), are the main causes of underdevelopment. They, therefore, advocate an increase in both domestic and foreign savings to increase investment.

Rostow (1960) used a growth rate equation, based on investment rate and capital output ratio, coupled with the belief in the leading sectors to propose that countries will eventually get to 'take-off' into sustained growth. Because the theory was based on Britain, Rostow's model country of growth, the overall relevance of Rostow's theory to Africa is indeed questionable. Rostow's theory has several weaknesses: insufficient empirical evidence concerning conditions needed for take-off; imprecise definitions; no theoretical ground for a society's movement from one stage to another; and the mistaken assumption that economic development in LDCs will parallel the early stages of the developed countries.

To be sure, this theory has been heavily criticised for its ambiguity in defining the stages and conditions of movement from one stage to another. It has been difficult to pinpoint the line of demarcation between the take-off stage and the drive to maturity. Likewise, for some advanced countries the take-off could not be identified. There is some evidence that the major impetus towards growth can occur at any stage and develop in a unique way to conform to the particular nature of the society. The specific characteristics for the different periods are often found in several of the stages for different countries. Finally, Rostow's theory has been criticised for not recognising that, because of differential factor endowments, technological or trading opportunities, follower countries may not successfully adopt the British model.

In Harrod-Domar's model, national output is determined by the ratio of saving to GDP and capital-output ratio.[2] The rate of growth of output is determined jointly by the national saving ratio and the national capital-output ratio. The growth rate of output ($\Delta Y/Y$) is directly related to the savings ratio (s/k) and inversely related to the capital-output ratio K. $\Delta Y/Y = s/k$ where Y is output (GDP), ΔY denotes the change in output; s is the saving-output ratio; and k is the capital-output ratio. Thus, the more of its national income a country saves, the more its output grows.

The linear stages models are criticised for ignoring important variables and focussing on the 'necessary condition'.

Gerschenkron (1962:40), who argued against the idea of Rostow's prerequisite for take-off, suggests a different development pattern (modelled after the Russian economy) for 'backward' countries—a '... process characterized by a great spurt in manufacturing output with heavy investment, much pressure on living standards, large-scale plants concentrated in heavy industries, coercive political institutions and lagging agricultural sector' (Crafts 1998:40). In fact, the examination of the stages of growth theories shows the reality of a non-existent typology of Western growth in economics that is relevant to Africa. As such, the stages of growth theory has little relevance to Africa.

The Structuralists

The structuralists—Arthur Lewis, John C. Fei and Gustav Ranis, and Holis Chenery—focus on the mechanism by which underdeveloped economies transform the structure of their domestic economies. For instance, Arthur Lewis, a pioneer development economist and Nobel laureate, developed a theory to explain the mechanism by which underdeveloped economies transform their domestic economies. As a structuralist, Lewis (and Fei-Ranis) extend Ragnar Nurkse's original idea and focus mostly on internal sources of underdevelopment and use a two-sector surplus labour model to show that the dualistic nature of developing economies, made up of urban (modern) and rural (traditional and agricultural) sectors, creates differential marginal products of labour (Lewis 1954:139-192; see also Nurkse 1953). This means that investment in the urban sector is necessary to reduce rural surplus labour through rural-urban migration.

G. Ranis and J.H.C. Fei (1964) extend Lewis's growth theory and 'set up a model with two turning points—when food supply begins to decline as labour is withdrawn from agriculture and when the marginal product of rural labour rises to the institutionally fixed urban wage' (Arida and Taylor 1998: 175). They explore the implications of population growth for greater productivity in industry as a key to increased per capita income. Like Lewis, they consider an economy that consists of two sectors, which may be thought of as agriculture and industry, traditional and modern, rural and urban, or non-capitalist and capitalist. Based upon the initial capital stock in the industrial sector, labour moves freely between the two sectors so as to equate wages in the two sectors. The capitalists in the industrial sector obtain profits which they save and invest, thereby increasing the capital stock and hence, the marginal product of labour (at any given quantity of labour). This in turn puts upward pressure on wages in the industrial sector, inducing a flow of labour in from the agricultural sector, mitigating the upward pressure on wages. The Lewis-Fei-Ranis model helps explain growth in Japan in the early part of the twentieth century. However, in the Japanese case, the capitalist wage rate was raised before all surplus rural labour was absorbed.

Hollis B. Chenery (1979) emphasises, in his patterns of growth model, both domestic and international constraints and recognises that increased savings and investment are necessary but not sufficient conditions for economic growth (see also Chenery and Syrquin 1975). Chenery identifies several characteristic features of the development process relating to the structure of the economy to which LDCs must pay attention, as well as the fact that LDCs are part of a highly integrated international system that can promote as well as hinder their development.

The structuralists have been criticised because of the inapplicability and irrelevance of their models to developing countries. One reason is because the pioneer, Lewis, was writing about the structural transformation of Great Britain.

Neo-Marxist Thinking, Dependency, and Self-Reliance

Dependency theory articulates the need for the developing regions in Africa, Latin America, and Asia to rid themselves of their endemic dependence on more advanced countries. Scholars have written much on dependency theory, but Paul Baran's *The Political Economy of Growth* (1957) marked the beginning of Marxist dependency theory and an attempt to develop a focus on the problems of the developing world. Baran tries to explain many of the difficulties capitalist developing countries encounter when dealing with development and believed that advantageous progressive coalitions would inevitably result from an alliance between the bourgeoisie and more moderate leaders of the workers and peasants.

André Gunder Frank (1969) divides societies into the centre (the developed countries) and the periphery (the developing countries). S.K.B. Asante (1986) defines dependency as 'a peripheral formation and relation in the world system through which former colonies and other underdeveloped countries are exploited economically, and their backwardness is maintained over time'. Asante describes the functioning of dependency based on the preservation of the status quo by the coalition of domestic privileged elite (such as the political and ruling group and the military) and external interests and forces. These groups constitute the main actors of dependency. Thus, imbalance in international trade and resource flows (sometimes called the North-South dichotomy) forms the core of dependency. It is believed that the 'periphery' (LDCs), due to their weak position, will suffer welfare losses and worsening trade relationship with the 'centre' (the industrial countries) if they trade. The totality of these arguments advanced by those who criticise trade between 'centre' and 'periphery' constitutes dependency theory.

The dependency school believes that international links between developing and industrialised countries constitute a barrier to development through trade and investment. Dependency is, essentially, considered to be the means of perpetuating underdevelopment. In other words, as long as the LDCs remain underdeveloped, they will be dependent.

International dependency thinking focuses mainly on external constraints to development.[3] Proponents of dependency argue that numbers, especially statistical averages calculated by structuralists, are of limited economic value. In their belief, unequal power relationships between the centre (more advanced countries) and the periphery (LDCs), render attempts by poor nations to be self-reliant and independent destined for failure.

Finally, they argue that advice provided by well-meaning but often uninformed, biased and ethnocentric international 'expert' advisers from developed country assistance agencies and multilateral donors does more harm than good. For example, the role of multinational companies (MNCs) or transnational companies (TNCs) is prominent in this regard, through the extraction and transfer of surplus by way of profit, repatriation or transfer pricing from the LDCs to the industrialised countries.

The dependency school is criticised for overemphasising external factors. Although LDCs may exhibit a temporal lack of advancement vis-à-vis the so-called advanced countries, to consider them backward is conceptually questionable. The whole notion of the centre-periphery theory, which Asante upholds, is under considerable debate among scholars.

The Neoclassical School

In the neoclassical exogenous model, the determinants of output growth are technology, labour, and capital. If savings are larger, then capital per worker will grow, leading to rising income per capita and vice versa. The neoclassical thinking can be expressed as the Solow-Swan model of the production function type $Y=F(N,K)$ which is expanded to

$$\Delta Y/Y = \Delta A/A + \Delta N/N + \Delta K/K$$

where Y represents total output, N and K represent the inputs of labour and capital, and A represents the productivity of capital and labour, and $\Delta Y/Y$, $\Delta A/A$, $\Delta N/N$, and $\Delta K/K$ represent changes in these variables respectively. The classical stationary state and diminishing marginal product of inputs are implicit in the model, while convergence is expected.

The Solow-Swan model, which typifies the neoclassical school, asserts that because of the diminishing marginal product of inputs, sustained growth is possible only through technological change (Solow 1956; see also Swan 1956). The notion of diminishing marginal product is rooted in the belief that as more inputs are used to produce additional output under a fixed technology and fixed resource base, additional output per unit of input will decline.

Solow examined the sources of growth analysis to determine the contribution of each factor to total growth (growth rate of the national product, of the labour force, and of capital). According to Solow high income countries have been able to sustain growth in per capita income over long periods of time because, in these countries, technological progress has allowed output per worker to continue to grow.

The neoclassical thinkers theorise that underdevelopment results from poor resource allocation due to incorrect pricing policies and excessive state intervention, hence the strong emphasis on structural adjustment involving reducing the size of government, privatisation, and exchange rate liberalisation. Notably, neoclassicism led to neoliberalism and so-called market fundamentalism. The less than satisfactory results of adjustment in Africa point to the failure of this line of thinking—or, at least, to the flaws in its conception and implementation with regard to Africa.

In short, the neoclassical school believes that increasing savings and capital formation and reducing domestic market distortions or barriers to foreign investment will bring about development through growth. Obviously, the lack of consideration for equity issues and distributive imperatives is a major shortcoming of the neoclassical theory. The theory does not discuss how changes in institutions and incentive mechanisms affect the variables. Of all the theories of growth and development, the neoclassical theory and the dependency theory have been the most significantly applied to Africa.

Endogenous Models

More recently, some economists are calling for a balance between the state and free market in a more endogenised growth model. The endogenous model that focuses on technological progress and innovation typifies this school of thought. The new growth theories (Frankel 1962; Lucas 1988; Romer 1990) believe that technological change is endogenous. They recognise the role of the private sector and free market enterprise as the engine of growth, but suggest an active role for public policy in promoting economic development. Even the World Bank is now advocating pragmatic policies and pragmatic orthodoxy, which allows for government intervention, regulation and arbitration.

The endogenous growth theory can be expressed as the AK model as $Y = AK$ where A is a factor that affects technology and K is the embodiment of physical and human capital. This suggests that technological change is endogenous and that education and knowledge generate external economies that cause the Solow $\forall$ to equal unity, resulting in increasing returns. This leads to sustained long-term growth, which suggests lack of convergence.

$Y = Ae^{iit}K^{\alpha}L^{1-\alpha}$ is reduced to $Y = Ae^{iit}K$

The endogenous growth theory discards the neoclassical assumption of diminishing returns to capital investment and accepts the possibility of increasing returns to scale in aggregate production. The theory also focuses on the role of externalities in determining the rate of return of capital investment. The assumption is that public and private investment in human capital generates external economies and productivity improvements that, in turn, offset the natural tendency for diminishing returns. The entire focus of endogenous growth theory explains the existence of increasing returns to scale and divergent long-term growth patterns among countries.

'In our view', state Philippe Aghion and Peter Howitt (1998:85), 'capital accumulation and innovation should be regarded not as distinct causal factors but as two aspects of the same process. For new technologies are almost always embodied in new forms of human and physical capital that must be accumulated if the technology is to be used'. In sum, several factors come together to determine the level of output in a country: government policy, economic behaviour, technology (which is determined by the expenditure on research and development), the rate of accumulation of factors of production (land, labour, capital, and entrepreneurship), and savings. The higher the rate of growth of output, the higher the savings.

As can be seen, to address inherent distortion and a myriad of imperfections and institutional dysfunctions, pioneers of development economics offered explanations—none of which were explicitly Africa-focussed. In his review of the *Handbook of Development Economics*, Albert Fishlow sums up these explanations as follows:

> ... W. Arthur Lewis and Raul Prebisch emphasized the divergence between the shadow and market prices of labor and foreign exchange respectively. Labor was too dear and foreign exchange too cheap. These distortions afforded scope for positive governmental action to subsidize absorption of labor by industry and to erect protective barriers against imports. Paul N. Rosenstein-Rodan pointed to the need for investment coordination and a big push if development were to occur. There was an obvious role for sectoral planning; the Mahalanobis model was an early formalization that became the basis for Indian policy for many years. Hirschman stressed the importance of investing in industries that employed 'dynamic linkages' to induce fuller utilization of underemployed resources. His unbalanced growth strategy exploited latent externalities and required an active state prepared to play an entrepreneurial role. Gunnar Myrdal insisted upon land redistribution and broad reform as essential components for Asian development; the inherited rural institutional structure militated against progress (Fishlow 1991: 1729).

Theories about how to develop Africa have come in various forms. Some suggest that eliminating government and allowing the free market to operate in an uninterrupted way will result in productive and allocative efficiencies and a self-regulating developed economic system. Others believe that government has a critical role to play in the development process, especially in regulatory realms and in providing the framework and enabling environment. Some argue that the development process is temporal and countries overcome burdens by going through the inevitable stages and become developed. Others contend that only through an infusion of a great amount of capital into the countries and an increase in the level of industrialisation, especially in the urban modern sector, can the rural agricultural sector experience a rise in the productivity of labour, which will bring about growth and development.

Those who focus on capital accumulation recommend saving more in order to invest more as a way to bring about development. Others emphasise getting the fundamentals right: human capital development, technology, outward-oriented policies that encourage exports, and import substitution. Yet some, in recognition of what they consider to be Africa's disadvantageous relationship with the developed world, recommend de-linkage from the central sources of exploitation and dependence and emphasise self-reliance. Still others recommend providing the society's basic needs as a means of engendering development.

Methodological Developments

Economic methodology mirrors economic theory and derives from it. Hence, economic methodology has been an extension of the theoretical constructs discussed in the previous sections. As is the case of economic theory, economic methodological approaches to the study of Africa have also been driven by prevailing Western or Eurocentric paradigms. Interestingly, the original interest in growth had little to do with underdevelopment (Basu 1997: 43). Indeed, the original interest centred on explaining the successes of wealthy Western nations. Economic growth was at the centre of this research interest and was studied mostly to explain the causes of growth in the Western world. Furthermore, until recently, economists (mostly of the orthodox school) tended to provide a uniquely economic answer to the question as to what causes growth to occur and why Africa is underdeveloped. Hence, research on Africa's development focussed on economic variables and development prescriptions that have remained largely economic in nature. Roughly, since the late 1980s, however, there seems to be new Africa-specific research and a new awakening to non-economic variables in the economic study of Africa. In fact, African economic development is beginning to enjoy a distinct attention in and of itself.[4] The fact is that because Africa is the least developed continent, it merits special attention. In his prominent article, 'The economics of development: a survey', Stern (1989:606) refers to '... the great diversity in the circumstances, attainments and difficulties across the world's countries'. According to Stern, making such simple distinctions as 'North and South, developed and underdeveloped, and so on' is extremely misleading. Hence, there is a need to minimise this high degree of diversity through a regional focus. A focus on Africa was designed to shed more light on the uniqueness of the African continent, discuss its development difficulties and their global implications, and establish Africa-specific remedies necessary to bring about development on the African continent. We now see issues like ethnic diversity, the colonial legacy, political instability, democracy, culture, and geography being raised within the mainstream of economic thinking as possible explicators of Africa's underdevelopment.

Alongside the methodological transformations that have occurred there is a shift in the conceptual thinking about economic development. Since the 1970s a new economic view has developed, ushering in the so-called dethroning of 'GNP' and a redefinition of development in terms of the reduction or elimination of poverty, inequality, and unemployment within the context of a growing economy (Todaro 1996). The emphasis of the World Bank shifted from 'growth' to 'redistribution', with a renewed recognition of the need aggressively to attack poverty and improve quality of life.

Cross-Country Statistical Analyses

Notwithstanding this new awakening, more eclectic approaches and models of growth have not been developed, but orthodox economists are beginning to test for the significance of other non-economic variables including historical, political, socio-cultural, geographical, environmental, and international factors. The starting point is the cross-country regressions that find the so-called Africa effect or the significant negative African dummy, which purports that being an African country has an adverse impact on growth (see Grier and Tullock 1989; Barro 1991; Levine and Easterly 1997; Gunning and Collier 1999). Stern (1989) provides invaluable insight into the origin and development of cross-country analyses of growth. In other words, the African dummy theory postulates that Africa is destined, by virtue of its geographical location, geographical characteristics, and isolation, to grow slowly. Bloom and Sachs (1998) do not find a significant African dummy and argue that Africa's unique geographical characteristics explain its dismal growth experience. Others, especially Paul Collier, take the position that policy choices made by African leaders have deepened Africa's lack of competitiveness and sub-par performance.

Graziella Bertocchi and Fabio Canova (2002) and Xavier Sala-i-Martín (1997) found that the colonial heritage explains Africa's growth, or lack thereof, and renders the African dummy insignificant. Gregory Price (2000) concludes that colonialism and colonial legacies adversely affect growth in former colonies in sub-Saharan Africa, even though differences exist among Francophone, Anglophone, and Luso-phone Africa. Robert Barro (1997; 1999) finds the existence of a nonlinear effect of democracy on growth. Paul Collier and Kwabena Gyimah-Brempong have found, through rigorous studies, that economic growth is unlikely to occur in the absence of political stability and democratic entrenchment (Collier and Hoeffler 2002; Gyimah-Brempong 2003).

Many economists have determined that ethnic and cultural diversity leads to slow growth and, in fact, may maintain a country in a state of low growth, especially if it is coupled with economic distress, significant income inequality, limited political rights and undemocratic systems. A number of economists (Easterly and Levine 1997; Rodrick 1997; Collier 1998) conclude that ethno-religious conflict and instability are bad for growth and development and Africa has been bedevilled by inter-ethnic conflict throughout its history.

Early on, G. W. Scully (1988: 653) concluded that 'nations that have chosen to suppress economic, political, and civil liberties have gravely affected the standard of living of their citizens'. Emphasis is placed on social capital and geography in the study of growth and development in Africa and elsewhere (Bloom and Sachs 1998; Frankel and Roemer 1999). Paul Collier and Jan William Gunning (1999) present a lack of social capital, lack of openness to trade, deficient public service, geography and risk, lack of financial depth, and high aid dependence as significant factors that have perpetuated underdevelopment. Missing from their analysis, however, is the historical legacy and external dimension. Perhaps none captures this better than the following statement from the World Bank (2000):

> The debate on Africa's slow growth has offered many explanations. Some factors—such as geography (tropical location, a low ratio of coastline to interior and the resulting high transport costs), small states, high ethnic diversity, unpredictable rainfall, and terms of trade shocks—are taken to represent 'destiny', or exogenous factors beyond the control of African policymakers. Others, such as poor policies (including trade and exchange rate policies, nationalization, and other restraints on economic activity) can, in principle, be changed. A second dimension distinguishes such factors depending on whether they are primarily domestic or external.

The study of Africa in the economics discipline is in flux and based on cross-country and often comparative studies. Notably, a consensus seems to be emerging that concludes that Africa's underdevelopment is caused by a complex mixture of factors—some of which lie in the continent's history of exploitation and colonialism, its postcolonial misgovernance and political instability, and unfavourable external relations.[5] The bottom line is that 'Africa's performance is influenced by its history and its geography. But sound policies and strong institutions can moderate exogenous factors, and Africa's economies will, like others, respond to better economic policies' (World Bank 2000:23).

On How Development can Occur in Africa

In recent times, the increasing focus on Africa in economics has not been limited only to the causes of Africa's underdevelopment; it has also been on how development can occur in Africa. If we accept the recent literature, the analysis of Africa's intractable development dilemma must be multifaceted or at least comprehensive—not dependent solely on an economic approach. In reality, however, we find that identifying the problem is one thing; prescribing appropriate remedies is another. With few exceptions, the underlying prescriptions and their *modus operandi* remain the same one-size-fits-all neoliberal structural adjustment programmes prescribed mostly by outsiders. Since the 1960s, Africa has suffered from faulty and inappropriate advice given by well-meaning but often uninformed, biased, and sometimes politically motivated 'expert' advisers from the developed world, usually representatives of the World Bank, the IMF, and the United Nations.

To this end, there are abundant recommendations on how to bring about economic development in Africa, from World Bank publications to texts and scholarly articles used in intellectual circles. Indeed, in 1991 the World Bank devoted its *World Development Report* to the 'Challenge of Development' in an attempt to explain how development occurs in the developed world and how it would occur in developing countries. In another publication, the World Bank (2000) asks *Can Africa Claim the 21st Century?* Each year, the World Bank publishes the *World Development Report*. It is therefore a difficult task to synthesise these myriad prescriptions in a short paragraph.

The prescriptions can be categorised into three groups: (i) those that are part and parcel of development theories presented in the preceding section; (ii) those that have been perennially prescribed by the multilateral organisations—the World Bank, United Nations, and IMF and their experts; and (iii) those found in the literature written by scholars and development practitioners. Largely, the generally recommended approach has been to target growth as a means of bringing about economic development. From the three categories of policy prescriptions, five general approaches to solving Africa's underdevelopment have been most utilised.

These five basic approaches, identified and summarised below, have been most often recommended and implemented over the years to bring economic growth and development to Africa. The first is the trickle-down approach, which is centred on the belief that economic take-off would occur after large amounts of foreign aid, private investment, and expanded trade opportunities and the benefits trickled down to the poorest members of each society. Many argue that this approach failed because of the concentration of economic resources in the hands of the rich, unrepresentative governments, and the exclusion of the majority of affected populations from economic decision-making. Also, when developing countries' economies were integrated into the international market place, they could not compete equitably.

Second, the basic human needs approach, based on development assistance and credit, was implemented but eventually led to Africa's current debt crisis. In this approach, it was believed that the best way to bring about development was by providing the basic human needs of food housing and medical care. Third, industrialisation through import substitution was attempted whereby countries such as Nigeria tried to replace imports with homemade goods. Import substitution was couched in terms of self-reliance and producing for local needs through regional integration and cooperation. In the 1970s, countries like Nigeria embarked on an import substitution industrialisation strategy supported by an oil boom. The underlying argument advanced by the United Nations and H. Singer (1950, quoted in Stern 1989: 630) was that '... the terms of trade facing developing countries for their traditional exports were deteriorating (i.e. the world prices of their exports—primary commodities—were declining relative to those for their imports—manufactures) so that as time progressed they would have to export more and more primary products to buy a given quantity of manufactures'.

To avoid this comparative disadvantage and trade deterioration, it was suggested that LDCs needed to both industrialise and control the increasingly expensive imports. Debt-financed growth subsequently created economic crises.

The fourth approach called for structural adjustment programmes based on imposed solutions of economic reforms, and the fifth approach advocated sustainable development based on long-term development. Africa's repeated failures are highlighted by this succession of approaches which, it is important to note, have done little to alleviate the continent's woes.

If the 1970s were the disaster years, the 1980s became Africa's lost decade. Africa was plagued by minimal industrialisation, increasing poverty, worsening economic conditions, and debt-driven austerity measures. The multilateral organisations, the IMF and World Bank, introduced stabilisation and structural adjustment programmes. Then, during the 1990s, the focus became self-reliance and the intensification of a regional strategy for African economic development. This period saw the strengthening of the Organisation of African Unity (OAU) and the formation of continental and regional organisations such as the African Economic Community (AEC), the Economic Community for West African States (ECOWAS), and, more recently, the African Union.

Targeting Economic Growth

As early as 1958, Albert Hirschman noted that poor countries should adopt development strategies that spur investment decisions. Since developing nations do not have enough of the skills needed to launch the 'big push,' the best approach, according to him, would be to deliberately unbalance the economy in line with a predetermined strategy. In this way, growth can then be encouraged to spread from one sector to another.

D. Byerlee (1973) has argued that labour-intensive agricultural development strategies can actually have forward and backward linkages for agricultural production, as well as have an increasing effect on non-agricultural employment through the processing and marketing of agricultural output. In like manner, Peter Kilby and Bruce Johnston (1971) found evidence that a labour-intensive strategy of agricultural development involving limited mechanisation (i.e. using locally fabricated small machines) had the greatest impact on non-agricultural employment, since the small machines were produced in the rural and urban small-scale sector by labour-intensive techniques. This is not the case with a strategy based on imported tractors or heavy machinery usage. Areas to look at include, but are not limited to, credit, land reform, relevant technology, economic linkages, and subsidies.

The World Bank (1991) argues that policies and institutions are crucial: 'A central issue of development ... is the interaction between governments and markets' (1991: 1). The requirements of rapid development include peace, economic integration—global integration in trade, investment, factor flows, technology, communication and global conditions and country policies. However, they write that '[i]ncreasing exposure to external influences undoubtedly puts the developing countries at risk' (1991:3).

In the specific case of Africa, the World Bank (2000) recommends improvement in governance, the reduction in poverty and inequality, investment in people, improvement in infrastructure, increases in agricultural and rural development, trade and regional policy reform, export diversification, and reduction in debt and dependence.

The IMF recommendations for improvement of growth performance in Africa involve an increase of the investment ratio of GDP; a government focus on essential services, infrastructure, and human resources; social development; and the maintenance of sound macro-economic policies in terms of reducing inflation, stabilising prices, and lowering deficits. The IMF also recommends implementing structural reforms through privatisation, financial sector reforms, trade liberalisation, and comprehensive and sustained policy reform.

The problem is that because of past failures and unpleasant experiences, African countries will look upon these new prescriptions with scepticism and suspicion. Because of the dismal results of previous prescriptions, the credibility of multilateral organisations is now in question. African countries believe that these organisations are either politically motivated or represent the interests of the developed world and their multinational corporations. One common theme among the recommendations of these multilateral institutions is the utter silence on the record, role, and responsibility of the international community, development agencies, and donor countries in the development equation of African countries. In other words, there appears to be a deliberate exclusion of the external dimensions of Africa's underdevelopment in both the analyses and proposals. In effect, what they are saying is: once African countries take care of the internal dimensions of their development failures, they will join the ranks of the developed world. Unfortunately, that is not so. Joseph Stiglitz (2001: 36)), Chief Economist at the World Bank from 1997 to 2000, talks about his first-hand knowledge of the dark side of globalisation as he writes of '... how so-called structural adjustment loans to some of the poorest countries in the world "restructured" those countries' economies so as to eliminate jobs but did not provide the means of creating new ones, leading to widespread unemployment and cuts in basic services'. Africa's lacklustre record in attracting direct foreign investment (DFI) underscores this contradiction.

Similarly, using the example of Kenya, where unfettered deregulation led to soaring interest rates, Stiglitz (2001:40) writes: 'Even after the United States experienced the ruinous consequences of financial deregulation, in the form of the savings-and-loans debacle, the IMF preached the gospel of rapid deregulation around the world, to countries far less able to withstand its negative consequences'.

Significant evidence of the IMF's overreach and problematic structural adjustment failures in Africa abound in the literature. Many recent publications (Korten 1995; Rodrick 1997; MacEwan 1999; Dunkley 2000; Ugarteche 2000) provide damning evidence of the gross failures of neoliberalism. Essentially, these authors have argued that neoliberal policies have been detrimental to economic development in developing countries. Oscar Ugarteche (2000) shows evidence of what he calls systematic crisis and worsening of LDC debt burden by IMF loans. In 2000, over half of the 54 African countries were severely indebted.

In sum, Africa needs resolute leadership, better governance, human and physical capital, investment, and international support. Overall, and based on existing literature, we can conclude that policies to promote growth include investment in physical capital, saving and investment, population control, and human capital development. Promoting growth also involves a decrease in unnecessary government regulation, which will increase total factor productivity and technical progress. In addition, governments must consciously encourage an increase in the rate of innovation and appropriate technology transfer.

On Trade, Regional Integration, and Globalisation

Another important element of the economics-African studies nexus is Africa's international economic relations, especially its relationship with the richer countries with regard to trade, private foreign investment, debt, and aid. This discussion, often couched in terms of neoliberal globalisation, prompts the question: Will globalisation as it is presently conceived and proposed in the neoliberal tradition be beneficial to African countries, and why? What are the implications and lessons of the current globalisation craze for African countries and what conclusions can we draw from these implications? These questions are important in light of the fact that as of November 2000, 41 of the 140 members of WTO were African countries, with the majority of them joining the organisation at its inception on 1 January 1995.

We need to understand globalisation's theoretical underpinnings and its relevance as the economics profession advances it in the African context. From an economic viewpoint, what could be considered a theory of globalisation is the extension of the classical trade theory; the sum total of which is that international trade and integration into the global economy contribute to economic growth, improved allocation of resources, and improved overall welfare.

Trade, Foreign Investment, and Debt

The neoliberal theory upon which the neoliberal vision of globalisation rests states that free movement of goods (free trade), services, and capital, unimpeded by government regulation, will lead to rapid economic growth. According to neoclassicism, this will increase global output and international efficiency because the gains from a comparative advantage-based division of labour and specialisation will improve overall welfare. In its dynamic form, neoclassicists argue that trade raises domestic levels of income, which in turn raise the level of saving. Since investment depends on saving and leads to growth, trade will therefore lead to growth. Likewise, the international mobility of financial capital will ensure that foreign capital will augment domestic saving and investment and lead to national economic growth.

The neoliberal position is not new. The role that trade and international cooperation play in fostering economic growth has been identified throughout the history of economic thought, from the mercantilist era through the classical period, to modern times. Trade, regional and global economic integration and cooperation are considered necessary for small fragmented economies to lower per unit production costs and to increase economic viability. Thus, integration of industrial production must accompany integration of markets.

Yet the reality is that, as in the general case of neoclassicism, neoclassical trade theories and integration theories are of little relevance to Africa because the fundamental neoclassical assumptions of full employment and perfect competition are absent, and the continent is instead characterised by market segmentation and information asymmetries. The problem, as the case of Africa illustrates, is that although trade may increase total global output, the equitable distribution of the gains from trade is far from guaranteed. This is because trade policy always has inter-personal, inter-sectoral, and inter-group re-distributive consequences.

Another criticism of the neoclassical-based trade theory is that it could be interpreted to mean that Africa and other developing countries 'should under welfare maximization and free trade continue to be producers of primary commodities, exchanging them for imports of manufactures' (Krueger 1984: 521). Hence, one cannot but conclude that the neoliberal foundations of globalisation are inadequate in the developing countries context and will lead to undesirable consequences. It seems, therefore, that therein lies the fundamental problem.

Sub-Saharan Africa remains an insignificant player in global trade, accounting for less than 1.35 percent of world exports of 5.2 trillion dollars and 1.5 percent of global imports of 5.3 trillion in 1998. Three major features characterise Africa's international trade: a highly volatile volume of trade history; lack of commodity diversification—primary products being by far the dominant export commodity; and export market concentration. The domination of African foreign trade by the European Community is historical, but the domination by primary products is a phenomenon that started in the early 1970s.

In adopting neoliberal reforms, one of the expectations of African countries is increased and unfettered capital flows from the rich countries in the form of direct investment, which they perceive to be extremely beneficial.[6] The reality, following over a decade of economic reform, is utterly disappointing. While recent trends suggest that the flow of DFI into developing countries is increasing, the amount of DFI that Africa receives is still very low. For example, in 1997 sub-Saharan Africa (SSA) received only 1.3 percent of the world's $394 billion total direct foreign investments (1.5 percent in 1996). In 1997, low- and middle-income countries received a total of $160,579 million, while SSA received only $5,222 million, or 3.3 percent, of the total (World Bank 1999).

African countries are currently facing serious external debt burdens that discourage foreign investment. Africa's external debt has more than doubled in the past two decades. From a mere $93 billion in 1980, Africa's external debt grew to $240 billion in 1991 and rose to $285 billion in 1993 (World Bank 1997).

Table 1: Africa's Crushing Debt Burden

	Percentage of African Countries	African Countries as Ratio of all Indebted Countries (%)
Severely Indebted (>Greater than 80% debt burden)	51.8	58.3
Moderately Indebted (60-80% burden)	24	37
Less Indebted (50-60% burden)	18.5	15.6

Source: World Bank 1997.

Although according to the World Bank Africa's total debt accounted for only 16 percent of the external debt of developing countries in 1993—just one third of Latin America's debt—it has the highest debt burden. In 1997, Africa's external debt almost reached the level of total regional GDP! This means that the debt/GDP ratio of the continent was close to 100 percent. In other words, Africa owed almost the same amount to foreign creditors as the total amount of goods and services it produced in that year. The sub-Saharan African debt burden (debt/GDP ratio) of 123.1 percent in 1993 raises serious concerns. In 1995 all sub-Saharan African countries, with the exception of Burkina Faso, had debt burdens that exceeded 60 percent. In 15 of the 30 countries classified by the World Bank as low-income countries, the debt burden exceeded 100 percent.

Africa's alarmingly high external debt burden constitutes a serious constraint to development because debt repayments absorb resources that could be channelled into domestic investment and development efforts. A high external debt burden discourages foreign investment because it creates a high risk environment characterised by capital flight, uncertainty among potential foreign investors about the possibility of profit repatriation, and higher taxes to service debts.

Globalisation

The advocacy of globalisation is mostly based on the benefits of free trade, which is believed to maximise internal and global welfare under laissez-faire regimes. For Africa it is argued that the need for global cooperation is both economic (to engender national, continental, and regional economic growth) and political (to foster and preserve independence and democracy). The main argument in favour of global cooperation is that trade has played an important role in the economic growth of many nations. To grow rapidly, therefore, it is argued that African countries must take trade seriously. Another argument in favour of global cooperation is that an absence of global cooperation causes a loss of markets, technology transfer, and capital, as well as the global interrelationships necessary to foster economic development. It appears that African countries must work harder to increase the flow of capital and technology into their countries.

Furthermore, global cooperation, economists believe, fosters political stability through induced democratic reforms and mutual political reinforcement by regional and global political organisations. Efficiency gains result from the use of scarce resources and improved quality of goods and services, improved resource allocation, and increased competition and product specialisation. Although losses may result (mainly from comparative and absolute advantages that will accompany a more global posture), openness, if properly engaged, will ensure net gains to participants in the form of cheaper imports, economies of scale, and increased competition.

Because of the human, environmental, social and political costs, some analysts reject neoliberalism simply on ethical and moral grounds. Notably, not all researchers agree with criticisms of globalisation (see Gilpin 2001; Sahn et al., 1997; Vásquez 2000). For instance, R. Gilpin (2001: 367) believes that 'Many of the problems alleged to be the result of economic globalization are really the consequences of unfortunate national policies and government decisions'.

Furthermore, contrary to the argument that neoliberal policies are inevitable, economists such as Arthur MacEwan (1999) use historical evidence to show that there is an alternative to neoliberalism and SAPs. According to him, free trade cannot be defended as an optimal policy on purely economic grounds because the choice is not necessarily between openness and autarky. Besides, globalisation 'is exposing a deep fault line between groups who have the skills and mobility to flourish in global markets and those who either don't have these advantages or perceive the expansion of unregulated markets as inimical to social stability and deeply held norms' (Rodrick 1997: 2). African countries 'form part of and participate in the programs of the (global) multilateral organizations (World Bank, IMF, etc.) They are heavily influenced by global phenomena over much of which they have little control. Also, the globalization adventure has been extremely costly to Africa even though there are potential benefits' (Nnadozie 2001: 25).

Economic Reform and Neoclassical Market Fundamentalism

The literature on African economic reform is mainly comprised of three distinct strands. The first strand, mostly generated by the international financial institutions (IFIs), tends to present a positive picture of the outcome of reforms (see IMF 1993; World Bank 1994). The second is from independent scholars, mostly Africanists (Heller et al., 1988; Chapelier and Tabatabai 1989; Obidegwu 1990; Haggard and Kaufman 1992; Havnevik et al., 1993), who have generated a spirited denunciation of the adjustment exercise as a total failure. The third category is literature that tries to provide the theoretical and analytical framework for understanding, analysing, and evaluating the reform process. Both the World Bank and the IMF have been presenting strong arguments for both the merits and the success of adjustment in the case of African countries. In a comparative sense, their arguments have been that the adjusting countries are better off than non-adjusting countries. This exaggerated optimism is exemplified by the following statement from The World Bank's *Adjustment in Africa* (1994: 7): 'African countries that have undertaken some reforms and achieved some increase in growth, the majority of the poor are probably better off and almost certainly no worse off'.

Criticism of the IMF and World Bank, their reform agenda, and their portrayal of the success of economic reform abound (see Haggard and Kaufman 1992). Based on a rigorous analysis of the World Bank's *Adjustment in Africa* (1994), Nguyuru H. I. Lipumba (1994: 40) describes the IMF paper *Economic Adjustment in Low-Income Countries* as 'more of a public relations exercise aimed at influencing the funding of the second [Enhanced Structural Adjustment Facility] (ESAF) than a serious attempt to analyze the impact of SAF/ESAF countries, particularly in Africa'. Joseph Stiglitz (2002) echoes the IMF's failures by drawing attention to the contradiction resulting from a change in its mission and ideology. According to him, the IMF was founded on 'the belief that markets often worked badly, it now champions market supremacy with ideological fervor' (2002: 12). In effect, Stiglitz opines that IMF-engineered privatisation destroyed jobs instead of creating them and has led to looting and a tremendous level of asset stripping.

Institutional, Organisational, and Infrastructure Dimensions

Like in other social sciences, much of the focus of economics on Africa has been theme-driven. Hence, we see a significant chronological focus on such familiar themes as structural adjustment, conflict, political instability, HIV/AIDS, democracy and democratisation, knowledge, and social capital. The frenzied, à la mode, theme-driven approach has also dictated the allocation of research dollars and efforts. There is also the issue of the esoteric and excessive mathematisation of economics. This mathematisation of economic methodology and the role that abstraction and esoteric modelling in economics have made economics inaccessible and unappealing to other disciplines.

Given recent developments in the continent and the intensification of globalisation, which has led to renewed interest in African studies, it is possible that the economics-African studies gap can be bridged. However, university leadership has a stake in defining the agenda. The question is: how many universities have courses in international business without any courses on Africa? Unfortunately, several do. Another problem is that foundations, which often dictate the agenda and therefore the focus of reputable research, mostly fund regional studies.

Organisations

Over the years, several national and sub-national professional organisations have emerged to provide the framework for African studies and to cater to the needs of Africanists. Prominent among them is the paramount national organisation of

Africanists, the U.S. African Studies Association (ASA) founded in 1957. There are also the regional organisations such as the Mid-America Alliance for African Studies (MAAAS) and the South East Africanists Association (SERSAS). Specialised professional organisations include the African Finance and Economics Association (AFEA), founded in 1988, which is an affiliate of the American Economic Association (AEA) and the American Finance Association (AFA). We also see an increasing number of African intellectual diaspora networks: the Association of Kenyans Abroad (AKA), the Moroccan Association of Researchers and Scholars Abroad (MARS), the Association of Nigerians Abroad (ANA), the South African Network of Skills Abroad (SANSA), and the Tunisian Scientific Consortium (TSC).

Curriculum

Several institutions have begun integrating and even emphasising economics in their African studies curriculum. But economics course offerings in African studies reflect an institutional interest in African studies (or a lack thereof), which in turn reflects the number of African studies faculty members. An examination of some African studies programmes in the United States shows a high degree of divergence in the level and manner of incorporation and integration of economics in the African studies curriculum. For instance, Howard University has eleven graduate courses that pertain to African economics or development. Four of those courses do not specifically focus on African economics or development but the course incorporates these themes. African studies at Boston University (undergraduate) offers twelve economics courses, five of which specifically focus on economic development. Cornell University's Institute for African Development (graduate) offers six courses in applied economics and management, three economic development courses included in rural sociology courses, eleven city and regional planning courses, and one related course—industrial and labour relations.

At the other end of the spectrum, the University of Illinois, Urbana Champaign, offers two courses in economics of Africa and development. Likewise, Ohio State University's undergraduate African studies programme offers three economic courses, two of which specifically focus on economic development. The University of California, Berkeley's undergraduate international and area studies (which incorporates African studies) offers two courses on *Political and Economic Development in the Third World* under the auspices of African-American studies. New York University's Africana courses at the undergraduate level include one economics course while Emory University's undergraduate minor in African studies includes no economics course.

What approach should be used in the study of Africa within the economics discipline? There is a need for an eclectic approach to studying African development to reflect the multidimensional nature of Africa's development challenges. First, as we have seen from the recent rethinking in mainstream economics, African economic development involves a wide variety of issues, ranging from smallholder farming to international finance. It touches on virtually every branch in economics: micro and macro, labour, industrial organisation, public finance, resource economics, money and banking, human capital, growth, trade, etc., as well as branches in history, sociology, and political science. Second, the study of Africa should deal with both the political and institutional framework in which economic development takes place. Third, the study of Africa in the economics discipline should consider the economic situations in African countries including their relationships to rich nations, using theoretical tools of classical, neoclassical, and heterodox economics, and empirical studies by economists and economic historians, in a comparative context. Finally, we should recognise the diversity of development experiences reflected in different African countries and acknowledge that the lessons of theory and history can only be applied within certain institutional and national contexts. The ingredients causing economic failure in one set of circumstances, in different circumstances might contribute to success.

Publications

Currently, there is a wide range of publications focussing on Africa in economics. These publications include trade books on the continent and on specific countries, textbooks on African economics, and journals dealing with various aspects of African economics and development. Yet, before the recent surge in Africa-centred economics publications, Africa was treated as part of the developing world in economics textbooks and journals. A look at the prominent economic development or comparative economics textbooks used at the college level—Michael P. Todaro, *Economic Development* (2000); E. Wayne Nafziger, *Economics of Developing Countries* (1990); Dwight Perkins et al., *Economics of Development* (2001), etc.—supports this assertion. These books are too broad and do not deal specifically with Africa. They deal with a broad range of developing countries with very diverse structures. They are mostly inaccessible to students who are not upper level economics majors.

Emmanuel Nnadozie's (2003) *African Economic Development* addresses the problems of the existing texts by focussing on the African continent and by ensuring that the chapter contributions are written by experienced scholars, including African-born experts with a deep understanding of Africa and its economic challenges. It presents major contributions to the study of African economic development in an easily accessible way—designed so that economics and non-economics professors can use it as a standard text dealing with African development issues.

In the area of academic and scholarly journals, some progress has also been registered. Here again, economic journals focussing specifically on Africa in North America and Europe did not emerge until the 1980s. Before this period the *Journal of Development Studies* was the first and one of the best-known international journals in the area of development studies since its founding in 1964. Others include *Journal of International Development; Journal of Economic Growth; Review of Development Economics; Journal of Economic Development; World Development; Progress in Development;* and *Economic Development and Cultural Change.*

Africa-focussed journals in which economics articles occasionally appear include the *Journal of Modern African Studies*, *African Studies Review*, *Journal of African Business*, *West Africa Review*, and *African Economic Review*. The *Journal of African Finance and Economic Development* (JAFED), produced by the African Finance and Economics Association (AFEA), and the *Journal of African Economies* (JAE), produced by the Centre for the Study of African Economies (CSAE) of the University of Oxford, are the two most visible economics journals devoted to the economic analysis of Africa.

JAFED's goal '... is to provide a forum for the exchange of ideas between academicians and practitioners and to disseminate the results of empirical and theoretical research, policy issues, and practical applications to as broad and audience as possible'.[7] JAFED, which began publication in 1998, focuses on a broad range of African financial and economic development issues. The JAE, which began publication in 1992, '... is a vehicle to carry rigorous economic analysis entirely on Africa, for Africans and anyone interested in the continent—be they consultants, policy makers, academics, traders, financiers, development agents'.[8]

Although one can discern a welcome degree of progress, the support infrastructure necessary for a well-developed Africa focus in economics is weak and insufficient, especially in comparison to other areas. Also, in spite of recognition of the need to develop economics as an integral part of African studies, actions have yet to match the rhetoric. But with globalisation issues and a resurgent South Africa, the future looks bright.

Conclusion

This essay has examined recent major theoretical and methodological developments and the current state of the field of economics as it concerns African studies to shed more light on the evolution and transformation of economic thought and how it relates to Africa. This analysis has been undertaken through the lenses of theoretical dimensions, methodological developments, and institutional, organisational, and infrastructure issues. The essay highlights the mutual neglect and unusual relationship that exists between economics and African studies. The essay shows that even though economics has a central role to play in Africa studies, this has not been the case. In turn, African studies has just begun to recognise the centrality of economics in the curriculum. Not only is the economic approach in and of itself germane to African studies, but economics can be used as a tool in the analysis of political, social, and institutional issues. That is, economics can constitute a centrepiece or method for analysing issues and problems. It is, therefore, important to make economics a central focus of African studies programmes. African studies programmes ought to have a strong economics component and the fact that Africa's repeated economic failures and persistent underdevelopment poses a serious challenge to the economic discipline should not be treated lightly.

The multiplicity of development theoretical thinking in the African context points to the current confused state of affairs and to Africa's role as the experimental laboratory of competing and often ruinous development ideologies, paradigms, and theories, imposed mostly from the outside. There has not been any home-grown, unified theory of African development that takes into consideration the continent's unique historical experience and legacy; the extreme levels of economic, socio-cultural, political diversity and demographic realities; resource endowment; and relations with the outside world.

Africa's development thinking has swung from one extreme to the other, which demonstrates how Africa has historically served as the ideological and experimental guinea pig for neoclassical orthodoxy's free market liberalism and neo-Marxist *dirigisme*. Only recently has there been some attempt to provide more realistic and less ideologically-driven thinking that recognises that the answer lies neither on the extreme left nor on the extreme right. Rather a cautious blend of the state and markets coupled with a deep understanding of the uniqueness and reality of Africa is necessary. Recently, the focus has been on two competing visions. One focuses on capital accumulation and the other on technological progress and innovation. The endogenous development theory, which focuses on technological innovation, seems to be winning for now.

From the foregoing discussion, we can see that African economics has focussed mostly on growth, development and economic conditions of African countries. There has also been work done in the area of African economic history. Yet, unlike history or even political science, economics has remained sidelined when it comes to African studies. Until the late 1980s and early 1990s, economics had not been embedded in African studies.

The original interest in growth has little to do with underdevelopment. Also, growth has been used as proxy for development and in some cases it has been treated as synonymous with development. Until recently, economists (mostly of the orthodox school) tended to provide a uniquely economic explanation for Africa's underdevelopment. Hence, economics research on Africa focussed on economic variables, and development prescriptions remained largely economic in nature. More recently, however, there seems to be a new awakening to non-economic variables in the African development equation. We now see issues like ethnic diversity, the colonial legacy, political instability, democracy, culture, and geography being raised within the mainstream of economic thinking as possible explicators of Africa's underdevelopment. Coupled with the prior economic fundamentalism has been the absence of courses and teaching materials on African development.

There have been improvements in the area of economic institutional, organisational, and curricular resources that provide support for African studies in response to the neglect of Africa in the economics discipline and economics in African studies. Undoubtedly, more needs to be done to fill the gap and improve upon the critical mutually reinforcing roles that economics and African studies can play.

Notes

1. A more comprehensive list of economics schools of thought include the classical theory of economic stagnation, Marx's historical materialism, Rostow's stages of economic growth, vicious circle theory, balanced versus unbalanced growth, the Lewis-Fei-Ranis model, Baran's neo-Marxist thesis, dependency theory, neoclassical counterrevolution, neoclassical growth theory, and endogenous growth theory.

2. Named after Roy Harrod and Evsey Domar.

3. For easy access to the essential features of the dependency theory, see Brewer, *Marxist Theories of Imperialism: A Critical Survey* (1980). Major dependency theorists include Cardoso, Celso, Bran, O'Brien, etc. For details on the 'unequal exchange', 'enclave' or 'terms of trade' arguments, see any economic development text such as Hogendorn (1992: 433-441), Nafziger (1990: 390-415).

4. African economic development can mean either the economic development of Africa—the process of increasing incomes, improving human welfare, and changing the economic structure of African societies—or the economics of African development—the application of economic analysis to the understanding of the economies of African countries. In the latter case (with which we are mostly concerned), it is the study of the processes and factors that bring about or prevent economic development in Africa.

5. Many of the variables that have been found to be important in cross-country growth analysis are relevant for Africa. Temple (1999) provides us with these variables: investment in physical capital, investment in human capital, investment in research and development, population growth, international trade, financial systems, macroeconomic policy, government size, infrastructure and public capital, income and wealth inequality, and social and political factors.

6. Such benefits include increased economic growth and a positive spill-over from transferring technology to domestic firms. See Caves (1982); Helleiner (1989); and Hadad and Harrison (1993). Furthermore, a foreign presence accelerates productivity growth (see Aitken and Harrison [1999]) and transnational corporations (TNCs) may have direct and indirect positive employment effects in manufacturing and services (Lal 1995; Chitrakar and Weiss 1995).

7. Obtained from the *Journal of African Finance and Economic Development* website, http://www.afea.org.

8. Obtained from the *Journal of African Economies* website, http://jac.oupjournals.org/.

References

Aghion, P. and P. Howitt, 1988, *Endogenous Growth Theory*, Cambridge Massachusetts: MIT Press.

Aitken, B.J. and A.E. Harrison, 1999, 'Do domestic firms benefit from direct foreign investment? Evidence from Venezuela', *American Economic Review* 89 (3): 605-18.

Asante, S.K.B., 1986, *The Political Economy of Regionalism in Africa: A Decade of the Economic Community of West African States (ECOWAS)*, New York: Praeger.

Baran, P.A., ed., 1957, *The Political Economy of Growth*, New York: Modern Reader Paperbacks.

Barro, R., 1991, 'Economic Growth in a Cross Section of Countries', *Quarterly Journal of Economics* 106: 407-43.

Barro, R., 1997, *Determinants of Economic Growth: A Cross-Country Empirical Study*, Cambridge, MA: MIT Press.

Barro, R., 1999, 'Inequality, Growth, and Investment', Cambridge, MA: National Bureau of Economic Research.

Basu, K., 1997, *Analytical Development Economics: The Less Developed Economies Revisited*, Cambridge, MA: MIT Press.

Bertocchi, G. and F. Canova, 2002, 'Did Colonization Matter for Growth? An Empirical Exploration into the Historical Causes of Africa's Underdevelopment', *European Economic Review* 46: 1851-71.

Bloom, D.E. and J.D. Sachs, 1998, 'Geography, Democracy, and Economic Growth in Africa', *Brookings Papers on Economic Activity* 2: 207-95.

Brewer, A., 1990, *Marxist Theories of Imperialism: A Critical Survey*, London: Routledge.

Byerlee, D., 1973, 'Indirect Employment and Distribution Effects of Agricultural Development Strategies: A Simulation Approach Applied to Nigeria', East Lansing, MI: Michigan State University.

Caves, R.E., 1982, *Multinational Enterprise and Economic Analysis*, Cambridge, MA: Cambridge University Press.

Chapelier, G. and H. Tabatabai, 1989, 'Development and Adjustment: Stabilization, Structural Adjustment and UNDP policy', UNDP Policy Discussion Paper, 24-25: New York: United Nations Development Programme.

Chenery, H.B. and M. Syrquin, 1975, *Patterns of Development, 1950-1970*, London: Oxford University Press.

Chenery, H.B., 1979, *Structural Change and Development Policy*. New York: Oxford University Press.

Chenery, H.B. and T. N. Srinivasan, 1988, *Handbook of Development Economics*, Vol. 1, Amsterdam: Elsevier Science Publishers.

Chitrakar, R. and J. Weiss, 1995, 'Foreign Investment in Nepal in the 1980s: A cost benefit evaluation', *The Journal of Development Studies* 31: 451-66.

Collier, P., 1998, 'The Political Economy of Ethnicity', Centre for the Study of African Economies, Institute of Economics and Statistics, University of Oxford.

Collier, P. and J.W. Gunning, 1999, 'Explaining African Economic Performance', *Journal of Economic Literature*, XXXVII (March): 64-111.

Collier, P. and A. Hoeffler, 2002, 'On the Incidence of Civil War in Africa', *Journal of Conflict Resolution* 46 (2): 13-28.

Crafts, N. F. R., 1998, 'Economic History', in M. Milgate, J. Eatwell, and P. Newman, eds., *The New Palgrave Dictionary of Economics*, New York: Palgrave Publishers, 37-42.

Dunkley, G., 2000, *The Free Trade Adventure: The WTO, the Uruguay Round and Globalism*, London: Zed Books.

Easterly, W. and R. Levine, 1997, 'Africa's Growth Tragedy: Policies and Ethnic Divisions', *Quarterly Journal of Economics* 112: 1203-50.

Fei, J.C. and G. Ranis, 1964, *Development of the Labour Surplus Economy: Theory and Policy*, Homewood, IL.: Irwin.

Fishlow, A., 1991, 'Review of *Handbook of Development Economics*', *Journal of Economic Literature* XXIX (December): 1728-37.

Frank, A. G., 1969, *Latin America: Underdevelopment or Revolution*, New York: Monthly Review Press.

Frankel, J., and D. Roemer, 1999, 'Does Trade Cause Growth?' *American Economic Review* 89, 379-99.

Frankel, M., 1962, 'The Production Function in Allocation and Growth: A Synthesis', *American Economic Review* 52, 995-1022.

Gerschenkron, A., 1962, *Economic Backwardness in Historical Perspective*, Cambridge, MA: Harvard University Press.

Gibbon, P., K.J. Havnevik, and K. Hermele, 1993, *A Blighted Harvest: The World Bank and African Agriculture in the 1980s*, London: James Currey.

Gilpin, R., 2001, *Global Political Economy*, Princeton, NJ: Princeton University Press.

Grier, K. B. and G. Tullock, 1989, 'An empirical analysis of cross national economic growth, 1951-80', *Journal of Monetary Economics* 24: 259-76.

Gyimah-Brempong, K., 2003, 'Political Instability and Economic Development in Africa', in E. Nnadozie, ed., *African Economic Development*, Amsterdam: Academic Press.

Haddad, M. and A. Harrison, 1993, 'Are There Positive Spillovers from Direct Foreign Investment?: Evidence from Panel Data for Morocco', *The Journal of Development Economics* 42 (1): 51-75.

Haggard, S. and R. Kaufman, eds., 1992, *The Politics of Economic Adjustment: International Constraints, Distributive Conflicts, and the State*, New Jersey: Princeton University Press.

Helleiner, G. K., 1988, 'Comments on "Comparative Advantage and Structural Transformation": A Review of Africa's Economic Development Experience', in T. Paul Schultz and G. Ranis, eds., *The State of Development Economics: Progress and Perspectives*, Cambridge, MA: Basil Blackwell.

Helleiner, G.K., 1989, 'Transnational Corporations and Direct Foreign Investment', in H. Chenery and T. N. Srinivasan, eds., *Handbook of Development Economics*. Amsterdam: North Holland.

Heller, P. S. et al., 1988, 'The Implications of Fund-supported Adjustment Programs for Poverty: Experiences in Selected Countries', Occasional paper No. 58, Washington, DC: International Monetary Fund.

Hogendorn, J.S., 1992, *Economic Development*, Vol. 2. New York: Harper Collins.

International Monetary Fund, 1993, 'Economic Adjustment in Low-Income Countries: Experience under the Enhanced Structural Adjustment Facility', Occasional Paper, No. 106. Washington DC: IMF.

Kilby, P. and B.F. Johnston, 1971, 'The Choice of Agricultural Strategies and the Development of Manufacturing', Paper presented at the Conference on Strategies for Agricultural Development in the 1970s, Palo Alto, CA.

Korten, D., 1995, *When Corporations Rule the World*, West Hartford, CN: Kumarian Press.

Krueger, A.O., 1984, 'Trade Policies in Developing Countries', in P. B. Kenen and R. W. Jones, eds., *Handbook of International Economics*, Amsterdam: North-Holland.

Lal, S., 1995, 'Employment and Foreign Investment: Policy Options for Developing Countries', *International Labour Review* 134 (4-5): 521-41.

Lewis, A., 1954, 'Economics Development with Unlimited Supplies of Labour', *Manchester School* 22: 139-91.

Lipumba, N.H.I., 1994, 'Structural adjustment policies and economic performance of African countries', Williamstown, MA: Center for Development Economics, Williams College, October.

Lucas, R.E., 1988, 'On the mechanics of economic development', *Journal of Monetary Economics* 22 (January): 3-22.

MacEwan, A., 1999, *Neo-Liberalism or Democracy: Economic Strategy, Markets and Alternatives for the 21st Century*, London: Zed Books.

Nafziger, E.W., 1990, *The Economics of Developing Countries*, 2nd edition, Englewood Cliffs, NJ: Prentice Hall.

Nnadozie, E., 2001, 'Africa at the crossroads of globalization', Unpublished paper.

Nnadozie, E., 2003, *African Economic Development*, Amsterdam: Academic Press.

Nurkse, R., 1953, *Problems of Capital Formation in Underdeveloped Countries*, New York: Oxford University Press.

Obidegwu, C.F., 1990, 'Adjustment programs and economic change in sub-Saharan Africa', Washington DC: The World Bank, 40-42.

Perkins, D. H., S. Radelet, D.R. Snodgrass, M. Gillis, and M. Roemer, 2001, *Economics of Development*, Fifth edition, New York: W. W. Norton & Co.

Price, G. N., 2000, 'Economic growth in a cross section of non-industrial countries: does colonial heritage matter for Africa?', Paper presented at the Allied Social Science Association Meeting, New Orleans, LA, January.

Rodrick, D., 1997, *Has Globalization Gone Too Far?*, Washington, DC: Institute for International Economics.

Romer, P.M., 1990, 'Endogenous technological change', *Journal of Political Economy* 98: S71-S103.

Rostow, W.W., 1960, *The Stages of Economic Growth: A Non-Communist Manifesto*, London: Cambridge University Press.

Sahn, D.E., P. Dorosh, and S. Younger, 1997, *Structural Adjustment Reconsidered: Economic Policy and Poverty in Africa*, Cambridge, MA: Cambridge University Press.

Sala-i-Martin, X., 1997, 'I just ran two million regressions.' *American Economic Review*, May: 178-83.

Schumpeter, J.A., 1934, *The Theory of Economic Development*, Cambridge, MA: Harvard University Press.

Scully, G.W., 1988, 'The institutional framework and economic development', *Journal of Political Economy* 96 (3): 652-62.

Sen, A., 1988, 'The concept of development', in H. Chenery and T. N. Srinivasan, eds., *Handbook of Development Economics*, Amsterdam: North Holland.

Singer, H., 1950, 'The distribution of gains between investing and borrowing countries', *American Economic Review* 40: 473-85.

Solow, R.M., 1956, 'A contribution to the theory of economic growth', *Quarterly Journal of Economics* 70 (February): 65-94.

Stern, N., 1989, 'The economics of development: a survey', *The Economic Journal* 99: 597-685.

Stiglitz, J., 2001, 'Thanks for Nothing', *The Atlantic Monthly* October: 36-40.

Stiglitz, J., 2002, *Globalization and Its Discontents*, New York and London: W.W. Norton & Company.

Swan, T.W., 1956, 'Economic growth and capital accumulation', *Economic Record* 32: 334-61.

Taylor, L. and P. Arida, 1998, 'Long-run income distribution and growth', in H. Chenery and T. N. Srinivasan, eds., *Handbook of Development Economics*, Amsterdam: North Holland.

Temple, J., 1999, 'The New Growth Evidence', *Journal of Economic Literature* 37: 112-56.

Todaro, M. P., 1996, *Economic Development*, Sixth edition, Reading, MA: Addison-Wesley Publishing Company.

Todaro, M. P., 2000, *Economic Development*, Seventh edition, Reading, MA: Addison-Wesley.

Ugarteche, O., 2000, *The False Dilemma. Globalization: Opportunity or Threat?*, London and New York: Zed Books Ltd.

Vásquez, I., 2000, *Global Fortune: The Stumble and Rise of World Capitalism*, Washington, DC: Cato Institute.

World Bank, 1991, *World Development Report 1991: The Challenge of Development*, New York: Oxford University Press.

World Bank, 1994, *Adjustment in Africa: Reforms, Results, and the Road Ahead*, Oxford: Oxford University Press.

World Bank, 1997, *World Development Indicators 1997*, Washington, DC: The World Bank.

World Bank, 1999, *World Development 1999/2000: Report: Knowledge for Development*, Washington, DC: The World Bank.

World Bank, 2000, *Can Africa Claim the 21st Century?* Washington DC: The World Bank.

Chapter 10

Trajectories of Modern African Geography

**Ezekiel Kalipeni, Joseph R. Oppong,
and Benjamin Ofori-Amoah**

This chapter reviews the state and the many trajectories of geographic research on Africa by scholars in Europe, North America and Africa. Since independence in the early 1960s, geographic research on Africa has been very vibrant and has evolved into a respectable discipline in both the social and natural sciences. While we briefly touch on works that go back to the 1960s in some of the sections, this chapter will largely focus on trajectories of African geographic research in the 1990s and recent years. During the 1980s research on Africa dwelt on the many crises, some real and some imagined, usually sensationalised by the media, such as the collapse of the state in Sierra Leone, Liberia, Somalia and Rwanda and the economic shocks of structural adjustment programmes. The 1990s witnessed momentous positive changes. For example, apartheid ended in South Africa and emerging democratic systems replaced dictatorial regimes in Malawi and Zambia. Persuaded that Africa had made progress on many fronts largely due to self-generated advances, some scholars began to highlight the positive new developments (Gaile and Ferguson 1996).

Due to space limitations, selecting works to include in this review was difficult. In many instances we stayed within five cited works (first authorship) for any one scholar to ensure focus on the most important works and to achieve a sense of balance in the works cited. Thus, research reviewed in this chapter should be treated as a sample of the variety and quality of geographical work on Africa. One major challenge was where to draw the boundary between 'geography', 'not quite geography' and 'by North American authors' versus others. In these days of globalised research paradigms, geography has benefited tremendously from interchanging ideas with other social and natural science disciplines. Thus, separating North American geographic research in the 1990s from other groundbreaking works that profoundly influence the discipline of geography is difficult. For example, while the *empirical subject matter* included agriculture, health, gender, and development issues, the related *theoretical paradigm* often included representation, discourse, resistance, and indigenous development within broader frameworks influenced by the ideas of social science scholars such as Foucault (1970, 1977, 1980), Said (1978), Sen (1981, 1990) and Scott (1977, 1987). This chapter engages these debates. Building upon Bassett's (1989) review of research in the 1980s, the chapter develops a typology for the growing research on African issues and related theoretical orientations by Africanist geographers (Table 1).

The reviewed works fall into the three main sub-disciplines of geography: human geography (by far the most dominant); physical geography, now commonly referred to as earth systems science or global change studies; and geographic information systems (GIS) (Table 1). Within these three main sub-disciplines, theoretical perspectives overlap (Watts 1993). In particular, the realisation that conventional narrowly focused disciplinary perspectives and approaches such as regional geographic approaches common in geographic research in the 1960s and 1970s (see for example, Hance 1975; De Blij 1964; Best and De Blij 1977; Udo 1978; Knight and Newman 1976) were inadequate to explain Africa's rapid and complex changes led geographers to embrace and even devise more complex and integrated interdisciplinary approaches. The most important of these transitions or developments in African geographical research during the 1990s include:

- Post-colonial/ post-structuralist/ postmodern approaches derived from the works of Said (1978), Foucault (1970, 1977, 1980), Sen (1981, 1990), and Scott (1977, 1987);

- Political ecology championed by Atkinson (1991), Bassett (1993), Blaikie (1994), Blaikie and Brookfield (1987), and Bryant (1992);

- Boserupian perspectives on population and environment promoted by Tiffen, Mortimore, and Gichuki (1994);

- Challenging environmental orthodoxies, particularly a reassessment of 'taken-for-granted' ideas about the environment championed by Leach and Mearns (1996), Fairhead and Leach (1996, 1998);

- Development from below/grassroots initiatives (Taylor and Mackenzie 1992);

- Recognition of the importance of indigenous knowledge;

- The impact of globalisation on economic development particularly in agriculture and industrial restructuring;

- Policy-oriented studies, for example the application of spatial allocation models and the ambitious Southern African Migration Project;

- Social geographies pertaining to gender and other issues; and

- Global environmental change research involving climatologists, geomorphologists, hydrologists and biogeographers utilising an integrative/ systems framework.

Table 1: Research Themes, Sub-Topics, and Theoretical Perspectives of Africanist Geographical Research

Research Themes	Major Sub-topics	Theoretical Orientation
Human Geography		
Population, Resources and the Environment	Population Growth and Agrarian Transformation Land in African Agrarian Change Resources and the Environment Gender and Resource Contestation Resources and Pastoral Conflicts Food and Hunger	Boserupian, Political Ecology, Political Economy, Post-Colonialism, Post-Structural, Feminist Perspectives
Population Dynamics	Fertility Mortality Migration Processes	Demographic Transition Model, Theory of Demographic Response, Political Economy
Development Discourse	The Power of Development Development Misconception	Postcolonial /Postmodern/Post-Structural, Feminist Perspectives, Sustainable/Green Development Approaches
Policy Oriented or Impact -Analysis Studies	The Human Factor Perspective Structural Adjustment Programmes (SAPs) Spatial Analysis	Modernisation, Dependency Perspectives, Core/periphery Concept, Human Factor Hypothesis
Urban and Regional Development	Industrial restructuring Informal Sector Studies Labour Segregation and Resistance	Neoliberal (Market Supremacy), Political Economy, Political Ecology, Globalisation
The Geography of Disease and Health Care	Disease Ecology HIV/AIDS in Africa Structural Adjustment and Health Geography and Health Care	Disease ecology, political economy, location -allocation models
Global Change and Earth Systems Science	Global change (Causes and Impacts) Hydrology of Wetlands Landscape Ecology	Global Climate Models, Earth Systems, GIS as a tool for monitoring global change
Geographic Information Systems	Vegetation Change Urban Morphology	Land use planning

The disciplinary subdivisions of human geography, earth systems science, and GIS, guided by the above theoretical approaches, form the organisational basis for the works reviewed in this chapter. Many other works do not fit neatly into the new developments but rather within previously established paradigms such as regional geography, spatial modelling, cultural ecology, and political economy. Wherever possible we attempt to distinguish between continuing and new lines of scholarship.

Population, Resources, and the Environment

Research in the 1990s in this area departed from the dominant neo-Malthusian approaches of the previous decades (see for example Morgan and Russell 1969; Timberlake 1986; Timberlake and Tinker 1986) which usually bemoaned the combination of rapid population growth and economic and environmental decline. Indeed, many geographers remain convinced that ecological degradation is a human-induced problem, but recent works have concentrated on exploring the role of population growth in agrarian transformation, the role of land tenure in agrarian change, farmer-pastoral conflicts, the environment, and issues of gender and resource contestation. The guiding frameworks for these recent works include the Boserupian perspective, political ecology and political economy.

Population Growth and Agrarian Transformation

A new body of literature stresses that increasing population densities induce positive agricultural transformation. The work by Turner, Hyden, and Kates *Population Growth and Agricultural Change in Africa* (1993), is of particular significance. Within the Boserupian tradition, this volume investigates the relationship between population growth in high-density areas of Africa and agricultural intensification, and concludes that population growth is just one of many factors that affect agricultural change. Differences in environment, market access, social institutions, land tenure, technology, and politics make it extremely difficult to establish a straightforward relationship between population growth, environmental degradation and agricultural intensification.

Using agricultural innovation in Kenya and the evolution of maize production in northern Nigeria as case studies, Goldman (1993) and Smith et al., (1994) highlight the synergistic effect of technology in a population-driven intensification process. Despite high population densities, agricultural intensification produced substantial increases in productivity and farmer welfare due to a good road system, high yielding varieties of maize, widespread adoption of fertilizer made possible in part by fertilizer subsidies, and a favourable market infrastructure. Smith et al. (1994) and Kull (1998) argue for quantum leap technologies in Africa to accelerate sustainable agricultural intensification, particularly in areas where the preconditions exist. They note that market production rather than population pressure *per se* has driven the agricultural transformation in the study areas, and it is highly unlikely that population growth alone could have produced these changes. Consequently, these works present a forceful argument for the introduction of appropriate technologies for agricultural transformations where conditions are favourable. However, such reliance on imported technologies, often financed by the World Bank and subsidised by the state, may be an unsustainable and possibly dangerous prescription as exemplified by World Bank-supported tube-well projects in Nigeria which have lowered the water table.

Perhaps the most influential work in the Boserupian tradition is Tiffen, Mortimore, and Gichuki (1994). In the hotly-debated book *More People, Less Erosion: Environmental Recovery in Kenya*, British and African geographers promote Boserupian ideas using Machakos District in Kenya as a case study (Tiffen and Mortimore 1994; Mortimore and Tiffen 1994). The central argument in the Machakos story is that even as population densities have increased, agro-pastoral productivities have increased and a degraded landscape has flourished with trees, terraces and productive farms. The underlying assumption is that population pressure gives rise to its own solution, namely, agricultural intensification.

Other scholars have contested the Machakos story from a number of angles. For example, Murton (1999) notes that an examination of the 'Machakos experience' of population growth and environmental transformation at household level shows neither a homogenous experience nor a fully unproblematic one. Data in Murton's study show how such changes in Machakos District have been accompanied by a polarisation of land holdings, differential trends in agricultural productivity, and a decline in food self sufficiency. Murton (1999) raises doubt about the universal relevance of the Machakos story and for that matter the Boserupian perspective as a model. Political ecologists have also criticised the Boserupian perspective, and cultural ecology analysis in general, for focusing on local dynamics while excluding relevant economic and political processes operating at broader scales.

Land in African Agrarian Change

Debates on indigenous land tenure systems versus privatisation intensified during the 1990s. Bassett and Crummey's work *Land in African Agrarian Systems* (1993) questions the traditional thought that indigenous tenure systems impede increasing agricultural productivity. The contributions in this collection challenge the notion that sweeping privatisation of land will reverse declining agricultural productivity. Instead, they reveal how land access, control, and management are embedded in dynamic social, political, and economic structures that fluctuate and change over time. The works of Fairhead and Leach (1996; 1998) about indigenous production systems and forest production or generation support the Bassett/Crummey thesis that indigenous land tenure systems may not obstruct resource conservation and sound agricultural practices. Similarly, Awanyo (1998) notes that the economic behaviour of cocoa farmers in Ghana is complexly linked to the politics of land tenure and cultural expectations and obligations, instead of price incentives and private tenure.

Other works examine conflicts between the state and the peasantry that arise over access to land. In both Zimbabwe and South Africa, disparity between black and white land ownership and control makes the 'land question' the most difficult resource issue, and its resolution the most important task of the respective postcolonial and post-apartheid governments (Weiner and Levin 1991; Masilela and Weiner 1996; Levin and Weiner 1997; Levin 1998; Zinyama 1992). Increasing issues of class, race, regionalism, and a general breakdown of the rule of law may be evidence of the failure of the Zimbabwe government's policy on land reform. While the works on Zimbabwe look at both colonial and postcolonial times, Mackenzie (1995; 1998) examines land and gender issues in a historical context, focussing on colonial Kenya. Moore (1998, 1999) also looks at conflicts over access to environmental resources and land between state administrators and peasants in a state-administered resettlement scheme bordering Nyanga National Park in eastern Zimbabwe. These insightful analyses show that struggles over resources, shifting political alliances, and competing agendas have encountered the salient differences of gender, generation, class, education and traditional authority.

Globalisation and Agrarian Change

The impact of globalisation on agrarian change in Africa is addressed under the rubric of contract farming—an arrangement between a grower and firm(s) in which non-transferable contracts specify one or more conditions of marketing and production (Little and Watts 1994). Watts (1994) compares the nature and origins of contract farming in developed and developing countries, including Kenya and Nigeria, and concludes that it illuminates the new configuration of state, capital and small-scale commodity production and a changing international division of labour. Thus, capital can dominate agriculture by not only expanding the frontier of capitalist enterprise but also through the establishment of elaborate networks of social regulation and control. Goodman and Watts (1997) extend our knowledge about the complexity and diversity of local and national levels of agrarian change in the context of global restructuring of the world's food and agricultural systems.

Using the Jahaly-Parchar project in Gambia, Carney (1994) also analyses the changes that can result from the introduction of contract farming and concludes that the project produced transformations that policy makers and project planners had never imagined. Attempts by donor agencies to entitle plots to women started a chain of conflicts that turned the household into a terrain of intense struggle, negotiation, and partial victories which have severely hindered the ability of contract farming to increase market surplus. Mather (1999) illustrates the impact of globalisation on agriculture, emphasising local market power and global market strategies pursued by large national and multinational corporations. These works claim that contract farming presents a new form of Third World agriculture being pushed by global restructuring. However, contract farming is not different from the way in which cocoa, tea, coffee, and other cash crops were introduced into African economies. Only the crops are different. It is doubtful whether the impact of this new trend on African agriculture will be different from what existing cash crops have done to Africa.

Resources, the Environment and Development

Many works utilising the political economy, political ecology and liberation ecology frameworks have tackled the perplexing issues of multinational corporations versus local resources, common property rights and indigenous knowledge, land for agricultural extensification versus wildlife conservation, and afforestation/ deforestation issues. For example, Watts (1996) relates the rise of home-grown politically-charged environmental movements, such as that led by the late Ken Saro-Wiwa in Ogoniland, Nigeria, to the larger landscapes of international exploitation and political economy. Stanley (1990) elaborates the contradictions of oil exploitation in the Niger Delta and the wider socioeconomic and environmental impacts of the industry.

Jarosz (1993: 1996) takes issue with blaming population growth and shifting cultivation for deforestation in the developing world. In Madagascar, Jarosz links discourse analysis with peasant resistance and response during the colonial period to argue that the colonial cash crop economy, rather than population growth, produced deforestation. This supports the works of Fairhead and Leach (1996; 1998) and Leach and Mearns (1996) which have challenged 100 years of received wisdom on the degradation of the African environment. Nevertheless, political ecology as an approach has been critiqued for overemphasising the deleterious effects of state and international policies. Besides, most works employing the framework sideline the 'ecology' in 'political ecology' in favour of the 'political'. Biophysical processes are often missing in the equation. In addition, others have also criticised it for having too little politics. Perhaps collaboration with geo-scientists might better articulate and redefine the application of the political ecology framework.

Neumann (1995, 1998) and Schroeder (1995) evaluate the paradox of remedial efforts in Tanzania and Gambia to restore, preserve and stabilise 'nature's' integrity through terracing, reforestation, or the creation of buffers. These studies show that despite the emphasis on the 'positive' incentives of profit-taking, participation and benefit sharing, many of the new integrated conservation and development projects in Africa have coercive elements, often constitute an expansion of state authority into remote rural areas, and do not benefit the majority. Two articles that focus on grassroots initiatives in control of resources are Matzke and Nabane (1996) and Barkan, McNulty, and Ayeni (1991). In Nigeria, Barkan, McNulty, and Ayeni show that hometown associations serve as a civil virtue, shadow state, bulwark against state power, local growth machine, intermediary broker of linkages, and expression of attachment to place. In Zimbabwe, Matzke and Nabane describe how local initiative in wildlife management has provided a new paradigm for local economic development in rural areas that lie close to national parks and wildlife preservation areas. This initiative, dubbed Communal Areas Management Programme for Indigenous Resources (CAMPFIRE) rationalises that people from wildlife producer communities should benefit from the wildlife that their land produces on a sustainable basis. The authors argue that CAMPFIRE has produced remarkable success—fencing has reduced loss of human life from animal attacks, and revenue generation and job opportunities have increased. The works of Neumann (1998), Matzke and Nabane (1996) and Barkan, McNulty, and Ayeni (1991) have contributed greatly to policy and social impact analysis. Neuman's work distinguishes between genuine empowerment and local control from top-down initiatives that masquerade as community development, exemplified by CAMPFIRE. *Development from Within* (1992), edited by Taylor and Mackenzie, provides an excellent critical appraisal of community development initiatives to preserve the environment. Using precise and historical understanding of specific places through local case studies, this volume addresses the tricky issue of mobilising village resources by and under the control of the rural poor themselves. Several other studies have explored women's environmental initiatives (for example, the Green Belt Movement in Kenya), and why gender matters greatly in assessing the success or failure of such bottom-up initiatives. Another important body of literature to which geographers have contributed significantly is the impacts of dams. Roder (1994), for example, examines the consequences of the Kainji Dam on the local population around Lake Kainji in Nigeria and shows that neither the predictions of great losses to the economy of the people, nor the expectations that they would take many decades to adjust to the lake, have come true. The people have met the changes and carried on with their lives.

The lessons from these works are clear. Community empowerment gives people an opportunity to manage their resources and make decisions about their own future. While this is not a new finding, the operational evidence of this in Africa is not very common. More of these studies will help instil the hope that grassroots Africa has much untapped potential for economic development.

Gender and Resource Contestation

The rise of post-structuralist, postcolonial, postmodern, and feminist critiques of development discourse (Crush 1995; Mackenzie 1995) has spawned an interesting set of case studies that examine the complex intersections among gender, agrarian change, environmental discourse, access to resources, and indigenous knowledge (Carney 1992, 1993a; Schroeder 1993, 1997; Rocheleau, Thomas-Slayter, and Wangari 1996). In these studies, the term 'resources' refers to household resources in both urban and rural areas. Carney links property rights and gender conflict to environmental change and reveals repeated gender conflicts over rural resources in Gambia as male household heads concentrate land holdings to capture female labour for surplus production. Schroeder's work in the Gambia questions agroforestry as an effective means of stabilising the environment because it does not always yield the intended results. Commoditisation of tree crops and incentives to enhance the rate of tree planting ultimately led to shifting patterns of resource access and control and produced gender conflict between husbands and wives due to multiple tenure claims to land.

Rocheleau, Thomas-Slayter and Wangari (1996) focus on women's struggle in Kenya to gain access to natural resources such as water and wood in their double burden of household production and reproduction. These works utilise political ecology, social institutions, situated knowledges and practices to argue that historical contexts and processes have been influential in creating environmental and social problems which, in turn, have resulted in the marginalisation and suffering of women in Kenya. Other scholars have explored the role of women in development and the changing conditions of women in rural and urban Africa. Johnston-Anumonwo (1997) offers a holistic approach to the study of gender issues in Africa and notes the many significant contributions women made to the overall development of the continent despite their marginalisation. Yeboah (1998) uses a Ghanaian case study and a novel geographical and historical framework to compare the economic status of the two genders and concludes that Ghanaian women are slowly closing the gender gap in economic status. Osei (1998) arrives at a similar conclusion in a study of the gender factor in rural energy systems in Africa and shows that while women dominate the rural energy system, they have not suffered any significant, negative socioeconomic impacts from being engaged in the system. However, both Yeboah's and Osei's conclusions contradict the majority of the literature which emphasises the barriers women face in trying to get fair access to resources and how this affects both their abilities to succeed and use the environment. Nevertheless, a common thread running though the works reviewed in this section is their insightful analysis of the role of local, national, and international forces in exacerbating the problems and burdens women face in their lives and the detailed examination of how women, households, and communities respond and adapt to these challenges.

Resources and Pastoral Conflicts

Several excellent studies within the political ecology framework have offered detailed analyses of agrarian and pastoral conflicts, stressing the embeddedness of these struggles in historical context, social relations, and linkages with wider geographical and social settings (Little 1992; Bassett 1993; Turner 1993; Heasley and Delehanty 1996; Bascom 1990a; Johnson 1993; Campbell 1991, 1993). Bascom (1990a) examines the factors that are bringing refugee cattle herds to extinction and jeopardising pastoralism as a way of life for Eritrean refugees. He attributes the demise of cattle herders to a dwindling amount of rangeland and the transformation of grazing rights, all of which have resulted from long structural processes.

Bencharifa and Johnson (1990) examine changes in pastoral farming in Morocco that promote and obstruct intensification. Increasing productivity, a decrease in the annual and inter-annual fallow cycle, a shift from a traditional extensive pastoral system to a much less nomadic life, and gradual abandonment of the tent as a primary residence for a permanent house and village location are all visible changes although quite inequitably distributed. Campbell (1991) examines the impact of socioeconomic and political conditions over the past century upon the coping strategies of the Maasai of the Kajiado District of Kenya and shows that both colonial and postcolonial development policies and strategies failed to recognise the complexity of society-environment interactions, which form the basis of Maasai pastoralism. Campbell calls for development strategies which enhance diversity and productivity of the Maasai economy to prevent their economic and social marginalisation.

Little (1992) looks at how the Lake Baringo area in Kenya changed from a food surplus to a food deficit area of famine, impoverishment, and ecological degradation. He questions conventional explanations by colonial officials and postcolonial ecologists that overstocking and the short-sightedness of pastoralists have damaged the ecological basis. His analysis goes beyond a 'blame the victim' paradigm to examine the complex web of external and internal factors in a historical context. A parallel study by Turner (1993) in the Sahelian belt of West Africa argues that the persistent reliance by environmental analysts on carrying capacity models oversimplifies range ecology and excludes social processes from causal analysis.

Bassett (1993) presents a case study of peasant-herder conflicts among the Senufo and Fulani of northern Côte d'Ivoire in the wider context of national and international forces. The study shows that the interactive effects of land use conflicts at three overlapping levels (local, regional, and national) continue to undermine both the expansion of Fulani livestock production and the intensification of agricultural systems in the savanna region. Heasley and Delehanty (1995) examine disputes over manure in Southwestern Niger, which reveal broad strategies for natural resource control employed by farmers and herders in a transitional and conflictual agropastoral economy. What needs to be emphasised is that most of these studies are about the value of the political ecology approach rather than about pastoralism *per se*.

Food and Hunger

Economic, agricultural, and development geographers who specialise in Africa have long known about the existence a 'lean' or 'hunger' season in many places (see for example Pedler 1955; Morgan 1969). This season is usually just before new food crops mature for harvesting. Prior to the 1980s, however, this was not considered to be a major problem and only a few geographers discussed it (see Pedler 1955; Hance 1967; 1975; 1977; Thomas and Whittington 1969; O'Connor 1971; Hodder 1973). Thus, while Pedler seriously examined the reasons why African farmers do not cultivate more food when demand was so high, O'Connor (1971) described the progress so far made by African countries to address the problem. The widespread famine in a number of African countries during the early 1970s and the early 1980s caused geographers to critically examine the food and hunger issues. These works, most of which adopted the political ecology approach, include the impact of drought on livelihood in the Sahel (Kates 1981), the political economy of famine in Nigeria (Watts 1983, 1987a, 1987b, 1989; Watts and Shenton 1984), the role of land concentration on food production in Zimbabwe (Weiner et al., 1985), and sources of change in pastoral sectors of Kenya and Ivory Coast (Campbell 1981, 1984;

Basset 1986, 1988; O'Connor (1991). The central message of all these studies is that famine in Africa was caused not only by the physical environmental factors but human factors as well (Basset 1989).

In the 1990s, food and hunger continued to occupy the attention of geographers but to a lesser degree than in the 1980s. These works include Bascom (1990b), Campbell (1990a; b), Zinyama, Matiza, and Campbell (1990) and Griffith and Newman (1994). Bascom's (1990b) work on the Sudan shows how state intervention favours large-scale commercial farming to the detriment of peasant agriculture. A common belief that emerged in the 1980s was the widespread use of wild foods in Africa to mitigate food shortages. Zinyama, Matiza and Campbell (1990) found that in Zimbabwe, wholesale dependence on wild foods during periods of food shortages was uncommon and that about 71 percent of the people interviewed in the seven villages in the low rainfall regions still relied on maize, millet, or sorghum as their staple. Major sources for this variation were continued availability of other sources of staple foods either through government food distribution or the generation of cash from other sources of rural occupation and remittances from relatives living in the urban areas. Another legacy of 1980s famine research was the establishment of the famine Early Warning Systems (EWS). Campbell's (1990a) work focussed on how to improve the accuracy of the database and argued for using indicators based on the observed responses of people vulnerable to food shortages. Incorporating the employed range of sequential coping strategies that vary between places, age groups, gender, and social status is critical.

Eliminating Hunger in Africa (1994) by Griffith et al., was born out of dissatisfaction with the progress made after the 1980s regarding the elimination of famine. The book combines new methods of data collection and analysis with a more sensitive critique that sees Africa's plight not in isolation but as part of a world order in which values and perceptions are important. Gaile's work shows that spatial analysis can be used to establish market distribution centres for the successful implementation of Kenya's food security programme (Gaile 1994). Ralston et al., (1994) highlight the role of transportation in the distribution of food aid, especially in landlocked countries in Africa. Little (1994) discusses the broader context of famine in Africa under the New World Order and argues that political and economic insecurity results in food insecurity. Listing the struggle for national integration, the acceptance of comparative advantage, and indebtedness as the main causes of political and economic insecurities in Africa, she concludes that what Africa needs is not charity but justice. Unless the Western perception of Africa changes food aid will not solve the food problem.

Other studies have used the micro-perspective approach by placing human systems within the context of their particular natural and social environment. Among these studies are household-level studies in urban Africa. For example, Drakakis-Smith (1990) and Drakakis-Smith, Bowyer-Bower, and Tevera (1995) examine the food impacts of structural adjustment programmes on the poor at the household level in Harare. Others have examined the impact of changing social and economic circumstances on household access to food by gender. Most of the studies under this rubric have been influenced by the work of Sen (1981, 1990) on entitlements, basic freedoms, social justice, and an equitable future for everyone. Other studies on the issue of food are more general and have dealt with US food aid policy (for example, Bush 1996; Kodras 1993). While these works have provided interesting perspectives, the food and hunger issue is more complex than the issues addressed here. We think that discussion on food and hunger in Africa should not focus narrowly on distribution from outside but also on internal production and provision of appropriate infrastructure and mechanisms.

Indigenous Environmental Knowledge

A growing literature addresses indigenous environmental knowledge and argues that rural peoples throughout the developing world understand their environment well, particularly its possibilities for sustaining livelihoods. Consequently, natural resource management practices reflect cultural appraisals of what is possible and desirable in a given setting. Katz (1991), focussing on children's environmental knowledge in Sudan—its means of acquisition and use—is an excellent example. Similarly, Nyamweru (1996; 1998) examines indigenous environmental knowledge about preservation of sacred groves in Kenya. Fairhead and Leach (1996) also show that the islands of dense forest in the Guinea savanna were actually created by local inhabitants around their villages and are not relics of previously extensive forest cover that has been degraded by population growth. Carney (1993b) highlights the rice cultivation technology brought to the New World by African slaves. This corrects the notion that Africa did not contribute any technological development to the New World.

While the literature is mute on the art of indigenous map-making in Africa, Bassett (1998) dispels the Eurocentric and pejorative view that Africans were incapable of making maps the same way Europeans did. Adopting an expanded definition of maps to include mnemonic maps, body art, the layout of villages, and the design and orientation of buildings, Bassett (1998) offers an intriguing overview of the range of maps existing in Africa's historical record and concludes that like those of other traditional cultures, African maps are social constructions whose form, content, and meaning vary with the intentions of their makers.

Population Dynamics

Parameters of population change such as the dynamics of fertility, mortality, and migration processes and how these relate to environmental change and resource scarcities have been relatively neglected by geographers, but Kalipeni (1995; 1996) attempts to fill this gap. Kalipeni (1995) adds a spatial dimension to the discussion of African fertility through a spatial-temporal framework for the demographic transition theory. His analysis shows that fertility levels in Africa have begun to decline and, some African countries—Zimbabwe, Botswana, Kenya, and Nigeria, for example—may be in the initial stages of an irreversible fertility transition.

The 1990s saw very little work on migration processes, and the primary focus was refugee movements from war torn areas and migration policy in Southern Africa (Crush 1998, 1999; Crush and James 1997; Crush, Jeeves and Yudelman 1991; Crush and Williams 1999; Hyndman 1999; Wood 1994). The most ambitious project is the Southern Africa Migration Project, a decade long study of many aspects of migration in southern Africa led by the Canadian geographer Jonathan Crush. This project is designed to formulate and implement new initiatives on cross-border migration in the region and promote public awareness of the role, status and contribution of foreign immigrants of African origin in South Africa. The project has great potential to influence important policy issues regarding what relationship should exist between post-apartheid South Africa and its neighbours.

Wood (1994) offers a framework for the causes of refugee flows and the conse-quences of such flows at the international and local scales. Hyndman (1999) adds a geographical dimension to the study of 'new' safe spaces and discourses emerging within humanitarian circles since the end of the Cold War. She argues that while camps continue to house refugees, the meaning and value of 'refugee' has changed dramatically and efforts to prevent people from crossing political borders to seek safety are increasing, producing a distinct geopolitical discourse and a new set of safe spaces. James Newman's (1995) book *The Peopling of Africa: A Geographic Inter-pretation* offers a refreshing synthesis of African precolonial migrations. This work uses the power of prose and narrates the population, human, and historical geogra-phy of precolonial Africa using concepts of space, region, and place to derive a coherent original synthesis of the richness and diversity of Africa from the begin-ning of humankind to the time just before European colonisation.

Development Discourse

Development discourse refers to the language, words, and images used by development experts to construct the world in a way that legitimates their intervention in the name of development. This approach seeks to establish the authority of experts and their opinions that this (and not that) is the way that the world actually is and ought to be. Geographers have contributed significantly in critiquing development discourse, particularly its characteristic language of crisis and disintegration, which gives justification for intervention. This critique arises out of the old suspicion of a hidden agenda behind the introduction and abandonment of development strategies in Africa as well as the perpetuation of development strategies and notions that are detrimental to Africa's development.

Most of these works have been influenced by Rostow's (1960) 'Stages of growth' theory; Gourou's (1961) 'Tropical world'; Dumont's (1966) 'False start in Africa'; Frank's (1969) 'Underdevelopment' in Latin America, Amin's (1972) 'Dependent development'; Bauer's (1972) 'Dissent on development'; Wallerstein's (1974) 'World systems theory'; Rodney's (1974) 'Underdevelopment' of Africa; Brookfield's (1975) 'Interdependent development'; Peet's (1977) 'Radical geography'; and Said's (1978) 'Orientalism'. Thus, utilising radical, postcolonial, postmodern, and feminist critiques the contributions of geographers to development discourse on Africa have had a twofold mission. First, they call on African people, governments, and policy makers to disabuse their minds of lies concerning Africa's development. Second they encourage them to critically examine development concepts, strategies, and theories before either adopting or abandoning them. While this may not be a new perspective, a number of influential interdisciplinary books have fruitfully engaged and critiqued this perspective. See for example Mabogunje's *The Development Process* (1980), Mehretu's *Regional Disparity in Sub-Saharan Africa* (1989), Taylor and Mackenzie's *Development from Within* (1992), Ofori-Amoah's *Saturation Hypothesis* (1995); Crush's *Power of Development* (1995), Corbridge's *Development Studies: A Reader* (1995), Adjibolosoo and Ofori-Amoah's *Addressing Misconceptions About Africa's Economic Development* (1988), and Godlewska and Smith's *Geography and Empire* (1994).

An important issue raised in this literature is the persistent (mis)representation of development and of Africa itself. For example, in *The Development Process*, Mabogunje (1980) is concerned with presenting a view from the periphery with a focus on 'what has to be done' in contrast to theoretical comprehensives that had characterised core-dominated development theories. Accordingly, he pays less attention to class analysis, which he argues does not have much relevance in most African societies in terms of its application and the solutions it offers for development. In *Regional Disparity in Sub-Saharan Africa* (1989), Mehretu also focuses on the principal socio-spatial constraints to development in Sub-Saharan Africa that has been largely ignored by development research. In his saturation hypothesis, Ofori-Amoah (1995) argues that all development theories have a tendency of being detrimental when applied to societies external to the origins of the theory and warns against indiscriminate adoption of such theories. Similarly, in *Geography and Empire* (1994) Rothenberg critiques *National Geographic* images and the complicity of geography as a discipline in perpetuating colonial and postcolonial myths about Africa and development. Indeed the articles by Bassett (1993; 1994; 1998) on colonial map making exemplify this point. Myers (1998) shows how Lusaka and Zanzibar were enframed by the plans developed by Eric Dutton, an officer in the service of colonial hegemony. Together these works offer a rich set of papers, which collectively explore the language of development, its rhetoric, and meaning within different political and institutional contexts.

Policy Orientation/Impact Analysis Studies

Over the past five decades, geographers have also contributed to an impressive collection of work on policy analysis in Africa. The nature and type of studies have depended on the policy that is in vogue. In general terms, some of these studies have been prescriptive while others have been very critical and have denounced the deleterious impacts of particular policies on African economies and livelihoods.

Prescriptive Studies

Prescriptive studies on Africa by geographers may be classified into three main categories. The first category emphasises the relevance of the geographer's spatial perspective in understanding and resolving problems of development and calls for the need to pay attention to this perspective. This work includes Taaffee, Morrill, and Gould's (1963) seminal work on the development of transportation in Ghana, Ominde and Baker (1971), Obudho and Taylor's (1979) spatial structure of development in Kenya, Mabogunje's (1980) spatial perspective of the development process, and Mehretu's (1989) regional disparity in Sub-Saharan Africa.

The second category emphasises the relevance of spatial analytical techniques in addition to the spatial perspectives of geography. Pioneered by Soja (1968) Riddell (1970) and Gould (1970) in their geography of modernisation studies of Kenya, Sierra Leone, and Tanzania, respectively these works use powerful multivariate statistical techniques to analyse the distribution aspects of development. As a method, spatial analysis fell out of favour among geographers during the radical critiques of the mid-1970s and the 1980s. In the 1990s, however, Mehretu and Sommers (1990; 1992), Gaile (1992; 1994), Gaile and Ngau (1995), and Ralston et al. (1994) reminded development geographers interested in Africa that modelling using spatial analysis, 'neoclassical style', is still valid for Africa, although structuralist development geographers have ruled out diffusion as a failure of the modernisation project. Indeed, critiquing growth centre strategy, Gaile (1992; 1994) and Gaile and Ngau (1995) have consistently argued that access issues that incorporate social capital, isolation effects, and institutional constraints can inform decision-making to address food security and poverty alleviation. Gaile's work in Kenya shows that spatial analytical techniques such as proximal areas, distance decay analysis and central place concepts of threshold and range provide a better strategy for rural-urban development.

Mehretu and Sommers (1990) also employ spatial analysis to explore the differences between developed and developing countries in national preferences and how competing preferences are resolved. Ralston et al.'s (1994) work, already mentioned, is in the same tradition. Wubneh (1994) interrogates the relationship between interregional disparities and political unrest in Ethiopia and attempts to analyse the impact of the policies and programmes of the socialist government on interregional disparities among Ethiopia's provinces. Despite its limitations, spatial analysis has great potential to contribute meaningfully to development, but its contributions have been in theory rather than in practice. Perhaps the major problem is that geographers often write from positions far removed from the exercise of power in Africa, and with the cutbacks imposed by structural adjustment programs (SAPs), little money is available to start implementing spatial optimisation projects.

The third category, consisting of a comparatively few studies (Adjibolosoo and Ofori-Amoah 1998; Ofori-Amoah 1995; 1996; 1998), has introduced a new prescriptive approach, the human factor (HF) perspective. The central message of this perspective is that Africa has a human factor problem that needs fixing before any meaningful development can take place. The human factor is defined as the spectrum of personality characteristics and dimensions of human performance that enable social, economic, and political institutions to function and remain functional over time.

Social Impact Assessment Studies

Although the work of geographers in Africa has informed policy-making in Africa, until very recently few have been directly involved in evaluating the social impact of policies. Part of this may be due to the fact that most of these works were either written as textbooks or their authors were content with describing what was happening at the moment without commitment to criticising and offering policy recommendations (See for example Fordham 1965; O'Connor 1971, 1991; Prothero and Barbour 1973; Udo 1982; Onyemelukwe and Filani 1983; Onyemelukwe 1984; Mountjoy and Hilling 1988; Gleave 1992). The few that somewhat addressed policy issues include Hance (1967, 1975, 1977), Hodder (1973), Mabogunje (1980), and Mehretu (1989). In *African Economic Development* Hance (1967, 1975, and 1977) identifies the obstacles in the way of African development and outlines opportunities that lie ahead. In *Economic Development in the Tropics* (1973), Hodder addresses several policy issues related to various sectors of the African economies. As already indicated, Mabogunje's (1980) and Mehretu's (1989) prescriptive studies also had several impact assessment implications for regional policies pursued in Africa.

By all measures, however, geographers working on Africa became more involved in social impact assessments of development policy in the 1990s and much of this research was dominated by structural adjustment programmes (SAPs). Among these are Mengisteab and Logan (1995), Ould-Mey (1996), Riddell (1992), Samatar (1993, 1994), Logan and Mengisteab (1993), Owusu (1998a, 1998b), and Carmody (1999). With structuralist and post-structural theoretical orientations these works invariably begin with a good background of the rationale for SAPs in Africa, and using selected case studies, highlight the failure of SAPs in resuscitating African economies. According to these studies, SAPs were prescribed at the beginning of the 1980s as the only solution for the internally generated economic stagnation by the International Monetary Fund (IMF) and the World Bank, the two major sponsors of SAP, together with their governmental supporters. This stagnation stems from market distortions, which in turn are due to overwhelming government intervention in the domestic economy. SAPs thus prescribe three groups of reforms: deflationary measures, which consist of the removal of subsidies and reduction of public expenditures, institutional changes in the form of trade liberalisation and privatisation, and expenditure-switching measures in the form of currency devaluation and export promotion.

After a decade of Africa's experience with SAP, the unanimous verdict is clear—while SAPs may enhance economic growth, they do not address the pertinent development issues facing African countries. In a comprehensive survey of 23 African countries that adopted SAPs, Logan and Mengisteab (1993) did not find significant differences in economic performance and social welfare between weak and strong SAP reformers. In Somalia, Samatar (1993) shows that liberalisation of the banana and rice economies reversed previous negative trends in production and improved profits in the industry, but nearly 75 percent of the earnings from exports went to overseas interests, depriving Somalia of an important source of capital. In Mauritania, Ould-Mey (1996) shows that SAPs have denationalised Mauritania—the country has almost lost its capacity to conceive, design, fund, implement, monitor and evaluate original development programmes. The nerve centre of decision-making has actually moved away from the state to international financial institutions and NGOs amidst accentuation of regional, ethnic, religious, linguistic and cultural adherence loyalties. In Zimbabwe, Carmody (1999) reports that instead of reviving and strengthening the textiles, clothing and footwear industries, SAPs contributed to their collapse.

Even the experience of Ghana, the 'star pupil' of SAP proponents, could not bear out a different verdict. Owusu (1998) shows that while SAPs led to huge export growth in the forest products sector that enabled the country to absorb the nation's annual debt interest payment, the traditional link between saw mills and domestic wood processors was broken and replaced by subcontracting to foreign firms. Furthermore, spatial integration was precluded and the programme has produced severe deforestation. Other adverse impacts of SAPs on the psychology, politics, education, economy, and social fabric of African countries are identified in the edited work of Mengisteab and Logan (1995). As Ould-Mey (1996) argues, SAPs were never intended to be a development strategy for Africa; their primary mission was to solve the internal economic problems of developed countries. This primary mission unfortunately has been further strengthened by two factors—the helplessness of African countries to withstand the pressure and the tendency for African governments to adopt the strategy as a metonym.

Urban and Regional Development

In as far as urbanisation is concerned geographers have had a long and successful tradition of examining the evolution of cities on the continent, both in pre- and postcolonial periods. Geographers have studied the many facets of urban development and the consequences of rapid urban growth in the face of declining economies. Examples of such works include Miner (1967); Hance (1970); Simon (1992); Aryeetey-Attoh (2003); Mehretu and Mutambirwa (2003). Hance (1970) offers an exciting reading about the general character of African urban systems, their problems, and possible solutions. The contributions in Miner's (1967) collection discuss a number of problems of African urbanisation with an emphasis on the processes of modernisation. Aryeetey-Attoh (2003) and Mehretu and Mutambirwa (2003) offer an excellent overview of sub-Saharan African cities in terms of their history, internal structure and the causes, consequences, and policy implications of the urbanisation process. Simon (1992) offers a lucid analysis of the essence of African cities, especially primate cities, from a political economy viewpoint.

During the 1990s many geographers in North America, South Africa, and Europe grappled with issues of urban development, industrial restructuring, the informal sector, labour, and regional development, particularly related to the South African transition. Rogerson (1999a) edited a special issue of *GeoForum* that examines the deconstruction of apartheid's migration regime (Crush 1999), migration and environment in Southern Africa (McDonald 1999) and re-regulating the citrus industry in local and global context (Mather 1999). Other works have focussed on labour for the mines and farms, the post-apartheid city, resistance through the construction of squatter camps, the informal sector, industrial restructuring and regional development, segregation, and urban protests (Watts 1997; Lemon 1995; Drakakis-Smith 1992; Rogerson 1996; 1999; Pickles and Weiner 1991; Pickles 1991; Hart 1998; Saff 1995; 1998; Bernstein 1996; Bond 1999). These works highlight the momentous changes within South Africa and its positioning within Africa. Until recently, many scholars and officials have found it convenient to treat South Africa as if it was not really part of Africa—its issues were treated as unique.

Pickles (1991) for example, shows that although industrial decentralisation fostered by the apartheid era stimulated increased levels of employment and production in rural areas, this was achieved at great expense to the state, ultimately resulting in poor working environments for those employed, and few benefits to rural communities. Weiner and Levin (1991) warn against planning the post-apartheid agrarian landscape, arguing instead for greater rural political mobilisation and participation in the reconstruction process. Rogerson (1996; 1999) argues for a coherent and comprehensive national urban and regional development strategy to avoid excessive conflict between the effects of implicit and explicit spatial interventions that exacerbate regional inequalities. Hart (1998) warns that a narrow focus on the industrial sector and agrarian dispossession due to global competition may undermine redistribution and equitable development in South Africa. Bernstein (1996) examines South Africa's attempts to transform its previously segregated and unequal cities in the light of a changing world economy and South Africa's role in a global marketplace. In the same vein, Bond's (1999) collection offers a set of articles that examine the uneven development of South Africa's cities and black townships and the struggle to correct these imbalances in the post-apartheid era.

While the bulk of the work on urbanisation and regional change is on the South African transition, works on other parts of Africa show some interesting changes in technology and industrialisation (McDade 1997; McDade and Malecki 1997; Spring and McDade 1998). Noting the pitiful performance of most African countries in industrialisation and manufacturing trends, McDade concludes that a conducive macroeconomic environment, adequate supply of capital, adequate infrastructure, and a motivated skilled labour supply are necessary for industrialisation to take off in sub-Saharan Africa.

In urban geography, Sanders (1992) attacks the Eurocentric bias of the study of African urbanisation in a very provocative essay and argues that while this is good for interdisciplinary reasons, it has not produced solutions to Africa's urban problems, nor shed any light on the nature of the urbanisation process. Consequently, the study of African urbanisation is an important development topic that requires a new debate within the realm of radical geography. On a slightly different note, Myers (1996) utilises the example of Zanzibar's Ngambo neighbourhoods to show how toponymy and boundary-making embody a complex spatial discourse on power in the urban landscape. Stock (1995: 193-236) and Aryeetey-Attoh (1997: 182-222) provide a detailed survey of cities in sub-Saharan Africa, their origin and growth, internal structures (with reference to selected cities), followed by the causes, consequences, and policy implications of the urbanisation process.

Employing the strategic concepts of place and space, two recent studies examine the evolution of the precolonial settlements of Kano in Northern Nigeria and the Oasis Sijilmassa in Morocco (Lightfoot and Miller 1996; Nast 1994; 1996). Nast (1996) attempts to marry critical geographical notions of landscape and spatial praxis with Foucault's (1977) notion of 'archaeology' to produce 'spatial archaeology'. Using the Kano palace of Northern Nigeria as a case study, Nast explores how slavery, gender, paternity and motherhood were socio-spatially constructed during a time of great regional change in Northern Nigeria circa 1500. In a similar fashion, Lightfoot and Miller (1996) offer a detailed archaeological study of the rise and fall of a walled oasis in medieval Morocco—the city of Sijilmassa. Moving to the twentieth century, Cooper (1997) examines gender with reference to women's housing strategies in Maradi, Niger. The strength of this work lies in its consideration of gender through the use of multi-disciplinary methodological approaches in which oral tradition, field reconnaissance, remote sensing, historical documentation, and archaeological fieldwork are combined to produce coherent narratives of place and space. Konadu-Agyemang (1991) examines the condition and spatial organisation of urban housing and the absence of squatter settlements in Ghanaian cities.

The Geography of Disease and Health Care

Medical geography research on Africa straddles the traditional lines of disease ecology (see May 1961) and geography of health care, with a clear trend toward situating health within its political and economic context. Partly due to its colonial legacy, spatial imbalances characterise the distribution of health facilities in African countries. Colonial health care tended to be curative, urban-based, and aimed to serve the needs of the colonial masters, their servants, and their immediate dependents. Postcolonial health care simply built on this spatial pattern, leaving as an intractable problem how to provide efficient and accessible health care particularly for rural residents. The concept of rural health centres as a necessary part of the health care delivery system was articulated clearly in the 1960s (Fendall 1963; King 1966; Roemer 1972). Yet the problem of poor rural access to health facilities persisted. Not surprisingly, spatial imbalance in access and distribution of health services was the hottest topic in the early 1980s. In Zambia (Freund 1986), Côte d'Ivoire (Lasker 1981), Nigeria (Okafor 1982; Stock 1985; 1986), Senegal (McEvers 1980; Menes 1980), Zaire (Schoepf 1986), researchers lamented the poor and unfavourable spatial distribution of access to health services.

The inverse care law (Hart 1971) maintains that those who need health care the most, usually have the least access to it. Although put forward to describe the situation of Great Britain, the law was widely applied to the African context. Consequently, several equity-oriented initiatives were undertaken during the 1970s and early 1980s, when a concern for disadvantaged groups was at the top of the international health agenda. The WHO (1978) advocated primary health care (PHC) while UNICEF promoted growth monitoring, oral rehydration therapy, breast-feeding, and immunisation. A substantial literature resulted from the evaluation of PHC programmes in African countries. A major facet of this was the declining use of rural health centres because of inadequate resources and poor services (Freund 1986; Van der Geest 1982; Lasker 1981). There is little reason to consult a health care provider who cannot offer treatment for most of people's health problems (Sauerborn, Nougtara, and Diesfeld 1989).

The 1994 World Bank volume *Better Health in Africa* summarised solutions to Africa's health care problems from the Bank's perspective. It argued that despite tight financial constraints, significant improvements in health are within reach in many countries, and recommended four major areas for action—health education, health care system reform to eliminate waste and inefficiency, cost-effective health packages, and finally, cost-sharing, or user fees. Vogel (1983), in *Financing Health Care in Sub-Saharan Africa*, argued for cost sharing and the elimination of health subsidies. Chastising the curative, urban-based health care systems that spent 70 percent or more of the health budget on rich urban residents to the neglect of the rural poor, Vogel argued that *free health care for all* translates into a relative neglect of the poorer rural population, particularly mothers and children. These two books make the case for cost-sharing programmes in African health systems.

Structural Adjustment and Health

The health implications of structural adjustment policies in Africa have been a subject of great interest (Turshen 1999, Stock 1995, Stock and Anyinam 1992, Logan 1995b, Oppong 1997a). Many writers dealt with the result of user fees on the health care system. Anyinam (1989) reports how user fees in Ghana drastically reduced access to biomedical health care, compelling users to forgo or delay treatment and seek alternatives to biomedical services. The impact was uneven and usually more severe in rural areas (Waddington and Enyimayew 1989).

Other work has examined the health and nutrition impacts of SAPs on mothers and infants, following from Cornia and Helleiner's (1994) groundbreaking study for UNICEF. Costello (1994) argues that most of the child mortality in World Bank tables should be viewed with suspicion because such data are based on extrapolation rather than direct measurements. Directly measured estimates for Zambia, Malawi, Botswana and Zimbabwe show an increasing trend in infant mortality starting from the 1980s through the 1990s. Other studies show a declining nutritional intake for mothers and children, which can be linked directly to structural adjustment programmes (Streefland, Harnmeijer, and Chabot 1994).

Turshen (1999) provides a scathing exposé of the health implications of structural adjustment and laments the emergence of the World Bank as the single largest donor in the health sector in Africa. In the light of Africa's high morbidity and mortality rates and the extensive record of World Bank policy failures, replacing tested and proven WHO initiatives such as primary health care with untested World Bank privatisation ideas is unjustifiable. Privatisation, by increasing costs, deters most of the ill from seeking care, causing them to die quietly at home, and thus delays awareness and response to new epidemics. In the concluding chapter of the book Turshen makes a strong case for linking health with its political and economic context and argues that investments in the private health sector are inefficient in Africa and detrimental.

Disease Ecology

John Hunter, premier disease ecologist, has done excellent work focussing on *filariasis* (elephantiasis) and *dracunculiasis* (guinea worm) in Ghana (Hunter 1992; 1996; 1997a; 1997b; 2000). Hunter (1997a) provides a breath-taking description of the transmission and health effects of the guinea worm, using a historical, political and ecological perspective to highlight the role of both the colonial and postcolonial administrations in the process. Hunter (1997b) calls attention to the 'walk-away syndrome' that commonly characterises donor-host projects. After infrastructure is established, programme advisors walk away with technical satisfaction while ignoring post-implementation issues. They assume erroneously that regional authorities have adequate technical and financial capacity and are sufficiently prepared to maintain the programme. Hunter et al., (2000) examine the dynamics of economic development and women's blood pressure in Zimbabwe. Frustrated with the static nature of the disease ecology framework, Mayer (1996) calls for a major shift to more exciting ones such as political ecology.

HIV/AIDS in Africa

HIV-AIDS is clearly the most serious health problem in Africa today. Initial work such as that by Caldwell (1995), Caldwell, Caldwell, and Quiggin (1989), Rushton and Bogaert (1989), and Rushing (1995) constructed theories based on the eccentricities of African sexuality, and in the case of Rushton and Bogaert, outright racial determinism. Others such as Barnett and Blaikie (1992) have been accused of over-generalisation (Oppong 1996). Geographers initially focussed on the spatial diffusion of the virus and its aetiology (Shannon, Pyle, Bashshur 1991). Gould (1993) traces the origins of the AIDS epidemic to African monkeys and argues that initial denial by African leaders in several countries escalated its spread. The two books by Gould (1993) and Shannon, Pyle, Bashshur (1991), both of which are conjectural in orientation, indirectly influenced the representations of Africa as a 'diseased continent'.

Recent geography research on HIV-AIDS in Africa has usually chosen a political economy or structuralist theoretical perspective (Oppong 1998b; Bassett and Mhloyi 1991), and typically recommends education with empowerment (Thiuri 1997). Good (1995) argues against intervention strategies that ignore poverty. Expecting people to abandon behaviour that brings pleasure and immediate gratification is unreasonable, especially when it brings them income or power, even while posing risks to personal and family health. Oppong (1998b) cautions against over-generalisation by arguing that HIV diffusion patterns probably reflect the spatial distribution and social networks of vulnerable social groups such as women compelled by economic difficulties into commercial sex work. Consequently, intervention and empowerment programmes that enable the vulnerable to protect themselves against the disease must supplement information-based campaigns.

Within the social sciences, the few books available on AIDS in Africa are more general in their treatment (Barnett and Blaikie 1992), utilise spatial rather than social analysis (Shannon, Pyle, and Bashshur, 1991), or encompass broader geographic perspectives within critical analytical frameworks (Bond, Kreniske, Susser, and Vincent, 1997). Given the strength of geography at village-level studies, a number of studies have examined the impacts of HIV-AIDS on community and household well-being (for example, Kesby 2000). Kesby study shows that unequal gender relations and poor communication between men and women about sexual matters within the community and household setting plays a central role in the rapid transmission of HIV. Yet analysis of how communication might practically be improved remains a critical area for investigation. Theoretically we are beginning to see a shift from AIDS as a Disease to AIDS discourse in the social and geographical analysis of African AIDS (Packard and Epstein 1991).

Frustrated by the facile, fashionable, and simplistic explanations of HIV-AIDS in Africa, Kalipeni, Craddock, Oppong, and Ghosh (2004) call for moving beyond epidemiology in order to avoid explanations that are grounded in racism, disciplinary blindness and shoddy research. The groundbreaking volume brings together international contributors including African scholars and activists from the social sciences to examine the disease from previously ignored angles. Presenting on the ground evidence and ethnographic cases, the volume emphasises that HIV transmission in Africa is rooted in local economies, deepening poverty, migration, gender, war, global economies and cultural politics. Consequently, HIV-AIDS in Africa cannot be stemmed without addressing these directly.

Geography and Health Care

Improving geographic accessibility to health services using location-allocation models has been a dominant thrust of research (Oppong 1996; Oppong and Hodgson 1994; Oppong 1997b; Oppong and Hodgson 1998). Data limitations notwithstanding and contrary to critics such as Phillips (1990), these works argue that given the substantial improvements in location-allocation modelling, it is possible to achieve spatial accessibility with better locational choices (Oppong and Hodgson 1994; 1998). Showing that optimal location of Maternal and Child Health (MCH) clinics in rural Nigeria would increase coverage substantially, Ayeni et al., (1987) conclude that proliferating locations of health service delivery facilities cannot eliminate inefficiencies of location. Also, the normal practice of reporting efforts to improve health services in rural areas by citing increases in the number of facilities is insufficient. Mehretu, Wittick, and Pigozzi (1983) used the p-median model with maximal distance constraint to find locations of health service sites in Burkina Faso. Logan's (1985) work in Sierra Leone comparing the distribution of rural health care facilities proposed by the government with a distribution that is achieved through modelling showed that a facility system based on the network of administrative centres is considerably more expensive (in terms of transportation cost) than a system that is based on a careful analysis of the actual distribution of the target population for a particular service. Oppong and Hodgson (1998) show that using an interaction-based location-allocation model to locate health facilities might help to reduce the spread of HIV-AIDS in West Africa because better equipped and staffed facilities would attract more users and reduce itinerant drug vendors (Oppong and Hodgson 1998).

Oppong (1997b) identifies lack of a spatial planning tradition, data limitations, bureaucracy, inherent technical problems (software and hardware), and the innovation diffusion process as the major obstacles impeding acceptance of LA models in health care planning in sub-Saharan Africa. He also cautions against reckless applications of location-allocation models. Ignoring important local variables such as the rainy season in modelling can produce elegant but useless results, while accommodating them, perhaps by simply editing the data, produces great results (Oppong 1996). Gore (1991a) has criticised the LA approach because it is guilty of spatial separatism—the notion that it is possible to identify, separate, and evaluate the spatial either as an independent phenomenon or property of events examined through spatial analysis. It ignores the political and social dimension of health facility location decisions.

African Traditional Medicine

The conflict between biomedicine and African traditional medicine has been another interesting focus of research. Some authors have focussed on the fierce struggle between the two as biomedicine contested the hegemony of indigenous medicine. Good (1991; 2004) examines how pioneer medical missions impacted the geography of health and social changes in colonial Africa and hindered the advancement of traditional medicine. Ademuwagun et al., (1979) report that traditional healers suffered from vigorous colonial repression, disdain by African graduates of colonial government and mission schools, and were considered savage and primitive. However, these tactics failed because they did not rid the continent of devastating epidemics (Janzen 1978). The struggle continues today (Good 1987). Some studies call for a revival of African traditional medicine because as Lasker (1981) reported from Côte d'Ivoire, many socioeconomic groups, not only the poor, use traditional medicine. Oppong (1998) argues that viewing African traditional medicine as inferior to western biomedicine is simply ethnocentric. Good (1991) provides an historical context and conceptual framework for investigating traditional medicine and offers a detailed research agenda for future research.

Global Change and Earth Systems Science

Tracking developments in the field traditionally called physical geography, which researchers increasingly call earth systems science or global change, was difficult because much of the work on Africa is published not in traditional geography journals but in specialised interdisciplinary ones. What needs to be emphasised at the outset is that there is a tremendous amount of work on the African physical environment by North American geo-scientists and their counterparts in Africa and Britain, conducting work in many countries and across several disciplines. The emerging idea of earth systems science as an integrative science has made the old fashioned term 'physical geography' obsolete so that people who used to call themselves physical geographers are now able to cross traditional disciplinary boundaries with ease and are often working on multidisciplinary team projects. Key areas of research include global change (causes and impacts), the hydrology of wetlands (mostly British research), and landscape ecology. Theoretical models include global climate models, earth systems, and Remote Sensing/GIS as tools for monitoring global change.

Geographers have played a key role in this largely interdisciplinary literature, particularly the causes and impacts of climate change in the Sahel, rainfall patterns, and El Niño effects in Africa (Nicholson 1999; Nicholson and Farrar 1994; Nicholson and Kim 1997; Nicholson et al. 1997; Lamb, Bell, and Finch 1998). Contrary to conventional wisdom, Nicholson and her co-researchers demonstrate that neither the Saharan boundary nor vegetation cover in the Sahel has changed in 16 years, and 'productivity' assessed by water-use efficiency of the vegetation cover remains unchanged (Nicholson et al. 1998). Tarhule and Woo (1997, 1998) and Woo and Tarhule (1994), analysing historical information on droughts, famines and rainfall data from northern Nigeria, conclude that the most disruptive historical famines occurred when the cumulative rainfall deficit fell below 1.3 times the standard deviation of long-term mean annual rainfall. Other works that have examined climate change and its effects on drought, rainfall variability and food production systems include Swearingen (1994), Campbell (1994), Fuller and Prince (1996), Hamly et al. (1998), and Ropelewski et al. (1993).

Sand transport, dune formation, desert landscapes, soil degradation, and river morphology studies have advanced rapidly, particularly due to Nickling, who has worked for almost 20 years in Mali and produced about a dozen papers on these topics (Nickling and Gillies, 1993; Nickling and Wolfe, 1994). Lancaster, Schaber, and Teller (2000) use orbital radar images of the central Namib Desert to show the extent of relict fluvial deposits associated with former courses of the Tsondab and Kuiseb rivers. In many studies, Dyer and Torrance (1993) examine soil potential and food production potential and suggest a wide range in food production potential throughout Ethiopia. European, particularly British, geographers and African geoscientists have been active in research broadly defined as physical geography. Following Adams's pioneering work on wetlands and downstream impacts of dams (Adams 1990, 1993), many hydrologists and ecologists are studying wetland ecology/hydrology. The Cambridge group led by Grove and Adams is actively examining the multifaceted physical geography processes affecting the continent. In a recent book, Adams, Goudie, and Orme (1996) detail the physical geography of Africa, its geomorphological and biogeographical aspects, and the impact of human agency on African environments at the local, regional and continent-wide scales.

Remote Sensing and Geographic Information Systems (GIS)

North American and European geography is undergoing an unparalleled revolution in spatial data analysis. Personal computers, remote sensing and global positioning systems have expanded the quantity and types of spatially referenced data on the human habitat and the physical environment. Besides, Geographic Information Systems (GIS) have eased the collection, management, and analysis of huge volumes of spatially referenced data. Thus, geographers can evaluate spatial processes and patterns and display the results and products of such analyses at the touch of a button.

GIS and remote sensing have grown as tools for studying environmental change in Africa. Nellis et al. (1997a) use Landsat thematic mapper (TM) digital data for the Southern District of Botswana to analyse variations in grazing intensity associated with rural land practices. Nellis et al. (1997b) use higher spatial resolution system, the SPOT HRV multispectral digital data, to analyse the urban morphology of Gaborone, the capital of Botswana. Such analysis could be used to compare the processes that structure cities in the developing and developed world. Anyamba and Eastman (1996) use the Normalized Difference Vegetation Index (NDVI) now being derived from satellite imagery to study climate trends within Southern Africa. Other studies in this vein include Fairhead and Leach (1996), Bassett and Zueli (2000), and Desanker (1995, 2001).

Conclusion

This review testifies to the liveliness of North American geographical research on Africa. Bassett's (1989) review of the 1980s contributions by North American geographers to Africanist research identified a number of insufficiently developed substantive areas including gaps in physical geography (geomorphology and biogeography), historical cartography, political and cultural geography, and regional geography. While these same topics continue to be under-represented as areas of research during the 1990s, Bassett's (1989) call to revitalise African regional and cultural geography seems to have been answered by the rise of several excellent and comprehensive textbooks (Stock 1995; Aryeetey-Attoh 1997; Newman 1995). Stock's (1995) and Aryeetey-Attoh's (1997) books provide a coherent thematic interpretation of the regional, cultural and development status of the continent. Newman (1995) follows the traditional regional geography approach in a powerful narrative of the many precolonial migrations and state formations throughout Africa. Another advance during the 1990s is the Rockefeller African Dissertation Awards programme, coordinated through the University of California, Berkeley with Michael Watts having a leading role. This program starts to address the difficulties many young African scholars face in getting solid training in methodologies appropriate for use in African settings, and in obtaining funding for African dissertation research. This important step may answer the critical question of where the next generation of African and Africanist scholars will originate.

One important neglected area by human geographers is the political and electoral geography of the continent. Transitions such as democratisation in quite a few countries and the collapse of organised authority in others (Liberia, Somalia, Democratic Republic of the Congo, Rwanda, etc.) have received precious little in the way of attention by geographers. With the exception of a few works such as those by Glassman and Samatar (1997), Samatar (1992), and Cliffe and Bush (1994), this area is ripe for research given the rapidly changing global order. Another area of neglect is the rapidly expanding area of remote sensing and Geographic Information Systems. Swedish, French, and other European geographers have been very active in this area in the African context. One of the few active American groups in this regard is the IDRISI group at Clark University. Although research on the physical geographic processes of the continent by North American geographers continues to lag behind, a few individuals were very active in this area during the 1990s. The lag is in part a reflection of lack of specialised training in this area in American universities.

Perhaps due to overreaction against the neo-Malthusian debacle, demographic factors have been completely ignored in recent research. As Goldman (1994) notes in his critique of Little's (1992) book, the major weakness of the literature that uses political ecology as its guiding framework is its muteness on the dynamics of population change and demographic factors. The human population has grown dramatically during the past 30 years throughout sub-Saharan Africa and this fact alone probably had major impacts on resource scarcities, out-migration, and wage employment, and made social conflicts more likely. In reading this body of work, however, most of the authors appear constrained by the political economy and political ecology frameworks and ignore population in their analyses either as a strong reaction against the neo-Malthusian hypothesis or for fear of being branded neo-Malthusian. Yet, excluding demographic factors in these important debates may produce shortsighted policy formulations.

In conclusion, geographical research on Africa adopted newer methodological and theoretical perspectives during the 1990s and in recent years. Several prominent geographers embraced and/or helped to advance postcolonial/post-structuralist studies of representation and resistance and critiques of development discourse (for example, Crush 1995; Pile and Keith 1997). Political ecology, indigenous knowledge, Boserupian perspectives on population, feminist analyses, globalisation, and the dramatic shift in South African geography in the post-apartheid era emerged as important research themes. In the twenty-first century, we predict intensified use of these newer interdisciplinary approaches and the development of novel approaches and theories, while discarding old and static methodologies.

Acknowledgments

We are grateful to the University of Illinois Research Board for the funding that made this project possible. We would like to thank Stella Sambakunsi, Sosina Asfaw, and Leo Zulu for their untiring library research. We are also extremely indebted to the anonymous reviewers, particularly the one reviewer who offered very detailed constructive suggestions. Without the assistance of these individuals, it would have been extremely difficult to write such a comprehensive and inclusive chapter. However, the ideas expressed in this paper and any errors belong to the authors. We are also grateful to Oxford University Press for the copyright permission to reproduce this paper in this volume in its current expanded version. An abridged version of this paper appeared as a book chapter: Kalipeni, E.; Oppong, J. R. and Ofori-Amoah, B. 2003. 'The Geography of Africa'. In Gary Gaile and Cort Willmott, eds., *Geography in America at the Dawn of the 21st Century*. Oxford: Oxford University Press, pp. 565-585.

References

Adams. W.M., 1990, 'Dam Construction and the Degradation of Floodplain Forest on the Turkwel River, Kenya', *Land Degradation and Rehabilitation* 1: 189-98.

Adams, W. M., 1993, 'Indigenous Use of Wetlands and Sustainable Development in West Africa', *Geographical Journal* 159 (2): 209-18.

Adams, W.M., A.S. Goudie, and A. R Orme, 1996, *Physical Geography of Africa*, London: Oxford University Press.

Ademuwagun, Z. et al., 1979, *African Therapeutic Systems*, Waltham, MA: Crossroads Press.

Adjibolosoo, S. and Ofori-Amoah, B., eds., 1998, *Addressing Misconceptions About Africa's Economic Development: Seeing Beyond the Veil*, Lewiston, New York: The Edwin Mellen Press.

Amin, S., 1972, 'Underdevelopment and Dependence in Black Africa', *Journal of Modern African Studies* 10: 503-24.

Anyamba, A.J. and R. Eastman, 1996, 'Interannual Variability of NDVI over Africa and its Relation to El Nino/Southern Oscillation', *International Journal of Remote Sensing*, 17 (13): 2533-48.

Anyinam, C., 1989, 'The Social Cost of the IMF's Adjustment Program for Poverty. The case of health care Development in Ghana'. *International Journal of Health Sciences* 19 (3): 531-547.

Aryeetey-Attoh, S., ed., 1997, *Geography of Sub-Saharan Africa*, Upper Saddle River, NJ: Prentice Hall.

Aryeetey-Attoh, S., 2003, 'Urban Geography of Sub-Saharan Africa', in S. Aryeetey-Attoh, ed., *Geography of Sub-Saharan Africa*, Second Edition, Upper Saddle River, NJ: Prentice Hall, 254-297.

Atkinson, T., 1991, *Principles of Political Ecology*, London, Belhaven Press.

Awanyo, L., 1998, 'Culture, Markets and Agricultural Production: A Comparative Study of the Investment Patterns of Migrant and Citizen Cocoa Farmers in the Western Region of Ghana', *Professional Geographer* 50 (4): 516-30.

Ayeni, B., G. Rushton, and M. L. McNulty, 1987, 'Improving the Geographical Accessibility of Health Care in Rural Areas: a Nigerian Case Study', *Social Science and Medicine* 25: 1083-94.

Barkan, J. D., M. L. Mcnulty, and M. A. O. Ayeni, 1991, 'Hometown Voluntary Associations, Local Development and the Emergence of Civil Society in Western Nigeria,' *Journal of Modern African Studies* 29 (3): 457-80.

Barnett, T. and P. M. Blaikie, 1992, *AIDS in Africa: Its Present and Future Impact*, Chichester, England: Wiley.

Bascom, J. B., 1990a, 'Border Pastoralism in Eastern Sudan', *Geographical Review* 80 (4): 416-30.

Bascom, J. B., 1990b, 'Food, Wages, and Profits: Mechanized Schemes and the Sudanese State', *Economic Geography* 66 (2): 140-55.

Bassett, M. T., and M. Mhloyi, 1991, 'Women and AIDS in Zimbabwe: The Making of an Epidemic', *International Journal of Health Services* 21 (1): 143-56.

Bassett, T. J., 1986, 'Fulani Herd Movements', *Geographical Review* 76 (3): 233.48.

Bassett, T. J., 1988, 'Breaking Up the Bottlenecks in Food Crop and Cotton Cultivation in Northern Ivory Coast', *Africa* 58 (2): 147-74.

Bassett, T. J., 1989, 'Perspectives on Africa in the 1980s', in G. Gaile and C. Willmott, eds., *Geography in America*, Columbus, OH: Merrill, 468-87.

Bassett, T. J., 1993, 'Land Use Conflicts in Pastoral Development in Northern Côte d'Ivoire', in Thomas J. Bassett and Donald Crummey, eds., *Land in African Agrarian Systems*, Madison, Wis.: University of Wisconsin Press, 131-54.

Bassett, T. J., 1994, 'Cartography and Empire Building in Nineteenth-Century West Africa', *Geographical Review* 84 (3): 316-35.

Bassett, T. J., 1998, 'Indigenous Mapmaking in Intertropical Africa', in D. Woodward and M. Lewis, eds., *The History of Cartography*, Vol. 2, Bk. 3: *Cartography in the Traditional African, American, Arctic, Australian, and Pacific Societies*, Chicago: University of Chicago Press, 24-48.

Bassett, T. J. and D. Crummey, eds., 1993, *Land in African Agrarian Systems*, Madison, Wis.: University of Wisconsin Press.

Bassett, T. J. and Zueli, K. B., 2000, 'Environmental Discourses and the Ivorian Savanna', *Annals of the Association of American Geographers* 90 (1): 67-95.

Bauer, P. T., 1972, *Dissent on Development: Studies and Debates in Development Economics*, Cambridge, MA: Harvard University Press.

Bencharifa, A and D. L. Johnson, 1990, 'Adaptation and Intensification in the Pastoral System of Morocco', in John G. Galaty and D. L. Johnson, eds., *The World of Pastoralism: Herding Systems in Comparative Perspective*, New York: The Guildford Press, 394-416.

Benyoussef, A. and A. F. Wessen, 1974, 'Utilization of Health Services in Developing Countries—Tunisia', *Social Science and Medicine* 16: 287-304.

Bernstein, A., 1996, *Cities and the Global Economy: New Challenges for South Africa*, Johannesburg: Centre for Development and Enterprise.

Best, A. C. G. and H. J. De Blij, 1977, *African Survey*, New York: Wiley.

Blaikie, P., 1989, 'Environment and Access to Resources in Africa', *Africa* 59 (1): 18-40.

Blaikie, P., 1994, 'Political Ecology in the 1990s: An Evolving View of Nature and Society', CASID Distinguished Speaker Series, No. 13. East Lansing: Center for Advanced Study of International Development, Michigan State University.

Blaikie, P. and H. Brookfield, 1987, *Land Degradation and Society*, London: Methuen.

Bond, G., J. Kreniske, I. Susser, and J. Vincent, eds., 1997, *AIDS in Africa and the Caribbean*, Boulder, CO: Westview Press.

Bond, P., 1999, *Cities of Gold, Townships of Coal: Essays on South Africa's New Urban Crisis*, Trenton, NJ: Africa World Press.

Brookfield, H., 1975, *Interdependent Development*, London: Methuen.

Bryant, R., 1992. 'Political Ecology: An Emerging Research Agenda in Third World Studies', *Political Geography Quarterly*, 11 (1):108-25.

Bush, R., 1996, 'The Politics of Food and Starvation', *Review of African Political Economy* 68: 169-95.

Caldwell, J. C., 1995, 'Understanding the AIDS Epidemic and Reacting Sensibly to it (Editorial)', *Social Science & Medicine* 41 (3): 299-302.

Campbell, D., 1981, 'Land Use Competition at the Margins of the Rangelands: An Issue in Development Strategies for Semi-arid Areas', in G. Norcliffe and T. Pinfold, eds., *Planning African Development*, Boulder, CO: Westview Press, 39—61.

Campbell, D., 1984, 'Response to Drought among Farmers and Herders in Southern Kajiado District, Kenya', *Human Ecology* 12 (1): 35-64.

Campbell, D., 1990a, 'Community-Based Strategies for Coping with Food Scarcity: A Role in African Famine Early-warning Systems', *GeoJournal* 20 (3): 231-41.

Campbell, D., 1990b, 'Strategies for Coping with Severe Food Deficits in Rural Africa', *Food and Foodways* 4 (2): 143-62.

Campbell, D., 1991, 'The Impact of Development upon Strategies for Coping with Drought among the Maasai of Kajiado District, Kenya', in *Pastoral Economies in Africa and Long-Term Responses to Drought*, Aberdeen: University of Aberdeen, 116-28.

Campbell, D., 1994, 'The Dry Regions of Kenya', in Michael H. Glantz, ed., *Drought Follows the Plough: Cultivating Marginal Areas*, Cambridge: Cambridge University Press, 77-90.

Carmody, P., 1999, 'Neoclassical Practice and the Collapse of Industry in Zimbabwe: The Cases of Textiles, Clothing and Footwear', *Economic Geography* 74 (4): 319-43.

Carney, J. A., 1992, 'Peasant Women and Economic Transformation in the Gambia', *Development and Change*, 2: 67-90.

Carney, J., 1993a, 'Converting the Wetlands, Engendering the Environment: The Intersection of Gender with Agrarian Change in The Gambia', *Economic Geography* 69 (4): 329-48.

Carney, J. A., 1993b, 'From Hands to Tutors: African Expertise in the South Carolina Rice Economy', *Agricultural History* 67 (3): 1-30.

Castro-Leal, F., J. Dayton, L. Demery, and K. Mehra, 2000, 'Public Spending on Health Care in Africa: Do the Poor Benefit?' *Bulletin of the World Health Organization* 78 (1): 66-74.

Cliffe, L. and R. Bush, 1994, *The Transition to Independence in Namibia*, Boulder, CO: Lynne Rienner.

Cooper, B. M., 1997, 'Gender, Movement, and History: Social and Spatial Transformations in 20th century Maradi, Niger', *Environment and Planning. D, Society & Space* 15 (2): 195-21.

Corbridge, S., ed., 1995, *Development Studies: A Reader*, London: E. Arnold.

Cornia, G. A. and G. K. Helleiner, 1994, *From Adjustment to Development in Africa: Conflict, Controversy, Convergence, Consensus?* Basingstoke: Macmillan.

Costello, A., 1994, *Human Face or Human Façade? Adjustment and the Health of Mothers and Children*, London: Centre for International Development.

Crush, J., ed., 1995, *Power of Development*, London and New York: Routledge.

Crush, J., ed., 1998, *Beyond Control: Immigration and Human Rights in a Democratic South Africa*, Cape Town: Queen's University/IDASA.

Crush, J., 1999, 'Fortress South Africa and the Deconstruction of Apartheid's Migration Regime', *Geoforum* 30 (1): 1-11.

Crush, J. and W. James, 1997, *Crossing Boundaries: Mine Migrancy in a Democratic South Africa*, Ottawa, Ontario: IDRC.

Crush, J., A. Jeeves, and D. Yudelman, 1991, *South Africa's Labor Empire: A History of Black Migrancy to the Gold Mines*, Boulder, CO: Westview Press.

Crush, J. and V. Williams, eds., 1999, *The New South Africans? The Immigration Amnesties and Their Aftermath*, Cape Town: IDASA/Queen's University.

De Blij, J. Harm, 1964, *A Geography of Subsaharan Africa*, Chicago: Rand McNally.

Desanker, P. V., 1995, *The Miombo Network: Framework for a Terrestrial Transect Study of Land-Use and Land-Cover Change in the Miombo Ecosystems of Central Africa: Conclusions of the Miombo Network Workshop, Zomba, Malawi, December 1995*, Stockholm, Sweden: International Geosphere-Biosphere Programme.

Desanker, P. V., 2001, *Africa and Global Climate Change*, Oldendorf/Luhe: Inter-Research.

Drakakis-Smith, D., 1990, 'Food for Thought or Thought about Food: Urban Food Distribution Systems in the Third World', in R. B. Potter and A. T. Salau, eds., *Cities and Development*, London: Mansell, 100-20.

Drakakis-Smith, D., 1992, *Urban and Regional Change in Southern Africa*, London: Routledge.

Drakakis-Smith, D., T. Bowyer-Bower, and D. Tevera, 1995, 'Urban Poverty and Urban Agriculture: An Overview of the Linkages in Harare', *Habitat International* 19 (2): 183.

Dumont, R., 1966, *False Start in Africa*, London: Andre Deutsch Ltd

Dyer, J. A. and J. K. Torrance, 1993, 'Agroclimatic Profiles for Uniform Productivity Areas in Ethiopia', *Water International* 18 (4): 189-99.

Fairhead, J. and Leach, M., 1996, *Misreading the African Landscape: Society and Ecology in the Forest Savanna Mosaic*, New York: Cambridge University Press.

Fairhead, J. and M. Leach, 1998, *Reframing Deforestation: Global Analyses and Local Realities with Studies in West Africa*, London: Routledge.

Fendall, N. R. E., 1963, 'Health Centers: A Basis for Rural Health Service', *Journal of Tropical Medicine and Hygiene* 66: 219.

Fordham, P., 1972, *The Geography of African Affairs*, Harmondsworth, UK: Penguin Books.

Foucault, M., 1970, *The Order of Things: An Archaeology of the Human Sciences*, London: Tavistock.

Foucault, M., 1977, *The Archaeology of Knowledge*, London: Tavistock.

Foucault, M., 1980, *Power/Knowledge*, Brighton: Harvester Press.

Frank, A. G., 1969, *Capitalism and Underdevelopment in Latin America: Historical Studies of Chile and Brazil*, New York: Monthly Review Press.

Freund, P. J., 1986, 'Health Care in a Declining Economy: The Case of Zambia', *Social Science and Medicine* 23 (9): 875-888.

Fuller, D. O. and S. D. Prince, 1996, 'Rainfall and Foliar Dynamics in Tropical Southern Africa: Potential Impacts of Global Climatic Change on Savanna Vegetation', *Climatic Change* 33 (1): 69-96.

Gaile, L., 1992, 'Improving Rural-Urban Linkages Through Small Town Market Based Development', *Third World Planning* 14 (2): 131-48.

Gaile, G. L., 1994, 'Thought for Food: Models and Policies for Food Security and Increased Agricultural Productivity', in D. A. Griffith and J. L. Newman, eds., *Eliminating Hunger in Africa: Technical and Human Perspectives.* Syracuse, NY: Maxwell School of Citizenship and Public Affairs, Syracuse University.

Gaile, G. L. and A. Ferguson, 1996, 'Success in African Social Development: Some Positive Indications', *Third World Quarterly* 17 (3): 557-72.

Gaile, G. L and P. M. Ngau, 1995, 'Identifying the Underserved of Kenya: Populations without Access to Small Towns', *Regional Development Dialogue*16 (2): 100.

Glassman, J., and A. I. Samatar, 1997, 'Development Geography and the Third World State', *Progress in Human Geography* 21 (2): 164-98.

Gleave, M. B., ed., 1992, *Tropical African Development,* London: Longman Scientific and Technical Publishers.

Godlewska, A. and N. Smith, eds., 1994, *Geography and Empire,* Oxford: Blackwell.

Goldman, A., 1993, 'Agricultural Innovation in Three Areas of Kenya: Neo-Boserupian Theories and Regional Characterization', *Economic Geography* 69: 44-71.

Goldman, A., 1994, 'Review of the *Elusive Granary: Herder, Farmer, and State in Northern Kenya*', *Professional Geographer* 46(1): 129-30.

Good, C. M., 1987, *Ethnomedical Systems in Africa,* New York: Guilford Press.

Good, C. M., 1991, 'Pioneer Medical Missions in Colonial Africa', *Social Science & Medicine* 32 (1): 1-11.

Good, C. M., 1995, 'Editorial: Incentives Can Lower the Incidence of HIV/AIDS in Africa', *Social Science & Medicine* 40 (4): 419.

Good, C. M., 2004, *The Steamer Parish: The Rise and Fall of Missionary Medicine on an African Frontier,* Chicago: The University of Chicago Press.

Goodman, D. and M. Watts, 1997, *Globalising Food: Agrarian Questions and Global Restructuring,* London: Routledge.

Gore, C. G., 1991, 'The Spatial Separatist theme and Problem of Representation in Location-Allocation Models', *Environment and Planning A* 23: 939-953.

Gould, P. R., 1970, 'Tanzania, 1920-63: The Spatial Impress of the Modernization Process', *World Politics* 22: 149-70.

Gould, P., 1993, *The Slow Plague: The Geography of the AIDS Pandemic,* Cambridge, MA: Blackwell.

Gourou, P., 1961, *The Tropical World: Its Social and Economic Conditions and its Future Status,* Translated by E.D. Laborde, London: Longman.

Griffith, D. A., J. L. Newman and W. A. Dando, eds., 1995, *Eliminating Hunger in Africa: Technical and Human Perspectives,* Syracuse: Syracuse University Press.

Hamly, M. E., R. Sebbari and P. J. Lamb, M. N. Ward, D. H. Portis, 1998, 'Variability of Rainfall Regimes ("Hydrological" Point of View)—Towards the Seasonal Prediction of Moroccan

Precipitation and Its Implications for Water Resources Management', *IAHS Publication* 252: 79-88.

Hance, W. A., 1967, *African Economic Development*, Revised Edition, New York: Frederick A. Praeger, Publishers.

Hance, W. A., 1970, *Population, Migration, and Urbanization in Africa*, New York: Columbia University Press.

Hance, W. A., 1975, *The Geography of Modern Africa*, Second Edition, New York: Columbia University Press.

Hance, W. A., 1977, *Black Africa Develops*, Waltham, MA: Crossroads Press.

Hart, G., 1998, 'Multiple Trajectories: A Critique of Industrial Restructuring and the New Institutionalism', *Antipode* 30 (4): 333-56.

Hart, J. J., 1971, 'The Inverse Care Law', *The Lancet* 1: 405-412.

Heasley, L. and Delehanty, J., 1996, 'The Politics of Manure: Resource Tenure and the Agropastoral Economy in Southwestern Niger', *Society and Natural Resources* 9: 31-46.

Hodder, B. W., 1973, *Economic Development in the Tropics*, Second Edition, London: Methuen & Co.

Hull, R. W., 1976, *African Cities and Towns before the European Conquest*, New York: Norton.

Hunt, C. W., 1996, 'Social Vs Biological: Theories of the Transmission of AIDS in Africa', *Social Science & Medicine*, 42/9: 1283-96.

Hunter, J. M., 1992, 'Elephantiasis: A Disease of Development in North East Ghana', *Social Science & Medicine*, 35/5: 627-49.

Hunter, J. M., 1996, 'An Introduction to Guinea Worm on the Eve of its Departure: Dracunculiasis Transmission, Health Effects, Ecology and Control', *Social Science & Medicine* 43 (9): 1399-1425.

Hunter, J. M., 1997a, 'Geographical Patterns of Guinea Worm Infestation in Ghana: An Historical Contribution', *Social Science & Medicine* 44 (1): 103-22.

Hunter, J. M., 1997b, 'Bore Holes and the Vanishing of Guinea Worm Disease in Ghana's Upper Region', *Social Science & Medicine* 45 (1): 71-89.

Hyndman, J., 1999, 'A Post-Cold War Geography of Forced Migration in Kenya and Somalia', *Professional Geographer* 51 (1): 104-114.

Janzen, J., 1978, *The Quest for Therapy in Lower Zaire*, Berkeley: University of California Press.

Jarosz, L., 1993, 'Defining and Explaining Tropical Deforestation: Shifting Cultivation and Population Growth in Colonial Madagascar (1896-1940)', *Economic Geography* 69 (4): 366-79.

Jarosz, L., 1996, 'Defining Deforestation in Madagascar', in Richard Peet and Michael Watts, eds., *Liberation Ecologies: Environment, Development, and Social Movements*, London and New York: Routledge, 148-64.

Johnson, L. D., 1993, 'Nomadism and Desertification in Africa and the Middle East', *GeoJournal* 31 (1): 51-66.

Johnston-Anumonwo, I., 1997, 'Geography and gender in sub-Saharan Africa', in S. Aryeetey-Attoh, ed., *Geography of Sub-Saharan Africa*, Upper Saddle River, NJ: Prentice Hall, 262-85.

Kalipeni, E., 1995, 'The Fertility Transition in Africa', *Geographical Review* 85 (2): 287-301.

Kalipeni, E., 1996, 'Demographic Response to Environmental Pressure in Malawi', *Population and Environment* 17 (4): 285-308.

Kalipeni, E. S. Craddock, J. Oppong, and J. Ghosh, eds., 2004, *HIV/AIDS in Africa: Beyond Epidemiology*, Oxford: Blackwell Publishers.

Kates, R., 1981, 'Drought in the Sahel: Competing Views as to What Really Happened in 1910-14 and 1968-1974', *Mazingira*, 5 (2) 72-83.

Katz, C., 1991, 'Sow What You Know: The Struggle for Social Reproduction in Rural Sudan', *Annals of the Association of American Geographers* 81 (3): 488-514.

Kesby, M., 2000, 'Participatory Diagramming as a Means to Improve Communication About Sex in Rural Zimbabwe: A Pilot Study', *Social Science and Medicine* 50 (12): 1723-41.

King, M., 1966, *Medical Care in Developing Countries: A Primer on the Medicine of Poverty and a Symposium from Makerere*, Nairobi: Oxford University Press.

Knight, C. G. and J. L. Newman, 1976, *Contemporary Africa: Geography and Change*, Englewood Cliffs, NJ: Prentice-Hall.

Kodras, J. E., 1993, 'Shifting Global Strategies of United States Foreign Food Aid, 1955-1990', *Political Geography* 12 (3): 232-46.

Konadu-Agyeman, K., 1991, 'Reflections on the Absence of Squatter Settlements in West African Cities: The Case of Kumasi, Ghana', *Urban Studies* 28 (1):139-51.

Kull, C. A., 1998, 'Leimavo Revisited: Agrarian Land-use Change in the Highlands of Madagascar', *Professional Geographer* 50 (2): 163-76.

Lamb, P. J., M. A. Bell, J. D. Finch, 1998, 'Variability of Rainfall Regimes ("Meteorological" Point of View)—Variability of Sahelian Disturbance Lines and Rainfall during 1951-1987', *IAHS Publication* 252:19-28.

Lancaster, N., G. G. Schaber, and J. T. Teller, 2000, 'Orbital Radar Studies of Paleodrainages in the Central Namib Desert', *Remote Sensing of Environment* 71 (2): 216-25.

Lasker, J. N., 1981, 'Choosing among Therapies: Illness Behaviour in the Ivory Coast', *Social Science and Medicine* 15A: 157-168.

Leach, M. and Mearns, R., 1996, *The Lie of the Land: Challenging Received Wisdom on the African Environment*, Oxford: James Currey.

Lemon, A., 1995, *The Geography of Change in South Africa*, Chichester, NY: J. Wiley.

Levin, R., 1998, 'Land Restitution, Ethnicity, and Territoriality: The Case of the Mmaboi Land Claim in South Africa's Northern Province', in E. Kalipeni and P. T. Zeleza, eds., *Sacred Spaces and Public Quarrels: African Economic and Cultural Landscapes*, Lawrenceville, NJ: Africa World Press, 323-56.

Levin, R. and D. Weiner, eds., 1997, *'No More Tears...' Struggles for Land in Mpumalanga, South Africa*, Trenton, NJ: Africa World Press.

Lightfoot, D. R. and Miller, J. A., 1996, 'Sijilmassa: The Rise and Fall of a Walled Oasis in Medieval Morocco', *Annals of the Association of American Geographers* 86 (1): 78-101.

Little, M., 1994, 'Charity versus Justice: The New World Order and the Old Problem of World Hunger', in D. A. Griffith and J. L. Newman, eds., *Eliminating Hunger in Africa: Technical and Human Perspectives*, Syracuse, NY: Maxwell School of Citizenship and Public Affairs, 23-38.

Little, P., 1992, *The Elusive Granary: Herder, Farmer, and State in Northern Kenya*, Cambridge: Cambridge University Press.

Little, P. D. and M. J. Watts, eds., 1994, *Living under Contract: Contract Farming and Agrarian Transformation in Sub-Saharan Africa*, Madison, WI: The University of Wisconsin Press.

Logan, B. I., 1985, 'Evaluating Public Policy Costs in Rural Development Planning: the example of Health Care in Sierra Leone', *Economic Geography* 61:144-57.

Logan, B. I., 1995a, 'The Traditional System and Structural Transformation in Sub-Saharan Africa', *Growth and Change* 26 (4): 495-523.

Logan, B. I., 1995b, 'Can Sub-Saharan Africa Successfully Privatize its Health Care Sector?', in Mengisteab, K. and B. I. Logan, eds., *Beyond Economic Liberalization in Africa: Structural Adjustment and the Alternatives*, London: Zed Books.

Logan, B. I. and K. Mengisteab, 1993, 'IMF-World Bank Adjustment and Structural Transformation in Sub-Saharan Africa', *Economic Geography* 69:1-24.

Mabogunje. A. L., 1980, *The Development Process: A Spatial Perspective*, London: Hutchinson & Co. Publishing Ltd.

Mackenzie, F., 1995, 'Selective Silence: A Feminist Encounter with Environmental Discourse in Colonial Africa', in Jonathan Crush,. ed., *Power of Development*, London and New York: Routledge, 100-14.

Mackenzie, F., 1998, *Land, Ecology and Resistance in Kenya, 1880-1952*, Edinburgh: Edinburgh University Press.

Masilela, C. and Weiner, D., 1996, 'Resettlement Planning in Zimbabwe and South Africa's Rural Land Reform Discourse', *Third World Planning Review* 18 (1): 23-43.

Mather, C., 1999, 'Agro-commodity Chains, Market Power and Territory: Re-regulating South African Citrus Exports in the 1990s', *Geoforum* 30 (1): 61-70.

Matzke, G. E. and N. Nabane, 1996, 'Outcomes of a Community Controlled Wildlife Utilization Program in a Zambezi Valley Community', *Human Ecology* 24 (1): 65-85.

May, J. M., 1961, *Studies in Disease Ecology*, New York: Hafner Publishing Co.

Mayer, J. D., 1996, 'The Political Ecology of Disease as One New Focus for Medical Geography', *Progress in Human Geography* 20 (4): 441-56.

McDade, B. E., 1997, 'Industry, Business Enterprises, and Entrepreneurship in the Development Process', in S. Aryeetey-Attoh, ed., *Geography of Sub-Saharan Africa*, Upper Saddle River, NJ: Prentice Hall, 325-44.

McDade, B. E., and Malecki, E. J., 1997, 'Entrepreneurial Networking: Industrial Estates in Ghana', *Tijdschrift voor Economische en Sociale Geografie, (Journal of Economic and Social Geography)* 88 (3): 262-72.

McDonald, D. A., 1999, 'Lest the Rhetoric Begin: Migration, Population and the Environment in Southern Africa', *Geoforum* 30 (1): 13-25.

McDonald, D. A., ed., 2000, *On Borders: Perspectives on Migration in Southern Africa*, New York: St. Martin's Press.

McEvers, N., 1980, 'Health and the Assault on Poverty in Low Income Countries', *Social Science and Medicine* 14G: 41-57.

Mehretu, A., 1985, 'A Spatial Framework for Redressing Disparities in Rural Service Delivery Systems', *Tijdschrift voor Economische en Sociale Geografie* 76: 363-373.

Mehretu, A., 1989, *Regional Disparity in Sub-Saharan Africa: Structural Readjustment of Uneven Development*, Boulder, CO: Westview Press.

Mehretu, A. and Mutambirwa, C., 2003, 'Cities of Sub-Saharan Africa', in S. D. Brunn, J. F. Williams and D. J. Zeigler, eds., *Cities of the World: World Regional Urban Development*, Lanham: Rowman and Littlefield Publishers, 293-330.

Mehretu, A. and Sommers, L. M., 1990, 'Towards Modeling National Preference Formation for Regional Development Policy: Lessons from Developed and Less Developed Countries', *Growth and Change: A Journal of Urban and Regional Policy* 21 (3): 31-47.

Mehretu, A. and L. M. Sommers, 1992, 'Trade Patterns and Trends in the African-European Trading Area: Lessons for Sub-Saharan Africa from the Era of the Lome Accords 1975-1988', *Africa Development* XVII (2): 5-26.

Mehretu, A., R. I. Wittick and B. W. Pigozzi, 1983, 'Spatial Design for Basic Needs in Eastern Upper Volta', *The Journal of Developing Areas* 17:383-394.

Mengisteab, K. and B. I. Logan, eds., 1995, *Beyond Economic Liberalization in Africa: Structural Adjustment and the Alternatives*, London: Zed Books.

Miner, H., ed., 1967, *The City in Modern Africa*, New York: Praeger.

Moore, D. S., 1998, 'Clear Waters and Muddied Histories: Environmental History and the Politics of Community in Zimbabwe's Eastern Highlands', *Journal of Southern African Studies* 24 (2): 377-403.

Moore, D. S., 1999, 'The Crucible of Cultural Politics: Reworking "Development" in Zimbabwe's Eastern Highlands', *American Ethnologist* 26 (3): 654-89.

Morgan, W. B., 1969, 'Peasant Agriculture in Tropical Africa', in M. F. Thomas and G. W. Whittington, eds., *Environment and Land Use in Africa*, London: Methuen, 241-272.

Morgan, W. T. W. and Russell, E. W., 1969, *East Africa: Its Peoples and Resources*, New York: Oxford University Press.

Mortimore, M. and Tiffen, M., 1994, 'Population Growth and a Sustainable Environment: The Machakos Story', *Environment* 36 (8): 10.

Mountjoy, A. B. and Hilling, D., 1988, *Africa: Geography and Development*, London: Hutchinson.

Murton, J., 1999, 'Population Growth and Poverty in Machakos District, Kenya', *Geographical Journal* 165: 37-46.

Myers, G. A., 1996, 'Naming and Placing the Other: Power and the Urban Landscape in Zanzibar', *Tijdschrift voor Economische en Sociale Geografie* 87 (3): 237-46.

Myers, G. A., 1998, 'Intellectual of Empire: Eric Dutton and Hegemony in British Africa', *Annals of the Association of American Geographers* 88 (1): 1-27.

Nast, H. J., 1994, 'The Impact of British Imperialism on the Landscape of Female Slavery in the Kano Palace, Northern Nigeria', *Africa* 64 (1): 34-73.

Nast, H. J., 1996, 'Islam, Gender, and Slavery in West Africa circa 1500: A Spatial Archeology of the Kano Palace, Northern Nigeria', *Annals of the Association of American Geographers* 86 (1): 44-77

Nellis, M. D., C. E. Bussing, T. L. Coleman, M. Nkambwe, and S. Ringrose, 1997a, 'Spatial and Spectral Dimensions of Rural Lands and Grazing Systems in the Southern District of Botswana', *Geocarto International* 12 (1): 41-47.

Nellis, M. D., C. E. Bussing, M. Nkambwe, and T. L. Coleman, 1997b, 'Urban Land Use and Morphology in a Developing Country Using SPOT HRV Data: Gaborone, Botswana', *Geocarto International* 12 (1): 91-95.

Neumann, R. P., 1995, 'Ways of Seeing Africa: Colonial Recasting of African Society and Landscape in Serengeti National Park', *Ecumene* 2: 149-69.

Neumann, R. P., 1998, *Imposing Wilderness: Struggles Over Livelihood and Nature Preservation in Africa*, Berkeley: University of California Press.

Newman, J. L., 1995, *The peopling of Africa: A Geographical Interpretation*, New Haven, CT: Yale University Press.

Nicholson, S. E., 1999, 'Historical and Modern Fluctuations of Lakes Tanganyika and Rukwa and their Relationship to Rainfall Variability', *Climatic Change* 41 (1): 53-71.

Nicholson, S. E. and Farrar, T. J., 1994, 'The Influence of Soil Type on the Relationships Between NDVI, Rainfall, and Soil Moisture in Semiarid Botswana. I. NDVI Response to Rainfall', *Remote Sensing of Environment*, 50/2: 107-20.

Nicholson, S. E., J. Kim, 1997, 'The Relationship of the El Nino Southern Oscillation to African Rainfall', *International Journal of Climatology* 17 (2): 117-35.

Nicholson, S. E., J. A. Marengo, J. Kim, A. R. Lare, S. Galle, and Y. H. Kerr, 1997, 'A Daily Resolution Evapoclimatonomy Model Applied to Surface Water Balance Calculations at the HAPEX-Sahel Supersites', *Journal of Hydrology* 189 (1-4): 946-64.

Nicholson, S. E., C. J. Tucker, and M. B. Ba, 1998, 'Desertification, Drought, and Surface Vegetation: An Example from the West African Sahel', *Bulletin of the American Meteorological Society* 79 (5): 815-29.

Nickling, W. G. and J. A. Gillies, 1993, 'Dust Emission and Transport in Mali, West Africa', *Sedimentology* 40 (5): 859-68.

Nickling, W. G. and S. A. Wolfe, 1994, 'The Morphology and Origin of Nabkhas, Region of Mopti, Mali, West Africa', *Journal of Arid Environments* 28 (1): 13-30.

Nyamweru, C., 1996, 'Sacred Groves Threatened by Development', *Cultural Survival Quarterly* Fall: 19-20.

Nyamweru, C., 1998, *Sacred Groves and Environmental Conservation*, Canton, New York: Frank P. Piskor Lecture, St. Lawrence University.

Obudho, R. A. and Taylor, D. R. F., 1979, *The Spatial Structure of Development: A Study of Kenya*, Boulder, CO: Westview Press.

O'Connor, A. M., 1971, *The Geography of Tropical African Development*, Oxford: Pergamon Press.

O'Connor, A. M., 1991, *Poverty in Africa*, London: Belhaven Press.

Ofori-Amoah, B., 1995, 'The Saturation Hypothesis and Africa's Development Problems: On the Nature of Development Theory and Its Implications for the Human Factor in Africa's Development', in S. B-S. K. Adjibolosoo, ed., *The Significance of the Human Factor in African Economic Development*, Westport, CT: Praeger, 15-24.

Ofori-Amoah, B., 1996, 'Human factor Development and Technological Innovation in Africa', in S. B-S. K Adjibolosoo, ed., *Human Factor Engineering and the Political Economy of African Development*, Westport, CT: Praeger, 111-24.

Ofori-Amoah, B., 1998, 'The Human Factor Perspective and Development Education', in V. G. Chivaura and C. J. Mararike, eds., *The Human Factor Approach to Development in Africa*, Harare: University of Zimbabwe Press, 34-43.

Okafor, S. I., 1982, 'Policy and Practice: The Case of Medical Facilities in Nigeria', *Social Science and Medicine* 16: 1971-77.

Ominde, S. H. and S. J. K. Baker, 1971, *Studies in East African Geography and Development*, Berkeley: University of California Press.

Onyemelukwe, J. O. C., 1984, *Industrialization in West Africa*, Sydney: Croom Helm.

Onyemelukwe, J. O. C. and M. O. Filani, 1983, *Economic Geography of West Africa*, Burnt Mill, UK: Longman.

Oppong, J. R., 1996a, 'Accommodating the Rainy Season in Third World Location—Allocation Applications', *Socio-Economic Planning Sciences* 30 (2): 121-37.

Oppong, J. R., 1996b, 'Review of *AIDS in Africa: Its Present and Future Impact* by Tony Barnett and Piers Blaikie. Guilford Press, New York, 1992. 193 pp.', *Social Science and Medicine* 43(2): 278-279.

Oppong, J. R., 1998a, 'A Vulnerability Interpretation of the Geography of HIV/AIDS in Ghana, 1986-95', *Professional Geographer* 50 (4): 437-448.

Oppong, J. R., 1998b, 'African Traditional Medicine: Dangerous, Anachronistics or Panacea,', in S. B-S. K. Adjibolosoo and B. Ofori-Amoah, eds., *Addressing Misconceptions About Africa's Economic Development: Seeing Beyond the Veil.* Lewiston, NY: The Edwin Mellen Press, 97-111.

Oppong, J. R. and Hodgson, M. J., 1994, 'Spatial Accessibility to Health Care Facilities in Suhum District, Ghana', *The Professional Geographer* 46 (2): 199-209.

Oppong, J. R. and Hodgson, M. J., 1998, 'An Interaction-Based Location-Allocation Model for Health Facilities to Limit the Spread of HIV-AIDS in West Africa', *Applied Geographic Studies* 2 (1): 29-41.

Osei, W. Y., 1988, 'The Gender Factor in Rural Energy Systems in Africa: Some Evidence', in S. B-S. K. Adjibolosoo and B. Ofori-Amoah, eds., *Addressing Misconceptions About Africa's Economic Development: Seeing Beyond the Veil*, Lewiston, NY: The Edwin Mellen Press, 84-96.

Ould-Mey, M., 1996, *Global Restructuring and Peripheral States: The Carrot and the Stick in Mauritania*, London: Littlefield Adams Books.

Owusu, J. H., 1998, 'Current Convenience, Desperate Deforestation: Ghana's Adjustment Program and the Forestry Sector', *Professional Geographer* 50 (4): 418-36.

Packard, R. M. and Epstein, P., 1991, 'Epidemiologists, Social Scientists, and the Structure of Medical Research on AIDS in Africa', *Social Science and Medicine* 33 (7): 771-94.

Pedler, F. J., 1955, *Economic Geography of West Africa*, London: Longmans, Green and Co.

Peet, R., ed., 1977, *Radical Geography: Alternative Viewpoints on Contemporary Social Issues*, Chicago: University of Chicago Press.

Phillips, D. R., 1990, *Health and Health Care in the Third World*, New York: John Wiley and Sons.

Pickles, J., 1991, 'Industrial Restructuring, Peripheral Industrialization, and Rural Development in South Africa', *Antipode*, 23/1: 67-91.

Pickles, J. and D. Weiner, 1991, 'Rural and Regional Restructuring of Apartheid: Ideology, Development Policy and the Competition for Space', *Antipode*, 23 (1): 2-32.

Pile, M. and Keith, M., eds., 1997, *Geographies of Resistance*, London: Routledge.

Prothero, R.M. and K. M. Barbour, eds., 1973, *A Geography of Africa: Regional Essays on Fundamental Characteristics, Issues, and Problems*, London: Routledge & Kegan Paul.

Ralston, B., Ray, J. and G. Harrison, 1994, 'Issues in the Transportation of Food Aid', in D. A. Griffith and J. L. Newman, eds., *Eliminating Hunger in Africa: Technical and Human Perspectives*, Syracuse, NY: Maxwell School of Citizenship and Public Affairs, 57-79.

Riddell, J. B., 1970, *The Spatial Dynamics of Modernization in Sierra Leone: Structure, Diffusion, and Response*, Evanston, IL: Northwestern University Press.

Riddell, J. B., 1992, 'Things Fall Apart Again: Structural Adjustment Programmes in Sub-Saharan Africa', *Journal of Modern African Studies* 30 (1): 53-68.

Rocheleau, D.E., B. P. Thomas-Slayter, E. Wangari, eds., 1996, *Feminist Political Ecology: Global Issues and Local Experience*, London: Routledge.

Roder, W., 1994, *Human Adjustment to Kainji Reservoir in Nigeria: An Assessment of the Economic and Environment Consequences of a major Man-made Lake in Africa*, Lanham, Maryland: University Press of America.

Rodney, W., 1974, *How Europe Underdeveloped Africa*, Washington: Howard University Press.

Roemer, M.I., 1972, *Evaluation of Community Health Centers*, Geneva: WHO.

Rogerson, C.M., 1996, 'Urban Poverty and the Informal Economy in South Africa's Economic Heartland', *Environment and Urbanization*, 8/1: 167-81.

Rogerson, C.M., ed., 1999, *South Africa: Different Geographies. Special Issue of Geoforum 30/1*, London: Pergamon Press.

Rogerson, C. M. and McCarthy, J. J., eds., 1992, *Geography in a Changing South Africa: Progress and Prospects*, Cape Town: Oxford University Press.

Ropelewski, C. F., P. J. Lamb, D. H. Portis, 1993, 'The Global Climate for June to August 1990: Drought Returns to Sub-Saharan West Africa and Warm Southern Oscillation Episode Conditions Develop in the Central Pacific', *Journal of Climate* 6 (11): 2188-2212.

Rostow, W. W., 1960, *The Stages of Economic Growth: A Non-Communist Manifesto*, Cambridge: Cambridge University Press.

Rothenberg, T. Y., 1994, 'Voyeurs of Imperialism: *The National Geographic Magazine* Before World War II', in A. Godlewska and N. Smith, eds., *Geography and Empire*, Oxford: Blackwell, 155-72.

Rushing, W. A., 1995, 'The Cross Cultural Perspective on AIDS in Africa', in W. A. Rushing, *The AIDS Epidemic: Social Dimensions of an Infectious Disease*, Boulder, CO: Westview Press, 59-90.

Rushton, J. P. and Bogaert, A. F., 1989, 'Population Differences in Susceptibility to AIDS: An Evolutionary Analysis', *Social Science and Medicine* 28 (12): 1211-20.

Saff, G., 1995, 'Residential Segregation in Post-apartheid South Africa: What Can Be Learned from the United States Experience', *Urban Affairs Review*, 30 (6): 782-808.

Saff, G., 1998, 'The Effects of Informal Settlement on Suburban Property Values in Cape Town, South Africa', *Professional Geographer* 50 (4): 449-64.

Said, E., 1978, *Orientalism*, London: Routledge.

Samatar, A. I., 1992, 'Destruction of State and Society in Somalia: Beyond the Tribal Convention', *The Journal of Modern African Studies* 30 (4): 625-41.

Samatar, A. I., 1993, 'Structural Adjustment as Development Strategy? Bananas, Boom, and Poverty in Somalia', *Economic Geography* 69 (1): 25-43.

Sanders, R., 1992, 'Eurocentric Bias in the Study of African Urbanization: A Provocation to Debate', *Antipode* 24 (3): 203-13.

Sauerborn, R., A. Nougtara, and H.J. Diesfeld, 1989, 'Low Utilization of Community Health Workers: Results from a Household interview Survey in Burkina Faso', *Social Science and Medicine* 29: 1163-74.

Schoepf, B. G., 1986, 'Primary Health Care in Zaire', *Review of African Political Economy* 36: 54-58.

Schroeder, R. A., 1993, 'Shady Practice: Gender and the Political Ecology of Resource Stabilization in Gambian Garden/Orchards', *Economic Geography* 69 (4): 349-65.

Schroeder, R. A., 1995, 'Contradictions along the Commodity Road to Environmental Stabilization: Foresting Gambian Gardens', *Antipode* 27 (4): 325-42.

Schroeder, R. A., 1997, '"Re-claiming" Land in The Gambia: Gendered Property Rights and Environmental Intervention', *Annals of the Association of American Geographers* 87 (3): 487-508.

Scott, J. C., 1977, *The Moral Economy of the Peasant: Rebellion and Subsistence in Southeast Asia*, New Haven: Yale University Press.

Scott, J. C., 1987, *Weapons of the Weak: Everyday Forms of Peasant Resistance*, New Haven: Yale University Press.

Sen, A., 1981, *Poverty and Famine*, Oxford: Clarendon Press.

Sen, A., 1990, 'Food, Economics, and Entitlements', in J. Dreze and A. Sen, eds., *The Political Economy of Hunger*, Oxford: Clarendon Press, 35-50.

Shannon, G. W., G. F. Pyle, and R. Bashshur, 1991, *The Geography of AIDS: Origins and Course of an Epidemic*, New York: Guilford Press.

Sharpston, M. J., 1972, 'Uneven Geographical Distribution of Medical Care: A Ghanaian Case Study', *Journal of Development Studies* 8: 205-222.

Simon, D. D., 1992, *Cities, Capital and Development: African Cities in the World Economy*, New York: Halstead.

Smith, J., Barau, A. D., Goldman, A., and Mareck, J. H., 1994, 'The Role of Technology in Agricultural Intensification: The Evolution of Maize Production in the Northern Guinea Savanna of Nigeria', *Economic Development and Cultural Change* 42 (3): 537-54.

Spring, A., and B. McDade, 1998, *African Entrepreneurship: Theory and Reality*, Gainesville: University Press of Florida.

Soja, E. W., 1968, *The Geography of Modernization in Kenya: A Spatial Analysis of Social, Economic and Political Change*, Syracuse, NY: Syracuse University Press.

Stanley, W. R., 1990, 'Socioeconomic Impact of Oil in Nigeria', *GeoJournal* 22 (1): 67-79.

Stock, R., 1982, 'Distance and Utilization of Health Facilities in Rural Nigeria', *Social Science and Medicine* 17: 563-570.

Stock, R., 1985, 'Health Care for Some: A Nigerian Study of Who Gets What, Where and Why', *International Journal of Health Services*, 15(3): 469-84.

Stock, R., 1986, '"Disease and Development" or "The Underdevelopment of Health": A Critical Review of Geographical Perspectives on African Health Problems', *Social Science and Medicine* 23 (7): 689-700.

Stock, R., 1995, *Africa South of the Sahara: A Geographic Interpretation*, New York: Guilford Press.

Stock, R. and Anyinam, C., 1992, 'National Governments and Health Policy in Africa', in T. Falola and D. Ityavar, eds., *The Political Economy of Health in Africa*, Athens, OH: Ohio University Center for International Studies.

Streefland, P., J. W. Harnmeijer, and J. Chabot, 1995, 'Implications of Economic and Structural Adjustment Policies on PHC in the Periphery', in J. Chabot, J. W. Harnmeijer, and P. H. Streefland, eds., *African Primary Health Care in Times of Economic Turbulence*, Amsterdam: Royal Tropical Institute, 11-17.

Swearingen, W., 1994, 'Northwest Africa', in Michael H. Glantz, ed., *Drought Follows the Plough: Cultivating Marginal Areas*, Cambridge: Cambridge University Press, 103-16.

Taafee, E. J., R. I. Morrill, and P. R. Gould, 1963, 'Transport Expansion in Underdeveloped Countries: A Comparative Analysis', *Geographical Review* 53: 503—29.

Tarhule, A. and M. Woo, 1997, 'Towards an Interpretation of Historical Droughts in Northern Nigeria', *Climatic Change* 37 (4): 601-16.

Tarhule, A. and M. Woo, 1998, 'Changes in Rainfall Characteristics in Northern Nigeria', *International Journal of Climatology* 18 (11): 1261-71.

Taylor, D. R. F. and F. Mackenzie, eds., 1992, *Development from Within: Survival in Rural Africa*, London: Routledge.

Thiuri, P., 1997, 'The Threats of AIDS to Women and Development in Sub-Saharan Africa', in Kalipeni, E. and Thiuri, P., eds., *Issues and Perspectives on Health Care in Contemporary Sub-Saharan Africa*, Lewiston, NY: Edwin Mellen Press, 73-114.

Thomas, M. F. and G. W. Whittington, 1969, *Environment and Land Use in Africa*, London: Metuen & Co. Ltd.

Tiffen, M. and M. Mortimore, 1994, 'Malthus Controverted: The Role of Capital and Technology in Growth and Environment Recovery in Kenya', *World Development*, 22 (7): 997-1010.

Tiffen, M., M. Mortimore, and F. Gichuki, 1994, *More People, Less Erosion: Environmental Recovery in Kenya*, Chichester, New York: J. Wiley.

Timberlake, L., 1986, *Famine in Africa*, New York: Gloucester Press.

Timberlake, L. and J. Tinker, 1986, *Africa in Crisis: The Causes, the Cures of Environmental Bankruptcy*, Philadelphia, PA: New Society Publishers.

Turner II, B. L., G. Hyden, and R. W. Kates, eds., 1993, *Population Growth and Agricultural Change in Africa*, Gainesville: University of Florida Press.

Turner, M., 1993, 'Overstocking the Range: A Critical Analysis of the Environmental Science of Sahelian Pastoralism', *Economic Geography* 69 (4): 402-21.

Turshen, M., 1999, *Privatizing Health Services in Africa*, New Brunswick, NJ: Rutgers University Press.

Twumasi, P. A., 1988, *Social Foundations of the Interplay Between Traditional and Modern Medical Systems*, Legon: Ghana Universities Press.

Udo, R.K., 1978, *A Comprehensive Geography of West Africa*, New York: Africana Publishing Co.

Udo, R.K., 1982, *The Human Geography of Tropical Africa*, Ibadan: Heinemann Educational Books.

Van der Geest, S., 1982, 'The Efficiency of Inefficiency: Medicine Distribution in Southern Cameroon', *Social Science and Medicine* 16: 2145-2153.

Vogel, R.J., 1994, *Financing Health Care in Sub-Saharan Africa*, Westport, CT: Greenwood Press.

Waddington, C.J. and K.A. Enyimayew, 1989, 'A Price to Pay: The Impact of User Charges in Ashanti-Akim District, Ghana', *International Journal of Health Planning and Management* 4:17-47.

Wallersdtein, I. M., 1974, *The Modern World-System: Capitalist Agriculture and the Origins of the European World-Economy in the Sixteenth Century*, New York: Academic Press.

Watts, M., 1983, *Silent Violence: Food, Famine & Peasantry in Northern Nigeria*, Berkeley: University of California Press.

Watts, M., 1987a, 'Drought, Environment and Food Security: Some Reflections on Peasants, Pastoralists and Commoditization in Dryland West Africa', in M. H. Glantz, ed., *Drought and Hunger in Africa: Denying Famine a Future*, Cambridge: Cambridge University Press: 173 -209.

Watts, M., 1987b, *State, Oil, and Agriculture in Nigeria*, Berkeley: University of California.

Watts, M., 1989, 'The Agrarian Question in Africa: Debating the Crisis', *Progress in Human Geography* 13 (1): 1-41.

Watts, M., 1993, 'The Geography of Post-Colonial Africa: Space, Place and Development in Sub-Saharan Africa', *Singapore Journal of Tropical Geography*, 14 (2): 173-90.

Watts, M., 1994, 'Life under Contract: Contract Farming, Agrarian Restructuring, and Flexible Accumulation', in Peter. D. Little and Michael J. Watts, eds., *Living Under Contract: Contract Farming and Agrarian Transformation in Sub-Saharan Africa*, Madison, WI: The University of Wisconsin Press, 21-77.

Watts, M., 1996, 'Nature as Artifice and Artefact', in Richard Peet and Michael Watts, eds., *Liberation Ecologies: Environment, Development, and Social Movements*, London and New York: Routledge, 243-68.

Watts, M., 1997, 'State Violence, Local Resistance and the National Question in Nigeria', in S. Pile and M. Keith, eds., *Geographies of Resistance*, London: Routledge.

Watts, M. J. and R. Shenton, 1984, 'State and Agrarian Transformation in Nigeria', in J. Barker, ed., *The Politics of Agriculture in Tropical Africa*, Beverly Hills: Sage Publications, 173-203.

Weiner, D. et al., 1985, 'Land Use and Agricultural Productivity in Zimbabwe', *Journal of Modern African Studies* 23(2): 251-85.

Weiner, D. and R. Levin, 1991, 'Land and Agrarian Transition in South Africa', *Antipode*, 23 (1): 92-120.

Woo, M. and A. Tarhule, 1994, 'Streamflow Droughts of Northern Nigerian Rivers', *Hydrological Sciences Journal* 39 (1): 19-34.

Wood, W. B., 1994, 'Forced Migration: Local Conflicts and International Dilemmas', *Annals of the Association of American Geographers* 84 (4): 607-34.

World Bank, 1994, *Better Health in Africa*, Washington DC: World Bank.

World Health Organization, 1978, *Primary Health Care*, Geneva: World Health Organization.

Wubneh, M., 1994, 'Discontinuous Development, Ethnic Collective Movements, and Regional Planning in Ethiopia', *Regional Development Dialogue* 15 (1): 120-44.

Yeboah, Ian E. A., 1998, 'Geography of Gender Economic Status in Urban Sub-Saharan Africa: Ghana, 1960-1984', *The Canadian Geographer* 42 (2): 158-73.

Zinyama, L., 1992, 'Local Farmer Organizations and Rural Development in Zimbabwe', in D. R. F. Taylor, and F. Mackenzie, eds., *Development from Within: Survival in Rural Africa*, London: Routledge.

Zinyama, L.M., T. Matiza, and D. Campbell, 1990, 'The Use of Wild Foods During Periods of Food Shortage in Rural Zimbabwe', *Ecology of Food and Nutrition* 24: 251-65.

Chapter 11

Psychology for a Contemporary Africa

Kopano Ratele

If asked, very many people around the world might and do maintain without hesitation that some or all of their accomplishments or failings were caused by an invisible hand, say of God. Some names for this and similar set of explanatory frameworks are Christianity or Islam. Another example: I think we will be hard-put to find even a handful outside of a certain class ˙of individuals who will attribute their divorces or hurtful relationships to invisible essences; here I am thinking of unconscious processes.

Other people, when questioned and if they feel 'safe' or confident to speak, might and do attribute similar failings to other ghosts, for instance evil magic cast by an envious neighbour and their achievements to a fortifying potion given to them by an *ngaka* (medicine man or woman) or something revealed by a *sangoma* (diviner). In the circles of my adult and working life, the first two explanations, which the majority of people around the continent and elsewhere in the world use, and which might be found when talking to a certain class of people, are often articulated in public and without shame. The last set of explanations, however, has largely gone underground, as it were, for to be successful and to believe that your success is because of invisible causes, in this case something that a *sangoma* said and did, to actually speak in such a manner makes you suspect, weird, for it is 'cultural' in a negative way, meaning primitive. An important and complicating matter which needs to be kept in mind when regarding these stories people live by: people who speak about *dingaka* (medicine men or woman) may also at the same time speak of God and the unconscious.

My aim with this chapter is to examine two primary concerns in psychology as they are thought of and get dealt with on the continent, with specific reference to South Africa. Furthermore, the chapter considers three other subsidiary and related matters: the question of the acclaimed scientificity of psychology, the notion of the individual, and delimitation of the discipline. I begin at the said primary issues, this being the relation of psychologies of or in Africa with the hegemonic form of the discipline, and the matter of proper phenomena for psychological investigation; otherwise put, is there space for looking at other sorts of elements of life and for thinking differently, both methodologically and theoretically, of psychology? I then proceed to a discussion of a number of common definitions of the discipline before indicating problems with some of the discourses these traditional definitions deploy, in particular when they are viewed in the light of the critical questions that face us on the continent, especially from sub-Saharan Africa. Following this the chapter is put to a discussion of what psychologists here and abroad in fact do in their private practices and in lecture halls, before indicating what I think local psychologists ought to be doing if psychology is to have a more self-conscious, critical and productive place in the present landscape on the continent in matters of personal, economic, social and political life.

The Universal Psychologist up the River

To a lesser or greater degree, two primary, critical concerns continue to trouble psychologists (but perhaps practitioners and scholars who keep their eyes on power and truth networks) in the poor countries—or more widely, psychologists outside of old Europe and the United States of America (US) in particular—but perhaps more so clinicians, counsellors and scholars who ply their skills and knowledge in countries in Africa. First off is this very relation: how to train students as well as what set of common practices to agree on, and at the same time define this set of educational moments and practises *as* an ethical, organic psychology—a psychology that is of necessity somewhat different to the received canon because it emerges out of the developing world in its inevitable relation to the theory and studies produced in and which are in conversation with the living conditions of the richer countries. The problem for psychologists from Africa is how, in other words, to mimic the powerful psychologies and heedlessly make claims about the *universal of the particular* in talking about the cognitive, affective and behavioural life of persons in his or her contexts of reflection.

Here is the problem: even with the most deconstructive thinkers the desire to understand the most general principles from our particular objects of study, of wanting to talk of a universal humanity from specific observations of the world, is always in mind. Appearing to foreclose this desire, one psychology teacher and author suggests that unlike their predecessors contemporary psychologists have become more sensitive culturally and politically, broadening the scope of their studies, sharpening their methodologies and opening their frames to include more human diversity. He claims that

> Psychological researchers of the past were mostly interested in the 'general' laws or principles of behaviour—the principles of perception or learning or motivation that all people share. In fact they assumed that those principles were so general that we could probably discover them by studying rats or pigeons or any other convenient species. When they studied some behaviour that required human subjects—language, for example—they still assumed that the principles were the same for all

people, so the research could focus on any convenient group of people. Most often, the research used students at US colleges (Kalat 1996: 28).

Although the mood of the times seems to have changed a lot in regard to using the white rat or US college freshmen to make inferences about humanity, evidence shows that psychological researchers, teachers and therapists still have some way to go to give up on their deeply-held wish to discover universal laws about human beings based on their studies of convenient samples. Nor have changes in the world and being witness to struggles for and eventual independence of former colonies, the movement of goods and people, global poverty and social justice movements' protest on television, high-tech and guerrilla wars, technological developments, and state and other terrorisms worked to halt orthodox scholars from getting grants to hypothesise about, study and discover universal truths on the essence and nature of human beings.

But for African intellectuals this desire for universality thrusts itself into the foreground with especial and vexing assertiveness. The problem of the universal truth is of course originally brought to the attention of and given salience in the minds of Africans by the fact that being physically, psychically, or politically located in this part of the globe they are thus more likely to be aware of the blind-spots, thoughtlessness, and arrogance of hegemonic ideologies that rule the world. The problem of African intellectuals and of psychologists specifically is of the same cut: these intellectuals will tend to be more aware of the global mainstream's arrogance of truth-claims. Thus African psychologists cannot but have to deal with Western mainstream psychology (with regard to the English-speaking world, this is a short-hand for the dominant version of psychological life emerging out of the United Kingdom (UK) and the US when it has made claims of universality). Among others, Mkhize (2004: 25) shows that it was 'in the quest to emulate the natural sciences that psychologists construed their discipline as an objective, value-free and universal science. Eager to demonstrate the universality of psychological processes such as motivation, perception and emotion, psychologists saw culture as an impediment'.

Admittedly, the problem of having to think their way past and out of the fair-ground of the ideas of psychology (such as that of a common, abstracted psyche and behaving individual) ironically becomes unavoidable, both as an intellectual and affective problematic, for African scholars and teachers precisely because of the undeniable achievements of psychology in infiltrating very many people's minds and into most locales of the globe. Many people around the world, even in some rural places, use the language of psychology: a friend might say she is experiencing a lot of stress from her work and family; one's unconscious makes him do things; a young man goes out to find himself; parents talk of their daughter developing her own personality. As a consequence of the power of the universal science, African practitioners are confronted on the one hand by this psychology's unthinking power as reflected in its foundational theses, and on the one hand held back, correctly, by a certain cautiousness from speaking of an abstract psyche or humanity. And power is always what is at the bottom of this; to paraphrase Hook (2004: 16), critical psychologists cannot but be preoccupied with the conjectures of psychology about the nature of humans for the knowledge produced by psychologists is not a neutral and objective reflection of how nature or humans beings are, but is rather constructed and disseminated by a specific group, in particular ways, for unspecified but certain interests. The knowledge of psychology, to put things in yet another manner, has never been disinterested, impartial, or without personal or group-informed suppositions.

The problem can be seen from another vantage point. And from here, the language that might be employed makes it somewhat clearer perhaps. This is, for instance, the language that speaks of identity, community connectedness, indigenisation, social embeddedness, Africanisation, or liberation; from this point, it is clear that the trouble for African psychologists is how to develop an identity by cultivating emergent or organic forms of the discipline without degenerating into exoticism. There has been a long growth in Africa of theoretical work around this issue. In a well-worn paper about what is known as the relevance debate, the author(s) argued that as

> everything in life should be regarded as political for the oppressed ... (and) the idea of being neutral a myth ... signifying non-commitment to social change ... (with) counseling (having) historically served the function of a 'repair shop' for capitalist society ... a more relevant or indigenous counseling psychology (has) to work to awaken the oppressed to political action ... (and) the counselor should conscientize all clients about the influence that socio-political factors have on their lives (Anonymous 1986: 87-88; see also Dawes 1986).

About the myth of non-partisanship and the enduring alienation of psychology from communities around it—the term community is a code for race, for African, for socially deprived sites, for historically dispossessed groups—a number of authors have commented that the practice of psychology, primarily the therapy work with white/affluent subjects, has attracted and needs to continue being seen as suspect, and as such those who have been conscientised about the effects and assumptions of disciplinary formations should keep working at developing practical logics that have the potential to render emancipatory services with and for those who need them (see Ngonyama ka Sigogo and Modipa 2004). With regard to therapy and counselling Ivey (1986: 24) once argued that the therapist who is critical or, thus, socially and politically sassed, 'is a sociotherapist before a psychotherapist precisely because a psychology which serves as an ideology critique cannot make the product of the mediated individual the first or even, for that matter, the last principle'. Others have simply asked: what forms of psychology and what images of persons would be appropriate for out time? (Foster 2004).

Again, as said, this problem of battling with universality, a certain kind of culturelessness, ahistoricity, or trans-society-ness when a party is only constructed as capable of the particular of course does not originate inside psychology. It is a problematic that haunts almost all disciplines as practised on the continent. Above all it is trouble that haunts almost all of the 'other' cultures in a developed world-led 'global village' that is surely hierarchically structured—the matter of it being how the periphery relates to the centre, of us and them, in Stuart Hall's terms, the discourse of the West and the Rest.

The second set of vexing questions to a psychologist in Africa is closely related to the first, and thus we can be brief. In short, these troubles revolve around issues of content and method in research, writing and teaching. In other words, critical psychologists working in Africa are bothered, rightly, about how they go about in trying to understand the world and, having do so, how to communicate this knowledge to those who may need it most, that is to say rather than to other practitioners or students of psychology. However, given the fact that we do psychology out of Africa (in a way, out-of-its-proper-place), one of the themes that does not want to go away is the question of what constitutes proper psychological phenomena in this context, how to talk about such phenomena, whether these phenomena are in fact the same as what researchers and theorists from the post-industrialised North write of and their textbooks speak of, and so what psychology to teach students and how.

What Is Psychology? Definitions, Histories, Family Resemblances

As a teacher of psychology and a potential middle-man and customer of multinational publishing houses, one of the many textbooks that has found its way to my bookshelves and referred to already defines psychology as 'the systematic study of behaviour and experience' (Kalat 1996: 6). Following this the book says something about the term psychology, how it is derived from the Greek for *psyche*, meaning *soul* or *mind*, and *logos* for *study*. The author then mentions the fact that like most disciplines the roots of psychology can be traced to philosophy but that the discipline has developed considerably since then, moving and spreading far from its philosophical origins, and that this is because of or has necessitated becoming more scientific in the process. Speaking of connections, this last and other psychology books make another association for the discipline, that with physiology, which, as becomes obvious in analysing these books, is a signal to the biological foundations and legitimation of the ruling bio-medical explanations in psychology.

While the text above does not mention the word science in the definition per se, there is veiled reference to it in the term 'systematic'. Additionally, chapter 2 of the text is, as in most psychology textbooks, on scientific methods that psychologists use to get to knowledge (Kalat 1996). Scientificity is very important to psychologists, a point obviously tied to the earlier one about general laws of human behaviour. Thus a definition that many psychology textbooks offer their students is that it 'is the scientific study of behaviour' (Wortman et al., 1999: 4). These last authors add that the behaviour studied by psychologists is 'both external observable action and internal thought'. These authors also indicate that an important implication of this definition that should not be missed is that psychology is a science not because of what it studies but because of how it studies what it does.

Dennis Coon (1998: 2) also maintains that it is because the mind (psyche) is difficult to observe that psychology gets to be defined as 'the scientific study of the human and animal behaviour'. Coon goes on to speak about the fact that the behaviour that he refers to is both that which is overt as well as covert behaviour, such as thinking and remembering.

Perhaps the most common definition of psychology is that it is 'the science of behavior and mental processes' (Davis & Palladino 1997: 3; see also Dworetzky 1997; Sdorow 1993). Davis and Palladino (1997) further state that although psychology stresses behaviour, the discipline encompasses the rich inner life that we all experience as well as the fact that psychological study covers dreams, daydreams and other inner experiences.

Turning to the continent, one of the leading South African psychologists, Lionel Nicholas, admits that there are many definitions of psychology with varying emphases but contends that 'all agree that psychology is the scientific study of behaviour' (2003: 2). I would have liked to but cannot here give full attention to the point to which that Nicholas gives a few lines: the standard history of the development of the discipline, in particular the role of for instance a figure such as Willem Wundt (1821-1894). Who is Wundt? (see Hunt 1993). He is the man for whose efforts in starting the exercise of delineating the field of psychology and for establishing the first psychological laboratory at Leipzig, Germany, is accorded the title of founder of the discipline. He is the professor of physiology and philosophy who broke away from all that to father a new science and therefore whose name deserves to be learnt by all who pass through psychology halls. He is the intellectual who realised that it is only through psychology that we could get to the real facts of consciousness, this interest being among those reasons that appear to have led him to campaign to make psychology a distinct and separate field of study from under philosophy or physiology. Wundt believed that psychology should be modelled after physics and chemistry, a foundation on which rests the scientific nature of psychology. The need to be scientific and systematic impelled Wundt to establish a laboratory for psychological studies. He is hence at the head of the long march, which started in December of 1879, we have made to understand the psyche of human beings everywhere, as well as being teacher to such a luminary as Stanley Hall, the first person to receive a doctorate in psychology in the US, the man who established the first psychology laboratory in that country, the founder of the first psychology journal, the first president of the American Psychological Association, in a word, another man who demands our respect for taking over from the Europeans to the US the inchoate science and bettering it. Now I must make clear one thing at least: that Wundt played an important role in the development of psychology. But it is critically important to show the problems about this telling of disciplinary formation. There is a problem that needs to be attended to about how the history of psychology is told to students, which is the progressivist narrative about cumulative and better knowledge, about one man leading the charge, giving the baton to another man, a narrative that banishes the everyday hesitations, glosses, contradictions, rivalries, but also the fears and ambitions informing intellectual production, the professional jealousies that make us do things and leave well along other matters. That is to say I think it is important to show the histories that lie underneath this rousing history of psychology (see, for example, Danziger 1990).

Notwithstanding, what I now want to turn fully to are the three other problematics in psychology: (a) the obvious one in the definitions above, that of science, (b) the implied one of the individual, and (c) end up at the topics that make up the field. I cannot do this before I indicate that contrary to Nicholas's (2004) recent confidence in psychological oneness, having for a long time been part of the most vocal critical elements against the psychology establishment in apartheid South Africa, it is not true that all psychologists agree about what psychology is, or what its proper object should be, and how those who claim the name of psychologist should look at the world. Firstly because, as Hook (2004) says, psychology is a field comprising diverse components, many of which bear only some family resemblance, at the level of methodology or conceptual frames. Secondly, because there are many other, and in the view of a rather sizeable number of African psychologists, better definitions of psychology and how they think of what they do. As an example, Manganyi (1991: 117), the father of conscious psychology, a while back was saying that 'a study on psychology and society ... should focus on the politics of experience, which is what I believe psychology is all about'. This assertion allows one to dispense with notions such as 'science of behaviour'. And taking off from this kind of thinking and a number of other writers, Mkhize (2004) opts to define psychology as cultural and social forms of knowledge arising out of the realities of the people and aimed at investigating their everyday behaviours and to address their needs. The most that can be said then is that there is the received, jingoistic view ruling the psychology world (Foster 2004). What is not heard enough is that psychology is not a unitary field, holding together disparate interests, changing interests, but some are more pronounced than others because they are part of power.

Science of the Individual

The idea of psychology as a science is then clear from the definitions that many psychologists claim for the discipline, choose to be untroubled by, or quietly go along with. 'Psychology emerged from philosophy as a self-designated science', a former president of the American Psychological Association once claimed in his address, as well as arguing that 'the science of psychology, because it deals with the fundamental understanding of behavior, serves as a core discipline for other social sciences concerned with human behavior' (Fowler 1990: 2). These are even today strong, bold words, it must be said. However, the notion of the science of psychology is not as unproblematic as it is made out to be in these definitions. Science and what counts as knowledge is a highly contested territory, something which orthodox scholars often neglect to mention to their audiences and readers, tending not to want to be bogged down by insignificant details like what is truth. Talking of one of the subdisciplines of psychology, the celebrated Turkish-born and US-educated social psychologists Sherif and his partner some time ago also claimed that 'policy makers, religious leaders, novelists, and commentators on the social scene cannot be held accountable for adhering to the ground rules of communicability and reproducibility of methods that permit verification—social psychologists are' (Sherif & Sherif 1969: 8). This of course was not quite true in the 1960s and is still false in the twenty-first century. Yet, it must be clear now, it is not such an old fashioned nor unique declaration that Fowler and the Sherifs were making, as can be seen in, for instance, an influential book (at least to newcomers to psychology) such as Baron and Byrne's (1997). These authors claim the status of science for social psychology by saying:

> Many persons seem to believe that the term science refers primarily to fields such as chemistry, physics, and biology. Such persons may find somewhat puzzling our view that social psychology, too, is scientific ... Although the topics that social psychologists study are very different from those in the physical or biological science, the methods we employ are similar in nature and orientation. For this reason, it makes sense to describe social psychology as basically scientific in nature (1997: 6-8).

Up to the present then it appears as if the scientific status of psychology remains as solid and unshakeable as ever (see for example, Atkinson et al., 1953; Halonen & Santrock 1999; Nairne 1997; Ruch 1984; Wittig & Williams 1984). But it was never said it was going to be easy, it should be admitted, and thus it is crucial to keep on reiterating and developing arguments that critical scholars have made in this regard. Also, to be sure, there have been gains made about this and about other conceptual and methodological frameworks: quantitative analyses might still rule the roost, but qualitative research is more widely accepted in the psychology fraternity; the ideas of 'race' and sex as social constructs are widely known; postmodernist explanations do not sound as strange as they did when Foucault, Kristeva, Derrida, and others were coming up with 'variables' such as knowledge-power, *différance*, discourse, deconstruction, abjection, and others. Collins (2004: 2) continues the work at the edifice of the science by repeating and extending the Nietzschean dictum for psychology students: 'all explanations are interpretations—those that deny this by making claims to universal scientific truth are simply made more dangerous by their attempt to hide their own perspective'. Moll (1993) told of how as a freshman psychology student in the 1970s the answer given to him and other students to the question of what is psychology was this very one: 'the science of behaviour'—an answer that, as suggested, we still give to our students today. Moll analysed three textbooks used at the University of the Witwatersrand. Moll's purpose was to show how the books, just as many psychologists, either take the notion of science for granted and are willing supporters of this notion, going along with the widespread pretence that the discipline is just like other sciences such as physics in its basic methodologies. Moll traced how while at some point some of the authors he looked at would betray an uneasiness (in later editions) about their claims and idea of what science is, the basic premise of a science would still be defended.

Manganyi, Mkhize, Moll, Collins, and other critical psychologists are saying that to tell psychology students that what they are studying is a science of behaviour, as the texts above do, is to foreclose their quest to learn about how science works and more generally their development as readers of and participants in their societies and the larger world. Telling psychology first year students that what they are studying is science (in the mould of chemistry rather than, firstly, the human sciences that it is)—which does not imply that psychology is not a science of a kind, but above all that in fact what they have to learn to reflect about is on struggle about science itself—is to bamboozle them into political and social disengagement, for as Foucault (2000) said it is the question of the political work that science does, the interweaving of effects of power and knowledge that needs questioning. And in making that quiet reference to the problem with the notion of ideology—and here we ought to incorporate under this that Popperian distinction between science and pseudo-science— Foucault (2000: 119) was saying the problem here 'does not consist in drawing the line between that which, in a discourse, falls under the category of scientificity or truth, and that which comes under some other category; rather it consists in seeing historically how effects of truth are produced within discourses that, in themselves, are neither true nor false'. Which leads to what in his influential work on the crisis of social psychology, the second and third rules (which applies to general psychology) Ian Parker (1989) suggested were that: (a) we have to let go of talking of *finding* and *discovering* and all other metaphors of revelation so favoured by psychological scientists of a certain kind when talking about human lives and social interaction and (b) that if we accept that there is no big truth out there, we have to find new 'criteria of goodness' away from the verification/falsification game and evaluate results of our work in terms of effects. I think 'the problem of what psychology' is a little clearer because of that more widely accepted idea that languages, and thus definitions and how histories are told, are never innocent but rather written all over with power.

We can turn now to the less obvious second notion in the idea of psychology, that of the individual. The individual lies at the centre of all the science of psychology as we have it. Once again, what the individual is and how he or she is to be understood is not a straightforward matter, with its own troubling aspects. This is what led Russel Spears and Parker (1996) to maintain that if there is an illusion that psychology thoroughly and determinedly sustains, it is that of individuality. It is also of importance to see the connection of the idea of the individual to that of the psyche, self, ego, I, as both a central concept of psychology apparatus and institutions, as well as the self as knower and only valid standpoint from which the world and other selves can be apprehended (see Franchi & Swart 2003). In other words, when authors say that psychology is the scientific study of behavioural and mental processes, what is being silently argued for as what needs to be taken for granted is that these mental processes occur in the head of the individual of course, and that behaviour is fundamentally defined by a person's ghostly essence.

This is a good point to enter how new psychology looks like. Also, disenchanted with orthodox explanations from psychology, groups of scholars have been trying to present a case for a different way of thinking about thinking (as an example for our purposes here, but we could also employ memory, motivation, intelligence, the unconscious, and other topics of psychology) and build a new psychology. In thinking about cognition, the received ideas are in error, these scholars have been saying. At least two problems present themselves with these traditional ideas of thinking: one methodological, the other pedagogic. The methodological problem is that thinking of thinking in this way makes psychology a strange scientific discipline because here it betrays itself as a science with nothing to observe save for ghostly entities. Thinking can only be hypothesised, never directly measured. The educational problem is that this view implies that the thinking of other people is ultimately unknowable, in spite of the centrality of a self that can know not just itself but other selves. The problem is that it seems thinking cannot be taught (which is wrong), but that it is something that develops mysteriously within an individual, as cognitive scientists tell us. According to Billig (1998a: 201), thinking is not 'a silent, individualistic and lonely activity which takes place mysteriously with the brain of the isolated individual as might be depicted in Rodin's famous sculpture of "The Thinker"'. For him and other rhetorical psychologists, the answer is simply that thinking is a social rhetorical activity, that it is teachable, and that we teach each other to think on a daily basis. In a phrase, thinking is inner speech, internalised conversation (Billig 1998a; see also Billig 1998b).

The larger argument Billig and others have been making about not just the topics of social, cultural, and psychological life, but also the disciplines that study and constitute that life, processes, states and concepts such as remembering, groups, identity, relationships, depression, ethnicity, motivation, consciousness as suggested above, as well as other phenomena like science, the individual, sex, 'race', culture and what psychology itself is, is that they are constituted through discursive activity and achieved in social interaction (see also, for instance, Antaki 1994; Danziger 1990; Duncan 1993). These scholars are mostly based in the very developed countries where the orthodoxy emanates, although there is a strong and growing presence in the South. These psychologists pushed discourse analytic and social constructionist frameworks and methodologies on a largely unsuspecting psychology community in the mid-1980s (Foster 2003), their interest being in studying how objects of psychological inquiry which orthodox psychology claims take place or grow 'inside' individuals are produced through discourse (see, also Durrheim 1997; Levett et al. 1997). People like Kevin Durrheim, Norman Duncan, Martin Terre Blanche, Hook, Billig, Antaki, Potter, Shotter, Margaret Wetherell, Parker, Ken Gergen, Sampson and Burman and others who formed part of the first and later surprise parties got some of their inspiration to do a different psychology from others, who were usually non-psychologists, folks like Ferdinand de Saussure, Vico, Ludwig Wittgenstein, Foucault, Derrida, Rom Harré, Erving Goffman, and so forth, but also from new movements such as the women's movement and feminist theory, developments around the postcolonies, postmodernism and post-structuralism. What this inspiration has led to is that where, for instance orthodox psychologists continue to treat objects like racism, self, or whiteness as identities or states individuals possess, discursive and constructionist psychologies have shown that these 'things' get produced in social relations and are achieved through language (Billig 1998b; Gergen 1995). Constructionist and discursive psychologies have been trying to show that psychological states or processes are activities and that people 'act' hatefully, racist, that they 'appear' motivated, and of course 'sound' American or foreign. That is to say, discourse analytic and social constructionist psychologies are interested in how people 'do' 'things' socially and accomplish them through language. Discourse-oriented and social constructionist psychologists are concerned with ways by which we come to account for ourselves and the world we live in, how our accounts result out of our relationships with others, as historically and culturally located (Burr 1995; Gergen 1985).

To then get back to the problem of the individual who goes out and thinks the world and him or her-self into existence on his or her own (that is, an entity that is seen as self-originating), and concomitant assumptions, it is that the possibility of other alternatives of living in and knowing the world and one's person may perhaps be excluded. This might be no problem at all in certain parts of the world, if we go with what is expressed in some of these texts, and thus something of little importance since a different world just does not seem to be conceivable. Also, perhaps for people whose historical burden has been social, cultural, political, and economic liberation, struggling for human recognition and justice, to be seen as one, unique, and a separate woman among many women, or a man with special attributes and internal life in this mass, is not be such as bad thing after all. But individualism has been shown by other psychologists, in Africa and in the North, to be a continuing problem that needs attention, both in the scholarly and teaching work and in living in the world outside of psychology. I think then the celebration of the individual in psychology, a celebration that is part of the problem posed by the dominant psychology in the context of Africa and the poor societies, is misplaced and even crass.

One thing that can then be said is that what psychology is all about is not commonly agreed upon. Indeed the very subject of what is psychology is one that there always has been a struggle over, right from the very inauguration of the discipline. But it must be noted that definitions of a discipline, its borders, identity, status, and methods rarely go uncontested and need struggling over. And the chance to transform a discipline presents itself especially in times of crisis (Parker 1989), which I think we have been experiencing in psychology in Africa from the start and continue to feel. Among other developments, the encouragement of interdisciplinary scholarship by research funding bodies has meant many an old border has been challenged or blurred with newer disciplines like cultural studies, bio-informatics, public health, and men's studies, and older ones like African studies, women's studies, international relations, and African American studies, for instance, which tend to be interdisciplinary in character, influencing interests in psychology and also being influenced by them.

Psychological Topics

Related to the matter of science and the individual in definitions of psychology is the scope of the discipline, a matter that was gestured to in the brief note to the delimitation of the discipline started at the inauguration of the field by Wundt. But to start with it should be said that the range of topics studied in psychology is potentially huge. Yet when one is about to open a new introductory text that has arrived on one's desk, one already knows what the book is likely to contain, and it is a list of about twenty topics. This has positive consequences as it banishes anxiety by indicating the borders and contents of the field. However, for intellectuals outside the main, developed and orderly centres where psychological knowledge is produced and disseminated from, intellectuals whose view of the social conditions of everyday existence and the play of power is often entirely different—one has the varied, intractable, terrorising, and hard to comprehend happenings in, for example, Sudan, the Democratic Republic of Congo, and Zimbabwe—this banishment of anxiety is not always rewarding as it signals that the territory and rules of the disciplinary game of psychology are cast in stone. For the psychologically trained scholar in Africa the well-known list of topics in undergraduate texts has the additional implication that what is true psychological knowledge has become so sedimented that there is only one choice if you want to play, regardless of the material conditions of life of the subjects in those places that he or she wants to make sense of: the choice is to join. That is to say, while psychology studies a range of topics having to deal with behaviour and mental processes, and US and Western European researchers and theorists have in fact covered a vast territory since the birth of the field, psychology seems to be a list of topics that begins with a chapter on what is psychology and another on scientific methods before going on to: the brain and biology, sensation and perception, altered states of consciousness, human development, learning, memory, cognition, emotion, language, intelligence, motivation, health psychology, personality theory, therapy, social behaviour, psychopathology and applied psychology. Sometimes a book might include a chapter on culture, gender, and/or sexuality. That psychology has grown and continues to find avenues for itself can be seen in the areas of specialisation that have come to include experimental psychology, neuropsychology, child, adolescent and adult development, cognitive psychology, social psychology, organisational or industrial psychology, educational psychology, counselling psychology and clinical psychology.

I am suggesting that psychology has the potential to be even bigger but more significantly of more efficacy and worth to us on the continent. I would say this usefulness, value, and potentiality starts with the issues that psychology would take up as suitable matter for the discipline. For example most psychologists do not seem to think that subjects such as homelessness, national identity, the land question, spatiality, governmentality, heteronormativity, political technology, freedom, evil, urban development, and anti-globalisation and social justice movements are proper areas of study for the discipline. These issues have received no attention at all. One reason for this state of affairs is that while other human sciences have had a go at some of these subjects, psychologists, even those outside of developed countries, seem not to want to touch these issues for the proper province of the discipline is the individual's (i.e. separate from society and culture) behaviour. That is also to say, and of critical importance, the idea that psychologists believe that the discipline is apart from, rather than a constitutive if reactionary part of, social, economic, cultural and political structures.

The principal reason for this neglect and apolitical stance though has to do with mostly US, and to some extent European, domination, of global psychological thought. US general psychology today surrounds us even more than when Serge Moscovici (1972) decried the state of European social psychology back then. And as indicated earlier, most of the ruling ideas in the world, about democracy or terror, truth and happiness, the soul, human functioning, and so forth trace the contours of US and, to a degree, Western European societies and cultures. However, talking of hegemonies, it is noteworthy that the US has by far the most number of students and practitioners of psychology amongst all countries. The number of psychologists in the US by the close of the last century was around 175,000 (see table below) (see also Nicholas 2003). The country with the second largest absolute number of psychologists, Germany, does not anywhere come close to that number, naturally. But such numbers tell only a part of the story. Another piece of the picture is given by the figures that show that it is not the US but rather the Netherlands (with 1290.3 psychologists per million population) with more opportunity for people to access mental and emotional health services and psychological understandings. Argentina is in second place (1069.4/1,000,000) and Finland is in third place (843.1/1,000,000) when countries are ranked along this measure (psychologists per one million of the population). The US comes in at number eight with 664.3 psychologists per million individuals. Only two countries from Africa, Uganda and South Africa, get a register when talking about psychology around the world. Uganda had 100 psychologists, meaning 4.7 psychologist per million of its population and South Africa had 4 341 or 97.3/1000 000.

Psychological Perspective

I wish to iterate in a different tongue an important point from the last section. Psychologists do study a range of topics, I have been saying, but that range has ossified and hampered us as time has gone by. Thus it is important to look at whether this is really what psychology is, or ought to be, and how to change it.

Table 1: Psychology Across the World

Country	Total No. of Psycho- logists 98	Membership of National Society (1998)	Population (million)(1995)	Psychologists per million population	GNP/ Capita
Argentina	37 000	100	34.6	1 069.4	8 100
Australia	12 000	100	18.1	663	18 000
Austria	4 000	12 500	8	500	24 630
Belgium	3 987	1 500	10.1	394.8	22 870
Bulgaria	4 500	500	8.8	511.4	1 250
Canada	16 000	4 300	29.5	542.4	19 510
China	3 500	3 500	1 221.5	2.9	530
Colombia	12 000	900	35.1	341.9	1 670
Croatia	1 200	-	4.5	266.7	2 560
Czech Republic	1 060	1 000	10.3	102.9	3 200
Estonia	600	58	1.5	400.0	2 820
Finland	4 300	1 500	5.1	843.1	18 850
France	30 000	1 100	58.0	517.2	23 420
Georgia	780	-	5.5	141.8	580
Germany	45 000	22 000	81.6	551.5	25 580
Greece	1 600	260	10.5	152.4	7 700
Israel	1 039	850	3.6	288.6	13 530
Italy	30 000	2 600	57.2	524.5	19 300
Japan	12 000	5 800	125.1	95.9	34 630
Korea	1 100	1 200	45.0	24.4	8 260
Mexico	11 500	1 025	93.7	122.7	4 180
Netherlands	20 000	8 000	15.5	1 290.3	22 010
New Zealand	1 700	700	3.6	472.2	13 350
Norway	3 200	3 526	4.3	744.2	26 390
Portugal	8 000	252	9.8	816.3	9 320
Romania	2 000	500	22.8	87.7	1 270
South Africa	4 341	1 337	44.6	97.3	1 930
Singapore	1 700	120	2.8	607.1	22 500
Slovenia	1 300	420	1.9	684.2	7 040
Spain	30 000	500	39.6	757.6	13 440
Uganda	100	100	21.3	4.7	190
USA	174 900	114 000	63.3	664.3	25 880
Venezuela	6 145	3938	21.8	281.9	2 760

Source: Adapted from the Health Professions Council of South Africa: Professional Board of Psychology (see also Nicholas 2003).

The first thing that persuades one to argue for the transformation of the discipline is that doubtless topics, however extensive or important or intriguing, have never made a subject area since in and of themselves topics do not really form a discipline.

Indeed, no amount of subjects of themselves can exhaust or constitute a discipline: new areas of interest will always arise to pursue, old topics will fall out of favour, and new ways of looking at old topics, and hence the list lengthens or contracts all the time. Although it is important to recognise this point: that psychology (and a similar argument can be put forward in respect of anthropology, sociology, or gender studies) has never been a bag of topics, nor a textbook commencing at what is psychology, scientific methods and biological bases of behaviour and closing with how psychology is applied, it is not the most important point. Of more weight is that disciplines are first and last ways of looking at the world and people. Disciplines are systems of interpretation. Psychology as any other discipline is constituted not by its subject matter but by how it sees and constructs and speaks of its chosen objects. Psychology is principally a window to the world. It is primarily a perspective about how to discourse or approach or frame things. Psychology is a form understanding the world, a mode of understanding that has to be seen as embedded in the sum of metaphysical, paradigmatic, epistemological, and methodological assumptions and technologies it develops and advances to make sense of its objects of interest. Like other fields of study, psychology is not, though it tends to mislead its readers, about sensations or motivation or cognition. At the bottom and eventually it is how it defines and understands these phenomena, and more generally human reality. A discipline is what, according to its loudest, luckiest, or most powerful of its exponents, counts as knowledge, and what models, according to those who are regarded as the best or the best-placed or well-born practitioners, are followed in pursuing their craft. In other words, it is how most or the privileged of those who work in the area approach their chosen topics that a field of study is principally built. Spears and Parker (1996) are talking of the same when they refer to psychology as an ideology and an activity of the adherents of the 'psy-complex' in Western societies and those caught in its grip. 'Psy-complex' is a term that the two borrow from Nikolas Rose to refer to that ensemble of discursive practices and ideologies that are socially reproductive, starting from the base up and from the individual out (Spears & Parker 1996: 1). Psychology, according to these authors, is more than a set of academic texts, departments, and journals, more than just topics, but rather filters out from university halls and professional journals and books and conferences out into the world of the everyday, its concepts like depression or schizophrenia getting taken up and used in a range of contexts from advertising to television sitcoms to glossy magazines and newspapers.

Psychologies of Culture

What needs further underlining from the preceding is that at times it appears that many psychological researchers are still interested more in legitimating their knowledge-claims than dealing with actual problems that face the cultures and societies in which they live and work. Perhaps this holds more for contexts other than the US and other developed societies though, because psychologists in the US have set the tune about what the discipline is or ought to be about, with the dancing left for researchers and educators from other parts of the world. Even in the US, the social and other psychologies that are legitimated and practised have tended to suit and address mostly the problems of the economically, socially, and politically, and culturally privileged group—the white male middle-class.

I have stated that what Henri Tajfel (1972) said about the identity crisis and social insecurity that European psychologists faced back in the 1970s applies to the developing countries and Africa even more. Talking of crisis it is well to note that what Parker (1989) said in respect to the crisis he saw in the sub-discipline of social psychology was that this looked like an ongoing crisis, a layered crisis. Tajfel (1972: 1) was saying that as practitioners of a discipline whose ostensible 'aim is the expla- nation of social life of individuals and of groups', the then European social psy- chologist, as a specific species of psychologist, was well-placed to contribute a great deal to the interpretation of social phenomena but was failing spectacularly. And so, for a profession professedly concerned with the study of human beings, so actually or potentially of great societal and personal importance to all of us, psychology in this continent then is hugely underachieving.

The point to end on is that for psychology to reach its potential must by defini- tion be of *a* place, *a* culture, *a* time, and *a* society. It must concern itself with a culture and society of real living people with bodies, living in specific communities, with particular histories, not abstractions, not hypothetical essences. What this im- plies is that if there is someone called a psychologist, sitting somewhere in Uganda or Botswana or Eritrea, writing wonderful pieces on people she or he has never interacted with in any way in any real sense of the term, and so full of abstraction of who these people are, and wants to pass these articles as saying something about real Africans, that expert cannot really want to be taken seriously. Again a lesson from the struggles of some European social psychologists' battle with the wholesale importation of US frameworks.

The real advance made by American social psychology was not so much in its empirical methods or in its theory construction as in the fact that it took for its theme of research and for the contents of its theories the issues of its own society. Its merit was as much in its techniques as in translating the problems of American society into socio-psychological terms and in making them an object of scientific enquiry (Moscovici 1972: 19).

If psychology has not grown out of the society or network of relations it seeks to address, regarding itself as the psychology of every individual and community on earth, universal in what it reveals, that is when there are likely to arise the dilemmas indicated, for then it is not a psychology of anybody, any one place or time—which is what orthodox psychologists would like us to believe, that psychology transcends history, power, culture. It is not. Since there can never be *the* history of oppression or liberation or the world, there was never nor possibly shall there ever be *the* human experience or behaviour, and thus there is little chance that there was ever *the* psy- chology of all humans (Wetherell 1996). Not merely because the employment of the category of human must always be regarded with suspicion, nor because we have to throw up our hands and write psychology off. It is because like most disciplines, a psychology that wants to be taken seriously by the culture and society it seeks to address will learn to be acculturated, socialised, aware of the assumptions and stories that cultures, societies and people live by. It does not mean that psychologists have to give up one set of rulers for a new set of masters. It might be hard to live without masters, but psychologists should learn to be distrustful of all powers, especially their own.

One of the things we believe is a psychology that wants to be taken seriously will seek to do certain things. Perhaps above all such a psychology must admit the existence of several, varying and contradictory 'theories of everyday living' that people hold on to on the continent: that God or Allah (*Unkulunkulu, Modimo*) is a strong story in people's lives, but that does not preclude them employing *badimo* (ancestors) or going to a *sangoma*. Psychology has to put more effort in studying these lives and go beyond just admission of the facts: it must be made to struggle for and defend the recognition of these disparate explanations. It must struggle with communities and people to defend the languages of their psyches and relations with the world, to create safe space for folks to speak and not be thought to be 'mad' or even just 'cultural' in that unfavourable way.

On another level, psychology has to step up to helping build Africa. For example, in thinking about self-perception and emotional life, about aggression or altruism or group relations, such a psychology will realise that it cannot just go blindly past slavery, colonialism, and apartheid in thinking about psyches. Any psychology that wants to be taken seriously will know it is important to work towards a just society and the flourishing of cultures as the practitioners engage in the work of helping our peoples to rebuild their sense of dignity, integrity, and relations with one another and with their societies. While its scholars get on with the work of building theory and doing research, they will also step out into communities to learn and help in how violence, trauma, the distortion, the injustice, the inequality are dealt with. But psychologists must also want to go beyond slavery, colonialism, ethnic wars, and white racism to see how humans can live better. It is the responsibility of students of psychology to our histories and ravaged cultures and societies that we are not to limit ourselves to thinking and working in little corners of the discipline even if we should always know how the centre works in relation to these corners. Being committed to a just world and ethical relations between people there is a responsibility to history and society that says we must admit that there is immense and driving want for a psychology that ought to work slowly, painfully, day by day towards opening our understanding one inch at a time and moving us to better national, regional, ethnic, racial, gender, economic, cultural, interpersonal and psychic relations.

References

Anonymous, 1986, 'Some Thoughts on a More Relevant or Indigenous Counselling Psychology in South Africa: Discovering the Socio-Political Context of the Oppressed.' *Psychology in Society* 5: 81-89.

Antaki, C., 1994, *Explaining and Arguing*, London: Sage.

Allport, G. W., 1968, 'The Historical Background of Modern Social Psychology', in G. Lindzey and E. Aronson, eds., *The Handbook of Social Psychology* Vol. 1, Second Edition, Reading: Addison-Wesley, 1-80.

Aronson, E., 1984, *The Social Animal*, Fourth Edition, New York: W. H. Freeman & Company.

Atkinson, R.L., R.C. Atkinson, E. E. Smith and E.R. Hilgard, 1953, *An Introduction to Psychology*, Ninth Edition, San Diego: Harcourt Brace Jovanovich.

Baron, R.A. & D. Byrne, 1981, *Social Psychology*, Third Edition, Boston: Allyn and Bacon.

Baron, R.A. & D. Byrne, 1997, *Social Psychology*, Eighth Edition, Boston: Allyn and Bacon.

Billig, M., 1998a, 'Rhetoric and the Unconscious', *Argumentation*, 12, 199-216.

Billig, M., 1998b, 'Keeping the White Queen in Play', in M. Fine, L. Weis, L. Powell and M. Wong, eds., *Off-White*, London: Routledge.

Burr, V., 1995, *An Introduction to Social Constructionism*, London: Routledge.

Collins, A., 2004, 'Summary: Theoretical Resources', in D. Hook, ed., *Critical Psychology*, Landsdowne: UCT Press.

Coon, D., 1998, *Introduction to Psychology: Exploration and Application*, Eighth Edition, Pacific Grove: Brooks/Cole Publishing Company.

Danziger, K., 1990, *Constructing the Subject: Historical Origins of Psychological Research*, Cambridge: University Press.

Dawes, A., 1986, 'The Notion of Relevant Psychology with Particular Reference to Africanist Pragmatic Initiatives', *Psychology in Society* 5: 28-48.

Davis, S. F. & J. J. Palladino, 1997, *Psychology*, Second Edition, Upper Saddle River, New Jersey: Prentice Hall.

Duncan, N., 1993, *Discourses of Racism*, Unpublished Doctoral Dissertation: University of the Western Cape, Bellville, South Africa.

Durrheim, K., 1997, 'Social Constructionism, Discourse, and Psychology', *South African Journal of Psychology* 27 (3), 175-182.

Dworetzky, J. P., 1997, *Psychology*, Sixth Edition, Pacific Grove: Brooks/Cole Publishing Company.

Foster, D., 1991, 'Introduction', in D. Foster, and J. Louw-Potgieter, eds., *Social Psychology in South Africa*, Johannesburg: Lexicon Publishers, 3-23.

Foster, D., 2003, 'Social Psychology', in L. Nicholas, ed., *Introduction to Psychology*, Lansdowne: University of Cape Town Press.

Foster, D., 2004, 'Liberation Psychology', in K. Ratele, N. Duncan, D. Hook, N. Mkhize, P. Kiguwa, and A. Collins, eds., *Self, Community and Psychology*. Lansdowne: University of Cape Town Press.

Foster, D. & J. Louw-Potgieter, eds., 1991, *Social Psychology in South Africa*, Johannesburg: Lexicon Publishers.

Foucault, M., 2000, *Power: Essential Works of Foucault 1954-1984*, Edited by J. D. Faubion, London: Penguin.

Fowler, R.D., 1990, 'Psychology: The Core Discipline. Presidential Address'. *American Psychologist*, 45: 1-6.

Franchi, V. E. and T. M. Swart, 2003, 'Identity Dynamics and the Politics of Self-Definition', in K. Ratele and N. Duncan, eds., *Social Psychology: Identities and Relationships*, Lansdowne: University of Cape Town Press.

Hook, D., 2004, 'Critical Psychology: the Basic co-ordinates', in D. Hook, ed., *Critical Psychology*, Landsdowne: University of Cape Town Press.

Hunt, M., 1993, *The Story of Psychology*, New York: Anchor Books.

Gergen, K., 1973, 'Social Psychology as History', *Journal of Personality and Social Psychology* 26: 309-320.

Gergen, K., 1996, 'Social Psychology as Social Construction', in C. McGarty and A. Haslam, eds., *The message of Social Psychology: Perspectives on Mind in Society*, Oxford: Blackwell.

Gergen, K. and M. Gergen, 1981, *Social Psychology*, New York: Harcourt Brace Jovanovitch.

Govender, P., 1999, 'Angry Parents end "Marriage Made in Heaven"', *Sunday Times*, 13 June.

Halonen, J. S. and J. W. Santrock, 1999, *Psychology: Context & Applications*, (International Edition), Third Edition, Boston. McGraw-Hill College.

Ivey, G., 1986, 'Elements of a Critical Psychology', *Psychology in Society* 5: 4-27.

Kalat, J. W., 1996, *Introduction to Psychology*, Fourth Edition, Pacific Grove: Brooks/Cole Publishing Company.

Levett, A., A. Kottler, E. Burman and I. Parker, eds., 1997, *Culture, Power and Difference: Discourse Analysis in South Africa*, London: Zed Books.

Manganyi, N. C., 1991, *Treachery and Innocence: Psychology and Racial Difference in South Africa*, Johannesburg: Ravan Press.

McDougall, W., 1908, *An Introduction to Social Psychology*, London: Methuen.

McGrath, J. E., 1970, *Social Psychology: A Brief Introduction*, London: Holt, Rinehart, Winston.

Mkhize, N., 2004, 'Psychology: An African Perspective', in D. Hook, ed., *Critical psychology*, Landsdowne: University of Cape Town Press.

Moll, I., 1993, 'Answering the Question: What Is Psychology?', *Psychology in Society* 1: 59-77.

Moscovici, S., 1972, 'Society and Theory in Social Psychology', in J. Israel and H. Tajfel, eds., *The Context of Social Psychology: Critical Assessment*. London: Academic Press, 17-68.

Mouton, J., 1996, *Understanding Social Research*, Pretoria: J. L. van Schaik Publishers.

Nairne, J. S., 1997, *Psychology: The Adaptive Mind*, Pacific Grove: Brooks/Cole Publishing Company.

Ngonyama, ka Sigogo, T. and O. T. Modipa, 2004, 'Critical Reflections on Community and Psychology in South Africa', in K. Ratele, N. Duncan, D. Hook, N. Mkhize, P. Kiguwa, and A. Collins, eds., *Self, Community and Psychology*, Lansdowne: University of Cape Town Press.

Nicholas, L., 2003, 'An Introduction to Psychology,' in L. Nicholas, ed., *Introduction to Psychology*, Lansdowne: University of Cape Town Press, 2-12.

Parker, I., 1989, *The Crisis in Modern Social Psychology—And How To End It*, London: Routledge.

Ross, E. A., 1908, *Social Psychology: An Outline and a Source Book*, New York: Macmillan.

Ruch, J. C., 1984, *Psychology: The Personal Science*, Belmont: Wadsworth Publishing Company.

Sdorow, L. M., 1993, *Psychology*, Second Edition, Madison, WI: Brown & Benchmark.

Sherif, M. and C. W. Sherif, 1969, *Social psychology*, New York/Tokyo: Harper & Row/John Weatheril.

Speake, J., ed., 1979, *A Dictionary of Philosophy*, London: Pan Books Ltd.

Spears, R. and I. Parker, 1996, 'Marxist Theses and Psychological Themes', in I. Parker and R. Spears, eds., *Psychology and Society: Radical Theory and Practice*, London: Pluto Press.

Tajfel, H., 1972, 'Introduction', in J. Israel and H. Tajfel, eds., *The Context of Social Psychology: Critical Assessment*, London: Academic Press, 1-13.

Terre Blanche, M. and K. Durrheim, 1999, 'Histories of the Present: Social Science Research in Context', in M. Terre Blanche and K. Durrheim, eds., *Research in practice*, Cape Town: University of Cape Town Press, 1-16.

Weiten, W., 1998, *Psychology: Themes and Variations*, Fourth Edition, Pacific Grove: Brooks/Cole Publishing Company.

Wetherell, M., ed., 1996, *Social Psychology: Identities, Groups and Social Issues*, London: Sage.

Wittig, A. F. and G. Williams, 1984, *Psychology: An Introduction*, New York: McGraw-Hill Book Company.

Worchel, S., J. Cooper, and G. R. Goethals, 1988, *Understanding Social Psychology*, Fourth edition, Chicago: The Dorsey Press.

Wortman, C., E. Loftus, and C. Weaver, 1999, *Psychology*, Fourth Edition, Boston: McGraw-Hill College.

II

Interdisciplinary Studies and African Studies

Chapter 12

Feminist Studies in the African Contexts: The Challenge of Transformative Teaching in African Universities

Amina Mama

Africans have long regarded education as a major route to liberation and development throughout the colonial and postcolonial periods. During the nineteenth century Pan-Africanists such as Africanus Horton called for the establishment of African universities, dedicated to the tasks of intellectual decolonisation. Twentieth century nationalists who saw independence as requiring the development and training of Africans to equip them to lead and run the emergent nation states took up this call. Those who emerged as leaders in the national liberation movements—men like Kwame Nkrumah, Julius Nyerere, Sekou Toure, Leopold Senghor and Kenneth Kaunda—were among the nationalist intellectuals who became political leaders, and who where then able to pursue the establishment of continental higher education institutions when the national liberation movements swept to power in the 1950s and 1960s. They set about transforming the colonial colleges and establishing hundreds of new institutions, with widespread popular support. Kenneth Kaunda said as much in the speech he made on the occasion of his installation as the first Chancellor at the University of Zambia:

> The University of Zambia is our own University in a very real sense. The story of how the people of this country responded to enthusiastically to my appeal for support is a very thrilling one. Humble folk in every corner of our nation—illiterate villagers, barefooted school children, prison inmates and even lepers—gave freely and willingly everything they could, often in the form of fish or maize or chickens, The reason for this extraordinary response was that our people see in the university the hope of a better and fuller life for their children and grand-children.—President

Kaunda, at the Chancellor's Installation Banquet, 12 July 1966, cited in Ajayi, Goma and Johnson (1996: 1).

From the 1960s onwards, the new African governments undertook massively to expand educational provision at all levels, treating the establishment of national universities as an essential aspect of becoming a nation. Mkandawire (2000:2) describes the intellectuals of the nationalist era as having a key role to play in the five major tasks of nationalism which he lists as 'de-colonization, national sovereignty, national development, democratization and regional co-operation'. No doubt it was this understanding that led African governments to build over 300 universities during the first four decades of political independence. There are currently over 600, augmented by the rapid establishment of a variety of smaller, private institutions.

African intellectual culture has therefore included a strong discourse on social responsibility. This is reflected in the founding declarations in the 1960s, and subsequently reiterated in resolutions which include the Dar es Salaam Declaration on Academic Freedom and Social Responsibility of Academics (1990) and the Kampala Declaration on Intellectual Freedom and Social Responsibility (1991). Politicians, policy-makers and intellectuals alike have assumed that the African intelligentsia would play a vanguard role in continental liberation and development. In so doing they have rejected the notion of ivory tower intellectualism implicit in the explicitly elitist academic cultures modelled by Oxford, Harvard and Yale. Scholars have been called upon not just to train the person power needed to staff the emergent nation-states and economies, but to provide critical analysis and solutions to the continent's many challenges—whether these required science and technology, social scientific or cultural work. Independent nations therefore invested heavily in establishing public universities.

This sense of social responsibility, of duty to the continent and its peoples has translated into a preference for interdisciplinary approaches, for locally relevant and locally grounded methodologies. It has led leading scholars to embrace the more critical elements of social theory, and doing so has enabled them to contribute significantly to radical schools of thought that have much bearing on theorising development and underdevelopment.

From a gender perspective, it is important to note that women in Africa have embraced higher education as least as enthusiastically as men, perhaps more so, given that it opened up respectable career possibilities that had hitherto been denied to them. The first generation of women leaders—women like Constance Cummings-John of Sierra Leone, Mabel Dove Danquah of Ghana, and Funmilayo Ransome-Kuti of Nigeria—all had backgrounds as professional educators, and strongly supported women's education (Mama 2003). Furthermore, in contrast to the handful of colonial colleges bequeathed to the region, independent Africa's universities were open to women from their inception. As a result, the overall numbers of African women attaining tertiary qualifications increased incrementally over the years, resulting in a pool of highly educated women educators, lawyers, doctors, public servants, businesswomen and so on. This is not to say that there was full equality, as marked gender disparities have persisted to the present day. Both student enrolment and academic staffing figures show that men have continued significantly to out-number women in all but the most conventionally feminine areas of study, and that these disparities are the most pronounced at the highest levels and in the more prestigious fields (see Mama 2003).

More broadly, suffice to say that it was through the strategy of investing sub-stantially in tertiary education that much of Africa was able to pursue the indigenisation of all its governmental, corporate and civil institutions, soon after independence had been achieved. This in turn saw the children of the educated elite spending their formative years in a postcolonial cultural and intellectual world in which their right to nationhood, to self determination and self realisation was as-sured. The right to the best education the world could offer was optimistically as-sumed and pursued.

Unfulfilled Promise

Given this background of commitment and investment it is necessary to ask ourselves why it is that, after five decades of independence, African higher education has been unable to fulfil its initial promise and make good on this early investment. Instead the continent has entered the twenty-first century—and the global knowledge economy—with the weakest higher education system in the world. Although somewhere between four and five million undergraduate students are enrolled in Africa' universities, this figure represents only a three percent uptake of the pool of people who qualify for entrance, the lowest rate in the world. Despite the fact that women have never been excluded from Africa's post-independence universities, only about 25 percent of those enrolled are women, and probably less than 19 percent of academic staff are women (Mama 2003; Teferra and Altbach 2003).

On the intellectual level, there is evidence to suggest that the methodologies, curriculum and teaching methods, indeed the intellectual cultures that define Afri-can research and teaching, fall far short of being grounded in and responsive to African conditions and agendas, not to mention the formal commitments to greater social inclusiveness along ethnic, gender and regional lines. This perspective was confirmed by the 50 or so participants at a two-day retreat on 'Visioning African Higher Education' held in Durban in 2003.[1] It was argued that African universities have yet to address the challenges of decolonisation and democratisation, and to fulfil their promise by developing a strong African intellectual culture. The need to question the received organisation of knowledge was emphasised, in terms of what was felt to be an outmoded and inappropriate disciplinary structure, the subject matter included in the curriculum, and in the approaches to teaching and research. It was further pointed out that these were largely derivative, having been developed under quite different conditions (in the West, during a period of capitalist expansion and affluence), and were yet to take on the challenges of African development, or the resource-deprived realities faced by those working in African universities..

Understanding the underdevelopment of African higher education and intellectual culture requires a critical analysis of both the material and intellectual processes that have constrained the realisation of African visions of higher education during the recent historical period.

Since the 1970s, public investment in higher education has been increasingly inadequate, largely due to the restrictions placed on African public investment by international financial institutions since the economic crisis of the structural adjustment era (see Federici et al. 2000; Zeleza 2003). By the 1980s Western financial institutions held the view that universities were a luxury that an impoverished continent could ill-afford, and African governments were directed to concentrate on basic literacy and numeracy. High level skills were to be provided by Western institutions, rather than by home grown intellectuals, an approach which has deepened dependency, and may well explain the continued underdevelopment (Mkandawire and Soludo 1999; Tadesse 1999). The unfavourable international economic regime has prevailed in the face of an ever-increasing public demand for higher education. The results are well known—national governments have continued to build universities, and to increase access, but they have had to do so in the context of severe resource constraints. These contradictory tendencies have plunged the system into crisis and so rendered the large-scale pursuit of education for liberation and development impossible.

In terms of intellectual production, Africa continues to be severely under-represented, producing less than 0.5 percent of the world's research publications at the present time (Teferra and Altbach 2003). Within this, the bulk are produced by a very small number of countries—Nigeria, Egypt and South Africa—leaving production being almost non-existent in many of Africa's 54 countries. African research production has declined dramatically in a manner that reflects the erosion of the public universities where the majority of researchers are institutionally located.

In what follows I argue that the scenario of unfulfilled promise may be the dominant one, but it is not the complete story. It is important to go beyond it to document and engage with the concerted attempts that have been made to sustain African intellectualism. Africa's radical scholarly tradition has survived and developed despite the dearth of resources within the academic mainstream. As a result some of the most important initiatives have taken place outside the universities, where it has been easier to subvert the disciplinary and pedagogical hierarchies that have tended to prevail in conventional and patriarchal academic institutions. Because so many of Africa's intellectuals have been forced or starved out of the universities, their survival has depended on the establishment of alternative knowledge sites, a process facilitated by international access and mobility of leading scholars. The establishment and development of independent scholarly networks and research centres, and the role that they have played within and beyond the universities illustrates this point. The growing importance of the largest social science network, the Council for the Development of Social Science Research in Africa, and the various roles that it has played at local and international levels is exemplary, and much could be learned from a thorough-going reflection on the experience of this body since the 1970s, including the major challenges it has faced.

However, for present purposes I develop this argument in relation to the particular emergence and development of gender and women's studies. My purpose in carrying out this exercise is to identify the conditions and forces that have facilitated and/or constrained this particular development, in order to consider the implications for Africa's intellectual development more broadly.

My starting point is the observation that the external over-determination of Africa's intellectual development/underdevelopment has not been complete. Rather, it has also been consistently challenged and resisted by the surviving elements of a strong progressive tradition within African intellectual development. Feminist thought is one of the elements within this progressive tradition. The emergence and development of gender studies within the universities owes much to successful mobilisations of women as intellectuals outside the universities, in a combination of scholarly and activist organisations. There is also evidence to suggest that these independent spaces engaged in feminist intellectual work have in turn influenced the universities, as manifest in the development of gender and women's studies as an academic field. It is a field that explicitly pursues social change, a critical stance in relation to dominant knowledges and the unequal and oppressive social relations that have characterised them. In contrast to those who insist that 'feminism' and 'gender' are Western imports, I suggest that while this is historically true of the conventional disciplines, it is less true of new transdisciplinary fields like gender studies. Gender studies is more a product of postcolonial African contexts than most disciplines because it has developed in response to local gender inequalities. Furthermore, gender studies as variously addresses the demands of policy-making and international development interventions, often from an activist perspective, and this ensures that the connections between theory, activism and policy-making are maintained.

Gender and Women's Studies in Africa

The establishment of the Association of African Women on Research and Development (AAWORD/AFARD) in Dakar in 1977 marks the beginning of steps to institutionalise gender and women's studies in post-independence African. Previous evidence of feminist intellectualism can be seen in the early writings and publications of women activists in the early twentieth century.[2]

AAWORD was set up during the United Nations Decade for Women, and the internationalisation of feminism has continued apace. The impact of feminism has been variously felt throughout the international development industry, within Africa's national governmental and regional structures, in civil society, within social movements, and in the cultural and educational sphere.

The establishment of other women's resource and documentation centres, nongovernmental organisations and networks throughout the 1980s and 1990s followed. The Women's Research and Documentation Centre, established at the University of Ibadan by the end of the 1980s, was one of a few university-based initiatives. Nonuniversity-based organizations engaged in educational and research work during this period include Women in Nigeria, the Zimbabwe Women's Resource Centre and Network formed in Harare; The Tanzania Media Women's Association (TAMWA); AAWORD/AFARD chapters in Lagos and Nairobi; The Tanzania Gender Networking Programme (TGNP); ABANTU for Development; and FEMNET, the Nairobi-based regional feminist education and training network. In South Africa the Durban-based AGENDA collective has engaged in feminist publishing since 1987, and the end of apartheid has seen the establishment of a number of other independent feminist organisations. These are all activist organisations which draw the link between knowledge and power, work collectively through networking and collaboration, and regard research, analysis and information as an integral part of activist strategy in the pursuit of women's liberation.

Over time, the commitment to intellectual activism within the African women's movement has deepened, giving rise to other new campus initiatives. The educational activities have also developed and spread. Women's organisations and gender and women's studies centres began holding dialogues and workshops in order to effect changes in consciousness and disseminate information beyond their own ranks. These were initially carried out within local communities, but since the 1990s, women's organisations and gender studies centres have been increasingly called upon to provide gender-training services.[3] Many have tried to address the demand for 'gender expertise' expressed by government and development agencies seeking to include a 'gender component' and later to 'mainstream gender' in development projects. For example, women's groups working on domestic violence would be invited to offer training to policy officers, in the hope that this would improve service delivery. The offering of short courses and training thus rapidly became instrumental in the context of endless development needs.

The fact that educational work on gender began in the women's movement suggests that in Africa, gender studies was initiated outside the universities by feminist activists, and only later taken onto the campuses. It took the efforts of feminist academics to institutionalise gender studies within the universities both as a legitimate course of study and a research area. This backdrop is important to an understanding of the conditions under which gender and women's studies in African universities have been relatively successful at maintaining a close and reciprocal engagement with feminist activism.[4] This may well be because the pool of women with tertiary education in Africa is so small, with the result that in a given national context it is the same women who are often simultaneously engaged in academic teaching delivery, off-campus activism, research, policy advisory and development work. However, it also relates to the broader African intellectual tradition, which as I noted above, has always stressed social responsibility over ivory tower intellectualism.

The first formally accredited academic course was the 'Women and Society' undergraduate course developed by feminist academics teaching in the Sociology Department at Ahmadu Bello University in Nigeria during the 1970s.

Responses to a survey carried out by the African Gender Institute in 2002 indicate there are over 30 different sites offering teaching in African universities. South African universities offer some form of gender studies at ten institutions: the Universities of Cape Town, Fort Hare, Kwazulu Natal, Pretoria, Stellenbosch, Western Cape, Rhodes, Venda, Transkei and the University of South Africa (UNISA). Of these most are recently established, and at the time only four had dedicated centres or units: the UNISA Institute for Gender Studies, the Universities of Venda and Pretoria Centres for Gender Studies, and the University of Cape Town's African Gender Institute. In Nigeria, seven of over forty universities offer courses in gender: Ahmadu Bello University, Lagos State University, Obafemi Awolowo University, University of Benin, University of Ibadan, University of Nigeria and Usmano Danfodiyo University. Elsewhere on the continent, courses have been established at Addis Ababa University in Ethiopia; Ahfad University in Sudan; Makerere University in Uganda; the Universities of Buea and Yaoundé in Cameroon; the Universities of Cape Coast and Ghana in Ghana; the University of Malawi; the University of Namibia; the University of Sierra Leone; the University of the Gambia, the University of Zambia; the University of Zimbabwe and the American University in Cairo, Egypt. Recent developments include the establishment of a new Centre for Gender Studies and Advocacy at the University of Ghana's Institute for African Studies, where previously there was a voluntary initiative (Development and Women's Studies, DAWS) that was driven by a collective of academics and activists. The Centre for Research and Training in Women and Development (CERTWID) has introduced a graduate course at Addis Ababa. There have also been renewed efforts to establish the first gender studies site in French-speaking West Africa at the University of Cheikh Anta Diop in Dakar.[5]

This profile suggests that probably individual faculty members located in mainstream disciplinary departments offer the majority of courses, but the number of stand-alone departments has also continued to grow. This suggests that feminist academics have so far been successful at resisting the imperatives of gender mainstreaming, which have often been seized upon by university men (and sometimes women) eager to withdraw even the limited institutional support and resources going to dedicated centres.

The AGI survey also indicated that sites for teaching and researching gender and women's studies are structured and administered in a number of different ways. Some institutions (17 out of 30) have departments, units or programmes dedicated to gender and women's studies teaching and research, while others (thirteen out of thirty) have gender components within traditional disciplines. Dedicated gender programmes, units or departments, for the purpose of this study, are defined as units which have gender teaching and/or research as their core function, and at least one dedicated faculty member. The African Gender Institute maintains a combination of local teaching from undergraduate to doctoral level and its continental programmes with 2.7 faculty and a meagre university budget. It therefore supplements this limited support through externally funded projects and contract posts. At the other end of the scale, Makerere represents a more conventional teaching department with twelve faculty, housed in a three-storey building complete with its own library and resource centre. Many other centres rely on the goodwill of faculty located in disciplinary departments but willing to take on the extra work of teaching gender studies, and some work with a combination (for example, the Western Cape has three dedicated faculty, but teaching is supported by input from colleagues in other departments).

What does the prevalence of formally recognised departments and centres mean in terms of teaching and research capacity? This question warrants a more detailed study than was possible in the above-mentioned survey. The existence of a dedicated gender studies unit might be taken as a superficial indicator of institutional commitment. However it is often the case that financial support is either minimal or nonexistent, with the department relying heavily on its capacity to attract external resources.[6] It is also telling to note that of the 17 dedicated units, only four have full departmental status within their institutions—the University of Makerere's Department of Women and Gender Studies, the University of Buea's Department of Women's Studies, the University of Cape Town's African Gender Institute, and the University of Zambia's Gender Studies Department. This limited institutional strength has major implications for accreditation of courses, and therefore the extent to which they are taken seriously as a contribution to the curriculum and the academic life of the university.

The levels at which teaching is offered are also of some interest. Contrary to the dictates of common sense, the field is top heavy, weighted in favour of postgraduate teaching, perhaps because administrations have assumed this to be a cheaper option in the context of limited faculty availability. From an intellectual perspective this is obviously an erroneous assumption, and not only because quality graduate programmes require experienced senior academics. Furthermore, the demands on academic staff are intensified where postgraduate entrants lack adequate preparation in gender theory and methodologies. Undergraduate preparation is demonstrably necessary in any field of study. However, only five universities on the entire continent can offer undergraduate degrees. Three of these are South African: Cape Town, Pretoria, and Western Cape. In the East African subregion, only Makerere's Department of Women and Gender Studies offers a full undergraduate degree, and in West Africa the University of Buea in the Cameroon Republic offers a first degree in Women's Studies. The limited availability of full degree programmes is only partly mitigated by the scattering of courses and modules on gender offered within existing disciplines.

At postgraduate level, twelve identified sites were found to offer masters programmes (six of these being in South Africa). Doctoral provision is also scarce, with only two sites offering doctoral degrees—the African Gender Institute in Cape Town and Makerere Department of Women and Gender Studies. Both of these are constrained by the small number of senior faculty available to supervise across a wide range of research areas. The implications of this top-heavy distribution are worth considering, as they place substantial pedagogical burdens on those accepting graduate students with limited undergraduate exposure. These are addressed in various ways and have resulted in some interesting curriculum innovations which cannot be detailed here. However, the fact remains that intellectually strong graduate programmes in gender studies, as for any other field, rely heavily on throughput from strong undergraduate teaching courses. This is confirmed by the experience of the post-graduate programmes initiated at the universities of Stellenbosch and the Witwatersrand in South Africa, both of which have since retracted.[7] The shortage of doctoral programmes seems to reflect the dearth of senior level teaching capacity, as there are hardly any full professors in gender studies, and those willing to supervise doctorates find themselves unable to accommodate the demand.

In the context of the decline and withdrawal of funding from higher education and research during the last two decades, the proliferation of work in G/WS presents something of an anomaly. Elsewhere I have suggested that it owes the uptake of feminism within the development industry has facilitated gender studies in Africa, to some extent conferring a degree of legitimacy (albeit an instrumentalist legitimacy) that has made it possible for women activists to take gender interests into the academic arena, and attract development funding not available to other disciplines (Mama 2004).

However, it is also clear that none of this would have led to gender studies had there not also been extensive mobilisation of women during the same period. Increasingly assertive women's movements have not only had an impact on the development industry, but also in nation states, as evidenced by the widespread establishment of machineries for women.[8] Gender activists from Africa have also become a strong presence in the international arenas of the United Nations (the Nairobi, Beijing and Beijing Plus 5 conferences), the Commission of the Status of Women (2005) and the World Social Forum during the last five years. While many of these initiatives are yet to be documented, the influence of women's activism can be seen in the public sphere, and this includes educational organisations, within which teaching and research in gender and women's studies has developed. The motivations for gender studies often make reference to the capacity needs of local and international governmental and non-governmental organisations, but addressing these places additional demands on faculty (Kasente 2002).

What are the prospects? The postgraduate shortage may change as more African women working in gender and/or women's studies obtain doctorates with each year that passes.[9] The steadily increasing numbers of faculty specialised in gender studies might also mitigate the undergraduate shortfall. However, the intense competition for limited resources tends to constrain the emergence of new and transdisciplinary courses of study, and favour the more entrenched academic status quo. In the long run, resource constraints have major implications for the both the intellectual content and strength of research and teaching programmes, in gender studies as much as in any other field.

Intellectual Content

To contribute to gender equality, as most of those involved in gender studies seek to do, requires an extensive, contextually specific knowledge base on gender relations and dynamics in all aspects of social life. Because gender relations pervade psychology and subjectivity, social relations, familial, community, economic and political institutions, they transcend the conventional disciplines, demanding transdisciplinary intellectual engagement, preferable rooted in explicit concerns that emanate from the dynamics of gender and gender struggles in particular contexts. In other words, understandings of gender in African contexts, even while they may make some use of paradigms that have some global currency or relevance, need to be grounded in the philosophies, lived realities, languages, popular discourses, cultural and sexual mores of the social contexts within which they are situated. It is these that afford African feminist thinkers with critical perspectives that emanate from their unique historic vantage point, and which are therefore able to engage with and influence the conditions of women, transform the oppressive aspects of African gender relations, while valuing and affirming positive aspects. Feminist thinkers are part of the broader communities of people who imagine and pursue liberatory ideas, cultural values and practices.

Gender studies takes many forms, ranging from the more minimalist and instrumentalist provision of technical services, to a concern with the broader epistemological concerns of transformative feminism suggested above. The research base available to the growing number of faculty teaching gender studies in African contexts is far from adequate, especially where the pedagogical objectives of the curriculum include feminist epistemology and praxis. To go beyond the provision of technical expertise, and deeper than the reductionism implicit in gender checklists and frameworks, requires much deeper knowledge. The annotated bibliography carried out by Lewis (2003) under the African Gender Institute's G/WS Africa programme lists no less than 1,600 entries, within which a significant proportion are by African scholars. However, it is worth noting that both this review, and its predecessor (Mama 1996), point to the overdetermination of the research field by Western scholarship both in terms of the quantity of publication, and in terms of the theoretical interests being articulated, despite the fact that both made a concerted effort to locate and procure research carried out by Africans scholars. The content of this burgeoning literature is too extensive and wide-ranging to be discussed here. However, it is worth noting that the content is concentrated in some areas, while others are neglected, and independent African research in controversial but strategically important areas is almost non-existent.

The main consequence of the Western monopoly on research funding is that African researchers are obliged to conduct research wherever they can, mostly through partnerships with Western scholars and institutions that are often far from equal, even within the relatively egalitarian and self-conscious arena of feminist studies. This works to alienate and fragment African intellectual labour, as research is carried out in the service of disparate external conceptual and institutional interests. Unless African feminist scholars are able to come together, to work together in teams and collaborative projects that allow a cumulative knowledge base to emerge and consolidate, the articulation of focused research agendas and development of African research and theory in gender studies will remain limited.

The continental programme 'Strengthening Gender Studies for Africa's Transformation' initiated in 2001 by the African Gender Institute has attempted to address the challenges by building a feminist intellectual community dedicated to developing a resource base that can support activism, teaching and research to advance women's equality in African contexts. This has required critical engagement with the intellectual politics of knowledge production, and the development of a set of strategies to strengthen the African resource base (feminist knowledge) and the teaching of gender in Africa. These objectives are being pursued using a combination of actual and virtual meetings and ICT networking strategies, and the development and dissemination of electronic and hard copy publications.

The first step involved reviewing the field and surveying both the intellectual and institutional capacity of gender studies in Africa, after which a continental workshop was convened to begin the collective process of setting out a strategic agenda, designing and planning and collaborative work. Participants at that meeting resolved to establish the Feminist Studies Network, which has grown from the 35 women who founded it to 130 members, the majority of whom are located in African institutions. Supported by a listserve, this has served as the main communication channel through which the previously scattered community of feminist-identified scholars keeps in touch with one another and engages in various debates.

The second main aspect of the programme involved developing a dedicated website, www.gwsafrica.org. This was set up to serve as a continental resource to support teachers and researchers in the field. It was envisaged that this would be collaboratively developed, serving as a major resource through which research, publications and relevant resources could be shared across the GWS community.

A third aspect saw the establishment of the first continental African gender and women's studies journal, *Feminist Africa*. Initially envisaged as a low-cost electronic journal, the feedback from the emergent community of feminist indicated the desirability of producing hard copy. As a result *Feminist Africa* is produced both as an open access online journal, and as a limited hard copy edition disseminated through the feminist scholarly network, university libraries and research organisations based on the continent. Now an accredited journal in its third year, *Feminist Africa* provides the only dedicated platform for feminist research carried out in Africa. It also profiles ongoing activism and carries debates taking place in Africa. It has been developed alongside the teaching resources posted on the GWSAfrica website, but includes a lengthy and rigorous editorial process that serves capacity development functions as well as ensuring the intellectual quality of the final product. So far both the reviews and the ongoing monitoring of web statistics indicate a high level of uptake within and beyond Africa, and a willingness to engage with the challenges of ensuring the development and dissemination of academic writing that is both African and feminist.

The final aspect of the programme addressed the challenges facing those teaching gender studies, in the intensely challenging contexts outlined above. This involved exploring ways of strengthening the involved curriculum, in terms of feminist epistemological concerns, quality and content. The strategy that was designed for this involved convening two specialised curriculum working groups and organising a series of workshops designed to identify priority areas for teaching, to develop the knowledge base by reviewing and critically engaging with the existing materials and developing new ones, and strengthen the pedagogical skills.

The core areas identified at the initial meeting were:

(i)   Sexuality;

(ii)   Culture and Identity;

(iii)   Politics;

(iv)   Policy;

(v)   Law;

(vi)   Feminist methodology;

(vii)   Women's movements; and

(viii) History.

The curriculum workshops were seminal events, as the participants realised that although they had been teaching G/WS for years, they had for the most part been working in isolation, or dependent on Western connections and literature. Prior to their involvement in the curriculum process, there had been no real opportunity for them to come together as African feminist scholars or to collectively reflect on their field of teaching.

The initial survey had demonstrated a dearth of teaching about sexuality, despite the salience of activism on various aspects—notably the fields of health and reproductive rights, sexual and domestic violence, sexual harassment and various sexually transmitted pathologies. It is a field identified as strategically important to any understanding of gender in African contexts, and yet heavily determined by powerful external agendas. The initial effort to compile and review African literature of this field foundered on the dearth of local research and perspectives, provoking a different strategy and an output that sought to present the field on different terms, and which required new research.[10]

The discussions around teaching and the quest to identify and develop African teaching resources compatible with the emergent feminist epistemology have given rise to new research, notably in the area of Sexuality and Higher Education Studies.[11] The 'Mapping African Sexualities' research project may be the first time a group of feminist scholars have engaged in a collaborative research venture designed to develop feminist methodologies for researching African sexual cultures. Six studies were commissioned in East, West and Southern Africa, to be carried out by locally-based researchers prepared to undertake in-depth transdisciplinary studies on subject matter that was identified during the curriculum process and developed in the initial research proposal. Given the social complexity of the subject matter, and what had been learnt about the teaching challenges in the curriculum workshop, it was decided to include a film-maker within the research team, with a view to experimenting with the production of audio-visual teaching resources as well as written research.

So far continentally-focussed teaching resources are most developed in the areas of Sexuality and the Law, for which brief review essays and resources have been provided on the GWSAfrica website. Further resources in the areas of Policy, Politics, Feminist Methodology, Women's Movements and History are still being developed.

The continental curriculum strengthening work is still underway, but the dialogues that have so far occurred have already given rise to new initiatives and courses, both within and beyond the curriculum group, as evidenced by ongoing discussions within the Feminist Studies Network and the G/WS listserve that services it.[12] In the longer term it is hoped that the curriculum work will be continued and expanded, and that some of the priority areas not yet addressed within this particular initiative will be taken up and addressed, either within the existing network of feminist scholars and G/WS sites, or among emergent ones.

Future Challenges

The institutional challenges reviewed here include the gender profile, the patriarchal institutional cultures of the higher education institutions, and the resources constraints facing all those engaged in the field. Faculty members with non-mainstream interests encounter great difficulty creating time and space for non-conventional teaching and independent research, and this situation seems set to intensify with higher education reform and the implementation of cost recovery, regardless of new donor funding interests.[13] In concrete terms the emphasis on counting up teaching hours and directing publication efforts into short pieces in accredited journals makes it ever harder for faculty (especially those at junior and mid-career stages) to spend time experimenting and taking the risks that are necessary to the development of innovative methodologies or alternative modes of intellectual output. Promotion prospects are compromised when faculty put in the much lengthier time that will produce coherent fields of knowledge, produce more innovative and/or substantial research, or decide to co-author, or to write books and monographs that count for less in the existing calculus. This has major implications for African contexts where collaborative work and innovation are essential both to the articulation of local perspectives and ideas, but also to the production of research capacity through mentoring and teamwork.

The growth of the field of G/WS in African contexts has been unprecedented, given the overall conditions prevailing within African higher education. The question that remains is whether the return of international donor interest in African

Higher Education will strengthen or undermine the field, and if so in what forms will it be supported or constrained. Whether international support can actually translate into more sustainable institutional commitments to gender studies, remains to be seen. So does the extent to which this in turn will allow space for the cutting edge work that has so far derived from feminist commitments to ongoing engagement in activism within and beyond the academy. I have argued that it is this which has so far driven growth and expansion of the field, as has been the case with other areas of radical scholarship, all of which have so far remained at the margins of African universities, sustained by alternative structures, when in fact they should be located at the centre of our higher education systems and intellectual endeavours.

Additional challenges arise from the nature of higher education reform as it is currently being implemented in African universities. So far this has tended to address gender equality largely in terms of increasing the numbers of women, through scholarships making available on a competitive basis, especially in the sciences, despite the fact that women actually tend to be concentrated in the humanities. Where reform has advanced in a manner that has allowed the establishment of a gender studies department as has been the case at Makerere, other challenges have arisen, notably the massive influx of large numbers of students and the doubling up of teaching loads to service public and private students (see Kasente 2002). It may also have implications for the intellectual agenda of those involved in teaching, and there are no public resources available to support graduate study or research. Other sites are experiencing the strictures of cost recovery, as was discussed above, and at this stage it is not clear how the new administrative and financial formulae will serve the expressed national political discourses and the mission statements that profess support for gender equity. The emphasis on numerical calculations, whether of teaching hours or head counts, have little to do with intellectual matters, yet there is evidence that they operate to constrain intellectual development in ways that are yet to be confronted.

Finally, a note on the intellectual challenges facing gender studies in Africa. Here the expansion of the field of teaching and research in gender studies appears to have had a limited impact on the wider intellectual environment, as this continues to take little or no cognizance of the theoretical and methodological implications of gender analysis and research (Pereira 2002). The question that this poses is whether a continent facing the developmental challenges that confront Africa can afford to ignore the centrality of gender as an organising principle in all aspects and spheres of social relations and institutions which are to date largely undemocratic and untransformed. Put more concretely, can a continent being decimated by a sexually transmitted pandemic continue to ignore the role of gender oppression and the related manifestations of sexuality in the spread of the disease, or in its consequences? Can a continent wracked by militarism and the concomitant outbreaks of conflict afford to neglect the dynamics of gender and the particular expressions of masculinity that have historically infused African politics and statecraft? Can a continent still failing to successfully address mass poverty afford to ignore the ongoing dynamics of gender in African economies, labour markets and livelihood prospects?

Notes

1. Sponsored by the Ford Foundation, see the Report of the Retreat (Mama and Hamilton 2003).

2. The writings of Doria Shafik and Huda Sharaawi in Egypt, Funmilayo Ransome Kuti in Nigeria, Charlotte Maxeke are examples, and many others can be found in the Women Writing Africa Series published by the Feminist Press.

3. Tsikata (2000) addresses the growth and limitations of gender training in the Ghanaian context.

4. South Africa because of the extreme divisions characterising relations between academics and social movements, exacerbated by the race, class and gender divisions presents a somewhat different scenario.

5. Personal communication with Takyiwaa Manuh , University of Ghana, Zenebeworke Tadesse of the AGI Advisory Board, and Fatou Sow of Cheikh Anta Diop University.

6. For example, the AGI existed for four years before a single salary came onto the payroll, and then stopped after only two additional posts had been established.

7. Personal communication with Amanda Gouws, Department of Political Science at Stellenbosch and Shireen Hassim, Department of Political Science at the University of the Witwatersrand.

8. Reviewed in the series of case studies carried out by Third World Network (TWN 2000).

9. For example, the Universities of Cape Town, Ghana and Makerere (and probably others) have all seen individual existing faculty return with doctorates in 2003, but restrictions on new hiring continue to pose a constraint and perpetuate brain drain.

10. The teaching resource on Sexuality was written up by Charmaine Pereira (2004), available at www.gwsafrica.org.

11. The 'Mapping African Sexualities Project' funded by Ford Foundation has so far produced a special issue of *Feminist Africa*, Issue no 5, available at www.feministafrica.org, other outputs forthcoming. Additional projects on 'Gender Sex and the Law' and Sexual Harassment in Nigerian Unviersities are being carried out by network members at Makerere and the Network for Women's Studies in Nigeria respectively. The 'Gender and Institutional Culture in African Universities' project is funded by the Association of African Universities, publication forthcoming.

12. These have been disseminated online and through CD-Rom within the network.

13. The Higher Education Partnership set up by a group of US Foundations to revitalise African higher education has committed a further 100 million dollars in 2005, but the agenda that this money will support in cash-starved universities is not yet clear or coherent.

References

Ajayi, J., L. Goma, and G. Ampah Johnson, eds., 1996, *The African Experience With Higher Education*, Oxford: James Currey/Accra: Association of African Universities.

Alexander, J. and C. Mohanty, 1997, eds., *Feminist Genealogies, Colonial Legacies, Democratic Futures*, London and New York: Routledge.

Bennett, J., 2002, 'Exploration of a Gap: Strategising Gender Equity in African Universities', *Feminist Africa* 1: 34-63.

Diouf, M and M. Mamdani, eds., 1994, *Academic Freedom in Africa*, Dakar: CODESRIA Book Series.

Federici, S, G. Caffentzis, and O. Alidou, eds., 2000, *A Thousand Flowers: Social Struggles Against Structural Adjustment in African Universities*, Trenton NJ: Africa World Press.

Feminist Africa, 2002, 'Intellectual Politics', Issue No. 1, African Gender Institute, Cape Town.

Feminist Africa, 2005, 'Women Mobilised', Issue No. 4, African Gender Institute, Cape Town.

Feminist Africa, 2005, 'Sexual Cultures', Issue 5, African Gender Institute, Cape Town.

Hountondji P., 2002, *The Struggle for Meaning: Reflection on Philosophy, Culture and Democracy in Africa*. Athens: Ohio University Press.

Jackson, C and R. Pearson, 1998, *Feminist Visions of Development*, London: Routledge.

Kasente, D., 2002, 'Institutionalizing Gender Equality in African Universities: the case of Women's and Gender Studies at Makerere University', *Feminist Africa* 1: 91-99.

Lewis, D., 2003, 'Feminist Studies in Africa Review Essay', www.gwsafrica.org.

Mama, A., 1996, *Women's Studies and Studies of Women in Africa*, Dakar: CODESRIA.

Mama, A., 2003, 'Restore, Reform, But do Not Transform: Gender Politics and Higher Education', *Journal of Higher Education in Africa* 1 (1): 101-125.

Mama, A. and G. Hamilton, 2003, 'Envisioning the African University of the Future: A Report of a Retreat on Higher Education', May 29–June 1, 2001, Durban, South Africa, Ford Foundation.

Mama, A., 2005, 'Gender Studies for Africa's Transformation', in T. Mkandawire, ed., *African Intellectuals: Rethinking Politics, Language, Gender and Development*, Dakar: CODESRIA, London: Zed Books, 94-116.

Mohanty, C., 2002, '"Under Western Eyes" Revisited: Feminist Solidarity through Anticapitalist Struggles', *Signs: Journal of Women in Culture and Society* 28 (1): 499-535.

Mudimbe,V. Y., 1988, *The Invention of Africa: Gnosis, Philosophy and the Order of Knowledge*, Bloomington and Indianapolis: Indiana University Press.

Pereira, C., 2002, 'Between Knowing and Imagining: What Space for Feminism in Scholarship on Africa?' *Feminist Africa* 1: 9-33.

Pereira, C., 2004, 'Teaching Resource on Sexuality', www.gwsafrica.org.

Sall, E., 2000, ed., *Women and Academic Freedom in Africa*, Dakar: CODESRIA Book Series.

Sawyerr, A., 2002, 'Challenges Facing African Universities: Selected Issues', Paper presented at the 45th annual meeting of the African Studies Association, Washington DC, 5-8 Dec.

Teferra, D. and P. Altbach, eds., 2003, *African Higher Education: An International Reference Handbook*, Bloomington and Indianapolis: Indiana University Press.

Zeleza, P. T., 2003, *Rethinking Africa's Globalization, Volume 1: The Intellectual Challenges*, Trenton NJ: Africa World Press.

Chapter 13

Conceptualising Gender in African Studies

Oyeronke Oyewumi

The last five centuries, described as the age of modernity, have been marked by a number of historical processes including the Atlantic Slave Trade and attendant institutions of slavery, and European colonisation of Africa, Asia and Latin America. The idea of modernity evokes the development of capitalism and industrialisation, as well as the establishment of nation states and the growth of regional disparities in the world system. The period has witnessed a host of social and cultural transformations. Significantly, gender and racial categories emerged during this epoch as two fundamental axes along which people were exploited and societies stratified.

A hallmark of the modern era is the expansion of Europe and the establishment of Euro/American cultural hegemony throughout the world. Nowhere is this more profound than in the production of knowledge about human behaviour, history, societies, and cultures. As a result, interests, concerns, predilections, neuroses, preju-dices, social institutions and social categories of Euro/Americans have dominated the writing of human history. One effect of this Eurocentrism is the racialisation of knowledge: Europe is represented as the source of knowledge and Europeans as knowers. Indeed, male gender privilege as an essential part of European ethos is enshrined in the culture of modernity. This global context for knowledge produc-tion must be taken into account in our quest to comprehend African realities and indeed the human condition.

In this chapter, my objective is to interrogate gender and allied concepts based on African cultural experiences and epistemologies. The focus here is on the nuclear family system, which is a specifically European form and yet is the original source of many of the concepts that are used universally in gender research. The goal is to find ways in which African research can be better informed by local concerns and interpretations. Concurrently, it is imperative that African experiences be taken seriously in general theory-building, as part of the effort to challenge the structural racism of global knowledge making institutions.

Gender and the Politics of Feminist Knowledge

Any serious scholarship on the place of 'gender' in African realities must of necessity raise questions about prevailing concepts and theoretical approaches. This is a result of the fact that the architecture and furnishings of gender research have been by and large distilled from Europe and American experiences. Today, feminist scholars are the most important gender-focused constituency and the source of much knowledge on women and gender hierarchies. As a result of their efforts, gender has become one of the most important analytic categories in the academic enterprise of describing the world and the political business of prescribing solutions. Thus, although our quest to understand cannot ignore the role of western feminists we must question the social identity, interests, and concerns of the purveyors of such knowledge. In accordance with this sociology of knowledge approach, Karl Mannheim (1936:4) states:

> Persons bound together into groups strive in accordance with the character and position of the groups to which they belong to change the surrounding world of nature and society or attempt to maintain it in a given condition. It is the direction of this will to change or to maintain, of this collective activity, which produces the guiding thread for the emergence of their problems, their concepts and their forms of thought.

Feminists as one such group have used their newly acquired power in Western societies to turn what were formerly perceived as the private troubles of women into public issues. They have shown how women's personal troubles in the private sphere are in fact public issues constituted by the gender inequality of the social structure. It is clear that Euro/American women's experiences and the desire for transformation have provided the basis for the questions, concepts, theories, and concerns that have produced gender research.

Feminist researchers use gender as the explanatory model to account for women's subordination and oppression worldwide. In one fell swoop, they assume both the category 'woman' and her subordination as universals. But gender is first and foremost a socio-cultural construct. Thus as the starting point of research we cannot take as given what indeed we need to investigate. If gender looms so large in the lives of white women to the exclusion of other factors, we have to ask, why gender? Why not some other category like race, for example, which is seen as fundamental by African Americans. Because gender is socially constructed the social category 'woman' is not universal, and other forms of oppression and inequality are present in society, additional questions must be asked: Why gender? To what extent does a gender analysis reveal or occlude other forms of oppression? Which women's situation does feminist scholarship theorise well? To what extent does it facilitate women's wishes, and their desire to account for their disadvantaged condition?

Many scholars have critiqued gender as a universal concept and have shown the extent to which it is particular to Anglophone/American and white women's politics, in the United States especially. Perhaps the most important critique of feminist articulations of gender as a foundational category of society is the one made by a host of African American scholars who insist that in the United States there is no way that gender can be considered outside of race and class. This position led to the insistence on the differences amongst women and the need to theorise multiple forms of oppression, particularly where inequalities of race, gender, and class are evident. Outside the United States, discussions have focused on the necessity of paying attention to imperialism, colonisation, and other local and global forms of stratification, which lend weight to the assertion that gender cannot be abstracted from the social context. Thus, other systems of hierarchy are relevant and must be taken into account.

In this paper, I want to add another dimension to the reasons why gender must not be taken at face value and specifically to articulate an African critique. First, I will explore the original sources of feminist concepts that are the mainstay of gender research. I wish to suggest that feminist concepts are rooted in the nuclear family. This social institution constitutes the very basis of feminist theory and represents the vehicle for the articulation of feminist values. This is in spite of the widespread belief among feminists that their goal is to subvert this male-dominant institution and the belief amongst feminism's detractors that feminism is anti-family. Despite the fact that feminism has gone global, it is the Western nuclear family that provides the grounding for much of feminist theory. Thus the three central concepts that have been central in feminist discourses: woman, gender, and sisterhood are only intelligible with careful attention to the nuclear family from which they emerged.

Furthermore, some of the most important questions and debates that have animated gender research in the last three decades make more sense once the degree to which they are entrenched in the nuclear family (which is both an institutional and spatial configuration) is appreciated. What is the nuclear family? The nuclear family is a gendered family par excellence. As a single-family household, it is centred on a subordinated wife, a patriarchal husband, and children. The structure of the family conceived as having a conjugal unit at the centre lends itself to the promotion of gender as a natural and inevitable category because within this family there are no cross-cutting categories devoid of it. In a gendered, male-headed two-parent household, the male head is conceived as the breadwinner and the female is associated with home and nurture. Feminist sociologist Nancy Chodorow gives us an account of how the gender division of labour in the nuclear family in which women mother sets up different developmental and psychological trajectories for sons and daughters and ultimately produce gender beings and gendered societies. According to Chodorow (1978: 12):

> The family division of labor in which women mother gives socially and historically specific meaning to gender itself. The engendering of men and women with particular personalities, needs, defenses, and capacities creates conditions for and contributes to the reproduction of this same division of labor. Thus the fact that women mother inadvertently and inevitably reproduces itself.

Gender distinctions are foundational to the establishment and functioning of this family type.

Thus, gender is the fundamental organising principle of the family, and gender distinctions are the primary source of hierarchy and oppression within the nuclear family. By the same token, gender sameness is the primary source of identification and solidarity in this family type. Thus daughters self-identify as females with their mother and sisters. Haraway (1991:138) in turn writes: 'Marriage encapsulated and reproduced antagonistic relation of the two coherent social groups, men and women'.

The nuclear family however is a specifically Euro/American form; it is not universal. More specifically, the nuclear family remains an alien form in Africa despite its promotion by the colonial and neocolonial state, international (under) development agencies, feminist organisations, and contemporary non-governmental organisations (NGOs) among others.

The spatial configuration of the nuclear family household as an isolated space is critical to understanding feminist conceptual categories. It is not surprising that the notion of womanhood that emerges from Euro-American feminism which is rooted in the nuclear family is the concept of wife since, as Miriam Johnson (1988: 40) puts it [In Western societies] 'the marriage relationship tends to be the core adult solidary relationship and as such makes the very definition of woman become that of wife', because the category 'wife' is rooted in the family. In much of white feminist theory, society is represented as a nuclear family, composed of a couple and their children. There is no place for other adults. For women in this configuration, the wife identity is totally defining other relationships are at best secondary. It seems as though the extent of the feminist universe is the nuclear family. Methodologically, the unit of analysis is the nuclear family household, which theoretically then reduces woman to wife. Because race and class are not normally variable in the family, it makes sense that white feminism, which is trapped in the family, does not see race or class.

Consequently, the fundamental category of difference, which appears as a universal from the confines of the nuclear family, is gender. The woman at the heart of feminist theory, the wife, never gets out of the household. Like a snail she carries the house around with her. The problem is not that feminist conceptualisation starts with the family but that it never transcends the narrow confines of the nuclear family. Consequently, wherever woman is present becomes the private sphere of women's subordination. Her very presence defines it as such.

Theorising from the confined space of the nuclear family, it is not surprising that issues of sexuality automatically come to the fore in any discussion of gender. Even a category such as mother is not intelligible in white feminist thought except if the mother is defined first as the wife of the patriarch. There seem to be no understanding of the role of a mother independent of her sexual ties to a father. Mothers are first and foremost wives. This is the only explanation for the popularity of that oxymoron: single mother. From an African perspective and as a matter of fact mothers by definition cannot be single. In many cultures, motherhood is defined as a relationship to progeny not as a sexual relationship to a man. Within the feminist literature, motherhood that in many other societies constitutes the dominant identity of women is subsumed under wifehood. Because woman is a synonym for wife, procreation and lactation in the gender literature (traditional and feminist) are usually presented as part of the sexual division of labour. Marital coupling is thus constituted as the base of societal division of labour.

Feminist sociologist Nancy Chodorow argues that even an infant experiences his or her mother as gendered being—wife of the father—which has deep implications in regard to the differential psychosocial development of sons and daughters. She universalises the experience of nuclear motherhood and takes it as a human given, thereby extending the boundaries of this very limited Euro/American form to other cultures that have different family organisations.

The Non-gendered Yoruba Family

Thus far I have shown that feminist concepts emerged out of the logic of the patriarchal nuclear family, a family form that is inappropriately universalised. In this section drawing from my own research on Yoruba society of southwestern Nigeria I present a different kind of family organisation. The traditional Yoruba family can be described as a non-gendered family. It is non-gendered because kinship roles and categories are not gender-differentiated. Significantly then, power centres within the family are diffused and are not gender-specific. Because the fundamental organising principle within the family is seniority, based on relative age and not gender, kinship categories encode seniority not gender. Seniority is the social ranking of persons based on their chronological ages. Hence the words *egbon* refers to the older sibling and *aburo* to the younger sibling of the speaker regardless of gender. The seniority principle is dynamic and fluid; unlike gender, it is not rigid or static.

Within the Yoruba family, *omo*—the nomenclature for child—is best translated as offspring. There are no single words denoting girl or boy in the first instance. With regard to the categories husband and wife, within the family the category *oko*, which is usually glossed as the English husband, is non-gender-specific because it encompasses both males and females. *Iyawo* glossed as wife, in English refers to in-marrying females. The distinction between *oko* and *iyawo* is not one of gender but a distinguishes between those who are birth members of the family and those who enter by marriage. The distinction expresses a hierarchy in which the *oko* position is superior to the *iyawo*. This hierarchy is not a gender hierarchy because even female *oko* are superior to the female *iyawo*. In the society at large even the category of *iyawo* includes both men and women in that devotees of the Orisa (deities) are called *iyawo* Orisa. Thus relationships are fluid and social roles are situational continuously placing individuals in context-dependent hierarchical and non-hierarchical changing roles.

The work of social anthropologist Niara Sudarkasa (1996) on the contrasting characteristics of African-based family systems and European-based forms is especially illuminating. She points out that the nuclear family is a conjugally-based family in that it is built around a couple—the conjugal core. In West Africa (of which the Yoruba are a part), it is the lineage that is regarded as the family. The lineage is a consanguinally-based family system built around a core of brothers and sisters—blood relations. She explicates:

> Upon marriage, couples did not normally establish separate households, but rather joined the compound of either the bride or groom, depending on the prevailing rules of descent. In a society in which descent is patrilineal, the core group of the compound consisted of a group of brothers, some sisters, their adult sons, and grandchildren. The core of the co-residential unit was composed of blood relatives. The spouses are considered outsiders and therefore not part of the family (Sudarkasa 1996: 81).

In the Yoruba case, all the members of the lineage as a group are called *omo-ile* and are individually ranked by birth order. All the in-marrying females are as a group known as *iyawo ile* and are ranked by order of marriage. Individually, an *omo-ile* occupies the position of *oko* in relation to the in coming *iyawo*. This insider-outsider relationship is ranked, with the insider being the privileged senior. The mode of recruitment into the lineage is the crucial difference—birth for the *oko* and marriage for the *iyawo*.

If there was one role-identity that defined females, it was the position of mother. Within the household, members are grouped around different mother-child units described as *omoya*, literally children of one mother—womb sibling. Because of the matrifocality of many African family systems, the mother is the pivot around which familial relationships are delineated and organised. Consequently, *omoya* is the comparable category in Yoruba culture to the nuclear sister in white American culture. The relationship among womb siblings just like that of sisters of the nuclear family is based on an understanding of common interests borne out of a shared experience. The defining shared experience that binds the *omoya* together in loyalty and unconditional love is the mother's womb. The category *omoya*, unlike sister transcends gender.

Omoya also transcends households, because matrilateral cousins are regarded as womb siblings and are perceived to be closer to one another than siblings who share the same father and who may even live in the same household. *Omoya* locates a person within a socially recognised grouping and underscores the significance of the mother-child ties in delineating and anchoring a child's place in the family. Thus these relationships are primary, privileged and should be protected above all others. In addition, *omoya* underscores the importance of motherhood as institution and as experience in the culture.

The Challenge of African Conceptualisations

The difficulty of applying feminist concepts to express and analyse African realities is the central challenge of African gender studies. The fact that western gender categories are presented as inherent in nature (of bodies) and operate on dichotomous, binarily opposed male/female, man/woman duality in which the male is assumed to be superior and therefore the defining category, is particularly alien to many African cultures. When African realities are interpreted based on these Western claims, what we find are distortions, obfuscations in language and often a total lack of comprehension due to the incommensurability of social categories and institutions. In fact, the two basic categories of woman and gender demand rethinking, given the Yoruba case presented above, and as I argued in my book *The Invention of Women: Making an African Sense of Western Gender Discourses*. Writings from other African societies suggest similar problems. A few examples follow.

Social anthropologist Ifi Amadiume (1987) writes about male daughters, female husbands, and the institution of woman marriage in Igbo society. These conceptions confound the Western mind and therefore should not be imprisoned by the feminist framework. In the novel *Nervous Conditions* set in Zimbabwe, Tsitsi Dangarembga (1989: 133) writing about Shona culture discusses the privileges of what she calls the 'patriarchal status' of aunt Tete, a character in the story: 'Now this kind of work was women's work, and of the thirteen women there, my mother and Lucia were incapacitated a little—Tete, having patriarchal status, was not expected to do much'. We gather that aunt Tete is a woman who has 'patriarchal status', which exempts her from women's work. The question then arises as to how the category 'woman' is constituted in Shona society. Who then is the woman who does women's work? What does it all mean within the social organisation of the society? Similarly, Sekai Nzenza-Shand (1997: 19), writing about her Shona family in her memoir *Songs from an African Sunset*, describes her mother's superior relationship to the *varoora* thus:

> In her maiden village, my mother was looked on as the great aunt, or an honorary man; the varoora gave her respect due to a father and my mother could command them as she wished. They therefore came to their 'husband's' village to support her in bereavement.

Is Nzenza Shand's mother a man (albeit an honorary man)? How do these constructions trouble our theoretically given categories? What does it all mean?

Coming back to West Africa, Ghanaian linguist, Kwesi Yankah (1995:89) in his monograph on the Okyeame—spokesperson for Akan chiefs—made the following observation: 'an Okyeame is traditionally referred to as the Ohene Yere, the chief's wife—it is generally applied to all Okyeame whether in appointive or hereditary positions'. He explains: 'even in cases where a chief is female and her Okyeame is male, the akyeame is still a wife and the chief a husband' (Yankah 1995: 89). This understanding clearly confounds the Western gendered understanding that the social role 'wife' is inherent in the female body. Finally, historian Edna Bay (1998:20) writing on the kingdom of Dahomey states:

> The king also married men. Prominent artisans and talented leaders from newly conquered areas were integrated into Dahomey through ties based on the idiom of marriage. Along with eunuchs and women of the palace, such men were called *ahosi*.

Male *ahosi* brought families with them or were granted women and slaves to establish a line.

The category 'women of the palace' mentioned in the quotation does not include daughters of the lineage. The females born into the lineage belong with their brothers in the category of lineage members, a grouping that derives from birthplace. These facts underscore the need to subject the category 'woman' to further analysis and to privilege the categories and interpretations of these African societies bringing them into ongoing global discourses of gender and allied concepts.

These African examples present several challenges to the unwarranted universalisms of Western feminist discourses on gender. From the cases presented, it is obvious that these African social categories are fluid, crossing anatomic boundaries. They do not rest on body type, and social positioning is highly situational. Furthermore, the idiom of marriage used for social classification in many African cultures is often not primarily about gender, as feminist interpretations of family ideology and organisation would suggest. Elsewhere I have argued that the marriage/family idiom in many African cultures is a way of describing patron/client relationships that have little to do with the nature of human bodies. Analysis and interpretations of Africa must start with Africa. Meanings and interpretation should derive from social organisation and social relations paying close attention to specific cultural and local contexts.

References

Amadiume, I., 1987, *Male Daughters, Female Husbands: Gender and Sex in an African Society*, London: Zed Press.

Bay, E., 1998, *Wives of the Leopard: Gender, Politics, and Culture in the Kingdom of Dahomey*, Charlottesville, VA: University of Virginia Press.

Chodorow, N., 1978, *The Reproduction of Mothering: Psychoanalysis and the Sociology of Gender*, Berkeley: University of California Press.

Dangarembga, T., 1989, *Nervous Conditions: A Novel*, Seattle, WA: Seal Press.

Haraway, D., 1991, *Simians, Cyborgs and Women: The Reinvention of Nature*, New York: Routledge.

Johnson, Miriam, 1988, *Strong Mothers: Weak Wives: The Search for Gender Equality*, Berkeley: University of Calfornia Press.

Mannheim, K., 1936, *Ideology or Utopia?* London: Routledge and Kegan Paul.

Nzenza-Shand, S., 1997, *Songs to an African Sunset: A Zimbabwean Story*, Melbourne and London: Lonely Planet Publications.

Oyewumi, O., 1997, *The Invention of Women: Making an African Sense of Western Gender Discourses*, Minneapolis: University of Minnesota Press.

Sudarkasa, N., 1996, *The Strength of Our Mothers: African and African American Women and Families: Essays and Speeches*, Trenton and Asmara: Africa World Press.

Yankah, K., 1995, *Speaking for the Chief: Okyeame and the Politics of Akan Royal Oratory*, Bloomington and Indianapolis: Indiana University Press.

Chapter 14

Contemporary African Art
and Western Exclusionary Politics

Nkiru Nzegwu

The West seems to believe that it alone is capable of assimilating other cultures without ceasing to be itself. In this bag are trapped those who still believe that Tarzan is the President of Tanzania. But an African artist can, without losing his identity, adopt elements of Western civilization which, without us, would not be as it is today.—Ery Camara, Senegalese curator (1991: 181).

The anthology, *Issues in Contemporary African Art*, for which an original version of this essay served as the introduction, grew out of a 1996 College Art Association panel enigmatically titled 'Hostage Crises: Contemporary African Art in Bondage'. Exasperated by the voyeuristic representation of contemporary African art by major blockbuster exhibitions, such as *Magiciens de la terre*, *Africa Explores*, and *africa now*, I conceived the panel to engage theoretically the deliberative side of contemporary African art that these exhibitions obscure. The goal was to challenge the narrow construction of this art as coterminous with signage and folk art. For a long time in the United States, contemporary African art was looked upon in some quarters as a bastardised version of traditional African art, and in others as an illegitimate child of European modernist art. Spurred by these negative attitudes, scholarship in the area of this art has lagged behind that of traditional art.

At the 1996 CAA panel, critical discussions were generated about works of art produced in some of the fifty-three countries of Africa since the 1960s. Like the panel, the anthology that derived from the panel examined how such works have been shaped by post-independence politics, an ebullient economy, cultural transformations, the forces of cosmopolitanism and urbanisation, civil strife, economic hardship, civil wars, life in refugee camps, peace and prosperity, professionalisation of art, and democracy movements. The authors who were part of the anthology, like many others in the field, share a deep concern about the intellectual ignominy that has befallen the study of contemporary African art in the United States. Their objective was to recover lost ground through critical art theory that is informed by artists' political standpoints and aesthetic choices, techniques of representation, cultural references, gender attitudes, identity concerns, and the particular histories of the cultures. In-depth research of this nature would expand our understanding of the relationship between art and historical memory, art and identity, art and decolonisation, and the varied formations of modernity in art. This approach to art history is convincingly resuscitative and absolutely necessary, since at the time the major journal, *African Arts*, and the professional organisation, the Arts Council of the African Studies Association (ACASA), that represent African art in the United States had yet to re-emerge from the ethnological closet into which they retreated over two decades ago.

In undertaking the study of contemporary African art, authors were engaged in a three-way dialogue with the artist, the history and politics of the artist's culture, and with the modernist art traditions of Europe. As such, a clarification of key nomenclature is in order to avoid mapping Europe's assumptions on to Africa.

In Africa art historiography, 'contemporary art' is a technical term that logically functions both as a chronological and theoretical marker. In a similar way but for different reasons, it parallels Europe's choice of the word 'modern' to reference and characterise its African-inspired works produced in the first half of the twentieth century. As used by Africans, 'contemporary art' distinguishes a body of works created since the beginning of the twentieth century with imported materials. As Salah Hassan (1993:6) notes, it 'denotes a wide range of artistic forms and traditions without real concerns for theoretical or methodological questions of definition'. This disregard for 'theoretical and methodological questions', which some have found troubling, is precisely the strength and difference of this art. In defying European principles of classification, and in unifying varied types of artistic forms under this rubric, contemporary African art asserts its autonomy and history. The paradox that some believe is created when what is created half a century ago is labelled 'contemporary', is no different from the paradox that occurs when what is created ninety years ago is represented as modern. The paradox dissolves once it is clear, as it should be to specialists, that like 'modern' in 'modern European art', the word 'contemporary' in 'contemporary African art' is a technical term.

Used loosely, 'contemporary art' adumbrates an assortment of styles ranging from realist landscapes, portraits and street scenes, to mythological and spiritual symbolism, and from arabesque to geometric and hard-edged abstraction. Included in this vibrant eclectic mix are neotraditional sculptures, ceramics, and textiles. However, when used strictly, the term narrowly refers to the paintings, sculptures and prints of formally trained artists, and marks a distinction between educationally trained and non-educationally trained artists. The ground of distinction is not education *per se*, but the precise technical understanding of forms, elements of design, and materials that follow from educational training.

A crucial difference between European modernism and contemporary art in Africa is that the latter has since its inception been engaged in political, social and historical matters of interest. From 1900 to the 1960s, Africa's contemporary art engaged in a visual argument with European artists and illustrators who were visually underscoring the brutish nature of Africans. During the nationalist struggle for independence, this art form participated in anti-colonial and anti-apartheid struggles and debates as politically motivated artists (Aina Onabolu and Ben Enwonwu from Nigeria, Kofi Antubam and Vincent Kofi from Ghana, Papa Ibra Tall and Ibra N'Diaye from Senegal, Gebre Kristos Desta and Skunder Bohossian from Ethiopia, Ibrahima El Salahi and Ahmed Shibrain from Sudan, and Gerard Sekoto and Mohl from South Africa) produced icons of liberation. In the post-independence period, as Hamid Irbouh (1998) argues in the essay, 'Farid Belkahia: A Morrocan Artist's Search for Authenticity', contemporary African art confronted the question of decolonisation, focussing specifically on how histories and ethnicities can be preserved in new forms. As well, it participated in the Cold War politics of regional realignment, in Ethiopia, through the revolutionary realist paintings of Mengistu Haile Mariam's period, and in Zimbabwe, through the North Korean-produced victory sculptures.

Although the chronological period defined by European modernism overlaps with the period of African contemporary art, and may suggest a causal connection, there are sufficient stylistic and philosophical differences that at its inception subvert the plausibility of this connection. Careful study reveals that contemporary African art derives from the radically different cultural, historical, and socio-political experiences of life in cities like Lagos, Dakar, Accra, Abidjan, Rabat, or Cape Town, as well as from macro-level socio-political processes that affect the nations at large. As the contributors of the anthology argued, these stylistic and philosophical differences include but are not limited to the construal of art as objects of either personal or historical memory, identity, embodiment, performative power, or resistance. Underscoring this issue of artistic autonomy, Ikem Okoye (1998) contends that Africa in the twentieth-century invented her own modernism and often in resistance to the force that casts her only as a victim.

In addition to being an act of naming and self-definition, the term 'contemporary African art' cannot be taken for granted. It highlights the impact of colonial trauma on our conception of time, space, and being. From the African centre in which this art is understood, the events of the twentieth century define a sharp rupture with, and a gradual decentring of, the normative socio-political order of historical times. In the formation of new identities and new social orders, the colonial event, which drew Africa into a different type of interaction with Europe from the second half of the nineteenth century, resulted in a quickening of time. This intermingling of European and African cultural values in the bowels of the continent generated momentous psychical force that gave a sense of contemporaneity to this period. In this heightened experiential state, time is reconceptualised and most of the twentieth century is transformed into one enduring present. This acceleration of time collapses and shortens it so that the issues of definition of identities of the early period are intrinsically replicated in the later period.

Interestingly, the social condition of this expanded contemporary moment is quintessentially Euro-'postmodernist' in character, rather than Euromodernist. It is acutely characterised by fragmentation of realities and knowledges, rejection of the epistemology of Eurocentrism, and the revelation of the pseudo-nature of the positivist concepts of universalism and objectivity. Buffeted by the Cold War super-power polarity of Americanism and Communism, social fissures emerged in the Third World that underscored cultural multiplicity, facilitated the coexistence of multiple ethnicities, encouraged resistance to hegemonic domination, initiated anti-imperialist struggles, supported transculturalisation of values, and disrupted the notion of history as progressive and linear.

Since the 1960s in Africa, intense debates have taken place about the interpreta-tion of contemporary African art and literature, and the appropriate criteria of evaluation that should be applied to them. These debates about issues of identity and distinctness have taken place in Nigeria, Senegal, Ghana, Britain, Morocco, South Africa, France, Germany, the United States, and Canada, and have engaged the attention of scholars, artists, and writers. Critically aware of the Eurocentric character of many so-called universal standards, African writers, artists, and schol-ars correctly insisted on the relevance of the category of culture to critical evalua-tion. At a time when sociological and cultural analyses were unfashionable in the West, and the formalist aesthetic theories of Roger Fry and Clement Greenberg were shaping the criticism of modern art in Britain and the United States, renowned writers such as Leopold Sedar Senghor, Willie Abraham, Chinua Achebe, the Nobel laureate Wole Soyinka, Ngugi wa Thiong'o, John Pepper Clark, Camara Laye, and Okot p'Bitek, and artists such as Enwonwu, Antubam, Ethiopian Gebre Selassie Adil, Tunisian Hatem El Mekki, Tall, Felix Idehen, and Sudanese Amir Nour, called into question the legitimacy of non-culturally mediated artistic criteria. Pointing out the epistemological importance of cultural paradigms, they underscored the rel-evance of socio-political experiences to intellectual and artistic production. In their view, no plausible general or universal account of art and artistic criteria can ignore the social context and status of the artists. Speaking in Senegal in 1966, at a collo-quium on Negro art at the First World Festival of Negro Arts, also known as Pre-mier Festival Mondial des Arts Nègres, Enwonwu (1968: 423) underscored this connectedness between art and culture. He asserted that 'without keeping in close touch with the rapid social, economic, educational, and even religious changes that have been taking place in the African countries', and without 'know[ing] the mind of the artist whose work [one is] writ[ing] about', one cannot offer valid artistic criti-cism. The upshot of this is that any evaluation of contemporary art must be both culturally and historically grounded.

Paradoxically, at the very moment that scholars in the United States are finally acknowledging what African artists and writers have long been asserting, Africa no longer exists on the intellectual map. Sliding back to the problematic Enlightenment ideas of Europe and Euro-America as the apex of intellectual and cultural progress, European and American scholars tend to overlook the contribution of Africans (and peoples from formerly colonised areas of the world) in exploding the myth of Europology. In this period of 'post-isms', American and European theorists consistently ignore the disruptive discourses of Third World writers, artists and scholars that critically challenge the attempt to stabilise the world along the hegemonic lines of American imperialism and European modernist paradigms. Within this context of new imperialisms, the legendary ignorance of Americans about the rest of the world shines through in art history as the marginalisation of Africa's visual culture. The marginalisation is noteworthy given Africa's provision of pertinent factual and counterfactual materials for radical theories of visual representation.

Lacking a fine sense of global history, art historians in the United States typically invoke a picture of reality that allows them to imagine African art as outside the modern. They imagine too, that, like the monkey in the rhyme, African artists are copy-cats, dutifully copying Euromodernist art, and submissively waiting for artists of European descent to pioneer a style before jumping up to try it. It never seems to occur to them that there is something seriously wrong with this picture, that, really, Senegalese, Tunisian, Egyptian, Sudanese, Ethiopian, Moroccan, Nigerian, Ghanaian, or South African artists must have issues of their own they want to pursue. Most baffling is how they miss the fact that if 'primitive' art had such a stupendous impact on European imagination, literally freeing it to comprehend visual abstraction after centuries of bondage to the naturalistic style, then Europeans do not own modernism regardless of fatuous attempts to do so. Against this backdrop of paradigm shifts, what art historians and artists in the United States understand as 'modern' is hardly intelligible, given that European modernist art is really a provincial extension of traditional African modes of representation. Since European modern art cannot be outside the limits of the art that shaped it, there is a need for a more informed understanding of the 'traditional African style' in its core.

The attempt to racialise Africa and to locate it outside the boundaries of the modern is propelled by the desire to reverse global history and the lines of appropriation. Of course, denying the centrality of Africa to modernism means that Europe is globally centred, and Africa, together with the works of its twentieth century artists, is displaced to the margins. From that site of marginality, it is then brought into theoretical discourse as emulators of European creativity. However, we should note that this inversion of historical relations so as to construct modernism into a European phenomenon prevents proponents from fully realising the metonymic potentials of art, and from seeing the superficiality of the concept of 'art for art's sake'. As Lassissi Odjo (2005:46) reminds us, 'the life-affirming, doxological essence of eudaemonistic Egyptian/African philosophy is profoundly at odds with the cumulative product of Cartesian philosophy'. By this he means that the dualistic ontology underlying Westernisation misrepresents art and the fullness of reality in which the injunction, 'art for art's sake', is a small elemental part (40). The reason for this is that creativity in African art did not originate in a Cartesian-type split between reason and unreason. Because creativity is informed by reason, African art can comprehend the infinity of possibilities in a way Euromodernist art does not.

The philosophic divergence between Africa and Europe in the construction of art and its modernity occurs on the ground of ontology. Unlike African artists who expanded the possibilities of art by deploying it in a number of ways, European and Euro-American art theorists and critics imposed a criterion of visuality and divested art of all its other possibilities. Operating with this parsimonious notion of art, they fabricated an equally parsimonious understanding of reality that made them oblivious to the century-long history of forms, concerns, terminologies, structures, and processes of contemporary African art. They are unable to see the convergence of strategies of cultural resistance and cultural transformation, as African artists perceived and interrogated their ethnicity, nationality, and relationship to the West.

So how should modernity be understood? In 'Formations of Modernity', Stuart Hall (1996a:10) offers a number of interesting features and defining strategies that free the concept of modernity from a Eurocentered framework, in which it has long been held hostage. The thrust of his argument is that modernity is a social process, and its formation began at different times in different societies, and occurs 'across several centuries in a low uneven way' with no precise cut-off points (Ibid). Displaying no singular logic of development, modernity did not assume the same forms or characteristics in all societies, but rather was conditioned by the peculiarities of each cultural context. This conceptual emancipation of modernity from the clutches of Europe's narcissism allows us to undercut teleological propulsion and to more vigorously interrogate what are the constitutive features of modernity in Europe and European art without necessarily treating Europe as *the* model. The recognition that modernity relates to a possible set of choices enables us to see that some of its identified features, such as innovation, stylistic experimentation, were taking place in other societies as well.

Hall's (1996b) enumeration of the formal traits of modernity offers a way to understand complex historical events without racialising the distinctive features of the period. By directing attention to the character of social processes, he brings to attention the specific spirit of modernity—dynamism, change, optimism, transformation, and forward movement—to displace older paradigms. Modernity or modernism (the spirit of modernity) is not coincident with Eurocentrism but with social processes, hence it is not equivalent or reducible to a European phenomenon. However, scholars who read modernity as European collapse the two to create an ideological space in which the two are synonymous. The weight of this tradition and literature provided the ground for Hassan (1993: 32) to assert that '"modernity" itself is a European construct that was articulated initially and most forcefully at the same time "traditional" Africa was being colonized'. While Hassan makes an important point about how modernity was construed by Europeans, and how they tried to sell this ideological viewpoint to Africans, he collapses their ethnocentric construction with the temporal nature of modernity itself. For this reason, he misses the fact that the interpretation of modernity he embraced was elaborated within Europe's hegemonic scheme of global history and prescribes European dominance for all who accept it.[1] Yet, a different, deeply structured temporal perspective exposes the fallacy of Europe's ideological construction of itself. The historical framework this perspective offers enables us to recover Africa's intellectual history and to step outside of Europe's ideological framework and exclusionary logic. Thus, to accept the current Europeanized version of art history is to accept a flawed account of creativity, and to miss the radical thrust of the comment of the Senegalese curator, Ery Camara (1991: 1), that 'without us [Africa], [Western civilization] would not be as it is today'.[2] It is also to miss the fact that the formal elements of modernism in art are basically the processes of experimentation, a radical shift to new stylistic forms, and a movement away from conventional modes of representation, whatever that might be.

Camara's comment provides the opportunity to consider and acknowledge the existence of a different conceptual framework that exposes the narrow limits of European conception of art. Cheikh Anta Diop's work on Western civilisation's dependence on Africa enables us to recover the totality of the African self and to discern ways of conceptualising the relationship between creativity and the creative process. Only by expanding the parameters of history can we see that the Cartesian legacy of dualism presents a false conception of reason and creativity. Thus, we need to pierce through centuries old layers of cultural amnesia to apprehend the transformatory power of creativity.

The issue of bondage to which the CAA Hostage panel alluded, and to which the essays in *Issues in Contemporary African Art* (Nzegwu 1998) are striving to end, has numerous causative factors. The most obvious is the dark stereotypical images of Africa's difference in First World imagination that fuels the imposition of asymmetrical power relationships with Africa. Bondage occurs when such simplistic negative images justify the erasure of any attempts to engage the complexity of life in different African nations. Writing in an issue of *TIME* (March 30, 1998), Johanna McGeary and Marguerite Michaels circulate such images and the embedded colonial power relationship. They state:

> The usual images are painted in the darkest colors. At the end of the 20th century, we are repeatedly reminded, Africa is a nightmarish world where chaos reigns. Nothing works. Poverty and corruption rule. War, famine and pestilence pay repeated calls. The land, air, water are raped, fouled, polluted. Chronic instability gives way to lifelong dictatorship. Every nation's hand is out, begging aid from distrustful donors. Endlessly disappointed, 740 million people sink into hopelessness. That portrait is real (1998: 35-6).

Within an epistemic context in which the predominant image of Africa is that of an undeveloped, problem-prone region, art historical scholarship is given short shrift as self-styled First World saviours, adventurers, and art collectors appear to map voyeuristic desires on the continent. Through monetary means they dictate to financially strapped individuals in rural areas and the by-ways what sorts of works they want the artists to produce. Scholarship is subsequently held hostage as these collectors galvanise their First World economic resources and publication outlets to present as authentic their voyeuristic view of Africa's art and culture.

The second causative factor of bondage can be traced to the origin of the academic discipline of African art history in the United States. Conceived and nurtured within anthropology, the handmaiden of imperialism, the study of African art was 'Othered' and consigned to the disciplinary domain of its birth mother, even when domiciled in art history departments. Forced to wear a troublesome anthropological garb, this history was forced to reflect the master narratives, metascripts, and methodological biases of the natal discipline. Consequently, the calibrated eye of anthropological difference initiated a quest for 'popular' cultural expressions that are represented as uniquely African and radically different from those produced in the West. Covertly implying that the art of Africa's trained artists is not part of popular culture, and that it is inauthentic, Africanist art historians haughtily dismiss the local criteria of evaluation in specific countries.[3] Instead they deploy a subjective criteria, and focus selectively on the low-grade commercial signs of barber shops, hairdresser's salons, and patent medicine sellers as well as on the garish scenes of Tarzan and the mythical Mami-wata (mermaids) painted in enamel on lorries and buses. In documenting and representing such objects as the authentic contemporary art of Africa, nowhere is it mentioned that similar low-grade commercial signs abound in major cities and small towns throughout the United States but are rarely represented as that nation's popular art. Indeed, the compulsion of certain scholars, collectors, and self-styled patrons to represent such works as the real contemporary art of Africa derives both from the exoticising gaze of anthropology, as well as from internalised First World prejudices about what appropriately constitutes contemporary art *for* 'primitive' Africa. While the abandonment of a more balanced global approach has led to the mystification of modern African cultures and societies, it definitely preserves intact the power differential between First World definers of Africa and Third World African artist-specimens.

The third and last causative factor to be considered has its location in the racially-inscribed arena of Euro-centred scholarship. Art historians typically privilege canonical epistemologies, symbolic systems, and aesthetic perceptions of certain cultures and conclude that Africa has nothing to offer. Consequently, they evince deep-seated hostility towards narratives about Africa that do not conform to their refracted stereotypes of the continent. A paradigmatic example occurred with the initial rejection of the panel proposal on 'Hostage Crises'. The reason offered was that 'a representative mix of subject areas and geographical distribution of session chairs' had to be maintained. Since geography was an important criterion for selection, the unstated implication was that there were panel proposals on the contemporary art of Africa, and that one of them was approved. But no such panel was approved. Implementing exclusion, the 'Hostage Crises' panel was rejected on the ground that it overlapped with two others, namely, 'Orientalism in Architecture: Extending Postcolonial Theory into Art History', and 'Diaspora, Modernism, and

Visual Culture'. Although one can readily see how postcolonial theory may be applied in African art history, it remains a complete mystery how the entire *oeuvres* of contemporary art on the continent of Africa could plausibly fit into the category of 'orientalism in architecture'. With regards to the other proposal that was set up in conflict, it is incomprehensible how anyone in the last decade of the twentieth century could construe Africa (the geographical mass) as synonymous with the category of diaspora. To the extent that Africa was perniciously collapsed into 'diaspora', it is not only a statement that the region lacks scholarly merit, but that a racist game of exclusion has suspended knowledge.

In the defence of canonical turf, Africa is held hostage by a poverty of vision and a poverty of knowledge, as well as the desire to excise it from art historical imagination. Thus, we need to be wary of reassuring public commitments to cultural diversity and multiculturalism, since they do hide discriminating attitudes. A high number of art historians in the United States are scornful of the visual expression of the cultures of Africa, Asia, Middle East, Latin America and other regions, and are driven to preposterous limits to erase it. This ambivalence towards genuine cultural diversity constitutes the masked face of First World imperialism that continually surfaces in art history in structuralist analyses, and in so-called radical post-structuralist preoccupations and deconstructionist demands. In every one of these theoretical approaches, the chosen criteria of interpretation, legitimacy and believability, ignore Africa, Asia, the Middle East, Latin America, as they privilege the exclusive voice of Europe and Euro-America.

I should state that in overturning the decision of the 1996 Program Chairs, the CAA Board reaffirmed its commitment to theoretical and multicultural diversification that reflects the disciplinary concerns of its membership. While this act is laudable we ought to remember that to the extent that panels on the contemporary art of Africa, Asia, or Latin America are eliminated at the preliminary stages of conference planning, no tangible proof exists of academic interest in this area. This means that one has to be vigilant and assume the onerous responsibility of alerting everyone when exclusionary practices occur. It is true that activisms are called for when contemporary African art intersects with the exclusionary politics the global art arena, but this state of affairs demonstrates the tenuous status of this art in the United States academy. The direct impact of this exclusionary politics on scholarship is poverty of knowledge about Africa, a situation that leads to the elision of vibrant theorisations on Africa's visual culture and aesthetics, and discourses on the complex interrelationships of art to memory, history, politics, tradition, spirituality, power, and identity.

Like the 1996 CAA panel, the book in which an original version of this essay was its introduction had a tumultuous history. Like the panel too, the *Art Journal* issue in which the essays were slated to appear faced cancellation. Following the positive response of the conference audience, I submitted a proposal with abstracts of papers to the editorial board of the *Art Journal*, for possible publication of an issue on contemporary African art. On approving the proposal the editorial board sched-uled publication for spring 1998. After extensive editorial work with contributors, procuring photographs and permissions from artists in South Africa, Senegal, Nigeria, and Ghana, and participating in a search for funding, the final manuscript was submitted to the editorial board. And then, extraneous considerations took over. Claiming that the journal had to make up for the previous neglect of artistic activity in contemporary Africa, the editor, whose idea of contemporary African art was shaped by André Magnin's aesthetic taste,[4] decided that the essays were too narrowly focussed on artists' relationship to modernism.[5] On her recommendation, the editorial board cancelled the issue without even reviewing the manuscript.[6] By that statement the editorial board colluded in exclusion and loudly stated that African art scholarship should take a back seat to voyeurism.

What is interesting is not the editor's predictable assumption that what African artists' are doing is related to [Euro]modernism, as she understands it. Nor is it the standard assumption that [Euro]modernism drives the creative engine. What *is* interesting is the readiness in which First World art historians unabashedly elevate ignorance to amazing heights to generate preposterous interpretations of phenomena and events of the Third World. Responding to the imperialism in the act as well as to the editorial board's double-standard, the South African contributor to the anthology, Ruth Kerkam, queried: 'Why is it that other topics in Western art have not had to have the same encompassing scope, but have been able to explore different issues in different decades in a lot more detail [and] will reappear in *Art Journal* publications again and again in different ways? Why do issues on contemporary American art not have to span modern and contemporary art all at once?'[7] Taking another critical tack Ikem Okoye ponders what one might 'say were a journal in South Africa or in Nigeria (producing an issue on American contemporary art) to engineer a similar rejection based somehow on the argument that contributors focussed too much on the American artist's relation to modernism. What kind of contemporary art exists in America outside the discourse that is in one way or another connected to modernity? Would we not have to exclude in this context all the artists that we might think of as postmodern?'[8]

What the two contributors are really pointing out is the incoherent nature of the editorial board's demands. To approve an issue on contemporary African art and then insist that the art discussed must be outside Africa's own modernity is to demand that Africa relocate outside time and history. That such a requirement is only placed on twentieth century African art and not on American art or European art of the same period exposes the racist nature of the demand.

Egregious as the cancellation of the *Art Journal* issue may be, there are others ways in which contemporary African art is policed and excluded. One way in which this occurs can be gleaned from the responses I received to a book prospectus on contemporary African art I circulated to publishers in the United States and England. In this case, the standard posture of resistance was that there is no market for such publications even though no critical anthology exists to serve the needs of instructors.[9] Most declined! Most interesting, however, was the subversive actions of the two editors who showed some interest. One commented positively on the theoretical orientation of the anthology, yet rejected the prospectus on the ground that it was not the sort of work they were publishing on Africa. The other requested the manuscript and sent it to a librarian to review, interestingly stating by that action that professional experience as a bibliographer certifies one to assert scholarly competence on contemporary African art.

It is often assumed that knowledge and objectivity govern the review and publications of academic books. But a panel at the 1996 African Studies Association in San Francisco has done much to dispel this notion. Participants compared the high rate of rejection of Africa-centred manuscripts against the high rate of acceptance of manuscripts with an externally-located perspective. From available evidence, they argued that political and racist machinations tele-guide publications on Africa, and that scholarship unduly suffers when facile knowledge displaces grounded knowledge as the yardstick for scholarly worth. Indeed, when the credential for becoming an expert on African affairs, or a respected contributor on African art to a leading art magazine in the United States, is a week-long safari trip, or an admirer of André Magnin's aesthetic taste, scholarship is held hostage by a *National Geographic* mentality. As Paul Tiyambe Zeleza 1994:183-182) succinctly observed, African studies 'is a reflection of relations of dominance of Africa by the West'; moreover 'the locations, identities, and ideologies of those who produce, categorize, disseminate, and safeguard knowledges on Africa, or any other region, have and will always matter'.

On the few occasions in which the standard Africanist interpretive gaze is employed to analyse contemporary art of Africa, artists' ethnicities are overemphasised in ways that minimise the impact of history, colonialism, nationalism, and modernity. Sacrificing nationality for ethnicity, or diversionarily playing off one against the other, or employing an ahistorical time-frame, results in a limiting view of the art of Nigeria, Tanzania, Senegal, or other African nations. This is best illustrated when white critics introduce the ethnic identity of African scholars to promote the idea that their evaluations of the art of other African cultural groups are suspect because they may be motivated by 'tribal' animosity (see Nzegwu 2002: 127-130). Such activities ignore the logic of modern African reality that promotes inter-cultural ties and cross-cultural understanding. When the search for ethnic authenticity is needlessly deployed to drive the theoretical engine, first, the contemplative and intellectual sides of Africa's contemporary art are negatively represented as contaminated by modernity; second, the modernity of Africans is denied; and third, Africans are forced into hermetically sealed oppositional 'tribal' bubbles. Against this epistemological scheme, inauthenticity becomes a policing tool that guards against the production of works devoid of overt ethnic markers and encourages naïveté. Since modernity is misattributed as European, White, Western, and sophisticated Africanists fall prey to false dichotomies and prejudicial beliefs that state what counts for authentically modern in African art are products of signwriters and roadside artisans.

Contrary to the assumptions of scholars for whom knowledge is unidimensional and flows from the West to the underdeveloped parts of the world, contemporary art criticism in the United States has much to learn from African art, which offers new concepts, alternative visions, and ways of thinking that fragments and subverts the hegemonic assumptions about creativity and art. Since 1970, innovative developments have been reshaping the artistic landscape of the nations of Africa, shifting the traditional conceptions of art, the artist, and the criteria of aesthetic evaluation. These shifts are the result of a plethora of recent local and global influences that include, but are not limited to, economic boom in certain countries, the unduly stringent fiscal policies imposed by the International Monetary Fund and the World Bank, the Soweto Uprising, anti-apartheid struggles, natural disasters like drought and famine, fratricidal civil wars, life in refugee camps, the AIDS epidemic, military dictatorships, Christian and Islamic fundamentalism, and democracy movements. Radically politicised, African artists have astutely responded to the prevailing vicissitudes of life defined by social and economic hardships, but are not limited by them. Unusual forms of visual representation have thrived as artists have continued to create works as direct, confrontationist, tormented, and soulful as their personal experiences. What do these experiences let us understand about human nature and creativity? What do they say about the role of creativity and art in human life?

The articles in *Issues in Contemporary African Art* (Nzegwu 1998) attempted to answer some of these important questions. In his essay 'Ajuju Azu Ndu II: (or Fishy Questions) on the Body of Contemporary Igbo and Izhon Sculpture: Sokari Douglas Camp and Chris Afuba', Ikem Okoye (1998) offers an answer that deconstructs the binary opposition of traditionality and modernity, and provides a troublesome entry and integration into the international art scene. By means of a series of probing questions he contests the difficulty contemporary art criticisms of the First World have with the legitimacy of contemporary African art practice. How does the contemporary African artist-as-subject enter, or become located in his or her work? How does the artist's declared ethnicity enter contemporary art that prefers, in the present romance with the idea of a globalised culture, to de-ethnicise its essence? And what does one imply if one labels as 'Yoruba', 'Igbo', or 'Izhon' twentieth century art of Africa that shares something with, say, English art by Barbara Hepworth or Bill Woodrow? Using Sokari Douglas Camp and Chris Afuba as examples, he contends that one is wrongly located within the space of Western epistemology when all that is recognised in one's vision is the apparent schism between Africa and the West. Since other epistemologies exist, Okoye suggests that a critique can be envisioned from a different space which fails to maintain the modern/tradition division. He argues that both *oeuvres* are not intelligible if it is assumed that modernity in African art is alien, and departs radically from the terms and traits of modernity in European, North American and Asian art. According to him, we must cease to assert that modernity was somehow a European invention exported to Africa, and begin to historicise Africa in the twentieth century in order to recognise that she invented her own modernity, quite often in resistance to the real force which casts her only as victim.

Hamid Irbouh (1998) extends this analysis to Morocco, as he looks at the process of decolonisation in North Africa and the creation of authenticity in modern art. Focussing on Farid Belkahia, he shows that Moroccan artists invented their own modernity in art by resolving the polarity of two artistic traditions—an indigenous tradition of craft and decorative design, and a tradition of art that relies on the teaching and vocabulary of Western art. Under colonial rule, and after independence, Moroccan artists posed the following question: 'how and to what extent could artists assert their identity through art?' Of the many viable options proposed to re-create 'authentic' Moroccan art, Belkahia exploited Morocco's visual heritage of decorative design. By evoking a discourse known as *al-asala wa al-mu`asara*, authenticity and modernity, he resisted and broke with the French/Western influence, automatically transplanting his work into a space within which popular culture could be articulated. According to Irbouh, Belkahia's art offers a study forum on how the struggle for decolonisation involved the employment of traditional materials and symbols, and transformed known materials and popular symbols and designs into complex ambivalent texts.

Moving southwards to Senegal, Elizabeth Harney (1998) investigates the politics of contemporary art in Senegal, and notes that works which often exhibit a rich, cosmopolitan mixture of formal and iconographic elements are not inauthentic forms of traditional art. In 'Art at the Crossroads: Senegalese Artists since the 1960's', she argues that rather than applying universal norms of criticism, one needs to focus upon local idioms that take into account Africa's place at the crossroads of colonialism and postcoloniality and acknowledge the cosmopolitan lifestyles, diverse referencing systems, and contributions of African artists to different modernisms and postmodernisms. Attending to how artists in Senegal draw on local notions of art, she shows how they redefine their activities and expand their definition of 'fine' art. She reveals that this redefinition has further enabled them to draw on local traditions of glass painting, and engage in sculptural activities that hitherto were hindered by religious and caste-related taboos. In stating her case, Harvey highlights the aesthetic choices, cultural references, personal visions, and voiced opinions of the artists, and recommends that scholarship would be served if future studies follow the debates around identity and artistry, which have occupied the artists.

Part two of *Issues in Contemporary African Art* (Nzegwu 1998a) consists of the works of Tanzanian-born artist, Shariff Ibrahim Noor (1998), and his approach to art and creativity within the contexts of his Muslim faith.[10] A citizen of the world, Noor employs an intellectualist scheme to synthesise his experiences in a context of enforced migration. *On Colors, Movement, and Light* is all about movement striving to transcend the frozen moments that typify most paintings. He finds that portraying movement is most effective with zebras whose stripes can be seen a mile away. The stripes have a protective function. When zebras run there is complete freedom of lines, swaying lines that dazes lions that cannot jump because of the hypnotic effect of the stripes. Noor's painting of zebras focuses on movement and creates movement: 'your eyes cannot stay in one place they keep on flying from one corner to another. You have this sense of disturbed zebras and movement'. He finds movement thrilling.

Part three shifts to studies of identity formation as it intersects with art production and history. Reflecting on the impact of gender on artist's identities in 'Transgressive Vision: Subverting the Power of Masculinity', I explore the transgressive nature of the relief sculptures of Ndidi Dike, Nigeria's foremost female uli artist (Nzegwu 1998b). In the context of the 1980s, in which women hardly sculpted, Dike's decision to become a sculptor assumed transgressive overtones, placing her in an adversarial relationship with a section of the populace who harbour outmoded ideas about the gender capabilities of women and men. Sometimes rebuked for being a feminist, the label simultaneously marks and circumscribes Dike's deviation from conventionally sanctioned behaviour. Indeed the negative connotation of the label exposes the latent sexism in Nigeria's art world. It also sets up a male-biased view of art in which women artists are expected to occupy a subordinate status. Interestingly, though, the transgressive nature of Dike's sculptor identity derives legitimacy, not from feminism as may be assumed, but from family lineage and the conceptual flexibility of Igbo gender identity. This conceptual flexibility and the cultural practices of women provide the requisite ground for subverting the near-total masculinisation of Nigerian art.

In the essay 'Artists in Zaria: Thirty Years after the Revolution', Sharon Pruitt (1998) returns to Ahmadu Bello University, Zaria, thirty years after the establishment of the Zaria Art Society and its philosophy of cultural consciousness by the Zaria rebels. The objective of this journey is to track the influence of that aesthetic philosophy among the later generations of painters and sculptors. She focuses on the centrality of the concept of the 'African self' in this philosophy and in the works of Gani Odutokun and Richard Baye, as well as on the underlying relationship between their art and the geographical location in which they were produced. Of all the former students of the art school, Pruitt selects Odutokun and Baye because they have been particularly influential in establishing the ideological and generational continuity of the artistic philosophy propagated in 1958, and because their works compel discussion and documentation.

Expatiating on the notion of memory underpinning historical construction, Ruth Kerkam (1998) argues in 'Remember, Remember: South African Art and the Role of Memory' that memory is crucial to the ways that we view history. She underscores its potential value as a counter-ideological strategy that could prevent a homogenous power structure from obliterating collective and individual stories. Treating history as manifold, interconnecting tales and threads that intertwine in a non-linear manner means, she argues that it will repeatedly refer to the past, loop around to the present, and point to the future. In her view, a plethora of differently constructed stories and memories would then facilitate the subversion of an official history that would otherwise smother difference and use amnesia as its own tool of power. She cautions against forgetting the old constructed memory of the apartheid regime, since it would be impossible to reconstruct a New South Africa, and if one were to forget the dismembered, it would be impossible to re-member.

Returning to the narrow limits of European modernism in art, Janet Hess (1998) problematises the accommodation of contemporary African art with established historical paradigms. In her essay 'An Irrational Eschatology: Nkrumahism, Post-Nkrumahism, and the Discourse of Modernity', she examines the relationship between statehood and contemporary art production in Ghana. She argues that the standard opposition to Greenberg's formalism invokes a phenomenological account of experience that inadequately accounts for the process of decolonisation, especially the relationship of Ghanaian art to the ideology of the state. According to her, it is an axiom of modern art studies that modernist discourse inadequately theorises the phenomenon of aesthetic experience. As a number of scholars have argued, the separation between form and aesthetics neglected the material conditions of the work in favour of an irrational and historicising eschatology. Yet, in her view the opposition presented to Greenberg's formalism, an opposition which has invoked the account of phenomenal experience provided by Maurice Merleau-Ponty, inadequately accounts for the phenomenon of contemporary African art.

Given the powerful impact of Magnin's construction of African art in art historical imagination, the anthology closes with a reprint of Dele Jegede's (1998) 'On Scholars and Magicians: A Critical Review of *Contemporary Art of Africa*', a review of Magnin's and Soulillou's edited book. He makes the pertinent point that it 'is an edifice to conceptual myopia, the morbid type that demonstrates a patronizing peevishness for any art produced by Africans who are versed in techniques that are believed to be the prerogative of the West. This explains why many of the major names in contemporary African art—on the continent, in Europe or in the United States, such as Skunder Boghossian, Magdalene Odundo, Sokari Douglas Camp, El-Anatusi—never made the Magnin list' (1998: 194).

Since the publication of *Issues in Contemporary African Art* in 1998 many more edited and single authored books have emerged on contemporary African art. Still the proliferation of these books does not imply that issues of hegemony and Western myopia have ceased. On the contrary, multiculturalism does come with its own pitfalls.

Notes

1. For a fuller and more extended critique of this notion of modernity see Nzegwu (1999).

2. Also, for an extensive argument of how the notions of Europe and the West were not only defined in opposition to the rest of the world but, in fact, are agglomerations of world cultures, see Stuart Hall (1996), 184-227.

3. 'Africanist' is used to refer to non-African scholars of Africa's history and culture. The term 'Africa scholars' refers to scholars who are Africans, but who may or may not be engage in the study of African history or culture.

4. Janet Kaplan, the editor of the journal, admitted this during a telephone conversation I had with her on learning of the cancellation of the issue, 31 October 1997.

5. This reason is from Kaplan's official letter of cancellation dated 24 October 1997.

6. The information that members of the editorial board did not read the manuscript was disclosed by the editor, who also asserted that this was a normal procedure. Her rationalisation for its normality was that the hectic schedule of members often precluded them from reviewing the manuscripts, and so they defer to her. Confirmation that members did not read the manuscript, and had relied on the editor's assessment, came from a member of the editorial board who stated that she did not receive the manuscript in the package sent to her. The confirmation was left on my answering machine.

7. This is from Kerkam's protest letter to the editorial board, 19 November 1997.

8. Okoye's response is also from his protest letter to the editorial board, dated November 1997.

9. A very conservative estimate of African and African-American scholars and artists who teach courses in contemporary African art is over sixty. While this may not be as high a figure as those teaching as some areas, it is equal to, if not higher than some highly specialised, narrow areas of European art. Also it is worth stressing that some of the professors in the art of Africa teach over six hundred students a year.

10. According to him, 'the lack of sculpture and painting in Zanzibar is not so much a result of Islamic influence as it is the result of unfamiliarity with the media. Prior to the introduction of art by the German and British, the Swahili culture, unlike communities in West Africa, did not emphasize figurative and representational art' (Noor 1998: 94).

References

Camara, E., 1991, 'Exchanged glances, crossroads', *Otro Pais: Escalas Africanas*, Las almas de Gran Canaria: Centro Atlantico de Arte Moderno.

Diop, C. A., 1991, *Civilization or Barbarism: An Authentic Anthropology*, Brooklyn, NY: Lawrence Hill Books.

Enwonwu, B., 1968, 'The African View of Art and Some Problems Facing the African Artists', In *1st World Festival of Negro Arts Colloquium on Negro Arts*, Paris: Editions Presence Africaine, 417-26.

Hall, S., 1996a, 'Introduction', in S. Hall, D. Held, D. Hubert, and K. Thompson, eds., *Modernity: An Introduction to Modern Societies*, Cambridge, Mass: Blackwell Publishers, 1-18.

Hall, S., 1996b, 'The West and the Rest: Discourse and Power', in S. Hall, D. Held, D. Hubert, and K. Thompson, eds., *Modernity: An Introduction to Modern Societies*, Cambridge, Mass: Blackwell Publishers, 184-227.

Harney, A. E., 1998, 'At the Crossroads: Senegalese Artists since the 1960s', in Nkiru Nzegwu, ed., *Issues in Contemporary African Art*, Binghamton, NY: International Society for the Study of Africa, 69-89.

Hassan, S., 1993, *Creative Impulses/Modern Expression*, Ithaca, NY: Africana Studies and Research Center and the Institute for African Development, Cornell University.

Hess, Janet, 1998, 'An "Irrational Eschatology": Nkrumahism, Post-Nkrumahism, and the Discourse of Modernity', in N. Nzegwu, ed., *Issues in Contemporary African Art*, Binghamton, NY: International Society for the Study of Africa, 173-186.

Irbouh, H., 1998, 'Farid Belkahia: A Moroccan Artist's Search for Authenticity', in N. Nzegwu, ed., *Issues in Contemporary African Art*, Binghamton, NY: International Society for the Study of Africa, 47-68.

Jegede, D., 1998, 'On Scholars and Magicians: A Critical Review of Contemporary Art of Africa', in N. Nzegwu, ed., *Issues in Contemporary African Art*, Binghamton, NY: International Society for the Study of Africa, 187-195.

Kerkham, R. M., 1998, 'Remember, Re-member: South African Art and the Role of Memory', in N. Nzegwu, ed., *Issues in Contemporary African Art*, Binghamton, NY: International Society for the Study of Africa, 155-172.

McGeary, J. and M. Michaels, 1998, 'Africa Rising', *TIME*, 30 March, 35-6.

Noor, S. I., 1998, 'On Colors, Movement, and Light', in N. Nzegwu, ed., *Issues in Contemporary African Art*, Binghamton, NY: International Society for the Study of Africa, 93-102.

Nzegwu, N., ed., 1998a, *Issues in Contemporary African Art*, Binghamton, NY: International Society for the Study of Africa.

Nzegwu, N., 1998b, 'Transgressive Vision: Subverting the Power of Masculinity', in N. Nzegwu, ed., *Issues in Contemporary African Art*, Binghamton, NY: International Society for the Study of Africa, 105-134.

Nzegwu, N., 2002, 'O Africa: Gender Imperialism in Academia', in O. Oyewumi, ed., *African Women and Feminism: Reflecting on the Politics Of Sisterhood*, Trenton, NJ: Africa World Press, 99-157.

Nzegwu, N., 1999, 'The Concept of Modernity in Contemporary Nigerian Art', in I. Okpewho, C. B. Davies, and A. Mazrui, eds., *The Africa Diaspora: African Origins in New World Self-Fashionings*, Bloomington: Indiana University Press, 391-427.

Odjo, A. Lassissi, Forthcoming, *Between the Lines: Africa in Western Spirituality, Philosophy and Literary Theory*, New York: Routledge.

Okoye, I. S., 1998, 'Ajuju Azu Ndu II (or Fishy Questions) on the Body of Contemporary Igbo and Izhon Sculpture: Sokari Douglas Camp and Chris Afuba', in N. Nzegwu, ed., *Issues in Contemporary African Art*, Binghamton, NY: International Society for the Study of Africa, 19-46.

Pruitt, S., 1998, 'Zaria Artists: Over Thirty Years after the Revolution', in N. Nzegwu, ed., *Issues in Contemporary African Art*, Binghamton, NY: International Society for the Study of Africa, 135-153.

Zeleza, P. T., 1994, 'African Studies and the Disintegration of Paradigms', *Africa Development*, XIX (4): 183, 182.

Chapter 15

The Study of African Religions: A Sketch of the Past and Prospects for the Future

Elias K. Bongmba

In this chapter, I provide a brief sketch of the study of African religions. There are more than thirteen major religions practised in Africa today.[1] I will only focus on Indigenous religions, called here African religions, Christianity, and Islam. I review highlights of some of the research and descriptions by scholars of these religions. Scholarly study of African religions has passed through several phases. The first phase is what I call the exploratory phase, during which anthropologists, colonialists, missionaries, and travellers studied African religions. Perhaps the most instrumental group of scholars were social anthropologists whose work was influential in creating an extensive library of African religions that have now become classics in the discipline and are still being used today.

The Nigerian scholar Bolaji Idowu (1973) has grouped scholarly activity during this first phase into three periods. First, there was a 'period of uncertainty'. Europeans regarded Africa as a dark continent that did not have any religion. They described African religious iconography or art objects as fetishism, cannibalism, and vulgar and repulsive idols (Idowu 1973: 87). This was followed by what Idowu called the 'period of resisted illumination', because some people in Europe were convinced that all people had some kind of religion. Scholarly writings by Andrew Lang and Father W. Schmidt on monotheism persuaded some scholars, but many thought Europeans took the idea to Africa (Idowu 1973: 91). The third period consisted of an 'intellectual dilemma' because researchers were convinced the idea of God was present in Africa but they also tried to reduce that idea to something less than what they thought existed in European societies.[2]

In the post-resisted illumination era, two developments influenced the study of African religions; the first was the emergence of sympathetic missionaries and the second was the rise of specific academic orientations that accepted the reality of

African religiosity. Both traditions laid the groundwork for the academic study of African religions and shaped the discipline through monographs that remain influential today. Some scholars interpreted local religions as *praeparatio evangelica*. Some scholars linked African monotheistic believes to Egyptian religion (Jan Platvoet 1996: 112). Several missionaries demonstrated an appreciation for local beliefs in the context of their missionary work. These included R.S. Rattray, W.C. Willoughby, and Edwin Smith, all of whom thought that there was one African religion.[3] Their writings shaped the development of the discipline in some African universities and Jan Platvoet (1996: 113) argues that Godfrey Parrinder (1969) who taught at the University College of Ibadan was a great proponent of this unified view of African religions.

Scholars from Britain and France shaped the disciplines with publications on African religions in different countries and communities (Ray 1976: 2-3; Werbner 1984). Radcliffe-Brown (1965) highlighted kinship and political organisations, Max Gluckman (1960) saw in the study of rituals a reversal and rebellion regarding rules set by the social structure (Ray 1976:8). Edward Evans-Pritchard (1956), perhaps the most influential member of this tradition, explored linguistic categories, and phenomenological and sociological analysis in his studies of the Azande and the Nuer people and mapped their religious life. The students he trained such as John Middleton (1992) on the Lugbara; Godfrey Leindhardt (1961) on the Dinka; Thomas Biedelman (1993) on the Kaguro/Swazi, and Wendy James (1988) on the Nuer, each published works on the religions tradition of an African community. Research studies by members of the Manchester University explored social process, conflict and resolution, situational analysis, perpetual succession, roles, situational selection, cross-cutting ties, cleavages, ritual, repetitive and processual change.[4] They studied society as a whole, but also considered individual actions as significant. They combined structural and historical approaches to study organisation, bureaucracy, and eventually states and economic processes. French ethnologists emphasised cosmological and philosophical ideas. As a result they focussed on symbolic and philosophical issues. Examples of studies of African religion from this tradition include Marcel Griuale's (1963) *Conversation with Ogotemmêli*, and Dominque Zahan's (1970) *The Religion, Spirituality, and Thought of Traditional Africa*.

The second phase was the indigenisation of the study of African religions by African scholars. The first group of Africans included J. B. Danquah, K. Busia, Jomo Kenyatta, Asare K. Opoku, E. Bolaji Idowu, John Mbiti, Gabirel Setiloane, and O. p'Bitek. Some of these scholars (Iduwo, Mbiti and Setiloane) were trained in theology, philosophy and anthropology.[5] They employed a diversity of methods, engaging in hermeneutics and fieldwork, to accomplish several things. First they sought to demonstrate that African religions had the same status as other world religions. Second, they argued that Africans worship one God; hence, the religions of African peoples were monotheistic. Third, some of them focused on the religions of their particular ethnic groups, the Akan, Yoruba, Tswana, and the Kikuyu. Idowu (1973) and Mbiti (1970, 1991) discussed African religions from a general perspective. While some of them taught religion, the two anthropologists in the group, Busia (1954) and Kenyatta (1959), were also political leaders in their countries. Kenyatta in his influential *Facing Mount Kenya* discussed not only traditional beliefs, *Arathi*, but also the African Initiated Churches (AIC), and the magical beliefs of the Kikuyu. Out of this group, it was p'Bitek (1971) who criticised scholars for employing Judea-Christian terminology and Hellenising African religions by using Greek concepts.

Platvoet (1996: 124) has criticised Idowu and other theologians and laments: 'some of them achieved paradigmatic status and established the unitary ATR, African Traditional Religion, an approach for the study, in [religious studies] departments, of traditional religions in Africa'. Platvoet is correct in calling into question views that give the impression that there is one indigenous religion in Africa, because scholars have noted differences. However, there is a place for general descriptions, broad definitions of terms and symbols presented in the work of Idowu. Idowu's (1962) first book, *Olodumare: God in Yoruba Belief,* focused on the Yoruba tradition. One could also argue that even with that work, Idowu's generalisations might have missed some of the nuanced perspectives that a focused study like Olupona's study of kingship rituals among the Ondo brings. A general view of the Yoruba world suggests only points of convergence among the different Yoruba communities and not absolute unity. While I share some of Platvoet's anxiety about witchcraft, the criticism that Idowu and later scholars believed in witches, even if later scholars appeal to Christian resources to deal with them, leaves something to be desired because recent studies of witchcraft do not focus on the empirical reality of witches, but on a social world created by the belief in them. I myself have argued that love (eros) understood as metaphysical desire is one way of responding to witchcraft (Bongmba 2001). While I am also cautious about any generalisation that indicates that there is a pan-African religion, I think that generalisation that is tempered by recognition of complexity does not make a work unscholarly. To reject arguments that develop points of convergence within indigenous religions in Africa because such arguments are grounded in theology might rule out a critical conversation partner. Critical theology need not always be the profession of one's faith.

During this second phase, some scholars took a historical approach to the study of African religions. One earlier historical approach was rooted in the notion that Africans were descended from Ham, the son whom Noah cursed for laughing about Noah's nakedness. No scholar of religion or even biblical scholar attaches any weight to that theory. Instead, scholars have turned to archaeological data, oral tradition, and political history, social and religious analysis to develop a historical sketch of religion in different societies. African religions are historical religions because the religious life of a particular community can be traced to its settlement and the components of African religiosity has been accessed through the study of mythology, rituals, social mores and moral ethos of different communities. The colonial project in Africa disrupted some of the historical information in areas where African religions were attacked and destroyed by the new religions. Many of the observers of the religions that reappeared in Africa during colonial times dismissed African religiosity by calling African religions pagan practices. Missionaries competed with rainmakers, tried to discredit them and destroy their equipment. Colonials destroyed shrines, executed priests, and suppressed cult activities (the Cult of Katawere in the Gold Coast, Ghana, the Mau Mau uprising, and the Bamucapi Regional Cult in southeastern Africa). Some African communities tried to protect their religious heritage by engaging the new comers in confrontation.[6]

The reconstruction of social histories of Africa has given researchers new tools to further probe the historical dimension of African religions. Scholars discussed the reconstruction of the history of African religions through studying oral traditions and archival materials at conferences at the University of Dar es Salaam in 1970 and in Malawi in 1971 (Ranger and Kimabo 1972). Matthew Schoffeleers (1978, 1992), M. L. Daneel (1970), and Jacob Olupona (1991) have published works that give a historical perspective on African religions.

Schoffeleers's studies of territorial and regional cults have indicated that these were concerned with the material and spiritual well-being of the population. Priests and members of the elite class led the cults and they guarded the ecology and fertility of the land through rain rituals. They also served the people through divination, healing, and information gathering. They went into decline when authorities rationalised ecology, turned chieftainship into a bureaucratic affair, alienated the people from the land, and introduced competition from Christianity. The Mbona Cult started in the Lower Shire Valley in the fourteenth century among the Mang'anja people. The mythic accounts of this cult explain why the Manga'nja people believe they belong where they live. They construct a new shrine every five years to avert trouble.[7] Scholars have documented the existence of the Nzila and Bituma cult in Zambia, the Mwari and Korekore cult in Zimbabwe, and the Mbona cult in the Lower Shire Valley of Malawi.

The third phase in the study of African religions is the global phase. Following the first conference of the African Association for the Study of Religions in Harare, in 1992, a new consensus emerged on two fronts; first, South African scholars could now collaborate with the other scholars of the continent, and second, the distinctions between insiders and outsiders in the study of religion in Africa were blurred because outsiders no longer dominated the discipline (Platvoet and Olupona 1996: 7). This is a development that was long in coming after pBitek's charge that westerners were Hellenising African religions. This assessment given by leading scholars of religion in Africa was not merely part of the rhetoric of globalisation, but reflected recent growth of the discipline and an increase in the number of African scholars engaged in the study of religions today who are part of the International Association for the History of Religions, the American Academy of Religion and the Society of Biblical Literature.[8] During the third phase, scholars have turned to the interrelatedness of religion to other aspects of life in Africa, stressing the experience and expression of religion in Africa (Blakely, Walter, and Dennis 1994). Scholars presented papers addressing various aspects of the experience and expression of religion in

Africa at a 1986 conference at Brigham Young University in Provo, Utah. They explored notions of the translatability of religion and religious texts, comparative studies, and religious instrumentality. On the continent itself colonial academic structures permitted the study of religion in Anglophone countries, a project that involved mostly the study of Christianity, while the Francophone countries did not promote such academic pursuits, except in former Belgian colonies that established faculties of theology and African Traditional Religions to promote Roman Catholic attempts at indigenisation (Blakely, Walter, and Dennis 1994: 13). Today, departments of religious studies have been established in Kenya, and with the transition to democracy in South Africa, departments of religions have replaced former theology departments in some universities.

Scholars have proposed different methodological approaches to the study of religion in Africa. Michael Bourdillon (1996: 139 ff.) has proposed a sociological analysis that employs *epoché* to listen critically to the other in order to provide a balanced analysis of the cultures of others. James Cox (1996) advocates the phenomenological *eidectic* approach that advances methodological conversion to a 'diatopical hermeneutics' that attempts to understand the perspective of another religion, including their belief in transcendent beings, without engaging in the non-scientific activity of theology.[9] Friday Mbon (1996) proposes a 'culture area' approach; religious studies would in his view demonstrate that there are different religions in Africa, a position which jettisons the unifying perspectives advocated by scholars like Idowu. In the South African context, Martin Prozesky (1996: 229 ff.) has called for greater emphasis on the social aspects of religion.

For future studies, I propose the critical dialogical pluralism approach. First, critical dialogical pluralism would employ among others, phenomenological approaches advocated by the history of religious tradition. That tradition's long cherished suspension of judgment in favour of objective scholarship has much to commend it because dispassionate scholarship is a necessary condition for the possibility of dialogue among the different religious communities. Second, critical dialogical pluralism would allow scholars to study religion together with the social sciences: psychology, sociology, anthropology, and political science. Theoretical developments in these fields have broadened our understanding of the religious imagination in individuals, the personal and communal and social *praxis* that have drawn on religious ideas, and the ritualisation of certain roles, virtues, and faith commitments.

Finally, critical dialogical pluralism should also include theological approaches to the study of religion in Africa. This is probably the most controversial approach in the African context for understandable reasons. Theology (Christian, and to a certain extent Islamic) has had a problematic relationship with religious studies in Africa because it has been seen as a statement of faith rather than dispassionate scientific analysis of religion. There is some validity in this charge because the varieties of theologies that have come down to us carry the marks of confessional anchorage, either as Catholic, Reformed, or Evangelical theology, to name only a few. Second, early African champions of indigenous religions were theologians whom their critics charged were Christianising African religions. These theologians at times employed categories from Christian theology to understand indigenous religions. The Christian perspective comes up in various places in the writings of Idowu (1962, 1973), Mbiti (1970), and Setiloane (1976).

The debate on the relationship between theology and religious studies is a global one that has been taken up by learned societies like the IAHR and the AAR. In Anglophone Africa, the early curriculum of what was considered religious studies exhibited the dominance of theology; and theological faculties dominated Francophone universities and South African universities. The challenge for theologians studying religion in Africa is whether theology as an academic discipline can be a partner in critical dialogue. I am convinced that theology that is representative of the broader culture and deconstructed away from a narrow Christian premise could be a partner in a critical dialogue on the religious experience in Africa. In order to do that the data for theological reflection must be drawn from religious experience. Theologians would also have to make sure that their claims are subjected to scrutiny in the academy. In addition, theologians have an obligation to listen to other perspectives on issues and areas that they have offered ideas. They cannot monopolise the discussion.

Critical dialogical pluralism would also strengthen studies of specific aspects of religious life in Africa. A good example here is what has happened in ritual studies over the years. The scholarly studies of rituals in Africa reached its plateau with Victor Turner's (1967, 1969, 1975) application of Arnold van Gennep's theories to Ndembu rituals.

Today, scholars have departed from nineteenth century perspectives that distinguished between rituals as action that are separate from thought (Bell 1997: ix). Furthermore scholars have expanded the study of rituals from Durkheim's (1995) emphasis on ritual as something that takes place in the *cultus*, to study ritualisation in secular places,[10] although many continue to see rituals in a sacred context, thus keeping alive a debate that goes back to the members of the *Annales School*, like Henri Hubert and Marcel Maus (Bell 1997: 15). In the late twentieth century, scholars paid attention to interpretation, cultural analysis, and exploration of meaning; an approach evident in African religious studies in the work of Victor Turner and Jean Comaroff (1985). These contextual interpretations present ritual as a drama where historical consciousness and *praxis* are articulated (Comaroff and Comaroff 1993). Rituals are now studied in a multidisciplinary context and scholars pay attention to the language employed to deal with the past, manage the present, and project the future in routinised activities that balance 'living and thinking' or thought and action (Lawson McCauley 1990: chapter 5; Claude Levi-Strauss 1981: 669-75, 679-84; Shils 1986: 736). In such a context, theological scholarship that employs hermeneutical and philosophical dimensions could contribute to a dialogue on meaning in the context of thought and action.

Finally, critical dialogical pluralism opens the door for developing research and teaching possibilities in various sub-disciplines across the curriculum and in the academy. The list includes religion and science, religion and politics, religion and literature, religion and the arts, religion and music, religion and film, religion, and media, and religion and medicine, and healing. There is a growing body of literature in this regard and the scholars employ interdisciplinary approaches to enable them to explore broadly how religion shapes or how those disciplines shape religious phenomena, thought and practice.

Christianity in Africa

Early studies of Christianity as an African religion focussed on the modern period and explored the dynamics of the African encounter with Christianity as a western religion in the context of colonialism. For a long time most studies of Christianity in Africa in western academies were undertaken from missiological perspectives. African Christianity was seen as an expansion of the Western Church. However, studies of Christianity in Africa by Africans and Africanists have focussed on Africa and employed a variety of approaches. First, some accounts have argued that Christianity in Africa is not really a Western religion because Christianity established roots on the continent before becoming a Western Religion. These perspectives have been taken both by theologians and historians of Christianity. This is the approach taken by Harvey Sindima (1994), Elizabeth Isichei (1995), Richard Falk, and Bengt Sundkler (2000). These studies trace the beginning of Christianity in Africa to accounts that Saint Mark preached in Egypt and the Ethiopian Eunuch took the gospel back to his home country after a pilgrimage to Jerusalem. In early North Africa religious diversity thrived and cities like Alexandria boasted a large scholarly community. It was here that the Septuagint translation of the Bible was made. The Church in Egypt grew and established working relationship with the Church in Ethiopia because the Patriarch of Alexandria appointed the *Abuna* of Ethiopian Church and of other churches in Nubia.

Historical studies trace the development of Christianity in early North Africa, its spread to Carthage, Libya, Nubia, and Ethiopia. The North African church also experienced the conflicts which pitted the church against various Roman rulers and thus experienced persecution. Following the persecution of the Emperor Diocletian, a controversy developed over what the church should do with those who lapsed during that persecution. The Donatists (after Bishop Donatus) argued that those who had lapsed could not be accepted while Augustine, who called for forgiveness, argued the Catholic position. Historical studies also highlight the development of monasticism in the deserts of North Africa following the devotional practices of the desert fathers who abandoned the world and went into the deserts to devote their lives to prayer. One of the most well-known of the deserts saints was Anthony, who with his sister lived an ascetic life. The other figure is Pachomius, born 292, who built a monastery in Tabennae. In addition to institutions, early Christian theology also developed in North Africa with the some of the earliest Church Fathers and theologians writing their theology on African soil. Tertullian and Cyprian of Carthage both wrote their theologies from Africa; Cyprian's work on the unity of the Catholic Church significantly shaped Catholic ecclesiology. He formulated the doctrinal position that remains central to the Catholic Church today, *nula ecclesiam, nula salu* (no salvation outside the church).

The most colourful of the early African theologians was Augustine of Hippo (354-430). He read law in Carthage, and proceeded to Milan to study rhetoric. Early in life, he followed the teachings of Mani that propounded a dualistic world view. Augustine had a long relationship with a mistress with whom he had a son. His mother Monica prayed for Augustine and had great influence on him. While in Milan, he converted to Christianity, was baptised in 386 and returned to North Africa, was ordained bishop of his hometown in 395 where he served his long and intellectually productive episcopacy. Augustine throughout his life engaged in controversies, taking what he believed to be the Catholic view. The bitterest controversy was with the Donatists, named after Bishop Donatus who succeeded Novatius, arguing that those who had lapsed during persecution could be forgiven and allowed to take the sacraments. The bishops who had lapsed could also preside over the sacraments because the power of the sacraments did not depend on the priest. Augustine directed more than a third of his writings against the Donatists. His other controversy was with the Irish Monk Pelagius. Augustine took sides against Pelagius, arguing what has become the standard doctrine of the church today regarding original sin.

Another African theologian who shaped Christian doctrine was Clement of Alexandria (150-215), who saw philosophy as a preparation to understand life in Christ. He taught the allegorical interpretation of scriptures. Clements's student, Origen, who was born in Alexandria in 185, later took over the leadership of the Catechetical School of Alexandria in 202. He believed in literal interpretation and at one point castrated himself in obedience to scripture. Origen attempted in the *Hexapla* to do what would be called today source criticism. Cyril, Patriarch of Alexandria (412-444), championed the notion of *theotokos* (Mary was bearer of God). Athanasius is well known for taking a position against Arius, a presbyter in Alexandria who argued that Jesus was neither human nor divine, but a semi-God who was dependent on the will of the Father. This position caused a division within the church and threatened peace in the Empire. Constantine, who had become a Christian in 313, called an ecumenical council of all bishops to meet in Nicea. The Council adopted Athanasius's position, stating that Jesus was both God and human (*homoousian*). Sindima has suggested that three other African Church leaders were popes: Victor (189-199), Melchiades (311-314), and Gelasius (492-496) (Sindima 1994). Although apostolic succession is traced back to Saint Peter, it was only with Gregory I that the Bishop of Rome assumed the rule that we have come to associate with the papacy.

The Church in North Africa was overrun by Muslims who conquered the area and established the Islamic faith in the seventh and eighth centuries. When the conquering Muslims came to Egypt, they experienced little resistance because the Egyptians were not happy with Byzantine rule. When Islam took over, Caliph Omar drew sharp boundaries between Christians and Muslims, and forbade Christians from constructing church buildings, imposed taxation on all people while exempting those who converted to Islam. Many Egyptian clergy entered the monastery. Berbers were later forced to become Muslims. Muslims advanced further south and attacked Ethiopia, but did not succeed in overrunning it. Christians attempted during the fourth crusade to take back North Africa but failed. In 1219 a Franciscan who attempted to evangelise Tunis succeeded. However, in 1220 Catholic Friars were killed in Morocco (Bauer 1994). Christianity remained the state religion in Ethiopia and from 1270 until 1527 the Ethiopian Monarchs defended the church against Arab attempts to penetrate into Ethiopia. Tekle Maimanot inspired a revival of Christianity and was called 'Saint of Ethiopia'. Muslims took over the Church in Dongola and turned it into a mosque in 1317.

Earlier studies provided little information about Christianity in Africa after the decline of Christianity in North Africa. Adrian Hastings's (1979) study, *The Church in Africa*, has filled that gap. Sundkler (2000) and Isichei (1995) also provide a study of that era. Hasting provides a rich exposition of Christianity in Ethiopia, mapping the relationship between church and state in what was Africa's only Christian Kingdom that was not conquered by Islam, or would not be colonised by Europeans. Christianity would come back to Africa during the period of European exploration. Europeans arrived at Meidera in 1420. In 1489, the local chief and several people were baptised, thus setting a pattern of conversion in which later missionaries would attempt to convert the ruler of the land in the hopes that the rest would follow their leader. In their first encounters, European Christians took slaves from Africa.

Scholars have linked modern African Christianity to the Western imperial project which involved Christianisation, civilisation and commerce; activities which some Westerners interpreted as a providential design (Comaroff and Comaroff 1991; Beidelman 1982, 1974; Etherington 1977). In the early phase of mission expansion churches were established in the Kongo from 1491 and the King of Kongo, Mbanza Kongo was converted to Christianity and took the title Alphonso I. A Christian presence was also established at Elmina in Ghana, Benin and Warri in Nigeria. During this first phase, Christian missions were not exempt from the slave trade, although many of its champions would later campaign for the abolition of slavery.

Some of the most multidisciplinary studies of modern Christianity in Africa have come from social scientists (Comaroff and Comaroff 1991, 1997; Elbourne 2002). These studies have taken different approaches to the study of modern missions and Christianity in Africa. First, some scholars have probed the conflicts and social upheavals that occurred with the coming of missionaries. Studies of modern Christianity in East Africa probe cultural clash exemplified in the circumcision debates (Welbourn and Ogot 1966; Ranger 1975). Scholars have analysed the methods, logic, and praxis of missionaries, especially the Victorian missionary when missionary activity was at its peak, especially in the Southern African context. At that time, missionary activity was already balkanised along denominational lines and major religious groupings. Catholic missionaries came from several missionary congregations such as The Marist Fathers, the Sheut Fathers, The Mill Hill Fathers, The

Society of the Divine Word, and the Xaverian missionaries. The Catholic Church with a reorganised Propaganda Fide under Cardinal Mauro Cappellari who was later elected Pope Gregory XVI decentralised missionary activity by allowing each congregation to be responsible for its own mission activity and established dioceses in the different mission fields. The Catholic Church condemned slavery in 1845. Different Orders were involved in mission work, including the Capuchins, Jesuits, and several Congregations of Nuns. Notable Catholic missionaries of the time included Charles Lavigerie who led the White Fathers, and Father Liebermann of the Holy Ghost Fathers.

Protestant missionaries came from several mission agencies. A London missionary society collaborated with the Jamaican black missionaries like Joseph Merrick. The English missionary Alfred Saker worked in Cameroon. Other mission organisations included the Society for the Propagation of the Gospel, the Baptist Missionary Society, formed in 1792, the Church Missionary Society, formed in 1799, the British Bible Society, formed in 1804, the University Christian Mission; the Church of Scotland Mission; the Glasgow Society, the Free Church of Scotland Mission, and The Wesleyan Methodist Society formed in 1813. Other denominations involved in mission work included the Methodists, Moravians, the Paris Evangelical Society, and the Basel Mission. Non-denominational agencies included the London Missionary Society that was formed in 1795; The Scottish Missionary Societies formed in 1796; the Board of Commissioners for Foreign Missions (ABCFM), formed in the United States, and other organisations that were founded in Paris, Leipzig, Bremen, and Berlin. In South Africa, well-known missionaries were Jack Van der Kemp, who was known for his support of local peoples, Robert Moffat who established the quintessential mission station at Kuruman, his famous son-in-law David Livingstone who abandoned missionary work for exploration, and Bishop John Colenso of Natal. Women were part of the missionary force from the beginning as wives, but later many single missionary women went out to Africa, notable among were Jane Waterston who started the Lovedale girl's boarding school in 1867, Mary Slessor of Calabar, and later in the twentieth century, Laura Reddig and Dr Helen Marie Schmidt in Cameroon.

Scholars have argued that the main object of missions was conversion and proselytisation.[11] The idea of conversion itself became a subject of inquiry and analysis. Perhaps the best-known discussion of the idea of conversion in the African context is Robin Horton's (1971, 1975) two essays on the subject. In a lengthy review of John Peel's (1968) book on the *Aladura*, Horton argued that in probing why people with a religious culture should embrace a religion dominated by the view that a Supreme Being is concerned about human morality, Peel had touched on a central issue on religious change, while at the same time demonstrating there were continuities between the old religion and the new. Horton (1971: 95) went on to argue that conversion was a development that would have taken place and Christianity was merely a catalyst. Other scholars have disagreed with this approach and

insisted that conversion is a religious phenomenon and that an intellectualist interpretation does not do justice to the phenomenon (Okorcha 1987).

Missionaries employed a number of strategies to convert people. They established social services such as education and literacy training, medical services, and
domestic science centres. In Cameroon, Dr George Dunger made education, health,
manual work, agriculture, and evangelism, all established on the foundation of the
word, the Bible, a blueprint for the church in Cameroon. He described the starting
of schools as the last hope for Baptist missions, but he also placed education in a
broader framework by describing education as a matter of Christian concern, an
'obligation to fellow humans, an expression of Christian grace and concern ... an
expression of my faith ... a concern for peoples' welfare as well as their faith' (Weber
1993: 84-85). In Cameroon, schools established by mission or voluntary agencies
received some support from the state and followed a curriculum set by the ministry
of education. Some of the schools were named after pioneer missionaries like the
all girls school in Limbe, Saker Baptist College, named after British missionary Alfred Saker; Joseph Merrick Baptist College at Ndu named after the black missionary from Jamaica, and Bishop Rogan College in the South West Province named
after a Catholic Bishop. In literacy and education, missionaries translated the bible
or parts of the bible and Western hymns into local languages. Some missionaries
who were linguists wrote grammars, dictionaries, and collected local stories. These
included specific works like Henry Bruton's (1802) *Grammar and Vocabulary of the
Susoo Language*, and comparative linguistic work like S.W. Koelle's (1954) *Polyglotta
Africanna*. Translation work continues today largely through a more professional
society, the Wycliffe Bible Translators. Other missionaries wrote treatises on different subjects, and perhaps the best example remains Placide Tempels (1959) who
worked in the Belgian Congo and published *Bantu Philosophy*. Recently, scholars have
picked up the theme of translation and this time focussed on the message and on
vernacular Christianity (Sanneh 1989; James 1988).

Health work was already part of the missionary enterprise in the nineteenth
century. The Universities Mission to Central Africa made medical services part of
their work by 1885 (Good 2004). The CMS sent Dr Hartord-Battersby to Nigeria
as missionary in the 1890s and he later started the Livingstone College in England to
train medical missionaries (Schram (1972: 143-144). A physician was the first CMS
missionary in the Sudan (Sanderson 1980: 161). The London Missionary Society
(LMS) did medical work as part of its outreach in South Africa (Lewis 1906;
Etherington 1987). Edith Koppin and Laura Reddig started medical work in Cameroon
in 1938 (Tih 1997, 1994).[12] The Health Board of the CBC operates two major
hospitals—BBH, and Mbingo Baptist Hospital, and over 35 health centres in urban
and rural areas of Cameroon.

Scholars have studied the idea of indigenisation through the three selves: self-
supporting, self-governing, and self-propagating, a concept articulated by Henry Venn
(Williams 1990: 17). These were ideals that took time to implement, and African
Christians fought the battles with mission agencies before they became national

churches that were not controlled by Western mission organisations. If one looks at what is happening on the continent today, it is evident that the church has also fallen on hard times as the state and the self-supporting vision of the church is a not a reality because many African churches still depend on Western Christian organisations and development aid to sustain their ministries.[13] Missionaries still work in Africa today as partners with the African churches. In areas such as health care, the term 'medical missions' has become obsolete, although there are people in African churches who play the role that missionaries played in the past.[14]

Other scholars have pointed to African agency in the appropriation and spread of Christianity. Many of them were former slaves who returned to Africa. Africans themselves were active in missionary work. In West Africa the list included: Ottobah Cugoana, Philip Quaque, Paul Cuffe, David George, Herbert Macaulay, Samuel Ajayi Crowther, and in Southern Africa Tioy Soga, Tom Bokwito, Harry Matecheta, the Lovedale evangelists William Koyi, Shadrach Ngunana, Mapasso Ntintili, and Isack Wauchope. Some of these Africans worked in places where missionaries could not go, and some like Samuel Ajayi Crowther who was consecrated Bishop and led the Niger Mission did not receive the respect due to him from whites who worked with him. One account that grounded the story of African Christianity among the elites was Jacob Ajayi's *Christian Missions in Nigeria 1841-1891* (1966), in which he showed how the mission establishment created a new group of leaders who shaped their societies and the work of the church. A further work in this regard was by another Nigerian scholar, Emmanuel Ayandele (1966), who described the impact of missionary work in Nigeria.

Following the Second World War as the process of decolonisation took place in Africa, African churches became autonomous institutions although they maintained close ties with Western mission agencies. Some churches formed national church councils and a united church was established, as in Zambia. However, in many countries Christianity was splintered into denominations and numerous independent churches. Two major pan-African organisations were established, the All African Conference of Churches, which was affiliated with the World Council of Churches, and the Association of Evangelicals of Africa and Madagascar. Both organisations were headquartered in Nairobi. African churches, many of them now independent, experienced a period of rapid growth so that by the 1970s John Mbiti (1984) argued that Christianity had become a religion of the South and was growing fastest in Africa. To meet the needs of the growing churches, seminaries were established in several countries to train ministers, especially in Nigeria, The Democratic Republic of Congo, Cameroon, Kenya, and South Africa, where ministers were also trained at universities. African churches continued to struggle with the integration of African culture into the church. Projects of indigenisation and acculturation were undertaken in music, liturgy, and theology. Vatican II had a major impact on Catholicism in Africa because it gave churches an opportunity to Africanise the liturgy.

With political independence in Africa, scholars of modern African Christianity assessed missions and the emerging church in Africa in two interdisciplinary studies.

The first study was a collection of papers presented at the Seventh International African Seminar held at the University of Ghana in 1965. The papers in the first part of the book discussed missions, the relations of missions to African communities, mission activities, and the motivation of missionaries, policies and methods. The second part addressed Christianity and African culture, highlighting the impact on traditional institutions, the rise of African Initiated Churches (AIC) and the ways of communicating the gospel. The last part addressed new problems such as family life, religion and socio-political issues and the predicament of the church in Africa that Professor E. Bolaji Idowu (1968: 435) summed up by saying, 'it is clear that she has not developed enough resources, in men (sic) and material, for the maintenance of her life'.

The second interdisciplinary study of Christianity in Africa evolved from several consultations. One was held on the Jos campus of the University of Ibadan (Fasholé-Luke, Gray, Hastings and Tasie 1978). This interdisciplinary collection of papers was structured in two parts; the first addressing religious and secular structures, with papers addressing structural issues in mainline churches and AICs. The second part of the book addressed continuities and conflicts with African indigenous religions. Writing in the introduction, Godwin Tasie and Richard Gray noted the collaboration between missionaries and colonial authorities, highlighted African agency, finances, grassroots activity, church state issues and conflicts, international connections, and relations with Islam. One issue they raised in the introduction was the relations between men and women, which Tasie and Gray (1978: 13) claimed were changing. They argued: 'if the change in social relationships between men and women is to be the greatest world revolution of the twentieth century, altering the nature of human relationships more profoundly than the Russian or Chinese revolutions or even the emergence of the Third World, then the churches in Africa are uniquely placed to take a major part in this'. This was a bold claim and today while some progress has been made on this front, there is every reason to believe that the church in Africa has not lived up to its potential in supporting equality between men and women.

In the 1980s scholars studied Christianity from a regional perspective, offering critical analyses of missionary work and the prospects of the church. Egyptian and North African Christianity was discussed in *The Roots of Egyptian Christianity* (1986), edited by Birger A. Pearson and James Goehring; three texts by Lamin Sanneh (1983), Kalu Ogbu (1980). Peter Clarke (1986) examined Christianity in West Africa. What these texts had in common was the fact that they provided a historical sketch of Christianity in the region, assessing the missionary impact, the status of Christianity in the region's different countries and offered appraisals of Christianity. Sanneh in his book studied the development of Christianity in West Africa from a religious perspective, arguing that modern missionary Christianity did not move into a vacuum, but into a religious world made up of indigenous religions and Islam. Kalu in the concluding essay in his edited book offered a critical and sober analysis of the contested issue at the time, the debate on the moratorium of missions. In postcolonial Africa, Bishop John Gatu called for a moratorium on missions to enable the African church to stand on its own. It is an idea that goes back to Edward Blyden who called for Africans to solve their own problems. Kalu (1980: 365-374) argued that as a call for self-reliance, the moratorium should be examined in the light of the church's mission and appropriate strategies brought about to make it work. Moratorium then was a call to end paternalism, increase collaboration by the churches of Africa, Asia and Latin America, oneness in Christ, and the indigenisation of Christianity. The idea of moratorium though separate, was close to the notion of the indigenous church addressed by Bolaji Idowu. This question of self-reliance would remain with the African church, and is even more pressing now when the church in Africa has again become dependent on outside sources to fund its development programmes in the wake of the decline of the post-neocolonial state.[15]

Regional studies of Christianity in East, South Central, and Southern Africa have explored missionisation, conflicts with culture, apartheid and the fight against apartheid. Scholarly work discussed the role of the Scottish Presbyterian Church in the conflicts in East Africa surrounding female genital cutting, the Christianisation of the *jando* rituals in Massasi, Christianity and women, the rise of independency in the wake of conflicts, and later expressions of Christianity (Ranger and Weller 1975). A recent study edited by Thomas Spear and Isaria Kimambo (1999) with most of the contributions from historians and only three contributions from scholars with a theological background, offered a broad-based assessment of Christianity in East Africa. Their study attempts to provide a social history, but the authors also examine the beliefs and practices of Africans in 'conversion, popular evangelism and the struggle for control, especially the critical role played by African teachers, catechists and translators in the process of interpreting Christianity and appropriating it to African religious and social concerns' (Spear 1999: 9). Spear argues that some of the essays in the book point the way to the future because they provide historical depth by examining developments in Uganda, religious conflict among the Kikuyu, the Holy Spirit Movement in western Kenya which gave rise to several independent churches, local perspectives on Christianity, church, state and societal issues today in East Africa (Spear 1999: 10-18).

Spear describes the unintentional collaboration between academic historians (Oliver, Temu, Strayer and Hansen) pioneering the study of Christianity and the revisionist perspectives given by Taylor, Pirout, Kiernan and Lema. It was church historians (Sundkler, Welbourn, Barret and Murray) who embraced independent churches as Christian. Academic scholars (Kimambo, Ranger, Sandgren, Robins, Larsson, Rasmussen and Hoehler-Fatton) have worked on religious history and church historians (Sundkler, Hastings, Waliggo, Githeirya, Ward and Bensen) have studied African religious thought in-depth (Spear 1999: 20). Spear notes that historians see history as the unfolding of human events and theologians see it as the outworking of a divine plan with a telos.

In Southern Africa a similar robust project has taken place and academic historians, anthropologists, social scientists, church historians, and theologians have studied Christianity in the region where white domination resisted change. Studies of

Christianity in Southern Africa have probed the missionary project and its praxis, highlight conflicts of interest as it collaborated with the marginalisation of blacks and rise of a dominant white class in the region. Independence came to Zambia, Botswana and Swaziland in the period of decolonisation and arrived late for Angola, Mozambique, Zimbabwe, and finally Namibia and South Africa. Historians, anthropologists and other social scientists have probed the ambiguous role of Christianity in the marginalisation and proletarianisation of the people of Southern Africa and the monster of apartheid, while church historians and theologians have documented the complicity in domination or the struggle mounted by the church to bring liberation (Chidester, Tobler, and Wratten 1997).

The list of scholars, historians, and theologians would be too long to list here for the Southern African region, but perhaps one of the best works that focuses on South Africa, but includes a variety of perspectives from many scholarly backgrounds, is Richard Elphick and Rodney Davenport's *Christianity in South Africa: A Political, Social, and Cultural History* (1997), which is not only richly documented, but also maps out the beginning of white settlement, enslavement of locals, arrival of Asians, the impact of Christianity on all aspects of life in South Africa, the pivotal role of theology in the creation of apartheid, and the central role of the church in the anti-apartheid struggle.

Scholars, theologians, and church leaders have addressed social issues that touch on cultural matters. One of those issues that has received scholarly attention by social scientist, but not by many scholars of religion and theologians, is marriage and family life. Aylward Shorter discussed marriage and family life in *African Culture and the Christian Church* and Michael Kirwen addressed the question of widowhood in his book *African widows* (Shorter 1974; Kirwen 1979).

Studies of church-state relations in Africa are a field that continues to receive attention and several new works have come out, especially in the light of developments in the post-neocolonial state. The apartheid situation in South Africa, the occupation of Namibia by South Africa, and the Unilateral Declaration of Independence by Ian Smith gave scholars a lot to research and write about. One of the earliest writings on this development from a non-theologian was Terence Ranger's (1962) essay, *State and Church in Southern Rhodesia 1919-1939*. Another study that came out of the region and dealt with Malawi was the study of John McCracken *Politics and Christianity in Malawi 1875-1940* (1977). Since then historians and theologians have written about Christianity and the apartheid state using the methodology of liberation and black theologies. Here one might mention John de Gruchy's book, *The Church Struggle in South Africa* (1970), and Norman Etherington's book *Preachers, Peasants and Politics in Southern Africa* (1978), and Charles Villa-Vicencio's *Theology and Violence* (1988). The *Journal of Theology in Southern Africa*, in over 25 years, carried critical theological perspectives on apartheid. The *Kairos Document* (1985) was a critical moment because in the tradition of the Barmen Declaration, a cross-section of theologians and church leaders in South Africa declared state theology in South Africa evil and called on churches to take a stand against it.

In the rest of Africa, one of the earliest studies in the post-neocolonial world was Tadesse Tamrat's (1972) study of church and state in Ethiopia and that of Donald Crummey's (1972, 2000) that discussed Protestant and Catholic missions in the same country. A later study was Adrian Hastings's book *A History of African Christianity 1950-1975* (1979), in which he discussed church-state relations in each decade from 1950 and concluded with an essay on politics and prayer. Lamin Sanneh (1996) presented another overview in *Piety and Power*. Other scholars have addressed church-state conflicts in specific countries (Henry Okullu (1974) in Kenya, Achille Mbembe (1988) in Cameroon, Carl Hallencreutz and Ambrose Moyo (1991) in Zimbabwe, Paul Gifford (1993) in Liberia, and John Nwafor (2002) in Nigeria. Recently many of the studies have discussed the role of the churches during the failed transition to democracy (Gifford 1995).

Scholarly studies of Christianity in Africa have also devoted attention to the rise and growth of African theology. The scholarly output in theology outweighs efforts in other areas of African Christianity because a majority of Africans who have earned advanced degrees in theology have published their research in that area. Theologians have also argued that for a church to indigenise as it needs its own theological voice. A number of forces, including the process of decolonisation, the emergence of speculative philosophy, especially Placide Tempels's *Bantu Philosophy*, and the influential work *Des Prêtes nous s'interrogent*, shaped theological developments in Africa. Theological debates focussed on the adaptation, inculturation and contextualisation of Christianity in Africa. In South Africa, a vigorous liberation theology and black theology rejected apartheid and worked in different ways for liberation. Concerns about critical theological discourse emerged at the Catholic University of Kinshasa which was founded in 1954, leading to critical and creative appropriation of theology in the African context.[16] Scholars like Mulago gwa Cikala (1965) studied African religiosity as part of his engagement with a theology of adaptation.[17] Adaptation theologians have proposed adopting key African religious concepts like ancestors for theological reflection. Fabien Ebousi-Boulaga has called for a reconstruction of Christianity through what he has called the Christic model which was ignored by the missionary project. Recently Elias K. Bongmba has employed theology to address intersubjective relations through his study of witchcraft. Many African theologians are members of the Ecumenical Association of Third World Theologians. Biblical scholars have studied the Bible in the context of poverty, violence, and apartheid; exmples include Itumeleng Mosala, *Biblical Hermeneutics* (1989), and Gerald West's *Biblical hermeneutics of Liberation* (1991). Recently, Musa Dube (2000) has called for a feminist postcolonial biblical interpretation.

Perhaps the most exciting theological development on the continent has been the emergence of the Circle of Concerned African Women Theologians who have taken on the question of patriarchy in the African church and have advocated pluralism in theology. Under the leadership of Mercy Amba Oduyoye, the Circle has pursued a new idea of community where all people are treated equally. Members of the Circle write theology that takes into account gender discrimination in the church today and also addresses the crisis that women face in Africa on all fronts (Njeroge 1997; Oduyoye 1997; Pemberton 2003; Monohan 2004). Oduyoye opened the debate with her 1986 publication, *Hearing and Knowing,* in which she called on African women to tell their own stories (Oduyoye 1986). The Circle carries out 'cultural hermeneutics' to explore the lives of women in several areas, including rituals, polygamy, leadership and ordination of women, and social injustice, which continues to put women in Africa at the bottom of society. Members of the Circle promote a 'two-winged theology' that brings women and men together to engage in critical theological reflection. The members of the Circle write about discrimination in the church that is based on certain aspects of culture and its rituals, read the Christian tradition in Africa from the perspective of women, and are now engaged in studying HIV/AIDS and its impact on African women.[18]

One area of Christianity that has not been explored in Africa as much as it has been in other fields through the studies of civil society, is the rise and growth of faith-based organisations (FBO) that have spread throughout Africa and are engaged in a variety of ministries, often competing with NGOs and private voluntary organisations. Traditional organisations like the All Africa Conference of Churches and its affiliate national organisations; the Evangelical Association of Africa and Madagascar, continue to carry out pan-African church ministries. These organisations have fallen on hard financial times because of economic decline on the continent. In the Catholic Church, the African synod that met in Rome from 10 April to 8 May 1994 under the leadership of Pope John Paul II, sought to revitalise the church. It focussed greatly on evangelisation, and addressed the international debt situation, but the final documents do not indicate that there was any substantial discussion of the HIV/AIDS pandemic, even though the Synod came nearly eleven years after the world first learned of the pandemic (Browne 1996). African Christianity faces its most challenging period and how it tackles the issues of the day will determine how it will fare in the future.

Christian Reform Movements in Africa[19]

Studies of Christian reform movements such as the African Initiated Church (AIC) emerged in the middle of the twentieth century with the publication of Bengt Sundkler's book *Bantu Prophets in South Africa* (1948). This was followed by George Shepperson's (1958) book that also addressed the questions of Christian independency. Social scientists dominated research on AIC except for research and publications that have been done in Southern Africa, Nigeria, Ghana, Kenya and Congo, where a number of theologians have done research and published books and essays on African Initiated Churches (AIC). Harold Turner (1966), John Peel (1968), F.B. Welbourn (1961), Welbourn and B.A. Ogot (1966) and David Barrett (1968) published important studies that provided in depth view of the new African churches.

Sundkler's pioneering work defined studies of Christian independency by introducing themes that would be explored by later research such as the motivations for independency, classification of churches, attention to felt needs and healing (Turner

1963, 1966, 1967; Fernandez 1964). There are more than 8000 AIC across Africa today and these are made up of churches that broke away from an existing church, of prophetic movements, healing churches and Pentecostal churches. Turner distinguished between the neo-traditionalist movements that depended on African traditional religious ideas, and Hebraist movements, which emphasised monotheism and the teachings of the Hebrew bible. It soon became very clear that the question of typology was an important issue because it generated debate among scholars. Some objected to typology, but continued to use it as a heuristic device. Harold Turner, James Fernandez and others discussed typology, but they moved on in their scholarship to explore specific movements in their socio-political context, noting that these churches were not only forms of resistance to hegemonic forces, but attempts at bringing reforms to the Christian tradition in Africa (F. B. Welbourn and B. A. Ogot (1966).[20] In an extensive study, Terrence Ranger (1986) mapped the scholarly study of religious movements and politics in Africa.

Researchers following Sundkler and Gerhardus Oosthiuzen have described the growth in South Africa of Ethiopian and Zionist Churches. The term 'Ethiopian' Churches refers to a spirit of independence because Ethiopia was not colonised. Ethiopian-type churches were called *Ibandla lase Tiyopia*. Members of these congregations, who saw Christian reform movements as political activity, were active members of the African National Congress. African Zionist Churches believed in and practised divine healing, baptism by immersion in the name of the Trinity, and the imminent return of Jesus. Their members wear robes, worship with bare feet, and carry holy staffs, symbols which Jean Comaroff has argued are not only used to follow the practices of the Hebrew Bible, but are employed as a critique of authority and structure of the older churches (Comaroff 1985: 219 ff). Two well-known Zionist churches are Engena Lekganyane's ZCC and *Ama Nazaretha* of Isaiah Shembe in Zululand. Shembe incorporated Zulu customs and the leader is called *inkosi*.

Several reform movements started during colonial times. Nehemiah Tile formed one in South Africa in 1884, and an Ethiopian-type church was formed in 1892 (Oosthuizen 1968: 32, 33). Former Methodists formed an Ethiopian-type church in 1894 in Johannesburg and in 1898 Simungu Bafazini Shibe left the American Zulu Mission to form the Zulu Congregational Church. In 1900, John Chilembwe set up his Ajawa Providence Mission and later called it the Providence Industrial Mission. Isaiah Shembe started *iBandla lama Nazaretha* (Church of the Nazarites) in 1911 after he had a spiritual experience in which he was called on to live a spiritual life. Elliot Kamwana Chirwa started his Watchtower movement in 1908 in Malawi. Prophet William Wade Harris was called in 1911 and he preached in Liberia and eventually moved to Côte d'Ivoire where he established a large following (Walker 1983; Haliburton 1973). By 1919, there were some twelve churches in Lagos called 'African' churches.

Charismatic and prophetic leaders led the second wave of African reform churches. In 1922, what would later become the Christ Apostolic Church started in Ibadan. It grew through the preaching of Evangelist Babalola. Josiah O. Oshitelu founded the Aladura Churches in Nigeria in 1925 and the focus of the church was faith, prayer, and fasting with an exciting programme of worship (Ayandele 1978). The Prophet Moses Orimolade Tunolase also started the Cherubim and Seraphim Church in 1925 in Lagos (Omoyajowo 1982). Simon Kimbangu was called by the Spirit during the epidemic of 1918 and he started preaching and healing in 1921. A movement was born that would later became The Church of Jesus Christ on Earth by the Prophet Simon Kimbangu (MacGaffey 1983; Martin 1976). Other Prophetic leaders who started movements during this period were Zakayo Kivuli of Kenya and Johane Maranke of Zimbabwe (Welbourn and Ogot 1966; Jules-Rosette 1975; Eboussi-Boulaga 1978; Sandgren 1989; Githieya 1997; Fabian 1971: 9).

At the time of decolonisation in Africa, a third wave of independency started. The Church of Christ of Africa broke away from the Anglican Church in 1963. Other churches that started at this time are the Mario Legio, the Lumpa Church, the Eden Revival Church in Ghana, and the Alice Lakwena movement in Uganda. David Barrett reported in 1985 that there were 7,170 independent churches in Africa. Scholars have articulated several reasons for the rise of AIC such as lack of love, poor race relations, nationalist feelings, and the influence of the Holy Spirit, the desire to indigenise the church, and negative missionary practices that displaced local culture.[21] AICs also sprang up because Africans desired the freedom to worship in an African style and meet their felt needs.

Church historians and theologians today study AICs as Christian reform movements, and argue that these churches have introduced a variety of practices that have revitalised the church in Africa (Makhubu (1988; Anderson 2001). Their members adopt believer's baptism, faith healing, new revelations, and the gift of speaking and interpreting in tongues, African values in worship, stress sacred sites, require an adherence to a moral code, and some permit polygamy. They have introduced several innovations. First, the new churches bring some new theological ideas (Ayegboyin and Ishola 1997: Chapter 18). The AICs take the role of the Holy Spirit seriously. Several leaders claim that they were called by the Spirit to start preaching (Kimbangu, the founders of the Roho Religion). Second, Shembe's Nazareth Church includes the Holy Spirit in their confession of faith and not Jesus: 'I believe in the Father, and in the Holy Spirit and in the Communion of the Saints of the Nazarites'. Third, the leaders claim that they heal people through the power of the Holy Spirit. In some churches, people still recognise the power of ancestral spirits. Fourth, Alice Auma believed in the power of spirit and used that power for a war of liberation in Uganda.

Second, AICs have introduced ecclesiological and liturgical reforms. The AIC churches have alternative church structures and some leadership positions are patterned after traditional structures. In the Harrist church, leaders sometimes come from the same family as did the traditional priests (Walker 1983: 92). The Aladura churches have reformed the church by making prayer and fasting central to church life. Shembe incorporated traditional Zulu dancing and music style to his church. In many of the churches, worshippers wear similar gowns. Third, AIC churches are involved with the social order. John Chilembwe established the Providence Industrial Mission to provide services for his people. Johane Masowe of Zimbabwe preached and healed in a racist society, encouraged his followers to work for self-sufficiency, and build schools to educate their children.

A large majority of AICs, except the Pentecostal ones, are committed to the preservation of African ideals. Perhaps the greatest contribution lies in the fact that they continue to use an aetiology of illness that is close to traditional thought and for that reason practise faith healing when mission congregations have all but abandoned it and instead have promoted western biomedical approaches. The HIV/AIDS pandemic has challenged some of the beliefs about health issues, but the idea of faith healing offers the opportunity to address healing in a holistic manner that allows for the acceptance of healing even if the cure for the physical ailment does not take place.

Some scholars argue that AICs have changed attitudes towards women in some cases. Women founded some of the churches and have played an important role in the development of the churches. Christianah Abiodun was one of the founders and leaders of the Cherubim and Seraphim in Nigeria. In some of the churches, women are ordained into different leadership positions. However, on some issues there is room for change in the churches. The way women are treated in Aladura churches when they are menstruating leaves a lot to be desired (Crumbley 1992, 2003).

M.L. Daneel (1999) has written about the work of AICs in Zimbabwe which are working to heal the environment by practising an environmental and eco-theology because they believe that earth-keeping is part of the salvation of the entire created order. The churches collaborate with traditional leaders, spirit mediums and politicians. The churches believe that environmental destruction is a sin and they stress that environmental destruction has caused ecological disaster. Churches must confess their sins in this regard and work for healing and environmental liberation. They hold rituals of tree planting because *Mwari* has commanded all people to care for the earth. They call Christ *muridzi venyika* (guardian of the land), and *nganga*, (healer) who saves and restores creation. The Holy Spirit is the *murapi venyika* (healer of the land). These churches encourage the planting of fruit trees and the conservation of wildlife and water resources.

Research on AIC has now turned to the spread of these churches in the new African diaspora. Studies by Rijk van Dijk and Gerrie ter Haar, have discussed the presence of African immigrant communities in Europe. Jacob Olupona has edited a book on African immigrant congregations in North America that is coming out in 2006 based on research done by African scholars in North America (Haar 2001; Olupona forthcoming).

Islam in Africa [22]

Studies of Islam in Africa indicate that it reached Africa before it expanded to other places in Arabia when the Arab general 'Amr bin al-'As took over Egypt (Mousa

1995: 129). It spread through trade routes in North and East Africa and through conquest. By the tenth and eleventh centuries, the teachings and practices of the religion had spread into many areas in Central and West Africa, attracting a wide following including kings and elite members of the society and greatly influenced the early empires of West Africa (Levtzion 2000: 63). Studies of Islam have discussed the establishment of mosques, Quranic schools where pupils learned Arabic, the *hadith* (traditions), *Shari'a*, (law), and the teachings of the religion (Sanneh 1977).[23] In North Africa Islamic clerics and rulers promoted a rigid monotheism. By the twentieth century, Islam was firmly established as a major religion in Africa, *ulamas, malams* and *marabouts,* and different categories of scholars and Sufi Orders leading the Islamic communities, teaching the word and carrying out reforms (Clarke 1982). They maintained a vibrant connection with the Middle East, and that connection was crucial because the Gulf states provided assistance to promote Islamic causes, especially during the process of decolonisation in places like Nigeria. Prominent Islamic leaders made pilgrimages to Mecca, the most notable being the pilgrimage of Mansa Musa.

Scholars have also traced the growth of Islam in East Africa, the process of Arabisation and Islamisation in Somalia in several towns, including Mogadishu (Martin 1974; Lewis 1965, 1969; Pouwels 1987). Islam grew in Somalia with a majority of the people becoming Sunni Muslims, although many people continued to observe their cultural beliefs. Later in the nineteenth century the Sufi brotherhoods established a presence in Somalia. Muslims also settled and spread the faith in Lamu, Kenya and further south as far as Mozambique (Trimingham 1964; Sperling 1985). A cultural fusion was taking place as settlers intermarried with locals but more importantly, a new culture and language, Swahili, emerged from the confluence of African and Arabic culture, the result of an urban and mercantile civilisation (Middleton 1992). The Swahili language has been instrumental in the growth of Islam, as its teachings became part of popular literature, as Swahili mythology and legends incorporated the teachings of the Prophet Mohammad (Knappert 1970). Arab economic influence under Omani helped the growth and spread of Islam into the hinterland in Tanzania, Kenya and Uganda. Contacts with the Gulf States and migrations from the Swahili Coast took Islam to the Comoros Islands.

Islam also arrived in South Africa through trade and later through mercenaries brought by colonials to the region. In Cape Town, the spiritual father of Islam was 'Abi din Taia Tjoossoep, Shaykh Yusuf of Macassar, who was from the Macassar region in Malaya (1626-99). Shaykh Madura and Tuang Sayyid followed his leadership. Their first students were prisoners, but it was with the coming of Abd Allah ibn Qadi that a community started to emerge. When Tuang Guru was released from prison, he established a mosque which Mousa (1995: 142) states served as a centre for social and political organisations. This was the beginning of an effective organisation that would also lay the ground for educational programmes and political organisation. When slaves were emancipated in 1834, it opened a new chapter in the growth of Islam. Mousa (1995: 134) has also argued that Islam grew in South

Africa through conversion, adoption, the purchase of slaves by Muslims and inter-marriage.

By the end of the eighteenth century, many Muslim exiles settled in South Africa. The conditions at the Cape were not very favourable to the Muslims, but they continued to grow in numbers. Muslims established houses of worship and an education system that provided learning for members of their community. Tuang Guru emerged as leader and when he died there was a leadership vacuum, but Shaykh Yusuf introduced mystical practices (*tasawwuf*). They also practiced *dhikr*, the repetition of divine names in liturgy. A folk Islam continued to grow in the Cape. In the Natal region, Indians who came to South Africa brought Islam with them and Sufi leaders Badsha Pir and Sufi Sahib. Badsha belonged to the Quadiryah Order and it is believed that he had powers to perform miracles. Sufi Sahib took over leadership after Badsha Pir and carried out reforms and expanded the building of mosques in Natal, at the Cape and in Lesotho.

Studies demonstrate that Islamic brotherhoods and orders have promoted the growth of Islam in Africa (Brenner 1984; Robinson 2000). Abd al-Quadir al-Jilani's order, the Quadiryah Mukhatariyas which was founded in Baghdad in the twelfth century has been present in Africa. Perhaps its prominent member was Shaikh 'Uthman dan Fodio, one of the best known mystics of the order, devoted his life to prayer and meditation and sought to follow the Prophet as closely as he could (Hiskert 1994). His devotional life attracted a great following and people consulted him for advice. The Shehu was a reformer of the faith, and carried out his reforms by condemning local religions and their gods and spirits. He also carried out a *jihad* of purification that had religious as well as political implications because his teachings and practices consolidated the Sokoto Caliphate (Johnston 1967: 111).

The Tijaniyah Order was founded by Ahmad al-Tijani. Two groups grew out of this order; the Hamalliyah which was founded by Shaikh Ahmad Hamallah and the Nassiyah also called the Ibrahimiyah which founded by Shaikh Ibrahim Niass of Senegal. The Order has followers in other parts of West Africa. The Sanusiyah Order was founded by Muhammade al-Sanusi and Muhammad 'Uthman al-Mairghani founded the Mirghaniyah Order. Students of Ibn Idris founded the Rashidiyah Order that is prominent in Somalia. Shaikh Amadu Bamba founded the Muridiyah Order in Senegal. French colonialists considered him a threat to the empire, even though Bamba never preached any violence. The Muridiyah order has Africanised Islam in Senegal and Africa, and become a symbol of resistance to power, and the image of Bamba has become an important icon in the urban landscape of Senegal (Roberts and Roberts (2003).

Scholars have also explored Islam as a way of life that offers 'a new language, new concepts of law and government, and new standards of dress and architecture' (Mousa 1995: 129). As a religion and faith, it has advanced through conversion. It was also associated with enslavement of Africans, but it was not associated with the colonial edifice as Christianity was. Muslims believe in and practise the five tenets of the religion, the profession of faith in Allah as the only God, saying prayers five times a day, fasting at the time of Ramadan, alms giving, and pilgrimage to Mecca. The spread, teachings, and practice of Islam in Africa benefited greatly from several Sufi orders. The orders have teachings, prayers, and litanies, and disciplines all exercised in relationship between the Sufi spiritual leaders and their disciples. The disciples in turn receive *Baraka* (blessing).

One of the most fascinating things in the study of Islam has been the recovery of Islamic scholarship that thrived in West Africa with centres of learning established at Timbuktu, Jenne, Takedda, Katsina and Gazargamu. Scholars who were trained in these centres served the community in various functions. Many of the scholars wanted to see an Islamic society and this concern generated some of the jihads of the eighteenth and nineteenth century. The most well-known jihads were those of Malik Sy which took place in 1690, and the jihads of Uthman dan Fodio which consolidated the Sokoto empire, and the jihad of al-Hajj 'Umar Tal, in Mali.

Islamic theology and law has developed with an emphasis on a belief in God and the written word. The different schools of Muslim laws have also maintained a tolerant attitude towards what is considered local culture (*urf*). Under the leadership of the Almoravid and Sanhaja led by Abdallah ibn Yasin, Maliki theology and law was introduced in parts of Africa. Maliki thought eventually reached the Sudan after the establishment of the Funji sultanate in the sixteenth century. The Maliki school's (*madhhab*) influence has stretched from the Sudan to Senegal. They specialise in the *Musatta*, of Malik ibn Anas, the *Tafsir al-Jalalayn* of Mahalli and Jalala al-Din al Suyuti, The *Risala* of Ibn Abi Zayd al-Qayrawani, and the *Mukhurusae* of Khalil ibn Isap al-Jundi. In other places in Africa legal influences include the Hanafis, Boharas, Khojas, and Ithna Asharis. Maliki thought took root in the Sudanic towns and developed its own perspective on law and theology by incorporating local customs. The judgments of the qadis were grounded on the divine law and local *ulamas* played an important role (Anderson 1955; Spaulding 1985; Honwick 1985; Pouwels 1978a, 1978b). Maliki law and theology later influenced the *Qadiriya* and the *Tijaniya*, and their influence led to greater interest in the *shari'a* in the region.

In East Africa, Islamic law and theology was studied in the Lamu Archipelago, and qadis were established in coastal towns as well as in rural Zanzibar. The most well known scholar in the region was Sayyid Ahmad who studied in Yemen and was for sometime the leading Shafi'i in Zanzibar. Shaikh Abdallah Bakathir was instrumental in spreading Shafi'i thought in East and South Africa.

In the post-neocolonial era, governments have often intervened in the interpretation of Islamic law, sometimes promoting local customs, or inducting local qadis into the judicial system of the state, the exception being Zanzibar and Northern Nigeria where Islamic law has been recognised, but even in Nigeria, the issue remains contentious. There is widespread belief in some quarters that strict adherence to Islamic law would undercut the rights of women.

Scholars have also studied social activism among Muslim scholars and the faithful in Africa. Abdulkader Tayob has argued that Islamic revivalism in South Africa today is being studied as a search for identity and a contribution to nation building

(Tayob 1996: 293). Muslims have also taken part in acts of civil disobedience. They formed organisations such as the South African Moslem Association, the Cape Malay Association and the Habibia Muslim Society. A Muslim Progressive Society was formed in 1942 and the Muslim Judicial Council was established in 1945 to take up social issues and provide relief to its members. In 1975, the Islamic Council of South Africa was formed and it became the umbrella organisation for Muslims. The Muslim Youth Movement of South Africa also promoted the study of Arabic and a modernisation project and kept a distance from the *ulama* (Mousa 1995: 148-9). The Islamic Brotherhoods of Egypt and groups in Pakistan influenced them. They also set up organisations that worked to promote the welfare of their members. Mousa argues that they lacked the religious language to articulate their positions during the crucial Soweto riots of 1976. However, during the 1980s they articulated a message of liberation condemning oppression (*zulm*), claimed that God takes sides with the poor (*mustad 'afin*), and called for justice (*adl*) and equity (*qist*). They placed all these goals in the context of a *jihad*.

Islamic politics and social norms have had a problematic relationship in some contexts in Africa. For example, conversion to the religion has meant that the new follower would abandon the practice of traditional religion. For local rulers this has often created a situation of conflict since the ruler had to abandon some traditional practices. Some have questioned the status of women under Islam because they have inferior rights to men. It is for this and other reasons that the Shari'a question in Islam has been contentious in Nigeria and Sudan. In both countries, a segment of the country advocates the institutionalisation of shari'a law as the legal instrument of the land. Opponents reject the imposition of Shari'a, arguing that it is a religious legal system that cannot be imposed on a secular state. In Nigeria, opponents point to the sentencing of Amina Lawal to death under Shari'a law for committing adultery, and remark on the gender biased aspects of Shari'a law and the kind of problems that the country could face were it to turn to a strictly religious order as a tool of governance. In addition to the shari'a issue, both Nigeria and Sudan have experienced violence that has been defined along Christian/Muslin lines (Falola 1998).

Future Challenges and Research Questions

Religion is alive and thriving in Africa. Scholars continue to discover that despite the changes that have taken place on the continent, Africans continue to adapt their religious life to meet daily challenges and celebrate their humanity. In a continent that some would rather write off, the religious life of the people demonstrates that one cannot dismiss the continent because it is vital, and that vitality is evident in its religious imagination. However, there is no denying that Africa is at the crossroads today and once more is looking to its symbolic resources to cope with the hand that has been dealt them by several forces, modernity, colonialism and its successor, what I call the post-neocolonial state, or maybe just simple fate. If one looks at the way things are today, one would almost say that African religions have a secure place and those who promote these traditions need not worry because they have a captive audience. Several issues call for further exploration.

(i) Religious Conceptualisation of the Spirit

If there is one religious symbol that all religious communities share that is divisive, but is employed constantly to claim divine anointing and legitimate alternative religious experience, it is the symbol of spirit. Scholars explored the idea of spirit in indigenous religions extensively (Evans-Pritchard 1961). Scholars have also paid attention to the reawakening of the spirit in African churches and AICs (Comaroff 1985; Gifford 1998; Meyer 1999). *Glossolalia* is alive and claims to be providing wealth and healing in the post-neocolonial state. Although some Islamic authorities condemn the spirits referred to in Islam as *jinn* or *shetani,* the persistence and good following that *bori,* and *zar* spirits possession cults continue to attract is an indication that spirits and spirit possession has a staying power and will continue to influence individuals (Lewis 1971; Lambek 1981; Boddy 1989; Murphy 1994). What needs probing here in my view is not only the nature and reality of the spirits, but the impact that belief in the power spirits has on the processes that shape interpersonal, economic, and political relationships.

(ii) Religion and the State

The concern I express here deals with religion and state in particular because in Africa it has become an issue and will remain an issue given the nature of politics in the post-neocolonial state. Religious leaders from different traditions have fought the excesses of power in Zimbabwe, Namibia, and South Africa. The crisis of the post-neocolonial state forced many religious leaders in Africa to rethink their often cozy relationship with the leaders of the post-neocolonial state. Some religious leaders worked with political leaders during the short-lived transition to democracy (Phiri 2001; Nwel 1995: 171, 178). Religious communities need to maintain a new vigilance in their relationship with the post-neocolonial state. The task ahead requires new calls for freedoms, human rights, justice, and the eradication of poverty. The present turn to manifestations of the spirit in Africa might actually be symptomatic of the failure of religious groups to carry out their prophetic task. Religious communities might put together a new ecumenical effort in each country to articulate the desires and aspirations of the African people to the politicians and work with them on a regular basis for justice.

(iii) Religious Violence: Towards a Culture Pluralism and Tolerance

Violence and genocide have held Africa hostage, and religion has been caught up in this violence, in some cases being the driving force. The violence that has rocked Nigeria and Sudan in the past may be symptomatic of conditions in the post-neocolonial state, but it is manifested immediately in religious intolerance. Religious communities have no choice but to rethink their priorities in light of the violence that many communities face in Africa. Religion can and ought to be a source and force of reconciliation. Religions communities in Africa must reorganise and promote peace building. Peace and peace building has now shifted from a political concern and become an area of study (Bongmba 2006: 173-174; Lederach 1999, 2004). Religious communities must work with warring parties to negotiate peace and religious leaders ought to be available to mediate.

(iv) Religion and Gender

The relations between men and women and the overall state of gender relations in society demand attention in all religious communities. It is no longer acceptable to assume that women were created to be helpers. Women and men are partners in a common human journey. Women have fought their subjugation in many ways, and for the struggle for equality to take place, religious communities ought to be places where radical equality begins. While there are many ways in which equality can be demonstrated, one of the ways to work and change the entire gender dynamics is for women to assume more leadership roles in religious life.

(v) Religion and Felt Needs

One of the reasons African Initiated Churches (AIC) sprouted throughout Africa was the fact that their felt needs were not being addressed in mainline or missionary churches. One of those felt needs has always been physical well-being. That quest for well-being has generated an eternal 'quest for therapy' (if I may use Jansen's well-known expression). In indigenous religions, this quest was structured in an aetiology that ascribed illness and healing to supernatural forces that work through several human intermediaries (diviners, *ngangas, nga mshep, sangomas*). People who shared this world view often had physical representations of the search for well-being and power in art objects (MacGaffey 1991; MacGaffey and Harris 1993; Bockie 1993: 132). The quest for power to overcome illness and disease has increased and if anything has been greatly compromised by the HIV/AIDS crisis that seems to make a mockery of all the beliefs that religious traditions share about illness, health and healing. How religious traditions proceed on this matter is going to be crucial for the future because one can no longer think that a utopian eschatology is enough. The 'quest for therapy' must proceed in an interdisciplinary manner drawing from spiritual resources which inspire the spirit to cope, while working for reforms in the public health sector.

(vi) Religion and the Occult: Witchcraft

One of the things that religious communities have to reckon with is the rising belief in the use of occult powers, especially witchcraft. Witchcraft beliefs remain strong in many communities and the belief in its power continues to pose a serious challenge to individual and communal well-being. It is clear now that whether one believes that something exists as witchcraft or not, the social world of witchcraft remains active, often manifesting itself in accusations, the visits to diviners, counter accusations, expulsions from the community, beatings, and some cases killings. Unfortunately, these beliefs continue to affect women disproportionately, and they are often the victims of great violence. The religious communities in Africa need to hold an inter-religious dialogue on the challenges posed by witchcraft and come up with ways of handling the matter in love (Bongmba 2001).

Notes

1. These religions include African Indigenous Religions, often called traditional religions, Christianity, Islam, Judaism, Sikhism, Parsee, Jainism, Chinese Religions, Buddhism, Baha'i, and Religions of the African Diaspora returning to Africa. See Jan Platvoet, and Jacob Olupona (1996: 16).

2. Bouquet (1933) argued that the idea of a high God among Africans was based on Deism.

3. See R. S. Rattray's works (1927a, 1927b); H. A. Junod (1912). P. A. Talbot (1969) argued that the religion of Africa resembled that of Egypt, but it must have suffered retrogression when contact was made with the northern Africans. The resemblances were found in the idea of a supreme Deity and different divinities. Also see W. C. Willoughby (1928).

4. Leading scholars were Max Gluckman Clyde Mitchell, Godfrey Wilson, Monica Wilson and Victor Turner (1967, 1969) whose work *Schism and Continuity in an African Society* powerfully signalled the methodological approach of the Manchester School.

5. There are other Africans who have studied African religions, whose work also shaped the field. These scholars were white South Africans who later became part of the British academic establishment. This group of scholars did field work in Africa and published widely on different aspects of African life. These scholars include Meyer Fortes, Max Gluckman, Isaac Shapera, Hilda Kuper, Monica (Hunter) Wilson, Audrey Richards, Elisabeth Colson and Max G. Marwick. Fortes, in particular, did pioneering studies of personhood and psychological dimensions of religious life as well as religion and morality in the African context. I suspect that the day will come when it would be possible to identify these academics as African scholars even though they lived and taught in British universities for most of their careers.

6. In East Africa, the Nyabingi Cult of the nineteenth Century, and in Tanzania, the Maji Maji movement of Kinjikitile, both used local medicines to resist the colonial presence. The Mambo Cult in Kenya, the Mwari Cult in Zimbabwe, and Poro in Sierra Leone also used their religious views to resist colonial authority.

7. Schoffeleers (1992).

8. There are three associations for the study of religion in Africa: The Nigerian Association of the Study of Religions (NASR), founded in 1976 and which joined the International Association of the History of Religions (IAHR) in 1980; The Association of the Study of Religions in South Africa (ASRSA) established in 1979 and joined IAHR in 1980; and the African Association for the Study of Religions (AASR) founded at the end of the 1992 conference in Harare and joined IAHR in 1995.

9. The terms 'diatopical hermeneutics' was proposed by Panikkar and Krieger who offer it as an alternative to conversion in a confessional sense through which one joins another religion. Such a conversion does not contribute to knowledge of two religions, the old religion and the new one that is embraced in conversion (Cox 1996: 155 ff).

10. In addition to Durkheim, other theorists like Max Müller, Edward Tyler, Herbert Spencer, James Frazer, Rudolf Otto, William James, E.O. James, made the connection between ritual and religion, and in much of the literature ritual is seen as the social manifestation of religion.

In other words in rituals, people act out their religious beliefs. On secular rituals, see Ronald Grimes (1982).

11. The idea of African conversion was the subject of an important study by Robin Horton (1971) in response to the work of John Peel (1968).

12. Today the member churches of Federation des Eglises et Mission Evangeliques du Cameroun (FEMEC) operate 137 health institutions in the country with 25 hospitals.

13. Paul Gifford (1998).

14. Hastings (1996: 258) has described the nineteenth-century missionary as a 'working man' He adds: 'He was an artisan, a worker with a skill, and even such clergy as went were seldom of a very different background. Even the rather grand Dr Philip was the same ... Missionaries of Philip's generation... were quintessentially Free Churchmen who received and expected from government at home little but an uneasy tolerance'. However, there were also university trained individuals and scholars who joined the ranks, including Newton Adams of the American Board of Mission, Bishop McKenzie, James Stewart, Robert Laws, William Elmsie, and Henry Callaway. Hastings (1996:265) has called Livingstone and Colenso the 'intellectual princes of the nineteenth missionary movement'.

15. In his assessment of Christianity in Africa, T. A. Beetham (1967: chapter 3) argued that the weakness of the church shortly after independence included missionary control, dependence on foreign funds, a large investment of resources in education, disunity, lack of a strong African ministry, polygamy, race relations, a slow process of indigenisation, etc.

16. Some participants in theological discourse employed the philosophical categories of Aristotle, (see Bahoken 1967; Lufuluabo 1966; Mulago1965: 37; Mudimbe 1991: 33).

17. Mulago's Centre d'Etude des Religions Africaines has contributed to the understanding of African religious thought through a number of publications and seminars on theology and philosophy, pp. 53 ff.

18. Some of the material here is taken from Elias K. Bongmba (2006: 148).

19. The discussion of the Christian Reform Movements in Africa draws from Elias K. Bongmba (2003).

20. These churches have also been called Independent churches, Prophetic Movements, New Religious Movements, and African Indigenous Churches.

21. Sundkler (1961: 17).

22. My short discussion of Islam has benefited from the work of scholars of Islam, especially Nehemial Levtzion (2000), Randall L. Pouwels (1987), J. S. Trimingham (1964), David Sperling (1985), Mervyn Hiskett (1994), Louis Brenner (1984), B. G. Martin (2003), Muhammad Sani Umar (2006) and many others.

23. Cheikh Hamidou Kane (1972) fictionalises the effectiveness of Quranic schools in his work novel *Ambiguous Adventure*.

References

Ajayi, J. F. A., 1965, *Christian Missions in Nigeria, 1841-1891: The Making of a New Elite*, Evanston: Northwestern University Press.

Anderson, A., 2001, *The African Reformation: African Initiated Christianity in the 20th Century*, Trenton, NJ : Africa World Press.

Anderson, J., 1955, *Islamic Law in Africa*, London: Frank Cass.

Ayandele, E., 1966, *The Missionary Impact on Modern Nigeria, 1842-1914: A Political and Social Analysis*, London: Longman.

Ayandele, E., 1978, 'The Aladura Among the Yoruba: A Challenge to the "Orthodox" Churches', in O. Kalu, ed., *Christianity in West Africa: The Nigerian Story*, Ibadan: Daystar Press.

Ayegboyin, D. and S. A. Ishola, 1997, *African Indigenous Churches: An Historical Perspective*, Lagos: Greater Heights Publication.

Bahoken, J.C., 1967, *Clairiéres métaphysiques afriaines*, Paris: Présence Africaine.

Barrett, D., 1968, *Schism and Renewal in Africa: An Analysis of Six Thousand Contemporary Religious Movements*, Nairobi: Oxford University Press.

Bauer, J., 1994, *2000 Years of Christianity in Africa: An African History*, Nairobi: Paulines Publications.

Beetham, T.A., 1967, *Christianity and the New Africa*, New York: Praeger.

Beidelman, T.O., 1974, 'Social Theory and the Study of Christian Missions in Africa', *Africa*, XLIV: 235-249.

Beidelman, T. O., 1982, *Colonial Evangelism: A Socio-Historical Study of an East African Mission at the Grassroots*, Bloomington: Indiana University Press.

Bell, C., 1997, *Ritual: Perspectives and Dimensions*, New York: Oxford University Press.

Benjamin, R., 1976, *African Traditional Religion: Symbol, Ritual and Community*, Englewood Cliffs, NJ: Prentice Hall

Blakely T. D., E. A. van B. Walter, and L. T. Dennis, eds., 1994, *Religion in Africa: Experience & Expression*, London: James Currey.

Bockie, S., 1993, *Death and the Invisible Powers: The World of Kongo Belief*, Bloomington and Indianapolis: Indiana University Press.

Boddy, J., 1989, *Wombs and Alien Spirits, Women, Men and the Zar Cult in Northern Sudan*, Madison: University of Wisconsin Press.

Bongmba, E.K., 2001, *African Witchcraft and Otherness: A Philosophical and Theological Critique of Intersubjective Relations*, Albany: State University of New York Press.

Bongmba, E. K., 2003, 'Christian Reform Movements', in P. T. Zeleza and D. Eyoh, eds., *Encyclopeadia of Twentieth-Century African History*, London and New York: Routledge, 77-83.

Bongmba, E.K., 2006, *The Dialectics of Transformation in Africa*, New York: Palgrave Macmillan.

Bouquet, A.C., 1933, *Man and Deity*, Cambridge: Heffer.

Bourdillon, M., 1996, 'Anthropological Approaches to the Study of African Religion', in J. Platvoet, J. Cox, and J. Olupona, eds., *The Study of Religions in Africa: Past, Present and Prospects*, Cambridge: Roots and Branches.

Brenner, L., 1984, *West African Sufi: The Religious Heritage and Spiritual Search of Ceerno Bokar Saalif Taal*, Berkeley: University of California Press.

Browne, M., ed., 1996, *The African Synod: Documents, Reflections and Perspectives*, Maryknoll: Orbis Books.

Bruton, E., 1802, *A Grammar and Vocabulary of the Susoo Language: to which are added Names of the Susoo Towns*. Publisher etc.

Busia, K.A., 1954, 'The Ashanti of the Gold Coast', in D. Forde, ed., *African Worlds: Studies in he Cosmological Idea and Social Values of African Peoples*, London: Oxford University Press.

Chidester, D., J. Tobler and D. Wratten. eds., 1997, *Christianity in South Africa: An Annotated Bibliography*, Westport, CT: Greenwood Press.

Clarke, P., 1982, *West Africa and Islam: A Study of Religious Development from the 8th to the 20th Century*, London: Edward Arnold.

Clarke, P., 1986, *West African and Christianity*, London: Edward Arnold.

Comaroff, J., 1985, *Body of Power, Spirit of Resistance: The Culture and History of a South African People*, Chicago: University of Chicago Press.

Comaroff, J. and J.L. Comaroff, 1991, *Of Revelation and Revolution: Christianity, Colonialism, and Consciousness in South Africa*, Vol. One, Chicago: The University of Chicago Press.

Comaroff, J. and J.L. Comaroff, 1993, *Modernity and its Malcontents: Ritual and Power in Postcolonial Africa*, Chicago: University of Chicago Press.

Comaroff, J.L. and J. Comaroff, 1997, *Of Revelation and Revolution: Christianity, Colonialism, and Consciousness in South Africa*, Vol. Two, *The Dialectics of Modernity on a South African Frontier*, Chicago: University of Chicago Press.

Cox, J., 1996, 'Methodological Considerations Relevant to Understanding African Indigenous Religions', in J. Platvoet, J. Cox, and J. Olupona, eds., *The Study of Religions in Africa: Past, Present and Prospects*, Cambridge: Roots and Branches.

Crumbley, D.H., 1992, 'Impurity and Power: Women in Aladura Churches', *Africa* 62 (4): 505-522.

Crumbley, D.H., 2003, 'Patriarchies, Prophets, and Procreation: Sources of Gender Practices in Three African Churches', *Africa* 73 (4): 584-605.

Crummey, D., 1972, *Priest and Politicians: Protestant and Catholic Missions in Orthodox Ethiopia 1830-1868*, Oxford: Clarendon Press.

Crummey, D., 2000, *Land and Society in the Christian Kingdom of Ethiopia: From the Thirteenth to the Twentieth Century*, Urbana: University of Illinois Press.

Daneel, M.L., 1970, *The God of the Matopo Hills: an essay on the Mwari cult in Rhodesia*, The Hague: Mouton.

Daneel, M.L., 1999, *African Earthkeepers Vol 2: Environmental Mission and Liberation in Christian Perspective*, Pretoria: UNISA Press.

de Gruchy, J.W., 1970, *The Church Struggle in South Africa*, Grand Rapids: E. B. Eerdmans Publishing.

Dube, M.S., 2000, *Postcolonial Feminist Interpretation of the Bible*, St. Louis, MO: Chalice Press.

Durkheim, E., 1995, *The Elementary Forms of Religious Life*, translated by Karen Fields, New York: The Free Press.

Eboussi-Boulaga, F., 1978, *Christianity without Fetishes: An African Critique and Recapture of Christianity*, translated by Robert Barr, Maryknoll: Orbis Books.

Elbourne, E., 2002, *Blood Ground: Colonialism, Missions, and the Contest for Christianity in the Cape Colony and Britain, 1799-1853*, Montreal: McGill University Press.

Elphick, R. and R. Davenport, eds., 1997, *Christianity in South Africa: A Political, Social, and Cultural History*, Berkeley: University of California Press.

Etherington, N., 1977, 'Social Theory and the Study of Christian Missions in Africa: A South African Case Study', *Africa* 47 (1): 31-40.

Etherington, N., 1978, *Preachers, Peasants and Politics in Southern Africa Preachers, Peasants and Politics in Southeast Africa 1835-1880*, London: Boydell and Brewer.

Etherington, N., 1987, 'Missionary doctors and African healers in mid-Victorian South Africa', *South African Historical Journal* XIX: 77-92.

Evans-Pritchard, E.E., 1961, *Nuer Religion*, Oxford: Clarendon Press.

Fabian, J., 1971, *JAMAA: A Charismatic Movement in Katanga*, Evanston, Ill.: Northwestern University Press.

Falk, P., 1978, *The Growth of the Church in Africa*, Grand Rapids, Mich.: Zondervan.

Falola, T., 1998, *Violence in Nigeria: The Crises of Religious Politics and Secular Ideologies*, Rochester: Rochester University Press.

Fasholé-Luke, E., R. Gray, A. Hastings and G. Tasie, eds., 1978, *Christianity in Independent Africa*, Bloomington: Indiana University Press.

Fernandez, J.W., 1964, 'African Religious Movements, Types and Dynamics', *Modern African Studies*, 2, 4: 531-549.

Gifford, P., 1993, *Christianity and Politics in Doe's Liberia*, Cambridge: Cambridge University Press.

Gifford, P., 1998, *African Christianity: Its Public Role*, Bloomington: Indiana University Press.

Gifford, P., ed., 1995, *The Christian Churches and the Democratisation of Africa*, Leiden: E. J. Brill.

Githieya, F.K., 1997, *The Freedom of the Spirit: African Indigenous Churches in Kenya*, Atlanta: Scholars Press.

Gluckman, Max, 1960, 'Rituals of Rebellion in South-East Africa,' in *Order and Rebellion*, New York: The Free Press.

Good Jr., C. M., 2004, *The Steamer Parish: The Rise and Fall of Missionary Medicine on an African Frontier*, Chicago: University of Chicago Press.

Griaule, M., 1963, *Conversations with Ogotemmêli: An Introduction to Dogon Religious Ideas*, London: Oxford University Press.

Grimes, R., 1982, *Beginnings in Ritual Studies*, Washington: University Press of America.

Grimes, R., 1984, 'Sources for the Study of Ritual', *Religious Studies Review* 10 (2): 134-145.

Haar, G. ter, ed., 2001, *Religious communities in the Diaspora*, Nairobi: Acton Publishers.

Hackett, R.I.J., 1996, Art and Religion in Africa, London: Cassel.

Haliburton, G.H., 1973, *The Prophet Harris: A Study of an African Prophet and his Mass-Movement in the Ivory coast and the Gold Coast, 1913-1915*, New York: Oxford University Press.

Hallencreutz, C. and A. Moyo, eds., 1991, *Religion and Politics in Southern Africa*, Uppsala: Scandinavian Institute of African Studies.

Hastings, A., 1979, *A History of African Christianity 1950-1975*, Cambridge: Cambridge University Press.

Hastings, A., 1996, *The Church in Africa, 1450-1950*, New York: Oxford University Press, 1994.

Headrick, R. and D.R. Headrick, eds., 1994, *Colonialism, Health and Illness in French Equatorial Africa, 1885-1935*, Atlanta, GA: African Studies Association Press.

Hiskert, M., 1994, *Sword and the Truth, the Life and Times of Shehu Usman dan Fodio*, Evanston, Ill: Northwestern University Press.

Hunwick, J. O., ed. and trans., 1985, *Sharia in Songhay: The Replies of al-Maghili to the Questions of Askia al-Hajj Muhammad*, London: Oxford University Press.

Horton, R., 1971, 'African Conversion', *Africa* 41 (2): 85-108.

Horton, R., 1975, 'On the Rationality of Conversion', *Africa* 45 (3-4): 219-35, 372-99.

Idowu, E.B., 1962, *Olodumare: God in Yoruba Belief*, London: Longman.

Idowu, E.B., 1968, 'Trends and Prospects in African Christianity', in C.G. Baëta, ed., *Christianity in Tropical Africa*, London: Oxford University Press.

Idowu, E.B., 1973, *African Religions: A Definition*, Maryknoll: Orbis Books.

Isichei, E., 1995, *A History of Christianity in Africa*, Grand Rapids, Mich.: Eerdmans Publishing Company.

James, W., 1988, 'Uduk Faith in a Five-tone Scale: Mission Music and the Spread of the Gospel', in D. Johnson and W. James, eds., *Vernacular Christianity*, New York: Lilian Barber Press, 131-145.

Johnston, H.A.S., 1967, *The Fulani Empire of Sokoto*, London: Oxford University Press.

Jules-Rosette, B., 1975, *African Apostles: Ritual and conversion in the Church of John Maranke*, Ithaca: Cornell University Press.

Junod, H.A., 1912, *The Life of a South African Tribe*, Neuchâtel: Attinger Fréres.

Kalu, O.U., 1980, 'Church, Mission and Moratorium', in O. U. Kalu, ed., *The History of Christianity in West Africa*, London: Longman, 365-374.

Kane, C.H., 1972, *Ambiguous Adventure*, London: Heinemann.

Kenyatta, J., 1959, *Facing Mount Kenya: The Tribal Life of the Gikuyu*, with an introduction by B. Malinowski, London: Secker and Warburg.

Kirwen, M.C., 1979, *African Widows: An Empirical Study of the Problems of Adapting Western Christian Teachings on Marriage to the Leviratic Custom for the Care of Widows in Four Rural African Societies*, Maryknoll: Orbis Books.

Knappert, J., 1970, *Myths and Legends of the Swahili*, London: Heinemann Educational Books.

Koelle, S.W., 1854, *Polyglotta Africana or a Comparative Vocabulary of nearly 300 words and phrases in more than One Hundred Distinct African Languages*, London: Church Missionary House.

Lambek, M., 1981, *Human Spirits: A Cultural Account of Trance in Mayotte*, Cambridge: Cambridge University Press.

Lawson, E.T. and R.N. McCauley, 1990, *Rethinking Religion: Connecting, Cognition, and Culture*, Cambridge and New York: Cambridge University Press.

Lederach, J.P., 1999, *The Journey toward Reconciliation*, foreword by Harold H. Saunders, Scottsdale, PA: Herald Press.

Lederach, J.P., 2004, *The Moral Imagination : The Art and Soul of Building Peace*, Oxford: Oxford University Press.

Levi-Strauss, C., 1981, *The Naked Man*, trans. John and Doreen Weightman, New York: Harper and Row.

Levtzion, N., 2000, 'Islam in the Bilad as-Sudan to 1800', in N. Levtzion and R. L. Pouwel, eds., *The History of Islam in Africa*, Athens: Ohio University Press, 63-91.

Lewis, I.M., 1965, *The Modern History of Somaliland, from Nation to State*, New York: Praeger.

Lewis, I.M., 1969, *Peoples of the Horn of Africa: Somali, Afar, and Saho*, London: International African Institute.

Lewis, I.M., 1971, *Ecstatic Religion: Anthropological Study of Spirit Possession and Shamanism*, Baltimore: Penguin Books.

Lewis, R.H., 1906, 'Medicine at Molepolole', *Chronicles of the London Missionary Society*, XV.

Liendhardt, G., 1961, *Divinity and Experience: The Religion of the Dinka*, Oxford: Clarendon Press.

Lufuluabo, F.M., 1966, *Perspective théologique bantou at théologie scholastique*, Malines: St. François.

MacGaffey, W., 1983, *Modern Kongo Prophets: Religion in a Plural Society*, Bloomington: Indiana University Press

MacGaffey, W., 1991, *Art and Healing of the Bakongo Commented by Themselves: Minkisi from the Laman collection*, Stockholm: Folkens Museum.

MacGaffey, W. and M. D. Harris, 1993, *Astonishment and Power*, Washington DC: The Smithsonian Institution Press.

Makhubu, P., 1988, *Who Are the Independent Churches?*, Johannesburg: Skotaville Publishers.

Martin, B.G., 1974, 'Arab Migration to East Africa in Medieval Times', *International Journal of African Studies* 7: 367-390.

Martin, B.G., 2003, *Muslim Brotherhoods in Nineteenth-Century Africa*, Cambridge: Cambridge University Press.

Martin, M-L., 1976, *Kimbangu: An African Prophet and His Church*, with forward by Bryan R. Wilson, translated by D. M. More, Grand Rapids, Mich: William B. Eerdmans Publishing.

Mbembe, A., 1988, *Afriques Indociles. Christianisme, Pouvoir et Etat en Societé Postcoloniale*, Paris: Karthala.

Mbiti, J., 1970, *Concepts of God in Africa*, New York: Praeger Publishers.

Mbiti, J., 1971, *Introduction to African Religion*, Second edition, Oxford: Heinemann Educational Books.

Mbiti, John, 1984, 'Christianity Tilts to the South: A New Challenge for Christian Ministry and Theological Education', *Indian Journal of Theology* 33 (Jan.): 1-9.

Mbon, F., 1996, 'Some Methodological Issues in the Academic Study of West African Traditional Religions', in J. Platvoet, J. Cox, and J. Olupona, eds., *The Study of Religions in Africa: Past, Present and Prospects*, Cambridge: Roots and Branches.

McCracken, J., 1977, *Politics and Christianity in Malawi, 1875-1940: the Impact of the Livingstonia Mission in the Northern Province*, Cambridge: Cambridge University Press.

Meyer, B., 1999, *Translating the Devil: Religion and Modernity among the E we in Ghana*, Edinburgh: Edinburgh University Press.

Middleton, J., 1992, *The world of Swahili: An African Mercantile Civilization*, New Haven, CT: Yale University Press.

Monohan, B.M., 2004, 'Writing, Sharing, Doing: The Circle of Concerned African Women Theologians', BA Honors Thesis, Boston College.

Mosala, I., 1989, *Biblical hermeneutics and Black Theology in South Africa*, Grand Rapids: W. B. Eerdmans Publishing.

Mousa, E., 1995, 'Islam in South Africa', in M. Prozesky and J. de Gruchy, eds., *Living Faiths in South Africa*, Cape Town: David Philip, 129-154.

Mudimbe, V.Y., 1991, *Parables and Fables: Exegesis, Textuality, and Politics in Central Africa*, Madison: University of Wisconsin Press.

Mulago, V., 1965, *Un visage africain du christianisme*, Paris: Présence Africaine.

Murphy, J., 1994, *Working the Spirits: Ceremonies of the African Diaspora*, Boston: Beacon Press.

Njeroge, N.J., 1997, 'The Missing Voice: African Women Doing Theology', *Journal of Theology for Southern Africa* 99 (November): 77-83.

Nwafor, J. C., 2002, *Church and State: The Nigerian Experience*, Frankfurt am Main: IKO Verlag.

Nwel, P. T., 1995, 'The Churches and the Democratic Upheaval in Cameroon 1982-1993', in P. Gifford, ed., *The Christian Churches and the Democratisation of Africa*, Leiden: E. J. Brill.

Oduyoye, M.A., 1986, *Hearing and Knowing: Theological Reflections on Christianity in Africa*, Maryknoll: Orbis Books.

Oduyoye, M.A., 1989, 'The Circle', in M.A. Oduyoye and M.R.A. Kanyoro, eds., *Talitha Qumi!: Proceedings of the Convocation of African Women Theologians*, Ibadan: Daystar Press.

Okorcha, C.C., 1987, *The Meaning of Religious conversion in Africa: The Case of the Igbo of Nigeria*, Aldershot: Avebury.

Okullu, H., 1974, *Church and Politics in Africa*, Nairobi: Uzima Press.

Olupona, J., 1991, *Kingship, Religion, and Rituals in a Nigerian Community: A Phenomenological Study of Ondo Yoruba Festivals*, Stockholm: Aimqvist & Wiksell International.

Olupona, J., ed., forthcoming, *African Immigrant Religions in America*.

Omoyajowo, J.A., 1982, *Cherubim and Seraphim: The History of an African Independent Church*, New York and Lagos: NOK Publishers.

Oosthuizen, G.C., 1968, *Post Christianity in Africa: A Theological and Anthropological Study*, Grand Rapids, Mich: William B. Eerdmans Publishing Company.

Oyewumi, O., 1997, *The Invention of Women*, Minneapolis: University of Minnesota Press.

p'Bitek, O., 1971, *African Religions in Western Scholarship*, Nairobi: East African Literature Bureau.

Parrinder, E.G., 1969, *West African Religion*, London: Epworth Press.

Pearson, B.A. and J.E. Goehring, eds., 1986, *The Roots of Egyptian Christianity*, Philadelphia: Fortress Press.

Peel, J.D.Y., 1968, *Aladura: A Religious Movement Among the Yoruba*, London: Oxford University Press.

Pemberton, C., 2003, *Circle Thinking: African Women Theologians in Dialogue with the West*, Leiden and Boston: Brill.

Phiri, I.A., 1997, 'Doing Theology in Community: The Case of African Women Theologians in the 1990s', *Journal of Theology for Southern Africa* 99 (November): 68-76.

Phiri, I.A., 2001, *Proclaiming Political Pluralism: Churches and Political Transitions in Africa*, Westport, CT: Praeger.

Platvoet, J., 1996, 'From Object to Subject: A History of the Study of the Religions of Africa', in J. Platvoet, J. Cox, and J. Olupona, eds., *The Study of Religions in Africa: Past, Present and Prospects*, Cambridge: Roots and Branches.

Platvoet, J. and J. Olupona, eds., 1996, 'Perspectives on the Study of Religions in Sub-Saharan Africa', in J. Platvoet, J. Cox, and J. Olupona, eds., *The Study of Religions in Africa: Past, Present and Prospects*, Cambridge: Roots and Branches.

Pouwels, R.L., 1985a, 'The Medieval Foundations of East Africa Islam', *International Journal of African Historical Studies* 11 (2): 201-226.

Pouwels, R.L., 1985b, 'The Medieval Foundations of East Africa Islam', *International Journal of African Historical Studies* 11 (3): 393-409.

Pouwels, R.L., 1987, *Horn and Crescent: Cultural Change and Transitional Islam on the East African Coast*, Cambridge: Cambridge University Press.

Radcliffe-Brown, A. R., 1965, 'Religion and Society', *in Structure and Function in Primitive Society*, New York: The Free Press.

Ranger T.O., 1962, *State and Church in Southern Rhodesia*. Salisbury: Historical Association of Rhodesia and Nyasaland, no. 4.

Ranger, T.O. and I.N. Kimambo, eds., 1972, *The Historical Study of African Religion*, Berkeley: University of California Press.

Ranger, T.O. and J. Weller, eds., 1975, *Themes in Christian History in Central Africa*, Berkerley: University of California Press.

Ranger, T.O., 1986, 'Religious Movements and Politics in Sub-Saharan Africa', *African Studies Review* 29 (2): 1-69.

Rattray, R.S., 1927, *Ashanti Religion and Art in Ashanti*, London: Oxford University Press.

Ray, B.C., 1976, *African Religious: Symbol, Ritual and Community*, Englewood Cliffs, N.J.: Prentice Hall.

Roberts, A.F. and M.N. Roberts, 2003, *A Saint in the City: Sufi Arts of Urban Senegal*, Los Angeles: Fowler Museum.

Robinson, D., 2000, *Paths of Accommodation: Muslim Societies and French Colonial Authorities in Senegal and Mauritania*, Athens: Ohio University Press.

Sanderson, L.P., 1980, 'Education in the Southern Sudan: The Impact of government-Missionary-Southern Sudanese Relationships upon the Development of Education during the Condominium Period, 1898-1956', *African Affairs* 79 (315): 157-169.

Sandgren, D.P., 1989, *Christianity and the Kikuyu: Religious Divisions and social Conflict*, New York: Peter Lang.

Sanneh, L., 1977, *The Crown and the Turban: Muslims and West African Pluralism*, Boulder, CO: Westview Press.

Sanneh, L., 1983, *West African Christianity: The Religious Impact*, Maryknoll: Orbis Books.

Sanneh, L., 1989, *Translating the Message*, Maryknoll: Orbis Books.

Sanneh, L., 1996, *Piety and Power: Muslims and Christians in West Africa*, Marynkoll: Orbis Books.

Schoffeleers J.M., ed., 1978, *Guardians of the Land: Essays on Central African Territorial Cults*, Gwelo: Mambo Press.

Schoffeleers, J.M., 1992, *River of Blood: The Genesis of a Martyr Cult in Southern Malawi, A.D. 1600*, Madison: University of Wisconsin Press.

Schram, R., 1972, *A History of the Nigerian Health Services*, Ibadan: Ibadan University Press.

Setiloane, G.M., 1976, *The image of God among the Sotho-Tswana*, Rotterdam: A. A. Balkema.

Shepperson, G., 1958, *Independent African*, Edinburgh: Edinburgh University Press.

Shils, E., 1986, 'Ritual and Crises', in Donald Cutler, ed., *The Religious Situation*, Boston: Beacon Press.

Shorter, A., 1974, *African Culture and the Christian Church: An Introduction to Social and Pastoral Anthropology*, Maryknoll: Orbis Books.

Sindima, H.J., 1994, *Drums of Redemption: An Introduction to African Christianity*, Westport, CT: Greenwood Press.

Spaulding, J., 1985, *The Heroic Age in Sinnar*, East Lansing, Mich: African Studies Center, University of Michigan.

Spear, T., 1999, 'Toward the History of African Christianity', in T. Spear and I.N. Kimambo, eds., *East African Expressions of Christianity*, Oxford: James Currey, 1-24.

Sperling, D., 1985, 'Islamization in the Coastal Region of Kenya to the End of the Nineteenth Century', in B. A. Ogot, ed., *Hadith 8: Kenya in the Nineteenth Century*, Nairobi: East African Publishing House.

Sundkler, B.G. M., 1948, *Bantu Prophets in South Africa*, London: Lutterworth Press.

Talbot, P.A., 1996, *The Peoples of Southern Nigeria: A Sketch of their History, Ethnology, and Languages, with an abstract of the 1921 census*, London: Frank Cass.

Tamrat, T., 1972, *Church and State in Ethiopia 1270-1527*, Oxford: Clarendon Press.

Tasie, G. and R. Gray, 'Introduction', in E. Fasholé-Luke, R. Gray, A. Hastings and G. Tasie, eds., *Christianity in Independent Africa*, Bloomington: Indiana University Press.

Tayob, A.I., 1996, 'Islamic Revivalism in South Africa: Identity Between Internal redefinition and Nation-Building', in J. Platvoet, J. Cox, and J. Olupona, eds., *The Study of Religions in Africa: Past, Present and Prospects*. Cambridge: Roots and Branches.

Tempels, P., 1959, *Bantu Philosophy*, Paris: Présense Africaine.

The Kairos Document: Challenge to the Church: A Theological Comment on the Political Crisis in South Africa, 1985, Grand Rapids, Mich: Eerdmans.

Tih, P.M., 1997, *A History of the Cameroon Baptist Convention Health Board 1936-1996*, Bamenda, Cameroon: Unique Printers.

Trimingham, J.S., 1964, *Islam in East Africa*, Oxford: Clarendon Press.

Turner, H., 1966, *History of an African Independent Church: The Church of the Lord (Aladura)*, 2 Volumes, London: Oxford University Press.

Turner, H. W., 1963, 'Chart of Modern African Religious Groups', in V.E.W. Hayward, ed., *African Independent Church Movements*, Edinburgh: House Press.

Turner, H.W., 1966, 'A Methodology for Modern African Religious Movements', *Comparative Studies in Society and History* 8 (3): 281-94.

Turner, H. W., 1967, 'A Typology for African Religious Movements', *Journal of Study of Religion in Africa* 1: 1-34.

Turner, V., 1967, *The Forest of Symbols: Aspects of Ndembu Ritual*, Ithaca, NY: Cornell University Press.

Turner, V., 1969, *The Ritual Process: Structure and Anti-Structure*, Chicago: Aldine.

Turner, V., 1975, *Revelation and Divination in Ndembu Ritual*, Ithaca, NY: Cornell University Press.

Turner, V. W., 1968 [1957], *Schism and Continuity in an African Society: A Study of Ndembu Village Life*, Manchester: Manchester University Press.

Umar, Muhammad Sani, 2006, *Islam and Colonialism: Intellectual Responses of Muslims of Northern Nigeria to British Colonial Rule*, Leiden: Brill.

Villa-Vicencio, C., ed., 1988, *Theology and Violence: The South African Debate*, Grand Rapids: W.E. Eerdmans Publishing.

Walker, S.S., 1983, *The Religious Revolution in the Ivory Coast: The Prophet Harris and the Harrist Church*, Chapel Hill: University of North Carolina Press.

Weber, C.W., 1993, *International Influences and Baptist Mission in West Cameroon: German-American Missionary Endeavor under International Mandate and British Colonialism*, Leiden: E. J. Brill.

Welbourn, F.B., 1961, *East African Rebels: A Study of Some Independent Churches*, London: SCM Press.

Welbourn, F.B. and B. Ogot, 1966, *A Place to Feel at Home: A Study of Two Independent Churches in Western Kenya*, London: Oxford University Press.

Werbner, R., 1984, 'The Manchester School in South-Central Africa', *Annual Review of Anthropology* 13:157-85.

West, G., 1991, *Biblical Hermeneutics of Liberation: Modes of Reading the bible in the South African context*, foreword by Norman Gottwald, Maryknoll: Orbis Books.

West, G.O. and M. Dube, eds., 2000, *The Bible in Africa: Transactions, Trajectories, and Trends*, Leiden: Brill.

Williams, C.P., 1990, *The Ideal of the Self-Governing Church*, Leiden: Brill Academic Publishers.

Willoughby, W. C., 1928, *The Soul of the Bantu: A Sympathetic Study of the Magico-Religious Practices and Beliefs of the Bantu Tribes of Africa*, New York: Harper & Row.

Zahan, D., 1970, *The Religion, Spirituality, and Thought of Traditional Africa*, translated by Kate Ezra and Lawrence M. Martin, Chicago: University of Chicago Press.

Chapter 16

Framing an African-Centred Discourse on Global Health: Centralising Identity and Culture in Theorising Health Behaviour

Collins O. Airhihenbuwa

The battle for African health in the context of culture and identity is moving from intellectual insurgency in theorising health behaviour to a reframing of the meanings of global health, particularly since recommendations in global health typically focus on what should be done for Africa. The battle for African health and Africa identity is typically expressed in the common mantra, 'the struggle continues', or as in a different expression in Nigeria; 'man no die, man no rotten'.

In this critical perspective, I will discuss the problems of current public health strategy as a failure of many Western and African scholars to understand public health as a voyage that is peopled with and anchored in the social contexts of cultural identity. Every voyage typically has a point of departure, the journey, and a destination. Unfortunately in public health and development, the destination is often thought of as modernisation and modernisation is assumed to be the result of development. In constructing theories of development, the point of departure is often believed to be economic growth. These theories when applied to Africa tend to offer prescriptions for development without raising questions about the non-viable political and economic structures that were horridly constructed by the colonial powers as they handed over power to their colonies (Keita 2005).

In measuring the achievements of a society, the point of departure is often constructed in the fields of humanities which include history, philosophy, and literature, to name three. It is through literature that many identities of people in distant locations are framed in the minds and imaginations of an author who may fictionalise their claims but in whose lenses readers ascribe meanings to people and places even before they venture there. Chinua Achebe reminds us of how Joseph Conrad's

Heart of Darkness has come to represent such a framing of African identity in a fictional imagination that Conrad imprinted in the Western mind. Thus literary imaginations have shaped, to a large extent, the points of departures, imaginary or real, for many about Africa. Where the humanities offer the points of departure, health and medical outcomes often offer the destination. Just as Westerners permitted themselves the literary license to frame African identity and humanity, medicine and health became the stamp of approval for the conclusions reached about the conditions of Africans. A celebrated flag bearer of this health and medical destination was Albert Schweitzer. His now popular dictum captures his supremacist's belief about Africans at the height of colonialism in which he professed: 'The African is indeed my brother, but my junior brother'. With the departure points and the destinations framed for Africans by non-Africans, African health scholars find themselves in an intellectual journey which appears more like intellectual quicksand with an endless struggle to transform a seemingly benign but a deceptively life-threatening landscape.

Thus addressing problems of health in Africa by Africans has been mostly a journey from neither a known African origin, nor a clear African destination. In the domains of health, while Africans continue to seek out the most recent health behaviour theory (commonly non-African) to frame African solution, several African solutions have been overlooked since these researchers can only find that which they were always schooled to look for—an African identity framed as a problem in the Western discourse on individuality. It is indeed the racialised forms of this discourse in Africa that prompted DuBois (1969) to pose the question to blacks in America: how does it feel to be a problem? When an identity is constructed to be synonymous with a problem, solutions cannot be sought from within 'the problem'. Hence solutions are believed to be hidden outside the contexts of the problems— identity. This logic, albeit skewed, established the foundation for how so-called 'experts' learned to import solutions into Africa from anywhere but Africa. Cornel West (1993) once lamented that many interventionists are fixated on searching for the door that hides the solution to the problem while in the meantime they walk by unnoticed several open doors of solutions. In what follows, I want to frame a journey, a theorising journey, in which Africans are able to define their points of departure and their destination for the voyage. I want to argue that the typical questions posed in the Western conventional approach to examining the issues of health in African countries, that focus on individual behaviour are inadequate. I argue, instead, that the critical questions about improving health conditions in Africa revolve around the affirmation of identity that are located within a context that define a person and his/her responsibility in a society. I want to further maintain that such question of affirmation could not be adequately addressed without the contributions of such luminary thinkers as Frantz Fanon (1958, 1968) and Cheikh Anta Diop (1991).

Public Health and Behavioural Research

As the outcome measures by which progress in society is defined and comparisons made with other nations, health and medical data occupy a central position in how a people are defined and solutions meted out for them. Health problems that have been defined in Africa have been based mostly on filling a void that is believed to exist in their humanity. Public Health as a profession that is grounded in practice has emphasised the need to understand the root causes of problems before engaging in how to frame the solutions. However, many of the strategies for public health in Africa are based not on understanding root causes but on examining the consequences of health problems at the individual level. Admittedly, individual level analysis of health problems should be a component of how one analyses the totality of the conditions of health. Such recognition should by no means translate into the privileging of individual behaviour over their cultural, social, historical, and political contexts. The common language by which the notion of behaviour is believed to be the key to unlocking the misery of health, is the language of 'universality.' The notion of a Western paradigm serving as an appropriate reference for Africa is very much anchored in the expressed or implied value placed on the universality of Western theoretical frameworks (Airhihenbuwa 1995). It is 'as though universality were some distant bend in the road which you may take if you travel out far enough in the direction of Europe or America, if you put adequate distance between yourself and your home' (Achebe 1988: 76). Thus the language of universality has greatly influenced how we understand and articulate our behaviour and practice.

Moreover, language also influences how we express our practice of and sub-scription to healing modalities within our cultural contexts. For example, in the fight against HIV and AIDS in Africa, some traditional healers have been reported to have wrongfully misrepresented their healing achievements by claiming to have a cure for AIDS. I have often wondered about this issue, not only because some physicians have also claimed to have a cure for AIDS (which does not summarily lead to a condemnation of all physicians), but because I know that the language of treatment has its root in chronic disease. In the past, before there was a treatable but non-curable disease like hypertension, the measure of success for all health care providers was to 'cure' a disease like measles. Most African healing traditions and their language of healing have their origin in that era where diseases were supposed to be cured. In a historical and political context where traditional healing has been demonised and not given the opportunity to evolve and its linguistic transformation that could better express its healing strategies has been stunted, one question should be asked. Could some healers (recognising that like some physicians, some healers exaggerate and misrepresent their healing skills) be referring to treatment when they say cure? After all, not many people outside of the health and medical professions in the United States or Europe, even though in regions of endemic chronic conditions, could make a distinction between the medical meanings of treatment versus cure. When healers say they cure a disease like HIV, do they have a language to express the term 'treatment'? Moreover, does their language offer terms and expressions that make a distinction between a treatment and a cure? In what follows, I want to critique the theoretical praxis of health behaviour research which is central to research in public health.

Public health scholars in the US have been calling for the need to examine the root causes of health problem rather than focussing on the behavioural outcomes at the individual level. The failure to reconcile what is advocated with what is practised has been due to two primary factors. The first is the challenge of how to transform a hegemonic gaze while under its influence. Since public health has promoted its *raison d'être* on the conventional theories and models of individual behaviour, its practitioners are incapable of extricating themselves from the proposed relocation of the goals of public health research and practice outside those theories for which their scholarship has been affirmed and rewarded. Without those theories that affirm their identities as public health practitioners in the first instance, they are exposed epistemologically. The second factor has to do with how to study Africans (and by extension people of African descent) without the fixation on the deficit framework by which scholars and educators were schooled in and nurtured on how to think about Africa. For many scholars, Africa is thought of as deserving of attention only to address crises or death. 'There is a saying according to which no one is listening until you make a mistake ... Bad news in Africa, is good news, elsewhere. Good news, in Africa, is no news, elsewhere' (Macamo 2005: 5). How we study African health issues is partly influenced by how we are introduced to health issues in Africa.

Studies in public health and health behaviour in Africa can be said to have grown from three basic traditions. The first tradition can be attributed to mental health research in Africa. The critical and insightful contribution of scholars like the former Deputy Director General of the World Health Organisation, Professor Adeoye Lambo, has greatly enriched our understanding of mental health treatment in Nigeria and indeed Africa. Lambo in his research drew attention to not only the immediate or proximate cause of a disease but also the ultimate cause (what today is referred to as root cause) of a disease. Proximate cause refers to disease signs and symptoms while ultimate cause refers to social, political, historical, and cultural conditions that produce vulnerability to the disease. Thus, to prevent a disease from reoccurring, one must address the ultimate cause. It is by understanding the ultimate cause that we are able to focus on the context of the disease rather than focussing on the individual behaviour which is often a manifestation of the broader problem. Lambo's earlier work in Ibadan placed collective efficacy, in terms of group identity, over self efficacy, in terms of individualism. Lambo found that families of mental patients and communities in which the patient lived were accepting of the patient such that it was not necessary to isolate the patient in an asylum or a clinical ward as was commonly practised in contemporary health facilities for the mentally ill.

The second tradition of the evolution of public health and health behaviour in Africa can be attributed to traditional healing. The wealth of knowledge of healers as major contributors to our knowledge of disease and healing has been documented by Bannerman, Burton, and Wen-Chie (1983). In additional to their healing achievements, healers offered communities information about behaviours that were thought to promote positive physical, emotional and spiritual health and those that were not. As I have cited in my book *Health and Culture: Beyond the Western Paradigm* (Airhihenbuwa 1995), some of healers' approach to surgical treatment was more advanced that those of modern medical practitioners of the time. A British medical missionary travelling in Baganda in modern-day Uganda observed in 1879 that the surgical technique employed by healers, such as the use of antiseptics, was evident of a sophisticated surgical technique developed and used by healers. This observation was made two years before Joseph Lister recommended the use of antiseptics in London. This observation leads to the conclusion that healers were using antiseptics before its adoption in modern medicine as we know it today.

The third tradition of the origin of public health and health behaviour research is rooted in environmental sanitation. This third tradition is shared with the origin of public health in the US and Europe and thus remains the most often cited source of public health in Africa (Basch 1999). The devastation created by mosquitoes in terms of the death toll on both Africans and foreigners gave the impetus to support a sanitation movement that was welcomed by everyone. However, when sanitation was effective, it was often because villages and cities made collective efforts to support and promote regulations around improving conditions that would reduce the likelihood of mosquitoes and other disease vectors breeding in the environment. Thus community collective action was central to success rather than individual behaviour such as the use of mosquito bed nets. Unfortunately, it is the individual action component of environmental sanitation that was emphasised in the literature and still promoted today rather than the community-oriented action that is supported by both the traditional healing and mental health treatment foundations of public health and health behaviour research.

On the issue of health behaviour as being central to public health research, behavioural health research has tended to focus on attitude and behaviour as the two most important characteristics of individuals. To understand attitudes, attitudinal change models were designed to focus on predictive indicators of individual's intention to take action about a given behaviour or an individual's attitude toward a particular behaviour. Behaviour in this case could range from using a condom to prevent a sexually transmitted infection like HIV, to one's attitude toward a diagnostic tool for heart disease. Models such as theory of Reasoned Action and Planned Behaviour, Health Belief Model, and Social Cognitive Theory represent this approach. Behaviour change models, on the other hand, tend to focus on the process and outcome of change so that each step of the process could be measured and evaluated. The Stages of Change model, Diffusion of Innovation, and many community and organisation change models fall into this category. In what follows, I offer a brief description of these models. For more details, see Airhihenbuwa and

Obregon (2000) for a description of these models and how they relate to individual level health behaviours.

The Health Belief Model (HBM) (Becker 1974) was developed in the 1950s to predict individual response to, and utilisation of, health/medical screening and other preventive health services. The HBM is based on rational-cognitive assumptions about an individual 'rational' decision-maker without accounting for the role of social contexts, including risk environments (Freimuth 1992). The Theory of Reasoned Action (Fishbein and Ajzen 1975) is a linear progression from attitude to action which assumes that a given behaviour will be determined by an individual's intention even though such presumptions are believed to be irrelevant to emotion-anchored responses that have been found to motivate initiation of behaviour to prevent HIV and AIDS (Michal-Johnson and Bowen 1992). The Social Learning/Cognitive Theory (Bandura 1986) postulates that an individual behaviour is the result of the interaction among cognition, behaviour, environment, and physiology. Although this model has been reported to be of relevance in HIV/AIDS communication campaigns in the United States (Freimuth 1992; Maibach and Flora 1993), there remains the question about its relevance in cultures where individual decisions are the result of group norms whereby being individualistic is going against the grain. It should be noted, however, that Bandura (1998) now advocates the need to focus on collective efficacy, which goes beyond self/individual efficacy. Other theories have included Rogers's Diffusion of Innovation, which focuses on the communication process by which a new idea or product becomes known and used by people in a given population. The latest revision (Rogers 1997) to this model has taken into account issues of cultural contexts based on findings from its application in Africa, Asia, and Latin America. Social Marketing is another framework which is applied as an organised approach to promoting the acceptability of a social idea. Among the criticisms of social marketing in HIV/AIDS are ethical concerns (Guttman 1997a) and the tendency to reduce public health issues to individual-level problems while defining solutions within 'information deficit' models. This becomes even more problematic in an African context.

While these theories and models have proven effective in certain societies for addressing certain diseases, they were concluded to be inadequate for communicating HIV/AIDS prevention and care messages in Africa, Asia, Latin America and the Caribbean (UNAIDS/Penn State, 1999; Airhihenbuwa, Makinwa, and Obregon 2000). In fact the assumptions (such as individualism as opposed to collectivism) on which these theories and models are based are foreign to many cultures where these models have been used to guide public health and communication strategies for HIV/AIDS prevention and care. We should not expect these models to be effective in how we understand the social contexts of behaviours, particularly in regions where commonsense knowledge of the world is quite different (Yoder 1997). A major gap in these models, I argue, is the absence of how to account for the strength of the social cultural infrastructure that shapes values and behaviours in African cultures.

Strengthening African Social Cultural Infrastructures

Social cultural infrastructure refers to those non-physical values that shape the moral and ethical codes by which relationships and expectations are defined, measured, and rewarded. Asked why the rural areas have a lower prevalence of HIV and AIDS, the responses by Africans include a poor data gathering method in rural areas that does not allow researchers to capture all the cases. Incidentally, I was told once that South Africans had used similar arguments in the past to explain why they have the highest case of HIV and AIDS in Africa. The blame game to explain one's unflattering position when measured by health outcome indicators has been true of cities like Nashville and Memphis both in Tennessee in the US, arguing for why STIs were higher in one city than another. A related issue has been the paradox of physical development and health outcomes. Again with HIV and AIDS, the geographic spaces with the best physical infrastructure are also the ones with the highest cases of HIV and AIDS.

On a regional level, South Africa and Botswana have higher cases of the disease (as well as some of the most dedicated researchers, activists, and practitioners fighting HIV and AIDS) than other countries in the region as well as other parts of Africa. On a national level Abuja, for example, has one of the highest cases in Nigeria compared to traditional regions or states like Oyo. A common explanation for the spread is that easy road access for movement contributes to spread of any human-to-human transmissible and infectious disease. The response may explain why it spreads among people who engage in behaviour that creates vulnerability. But it does not explain why it does not spread in certain regions. Nor does it explain why the same modern physical infrastructure and its attendant privileging of modern communication (i.e., TV and the internet) does not offer the expected changes in behaviour to address the problems created by the availability of these modern communication infrastructures. Finally, the low incidence in rural areas does not explain while rural folks with shared cultures may engage in behaviour that protects them from infection.

I argue that many rural areas have a well-established social cultural infrastructure that offers some social protection for their members. It is for this reason that many (including persons living with HIV and AIDS) self-repatriate to their villages when all else has failed in their environment with modern physical infrastructures. The reality remains, the increasing rate of rural cases of HIV notwithstanding, rural areas have lower cases in general. One reason, I would argue, is their social cultural infrastructure which has helped to nurture some sense of collective identity in the face of foreign assault on their cultural values. The assumption is that the disease should be there and if it is not, it is because the villagers are protected by the backwardness of their physical infrastructure rather than being protected by the strength of their social cultural infrastructure. Even then, many sick people end up going back to their village when they become desperate and in need for culture-based support.

A recent report from Senegal has revealed that men who are in polygynous marriages have lower infection rates than their counterparts in monogamous marriages. While this was not meant to promote polygyny, the findings support the long established prevention campaign of Zero Grazing that was pioneered in Uganda many years ago. This concept of zero grazing recommends that sexual activities be restricted to the circle of marital relationships. The concept was advanced in recognition that it is when members of a marital unit engage in sexual activities outside their unit that the entire unit is subjected to the threat of HIV. Recent argument on the role of commerce in women's agency, mostly in urban areas, would suggest that zero grazing, whether or not in polygynous marriages, is more likely to be practised in rural than urban areas. As Nyamnjoh (2005) argued, the competing demands brought about by commercialisation have led women, young and old and mostly in urban areas, in different African countries, to normalise having different men fulfilling their basic, educational, and sometimes professional needs.

Another aspect of social cultural infrastructure is the currency of language in education and commerce in Africa. The devaluation of national monetary units in Africa has tended to occur, *pari passu*, with the devaluation of African languages. Some of the key agents of the devaluation of African languages are the African professional elites. The importance of promoting African languages in centring African agency to define the gateway for African identity is even more critical today. In *Decolonizing the African Mind* (1989), Ngugi wa Thiong'o argued that the most devastating form of a weapon of mass destruction is a cultural bomb that is unleashed when the language of a people is systematically devalued. In *Hopes and Impediments*, Chinua Achebe offers the following quotes from a Japanese colleague: 'My grandfather graduated from the University of Tokyo at the beginning of the 1880s. His notebooks were full of English. My father graduated from the same university in 1920 and half of his notes were filled with English. When I graduated a generation later my notes were all in Japanese...' (1988:160).

Experience in African countries today will show that the trends are moving in the opposite direction of what Japanese educational systems offered to the Japanese. In secondary school in Nigeria in the 1970s, we were punished for speaking Edo during school hours and required to pay a monetary fine. At least we were able to speak our language with our parents at home and in the market place while engaging in commerce. Today, the schools may no longer have to concern themselves with the bad old days. Many African children of today are being raised within their African cultural environment so that they do not speak their African languages. It is not unusual for children in secondary schools and universities not to speak or understand their own parents' language even if they grew up within their own culture, unless, of course such a child was educated in the rural areas. Many of the children of African professional elites today, particularly university professors, do not speak the language of their parents. It is not unusual for a young adult, whose parents are both Yoruba and live in Ibadan, for example, are unable to speak or understand a word of the Yoruba language. This is true of many other ethnic groups in different African countries. This has implications in developing effective approaches and strategies to address African health issues.

Framing the Journey for a Destination

It is when an agreed-upon destination has been defined that the voyage can be planned and framed. Included in the plan is the reason for the journey in the first place, who should drive the vehicle for the journey and why; who are the co-travellers and their roles (formative evaluation); what are the various points and locations for resting (process evaluation points); and what is the ultimate destination and how do we know when we arrive there (outcome evaluations).

For the purpose of explicating the limitations of the conventional social psychological models in addressing health problems, I will use some theorising around HIV and AIDS in Africa to explain. The very notion of stigma was introduced into social science in the 1960s by Ervin Goffman (1963). This sociologist's research focussed on the notion of deviance, and how individuals may suffer ostracism from society due to their health condition. In 2003, Richard Parker and Peter Aggleton (2003) published an article in which they expanded the appropriation of stigma beyond individual 'deviance' to begin to examine the location of power in relation to stigma. They argued that a broader conceptualisation of stigma should be anchored in the seminal work of the French philosopher, Michel Foucault (1990). However, as I have noted elsewhere (see Airhihenbuwa 2005), Foucault, in his writings did not address the question of racism or, specifically, the marginalisation of African identity. I do not argue that he should have, I am simply noting that he did not. Thus, while Foucault's work is instructive in understanding the location of power, it does not offer us an analysis, in this instance, of understanding stigma in a context in which being an African has been stigmatised before the advent of AIDS.

Stigma manifests itself in different forms and through different experiences in society. Running away from one's language by refusing to teach one's children about it, running away from one's history limits the instruments of one's culture such as language and governance, running away from one's healing modality in the ways that demonises one's healing traditions, are all deeper forms of stigma. The call to examine root causes as advocated in public health requires that we examine the impact of the stigma of African identity and affirmation on the question of a condition for which there are limited healing language to accurately capture it as a syndrome—a collection of a weakened state of the balance in health. How we address health and issues of development in Africa should not be based on Western solutions. It is for this reason that a report entitled *Our Common Interest* sounded a warning to us all. 'In the West development is about increasing choice for individuals; in Africa it is more about increasing human dignity within a community. Unless those who shape Africa's development make this integral to the way they formulate their policies they will fail' (Commission for Africa 2005). In what follows, I will offer a cultural model that

I developed in 1989 and have modified ever since to underscore the need to focus on the question of identity in public health research—more pointedly, the need to begin every project with the positive rather than the negative as conventional behaviour models typically directs.

A Public Health Model for Strengthening the Social Cultural Infrastructure in Africa

PEN-3 is a cultural model that was developed in the late 1980s (Airhihenbuwa 1989) to guide cultural approaches to health issues and problems in Africa. It has been applied to child survival intervention in Nigeria (Airhihenbuwa 1993,1995), and HIV/AIDS in Zimbabwe (Gwede and McDermont 1992); intervention research related to cancer (Erwin, Spatz, Stotts, Hollenberg, Deloney 1996; Paskett, Tatum, D'Agostino, Rushing, Velez, Michielutte, Dignan 1999); cardiovascular risks reduction intervention research (Walker 2000); and cultural meanings of female condom use in South Africa (Webster 2003). Others have also used PEN-3 to describe the planning, implementation, and evaluation of health interventions (Green and Krueter 1999; Huff and Kline 1999). The model is composed of three primary domains: Cultural Identity, Relationships and Expectations, and Cultural Empowerment. When a health issue is identified, such as HIV/AIDS related stigma, a 3x3 table is created to group the interaction between the domain of Relationships and Expectations with the domain of Cultural Empowerment. These two domains are discussed first, followed by a discussion of the third domain of Cultural Identity. The Cultural Identity domain is used to determine the point of intervention entry.

Figure 1: The PEN-3 Model

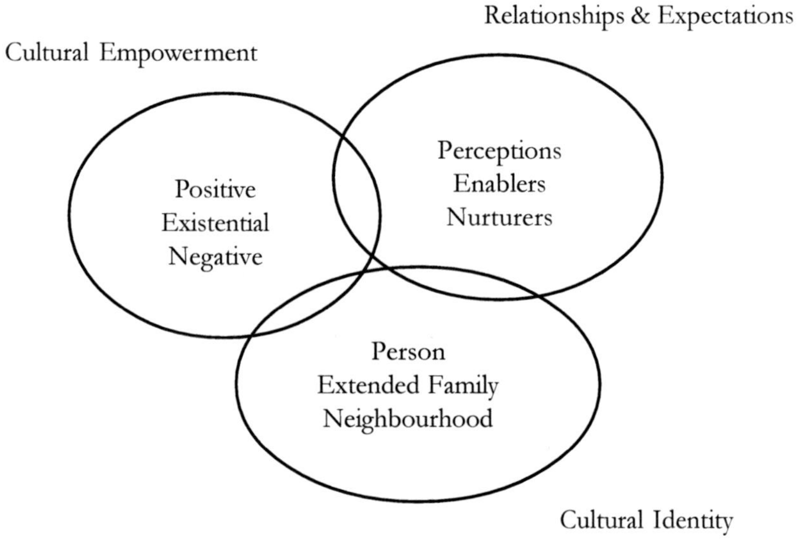

Relationships and Expectations

The meanings of behaviour are commonly based on the interaction between the perception we have about that behaviour, the resources and institutional forces that enable or disenable actions, and the influence of family, kin, and friends in nurturing the behaviour. The three categories of Relationship and Expectation are: *PERCEPTION*—knowledge and beliefs and values in decision-making that are either focussed on individuals or groups, the complementarity of emotion and rational cues to behavioural actions. An example for this component is the knowledge or belief that HIV has a spiritual message delivered as a punishment from God or being bewitched. *ENABLERS*—resources and institutional support, socioeconomic status, wealth (assets over liability) as a measure of resources and power, costs and availability of services such as drugs for treating HIV. An example for this category could be the depletion or absence of condoms for use in preventing HIV. *NURTURERS*—supportive or discouraging influences of families and friends particularly as they relate to shaming and distancing from family members. An example is nurturing a culture of home based care on the one hand and on the other hand a patriarchal practice of subordinating a widow's agency to the authority of her in-laws as in wife inheritance.

Cultural Empowerment

Culture and empowerment are two words that are almost never used as a coupling term because of the ways in which culture is often represented as a barrier, and empowerment is represented as a strength. The domain of cultural empowerment is thus an affirmation of the possibilities of culture, which range from positive to negative.

Culture can be empowering in the sense that culture represents the continuum of good, indifferent, and bad (Airhihenbuwa and Webster 2004). The goal of cultural empowerment is to ensure that an intervention accentuates the positive rather than focussing only on the negative. This model insists that regardless of the point of intervention entry, the positive aspects of behaviour and culture must be identified as the first priority since every culture has something positive about it. Otherwise the interventionist could become a part of the problem (Airhihenbuwa 1999). The cultural empowerment domain is thus composed of three categories. *POSITIVE*—values and relationships that promote the health behaviour of interest. An example is the traditional healing modality given that each culture has its strategy for dealing with health problems including sexually transmitted infections. An example of this category is *ukhusoma* (a Zulu term for the cultural practice of non-penetrative sex). *EXISTENTIAL*—values and beliefs that are practised in the culture but pose no threat to health. Interventionists should not blame these values for failed interventions. An example is what Airhihenbuwa (1999) refers to as *language elasticity* in terms of the various codes and meanings of languages whereby language of flexible principles should not be judged with the rules of language of rigid principles.

Even the same language, such as English, that may be spoken in different parts of the world have different meanings that are culturally coded. Another existential quality is oratory or orality in terms of interventions that should ensure consistency between the communication strategy and that used in the culture. For example, there are some common characteristics of many African cultures such as the value of the extended family. However, there are also different political experiences, such as in apartheid South Africa that directly affect the present representation of South African culture. For example, racism is an important factor to be considered in the internal politics and social arrangement in South Africa compared to other African countries. *NEGATIVE*—values and relationships that surround behaviour, including the policy environment, income and wealth of individuals, communities and society; the position of women in society relative to decisions about sexuality; and the spiritual contexts of the health behaviour in question. Examples of this category include a caste system that may privilege certain families over others regarding leadership, or the militarisation of the language of interaction and behaviour that has resulted from years of military dictatorships in a country like Nigeria.

Cultural Identity

Culture represents a shared pool of collective consciousness. It represents shared historical and political memories that position us to define the future from the possibilities of the present.

In the application of PEN-3, as will be discussed later, the interventionist first creates a 3x3 table. Having completed the categories in the table, it is necessary to identify the point of intervention entry with the understanding that there could be multiple entry points for addressing the social contexts and behaviours that have been identified for promotion or change. This process removes the assumption that all interventions should focus on the individual, thus leading to the development of bill boards and other media messages that may not address the context of behaviour change. The three components of the domain of cultural identity are: *PERSON*— the degree to which the cultural context and language of the culture focuses on seniority (as with the Edos and the Yoruba of Nigeria) rather than gender (as in English and French) (Oyewumi 1997). As Gyekye (1997) has argued, there is a difference between a person and an individual in African languages. An individual is the person whose behaviour and values are considered unacceptable by the collective.

EXTENDED FAMILY—intervention may need to focus on gender and generation depending on the focus of the intervention, on consumption patterns relative to the role of food in maintaining good health, and communication channels relative to the direction of communication, particularly in cases where an older person believes that they cannot discuss sex with a younger person. For example, recent surveys have shown that mother-in-laws in some African cultures discourage their pregnant daughter-in-laws from using the available health care facilities. In an ethnographic study to understand this practice in Senegalese cultures, Professor

Cheikh Niang of the Cheikh Anta Diop University in Dakar found that these mothers-in-law saw themselves as totally responsible for the welfare of their pregnant daughter-in-law. The value is so strong that the mothers would pray to God that rather than anything happening to their daughter-in-laws, they ask God to take their own lives instead. The strong belief in their responsibility and the related lack of confidence in the health centres lead these women to discourage their daughter-in-law from using such centres. In particular, the mothers have no control over the kind of care offered at these centres.

NEIGHBOURHOOD—this relates to a community's capacity to decide on bill board advertising and communication in their community, or the economic status and power structure of the community in dealing with HIV education with a culturally appropriate strategy.

The PEN-3 Model can be used effectively to address HIV-related stigma, which continues to impede prevention and control efforts in Africa communities as in other places. What follows is a description of HIV-related stigma and its impact. Stigma examples are used to show how PEN-3 Model might be used to guide interventions.

Application of the PEN-3 Model

The first step is to develop a 3x3 table to produce nine categories. This is done by crossing the components of the domain of Cultural Empowerment (i.e., positive, existential, negative) with the domain of Relationships and Expectations (i.e., perception, enabler, nurturer).

The following are the nine categories and HIV-specific examples from African lessons learned:

(i) *Positive Perception*—An interventionist who is not able to identify the positive aspects of a culture relative to a given disease has no business being in such cultural contexts because he or she ends up blaming the culture for their failure at the end of the programme.

(ii) *Existential Perception*—Family and/or community are stigmatised and may also be protected if an individual family or community member is HIV-positive. Adoption as a practice has often been used to describe the caring for a child by parents who are not the child's biological parents. When addressing issue of adoption in African cultures, it is not unusual for some cultures to be referred to as not believing in adoption. However, the very notion of extended family means that adoption becomes a normal feature of such arrangements even though those parents in extended families caring for a non-biological child may not consider those children as adopted.

(iii) *Negative Perception*—Myths and misconceptions about HIV lead to discrimination and human rights abuses. Mothers who claim that their child died of witchcraft when AIDS was the actual cause of death are considered ignorant of HIV knowledge and the means of transmission. In a climate of stigma, it is quite plausible for a mother to defer to a culturally acceptable explanation for a child's death even when she is aware of the actual cause.

(iv) *Positive Enablers*—The role of government policy has been noted in the success of the consistent low incidence and prevalence of HIV/AIDS in Senegal and the continuous decline of new cases of HIV in Uganda and more recently Zambia.

(v) *Existential Enablers*—It is now evident that traditional healers in Senegal have developed a treatment regimen for successfully treating HIV. In South Africa a drug named UBEJA was discovered by traditional healers and has proven effective in treating some persons living with HIV and AIDS.

(vi) *Negative Enablers*—The refusal of governments to support healers clearly presents a disenabling environment for effectively addressing HIV/AIDS. An enabling environment is critical to effectively reducing and eliminating the stigmatisation of traditional healers in Africa.

(vii) *Positive Nurturers*—While much emphasis has been placed on the prevention of sexual transmission of HIV, cultural practices such as *Ukhusoma* (a Zulu word for non-penetrative sex) has received little or no attention in the literature as a way of promoting cultural practices that promote positive sexual relationships.

(viii) *Existential Nurturers*—Home based care has become an important aspect of HIV/AIDS care and support that is anchored in cultural practices of supporting and caring for a sick relative at home. This kind of service continues to be provided by family members, often with little or no support from government and other local resources; not even support for the protection of care givers in the families to prevent HIV transmission is available.

(ix) *Negative Nurturers*—Stigma, as a negative nurturer, discourages testing for HIV, promotes a false sense of security by encouraging unsafe sexual behaviour, and forces infected persons underground, which leads to isolation from social support and available treatment that could enabled the infected to live with the disease in dignity.

Having framed relevant socio-cultural issues into these nine categories, a collective decision must be made among the researchers and members of the community to prioritise the point of intervention entry given what research results show about the context of prevention that is likely to lead to a significant change in controlling the epidemic. In the examples cited above, a collective decision would be made based upon whether changes in any of the examples given will take place at the level of a person, the extended family, or the neighbourhood and community. In a conventional model, we often begin the intervention by discussing the individuals. In the PEN-3 Model the identity component is the last component because it is the nature and context of the issues that drive which of the identity categories have the most impact in reducing the spread of HIV/AIDS. For example, the explanation of witchcraft as the cause of HIV could not be effectively examined simply at the individual level. An examination of the belief would involve a qualitative evaluation of the cultural contexts of such a belief and the role of a disenabling environment may play in the construction of HIV meanings at the individual level. In the final analysis, people's behaviour reflects their explanation of several factors in their environment.

The Destination—Framing the Cultural Contexts of Health in Africa

We are fortunate to have luminary scholars like Fanon and Diop who offered us our gateways for entering writing, reading, and thinking about Africa. Fanon's professional location as a psychiatrist offered tormenting as well as healing insights into the question of African (including the diaspora) identity at a time when his colleagues focussed on the psychology of individuality (Airhihenbuwa 2005). Indeed, when he addressed the location of power and difference produced by colonisation, the focus of his inquiry was the dislocation of affirmation of identity of Africans. Cheikh Anta Diop was born in Senegal and lived there until his death. As an Egyptologist and anthropologist, he became an intellectual beacon for many Africans attempting to understand the question of African identity and the framing of questions around what is considered to be normal or abnormal behaviour. More recently, in the CODESRIA book entitled *African Intellectuals*, this generation of African thinkers continues to illuminate the need to centralise African identity in African research. The editor of the book, Thandika Mkandawire (2005: 3), echoed Joseph Ki-Zerbo's call for African intellectuals to speak up and not remain silent since the imposition of development agenda on Africans gained momentum because of 'how intellectuals often accepted the Faustian bargain of being part of the exhilarating project in exchange for remaining silent, since one could only be "organic" by not being intellectual'.

Researching public health in Africa should make the question of identity and belonging central. This means the question of identity should become salient for a broader exercise in theorising for health promotion and disease prevention. In this way, studying health issues, for example, is located within a broader context to examine the impact of the history, politics and language on contemporary Africans. It is in this context that a cultural framework for analysing the context of health behaviour is instructive. A cultural framework offers us the possibility to map our departure, our journey, and our destination in health.

References

Achebe, C., 1988, 'Colonialists and Criticism', in *Hopes and Impediments: Selected Essays*, New York: Anchor Books.

Airhihenbuwa, C.O., 1989, 'Perspectives on AIDS in Africa: Strategies for Prevention and Control', *AIDS Education and Prevention* 1 (1): 57-69.

Airhihenbuwa, C.O., 1993, 'Health Promotion for Child Survival in Africa: Implications for cultural appropriateness', *International Journal of Health Education* 12 (3): 10-15.

Airhihenbuwa, C.O., 1995, *Health and Culture: Beyond the Western Paradigm*, Thousand Oaks, California: Sage.

Airhihenbuwa, C.O., 1999, 'Of Culture and Multiverse: Renouncing "The Universal Truth" in Health', *Journal of Health Education* 30: 267-273.

Airhihenbuwa, C.O., 2005, 'Theorizing Cultural Identity and Behaviour in Social Science Research', *CODESRIA Bulletin* 3 & 4: 17-19.

Airhihenbuwa, C.O., B. Makinwa, R. Obregon, 2000, 'Toward a New Communications Framework for HIV/AIDS', *Journal of Health Communication* 5 (supplement): 101-111.

Airhihenbuwa C.O. and J. D. Webster, 2004, 'Culture and African Contexts of HIV/AIDS Prevention, Care, and Support', *Journal of Social Aspects of HIV/AIDS Research Alliance* 1: 4-13.

Bandura, A., 1986, *Social Foundations of Thought and Action: A Social Cognitive Theory*, Englewood Cliffs. NJ: Prentice-Hall.

Bannerman, R.H., J. Burton, C. Wen-Chieh, 1983, *Traditional Medicine and Health Care Coverage: A Reader for Health Administrators and Practitioners*, Geneva: World Health Organization.

Basch, P.F., 1999, *Textbook of International Health*, Second Edition, New York: Oxford University Press.

Becker, M.H., 1974, 'The Health Belief Model and Personal Health Behavior'. *Health Education Monographs*. Vol. 2, No. 4.

Commission for Africa, 2005, *Our Common Interest—Report of the Commission for Africa*, 21–79, http://www.commissionforafrica.org/english/report/introduction.html#report

Diop, C.A., 1991, *Civilization or Barbarism: An authentic anthropology*, Brooklyn, NY: Lawrence Hill Books.

Diop, W., 2000, 'From Government Policy to Community-Based Communication Strategies in Africa: Lessons from Senegal and Uganda', *Journal of Health Communications* 5: 113-118.

Du Bois, W. E. B., 1969, *The Souls of Black Folk: Essays and Sketches*, Second Ed., Greenwich, CT: Crest Books.

Erwin, D.O., T.S. Spatz, C. Stotts, J. A. Hollenberg, and L. A. Deloney, 1996, 'Increasing Mammography and Breast Self-Examination in African American Women Using Witness Project Model', *Journal of Cancer Education* 11 (4): 210-215.

Fanon, F., 1958, *Black Skin, White Mask*, London: Penguin.

Fanon F., 1968, *The Wretched of the Earth*, New York: Grove.

Fishbein, M. and Ajzen, I., 1975, 'Belief, Attitude, Intention, and Behavior: An Introduction to Theory and Research', Reading, MA: Addison-Wesley.

Foucault, M., 1990, *The History of Sexuality: An Introduction*, Vol. 1, New York: Vintage Books.

Freimuth, V. S., 1992, 'Theoretical Foundations of AIDS Media Campaigns', in T. Edgar, M. A. Fitzpatrick, V. S. Freimuth, eds., *AIDS: A Communication Perspective*, Hillsdale, New Jersey: Lawrence Erlbaum Associates, 91-110.

Gisselquist, D., J. J. Potterat, S. Body, F. Vachon, 2003, 'Let It Be Sexual: How Health Care Transmission of AIDS in Africa was Ignored', *International Journal of STD and AIDS* 14: 148-161.

Goffman, E., 1963, *Stigma: Notes on Management of Spoiled Identity*, New York: Simon and Schuster.

Green, L. W. and M. W. Kreuter, 1999, *Health Promotion Planning: An Educational and Ecological Approach*, Mountain View, CA: Mayfield Publishing.

Guttman, N., 1997a, 'Beyond Strategic Research: A Value-Centered Approach to Health Communication Interventions', *Communication Theory* 7(2): 95-124.

Guttman, N., 1997b, 'Ethical Dilemmas in Health Campaigns', *Health Communication*, 9 (2): 155-190.

Gwede, C., and R.J. McDermott, 1992, 'AIDS in Sub-Saharan Africa: Implications of Health Education', *AIDS Education and Prevention* 4 (4): 350-361.

Gyekye, K., 1997, *Tradition and Modernity: Philosophical Reflections on the African Experience*, New York: Oxford University Press.

Huff, R.M. and M.V. Kline, 1999, *Promoting Health in Multicultural Populations: A Handbook for Practitioners*, Thousand Oaks, CA: Sage Publications.

Keita, Lansana, 2004, 'Philosophy and Development: On the Problematic of African Development: A Diachronic Analysis', *African Development* 29 (1): 131-160.

Lambo, T.A., 1978, 'Psychotherapy in Africa', *Human Nature* 1 (3): 32-39.

Macamo, Elisio, 2005, 'Against Development', *CODESRIA Bulletin* 3 & 4: 5-7.

Maibach, E. and J.A. Flora, 1993, 'Symbolic Modeling and Cognitive Rehearsal: Using Video to Promote AIDS Prevention Self-Efficacy', *Communication Research* 20 (4): 517-545.

Michal-Johnson, P. and S.P. Bowen, 1992, 'The Place of Culture in HIV Education', in T. Edgar, M. A. Fitzpatrick, and V. S. Freimuth, eds., *AIDS: A communication Perspective*, Hillsdale, NJ: Lawrence Erlbaum Associates, 147-172.

Mkandawire, T., ed., 2005, *African Intellectuals: Rethinking Politics, Language, Gender and Development*, CODESRIA: Dakar, and London: Zed Books.

Ngugi Wa Thiong'o, 1986, *Decolonizing the Mind: The Politics of Language in African Literature*, London: James Currey/Heinemann.

Niang, C. I., P. Tapsoba, E. Weiss, M. Diagne, Y. Niang, A.M. Moreau, D. Gomis, A. S. Wade, K. Seck, and C. Castle, 2003, 'It's Raining Stones: Stigma, HIV Vulnerability Among Men Who Have Sex With Men in Dakar, Senegal', *Culture, Health and Sexuality* 5: 499-512.

Nyamnjoh, F., 2005, 'Diskettes and Thiofs', *Africa* 75 (3): 295-324.

Olukoshi, A. and F. Nyamnjoh, 2005, 'Rethinking African Development', Editorial. *CODESRIA Bulletin* 3 & 4: 1-4.

Oyewumi, O., 1997, *The Invention of Women: Making an African Sense of Western Gender Discourses*, Minneapolis: University of Minnesota Press.

Parker, R. and P. Aggleton, 2003, 'HIV/AIDS Related Stigma and Discrimination: A Conceptual Framework and Implications for Action', *Social Science and Medicine* 57: 13-24.

Paskett, E.D., C.M. Tatum, R. D'Agostino Jr., J. Rushing, R. Velez, R. Michielutte, and M. Dignan, 1999, 'Community-based Interventions to Improve Breast and Cervical Cancer Screening: Results of the Forsyth County Cancer Screening (FoCaS) Project', *Cancer Epidemiology, Biomarkers & Prevention* 8: 453-459.

Petros, G., C.O. Airhihenbuwa, L. Simbayi, S. Ramlagan, B. Brown, in press, 'HIV/AIDS and 'othering' in South Africa: The Blame Goes on,' *Culture, Health, and Sexuality*.

Rogers, E.M., 1995, *Diffusion of Innovations*, Fourth Edition, New York: The Free Press.

UNAIDS/PennState, 1999, *Communications Framework for HIV/AIDS: A New Direction*, A UNAIDS/PennState Project, eds., C. O. Airhihenbuwa, B. Makinwa, M. Frith and R. Obregon, Geneva: UNAIDS.

UNAIDS, 2002, *Report on the Global HIV/AIDS Epidemic*, Geneva: UNAIDS

Walker, C., 2000, 'An Educational Intervention of Hypertension Management in Older African Americans', *Ethnicity and Diseases* 10: 165-174.

Webster, J.D., 2003, Using a Cultural Model to Assess Female Condom use in Mpumalanga, South Africa, Doctoral dissertation, Pennsylvania State University.

West, C., 1993, *Keeping Faith: Philosophy and Race in America*, New York: Routledge.

Yoder, P.S., 1997, 'Negotiating Relevance: Belief, Knowledge, and Practice in International Health Projects', *Medical Anthropology Quarterly* 11 (2): 131-146.

Chapter 17

Re-thinking Communication Research and Development in Africa

Francis B. Nyamnjoh

Development for Africa is fraught with a multiplicity of exogenously generated ideas, models and research paradigms, all with the purported goal of 'alleviating' or bringing about 'the end of poverty ... in our lifetime' (cf. Sachs 2005). This discourse, which like fashion, goes round in circles, is carried on mainly by 'development' agents and 'experts' (mainly social and pseudo-social scientists moonlighting through consultancies) and who often limit the question of development to the problematic of achieving growth or 'the end of poverty' within the context of neoliberal economic principles. Notwithstanding the rise of 'alternative development' thinking and practice, the problem is rarely studied in a holistic manner. This is especially true of Africa, where problematic 'expectations of modernity' (Ferguson 1999) have engendered technicised, disembedded, depoliticised and sanitized approaches to 'development' as a unilinear process of routinised, standardised, calculable and predictable practices (Ferguson 1990). There is more emphasis on teleology and analogy than on the systematic study of ongoing processes of creative negotiation by Africans of the multiple encounters, influences and perspectives evident throughout their continent. Africans are actively modernizing their indigeneities and indigenising their modernities, often in ways not always obvious to scholarly fascination with dichotomies.

One of the important aspects of economic growth and development is investment in human capital, or more simply put, investment in education. But education is not just the inculcation of facts as knowledge but also a set of values that in turn appraise the knowledge being acquired. When the values are not appropriate for progress as understood by those who have sacrificed in pursuit of that education, the knowledge acquired becomes a cosmetic irrelevance. Using the example of African communication researchers educated in tune with exogenously induced (largely Western) cultural values, I argue that communication research steeped in Western expectations of modernity (Ferguson 1999) has only resulted in mimicry and insensitivity to the very socio-cultural realities necessary for effective communication and the negotiation of change and continuity (Nyamnjoh 2004a&b). The result is that the knowledge needed for African development is rendered irrelevant by the dysfunctional set of values imbibed and reproduced by African 'communication researchers', 'development experts' and the policymakers they influence (Moemeka 2000; Okigbo & Eribo 2004). In this regard, domesticated development in Africa is greatly hindered, even as the evangelicals of universalism claim ever more mileage and converts for their one-best-way development model. Hence, the need to seriously revisit the dominant epistemological underpinnings of prevalent development research and assumptions, that are not always sensitive to the complex realities of Africans as laboratories for negotiating conviviality amongst competing traditions, identities and ideas of progress (Nyamnjoh 2004a&b, 2005a).

For over five decades Africa has attempted to build 'nation-states' and pursue development along the path traced out by Western experience. The continent's postcolonial leaders have been persuaded by arguments which present the 'nation-state' as the only form of political unit 'recognised' and 'permitted' in 'the modern world' (Smith 1986:230; Deutsch 1969:171-2; Wallerstein 1964:4), and the modernisation thus inspired as the unilinear route to development. Today, as xenophobia and autochthony claim centre-stage even as globalisation is celebrated, researchers are unanimous that the attempt by African states to build 'nation-states' or to develop *'à l'européenne'* has met with little success in the short term, and that from current trends, there is hardly any reason to think that things would be different in the long term. This paper sets out to examine the workable link forward between communication research and development in Africa. But to do this properly, it first tries to answer why development has failed to occur despite multiple efforts and to evaluate the sort of communication research that has had little success in the African continent.

This contribution highlights two factors responsible for the failure of both communication research and development to make a positive and sustained impact on Africa in the last 50 years. The first factor is that the continent has relied on a notion of development and on development agendas that are foreign to the bulk of its peoples, both in origin and objectives, and that have not always addressed the right issues or done so in the right manner. The second reason is that development communication researchers have adopted research techniques designed to answer to the needs of Western societies and which do not always suit African cultures or societies that are in the main rural and non-literate. This means that for most of the time communication scholars have either been asking the wrong questions altogether or asking the right questions to the wrong people. The paper seeks to establish to what extent communication researchers and the media have been willing colluders in modernisation, trying to convince local people that this is good for them, the right thing to do, the central value, the one-best-way. It contends that the communication scholars have hardly had the financial, cultural and intellectual independence to set their own agendas in the service of the African masses.

The exogenously induced development agendas have often established an inappropriate sense of problems. Good communication has been presented as a means of being able to break through blockages (backward attitudes and practices, customs, traditions, and philosophies) with knowledge. The question as to *whose* knowledge for *what* purpose has seldom been asked. The assumption has been that there can never be any such thing as the transmission of wrong (inappropriate, unwanted or unsolicited) knowledge through the media by agents of modernisation. Few ever query whether the knowledge is correct; as the government, development agencies and the development experts have the same idea that they know best the people's problems and what to prescribe as solutions. Little or no attention is paid either to background or indigenous knowledge or to the need for active local participation in the conception, design and execution of development projects.

Even today when some may claim the situation is better, the attitude remains that of coming from the outside and knowing what is best in matters of local development. As Kasongo (1998:116) has argued, even when some participation by intended beneficiaries is claimed, this is usually 'token', 'mobilised' or 'directed' participation by external agents. As he writes, 'the much publicised participation of the intended beneficiary communities in their development takes but the form of selecting between choices already established by the benefactors. The key decisions regarding what the projects will deliver to the communities thus purported to be in need, remain prerogatives of the benefactors' (Kasongo 1998: 25). This illusion of choice and participation is well captured in the illustration: 'You will now decide for yourselves by majority vote. Do you want a clinic, a school or a bore hole?' (Kasongo 1998: 115). Nothing seems to start from the base, or from grassroots research, even when those targeted by behaviour and attitude change communication are at the grassroots. There is much talking at, talking on, talking past and talking to, but little talking with the African masses targeted by the media and research evangelists.

Thus it is hardly surprising that many attempts at development have been an utter and unmitigated disaster year after year for five decades, and that today Africans are by every standard much worse off than they were in the 1950s (Nyamnjoh 2005b; see also various UNDP human development reports). The pursuit of modernisation and consonant World Bank and IMF strategies for development have proved inappropriate in Africa; indeed, it has been argued that this pursuit has served to excuse Western penetration and exploitation. I remember in 1994, invited to present a paper on sustainable development, arguing that this idea (or any of its other aliases) was another World Bank initiative, and that there was little reason for optimism that things would work this time, especially as when examined in detail the whole idea of sustainable development was nothing but modernisation theory in camouflage. For one thing the agenda was still from outside 'experts', which meant that the targeted populations might not have had the opportunity to scrutinise and prioritise it. Sustainable development stressed long-term effects, and how to go about things in order to guarantee success and accountability, but was mute on the *why* of it all. The basic assumption here, like in modernisation theory, was that 'modern' or 'forward looking' people act in a rational and informed manner and that success inevitably results from careful planning. This 'rationalist and positivist' approach where everything can be measured and uncertainty eliminated is hardly a reflection of real life.

This obsession with calculability not only mistakes short-term effectiveness for long-term effects, its focus is often too narrow to recognise other forces at play, as it assumes that only what can be counted counts. This quantitative obsession in which quality is sacrificed as unmarketable has not exactly disappeared with the new initiatives around millennium goals and poverty eradication. These are clearly stand-ards set by the World Bank and like-minded others schooled to limit indicators of scientific rationality to the mathematical and the statistical for measuring success in the battle against poverty. Not only is there the possibility that the wrong things will be measured (which has been largely the case with modernisation in its various guises), but implicit is the assumption that should sustainable development or pov-erty eradication fail to materialise, the blame could be assigned to the inability of the backward-looking people targeted by development initiatives (structural adjustment programmes, poverty reduction strategy papers, millennium development goals, etc.) to free themselves of constricting customs, false beliefs and unaccountable govern-ments, and to embrace good governance and the rational culture, the one-best-way of managing social change as 'successfully' experienced in the prescriptive West. For example, Summers and Thomas (1993: 243) argue in support of the World Bank and IMF that 'nations shape their own destinies' and 'poor domestic policies, more than an unfavourable external environment, are usually to blame for development failure'. Supported and financed by the World Bank and the IMF, it is hardly sur-prising that such neoliberal attempts to minimise the impact of external forces and unequal power relations amongst states guarantee that globalisation shall, its rhetoric of flows and flexible mobility notwithstanding, ensure that devalued African labour does not graduate from its geographies of poverty that flexible accumulation makes possible for multinationals to exploit with impunity (Amin 1999a&b 2005).

African Development in the Image of Modernisation Theory

Current calls to re-think African development are in tune with past efforts in this regard, just as current poverty eradication initiatives share much in common with the modernisation theory that has assumed the status of a dinosaur in what Mamdani (1996: 12-13) has termed scholarship by analogy. As Laburthe-Tolra and Warnier (1993: 6-8) have pointed out, following the Second World War the gap between the rich, fast-growing industrialised countries and countries of the Third World buried in their poverty and underdevelopment became evident. Western sociologists saw in the success of the Western countries the result of a modernisation process. By modernisation Western theorists understood the process of change towards the types of social, economic and political systems which developed in Western Europe and North America from the seventeenth to the nineteenth centuries, and which subsequently spread to other regions of the world. According to this definition, modernisation touches on all aspects of existence: social and political organisation, family, kinship, belief systems, and economy. It possesses an original model: that of Europe and North America. This model is placed under the sign of scientific rationality, inherited from the century of Enlightenment and perceived as universal. Consequently, it is potentially detachable from the civilisation in which it was born. It promises the only rational way, the-one-best-way, therefore the universal way of doing anything. The Modernisation Model is generally seen to be spreading beyond its area of origin through diffusion, thanks to its scientific rationality, which imposes itself on particular civilisations founded on other systems of thought, qualified as 'pre-scientific', 'pre-logical', or simply 'irrational' (Lerner 1958: 45). Modernisation is thus seen as a giant compressor determined to crush every other civilisation in order to reduce them to the model of the industrialised West. That is the reason why modernisation theory can also be termed *the theory of the convergence of civilisations* since every other civilisation is considered to be moving towards this unique model. A reasoning very much in tune with the prevalent colonial belief that 'European civilisation was the culmination of all human progress and that the new African nations could have no better pattern and should aim at nothing different' (Ajayi 1966: 606). Modernisation is also seen as a process of change and innovation, where what is new is perceived as progress, regardless of its real impact on the recipient individuals and communities, as emphasis is on measuring effectiveness, not on effects which may not always be measurable even if more relevant. A modern society is that which is (quantitatively, not qualitatively) forward looking, not backward-looking.

Thus according to modernisation theorists, since the purely participant society is more or less a utopia, it is only appropriate that the societies of the West, which happen to be the most modern, serve as models or pacesetters for the emerging nations. Westernisation is therefore their prescription for difficulties in development in Africa. By assuming a unilateral path in development, such theorists imply that the problems of political instability, cultural pluralism, and socioeconomic underde-velopment in Africa can only be overcome through the infusion of 'rationalist and positivist' Western policies, institutions, and values. Africa's only chance is in seeking to become like the West, since 'modernism, dynamism and stability tend to go to-gether' (Lerner 1958: 84).

Since independence, keen to cover mileage on the unilinear path to the universal civilisation into which they have bought, African educational systems have excelled at the sort of mimicry Okot p'Bitek (1989) decries in *Song of Lawino*. If ancestors are supposed to lay the path for posterity, inviting Africans to forget their ancestors has been an invitation for them to be born again and socialised afresh in the image of the West, using Western-type academic institutions and rituals of ancestral wor-ship. In general, the extraverted nature of African scholarship has favoured the Western knowledge industry tremendously (Teferra & Altbach 2003; Zeleza &

Olukoshi 2004; Odhiambo 2004). It has allowed Western intellectual traditions and practitioners to write themselves into the past, present and future of Africa as civilisers, saviours, initiators, mentors, and arbiters (Chinweizu 1987; Mudimbe 1988; Schipper 1990; Ngugi wa Thiong'o 1986; Crossman & Devisch 1999; Mbembe 2000: 7-40; Magubane 2004). Europe and North America have for decades dominated the rest of the world with their academic traditions and products. In the social sciences, the West has been consistently more 'advanced' and 'expansionist' than the 'underdeveloped' and 'dependent' regions of the world. In the late 1980s, American social science, in its 'unrelenting one-way traffic', was able to penetrate regions and countries with cultures as different from its own as those of Africa, France, India, Japan and the Republic of Korea (Gareau 1987: 599).

Seen in terms of modernisation theory where those who 'know best' about the one-best-way arrogate to themselves the right to prescribe, it is hardly surprising that the study of Africa continues to be dominated by perspectives that privilege analogy over the historical processes that should qualify Africa as a unit of analysis in its own right (Mamdani 1996: 12-13; Zeleza 1997). Although research on and in Africa has shaped the disciplines and our convictions of a supposedly universal truth (Bates et al., 1993: xiii-xiv), the quest for such universality has meant the marginalisation of African alternatives. What obtains has been nothing short of an epistemological imperialism that has facilitated both a Western intellectual hegemony and the silencing of Africans even in the study of Africa (Chinweizu 1987; Mafeje 1998: 26-29; Copans 1990: 305-395, 1993; Mkandawire 1997; Zeleza 1997; Obenga 2001; Amin 2005). This makes the situation particularly precarious for young and upcoming African scholars, who are confronted by histories they cannot just ignore and write as if debates had never previously taken place. Epistemologically, they are compelled to start by knowing what is documented already, for them to see if there are any differences from or similarities with the African perspectives envisaged (cf. Owomoyela 2001).

Understandably missing have been perspectives of the silent majorities (because of whose backwardness, or should we say inadequate modernisation, that is, Westernisation) find themselves deprived of the opportunity to tell their own development predicaments in their own ways or even to enrich defective accounts by others of their own life experiences. Correcting this entails doing more than paying token attention to the popular epistemologies from which ordinary people draw on a daily basis, and the ways they situate themselves in relationship to others within these epistemologies (p'Bitek 1989; Hountondji 1997; Nyamnjoh 2004a&b; Okere et al. 2005). The implication for African countries of taking their political, cultural, economic and intellectual cues from the West, as modernisation theorists suggest, is the risk of losing any political autonomy, cultural identity, economic independence and intellectual creativity that they may have. Yet as others argue below, these very qualities are the necessary preconditions for development in tune with the expectations, dignity and humanity of Africans.

Modernisation Theory as a Stubborn Illusion

Modernisation theory has mastered the art of recycling, camouflaging or disguising itself under various labels, as its disciples refuse or are simply incapable of changing their spots. Any alternative to modernisation theory today when globalisation has become its latest camouflage, should seek to build upon past critiques of its models of development. In this light, a number of criticisms are possible. This theory was designed originally to account for social change in the West during the emergence of capitalism. Its assumption that 'traditional' societies will (and should) converge on modern Western forms is ethnocentric. As a theory it does not correspond very well with the empirical facts, and tends to confuse ideal types with reality (Portes 1976).

It is the belief in and quest for homogeneity, the expressed or implied assumption that other societies should reproduce Western systems and institutions regardless of feasibility or contextual variations, which proponents of alternative perspectives have criticised in modernisation as the theory of homogenisation, as the West claims monopoly over 'freedom of imagination' (Chatterjee 1993:13). By restricting the concept of the rise of nations to that of the birth of capitalism, Western researchers have developed concepts and theories that extrapolate the parochial European experience (considered as 'normal'), and that 'reduce' the experiences of Africa, Asia and Latin America to those of the West (Abdel-Malek 1967: 250; Chatterjee 1993; Amin 2005). Instead of restructuring, modifying, enriching and remodelling their concepts and theories in order to accommodate the broader experiences and contextual variations of the contemporary world, these researchers have stubbornly insisted on Western intellectual hegemony or the comforts of studying down (Abdel-Malek 1967: 259; Portes 1976: 55-6; Gareau 1987: 596-7; Riggs 1987: 607-9). As Abdel-Malek (1967: 250-64) puts it, the European origins of the social sciences lead to Euro-centrism, whereby 'the world is conceived in the image of Europe' to which others are expected to conform, and where exceptions are not tolerated. This is very much in evidence in the current proliferation of 'scholarly' prescriptions on the so-called 'failed states of Africa', as blame is systematically taken away from the problematic assumption that 'nation-states' are possible and that they could be anything but dysfunctional in the current neoliberal configuration of global power relations, and that Africans are at fault for not attaining functional nation-states. And so, everything must be done to bring about 'functional states' in Africa, even if this entails placing 'failed' or 'dysfunctional' states under some kind of 'international trusteeship' (see Ellis 2005).

In the light of the weakness of African states vis-à-vis Western states and institutions in particular, many scholars recognise the need to form large economic, political and military units as Africa's only chance of effective intervention in the world today and of winning respect as real partners. They call for a break with 'the narrow ideology of the nation' inherited from nineteenth century Europe (Amin 1985: 107; Doumou 1987: 57; Goulbourne 1987; Cobban 1969: 124-9; Gabou 1987: 76-85; Hadjor 1987: 139). And some would argue that, their shortcomings notwithstanding, the African Union and NEPAD constitute the baby steps towards an eventual realisation of this dream.

The issue of popular democratic participation as a prerequisite for economic development has remained a recurrent theme in the literature on Africa since the 1980s (Goulbourne 1987; Hadjor 1987; Nyong'o 1987; Soyinka 1994; Olukoshi 2005). Observers of the liberal democratic process in Africa, especially since the 1990s, have borne witness that enfranchisement does not necessarily lead to empowerment and universal suffrage does not guarantee access to political decision-making (Ake 2000). Political equality almost everywhere has been confined to the right to vote, as autocrats have chosen to ignore the right of most to be voted for or to enjoy civil liberties in between elections. Although statements have been made to the contrary, ordinary people and alternative social and political organisations continue to face enormous difficulties exercising their rights: to hold and express opinions contrary to those held by the state and its leaders; to assemble freely and organise themselves in accordance with the law; to disseminate views and suggest alternative political strategies that may be contrary to those held by the leadership; and to expect protection from the state against the excesses of its own zealots (Goulbourne 1987: 46; Englund 2002; Fawole & Ukeje 2005; Nyamnjoh 2005a). Despite the rhetoric and alleged reality of liberal democracy, the state remains 'an interfering irritant, a source of corruptly obtained advantage or a massive irrelevance for many people' (Barnett 1997: 45), floating with impunity above civil society like a balloon in mid-air (Hyden 1983: 19), extracting loyalty and pleasure, exercising corrupt control at all levels of everyday life (Mbembe 2000). To Claude Ake, for all but a few, the postcolonial state 'is alien and remote, uncaring and oppressive'; it is encountered by ordinary people 'as ruthless tax collectors, boorish policemen and bullying soldiers, corrupt judges cynically operating a system of injustice, a maze of regulations through which they have to beg, bribe or cheat their way every day'; and has forced most of them to commit their loyalties to their home villages or ethnic groups (Ake 2000: 114). And who is to blame when a dress made to fit the slim, de-fleshed Hollywood consumer model of a Barbie doll-type entertainment icon cannot fit the body of a full-figured person, rich in all the cultural indicators of health Africans are familiar with? Curiously, under modernisation theory, neither the tiny dress nor its designer, nor the person who made a gift of it is to blame, as the assumption is that the Barbie-doll figure is everyone's dream and aspiration, the one-best-way of being (Nyamnjoh 2005c, 2005a: 25-39).

In the mid-1980s Goulbourne made an observation which is still very relevant. He noted that African governments have often justified repression with 'spurious arguments', one of which claims that to ensure 'rapid development it was necessary first to put controls in place', because any political differences were likely to divert attention from development, the main national pursuit. This view gives the impression that the leaders intended to tackle the issue of national development with total seriousness, and that it was only appropriate to 'consider putting aside some less pressing issues' for its sake. It was unwise for a country with limited resources, 'to dissipate its energies in the niceties, or luxuries, of allowing all and sundry to put their views about national matters when the task of prosecuting development is the national project over which independence was fought'. But as Goulbourne maintained, the very exclusion of a 'high degree of popular democratic participation' is in itself an obstacle to national development. 'Were democracy indeed the problem, its repeated suppression should have brought about rapid economic development' (Goulbourne 1987: 36-7). Soyinka is known for his critical views about the 'near-mystical linkage' which African leaders have tended to make between human rights and development, daring to imply that it is immoral to withhold aid from them because they withhold rights from their citizens. Soyinka compares this attitude to that of a mendicant mother, who with one hand 'holds out her beggar's cup to you', while 'the other is busy dealing vicious blows to the head of the wretched bundle that complements her own misery'. He purges the African intelligentsia of any claim to innocence, and accuses them of often providing the 'conceptual noises which legitimate' the costly rounds of 'competitive alienation' that African leaders impose on their peoples (Soyinka 1994: 7-9).

Writing in the late 1980s, Peter Anyang Nyong'o blamed African policy-makers for failing to understand the structural character of the national and international milieu in which they operated, and for the rigid suppression of the contending social forces in their own societies. Dependency notwithstanding, he believed that the lack of accountability on the part of those in power exacerbated the failure to bring about 'more positive social transformation and more auto-centred processes of accumulation'. He found 'a definite correlation between the lack of democratic practices in African politics and the deteriorating socioeconomic conditions' (Nyong'o 1987: 19). He stressed the need for a state capable of planning an 'inward-looking, self-centred and self-sufficient development' (Nyong'o 1987: 24); but one which at the same time must be controlled by and accountable to the popular forces which have been marginalised in the contemporary political arena, despite the enormous contributions they made to 'the national democratic struggles for independence' (Nyong'o 1987: 20). Armed with these convictions, Peter Anyang Nyong'o could not have had a better opportunity to prove himself when he joined the post-Moi government of Kibaki in 2002 as minister of Planning and National Development.

Also of increasing concern to African scholars is the missing or often inadequately stressed link between culture and development. Writing on this issue, Mazrui not only sees an inevitable link between culture and development in Africa—especially as 'Africans have demonstrated that they respond more to *socio-cultural* ideologies than to *socio-economic* ideologies'—but argues that instead of seeking the political kingdom first as prescribed by the late Kwame Nkrumah, Africans 'need to seek first the cultural kingdom, in the hope that much else will be added unto it' (Mazrui 1994: 127-136). For his part, Nyong'o argues that although 'the colonization of Africa was a serious challenge to African cultural autonomy', the emphasis by the postcolonial African leadership on the primacy of politics and their fascination with things foreign has meant that 'cultural changes in many African societies are not always deeply rooted in the local soil or home-grown'. He concludes that governments must show their commitment and seriousness 'to the development of their peoples by coming to terms with local cultures', and by seeking 'effective and meaningful domestication of the theory and practices of modernization' (Nyong'o 1994: 429-446).

Communication Research and Development

According to the Modernisation Theory, for traditional Africa to develop people had to change their attitudes and ways. To achieve this, they needed vast amounts of information and persuasion which could only be obtained through the mass media, 'the great information multipliers' (Schramm 1964: 246-7). This conception of development gave rise to a type of communication research that focussed mainly on the *effectiveness* of the techniques of persuasion, diffusion and adoption of innovations (Rogers 1962; 1973). Researchers influenced by this approach have tended to see social structure as an impediment to development and the traditional power elite as gatekeepers against modernisation. When such researchers seek to understand the social structures of the societies they study, it is in order to determine how best these structures could be replaced by 'modern' ones (Rogers 1973). Most prevailing uses of communication in development have relied heavily on this theory of 'exogenously induced change' which suggests that some societies are 'static' and that such 'static societies are brought to life by outside influences, technical aid, knowledge, resources and financial assistance and (in a slightly different form) by the diffusion of ideas' (Golding 1974: 43).

Some examples of the use of communication in this connection have been analysed. In 1977, under the auspices of UNESCO, Diaz Bordenave (1977) published the results of a critical evaluation of projects in ten countries where different mass media were used to promote rural development. The countries in question were Colombia, Brazil, India, Senegal, Peru, Iran, Tanzania, Canada, Tobago and the Philippines. Diaz Bordenave looked at the origin, background and reasons for each of the projects. He discovered that in none of the ten case studies did the request for a rural development programme using communication originate with the rural populations most concerned. A usual pattern was for a government to decide on a development scheme and then search out a locale and a team to carry out a communication programme to promote the scheme. Another was for an international agency or group to become interested in a communication technique or a development problem currently arousing interest and then find a country willing to embark on a programme centred on this technique or problem. In the light of these inadequacies, Diaz Bordenave argued for countries, bilateral, and international organisations to take a closer look at overall priorities in rural development and at communication resources so as to determine where rural development communication efforts are most needed and would have the greatest effect. Concerning sponsorship, he remarked that communication agencies involved with development programmes were often more interested in testing and promoting new 'hardware' than in analysing the realistic needs of the populations under study. In some of the case studies, the sponsors did not devote enough time to specify clearly what they really wanted and why, and thus found it difficult to prevent or attenuate divergences in opinion and expectation between sponsors. Government support in one form or another was the norm.

Most criticisms of development communication theories (see Servaes 1983, 1986, 1994; Kasongo 1998; Moemeka 2000; Okigbo & Eribo 2004) are similar to criticisms of Modernisation Theory in general. Their Western-centredness, their neglect of the international dimensions of both communication and development, and their emphasis on the attitudes rather than the structures that account for underdevelopment, have been heavily criticised. Development communication studies have tended to emphasise 'person-blame' rather than 'system-blame', and have failed to recognise that 'In the circumstances of many developing countries, existing patterns of power and exploitation mean that poor people have little reasonable prospect of self-betterment; and an attitude of fatalism may be the only realistic one' (Hartmann et al., 1989: 28). As Mamdani (1972) observed in the *Myth of Population Control*, a critical re-study of an earlier American-sponsored survey of birth control practices in a region of India that had reached problematic conclusions, it takes a critical predicament-oriented study to understand that people are not poor because they have large families. They have large families because they are poor. The tendency by researchers has been to treat all 'progressive change as unproblematic' and to assume that every innovation communicated is necessarily beneficial to the populations they affect. But as Hartmann et al. (1989: 255-69) argue, 'Changes that benefit one section of the community may leave others untouched or even damage their interests' (1989: 255).

Hartmann et al. (1989: 256) thus advocate the inclusion of 'social structure and structural conflict in discussions of development', and criticise the widespread tendency to 'treat the people as an amorphous mass' and to encourage a false sense of 'harmony of interests'. The rural population for example, are often credited with a harmony of interests that is more mythical than real. In their study of India, Hartmann et al., realised that not only are village societies 'highly differentiated in terms of access to resources and by caste and other divisions', but that they are 'characterised by competition for resources among different interest groups'.

Hartmann et al. (1989: 257-63) have also criticised the tendency in this model to consider those targeted by communication for development 'as essentially passive, an audience to be manipulated into compliance with the development nostrums of those who know best'. Such a tendency has made of the advertising campaign (social marketing) the dominant model for development communication, where everything is seen in terms of 'injecting' the development 'message' into communications directed at the 'target audience', as though development were a commodity to be sold like beer, soap or any other'. Communicating development 'is seen as an essentially mechanical process' in which the individual audience is treated both as passive and as detachable from the social context. This approach is reflected in communication studies, where the lion's share of research has gone to 'assessing audience response to deliberately persuasive 'messages' of the campaign type,' with emphasis on 'the KAP formula—knowledge, attitude, practice—which is deemed to be the sequence in which effects occur'. Yet the effects of communication are much larger than the rapid spread of information, and could include the gradual socialisation into alternative ways of seeing and doing. Like individuals and communities everywhere, Africans targeted by development communication 'may welcome, accept or collude in some cases, but in others they may ignore, select, reshape, redirect, adapt and, on occasions, even completely reject [media content]. Even when the same material is available to all and widely consumed, the eventual outcome may vary considerably both within and between countries' (Halloran 1993: 3).

In view of the rising disenchantment with the fact that modernisation has encouraged an orientation of mass media and communication that 'is essentially vertical, directive, aimed at manipulation and indoctrination', Diaz Bordenave (1977: 21-22) recommends Paulo Freire's 'pedagogy of the oppressed' as a way out. Freire argued that the mere transfer of knowledge from an authoritative source to a passive receiver does not promote the receiver's growth as an autonomous person conscious of the need to contribute to and influence his society. He proposed a 'pedagogy of the oppressed' wherein the emphasis is on participation, democracy and dialogue. Freire's approach suggests that not only may exogenously induced research methods be inappropriate to African conditions, but also that strict adherence to dominant research models may preclude the asking of the really important questions (see also Masilela 2000).

Halloran, using the example of comparative international research, which is quite common in development communication studies, echoes this point. Such research is by nature very difficult to conduct, but certain assumptions in orthodox research tradition have made it even more so. At the heart of the problem is the failure to recognize that social research is embedded in cultural values and that the fundamental differences (culture, language, demographic structure, experience, expectations, etc.) which obtain in different societies preclude the use of carbon copy survey or interview methods which assume that genuine comparability can be achieved only by administering the same questions in the same way in all participating countries. 'One has only to take note of the relationship between language and culture to realise that this approach is patently absurd' (Halloran 1981: 9). Thus methods of data collection no matter how appropriate in one context (say Western), are not necessarily so in another (say African). In adopting our research methods in development communication in Africa, how much attention have we paid to the continent's fundamental cultural, linguistic and demographic diversities, specificities, experiences and expectations?

The conventional quantitative techniques of data collection are not always adapted to the realities of Africa, much as we might like to use them. The cultural, linguistic and social cleavages in Africa are such that a researcher must exercise special care when applying research methods developed to suit the needs and expectations of mainly Western societies. Take the questionnaire for example. It can only be administered selectively, given the widespread rate of illiteracy in Africa. In the case of Cameroon, if the results of the 1987 census are to be believed, almost 50 percent of the entire population can neither read nor write French and English, the official languages. Of the 45 percent or so who have been to school, less than 20 percent have gone beyond primary level. Indeed less than three percent of the population have been educated further than secondary school. This not only seriously questions the use of questionnaires drawn up in French and English, but also their relevance as a research method in a largely oral society. And Cameroon is amongst the most literate societies in Africa. Translation is arguably a way out, but given Cameroon's mosaic linguistic situation and ethnic complexities, as well as the fact that many words and concepts in French and English do not have ready equivalents in indigenous languages, it is hard to see of what significant use translation could be. And if one were to stubbornly insist on using the questionnaire, these drawbacks notwithstanding, it would be a case of attempting to extrapolate or generalise from a most unrepresentative sample; so that any decision taken as a result of any such study is most unlikely to have grassroots support or endorsement. The elitist nature of such research methods compounds rather than alleviates the marginalisation of the African masses. And should one be surprised if development did not result from such research?

It is in this regard that as far back as 1963 Cheikh Anta Diop perceptively suggested a multi-methodological approach in African sociological research. He questioned the tendency to make *a priori* distinctions between sociological and anthropological methods and to equate the latter with the study of 'primitive' or 'archaic' societies. Every research situation, he maintained, should determine its methods. He argued that nowhere else better than in the study of African societies, can anthropology and sociology combine their methods and collaborate more effectively; for in Africa where indigenous elements co-exist with Western ones, changes are in process that are only inadequately understood with research methods drawn from both disciplines (Diop 1963: 181). Such methodological buffets offer better prospects than the insensitive insistence that certain methods must go with certain disciplines or certain types of inquiry.

Anthropology and its methods have certainly served to foster imperialist appropriation of Africa, but as a discipline, it has undergone critical self-appraisal and re-orientation that should be instructive for communication research, other disciplines and fields of study interested in Africa, especially in the age of flexibilities and contestations of essentialisms. Anthropology has progressed from functionalist models of evolutionary change through binary oppositions of structuralism, to an understanding of 'cultural and social organisation as dynamic rather than fixed or determined by a set of essentials' (Gardner & Lewis 1996: 51-52). Discussing anthropology and development, Gardner and Lewis have argued that both have little choice but to re-focus to enrich each other in our era of flexibilities and fluidities. Postmodernism, they argue, has contributed the celebration of difference and diversity to understanding of development processes and the relevance of anthropology therein. The result has been a demise of the unitary- or meta-narratives that accounted for the dominance of modernisation and dependency paradigms from the 1960s to the 1980s. Unitary theories of development have 'reached a profound impasse', as 'Emphasis on diversity, the primacy of localised experience and the colonial roots of discourses of progress, or the problems of the Third World, have radically undermined any attempt at generalisation' (Gardner & Lewis 1996: 22).

Far from being neutral and selfless, Gardner and Lewis argue, development and anthropological representations of development processes are embedded in power relations. To them, development is 'an enormously powerful set of ideas which has guided thought and action across the world' for the best half of the twentieth century. It 'involves deliberately planned' political, economic and social change, and continues to affect the lives of millions of people around the world, regardless of what critiques think or say of it (Gardner & Lewis 1996: 2). They perceive development as 'a series of events and actions, as well as a particular discourse and ideological construct' that are 'inherently problematic', and in certain regards, 'actively destructive and disempowering' (Gardner & Lewis 1996: 25). Far from being simple, homogenous, wholly monolithic, static and encompassing, as is often thought, development decision-making, policy and practice actually comprise 'a variety of countervailing perspectives and practices, as well as a multiplicity of voices' (Gardner & Lewis 1996: 78). In other words, 'development discourse is heterogeneous, contested and constantly changing'. Hence their conclusion that development processes 'are working in several directions at once—both towards and against change. At times and in some ways the dominant discourse and the power relations it involves are maintained; at other times, in other ways, they are challenged and slowly transformed'. For, 'contrary to the impression given in much contemporary analysis, discourses of development are not all the same; nor indeed are they fixed. Instead, they are constantly being contested and are therefore open to change'. Also, just as development 'does not involve a unitary body of ideas and practices,' so too developers 'are not a unitary body of people', and should not be treated as such, as has often been the case (Gardner & Lewis 1996: 125-128).

Gardner and Lewis recognise the need for a new anthropology of development that serves 'to deconstruct the knowledge of developers as well as those "to be developed"'. For 'development plans are often far from rational, and relationships within development institutions are as hierarchical, unequal and culturally embedded as any of the societies usually studied by anthropologists. The interface between developers and those to be developed is not simply a case of binary oppositions: modern ("scientific") versus traditional ("indigenous") thought. Instead, the paradigms within which developers work are as contextually contingent, culturally specific and contested as those of the social groups whom they target' (Gardner & Lewis 1996: 154-155). They suggest that in this process anthropologists could use gender and poverty as their stopping points to endless cultural relativism (Gardner

& Lewis 1996: 24-25). In and of development, anthropologists could 'help change the representations that development institutions produce', as being involved would facilitate both the adoption of anthropological perspectives by various development actors, and the shifting of 'discussions away from 'development' and towards a focus upon social relations of poverty and inequality'. They see 'the anthropological eye' and its focus on particular issues to be 'invaluable in the planning, execution and assessment of positive, non-oppressive developmental interventions' (Gardner & Lewis 1996: 76-78).

Gardner and Lewis invite anthropologists to challenge 'the social and political relations of poverty, through generating and applying anthropological insights' (Gardner & Lewis 1996:25). Anthropologists, they argue, 'can suggest alternative ways of seeing and thus step outside the discourse, both by supporting resistance to development and by working within the discourse to challenge and unpick its assumptions'. They note as encouraging the fact that 'anthropologists are increasingly picking away at development agencies, infiltrating their decision-making bodies, lobbying them from the inside and contributing to their reports'. However, the risk remains, of 'the dominant discourse co-opting anthropological concepts by translating them into simplified and homogenising categories' (Gardner & Lewis 1996: 76-77), given that 'ideas which start their life as radical alternatives all too often become a neutralised and non-threatening part of the mainstream'. 'Thus, although challenged by alternative perspectives, the extent to which the discourse has so far been significantly transformed is open to question' (Gardner & Lewis 1996: 103-104).

Whatever the risks of cooptation, they argue, the attitude and outlook which anthropology promotes is a lesson worth learning: 'a stance which encourages those working in development to listen to other people's stories, to pay attention to alternative points of view and to new ways of seeing and doing'. It is an attitude and outlook that continually question generalised assumptions that researchers and development agents might wittingly or unwittingly draw from their cultures and seek to apply elsewhere, and call attention to the various alternatives that exist in marginalised cultures. The lesson that anthropology could offer the development communication research 'is a continuous questioning of the processes, assumptions and agencies involved in development', while at the same time playing the role of 'unpicking, analysing and changing development practice over time' (Gardner & Lewis 1996: 167-168).

Alternative Communication Research in Africa

As Servaes and Arnst (1994: 2-3) have argued, it is about time that the poor and the illiterate, who 'have always been researched, described and interpreted by the rich and educated', became actively involved in, and why not take over, research on their predicaments, especially, as often, 'they best know their situation and have a perspective on problems and needs that no outsider can fully share'.

This call for participatory research is in tune with the call for more representative communication systems and the need for group, local or community media, in the face of increasing centralisation and synchronisation (UNESCO 1980: 55-7). Since the 1970s in Latin America for example, researchers have expressed the need for an 'alternative communication' system that is democratic, participatory and decentralised, and that is rooted in the masses who are currently marginalised by a communication system that serves the preponderant interests of the transnational corporations and the dominant internal economic and political power groups (White 1980; Diaz Bordenave 1977; White & Mcdonnell 1983; Reyes Matta 1986; Simpson Grinberg 1986). It is a type of communication that would serve the interests of 'the oppressed sectors of society at the national level, and the dominated countries at the international level', one that guarantees 'a process of dialogue and widespread creativity' (Reyes Matta 1986: 190-1).

To attain this alternative communication, Simpson Grinberg (1986: 183) for example, reiterates Golding's call for research (Golding 1974), by stressing 'the need to study the current extent and impact of native communication systems that pre-date the coming of the mass media' to the Third World. The 'marrow of alternative communication', he writes, 'is the decentralization of communication power, which implies a decentralisation of the technological know-how' (Grinberg 1986: 184). In White's (1980: 3) words, "*Communicación popular*" does not consist merely of an incorporation of "many elements of the folk culture"', but must be seen above all, as 'an attempt to set up communication channels independent of the hierarchy of intermediaries'. This entails a system of communication that is managed by the people, is horizontal, decentralised at every level, participatory, and free from the shackles of domination by either external or internal forces. Writing about the whole of the developing world, Hamelink calls for an emancipatory science (Hamelink 1983a), and prescribes 'dissociation' as the only real alternative to the process of 'cultural synchronization' perpetuated by the industrialised states, and as the sole guarantor of the autonomy and self-reliance 'essential for a process of independent development' (Hamelink 1983b).

The main characteristic of participatory communication is that the media arise from and are controlled by the locality. It comprises peasants or worker groups addressing themselves or other groups with similar concerns and aspirations. The media are socially horizontal in that they do not go 'up' to a communication centre controlled by higher-status individuals and then back 'down' again to other lower-status groups but direct from one lower-status group to another. The language of communication is the language of the people, freely chosen by them to communicate amongst themselves; it is not introduced or imposed by any outside leadership. If sympathetic specialists or professionals offer any expertise, it is purely technical and strictly on the terms of the locals (White 1980: 4; Criticos 1989: 36-7; Moemeka 2000).

For participatory communication to take root in Africa, there is the need for participatory research into how best to realise this aim. For, to adapt Hadjor (1987: 38-40), only through 'an intimate acquaintance with everyday life and the experience of the masses', can the communication researcher recognise 'what people want and how much they want it', and so be able to recommend what is necessary towards sustainable development or poverty eradication. Servaes and Arnst (1994: 4-5) consider participatory research as an educational process that is 'cyclical, continuous, local, and accessible', in that it comprises three interrelated facets namely: (i) 'collective definition and investigation of a problem by a group of people struggling to deal with it'; (ii) 'group analysis of the underlying causes' of the said problem; and (iii) 'group action to attempt to solve the problem'.

This sort of research has a lot to borrow from anthropology as discussed by Gardner and Lewis (1996) above, especially as anthropology is noted for the long periods its practitioners take to understand, in a multifaceted way and in detail, the communities or institutions they study. In addition to the attitude, outlook and other indicators highlighted by Gardner and Lewis above, Laburthe-Tolra and Warnier (1993: 367) talk of 'prolonged familiarity, within, in a face to face relationship and communication with a group, a region, a political, linguistic or residential community,' as the most distinctive characteristic of anthropological studies. Unfortunately, most people and organisations who recognise and appreciate the originality of the anthropological approach, have failed to recognise what accounts for that originality: the prolonged familiarity within a given community which is only possible if the researcher can get him/herself accepted into the group of study, and participate in its daily life. Only by so doing can the researcher uncover the solidarity that accounts for the dynamism of the group, or the tensions and conflicts that perpetuate underdevelopment. Findings from such research would certainly contribute towards the organisation of local or community activity that 'enlists the active participation of the people most in need of better opportunities' (Hartmann et al. 1989: 268).

Doing participatory research requires re-socialising and reappraising certain alternatives that we have either ignored in the past or simply never really thought of. It means that we must increasingly question certain basic assumptions, conventional wisdom, academic traditions and research practices, which we have uncritically and often unconsciously internalised, but which remain largely ill-adapted to our research contexts. We need to critically examine such 'canned' (Ramos quoted in Gareau 1987: 603) communication research methods imported from Europe and North America and see how they could best be harnessed or domesticated to serve Africa in its quest for sustainable development and poverty eradication.

The bulk of communication research on the continent remains heavily coloured by the American tradition where the tendency has been and remains 'to assume uncritically that social action can be understood mainly in terms of individual beliefs and attitudes', while largely ignoring in which ways such 'attitudes may be the product rather than the cause of economic conditions and power relationships'. Such 'simplistic psychologism ... takes insufficient account of the social and political dynamics of change and lacks an adequate conception of the relationships between ideas and actions, between culture and social structure'. It has produced the false belief that 'ideas may be manipulated more or less independently of structural factors' (Hartmann et al. 1989: 23).

What America has exported to Africa has been summarised by Kunczik (1993: 39) as research that emphasises the collection of 'commercially and politically quickly usable, methodically unexceptionably obtained facts, without reflecting further on them'. The result is usually 'a cornucopia of individual findings gained with the aid of sophisticated research instruments; findings that, because of the absence of a comprehensive theoretical framework, cannot be integrated'. The focus is on 'discovering short-range, quick and dependably identifiable effects', while 'the consideration that the mass media are part of an over-all social framework is completely ignored. The approach deals simply with the reactions of isolated individuals or groups to specific communications'. As Kunczik further points out, the emphasis on 'miniature surveys of little experiments that are quickly, routinely evaluable and usable whether for publication or for practical purposes' socialises the communication researcher in favour of 'an 'atomistic' perspective that does not take into consideration the over-all social aspects. Questions of how the research results can contribute to progress in the field, or how they can be integrated within a comprehensive theoretical framework, are generally ignored (Kunczik 1993: 40-41).

Such narrowly focussed and superficial studies fall within what Halloran has termed 'conventional research'. This is a type of research that stresses efficiency and practicality, is mostly atheoretical in nature, hardly relies on well-formulated or tested hypotheses, and is usually aimed at resolving a precise policy or commercial problem. Hence, it tends to be more concerned with sampling than with conceptualisation, and with description than with analysis. It is piecemeal in approach, scarcely integrated, and does not emphasise continuity. 'Irrespective of the nature of the social phenomenon under investigation, the final research report is usually confined to quantitative statements about amenable but relatively superficial aspects of a complex issue' (Halloran 1974: 8). Its 'positivistic/behaviouristic' approach has tended to blind its practitioners to the 'value assumptions ... implicit in every research question and that ... enter into the formulation of every research design' (Halloran 1983: 274). The researchers in this tradition hardly bother to redefine the research problem brought to them by governments and other agents of development; and their research tends to serve the 'interests that pay for it and find it useful in optimising their security and profitability' (Smythe & Dinh 1983: 118-121).

Conclusion

Some familiar with the culture of branding that characterises consumer capitalism where difference is less in the content of a product than in the fact that it is patented and identified under a unique brand name, are bound to question why in the twenty-first century where 'globalisation' is the latest brand in town, one should be discussing African development under an outdated conceptual model as 'modernisation theory'. It is not because the modernisation hydra loses a tentacle or two in a bout with a poorly organised and less self-confident rival, that its creative self-reinvention should be counted for dead. Just as leopards, scholars seem glued to their conceptual spots even when harkening to the rhetoric of theoretical re-orientation, especially when such spots feed on and are comforted by prejudices of relative superiority and ambitions of dominance as informed by race, culture, geography, class or gender.

However, my choice to discuss 'modernisation theory' is motivated less by brand loyalty than by reluctance to be swept away by appearances. A closer examination of the content beneath the brand name leaves little doubt that globalisation is nothing but a misleading label for the same basic modernisation package. Like a hydra modernisation has simply refused to lose out on the brand war by repairing and multiplying itself so profusely that even its staunchest critics are inclined to mistake its pluralism for diversity. It refuses to die simply because it has been decreed dead by analysts to whom rhetoric has always mattered more than reality. More importantly, modernisation is nurtured and sustained by vested political, economic, cultural and intellectual interests, which find in it an outlook, a way of life, a civilisation that all must be deployed to defend, maintain, reproduce and disseminate aggressively and deafly round the globe. Its survival and triumph lies in its ability to standardise and routinise research and scholarship, so that emphasis is shifted from thinking to doing, and from quality to quantity. Given such formidable forces at its service, it is hardly surprising that the touch and go, bite and blow attacks by those whose ways of life it assaults with intentions of cooption or annihilation, have only toughened its resistance and ingenuity.

As a branded methodological import from America, modernisation has survived in Africa more because it suits the purposes of its agents than because of its relevance to understanding the African situation. Those who run international development programmes along the Western model inspired by Modernisation Theory, 'are not interested in challenge, stimulation and provocation at any level' (Halloran 1981: 18). They want their programmes to go on without disturbance, and would only select as researchers or accept only those research questions and findings that confirm their basic assumptions on development in Africa. But the development communication researcher has the responsibility to challenge such unfounded assumptions based on vested interests and hidden agendas. This is by no means an easy task, especially since we rely on these very agents of development to fund our research. As Halloran observes in general, anyone in a position of power and control would hardly accept research that is critical of them. They therefore are more likely to sponsor only such research that would produce results that justify their position and/or help them in their defence when challenged (Halloran 1981: 20). To paraphrase Susan George (quoted in J. Barry Riddell 1992: 723), it matters not how many 'mistakes' mainstream researchers or development theorists make, for 'protected and nurtured by those whose political objectives they support, package and

condone, they have a licence to go on making them, whatever the consequences...'
Thus 'research frequently tends, in some way or other, to reflect the values and
reinforce the system within which it is conceived, supported and executed. In fact, in
some countries, it is deliberately intended that it should do this and it is important to
look at research as a possible form of social control' (Halloran 1981: 14). As development communication researchers, we cannot afford to be partial, blind or naive
whatever the pressures on us, and regardless of our level of misery and need for
sustenance. Thus for communication research to contribute towards a genuine,
multifaceted liberation of the African, we ought to start not by joining the band-
wagon as often we do, but with an insightful scrutiny of the whole idea of sustainable development or poverty eradication—its origin, form, content, assumptions,
practicability and articulation; and then be able to decide whether to accept, reject or
modify it.

Thus depending on the national, regional or cultural context wherein they operate, social scientists 'adopt contrary research designs and methodologies' (Gareau
1987: 598). This writer sees the social sciences as marked by profound ideological
conflicts, and their practitioners as looking in different places for evidence, and
using contrasting methods to determine whether or not they have found it (Gareau
1987: 598). Gareau's global view of social science thus 'sees its initiates as undergoing divergent professional socialization processes, reading different bodies of literature, and often coming to contrary conclusions' (Gareau 1987: 598). And thanks to
unequal power relations, some countries (the USA for example) and regions (Europe and North America—the West) have succeeded more than others in rendering
their 'social science sects' more visible and dominant globally, without necessarily
being more legitimate. Hence, as Schiller (1977) has pointed out, America for example, has used its rhetoric of 'Free Flow of Information' as a 'highly effective ideological club' to promote its political, economic and cultural values by whipping 'alternative forms of social organization' into a ridiculous defensiveness. This is certainly
comfort enough in our quest for development perspectives in tune with African
predicaments through scholarship stripped of mimicry.

References

Abdel-Malek, A., 1967, 'Sociologie du Développement National: Problèmes de Conceptualisation',
    Revue de L'Institut de Sociologie 2(3): 249-64.

Ajayi, J. F. A., 1966, 'The Place of African History and Culture in the Process of Nation-building
    in Africa South of the Sahara (1960)', in: I. Wallerstein, ed., *Social Change: The Colonial Situation*,
    New York: John Wiley & Sons, 606-16.

Ake, C., 2000, *The Feasibility of Democracy in Africa*, Dakar: CODESRIA.

Amin, S., 1985, *La Déconnexion: Pour Sortir du Système Mondial*, Paris: Éditions La Découverte.

Amin, S., 1997a, 'Reflections on the International System', in Golding, P. and P. Harris, eds., *Beyond
    Cultural Imperialism: Globalization, Communication & the New International Order*, London: Sage,
    10-24.

Amin, S., 1997b, 'L'Afrique et le Développement,', *Jeune Afrique Economie* 3 Février (234): 36-43.

Amin, S., 2005, 'The Driftages of Modernity: The Case of Africa and the Arab World', in Boron, A. A., and G. Lechini, eds., *Politics and Social Movements in an Hegemonic World: Lessons from Africa, Asia and Latin America*, Buenos Aires: Clacso Books, 79-116.

Barnett, T., 1997, 'States of the State and Third Worlds', in Golding, P. and P. Harris, eds., *Beyond Cultural Imperialism: Globalization, Communication & the New International Order*, London: Sage, 24-48.

Bates, R., V.Y. Mudimbe, and J., O'Barr, eds., 1993, *Africa and the Disciplines*, Chicago: The University of Chicago Press.

Chatterjee, P., 1993, *The Nation and Its Fragments: Colonial and Postcolonial Histories*, Princeton, New Jersey: Princeton University Press.

Chinweizu, 1987, *The West and the Rest of Us: White Predators Black Slavers and the African Elite*, Lagos: Preo Press.

Cobban, A., 1969, *The Nation State and National Self-Determination*, London: Collins.

Copans, J., 1990, *La Longue Marche de la Modernité Africaine: Savoirs, Intellectuels, Démocratie*, Paris: Karthala.

Copans, J., 1993, 'Intellectuels Visibles, Intellectuels Invisibles', *Politique Africaine* 51, (Octobre, 7-25.

Criticos, C., 1989, 'Community in Media', in C. Criticos, ed., *Experiential learning in Formal and Non-Formal Education*, Durban: Media Resource Centre, Department of Education University of Natal, 35-45.

Crossman, P. and R. Devisch, 1999, *Endogenisation and African Universities: Initiatives and Issues in the Quest for Plurality in the Human Sciences*, Leuven: Katholieke Universiteit Leuven.

Deutsch, K.W., 1966 [1953], *Nationalism and Social Communication*, London: The M.I.T. Press.

Deutsch, K.W., 1969, *Nationalism and its Alternatives*, New York: Alfred A. Knopf.

Diaz Bordenave, J. E., 1977, *Communication and Rural Development*, Paris: UNESCO.

Diop, C.A., 1963, 'Sociologie africaine et méthodes de recherche', in *Présence Africaine* 48: 180-186.

Doumou, A., 1987, 'The State and Popular Alliances: Theoretical Preliminaries in the Light of the Moroccan Case', in P. A. Nyong'o, ed., *Popular Struggles for Democracy in Africa*, London: Zed Books, 48-77.

Ellis, S., 2005, 'How to Rebuild Africa', *Foreign Affairs* 84(5): 1-14.

Emmanuel, A., 1972, *Unequal Exchange: A study of the Imperialism of Trade*, New York: Monthly Review Press.

Englund, H., ed., 2002, *A Democracy of Chameleons: Politics and Culture in the New Malawi*, Uppsala: Nordiska Afrikainstitutet.

Fawole, W. A. and C. Ukeje, eds., 2005, *The Crisis of the State and Regionalism in West Africa: Identity, Citizenship and Conflict*, Dakar: CODESRIA Books.

Ferguson, J., 1990, *The Anti-Politics Machine: 'Development', Depoliticization and Bureaucratic Power in Lesotho*, Cambridge: Cambridge University Press.

Ferguson, J., 1999, *Expectations of Modernity: Myths and Meanings of Urban Life on the Zambian Copperbelt*, Berkeley: University of California Press.

Gabou, M.L., 1987, *The Crisis in African Agriculture*, London: Zed Books.

Gardner, K. & D. Lewis, 1996, *Anthropology, Development and the Post-Modern Challenge*. Pluto: London.

Gareau, F.H., 1987, 'Expansion and Increasing Diversification of the Universe of Social Science', *International Social Science Journal* (114): 595-606.

Golding, P., 1974, 'Media Role in National Development: Critique of a Theoretical Orthodoxy', *Journal of Communication* 24(3): 39-53.

Goulbourne, H., 1987, 'The State, Development and the Need for Participatory Democracy in Africa', in P.A. Nyong'o, ed., *Popular Struggles for Democracy in Africa*, London: Zed Books, 26-47.

Hadjor, K. B., 1987, *On Transforming Africa: Discourse with Africa's Leaders*, Trenton and London: Africa World Press and Third World Communications.

Halloran, J. D., 1974, *Mass Media and Society*, Leicester: Leicester University Press.

Halloran, J. D., 1986, 'Beyond Development Communication: The International Research Experience', Paper presented at the AMIC-WACC-WIF Consultation: Singapore, 18-22 November.

Halloran, J. D., 1993, 'The European Image: Unity in Diversity—Myth or Reality', A Presentation at the IAMCR Conference, Dublin, June 1993.

Hamelink, C. J., 1983a, 'Emancipation or Domination: Toward a Utopian Science of Communication', *Journal of Communications* 33(3): 74-9.

Hamelink, C. J., 1983b, *Cultural Autonomy in Global Communications: Planning National Information Policy*, London: Longman.

Hartmann, P., Patil, B. R., Dighe, A., 1989, *The Mass Media and Village Life: An Indian Study*, New Delhi: Sage Publications.

Hountondji, P., ed., 1997, *Endogenous Knowledge: Research Trails*, Dakar: CODESRIA.

Hyden, G., 1983, *No shortcuts to Progress*, London: Heinemann.

Kasongo, E., 1998, Are Africa's Development Failures due to Cultural Irrationality or the Development Manner? Towards a Theory of Sustainable Community Development through Communication, PhD thesis, University of Natal, Durban, South Africa.

Kunczik, M., 1993, *Communication and Social Change*, Bonn: FES.

Laburthe-Tolra, P., and J.-P. Warnier, 1993, *Ethnologie, Anthropologie*, Paris: PUF.

Lerner, D., 1958, *The Passing of Traditional Society: Modernizing the Middle East*, New York: The Free Press.

Mafeje, A., 1998, 'Anthropology and Independent Africans: Suicide or End of an Era?' *African Sociological Review* 2(1): 1-43.

Magubane, Z., 2004, *Bringing the Empire Home: Race, Class, and Gender in Britain and Colonial South Africa*, Chicago: The University of Chicago Press.

Mamdani, M., 1972, *The Myth of Population Control*, New York: Monthly Review Press.

Mamdani, M., 1996, *Citizen and Subject: Contemporary Africa and the Legacy of Late Colonialism*, London: James Currey.

Masilela, T.S.B., 2000, 'Walking with Paulo Freire: Political/development Communication and Alternative Media in Africa', in Servaes, J., ed., *Walking on the Other Side of the Information Highway: Communication, Culture and Development in the 21st Century*, Penang: Southbound: 35-145.

Mazrui, A., 1994, 'Development in a Multi-Cultural Context: Trends and Tensions', in: I. Serageldin and J. Taboroff (eds.), *Culture and Development in Africa*, The World Bank: Washington (pp.127-136).

Mbembe, A., 2000, *De la Postcolonie: Essai sur l'Imagination Politique dans l'Afrique Contemporaine*, Paris: Karthala.

Mkandawire, T., 1997, 'The Social Sciences in Africa: Breaking Local Barriers and Negotiating International Presence', The Bashorun M. K.O. Abiola Distinguished Lecture Presented to the 1996 African Studies Association Annual Meeting, *African Studies Review* 40 (2): 15-36.

Moemeka, A., 2000, *Development Communication in Action: Building Understanding and Creating Participation*, Maryland: University Press of America.

Ngugi wa Thiong'o, 1986, *Decolonising the Mind: The Politics of Language in African Literature*, London: James Currey.

Nyamnjoh, F. B., 2004a, 'A Relevant Education for African Development—Some Epistemological Considerations', *Africa Development* 29 (1): 161-184.

Nyamnjoh, F. B., 2004b, 'From Publish or Perish to Publish and Perish: What "Africa's 100 Best Books" Tell Us about Publishing Africa', *Journal of Asian and African Studies* 39 (5): 331-355.

Nyamnjoh, F. B., 2005a, *Africa's Media, Democracy and the Politics of Belonging*, London: Zed Books.

Nyamnjoh, F. B., 2005b, 'Fishing in Troubled Waters: Disquettes and Thiofs in Dakar', *Africa* 75 (3): 295-324.

Nyamnjoh, F. B., 2005c, 'Africa in 2015: Interrogating Barbie Democracy, Seeking Alternatives', *Democracy & Development—Journal of West African Affairs* 4 (2): 107-112.

Nyong'o, P.A., 1987, 'Introduction', in P. A. Nyong'o, ed., *Popular Struggles for Democracy in Africa*, London: Zed Books, 14-25.

Obenga, T., 2001, *Le Sens de la Lutte Contre l'Africanisme Eurocentriste*, Paris: Khepera and L'Harmattan.

Odhiambo, E. S. A., 2004, 'Africa's "Brain Gain": Whose Shibboleth?' Paper prepared for Africa's Brain Gain Conference, 19-22 December, Nairobi, Kenya.

Okere, T., Njoku, C. A., and Devisch, R., eds., 2005, (Special issue, 'All Knowledge is First of all Local'), *Africa Development* 30 (3).

Okigbo, C. and Festus Eribo, F., eds., 2004, *Development and Communication in Africa*, Lanham, Rowman and Littlefield.

Olukoshi, A., 2005, 'Changing Patterns of Politics in Africa', in Boron, A. A., and G. Lechini, eds., *Politics and Social Movements in an Hegemonic World: Lessons from Africa, Asia and Latin America*, Buenos Aires: Clacso Books, 177-201.

Owomoyela, O., 2001, 'From Folklore to Literature: The Route from Roots in the African World', in I. Okpewho, B. C. Davies, and A. A. Mazrui, eds., *The African Diaspora*, Bloomington: Indian University Press, 275-289.

P'Bitek, O., 1989, *Song of Lawino*, Nairobi: East African Educational Publishers.

Portes, A., 1976, 'On the Sociology of National Development: Theories and Issues', *American Journal of Sociology* 82 (1): 55-85.

Reyes Matta, F., 1986, 'Alternative Communication: Solidarity and Development in the Face of Transnational Expansion', in R. Atwood and E.G. McAnany, eds., *Communication & Latin American Society: Trends in Critical Research, 1960-1985*, Wisconsin: The University of Wisconsin Press, 190-214.

Riddell, B.J., 1992, 'The new Face of Imperialism and Africa's Poverty', *The Journal of Modern African Studies* 30 (4): 721-725.

Riggs, F. W., 1987, 'Indigenous Concepts: A Problem for Social and Information Science', *International Social Science Journal* 114: 607-17.

Rogers, E. M., 1962, *Diffusion of Innovations*, New York: The Free Press.

Rogers, E. M., 1973, 'Social Structure and Social Change', in G. Zaltman, ed., *Processes and Phenomena of Social Change*, New York: John Wiley & Sons, 75-87.

Roncagliolo, R., 1986, 'Transnational Communication and Culture', in R. Atwood and E.G. McAnany, eds., *Communication & Latin American Society: Trends in Critical Research, 1960-1985*, Wisconsin: The University of Wisconsin Press, 79-88.

Sachs, J., 2005, *The End of Poverty: How we can make it happen in our lifetime*, London: Penguin Books.

Schiller, H. I., 1977, 'The Free Flow of Information—For Whom?', in G. Gerbner, ed., *Mass Media Policies in Changing Cultures*, London: John Wiley and Sons, 105-15.

Schipper, W. J. J., 1990, 'Homo Caudatus: Imagination and Power in the Field of Literature', in W. J. J. Schipper, W. L. Idema, and H. M. Leyten, *White and Black: Imagination and Cultural Confrontation (Bulletin 320)*, Amsterdam: Royal Tropical Institute-Amsterdam, 11-30.

Schramm, W., 1964, *Mass Media and National Development: The Role of Information in the Developing Countries*, Stanford: Stanford University Press.

Servaes, J., 1983, *Communication and Development*, Leuven: Acco.

Servaes, J., 1986, 'Communication and Development Paradigms: An Overview', in: *Media Asia* 13 (3): 128-36.

Servaes, J. and R. Arnst, 1994, 'Participatory Communication in the Research Process', Paper for the Ninth ACCE biennial conference 'Media and Sustainable Development in Africa', Accra, Ghana, October 16-23.

Simpson Grinberg, M., 1986, 'Trends in Alternative Communication Research in Latin America', in R. Atwood and E.G. McAnany, eds., *Communication & Latin American Society: Trends in Critical Research, 1960-1985*. Wisconsin: The University of Wisconsin Press, 165-189.

Smith, A. D., 1986, 'State-Making and Nation-Building', in J. A. Hall, ed., *States in History*, Oxford: Basil Blackwell, 228-63.

Smythe, D. W. & Dinh, T. V., 1983, 'On Critical and Administrative Research: A New Critical Analysis', *Journal of Communication* 33 (3): 117-127.

Soyinka, W., 1994, 'Democracy and the Cultural Apologia', *Afrika Spectrum* 29 (1): 5-13.

Summers, L. H. and V. Thomas, 1993, 'Recent Lessons of Development', *Research Observer* 8 (2): 241-254.

Teferra, D. and P. G. Altbach, eds., 2003, *African Higher Education: An International Reference Book*, Bloomington: Indiana University Press.

UNESCO, 1980, *Many Voices, One World: Towards a new more just and more efficient world information and communication order*, London: Kogan Page.

Wallerstein, I., 1964, *The Road to Independence: Ghana and the Ivory Coast*, Paris: Mouton.

White, R. A., 1980, '"Communicaciön Popular": Language of Liberation', *Media Development* 27 (3): 3-9.

White, R. A. and J. M. Mcdonnell, 1983, 'Priorities for National Communication Policy in the Third World', *The Information Society Journal* 2 (1): 5-43.

Zeleza, P. T., 1997, *Manufacturing African Studies and Crises*, Dakar: CODESRIA Books.

Zeleza, P. T. and A. Olukoshi, eds., 2004, *African Universities in the Twenty-First Century* (Volumes 1 and 2), Dakar: CODESRIA.

Chapter 18

African Cultural Studies and Contemporary African Philosophy

Lewis R. Gordon

The presence and impact of cultural studies in the First World academies are both undeniable and ambivalent. They are undeniable because there is no major university in any of the regions that comprise this geopolitical unit without scholars or programs devoted to the study of human phenomena under the rubric of 'cultural studies'. Their reality is met by ambivalence, however, because of the ongoing battles over questions of rigour and disciplinarity in the Western academy. Even where cultural studies is present, and may even be having great impact, it may meet opposition as a legitimate, *academic* field of inquiry. This is primarily because of the tendency of such scholars to focus on 'popular' culture, the consequence of which, from a more traditional, academic perspective, is the appearance of 'fluff' or less enduring work. Moreover, the political history of cultural studies is one that often valorises working-class and *lumpenproletariat* communities across racial and ethnic lines, and, when wedded to postmodern developments, it extols so-called 'marginalised' groups, the result of which has been an alliance with identity politics and the politics of difference that at least lays claim to favouring such groups.[1] The backlash marked by the term 'political correctness' has been the result of this association (see Butler 2002; Gordon 1997, esp. 92-100).[2]

Identity politics and the politics of difference that locate Africans and the African diaspora on the 'margins' find themselves at the outset situated by the confines of white normativity. By white normativity, I mean the centring of whiteness as the perspective on and of reality. In an African-centred world, the question of African marginality would make no sense. It would mean, literally, for the African to look at the African self wholly from the perspective of the non-African. This is not to say that such an exercise does not ever occur. Nor is it to say that it doesn't often occur.

The geopolitical reality of the present is that beyond highly localised and immediate realities of day-to-day living, where one's customs tend to prevail, the notion of a globally centric self-understanding outside of the First World nations is absent except in cases of nearly delusional or fanatic indoctrination of past ages.[3] The late twentieth-century and early twenty-first century conflict both within Islam and between Muslim and non-Muslim communities is indication of at least one effort to assert an alternative centre that conjoins word and deed.

The question of identity, difference, and centring in academic circles is, however, more conditioned by discourses of First World nations, and even in the case of Islam, the formulations still work within predominantly secular—read European and Modern—practices and processes of legitimation. In other words, scholarship itself is conditioned by the centring of Modern European academic culture. For the African academic who decides to study things and people African, this identity of being in effect a Western European academic and an African has led to reflections on the political and epistemological meaning of the 'Westernised African'.[4] The anxiety of this African figure is that although he or she appears as an amalgam of at least two (often several) cultural perspectives, his or her legitimating practices—how the scholar advances truth and reality—tends to be indisputably non-African, which exemplifies a form of African subordination. The message is often clear: Whatever Africa 'was', its future is a different Africa, one that is a fusion with the legacies of Europe and Asia with the latter two carrying greater normative force. It is an anxiety shared by the African diaspora, as evidenced by George Lamming's (1970) remarkably poignant novel, *In the Castle of My Skin*, where the author reflects upon a world that constitutes him while simultaneously being a world that is to be washed away by the torrents of history.

The source of such cultural anxiety comes, of course, from the relation of messengers to messages. Must it be the case that the messenger's identity be constitutive of the message? The answer is at first obviously negative where the message is treated as pre-formed and intact and simply 'delivered' by the messenger. But there is an insight from the mythopoetics of cultures all over the world, whether by way of tricksters such as the Yorubu Esu-Elegbara in Africa, the clever spider Anancy in the Caribbean, the signifying monkey in African America, or Hermes the trickster and messenger in Ancient Greece and the namesake of the academic technique of 'Hermeneutics'—namely, the messenger *affects* messages whether by embellishing them, by rendering them ambiguous, or by lying.[5] Thus, whatever the initial message may have been, its delivery and meaning is at the mercy of the messenger. Many of the disciplinary and intellectual programmes in the contemporary academy emerged out of the revolution in knowledge production that took place in Europe and then in conjunction with its colonies known as the emergence of modern science. What the African intellectual faces in the modern academy, then, is that both the message and the messenger boil down to the same story of a European *hegemon*.

Africa in Cultural Studies

Cultural studies has been an academic enterprise from its inception, and it, for the most part, continues to be so. This fact means that it comes to the African intellectuals as an ally by virtue of their relation to the European centre while at the same time functioning as one among many bits of flame of what Mary Wollstonecraft Shelley calls the 'modern Prometheus' (modernised Greek) instead of Osiris (Ancient Egyptian) or, say, Onyam' (Akan).[6] The standard history of cultural studies begins in Birmingham, at the Centre for Contemporary Cultural Studies in 1964, under the leadership of Richard Hoggart, author of *The Uses of Literacy*. The programme offered an interdisciplinary approach to the study of culture through the resources of Marxist social theory. Its history is marked by several forays into conflicts with structural Marxism as developed by Louis Althusser on the one hand, and the advancement of Gramscian Marxism, particularly Antonio Gramsci's notions of hegemony and organic intellectuals, through the leadership of Stuart Hall, on the other (Morley et al., 1996). Yet its intellectual history preceded the 1964 founding of the institute by way of the emergence of the New Left and the role of E. P. Thompson, Raymond Williams, and Stuart Hall in developing a leading voice by way of founding the *New Left Review*. It is without question, however, that it is with Stuart Hall's leadership and through his charisma that both the centre and the movement that constituted British cultural studies achieved international prominence and led to the development of cultural studies programmes in universities worldwide.

The place of Africa in the development of cultural studies has ironically been peripheral. This is perhaps due to the influence of Caribbean and South Asian immigrants in Britain, and in North America it is connected to the impact of the Atlantic Slave Trade, the unique forms of invisibility faced by indigenous populations, and the ongoing tides of immigrants from the Caribbean and Asia. The main exception in this regard has been the unique history of South Africa (Cooper and Steyn 1996). The anti-apartheid struggle led to a variety of exiled intellectuals—black, coloured, Asian, and white—the result of which was a concomitant development of discourses and praxes highly sympathetic to the New Left foundations of the Birmingham groups and yet attuned to new and ever-evolving questions of race that initiated linkages with North American and Caribbean communities.[7] The influence of Steve Bantu Biko (2002; see also Sanders 2002), with his ecumenical conception of Black Consciousness, is a key example of this development. At this stage, cultural studies became a partner with what has become known as postcolonial studies, but the African element, even the South African one, was soon eclipsed by the Middle Eastern and South Asian tides primarily due to the enormous impact of Edward Said's (1979) *Orientalism* and the influential work of Gayatri Spivak and subsequently Homi Bhabha.[8] By the 1980s, the question of postcoloniality became almost exclusively devoted to constituencies along the lines of those scholars' research interests, but the question of cultural studies from the Birmingham perspective continued its development and moved across the Atlantic as Stuart Hall and some of his best proteges—namely, Kobena Mercer, Hazel Carby, Paul Gilroy, and Isaac Julien—made their mark in such influential United States institutions of higher learning as the University of California at Santa Cruz, Yale University, and New York University. The impact of their work, conjoined with the already budding African American cultural studies movements led by Houston Baker, Jr., Henry Louis Gates, Jr., Cornel West, and bell hooks/Gloria Watkins, culminated in bodies of work emanating primarily from three institutions each of which enjoyed having a heyday in the field: Yale in the early through mid-1980s; Princeton in the late 1980s through early 1990s; and then Harvard University for most of the 1990s.[9] Throughout the 1990s, there was, however, an unusual, ongoing community of scholars focussing on the study of the African diaspora with unique attention to Africa, and that group was the New York University Africana Studies programme under the leadership of Manthia Diawara. That group distinguished itself by its excellent work on African and African diasporic cinema, its ongoing development of Francophone African cultural studies, and its inclusion of such eminent Africana literary giants in its alumni as Ngugi Wa Thiong'o and Kamau Braithwaite, which marked a decisive moment in the study of African literary culture.

In the meantime, there continued to be a group of young scholars devoted to fusing the Marxist brands of cultural studies with questions of postcoloniality in Africa and the Anglophone Caribbean. This group was particularly concerned with the seeming occlusion of the question of Africa as a site of postcolonial discourse. Its members include such scholars as Benita Parry, Neil Lazarus, and Laura Chrisman.[10] This group is, in many ways, critical of the developments that occurred in the later Birmingham group because of the more postmodernist tendencies of the latter evidenced by their focus on such thinkers as Gilles Deleuze, Jacques Lacan, Jacques Derrida, and their often very critical and at times derisive views of black liberation movements.[11]

While such developments were emerging in cultural studies and questions of Africa, another discourse was also evolving, and its roots were in the late 1960s and early 1970s. That development we could call *Contemporary African philosophy*. Its beginnings were through theological auspices in stream with the growing liberation theologies of the last half of the twentieth century. Unlike the cultural studies turn, its aims were more explicitly systematic and foundational, and although it has not enjoyed as much popularity as the cultural studies movement, it has in its own way occasioned a revolution in the thinking about Africa in late modernity. It is to that movement I shall now turn.

Contemporary African Philosophy

The second half of the second Millennium ACE has been marked by the unquestionable emergence of European civilisations as the dominant imperial forces whose reach span economic, epistemological, and cultural realms. Accompanying that expansion has been a sustained query on the European self the consequence of which is, literally, *the European self.* Prior to such emergence, there was no self-identified Europe. This process of forming the notion of a geopolitical self is, however, symbiotically linked to the negation of that self; that is to say that the process of determining 'what' constitutes Europe and things European requires formulating what does *not* constitute such phenomena. The tale of the unfolding of such identity is known as European modernity, and with it a simultaneous tale of what Enrique Dussel calls its 'underside' of the geopolitical significance of 1492. Although there is an African tale that preceded 1492 by virtue of the Portuguese forays along the West African coast as early as the 1420s, the Columbus phenomenon marks a new stage in the march of European global supremacy.[12] It is with the Columbus voyage that the notion of the 'new' came into the equation, which renders the African element paradoxically a chart of discovery about things 'old'. Peoples of Africa and Europe have, after all, been in communication with each other for ages, and the presence of the Moors in Portugal and Spain was, in many ways, a function of that ongoing relationship of conquerors today and the conquered tomorrow. What was different, however, in the developments from the fifteenth century onward was that such conflicts were no longer between some peoples of one continent and those from another, but between entire peoples of the continents and those of other continents. In short, it became *Europeans* conquering, enslaving, and colonising *Africans, American Indians,* and *Australian Aboriginals*; not, in other words, the Spaniards, French, or English against those other peoples. Rationalisations accompanied this development, and those rationalisations led to the emergence, first, of 'damned' people through Biblical rationalisations of children of Ham, Noah's cursed son; and then naturalistic explanations that later culminated in questions of who constitutes the truly human and who does not. Increasingly, discourses on the human began to emerge the consequence of which became the human sciences in general and anthropology in particular.

African peoples in the midst of all this rationalisation began to discover that they had an identity imposed from *without*—namely, the continental identity of being African. They also discovered a similar racial identity similarly imposed—that of being either *black* people or *primitives*.[13] And they began to discover that beyond the dignity afforded by the localism of their ethnic identities—Asante, Fanti, Yoruba, Ibo, Masai, Twa, etc.,—they were regarded in European and Asian regions as less than human. Their humanity challenged, they began modes of resistance that included not only slave revolts the most dramatic of which was the Haitian Revolution in the New World, but also ways of advancing their humanity through the formation of discourses that constitute things human in the first place. The slave narratives of the eighteenth and nineteenth centuries are key exemplars of such acts of epistemic resistance.[14] Whether Quabno Cugoano and Wilhelm Amo in the eighteenth century or Frederick Douglass and the Reverend John Jasper in the nineteenth, they all culminated in the question of what constitutes being human.[15]

For people whose humanity have long been denied, the value of philosophical anthropology became their *philosophia prima.*

A consequence of the differentiation of the European self from the African one raises the question of the degree of difference between peoples on the two continents. How radically different from each other are Europeans and Africans? Given the racial subtext of this question—wherein the Northern and Eastern Semitic peoples are not often the subject of such a query—we could translate the question into how different are whites in Europe from blacks in Africa. European thinkers have not been unanimous in their response to this question. Thomas Paine argued that the differences were superficial enough not to warrant the practice of slavery, whereas David Hume and Immanuel Kant argued that they were substantial enough not to take seriously the status of blacks as human beings.[16] G. W. F. Hegel (1956), in the introduction to his *Philosophy of History* presented the most influential support for radical, substantial difference by virtue of his claim in the introduction that history didn't even pay a courtesy visit to the black peoples of Africa. Even the virtue of religiosity should not be ascribed to Africans, in Hegel's view, for genuine religion requires a movement of spirit (*Geist*) and the emergence of consciousness, whereas Africans, as he saw them, were capable only of sorcery and the primitivism of magic. The impact of the Hegelian view becomes acute when the question of philosophy is raised in the African context, for the movement of History for Hegel is also the unfolding realisation of Reason; thus, to search for the practice of reason as manifested in philosophy in the place that exemplified the antipode of reason was a contradiction of terms. Philosophy was for a long time since rejected by Europeans as existing in Africa not on the basis of empirical evidence but on the conviction that *it could not exist there by virtue of its indigenous people.*[17]

The result of the Hegelian thesis was much ignoring of Medieval African thought and the complex intellectual history of various African nations well into the mid-twentieth century. Much of the continued failure to examine Africa in this light is premised upon the ongoing misrepresentation of Africa as a continent without indigenous forms of writing.[18] Although philosophy does not rely on writing for its performance and existence, its place in intellectual history (of any kind) has been much facilitated by the existence of written texts. The current research on Abyssinian Medieval philosophers is a function of their having left a legacy of written texts, and the effort to write down the origination narratives of many oral traditions worldwide is a function of the declining numbers of individuals with both the time and devotion to maintain such vast reservoirs of their cultures in their individual memory.[19]

The 'Westernised African' returned, then, as academics raised in their local traditions but trained in another.[20] This African academic usually faces two major tasks. The first is translation, where the task is to articulate the tenets of the traditional African culture in Western academic terms. This is a project geared not only at the non-African academic, but also at fellow African academics, for the language of the academy becomes one of the many languages they face mastering in their life's journey. The second task is to formulate theories, interpretations, and criticisms of their own. This latter aim could be in the language of the Western academy, but it need not be so. An influential and much criticised text that exemplifies these two tasks is John S. Mbiti's (1990 [1969]) *African Religions and Philosophy*. Mbiti offers in that work a systematic account of the structures of Bantu-speaking societies through an analysis of their conception of time. The importance of such a focus emerges from a basic philosophical insight: there are no values without temporality. Eternal creatures, for instance, neither come into time nor go out of it, which presents serious metaphysical problems, not only as to whether they can 'act', but also whether their behaviours could translate into meaningful ones. Creatures who gain immortality face a similar dictate, only they have the addition of having been born. Yet, there is no accident that many civilisations portray such mythic creatures as monsters. Not being able to die takes meaning from their lives and makes what is insignificant to them behaviours that for the rest of us—mortal and hence finite—monstrous. Values are thus linked to the fact that we are born, we live for a time with knowledge of an accumulated past and awareness that we will eventually die, and even if we don't worry much about our own death, the eventual death of our loved ones is sufficient to stimulate much concern.[21] One could go further and present a transcendental phenomenological version of this argument thus: There is no consciousness without intentionality, where consciousness is consciousness *of* something, but 'something' cannot be apprehended without maintenance of it if but for a nanosecond. Such notions as sustaining a thought or a concept requires temporality, which makes time a necessary condition of consciousness.[22] Since there is no point in talking about the values of a community without members of that community being conscious, then the argument for the temporal advances through to the question of community. Mbiti's concerns with meaning require such a philosophical manoeuvre.

Mbiti's argument, of which much criticism has been made, is that the metaphysics and cosmology of Bantu-speaking peoples is premised on the view that all being, all actuality, flows from God, which means that nothing ever 'is' until the forces that constitute God's ongoing unfolding of reality occur.[23] What that means is that there is no future until the future occurs, which means for it to be, it must become the present and then the past. In Mbiti's words (1990: 17),

> The future is virtually absent because events which lie in it have not taken place, they have not been realized and cannot, therefore, constitute time. If, however, future events are certain to occur, or if they fall within the inevitable rhythm of nature, they at best constitute only *potential time* not *actual time*. What is taking place now no doubt unfolds the future, but once an event has taken place, it is no longer in the future but in the present and what is past. It moves 'backward' rather than 'forward'; and people set their minds not on future things, but chiefly in what has taken place.

Mbiti's argument can easily be misread to entail that Bantu-speaking people have no conception of time. What the argument does reveal is a theory of temporal realism. What this means is that the unfolding of events are all that constitute reality. But more, if the *source* of such an unfolding constitutes the densest exemplification of reality—namely, God—then each subsequent event is of less ontological potency than its predecessor. In effect, there is a kind of metaphysical 'fall' or 'drying up' of the real to the eventual unreal. The significance of this schema becomes apparent in one striking value in many African axiologies: The importance of ancestors.[24] That ancestors precede us affords them a greater place both in the ontology and its accompanying order of values. Our parents are not simply more experienced than we are; they are more valuable than we are, and so are we in relation to our children. (This does not mean that we cannot value our children through loving them, and it can easily be argued that our children's appreciation of us should be a function of the enormous value of the love we offer them).

For our purposes, the importance of Mbiti's argument is that he has tapped into a concept that is a unique development in contemporary (and perhaps all) African philosophy, and because of this development, that philosophy's relation to the human sciences and consequently the study of African culture. Although there are many meta-philosophical analyses of philosophy in the African context, many of which offer their advancement and criticisms of such developments as ethno-philosophy, sage philosophy, 'professional' philosophy, and praxis philosophy, a striking feature of African philosophy that is often not discussed is African philosophers' near obsession with the past.[25] These philosophers, even the analytical ones among them, take on the past with the zeal of the proverbial drowning man. There is the very practical question of reconstructing what anti-black and Eurocentred scholars have claimed never existed. But this does not explain the peculiarity of the sense of normative urgency African (and Africana) philosophers bring to their historical work, the zeal. Many of us know, that is, that racists attitudes belie the significance of proof that contradicts their racist attitudes; they collapse such evidence into the realm of 'exceptions' to the point of there being no amount of sufficient evidence that could collapse their position the fall of which, for those who hold onto them in the realm of 'reason' and philosophy, means the end of the world.[26] Their relationship to history must be connected to something that matters, in a normative sense, *to them*, within *their* system of values. I suspect that this is so because the past does not function for many of them as it does for, say, a European intellectual historian. For such an historian, the project is the articulation of *his* or *her* narrative about 'what' happened or 'what' was argued. But for the African philosopher and intellectual historian, the narrative is about ancestors and their deeds and thoughts and their suffering. If part of their suffering was their 'disappearance', which may be in effect similar to the wrong of an improper burial, then the act of getting the past right is also a corrective act of justice through the resources of truth. It makes the role of the African philosopher, whether that philosopher likes it or not, more than secular notions of method and procedure. It is no wonder that Frantz Fanon, an African diasporic thinker looking at the damage of colonialism and racism, announced the suspension of method in his investigations. For him, method sometimes get in the way of the resounding truth of the value of human existence.[27] The African philosopher thus faces the twofold and symbiotically related themes of identity and liberation. The first raises the question of who and what is the subject and the second of the purpose or aim of the first. Many African philosophers take the position that the answers to both lie in the past as groundwork of the present on which the future must be built.

What we find at the heart of this view is a peculiar conception of agency that transcends stoic resignation. The result of this peculiar view of agency is a unique form of constructivism that I shall here simply call *inventionism*. The unique addition of African philosophy to which I have been alluding is the power of African philosophers' advancement of the concept of invention. It is to that I shall now turn and provide a brief outline of what I mean.

The problem of invention in African philosophy comes to the fore in V. Y. Mudimbe's (1988) seminal work *The Invention of Africa: Gnosis, Philosophy, and the Order of Knowledge*. Nearly every major work in contemporary African philosophy since the late 1980s has been influenced by Mudimbe's discussion of invention. According to Mudimbe (1988: ix), Africa is not only a continent but a mode of discourse that exemplifies what he calls a form of *gnosis* or way of knowing:

Specifically, *gnosis* [from the Greek *gnosko*, which means 'to know'] means seeking to know, inquiry, methods of knowing, investigation, and even acquaintance with someone. Often the word is used in a more specialized sense, that of higher and esoteric knowledge, and thus it refers to a structured, common, and conventional knowledge, but one strictly under the control of specific procedures for its use as well as transmission. *Gnosis* is, consequently, different from *doxa* or opinion, and, on the other hand, cannot be confused with *episteme*, understood as both science and general intellectual configuration.

Gnosis is not as rigid a concept as the early Michel Foucault's notion of *episteme*. It is instead sufficiently broad in its reach to be a way of knowing that constitutes and maintains new forms of life. It is in this sense that Africa is 'invented'. It is invented by the systems of knowledge constituted by the process of conquest and colonisation on the one hand, and it is also constituted by the processes of resistance born out of those events the consequence of which is an effect on both on each other. In both instances, the gnostic practices could function at subterranean levels. Colonial practices, for example, emerge at the heart of modern gnostic practices that make no claim of colonial intent even to the point of being, in some cases, explicitly *anti-imperial*. The struggle for liberation, for instance, is difficult precisely because of its location within such gnostic practices, the result of which is the proliferation of more endemic identities and values, which in this case means more 'Africanisms'. He concludes that 'Even in the most explicitly "Afrocentric" descriptions, models of analysis explicitly or implicitly, knowingly or unknowingly, refer to the same order' (p. x).

Mudimbe's argument could easily be criticised as an exemplification of the practices it rejectss because of its obvious genealogical post-structural form. The similarities here between Foucault's archaeological and genealogical writings could be such that one could see the influence of the power/knowledge of the latter on Mudimbe's gnosis/colonialism argument, and Mudimbe uses the term 'archaeology' to describe his approach to the study of African gnosis (p. x). Yet, we may ask why must it be the case that an African thinker's affinities with a European thinker mean a *causal* relationship in which the latter has an effect on the former. The argument I have suggested on which the turn to invention is based suggests a different read in which Foucault's relation to Mudimbe is more associational than causal. For in the end, what is absent in Foucault's analysis but present in Mudimbe's is (i) the historical significance of *outside* imposition and (ii) the ontological weight of the past as manifested in African gnosis. Invention for Mudimbe is, in other words, more weighted down in *reality* by the ancestors than the more epiphenomenal notions that tend to accompany European post-structural readings of historical events (Mudimbe 1994: xv). What's more, for the European, or at least the Modern and postmodern European, the present stands in a peculiar relationship with the past— one without commitment and against authority; sociologically, each generation presumes itself to be the judge of the past simply by living in the present. But in the African context, it is reversed. The past, having legitimation and ontological priority over the present, is more than the foundation of the present; it is also the judge of the present. Most Europeans and Euro-Americans often see themselves, at best, as thus 'owing' the future; whereas most Africans stand in a constant debt to the past.

Kwame Gyekye (1995: xxiii-xxxii) picks up on this aspect of Mudimbe's work when he criticises K. Anthony Appiah's appropriation of Mudimbe's term. Appiah used the term to argue for a theory of maximum difference between African ethnic groups in his very popular and influential book *In My Father's House*.[28] The notion of a common black people of Africa is, in his view, not only an invented fiction, but also a racist one whose fault rests with New World pan-Africanists Alexander Crummell and W.E.B. Du Bois. After taking issue with Appiah's failure to hold Europeans accountable for the colonisation of and imposition of modern antiblack racism onto Africa, Gyekye's response is that Appiah's claim of maximum difference and disunity of African peoples is empirically false and Appiah contradicts himself on this theme in various instances of his analysis. Drawing primarily on the work of Igor Kopytoff and Philip Curtin et al., Gyekye points out that many African communities south of the Sahara are descendants of cultures that once inhabited the northern fertile regions many thousands of years ago (Kopytoff 1987; Curtin et al., 1978). These and many other scholars who have actually conducted comparative studies of African ethnic groups marvel at the commonalities they discover (Shaw, et al. 1993; Finch 1996). He concludes: 'It would be methodologically aberrant, unscientific, and intellectually facile to just shrug off the conclusions of these elaborate empirical investigations of the cultures of African peoples' (Gyeke 1995: xxvii). With regard to contradictions, he posits: 'Also, can Appiah say, "Most Africans, now, whether converted to Islam or Christianity or not, still *share* the beliefs of their ancestors in an ontology of visible beings" [p. 134 of *In My Father's House*, Gyekye's emphasis], and at the same time absolutely deny "a metaphysical unity to African conceptions" ([p. 81) or "*an* African worldview"?' (xxvii). Finally, he rejects Appiah's argument that any cultural borrowing of a group is evidence of traditions that are not theirs. Gyekye's response:

> It can hardly be doubted, I think, that cultural borrowing is an outstanding *historical* phenomenon in the development of all human cultures ... Given this historically justifiable assumption, I find it difficult to endorse Appiah's skepticisms regarding the possibility of identifying some precolonial system of ideas or values of a particular African people as (part of) *their* tradition ... (xxviii).

He concludes by advancing his own view of what he calls a 'weak sense of the idea of unified cultural life,' which

> ... does not imply or suggest a monolithic cultural life for a people who live in what may be described as a shared cultural environment. Rather, it allows for the expression of individual or group sentiments, preferences, tastes, and different ways of responding to local or particular experiences. Social stratification, occupational differences, and differences in individual talents, endowments, desires, and aesthetic perceptions insistently constrain the homogenization of particular forms of cultural life even in the same cultural milieu. To say this, however, is of course not to deny that people belonging to the same cultural environment would generally share certain cultural values—a proposition that logically derives from the notions of culture and community (xxxii).

Internal to African communities, then, there is a creative, dynamic process of cultural formation the consequence of which is both commonality and the unfolding of creative possibilities of individual expression. What this means for Gyekye is that Africa is not simply *invented* but that it continues *to be invented* and reinvented. The role of African philosophy is one of nuanced critique of and systematic inquiry into the general principles that constitute the fundamental thought and values of African peoples (4).

Mudimbe's and Gyekye's formulations of invention are not, however, the final story of invention in African philosophy. Oyewumi, a social theorist working from within the Yoruba tradition, has recently advanced a provocative conception of invention in which she argues for a more *radical* use of invention. In her award-winning *The Invention of Women*, she issues a critique of anti-essentialism and constructivism in Western feminist thought. If gender is constructed as the proponents of such thought claim it is, then why should it follow that gender (i) be constructed the same way everywhere and (ii) why should it have been constructed at all everywhere? Could there not be some societies in which gender has never been constructed? By working through sociolinguistics, Oyewumi (1997) offers an analysis of Yoruba society in which gender, she claims, isn't basic but other factors of social life, such as trading, are. The difficulty in seeing how Yoruba society was historically invented by the Yoruba and how subsequent invasion of different social practices constitute a recent engendered discourse is a function of what she describes as a Western obsession with the body and visual perception (see pp. 1-17). In societies that don't centre such perception, the identities that emerge from social relations premised upon other senses—such as hearing, smelling, and touching—may be radically different and in some cases, as with gender, not present. Gender and sexual difference are, after all, ways of differentiating types of human bodies; without focus on the bodies, the necessity of such terminology is eliminated and perhaps more fluid instead of fixed relations emerge.

In her critical engagements with other African philosophical writers, Oyewumi is not as generous as Gyekye in her reading of Mudimbe's use of invention. She writes:

> As a prologue to his acclaimed book *The Invention of Africa*, Mudimbe disseminates what he calls the 'good news'—that the African now has 'the freedom of thinking of himself or herself as the starting point of an absolute discourse' [Mudimbe 1988: 200]. His claim is surprising given that the content of his book does not derive epistemologically from Africa and is heavily dependent on European thought. This is hardly the multicultural heritage that Appiah wants us to believe obtains in African studies. It is clearly a Western heritage and explains why Ogún does not stand a chance against Zeus and why Africa remains merely an idea in the minds of many African scholars. Of course, in reality Africa continues to unfold in the march of history. The original human history at that! (Oyewumi 1997: 27).

A curious feature of Oyewumi's text is the absence of any discussion of ancestral obligation or even ancestors. It is perhaps this absence that occludes, in her analysis, my reading of Mudimbe and Gyekye's notions of invention. Oyewumi's is a radical constructivism, yet her argument suggests that something is lost by European influences on our readings of Yorubaland's past. For her, history, too, is invented (and I shall presume that so, too, are notions of ancestors by African peoples themselves), which leads to an affected discourse of the past. The conception of invention she favours, in this regard, is one of 'invented traditions'. On this concept, she writes:

> I deploy it to acknowledge the implication of the present in the past, rather than making a 'presentist' claim that the past is solely fabricated to reflect present interests ... The notion of invented traditions does not necessarily imply dishonesty; the process is usually much more unconscious. In fact, it is a testament to the immediate nature of evidence and the positionality of any particular recorder of the past ... What is permissible is culture-bound. The idea expressed in the notion of permissibility is that the extent to which the past is malleable for present purposes is limited. Although many things can change, some things must remain the same (p. 81).

This passage strikes me as Oyewumi's argument ultimately sharing more affinity with Gyekye's because, as he, she wants to draw upon what was invented by African people outside of the discourses that were a function of Western imposition. This conclusion is clearly so when she writes:

> Since the colonial period, Yoruba history has been reconstituted through a process of inventing gendered traditions. Men and women have been invented as social categories, and history is presented as being dominated by male actors. Female actors are virtually absent, and where they are recognized, they are reduced to exceptions (p. 82).

Notice that Oyewumi's argument does not entail the rejection of a feminist response to Africa's historical present, which her argument here suggests is perhaps even required given the occlusion of 'female actors.'[29] But, like Sylvia Wynter, who has developed her own brand of Caribbean poststructuralism, she is concerned with the power of language and the social realities maintained by the use of those linked to one order of knowledge over others.[30] Oyewumi thus demands a more radical interpretation of invention because she regards the consequences of failing to do so to be detrimental to the people who have been invented as invisible or abnormal beings. The consequence of Western inventions, in other words, is not only Western normativity, but also its accompanying baggage of white and male normativity.

Yet not all contemporary postmodern African philosophers see radical invention as the way to go. A danger, as Elias Kifon Bongmba sees it, is that of moral and epistemological relativism. In *African Witchcraft and Otherness: A Philosophical and Theological Critique of Intersubjective Relations* (Bongmba 2001), he criticises notions of radical constructivism and radical difference on ethical grounds. He agrees with the inventionists that the relationship the West has had with Africa has been such that, as conventional wisdom has it, unshackling the colonial relationship of the African as experience for white theoretical reflection demands much ontological, epistemological, and political resistance. Western intellectuals, after all, often considered themselves the custodians of bringing the light of reason to the understanding of African experience. The result has been a terrible situation in African studies. African studies is in much of its appearance a white-dominated field of study.[31] The consequence is that it has been difficult for black scholars to play roles beyond those of ethnographic informants. In philosophy, long regarded as the Queen of the Humanities, the situation has been similarly anxious: The inclusion of black *philosophers* often raised the problem of the *particularity* of Western philosophy in spite of its avowed universality (Gordon 1995a: 144-5). Even Emmanuel Lévinas, upon whose work much of Bongmba's ethics is based, suffered from such centrism in his well-known effort to forge a Graeco-Semitic torch for humanity's night. Bongmba thus admits that his and other African scholars' task is manifold: To think through ideas in fields saturated by many practitioners who neither expect nor want people like him to think.

Bongmba begins *African Witchcraft and Otherness* by demonstrating the problem with simply applying wholesale the term 'witchcraft' to activities by African peoples that may range from judgments on natural gifts to efforts to initiate supernatural occurrences. We find here an instance of the classic problem of cultural translation and indeterminacy. Although even among Europeans there is a rich language to deal with such phenomena beyond the terms of 'witchcraft,' their application to African activities has been reductive, and indigenous African communities, in their effort to translate their activities to European communities, simply use the misguided European terms. Thus, a colloquialism of 'witchcraft' emerges where in fact *witchcraft* as understood in the West is absent. In English, for instance, we have terms such as 'genius' (whose roots by the way are obvious in such a word as 'genii'), 'gifted', 'wizard', 'sorcerer', 'magician', 'witch', and 'warlock'. Bongmba shows that at least among the Wimbum, the Cameroonian ethnic group of which he is a member, such terms as *bfiu*, *brii*, and *tfu* should not be lumped together under the term 'witchcraft' because only the last comes close to Western analogues. The first, for instance, refers to a special skill to do extraordinary things. Could one imagine Albert Einstein, Jimmy Hendrix, and Michael Jordan referred to as 'warlocks', instead of geniuses or gifted? But in effect, that is what is going on in some scholarly treatments of these communities. At this point of his analysis, he is in stream with Oyewumi and the other inventionists.

After pointing out the complexity of translating African terms into European ones, Bongmba then makes a move that further challenges establishment approaches to the study of Africa and African religions. He offers a *critique* of how activities associated with such phenomena as *tfu* are manifested in contemporary Africa. To understand why he makes this move, one need reflect on the two extremes in Western approaches to the study of African communities. On the one hand, there is the old-style civilisation versus primitivism approach. There, the criticism was that Africans were primitive, backward peoples who need to move forward through the adoption of Western values usually by way of Christianity. It is this conviction that motivated Christian missionaries to look into the interstices of what they considered to be the African mind and search for an ethnophilosophy; by so doing, they could find the key for syncretic adaptation and the creation of Afro-Christian practices.[32] In response to that view, another extreme emerged: Be good ethnographers and simply describe; do not judge or criticise the communities. A problem with this latter approach is that a form of relativism emerges that destroys intersubjective relations; it is, in effect, a form of not meeting another human community *as a human community*. Writes Bongmba (2001: xix):

> I question the anxiety scholars have about any attempt to criticize local African practices. If scholars feel awkward about critical discourse on Africa, then contemporary African scholarship has touched Africa with a 'fatal kindness,' to borrow a metaphor from Friedrich Schleiermacher (*African Philosophy and Witchcraft*).

On the basis of rejecting 'fatal kindness', Bongmba parts company with most works *on* the study of witchcraft, and advances a critical philosophy *of* witchcraft. This approach raises the problematics of the human sciences and offers an interdisciplinary methodology anchored in the critical resources of lived experience. By 'critical philosophy' is here also meant a phenomenological investigation guided by ethical engagement, which here means both taking seriously what members of a community say and speaking truthfully with that community—that is, engaging the community in genuine *dialogue*. He takes this dialogical point of departure to expand his analysis by adding the resources of Lévinasian studies and ethics. There, he offers a reading and application of Lévinas's thought that is more *socially* rich than Lévinas's formulations. Although he builds much on Lévinas's claim of the 'face-to-face' dimensions of ethical encounter, where the Other exemplifies an ethical *cry*, it strikes me that the social resources to which he appeals in his discussion of the Wimbum are more thick than Lévinasian one-to-one formalism affords. Bongmba's critical conclusion on *tfu*, the closest activity to witchcraft in the Western sense, is that Wimbum theology should adopt a theory of desire without consumption or totalisation. The absence of totalisation means room for positive critical engagement between Western and traditional African communities on questions of ethical life.

The question of ethical life raises questions of the kind of normative thought is needed in the African context. Frantz Fanon (1963), it is well known, argued in *The Wretched of the Earth* that discussion of ethics before political resolutions lead to reassertions of what he calls 'the Graeco-Latin pedestal'. He would no doubt be very critical of Bongmba's ethical turn, but some readers of Fanon have argued for a consolidation of Fanonian and Lévinasian engagements with ethics (Maldonado-Torres 2001). Drawing upon philosophical hermeneutics, Tsenay Serequeberhan (1994) has argued that the kind of emancipatory politics needed to precede ethics is one that is governed by the spirit of interpretation and criticism. A problem with hermeneutical approaches, however, is the kind of suspension they have on questions of truth. What happens to the 'ancestors' when even they stand as indeterminate functions of open textual interpretation? Serequeberhan (2000) seems to have realised this critique because he subsequently wrote an existential engagement with this question under the title *Our Heritage: The Past in the Present of African-American and African Existence*.

The question of ethical relativism has also been taken up by Kwasi Wiredu (1996) in *Cultural Universals and Particulars*, his work on relativism and problems of human rights in the African context. Working methodologically through the resources of pragmatism, linguistic analysis, and the impact of biology, Wiredu argues against relativism primarily through appeals to *reductio ad absurdum* arguments couched in a sober faith in the unyielding force of reality. The problem with arguments in favour of radical invention and their consequent relativistic appeals is that they function like ancient logical paradoxes that deny the reality of time, distance, and motion. One simply need take a walk. Although bad translations do emerge, the fact of the matter is that different communities of people do manage to communicate with each other, and since they are able to do so, there must be cultural universals (p. 21). That there are *no* instances of radical incommunicability—for even where a term cannot be translated from one culture into another, the logical response has always been simply the adaptation of that new term to the stock of words in the other culture—its cause must be in human beings rather than a contingent consequence of human behaviour. For Wiredu, this means we must take biology more seriously as a foundation of this aspect of human behaviour (pp. 34-41). With regard to cultural relativism, his argument suggests that its proponents are taking what should be a natural consequence of contingent human forces—that different communities will have their own histories and develop different ways of life and languages—to entail untranslatable human difference. Human communities are founded on communication, however, which means that there are underlying norms of thought that come into play not only within communities, but also between communities. His reflections are illuminating:

> Consider the implications of this last result [that the whole species must have some norms of thought in common]. It cannot be history, culture, or ideology that accounts for this commonality, for these are the causes of the diversity rather than the unity of the species. And, in any case, they all presuppose that very same commonality. Why? Because the norms of thought that make it possible for us to think and make history and everything else are the same conditions that make social interaction with others (of whatever identities) possible. It is, I suggest, nothing other than our common basic biology that underlies the particular mental affinity of all the members of the human race with which we are concerned (p. 34).

The post-structural commitments of some inventionists have unfortunately led to antipathy on their part toward offering the biological as a category of analysis. This is because of the historical-centrism of many such proponents. For they would argue that the notion of the biological is itself a socially-conditioned category. This is certainly Oyewumi's (1997: 9) position:

> That many categories of difference are socially constructed in the West may well suggest the mutability of categories , but it is also an invitation to endless constructions of biology—in that there is no limit to what can be explained by the body-appeal. Thus biology is hardly mutable; it is much more a combination of the Hydra and the Phoenix of Greek mythology. Biology is forever mutating, not mutable. Ultimately, the most important point is not that gender is socially constructed but the extent to which biology itself is socially constructed and therefore inseparable from the social.

Biology is, in other words, simply part of an epistemic ordering of life. But is this so? We find in this kind of argument a fallacy that emerges in many social constructivist arguments. The fallacy involves confusing the conditions of meaning with that which is meant by a particular term or sentence. That meaning must be social is clearly a consequence of its being part of language and communication, and, as Ludwig Wittgenstein (1967: Section 243) has shown, in principle understandable and thus communicable and therefore depend on a set of rules and norms that are *not* 'private.' But being of the social does not mean referring to the social. Signification can be such that it points, as most semioticians have observed, beyond itself.[33] The fallacy is, in other words, much like taking a pointing finger to be the thing it is pointing at instead of looking at that to which it points. Of course the biological is a function of social reality and is an episteme. But it does not follow that the biological *is* social.[34]

Wiredu's argument is, in fact, compatible with an inventionist position. For his claim is that we are creatures in whose biological makeup is the propensity to invent the plethora of activities that constitute the social world. *Within* that world is a multitude of meanings that mark cultural variety from communities to communities of members of the same species—namely, *homo sapiens sapiens*. Wiredu thus brings the human science question back into the discussion of studies of Africa, and he does so by advancing a philosophical anthropology that engages developments across the varieties of human and life sciences. Like Gyekye, he does not wish to ignore empirical evidence, and since he is not using natural science as the final arbiter but only a factor in the course of the argument, his position isn't reductive nor positivist.

Many of Wiredu's conclusions have been similarly advanced in the phenomenological tradition, proponents of which would immediately see similarities not only between Wiredu's position and Alfred Schutz's *Phenomenology of the Social World*, but also the arguments I have expanded in my discussion of human science and notions of problem people in *Existentia Africana* (Gordon 2000) and those developed much earlier in South Africa by Noel Chabani Manganyi (1973, 1977). In the expansion of the question of invention in African philosophy to that of African diasporic philosophy, the strongest recent developments are, no doubt, Paget Henry's (2000) *Caliban's Reason: Introducing Afro-Caribbean Philosophy*, and the work of Nkiru Nzegwu.[35] Henry begins his text with a discussion of the important contributions of traditional African thought (the ancestors) to the formation of Afro-Caribbean communities, which he regards as creolisations of Africa, Asia, and Native America, and then he advances a conception of philosophy in which the consequence of critical, systematic reflections on reality is the formation of a community's self-consciousness—the spirit of its culture—in a tension of what he calls *historicist* and *poeticist* prescriptions. These two prescriptions/approaches are the return of the liberation and identity themes, for the historicist wants to change the world and the poeticist argues for understanding the self that is to be changed, whether through resources of imagination for the semiosis of things cultural. That both can be reconciled is evidenced by such thinkers as Leopold Sénghor, Aimé Césaire, C. L. R. James, and Frantz Fanon, each of which appealed to liberatory thought through poetic resources. It seems that the living great Afro-Caribbean thinkers are mostly of the poeticist bent as witnessed by Sylvia Wynter, Wilson Harris, Eduoard Glissant, Kamau Braithwaite, Derek Walcott, Jamaica Kincaid, Maryse Condé, and George Lamming's contemporary appeal. Among the Africans, the same could be said with regard to Ngugi wa Thiong'o, Chinua Achebe, Ama Atta Aidoo, and Wole Soyinka. There is irony here, for the historicists are either mostly dead, and the few who are alive and have not taken heed of recent developments seem 'outdated'.[36]

Nzegwu charts the complexity of West African history and art and demonstrates the fallacy of simply applying West African cultures, intact, to the New World African diasporic condition, which, like Henry, she regards as creolised communities with unique historical and political developments. She adds, however, that a unique influence is the impact of European ontological categories that include the primacy of the body as the location of identity. The geopolitical-epidemiological consideration to bear in mind in West Africa, however, is the constraining force of malaria on the scale of white settlements, which made it difficult to maintain a body-racial politics in that region. What needed to be *invented*, in her view, was the notion of *cultural* and *technological* inferiority—namely, the notion of primitivism. The result is the hegemony of European culture as 'modern', which has an affect not only on the value of West African cultures, but also on their *study*. Her conclusion on what her analysis offers warrants a lengthy quotation:

> The epistemological consequences of taking seriously the radically different histories of Africa and the United States are having far-reaching effects. For one, the experiences of colonial racism and the politics of area studies in the United States are increasingly forcing African scholars to interrogate the motives of scholars who purport to be responsive to the best interests of Africa and Africans, yet who end up creating an alienated discourse *of* Africa rather than *about* Africa. This interrogation is primarily a response to the invidious de-Africanization that results from the works of both the old-time Africanists and the New Africanists, whose knowledge of Africa tends to be breathtakingly superficial. The consensus of opinion is that this de-Africanization process is a colonial strategy that has effectively been used for decades to gain control of the production of knowledge about Africa. In de-Africanization, the conceptual categories of the different African nations are obscured, then the political, economic, social, and philosophical issues are conducted on the basis of Western Categories and interests. If Africa were really placed at the center of such analyses, as it rightly should, it is debatable that old-time and new Africanists would begin with the currently used set of research issues and assumptions (Nzegwu 1999a: 135).

To Conclude

Yet, Africana philosophy—African, African American, and Afro-Caribbean philosophy—is thriving, and it seems to have been able to negotiate its place between the historicist-poeticist divide and the unyielding misrepresentations by mainstream or Eurocentric approaches to human studies.[37] One could argue that this is because of how squarely it has placed at the forefront not only the question of how Africana peoples should be studied, but also the constitutive question of the grounding of such peoples in the first place—namely, their humanity. The impact of this turn cannot be underestimated since it is raising a question that crosses disciplinary divides as hoped for by the cultural studies considerations with which this chapter began. In the anthropology of Africa, the impact of at least philosophical language, particularly in the foundational rationalisations of ethnographies of peoples on the continent, has clearly been advanced through fusions of Marx and Foucault by leading scholars in the field such as John and Jean Comaroff.[38] The philosophical challenge of contemporary African philosophy, more so than African cultural studies, is whether they and other social scientists—those in history, political science, and sociology—and scholars in the humanities who study Africa will draw upon the insights and intellectual resources of contemporary African philosophical thought. For it is the case that the natives have transcended the status of informants and now offer an opportunity to co-invent a new relationship beyond African studies as white hegemony the achievement of which would be, at least in part, a genuinely new world.

Notes

1. The reader may wonder about the difference between identity politics and the politics of difference. The former is a politics often grounded in standpoint epistemology, where there are special claims advanced on the basis of what one uniquely knows by virtue of one's identity. Some scholars have formulated identity politics in terms of the so-called politics of recognition, where a subordinate group seeks acceptance, whether politically or culturally, by a dominant group. The politics of difference, on the other hand, focuses on retaining one's identity beyond questions of recognition. The aim, in other words, is not to be assimilated into a centred body of normative dictates but to be respected as unassimilable. There is, as well, another kind of politics of difference premised uniquely on the question of psychoanalytical difference usually conditioned by sexual difference. Here, the politics of difference usually refer to women or people outside of sexual normativity without specifying feminism or queerness. Since cultural studies focuses on all these categories, I have chosen to say both identity politics and the politics of difference.

2. For an excellent summary of postmodernism and its political themes in regard to the study of culture, see Butler (2002). See also Gordon (1997), chapter 5, especially pp. 92-100.

3. I take this insight as one of many in Frantz Fanon's (1967) classic early reflections history from the question of the colonised self, *Black Skin, White Masks*, Introduction, chapter 5, and 'By Way of Conclusion'.

4. The discussion emerges among many prominent African writers. See, for example, Appiah (1992); Diawara (1998); and Tsenay (2000).

5. Much has been written on this question. For the most influential text on the African and Africana dimensions, see Gates, Jr. (1988) and for the European tradition, see Gadamer (1990).

6. I am speaking, of course, of Mary Wollstonecraft Shelley's classic novel, *Frankenstein, or the Modern Prometheus* (1999), see especially her preface, where she explains her Protagonist, Frankenstein, to exemplify the fate of the tragic Greek god Prometheus, who brought fire to humankind. Frankenstein, too, is a metaphor for Modern European scientists who bring the 'fire' of modern science to humanity. Like Jean-Jacques Rousseau, however, Shelley was aware of the dialectical qualities of the enlightenment, which she brilliantly portrayed in her protagonist's realisation of the monstrosity that constituted his effort to take God's place, a monstrosity that in part was conditioned by his own failure to take responsibility for it. On his formulation of the dialectics of enlightenment, see 'Discourse on the Sciences and Arts or The First Discourse', in Rousseau (1990).

7. See Sanders (2002), especially chapter 2 for some of these themes of bringing the story of the anti-apartheid struggle to Europe and elsewhere beyond Africa are discussed.

8. For this history, see Ahmad (1992). See also Williams and Chrisman (1994).

9. A volume that conveys many of these developments is Dent (1992).

10. Chrisman is already cited in several places in this chapter. Lazarus and Parry are prolific and influential in their own right, and they and other like minded writers can be found in Bartolovich and Lazarus (2002).

11. Perhaps the best summary of this critique is Laura Chrisman's 'Journeying to Death', *Race and Class*, which is her critique of Paul Gilroy's (1993) *Black Atlantic: Modernity and Double Consciousness*. See also *Her Majesty's Other Children*, chapter 5 (Gordon 1997a).

12. This is well known, but see for example, the website: http://www.ucalgary.ca/applied_history/tutor/eurvoya/africa.html.

13. See, for example, Nkiru Nzegwu (1999). Following Nzegwu, I here say 'black' and 'primitive' since the former was not always the operating factor of race, especially in West Africa, where whites were considered inferior at the level of the body but superior with regard to technological mastery the consequence of which was the notion of African technological and cultural primitiveness (pp. 134-135). For a discussion of the construction of the primitive beyond the West African context, see also Mudimbe (1988: 72-75).

14. For an excellent recent discussion of the Haitian Revolution and its impact on the development of historical narratives of resistance, see Sibylle Fischer (forthcoming).

15. See Quobna Ottobah Cugoano (1999); Wilhelm Anton-Amo (1729) and, for commentary, W. Abraham (1964: 60–81); and for the Reverend John Jasper, see *Two Early African American Philosophers*, ed., with an introduction by Robert Redding, Jr. and a foreword by Lewis R. Gordon (Forthcoming).

16. See Thomas Paine (1987). Relevant selections from Hume's and Kant's writings are reprinted in *Race and the Enlightenment: A Reader*, ed. by Emmanuel Chukwudi Eze (1997: chapters 3-4).

17. The response to the important role of ancient Egypt is well known: Make it, in its origins, Asiatic in spite of all the evidence that demonstrates otherwise. The debate continues. See Martin Bernal (2001) and for a detailed critique of the civilisation-not-out-of-Africa thesis, see Charles Finch (1996).

18. Even in the age of deconstruction, wherein every aspect of reality, including culture itself, is treated as a form of writing, this misrepresentation presents Africa as a form of limit unless the divide between inscription and metaphors of inscription is completely blurred. Beyond that, as well, is the problem of the many roles of deconstruction articulated by Jacques Derrida (1981), at least in his classic essay 'Plato's Pharmacy', where the multitude of simultaneous economies of psychoanalysis, Marxism, and semiotics interplay as an anxiety over the father, authority, and speech, appears both Eurocentric and culturally relative in relation to this question of African thought since it requires a variety of values premised upon family structures and sexual anxieties that are alien to many traditional African societies wherein the economy of even polygamy has strong matrilineal injunctions. On this matter of matrilineality, see, for example, Nkiru Nzegwu's (1996) 'Questions of Identity and Inheritance: A Critical Review of Anthony Appiah's: *In My Father's House*'.

19. See, for example, Teodros Kiros (forthcoming).

20. I write 'traditions' because I know of no African who has been raised in a single tradition. There is much creolisation of various indigenous groups in Africa, either literally through mixed ethnic relationships or through cultural intermixture in which there is often great knowledge (including linguistic mastery) of at least two cultures.

21. The obvious similarity here with existential treatments of value as a function of our consciousness of our own finitude is not accidental. Although the theological underpinnings of Mbiti's arguments are Christian, it can easily be shown that the common ground through which his

theology meets his traditional African upbringing is an existential one. For an outline of this type of argument, see Paget Henry (1997).

22. The origin of this argument is, by the way, in Kant's classic response to Hume's attack on necessity. For Kant's argument, see *The Critique of Pure Reason* (1998) and for Hume's, see *A Treatise of Human Nature* (2000).

23. For criticisms of Mbiti's conception of time, see especially Kwame Gyekye (1995). See also discussions of Mbiti by Barry Hallen (2002) and D.A. Masolo (1994).

24. The question of ancestors is perhaps the most dominating feature of African ethics, and it is analysed in nearly every work on African philosophy. I won't focus on it in each of the subsequent texts I discuss, but it appears in all but one of them—namely, the radical inventionist. For more discussion of my views on this subject, see Lewis R. Gordon (2002).

25. For an excellent recent summary of these conceptions of African philosophy—sage philosophy, ethnophilosophy, 'professional' philosophy, and praxis philosophy—see Barry Hallen's (2002) *A Short History of African Philosophy* and D. A. Masolo's (1994) *African Philosophy in Search of Identity*.

26. On this matter of tenacious racism and its relationship to orders of rationality, see Lewis R. Gordon (1995a: Part II) and (1995b: chapters 2 and 3).

27. 'It is good form to introduce a work in psychology with a statement of its methodological point of view. I shall be derelict. I leave methods to the botanists and the mathematicians. There is a point at which methods devour themselves', Frantz Fanon (1967: 12).

28. Criticisms of this book abound. For criticism of its logicism, see Paget Henry (1993); for criticism of its Eurocentric patriarchy, see Nkiru Nzegwu (1996a); for criticisms of its race theory, see Lewis R. Gordon (1995), Part II; and for criticisms of its attack on a black-based pan-Africanism, see Lewis R. Gordon (1997a).

29. For contemporary African feminist philosophical work, see Safro Kwame (1995); Nkiru Nzegwu (2006).

30. See Sylvia Wynter (1996, 1997) and Paget Henry (2000). Wynter, unlike Oyewumi is more sympathetic to Mudimbe's views, which she makes explicit in these essays.

31. For recent discussion, see Michael West (Winter 1996).

32. Scholarly treatment of this effort abounds, but see especially Josiah Young (1992). The most famous instance of this practice was, by the way, Father Placide Tempels's (1959) *Bantu Philosophy*.

33. See Kwasi Wiredu (1996), *Cultural Universals*, pp. 15-16, and for a general discussion of semiotics, see Deely (1990).

34. I criticise this fallacy also as a form of disciplinary decadence, where a particular discipline is advanced as the ontological arbiter of all other disciplines without opening itself to the possibility of its limits. Sociologism is such an instance, where the sociologist rejects the conclusions of other disciplines for not being sociological ones. We see this in Oyewumi's argument, but it emerges also in Paul Gilroy's (2001: 29) *Against Race*, where Gilroy rejects genomics research for not making sociological conclusions on race: 'Prompted by the impact of genomics, "race," as it has been defined in the past, has also become vulnerable to the claims of a much more elaborate, less deterministic biology. It is therefore all the more disappointing that much influential recent work in this area loses its nerve in the final furlong and opts to remain ambiguous about whether the idea of "race," can survive a critical revision of the relationship between human beings and their constantly shifting social nature'.

35. Nzegwu's work consists of an impressive array of articles, art history, and feminist politics, as well as work as a poet and visual artist, and her leadership as president of the International Society for African Philosophy and Studies. Her philosophical ideas appear in her volume, *Family Matters: Feminist Concepts in African Philosophy of Culture* (2006). See also her anthologies *Contemporary Textures: Multidimensionality in Nigerian Art* (1999) and *Issues in Contemporary African Art* (1998).

36. For an excellent recent treatment of great black historicists, all of who are unfortunately dead, see Bogues (2003).

37. Evidence for this claim of Africana philosophy thriving consists of the several book series housed by influential publishers, the several societies worldwide, and the many journals and newsletters devoted to its study. A good source on such developments is the award-winning *Journal of Africana Philosophy*, housed at De Paul University.

38. See especially their introduction to the second volume of their now classic work (Comaroff and Comaroff 1997), *Of Revelation and Revolution*, where, too, the question of invention is explored through the missionaries' efforts at Christianising of the indigenous population.

References

Abraham, W., 1964, 'The Life and Times of Wilhelm Anton Amo', *Transactions of the Historical Society of Ghana*, 7, 60–81.

Ahmad, A., 1992, *In Theory: Classes, Nations, and Literatures*, London: Verso.

Amo, A.-W., 1729, *De Jure Maurorum in Europa*, Dissertation: University of Halle.

Appiah, K. A., 1992, *In My Father's House: Africa in the Philosophy of Culture*, New York: Oxford University Press.

Bartolovich, C. and N. Lazarus, eds., 2002, *Marxism, Modernity and Postcolonial Studies*, London: Cambridge University Press.

Bernal, M., 2001, *Black Athena Writes Back: Martin Bernal Responds to His Critics*, edited by D. C. Moore, Durham: Duke University Press.

Biko, S., 2002, *I Write What I Like: Selected Writings*, New Edition, foreword by Lewis R. Gordon; ed. with a personal memoir by A. Stubbs; preface by D. Tutu; introduction by T. Mpumlwana, Chicago, IL.: University of Chicago Press.

Blyden, E., 1908, *African Life and Customs*, London: C. M. Phillips.

Bogues, B. A., 2003, *Black Heretics, Black Prophets: Radical Political Intellectuals*, New York: Routledge.

Bongmba, E. K., 2001, *African Witchcraft and Otherness: A Philosophical and Theological Critique of Intersubjective Relations*, Albany: State University of New York Press.

Butler, C., 2002, *Postmodernism: A Very Short Introduction*, Oxford: Oxford University Press.

Carby, H., 1999, *Cultures in Babylon: Black Britain and African America*, London: Verso.

Chrisman, L., 2000a, 'Journeying to Death: Gilroy's *The Black Atlantic*', in K.O. Comedia, ed., *Black British Culture and Society: A Text Reader*, London: Routledge, 453-464.

Chrisman, L., (2000b, 'Rethinking Black Atlanticism', *The Black Scholar* 30 (3-4), 12-17.

Comaroff, J. and J. Comaroff, 1997, *Of Revelation and Revolution*, Volume 2: *The Dialectics of Modernity on a South African Frontier*, Chicago: University of Chicago Press.

Cooper, B. and A. Steyn, eds., 1996, *Transgressing Boundaries: New Directions in the Study of Culture in Africa*, Rondebosch, South Africa: University of Cape Town Press in association with the Centre for African Studies and in Athens, Ohio: Ohio University Press.

Cugoano, Q. O., 1999, *'Thoughts and Sentiments on the Evil of Slavery' and Other Writings*, edited with an introduction and notes by Vincent Carretta, New York: Penguin Books.

Curtin, P., S. Feierman, L. Thompson, and J. Vansina, 1978, *African History*, London: Longman.

Deely, J., 1990, *Basics of Semiotics*, Bloomington: Indiana University Press.

Dent, G., ed., 1992, *Black Popular Culture: A Project by Michele Wallace*, Seattle: Bay Press.

Derrida, J., 1981, *Dissemination*, Translated with an introduction and additional notes by Barbara Johnson, Chicago: University Press.

Diawara, M., 1998, *In Search of Africa*, Cambridge, MA: Harvard University Press.

Fanon, F., 1963, *The Wretched of the Earth*, Translated by Constance Farrington, New York: Grove Press.

Fanon, F., 1967, *Black Skin, White Masks*, Translated by Charles Lam Markmann, New York: Grove Press.

Finch, III, MD, C., 1996, *Echoes of the Old Darkland*, Decatur, GA: Khenti, Inc.

Fischer, S., Forthcoming, 'Unthinkable History? Some Reflections on the Haitian Revolution, Historiography, and Modernity on the Periphery', in L. R. Gordon and J. A. Gordon, eds., *A Companion to African American Studies*, Malden, MA: Blackwell Publishers.

Foucault, M., 1973, *The Order of Things: An Archaeology of the Human Sciences*, New York: Vintage.

Foucault, M., 1979, *Discipline and Punish: The Birth of the Prison*, Translated by Alan Sheridan, New York: Vintage.

Gadamer, H-G., 1990, *Truth and Method*, Second Edition, Revised translation, Joel Weinsheimer and Donald G. Marhsall, New York: Crossroad.

Gates, Jr., H. L., 1988, *The Signifying Monkey: A Theory of Afro-American Literary Criticism*, New York: Oxford University Press.

Gilroy, P., 1993, *The Black Atlantic: Modernity and Double Consciousness*, Cambridge, MA: Harvard University Press.

Gilroy, P., 2001, *Against Race*, Cambridge, MA: Harvard University Press.

Gordon, L., 1995a, *Bad Faith and Antiblack Racism*, Amherst, NY: Humanity Books.

Gordon, L., 1995b, *Fanon and the Crisis of European Man: An Essay*, London: Routledge.

Gordon, L., with T. D. Sharpley-Whiting and R. T. White, 1996, *Fanon: A Critical Reader*, Oxford: Blackwell Publishers.

Gordon, L., 1997a, *Her Majesty's Other Children: Sketches of Racism from a Neocolonial Age*, Lanham, MD: Rowman & Littlefield.

Gordon, L., ed., 1997b, *Existence in Black: An Anthology of Black Existential Philosophy*, New York: Routledge.

Gordon, L., 2000, *Existentia Africana: Understanding Africana Existential Thought*, New York: Routledge.

Gordon, L., 2002, 'Moral Obligations across Generations: A Consideration in the Understanding of Community Formation', in P. Alperson, ed., *Understanding Communities*, Oxford: Blackwell Publishers, 116–127.

Gyekye, K., 1995, *An Essay on African Philosophy: The Akan Conceptual Scheme*, Philadelphia: Temple University Press.

Hallen, B., 2002, *A Short History of African Philosophy*, Bloomington: Indiana University Press.

Hegel, G. W. F., 1956, *The Philosophy of History*, With prefaces by Charles Hegel and the translator, J. Sibree, and a new introduction by C. J. Friedrich, New York: Dover Publications.

Henry, P., 1993, 'African Philosophy in the Mirror of Logicisms: A Review Essay', *The C. L. R. James Journal* 4 (1).

Henry, P., 1997a, 'African and Afro-Caribbean Existential Philosophies', in L. R. Gordon, ed., *Existence in Black: An Anthology of Black Existential Philosophy*, New York: Routledge, 11-36.

Henry, P., 1997b, 'Rastafarianism and the Reality of Dread', in L. R. Gordon, ed., *Existence in Black: An Anthology of Black Existential Philosophy*, New York: Routledge, 157-164.

Henry, P., 2000, *Caliban's Reason: Introducing Afro-Caribbean Philosophy*, New York: Routledge.

Hoggart, R., 1992, *The Uses of Literacy*, New Introduction by Andrew Goodwin, New Brunswick, NJ: Transaction Publishers.

Hume, D., 2000, *A Treatise of Human Nature*, eds., D. F. Norton, M. J. Norton, Introduction by D. F. Norton, Oxford: Oxford University Press.

Kant, I., 1998, *Critique of Pure Reason*, Translated and edited by P. Guyer, A. W. Wood. New York: Cambridge University Press.

Kiros, T., Forthcoming, 'Zara Yacob and Traditional Ethiopian Philosophy', in K. Wiredu, ed., *Encyclopedia of African Philosophy*, Malden, MA: Blackwell Publishers.

Kopytoff, I., ed., 1987, *The African Frontier: The Reproduction of Traditional African Societies*, Bloomington, IN: Indiana University Press.

Kwame, S., 1995, 'Feminism and African Philosophy', in S. Kwame, ed., *Readings in African Philosophy: An Akan Collection*, Lanham, MD: University Press of America, 251-271.

Lamming, G., 1970, *In the Castle of My Skin*, Introduction by R. Wright, New York: Collier.

Maldonado-Torres, N., 2001, 'The Cry of the Self as a Call from the Other: The Paradoxical Loving Subjectivity of Frantz Fanon', *Listening: A Journal of Religion and Culture* 36, (1): 46-60.

Manganyi, N. C., 1973, *Being-Black in-the-World*, Johannesburg: Ravan Press.

Manganyi, N. C., 1977, *Alienation and the Body in Racist Society: A Study of the Society that Invented Soweto*, New York: NOK Publishers.

Masolo, D. A., 1994, *African Philosophy in Search of Identity*, Bloomington, IN: Indiana University Press.

Mbiti, J., 1990, *African Religions and Philosophy*, Reed Educational & Professional Publishing, Limited.

Mercer, K., 1994, *Welcome to the Jungle: New Positions in Black Cultural Studies*, New York: Routledge.

Morley, D., K-H. Chen, S. Hall and D. Morley, eds., 1996, *Stuart Hall: Critical Dialogues*, New York: Routledge.

Mudimbe, V. Y., 1988, *The Invention of Africa: Gnosis, Philosophy, and the Order of Knowledge*, Bloomington: Indiana University Press.

Mudimbe, V. Y., 1994, *The Idea of Africa*, Bloomington: Indiana University Press.

Nzegwu, N., 1996a, 'Questions of Identity and Inheritance: A Critical Review Anthony Appiah's: *In My Father's House*', *HYPATIA: A Journal of Feminist Philosophy* 2 (1): 176–199.

Nzegwu, N., 1996b, 'Philosophers' Intellectual Responsibility to African Females', *American Philosophical Association (APA) Newsletter* (November), 130-135.

Nzegwu, N., ed., 1998, *Issues in Contemporary African Art*, Binghamton: International Society for the Study of Africa.

Nzegwu, N., 1999a, 'Colonial Racism: Sweeping out Africa with Mother Europe's Broom', in S. E. Babbitt and S. Campbell, eds., *Racism and Philosophy*, Ithaca, NY: Cornell University Press, 1999, 124-156.

Nzegwu, N., 1999, *Contemporary Textures: Multidimensionality in Nigerian Art*, Binghamton: International Society for the Study of Africa.

Nzegwu, N., 2006, *Family Matters: Feminist Concepts in African Philosophy of Culture*, Albany, NY: State University of New York Press.

Oyewumi, Oyeronke, *Invention of Women: Making an African Sense of Western Gender Discourses*, Minneapolis: University of Minnesota Press.

Redding, Jr., R., ed., Forthcoming, *Two Early African American Philosophers*, Foreword by Lewis R. Gordon.

Rousseau, J-J., 1990, 'Discourse on the Sciences and Arts or the First Discourse', in J-J. Rousseau, *The First and Second Discourses, together with Replies to Critics and 'Essay on the Origin of Languages'*, Newly edited, translated and annotated by Victor Gourevitch, New York: Harper Torchbooks, 1-27.

Said, E., 1979, *Orientalism*. New York: Vintage.

Sanders, M., 2002, *Complicities: The Intellectual and Apartheid*, Durham: Duke University Press.

Shaw, T., P. Sinclair, B. Andah, and A. Okpoko, eds., 1993, *The Archaeology of Africa: Food, Metals, and Towns*, New York: Routledge.

Shelley, M. W., 1999, *Frankenstein, or the Modern Prometheus*, Cambridge: Chadwyck-Healey.

Schutz, A., 1962, *Collected Papers*, vol. 1, *The Problem of Social Reality*, Edited with an introduction by M. Natanson and a preface by H. L. Van Breda, The Hague: Martinus Nijhoff.

Schutz, A., 1970, *The Phenomenology of the Social World*, Translated by George Walsh and Frederick Lehnhert, with an introduction by George Walsh, Evanston: Northwestern University Press.

Temples, P., 1959, *Bantu Philosophy*, Translated by C. King with foreword by M. Read, Paris: Présence Africaine.

Tsenay, S., 1994, *The Hermeneutics of African Philosophy: Horizon and Discourse*, New York: Routledge.

Tsenay, S., 2000, *Our Heritage: The Past in the Present of African-American and African Existence*, Lanham, MD: Rowman & Littlefield.

West, M., 1995, 'Summary Report of "Ghettoizing African Studies?": The Question of Representation in the Study of Africa—a Roundtable Held at the 38th Annual Meeting of the African Studies Association, November 4, 1995', *ACAS Bulletin* no. 46 (Winter 1996). Also at http://www.prairienet.org/acas/bulletin/bull46toc.html.

Williams, P. and L. Chrisman, eds, 1994, *Colonial Discourse and Post-colonial Theory: A Reader*, New York: Columbia University Press.

Wiredu, K., 1996, *Cultural Universals and Particulars: An African Perspective*, Bloomington: Indiana University Press.

Wittgenstein, L., 1967, *Philosophical Investigations*, Translated by G. E. M. Anscombe, Third Edition, Oxford: Blackwell.

Wynter, S., 1996, 'Is "Development" a Purely Empirical Concept or also Teleological?: A Perspective from "We the Underdeveloped"', in A. Y. Yansané, ed., *Prospects for recovery and sustainable development in Africa*, Westport, CT: Greenwood Press, 299-316.

Wynter, S., 1997, 'Columbus, the Ocean Blue, and Fables That Stir the Mind: To Reinvent the Study of Letters', in B. Cowan and J. Humphries, eds., *Poetics of the Americas: Race, founding, and Textuality*, Baton Rouge: Louisiana State University Press, 141–164.

Young, III, J., 1992, *A Pan-African Theology: Providence and the Legacies of the Ancestors*, Trenton, NJ: Africa World Press.

Chapter 19

Useless Provocation or Meaningful Challenge? The 'Posts' Versus African Studies

Kwaku Larbi Korang

There are two ways to lose oneself: by segregation in the particular or by dilution in the 'universal'.— Aimé Césaire

African Studies Today: 'Rejectionists' and 'Accommodationists'

A cleavage is apparent in African studies today, a line dividing those who denounce the 'posts' and reject their Africanist validity from those who, if they do not embrace the 'posts' wholly, are nevertheless willing to negotiate an Africanist accommodation with their protocols of critical and cultural understanding. 'East is East and West is West, and never the twain shall meet': Kipling's proposition of two positions radically at odds with each other could be an apt characterisation of the position of the hardline 'rejectionists'. These belong to what I refer to in this essay as the strongly Africanist/nationalist camp. And we see their rejectionist position strongly and impressively articulated at length, recently, by the leading Africanist Paul Tiyambe Zeleza in his essay, 'The "Posts", History and African Studies' (2003: 229-93). Zeleza cites, vigorously endorses, and augments the critiques of others regarding the universalist pretensions and globalist ambitions of 'post' theorising and cultural critique (for example, Ahmad 1992; McClintock 1996; Mukherjee 1990; Shohat 1996). And he dismisses what he characterises as the vapid, 'apolitical posturing' and 'historical fatigue' (2003: 230) of intellectuals who answer to one or the other of its dominant manifestations in contemporary scholarship: postmodernism and postcolonialism.

Zeleza's 'anti' posture towards the 'posts' recalls a suspicious Wole Soyinka (1976: x), in another context, rising up in arms against what he saw as sneaky neo-global knowledges that threatened to rob unwary Africans of autonomously validated self-apprehension:

[W]e ... Africans have been blandly invited to submit ourselves to a second epoch of colonisation—this time by a universal-humanoid abstraction defined and conducted by individuals whose theories and prescriptions are derived from the apprehension of *their* world and *their* history, *their* social neuroses and *their* value systems.

Soyinka concludes, 'It is time, clearly, to respond to this new threat, each in his own field'. And for those in the community of Africanist scholarship who would see in this a call for vigilant intellectual policing of the borders of 'Africa', upstart, Johnny-just-come 'post' scholarship must be rejected for an irreverence and insensitivity to the *situated* difference of African(ist) knowledge. This is '*the* African difference' (Owomoyela 1996), they would like to remind the upstarts, that has been consolidated in a century and half of passionate inquiry into a sustainable practical 'idea of Africa' (Mudimbe 1994).

In the light of this, what use, the rejectionists would argue further, is the blanket universalist proposition by Gayatri Spivak (1991: 172), the preeminent Indian-born postcolonial critic, that 'the deconstructive position ... has its historical case in postcoloniality'? Especially when 'Africa', drawn into a 'postcoloniality' Spivak understands in the postmodernist terminology of post-structuralism, finds itself opened up to a deflationary critique that robs it of a meaningful and purposive foundation of knowledge to stand on? Thus Spivak's sceptical reading of 'Africa' in her postmodernist postcolonialism:

> *Africa*, a Roman name for what the Greeks called 'Libya', itself perhaps a latinization of the name of the Berber tribe Aourigha (perhaps pronounced 'Afarika'), is a metonym that points to a greater indeterminacy: the mysteriousness of the space upon which we are born. *Africa* is only a time-bound naming; like all proper names it is a mark with an arbitrary connection to its referent, a catachresis. The earth as temporary dwelling has no foundational name (170).

Opening up the relativity in time of the concept 'Africa' and its shifting, unstable spatial reference, Spivak is out to show that there is no natural, unproblematic connection between this sign and its (geo-historical) referent. It follows for her, therefore, that one cannot lay claim in 'Africa' to a transcendent cultural and political referent, either. Hence, those who wishfully project 'Africa' in African modernist cultural and political nationalism must learn the sobering postmodern lesson that 'Nationalism can only ever be a crucial political agenda against oppression. All longings to the contrary, it cannot provide the absolute guarantee of identity' (170). 'Africa' must emerge for Spivak, therefore, in the language of textuality, undecidability, and ambivalence beloved by post-structuralist critics, as a representation always already haunted and vitiated by *différance*, aporia, and catachresis.

It is deflationary critique of this kind that has provoked the rejectionist response in the community of Africanist scholarship—a response which says, as it were, 'Let them keep theirs and let us keep ours'. And, as Pius Adesanmi confirms in 'Africa, India, and the Postcolonial', who are 'them' and what is 'theirs' appears in an Africanist perception about a (postmodernist) postcolonialism that (a) its iconic intellectuals are 'cosmopolitan' Indians located by and large in metropolitan academies and institutions; and that (b) its privileged object is India. The verdict, as critics like Zeleza make the Africanist case against the 'posts', then, appears to be: 'What is good for India is not necessarily what is good for Africa'. In Zeleza's (2003: 248-249) assessment:

> Compared with their Indian counterparts, 'cosmopolitan' African scholars tend to be less dismissive of nationalism because of Africa's special position as the ultimate negative other of Europe, borne out [by the experience of] the Atlantic Slave Trade, which demands constant discursive redress. Also, African nationalisms were articulated at national, regional, and international levels through Pan-Africanism and Pan-Arabism, and often involved protracted armed liberation struggles, which mean that the nationalist imaginary was not chained to the performance of one particular territory or the interests of the elites, so that hope could always be transferred from one failed country to another, or into the possibilities of the masses being mobilized again as they had been during the liberation struggles. Indeed, the very failures of decolonization, which have been recorded with such a deep sense of anger and betrayal by African writers, were blamed less on the nationalist agenda itself than on the unwillingness or inability of the political class to implement it, abetted by international conditions and inequities.

The case is eloquently made here for African exceptionalism. Rejecting the intellectual moves that would make Africa go the 'cosmopolitan' way of India in the 'posts', Zeleza, we might justly say, hands us a latter-day version of the old nationalist/Pan-Africanist slogan 'Africa for the Africans!'

In contrast to the uprising tendency in African studies that is articulated in a pure resistance against perceived alienating and dangerous contaminations of 'Africa' by foreign theory, there is the accommodationist tendency. This is dominantly represented by the work of V. Y. Mudimbe, Kwame Anthony Appiah, and Achille Mbembe. This latter tendency in the community of African scholarship acknowledges Africa's objective and inescapable situatedness on the material and cultural terrain of 'The Postcolonial and the Postmodern' (Appiah 1992). Africa, in the view of this tendency, has been economically absorbed and culturally assimilated by the metropolitan West into an imperial-colonial modernity. As a direct consequence, Africa today, in the colonial aftermath, is a part of—and nothing apart from—the internationalised commodity exchanges and the 'borderless' transnational cultural and intellectual circuits marked in contemporary understanding by the admittedly disputed designations 'postcolonial' and 'postmodern'.

In assessments of this kind Appiah and others in the Africanist community of scholarship have warranted the 'posts' an objective African habitation. These cultural critics, in doing so, have sought to define an intellectual mission also—a mission conceived in a desire and a project to *properly* Africanise the 'posts'. Zeleza clues us into the motivations behind this scholarly move in African (cultural) studies in the citation above when he points out the 'special position' of Africa 'as the ultimate negative other of Europe'. Europeans, we will recall, produced this image of Africa to justify their colonial domination of that continent, an image that has proved durable, still doing useful service in the colonial aftermath for the West in its relations with Africa. Insofar as Zeleza acknowledges that this is a situation 'which demands constant discursive redress', he alludes to a Western-dominated global discursive and representational terrain embroiled in contestation (see in this regard Ashcroft et al. 1989; Said 1993). The West aspires to cover the world, and in pursuing this aspiration it has caused the Rest to disappear into a self-absorbed monocentrism, monolingualism, monologism, and monovision that it mistakenly refers to as the Universal (see Achebe 1989; Chinweizu et al. 1983). In the circumstances, for the Rest dominated by the West, 'redress' has come to be an imperative call for the global representational terrain to be *dialogically* opened up in order that the West's others might see their different visages reflected in the same: the Universal.

The call from the ex-colonial margins, therefore, is for the West's pernicious images of non-Western otherness, blankness (or human non-presence), unintelligibility, and muteness to be contested and revised. It goes without saying that for Africa, represented in the Western imagination as the ultimate other, the repository of Nothingness, the domain of untranslatable cultural non-sense, the dialogic proposition has a special historical and existential urgency: Africa must 'constantly'—Zeleza's word—seek world-recognition for a *présence africaine*. And, in this making of Africa an intelligible and intelligent presence in the world—which amounts to an African cultural politics of world recognition—the African intellectual is especially enjoined to perform an on-behalf-of function for Africa. Contesting the West's image of the continent, the representative intellectual must demonstrate that Africa is not cultural non-sense but has cross-cultural intelligibility (or is translatable into humanistic common sense). She/he must show that Africa's being has a world-significance on a competitive humanistic par with that of her detractors. Granted 'Africa for the Africans!' has its place; but there is a compelling pressure on Africa to unfold her being on a *world* stage.

The cultural politics that will project a global Africa is by no means problem-free. Africanist intellection going global must come up against the objectivities of an imperial-colonial history that has ensured that the terrain on which it prosecutes its cultural politics is dominated by the West. The West's relative upper hand in the unequal cultural exchanges between itself and the Rest have warranted the languages of the West the status, power, and global reach of world languages. Insofar as her/his cultural politics is about Africa in *world* recognition, therefore, the intellectual is in a paradoxical situation: she/he finds that African intelligibility as a world proposition is to be effected through a world language and its protocols and idioms of cultural and critical intelligibility. If the West must be contested, its monologism and monocentrism displaced by the Rest, then an imperial history has predetermined, and its contemporary legacies continue to determine, that the contestation and displacement will more or less proceed in terms of a dominant West's linguistic, discursive, and representational hegemony. And since the 'posts', cognitive formations manufactured in, and disseminated from, the academies and cultural institutions of the West, happen to be contemporary manifestations of this cultural hegemony, the accommodationists will argue that there is historic and existential validation for the non-Western intellectual's cognitive (self)-positioning within this hegemony. Hence, for the accommodationists, the stringent posture of resistance adopted by the rejectionist Africanists is a symptom of bad faith. For these rejectionists can proclaim their resistance in purist terms because they have either ignored or underplayed the Western cognitive and discursive hegemony in which their own nationalist/modernist rhetoric and critical cultural work are unavoidably implicated (see Appiah 1992: 59, 149; Kanneh 2000: 48; Miller 1990: 70; Mudimbe 1978: 185).

If the Africanist intellectual is always already positioned within the hegemony of the West, does that mean that she/he is simply colonised, as Soyinka, for instance, would understand the matter? It is Spivak who has captured the dilemma of the non-Western intellectual vis-à-vis the West's hegemony well in her observation that: 'Postcolonial persons like ourselves from formerly colonized countries are able to communicate to each other (and to metropolitans), to exchange, to establish sociality, because we have had access to the so-called culture of imperialism'. But, then, when she goes on to ask: 'Shall we assign that culture a measure of "moral luck"?' her response is, 'I think there can be no doubt that the answer is "no"'. Nonetheless she finds this 'no' coming from the 'postcolonial person' problematic. For she/he says it to 'a structure one critiques yet inhabits ... intimately' (1991: 172). Spivak's 'post' knowledge of the situation of the intellectual who will contest the West reveals this intellectual's contestation in the light of something veritably impure and compromised. In 'postcoloniality,' she implies, resistance can ever only be, ambivalently, resistance-in-accommodation.

Should we acknowledge the justness of Spivak's ambivalent proposition, then, we may, perhaps, be readily willing to side with the accommodationist Africanists. These are the ones who, 'posting' African intellectual work beyond 'Africa for the Africans!' will project their 'Africa' into, and/or model it in, the contemporary terms of the West's hegemony, the 'posts'. This would be a matter *within* that hegemony, as Appiah would have it, of 'space-clearing'—that is to say, a matter of making room within the 'posts' to bring a *présence africaine* intelligibly into view in a world frame.

It would be a matter also of 'Africa' modelled in the 'posts' as a 'praxis of infliction,' a project whose necessity Adesanmi (2004) makes an eloquent case for in his essay. By praxis of infliction, Adesanmi invokes a Promethean intellectual energy whose exemplary form he sees in the activity of the 'cosmopolitan' Indian intellectuals alluded to above. These intellectuals have appropriated the 'posts', and successfully resituated them as iconically 'Indian' formations. In that they have put 'India' in a pole position in the contemporary global intellectual exchanges organised under the rubric of the 'posts'. In Adesanmi's view, therefore, African intellectual work will do well to 'Indianise' itself—that is, in an emulation of the ways 'cosmopolitan' Indian intellectuals have purchased world recognition for India in their strategic turning of the hegemonic tables on the West.

In the foregoing I have attempted a brief review of the positions in the Africanist debate over the relation/non-relation of 'Africa' to the 'posts'. The reader might legitimately wonder: If this writer, as an African and Africanist intellectual, is himself impacted by the debates, which side is he on? Is he on the side of the strongly nationalist/Africanist rejectionists who will resist the 'contamination' of the 'posts' with might and main, or of the weakly nationalist/Africanist accommodationists who will embrace them?

My purpose in this essay, I should point out, is not to adjudicate in an absolutist manner between the politically correct and the politically incorrect in the debates, and hence to come out on the side of the one position over the other. The reason should be the obvious one that African intellectual and cultural-political work is an overdetermined affair: it necessarily must unfold in manifold orders of engagement. It is true, as Biodun Jeyifo (1992: 356) acknowledges, that 'much of postcolonial African ... critical thought involves the exploration of Africa's place in the world'. In Jeyifo's assessment, however, the postcolonial proposition which posits Africa-for-the-world cannot and must not overlook what he sees as 'the most important issue in African cultural politics', which 'is the relationship of Africa to itself, the encounter of African nations, societies, and peoples with one another'. And this proposition that Africa-for-itself matters most in Africanist cultural-political work amounts to a strong validation of the strongly nationalist (and rejectionist) position.

To be 'rejectionist' or to be 'accommodationist', therefore, is not a question easily answered in the opinion of this writer. In what follows below, I have chosen to be *both* in critical readings of two case studies, as it were, of the 'posts' in African intellectual and cultural-political work. I propose these readings as demonstrations of where and when it may be useful to align 'Africa' with the 'posts' and where and where it may not be. One of the cases has to do with 'Africa' in what I have alluded to above as a problematic of world recognition. And this is 'Africa' as represented in Appiah's aforementioned piece, 'The Postcolonial and the Postmodern' (a chapter in his 1992 book *In My Father's House: Africa in the Philosophy of Culture*). I bring an elaborate reading to Appiah's space-clearing manoeuvres with 'Africa' as he navigates within and between the postcolonial and the postmodern. Appiah's nuanced manoeuvres—we hear him, in Spivakian postcolonial ambivalence, simultaneously saying, by way of 'Africa,' a reasoned 'yes' and a critical 'no' to the 'posts'—makes, perhaps, the strongest case yet for the accommodationist position in the debates about the 'posts' and 'Africa'. My critical posture in that regard is to go along with, and in endorsement of, Appiah's accommodationist manoeuvres.

In the other case study I address the work of an African intellectual who has taken up the tenets of postmodernism to mount a postcolonial challenge to the modernist protocols of African self-recognition (i.e., the nationalist proposition of Africa-for-itself). I refer to Dennis Ekpo's (1995) 'Towards Post-Africanism', and its deconstructive critique and rejection of what its author sees as the Enlightenment

and modernist categories upon which 'Afrocentrism' or, alternatively, 'Africanism'—
which Ekpo sees as *the* dominant cognitive paradigm of African self-knowledge—
has been constructed. Ekpo goes on to advocate a paradigm shift for 'Africa', calling
for a reconstruction of African self-knowledge and institutional renewal on the basis
of the cognitive and affective tenets of an Africanised postmodernism—or 'post-
Africanism'. Looking at Ekpo's conclusions, one may well wonder with his Nigerian
compatriot Oyekan Owomoyela (1994) (in the rejectionist camp): 'With Friends
Like These Who Needs Enemies?...' As I take a critical look immediately below at
what I see as a spectacularly failed example of accommodationist endeavour in
African studies, therefore, my dominant impulse is to seek a reaffirmation of the
strongly nationalist/rejectionist position.

Scattering 'Africanism' to the Wind: Africa and Post-Africanity

Ekpo begins his critique of 'Africanism' and the 'Afrocentric' paradigm on a historical
note. He points out how the colonial African intelligentsia who had come under
pressure to counter colonialist denigrations of Africa had seen their intellectual and
existential tasks in terms of a nationalist affirmation that would rehabilitate the
continent in models of a coherent modernist self-consciousness. According to him,
the invention of an 'Africanism' provided an

> umbrella doctrine [under which] totalities, labels, and paradigms such as African
> identity, African nation, African rationality, African personality, African authenticity,
> etc. were created and turned into metacodes of modern African self-awareness. In
> this discourse of Africanity, the modern African subjectivity was formed (1995: 126).

In Ekpo's estimation, however, such nationalist and fundamentalist projections of
an African modernity have proved postcolonially unworkable. Historical outcomes
in the African postindependence era have made it obvious that the 'lived, everyday
realities of Africa, including its irreconcilable and natural differences, incompatibilities
and obscurities were magically frozen or simply palmed' by Africanism (p.126).

There is a fatal mismatch therefore, as Ekpo believes, between Africanist thought
and the recalcitrant objectivity of the 'Africa' it would seek to knowledgeably comprehend and master. In that case there is a postcolonial imperative that tasks the
African intellectual to conduct, in Jean Franco's words, 'a skeptical reconstruction
of past errors' (quoted in Gikandi 1992: 381). This is the basis of the keen self-
reflexivity Ekpo brings to the modernist problematic of African self-consciousness.
He presents himself as the African intellectual who is compelled to undertake a
critical genealogical and archaeological inventory of his intellectual heritage as a
starting point of positing continental alternatives. Ekpo's questions might be resolved broadly thus: What are the structural and cognitive first principles undergirding
the relations between the European coloniser and the native African intelligentsia
laid down in the imperial-colonial past? And how might these foundational principles
account for the compromises and failures of an intelligentsia-led project of African
modernity in a postcolonial era?

In Ekpo's view, 'Africanism' is epistemologically predetermined and overdetermined. And this is so to the extent that, in the colonial situation, the enlightened native who sought to resist the coloniser came under an irresistible compulsion to use the master's tools not only to dismantle the master's house but to apply them in building his/her own. As he points out: '[T]he European Logos ... through the agency of colonial culture provided the context in whose pre-comprehension and pre-structuring suppositions ... Africa became thematized as a problem' (1995: 123-124); there was a colonial 'superimposition of a logocentric rationality on native minds' (p. 122). In the light of this, Ekpo sees abiding 'isomorphisms between European cultural modernity and modern African thought' (p. 123).

This development has led to a 'crisis in modern African thought today'. There should be no surprise in this since the founding categories of Africanist thought 'being logocentrically mediated ... their purported origin from, their coincidence with, or even their real concern with, an original pre-logocentric Africa, are a priori excluded or deferred and at best express a mere desire'. Thus the 'modern African mind is held captive even in its most strident posture of African authenticity' (p. 127). Africans having locked themselves up in a seemingly hermetic prison-house of Western concepts,

> [T]his means ... that the foundational concepts of our modern consciousnesses are mostly incongruous totalities, false positivities or misleading labels. ... The proto-Africanist ambitions of certain strands of modern African thought can then be shown to be an exercise in self-delusion. Such thinking can subsist merely as a utopian ideology or poetry. (p. 127)

Ekpo, therefore, diagnoses the disease as cognitive bad faith on the part of African intellectuals, resulting in a 'performative impasse of the modern African thought systems' (p. 123).

In what lies the cure, then? Where is salvation to come from? And towards what practical model of a new, unillusioned continental 'mind' does Ekpo's prognosis of African salvation look? The answer on all counts is (Western) postmodernism. Postmodernism appears in Ekpo's thought first as gifting African modernity with a mode of radical autocritique: '[T]he change of knowledge/critical paradigms occasioned by postmodern reflexivity offers perhaps the shortest route to the structural and conceptual snares ... undermin[ing] the efficacy and creativity of the modern African mind set'; hence a 'deconstructionist or postmodernist re-reading' is called for if we are to 'de-obstruct the modern African mind set' (p.127). Such 'de-obstruction' will steer African thought and practice away from the constricting channels laid for them by the dominant—and self-deluded, as Ekpo will have it—fundamentalist blueprints of 'Afrocentrism'. 'Translated into practical applications in politics, development, social engineering, etc.,' as he assesses, 'Afrocentric thoughts have so far engendered mostly confusions, instability, aberrations, failures and woes' (p. 127).

It is in the light of these practical failures that Ekpo endorses for Africa a radical 'postmodern cynicism', which he clearly believes is at the cutting-edge of rethinking practice in ways that accord with the hard-nosed realities of the contemporary world. As he argues: '[N]ot only are we [Africans] caught up in the implacable systemic rationality of the western economic power complex but our very capacity to develop and modernize depends solely on our ability to come to terms with the postmodern systemic imperatives of this power complex' (p. 131). There is no point, then, as an Afrocentric nationalism has been wont to do, to indict the imperial and neocolonial impulses of the West 'from the moral-humanist interpretation of history'. For:

> What the postmodern unmasking of western historical forms of power reveals is that the West, by the time of imperial capitalist expansion, had already abandoned the moral-humanist mode of legitimation (Legitimation by Grand Tales) and adopted the logic of systematic rationality—the logic of legitimation by the success, efficacy and maintenance of systems ... The question was not whether it was right or wrong to colonize Africa, but whether it could be done. In other words, it was purely a technocratic problem. Accordingly, any indictment of the West couched in terms other than those of the power signs or systems logic of the West is bound to produce little or no real effect on its target. It is not for nothing that one talks of 'postmodern cynicism' as the distinctive character of the technocrative logic of modern European reason/power. (p. 130)

Given the cultural trap in which Africa is ensnared by the West; given the formidable economic power complex under the latter's control, the only realistic resolution for Ekpo—and it is a realism he resolves as postmodern—is to join them in the game if you can't beat them. What is called for is an 'extramoral re-conceptualisation' of the terrain of struggle that pits Africa against the West. On this refigured terrain, Africa is enjoined to 'play a double-game by feigning obedience to the "Master's rules" while at the same time taking advantage of little openings to outwit him' (p.133). In order to 'beat the Master at his own game or at least to play as well as he', Ekpo's postmodernist imperative enjoins the African mind to immerse itself 'in the West, not in order to know it, but through guile, to master its various knowledge/power games strictly in accordance with the Master's knowledge rules' (p.133).

> [F]rom this power game perspective ... the whole cognitive tradition ... from which the modern African mind construed itself and its perceptions of the West, is shown to be neither true nor false, merely another power game but one which is no longer useful because it is powerless. If all knowledge is power game, then the only knowledge that matters is precisely one that enables me to gain power and to ensure the maintenance of my system ... By accepting and adopting this alternative strategy, we will already have overthrown Afrocentricism [sic]; we will be standing already in post-Africanity (p.134).

A number of objections may be entered against Ekpo's post-Africanist effusions. First, taking its measure on its own post-structuralist ground, the argument *against* Afrocentrism and *for* post-Africanity remains inconsistent. In spite of Ekpo's deconstructive dismemberment of the Western logos in his argument against, this logos returns, preserved for Africa *in* (a reformed) Africanist thought, in the form of the postmodern West valorised as a knowable *positivity* and imitable *totality*. The West is re-centred again, even more securely in a would-be post-Africanity, in spite of its apparent displacement. The West is not only the source of the African disease, it *only*, it appears, must be the source of the cure. As for the agenda in which Ekpo asks for 'de-totalized, polycentric interpretations of the African world' (p.129), this seems to have disappeared by the end of the essay. For Africa, read into the games-manship of a new, postmodern Occidentalism, encounters itself in the image of the West as one totality encountering, and compelled to figure itself out of, another.

Secondly, Ekpo caricatures African modernity by reducing it, in cognitive and socio-cultural practice, to an unreconstructed Afrocentrism. He appears to be out to see all ideologically mutable Africanist efforts in intellectual and cultural work as 'torsions within the same anxiety' (Foucault 1988: 16). This reading lacks historical depth and intellectual rigour. For it places the Guinéan (Bissau) revolutionary leader Amilcar Cabral on a par with, say, Mobutu Sese Seko, the Congolese kleptocrat. That there are identifiably progressive Afrocentrisms, and that we can tell the pro-gressive from the obscurantist versions, is a point that must be insisted on. Thus, for instance, Cabral's notion of a 'return to the source' in Guinea Bissau produced a systematic and practical Afrocentrism which raised the revolutionary awareness of the peasantry of that country. Newly empowered by their nationalist self-awareness, the revolutionary masses of that country carried the anticolonial battle to their Portuguese colonisers and succeeded in overthrowing their rule.

On the other hand, Mobutu's doctrine of *authenticité*, or African authenticity, in the Congo (Zaire under Mobutu) can be dismissed as the cynical ploy of a politician to perpetuate his oppressive rule. Ekpo's blanket postmodernist condemnation of Afrocentrism does not allow us to establish this vital difference. It is imperative we should be able to affirm something in 'Africa' without neglecting to be critical of Africanist shortcomings. If becoming postmodernist enjoins us to throw the Africanist baby out with the bath water, however, then what remains of, and on what basis do we validate, the claim that we are African?

We also find an implicit rejection by Ekpo of any moralism in accounting for Africa's current impasse. Were one to argue, for instance, that Africa has been betrayed by the greed of her leadership, this will not do for Ekpo because it spon-sors a 'do the right thing' analysis of the kind which lays blame on, and seeks the reformation of, the psychology of individual and/or social, racial group. Such mor-alism Ekpo rejects utterly: it is *efficient* doing, the West's *forte*, and not *right* doing, that matters above all. Two consequences follow from this expunging of the moral-humanist proposition from Africanist critique and self-understanding. In an era of 'postmodern cynicism,' not only is God—the logocentric God of a high Human-ism—dead in Europe, as Nietzsche declared; the final nail in Humanism's coffin is to be planted by Africa. Projected heroically beyond good and evil, Ekpo's Nietzchean post-Africanity is affirmed *only* in its successful mimicry of a soulless postmodernist technocracy. Instrumental reason, the European invention which had been discovered and decried by Max Weber, is thus installed by Ekpo as Africa's postmodern godhead.

One ought to question the worth for Africa of this postmodern cynicism that upholds one supreme value—efficiency. The classic case of the postmodern cynicism advocated by Ekpo in twentieth century Europe would be Adolf Hitler. Hitler did not ask whether killing millions of Jews ought to be done but whether it could be done, and if so how efficiently. The resolution of the question was a purely technocratic one; it was the end that justified the means. We have to wonder what an African intellectual is asking for if he insists that morality and humanism should have no place in the technocratic world of post-Africanity. From a cynical postmodern perspective, genocide can only be seen and justified as the efficient management of human resources through the culling of 'excess' or 'deviant' populations. In the name of efficiency, postmodern cynicism, in other words, would normalise the horrors of Rwanda and apartheid South Africa. What is more, if it is ends that solely justify means, then Ekpo and his Nigerian compatriots should have no valid moral case against the murderous Sani Abacha regime. This cold and remorseless postmodern logic, surely, has to be rejected out of hand! And we should reject it on Africanist ground in the insistence that morality and humanity ought to be part of the meaning of Africa.

Finally, there is the mandarin, self-assured tone running through what after all is a non-Westerner's advocacy on behalf of the West for Africa. Ekpo's post-Africanist Occidentalism is not troubled at all by the existential import of its critical convictions. Certainly, not in the manner in which we find the same, for instance, in the writing of another Africanist with postmodernist leanings, V. Y. Mudimbe. In Mudimbe's assessment:

> But truly for Africa to escape the West involves an exact appreciation of the price we have to pay to detach ourselves from it. It assumes that we are aware of the extent to which the West, insidiously perhaps, is close to us; it implies knowledge, in that which permits us to think against the West, of that which remains Western. We have to determine the extent to which our anti-Occidentalism is possibly one of its tricks directed against us, at the end of which it stands, motionless, waiting for us (quoted in Ngate 1988: 11-12).

There is existential anguish displayed in this passage and elsewhere in his writings which, in the end, is Mudimbe's saving grace. And what this anguish reveals is that the subjectivity of the African intellectual, however ambivalent, ought to be a site of struggle and not easy compromise. It must operate, in this sense, in the Benjaminian mode of 'pessimism of intellect, optimism of will'. It is the optimism that shows when Mudimbe *the nationalist* supersedes Mudimbe *the postmodernist*, as he declares confessionally at the end of *The Invention of Africa*:

> I believe that the geography of African gnosis ... points out the passion of a subject-object who refuses to vanish. He or she has gone from the situation in which he or

she was perceived as a simple functional object to the freedom of thinking of himself or herself as the starting point of an absolute discourse. It has also become obvious, even for this subject, that the space interrogated by series of explorations in African indigenous systems of thought is not a void (1988: 200).

More Faust than Prometheus, Mudimbe may trouble and push 'Afrocentrism' to the breaking point, but he does not renounce it. The Promethean Ekpo, on the other hand, binds Africa over too quickly to the West.

Africa in the World, the World in Africa

When all is said and done, Ekpo's error-prone postmodernist advocacy has at least one merit: it alerts us to the important and substantial question of how Africanists must construe a normative 'Africa' in cultural knowledge and socio-political practice. That is, are we to assume a normative 'Africa' that is always already guaranteed such that this absolute 'Africa' is the type of subject/object of which we can ask the same questions, and which we can task cognitively and practically to perform the same jobs eternally, world without end? Or ought we to define and position 'Africa' contingently and relationally—hence an 'Africa' open to the modifying pressures of time and of its global situation?

I raise these questions—questions I will return to in my conclusion—as I shift the locus of the chapter's discussion of Africa *against* and *for* the 'posts' from the imperative demands of Africa-for-itself (the strongly nationalist proposition) to the imperative demands of Africa-for-the-world (the weakly nationalist proposition). In the latter proposition, if we go by Appiah's posture in 'The Postcolonial and the Modern', not only must 'Africa' interrogate the 'world', 'Africa' must also submit to being interrogated by the 'world'. And in this dialectic, the normativity of Africa that the Africanist brings to critical cultural work can hardly emerge in one exhaustive aspect. As Appiah's accommodationist manoeuvres in the worldly 'posts' persuasively demonstrate, a world-bound Africa—that is, an Africa that aspires to worldly intelligibility and, in that, to world recognition—is enjoined to be both nationalist and *post*-nationalist (and this post-nationalism emerges especially in Appiah's inclusive humanism).

If Appiah's focus, therefore, is on 'Africa in the philosophy of culture', as his book *In My Father's House* is subtitled, this focus is one in which he self-consciously projects 'Africa' beyond 'Africa for the Africans!' into what he refers to generally as 'our human modernity' (1992: 144). The reference and claim to what is *ours* thus marks Appiah's postnationalist and humanist terrain. That terrain is much wider, and his prize much bigger, than Africa, a locale that he produces historically and logically as a part of the cultural-intellectual, ideological, and commodity exchanges of international modernity. A peripherally modern Africa may not be exactly at the centre of these exchanges but Appiah's procedures are informed by the understanding that 'center and periphery are mutually constitutive' (1992: 54); and that 'We must not overstate the distance from London to Lagos' (76). Appiah certainly acknowledges (Africa as) Difference, but he proceeds also in a mode of demonstrating that by the force of a globally shared history, of institutions and imaginaries coordinated imperially across space and time, local differences look to, and *demand a critical articulation in*, the Same.

Against the shibboleths of nationalist exceptionalism, therefore, the 'post' Appiah brings to African difference is expressed in a philosophical thesis and critical practice of Africa's *translatability* into a 'commonwealth' of a modern, transnational culture. The case against African exceptionalism is made by Appiah in indirect fashion. It involves a turning of the tables on the Weberian account of modernity, an account which reserves 'rationalisation'—the quality of a reflexive, calculating reason—for Western civilisation as this civilisation's salient mode of being exceptional. Comparatively, therefore, a non-West, Africa included, is radically different from the West because its tradition-bound cultures remain 'enchanted,' still wedded to 'irrational'—or 'pre-rational,' if one wants to be generous—structures of religious faith, mythic knowledge and understanding, charismatic authority, and so on. On the other hand, for Weber writing in the early twentieth century, the culture of Western civilisation was, if not already so, on its way to encountering its ultimate fate, which is total 'disenchantment'. Tradition-bound structures in thought, affect, and practice were bound to disappear, displaced by the operations of what Weber called instrumental reason. Despite Weber's confident prediction, however, the de-traditionalising of the West, and the cultures it has influenced, is exactly what has not happened. The reverse, as Appiah notes, is true; and so

> [T]he beginning of postmodern wisdom is to ask whether Weberian rationalization is in fact what has happened. For Weber, charismatic authority—the authority of Stalin, Hitler, Mao, Guevara, Nkrumah—is antirational, yet modernity has been dominated by such charisma. Secularization seems hardly to be proceeding: religions grow in all parts of the world; more than 90 percent of North Americans avow some form of theism; what we call 'fundamentalism' is as alive in the West as it is in Africa and the Middle East and the Far East: Jimmy Swaggart and Billy Graham have business in Louisiana and California as well as in Costa Rica and Ghana (145).

Appiah, out to show 'why the rationalization of the world can no longer be seen as the tendency either of the West or of history' (144), is after a 'radically post-Weberian conception of modernity' (145). And the implication is that the account of modernity, conducted through rationalisation and reason, cannot rest on the simple epistemological dichotomies of haves and have-nots. Weber slides too easily from content to form; that is, rationalisation and reason as given Western content reveal the form of the modern as such. Yet the retention of tradition and burgeoning of traditionalism the world over reveal that, culturally speaking, we are all universally traditional in form and kind. In what we might resolve as a contingent proposition, it is in the *degree* to which a Weberian content 'overrides' (traditional) form that we can tell a mainstream modern (the West) from its marginal counterpart (a non-West). Difference in (contingent) degree, then, not in (essential) kind. Thus, freed by

Appiah from essence-conferring form, as given in the Weberian account, modernity as content is able to speak with an African accent, from within African (traditional) form, too. (Appiah chooses to call this African modernity 'neotraditional' to illustrate how a modern content witnesses to a resilient African form.)

Appiah's post-Weberian effort aims to clear the thick undergrowth that obscures Africa's habitation in the conceptual forest of the modern, and thus to unlock the 'sympathetic' epistemologies making for adequate translation that would give African Difference a valid residence in the Same. As we will see below, in Appiah's rehabilitation of an ethical universal, a modernist humanism, self-consciously activated within the 'post', does epistemological service in this sympathetic crossing over of Difference into the Same—or translation. But Appiah's appeal to a post-Weberian humanism is in essence a critical one: it rests on the understanding that such humanism cannot simply assume its adequacy as it did in an earlier time of innocence when its dominion and centrality went unchallenged. Humanism's appeal as valid mode of knowing and representing—to the extent that the assumptions behind an older humanism are badly bruised and battered—has to be a *negotiated* one. Hence Appiah's deference to the currency and challenge of postmodernism and postcolonialism as dominant modes of contemporary knowledge, themselves central in interrogations of totalising humanist myths and narratives of modernist legitimation, such as the global triumph of (Western) Reason, etc.

In effect what this means is that a humanistic Same, postulated for and in Appiah's Africa, must look at itself in the comparative light of—and figure something of itself out of a place and relationship between—the two 'posts'. If the critical objective is a crossover that places this Africa in a translation and transaction between home and world, local and global, this crossover is also to be negotiated in a placing of Africa comparatively and *selectively* between the postmodern and the postcolonial. Appiah's Africa, tasked to traffic between the two in translation and transaction, both draws on them in useful appropriation and donates itself to them in an extension of a human(ist) pool of knowledge. Africa in this mode is also engaged in interrogating and being interrogated by the postcolonial and postmodern in reciprocal and fraternal correction, while also rejecting what is unworkable in them, for itself and the humanity it sponsors, in wholesome critique.

What is at stake in this undertaking is spelt out in the following terms: 'The role that Africa, like the rest of the Third World, plays for Euro-American postmodernism ... must be distinguished from the role postmodernism might play in the Third World' (157). The first of these roles—Africa's place in Euro-American postmodernism—is in some sense settled, though hardly in a way, and on terms, as Appiah demonstrates, that we can be happy with. As for the second—postmodernism's place in Africa's relations with itself—according to the critic, it is 'too early to tell [and] what happens will happen not because we pronounce upon the matter in theory but out of the everyday changing practices of African cultural life' (157). If the first calls for a diagnostic critique, the second calls for critical prognostication (a 'prophetic' criticism), both conducted within the humanistic viewpoint that Appiah favours. It is within the humanist strategy that, in the first instance, the critic brings his reader to assess (a) a postmodernist relativism by which the West privileges Difference over Same; and (b) an uncritical universalism, both working together to assimilate the Other subserviently to the Western Self, its needs and desires. The question Appiah asks out of, and through, Africa, then, is: What are the implications of this relativism/pseudo-universalism, coming out of a postmodern West, for the marking and identification of subjects and objects which inhabit the other 'post'—that is, the postcolonial? And he asks this confident that what he has to say 'will work elsewhere in the so-called Third World and that, in some places, it certainly will not' (147).

As Appiah searches for the answer to the impact of the West on African subjects and objects, then, he must open Africa up to the question of the terrain and trajectory of the postcolonial, too. In what and where, Appiah asks, are African subjects and objects (to be) marked as postcolonial? And for the critic this is essentially about making sense of African postcoloniality in three dimensions of time, space, and subjectivity. The 'post' marks Africa in a time after the colonial; and it marks the productive activities of Africa, cultural and other, as occurring in a space worked over by colonial processes. And yet, for Appiah, if all cultural objects appearing in the aftermath of the colonial can be subsumed under the temporal and spatial label postcolonial, not all the persons accounting for these objects are, in a relevant subjective sense, postcolonial. Thus, two kinds of cultural subjectivity appear in postcolonial space-time: first, those who are subjectified as (post)colonial—the *'comprador* [African] intelligentsia' (149), who have been brought up in, and professionalised according to, the ways of the West, fed on its epistemologies and ideologies of action, and for whom, therefore, Western modes of thought and action have become, and anxiously so, a second nature. If this West-in-Africa occupies the ground of 'high culture' and politics on the continent, there are those Appiah identifies with 'mass culture' (148), who are not—or perhaps who are less (anxiously)—subjectified as postcolonial, in the special sense in which Appiah uses the term to capture a Westernized subjectivity in Africa.

Nevertheless—and this complicates the picture somewhat—given the post-Weberian logic sponsoring Appiah's perspective, the subjectivities of both elite and masses in Africa are modern. And the cultural objects they produce—literature in the case of high culture, folk art in the case of mass culture—participate in globally postmodernising processes of international consumption and exchange. As Appiah notes, '[B]ecause contemporary culture is, in certain senses ... transnational, postmodern culture is global' (144). In one of the senses in which Appiah produces contemporary culture, the postcolonial products of elite and masses are similarly positioned in (the condition of) postmodernity. Postmodernity here does service as the name of a global market, which is Western-controlled, and governed by what Frederic Jameson, quoted by Appiah, calls the commodity 'logic of late capitalism'. It is to this postmodernist logic of commodification—which, in a thoroughgoing way, brings into being a 'social functionality of culture'—that Appiah addresses a market-driven aspect of the (many-sided) question of relativism. He shows that there is an urge in the West to differentiate (aesthetic) products, confer on them a unique, saleable identity that not only marks them *off* in time and space from other products but also, consequently, marks them *up* in market value. A highly self-con-scious Western ideology of the market explains the differentiation of the domains of concept and practice in which these products are created and consecrated. Hence *post*modernism must succeed and supersede an antecedent modernism even though when we look at various domains of their practice, and at the qualitative features of their products, the 'break' between the two might appear to be more ideologically willed than substantive. If 'Modernity has turned every element of the real into a sign, and the sign reads "for sale"' (145), for Appiah its 'post' is to be understood in ideology and practice as a 'space-clearing gesture' which permits new relations of value to appear (and profits, we might add, to accumulate).

> Postmodernism can be seen, then, as a new way of understanding the multiplication of distinctions that flows from the need to clear oneself a space; the need that drives the underlying dynamic of cultural modernity. Modernism saw the economisation of the world as the triumph of reason; postmodernism rejects that claim, allowing in the realm of theory the same multiplication of distinctions we see in the cultures it seeks to understand (145-146).

But if the space-clearing gesture is, vitally, in process within the space of the West, what status does the process confer on the postcolonial aesthetic object, from Africa, incorporated into the exchange relations between centre and periphery? Objectively speaking, how is this object 'translated'—i.e., assimilated (or made the same)—into the metropolitan logic of aesthetic and cultural commodification; that is, the functionality of social marketability postmodern ideology brings to cultural production? And looking at this ideology, how *well*, if at all, does the African, and therefore non-Western object translate? Again, what does this translation, subject to postmodernist 'terms of trade' of Western imposition, project on to the creative subject behind the postcolonial object?

Appiah finds that the postmodernist value of the postcolonial object, inherited unchanged from Western modernism, is still negotiated through an aestheticised Primitivism (which canonises into *art* African folk expression once seen as merely crude and rude). The value of traditional African art may appear to be fixed extrin-sically, according to allegedly disinterested (i.e., universalist, all-inclusive) aesthetic criteria. But an ideological sleight of hand operates here, for ultimately the art ob-ject's value is very much made out of what is seen as intrinsic to it and what is exclusive about the site of its production. The Malian novelist Yambo Ouologuem has treated this issue extensively and sceptically in his novel *Bound to Violence*. And Appiah, in approving citation of Ouologuem, notes: '[A]n ideology of disinterested aesthetic value—the "baptism" of "Negro art" as "aesthetic"—meshes with the international commodification of African expressive culture, a commodification that requires, by the logic of the space-clearing gesture, the manufacture of Otherness'

(156). The art object, and the African subject who accounts for its production, must preserve a pure difference from what is Western or Western*ised*, be baptised as authentic as such, even as they enter vitally into postmodern cross-border exchanges that confound both authenticity and pure difference. As Appiah sees it, Africa, forcibly confined to unchanging tradition is made the *outsider* inside, the incommensurable other of the (post)modern, which is also, absurdly, *within* its frame.

The principle at work here is an instance of what Doreen Massey analyses elsewhere in terms of a differential 'power-geometry' in global relations. By this she means to point to

> power in relation *to* the [transnational] flows and movement ... [where] some people are more in charge of it than others; [where] some initiate flows and movements, others don't; [where] some are more on the receiving end than others; [where] some are effectively imprisoned by it (quoted in Hall et al., 1996: 624).

Consider, in this light, Appiah's reading of who has the authoritative last word as he compares the contributions to a 1987 exhibition, organised by the Center for African Art in New York, by two men, one 'postmodern,' the other 'traditional'. These two were the American David Rockefeller, collector of African art, and Lela Kouakou, diviner and producer of African art, a man who belongs to the Baule ethnic group of Côte d'Ivoire. The show, whose curator was a Susan Vogel, was entitled 'Perspectives: Angles on African Art' and the two were appointed, along with seven others, as 'co-curators' charged with selecting ten items, out of a hundred from across Africa, for the show. Rockefeller is quoted as saying about one of the art objects: 'I thought it was quite beautiful ... the total composition has a very contemporary, very Western look to it. It's the kind of thing that goes very well with contemporary Western things'. In this and others of Rockefeller's responses, we have, Appiah notes, 'a microcosm of the site of the African in contemporary— which is, then, surely to say, postmodern—America'; Africa's place and utility emerge then in postmodern 'considerations of finance, of aesthetics, and of décor' (Appiah 1992: 138).

On the other hand, the critical competency of Lela Kouakou is denied any such catholic and cosmopolitan perspective. From the start, he was assumed to be 'a man familiar only with the art of his own people', and for this reason 'only Baule objects were placed in the pool of photographs' he was required to choose from. The curator explained:

> Showing him the same assortment of photos the others saw would have been interesting, but confusing in terms of the reactions we sought here. Field aesthetic studies, my own and others, have shown that African informants will criticize sculptures from other ethnic groups in terms of their own traditional criteria, often assuming that such works are simply inept carvings of their own aesthetic tradition (p.137).

Clearly, the relativist principle invoked here is to ensure that Kouakou is spoken for by Vogel: that he would have been confused is hypothetical, not empirically proven. Not only that: if he is allowed to speak (in critical judgement) at all, this permission to speak is granted within a severely restricted framework. He must come to speech only as a 'tribesman' within the postmodern frame (*in* it but not *of* it). For the postmodern American, on the contrary, the following is true: 'David Rockefeller is permitted to say *anything at all* about the arts of Africa because he is a *buyer* and because he is at the *center*' (138). Between Vogel's postmodernist relativism—the gesture of apparent respect for Difference—and Rockefeller's universalism—the apparently 'charitable' gesture of inclusion—we see two masquerades of Western ethnocentrism that work together to maintain a strategic control over the productions of the Other and their circulation. Lela Kouakou, 'who merely makes art and who dwells at the margins', Appiah concludes, 'is a poor African whose words count only as parts of the commodification ... of Baule art' (138). Relativism, bemoaning African lack (as in Vogel's statement), privileges the West as the supreme term in African translation; universalism, as another strategy in that translation (as in Rockefeller's), reduces Africa to an objective complement of—an element that merely blends into— the West. Both strategies make Africa a candidate of assimilation on purely Western terms.

For Appiah, therefore, even as it crosses over objectively, Africa remains a victim of ideologically motivated and commercially inspired mistranslation, the exoticised Other which is a part of (hence Same) yet somehow apart and distant from (hence radically Different). Lela Kouakou may be allowed a space to speak, his opinion allowed to mingle with those of Westerners and the Westernised; yet, from Appiah's critical humanist perspective, this postmodern orchestration of voices amounts to a communicative short-changing of the 'traditional' African and not to genuine human exchange.

Clearly for Appiah, this postmodern reification of Difference that rests on a manipulative denial of the Same for others must be resisted. But does this mean, then, that the 'post' in postmodernism has no relevance for Africa? For Appiah the answer is both 'yes' and 'no'—and he makes the answer contingent on where in postcolonial Africa one is looking. 'Both village and urban dwellers alike, bourgeois and non-bourgeois', he reminds us, 'listen, through discs and more importantly, on the radio, to reggae, to Michael Jackson, and to King Sunny Ade' (p.148). In short, it is part of Africa's postcolonial condition to be marked by the transnational trajectories of the modern/postmodern. However, Appiah insists on a critical differentiation within this shared condition:

> All aspects of contemporary Africa life—including music and some sculpture and painting, even some writings with which the West is largely not familiar—have been influenced, often powerfully by the transition of African societies *through* colonialism, but they are not all in the relevant sense postcolonial. For the *post* in postcolonial, like the *post* in postmodern is the *post* of the space-clearing gesture ... and many areas of contemporary African cultural life—what has come to be theorized as popular

culture, in particular—are not in this way concerned with transcending, with going beyond coloniality. Indeed it might be said to be a mark of popular culture that its borrowings from international cultural forms are remarkably insensitive to—not so much dismissive as blind to—the issue of neocolonialism or 'cultural imperialism'. This does not mean that theories of postmodernism are irrelevant to these forms of culture: for the internationalization of the market and the commodification of artworks are both central to them. But it *does* mean that these artworks are not understood by their producers or their consumers in terms of a postmodern*ism*: there is no antecedent practice whose claim to exclusivity of vision is rejected through these artworks. What is called syncretism here is made possible by the international exchange of commodities, but is not a consequence of the space-clearing gesture (p.148).

It is in the 'post' as a 'space-clearing gesture', one that challenges an 'antecedent practice which claims exclusivity', that Appiah, looking towards a specific mode of self-critique, makes room for a joining of the postmodern and the postcolonial together in Africa. Where it is appropriate to do so, the critic claims, is the domain where the distinction between high and mass culture in Africa 'is powerful and pervasive': in European-language African writing. It is in this writing (produced by those with a Westernised subjectivity) that we find 'a place for consideration of the question of the *post*coloniality of contemporary culture' (149).

What does the 'post' in African writing gesture beyond? What is the antecedent of this 'post'? Appiah's answer takes us to the promotional novels written to legitimate the elite practice of African nationalism, a nationalism mediated by ideologies of modernisation. The narrative convention of realism, borrowed from European eighteenth- and nineteenth-century literary nationalism, underwrote the attempt by a first generation of modern African novelists to recreate a common cultural past. The purpose was to fabricate therein a shared and useable tradition to energise the African anti-colonial struggle and to lay cultural foundations for the new nations that were being struggled for. Achebe's *Things Fall Apart* and Camara Laye's *L'Enfant noir*, classics of the 1950s, are conceived in this mode.

However, the promotional nationalist writing was not to last. Appiah's reading of Ouologuem's *Bound to Violence*, published in 1968, shows that by this time writerly enthusiasm about the nation was on the wane. The effort to naturalise nation and nationalism had been rendered unsupportable because 'The national bourgeoisie that took on the baton of rationalization, industrialization, bureaucratization in the name of nationalism, turned out to be a kleptocracy'. If this elite showed any enthusiasm for 'nativism', it was simply because they needed a justification of their 'urge to keep the national bourgeoisies of other nations—and particularly the powerful industrialized nations—out of their way'. Nativism could also fit in very well with the nefarious designs of 'traditional and contemporary elites who require a sentimentalized past to authorize their present power' (156). Thus, in the light of these negative developments, Appiah thinks that postcoloniality has also 'become a condition of pessimism' (155).

The pessimism that infects *Bound to Violence* is not only expressed in theme; the form of the novel, according to Appiah, challenges the conventional realist techniques and presuppositions of its forebears of the first stage. Hence this novel of the second stage is, as Appiah puts it, 'postrealist', as such allowing its author to 'borrow, when he needs them, the techniques of modernism which, as we have learned from Fred Jameson, are often also the techniques of postmodernism' (p.150). Insofar as Ouologuem rejects a realist aesthetic, ideologically he also rejects nativism, the sentimental content of African nationalism. In this light he is 'postcolonially postnationalist as well as anti- (and thus, of course, post-) nativist' (p.152).

And yet—and this is important for the humanist in Appiah—if postmodernism is postrealist also, the motivation behind Ouologuem's postrealism is not of the same order as that of 'postmodern writers as, say, [the American Thomas] Pynchon' (p.150). Appiah notes:

> Because [*Bound to Violence*] is a novel that seeks to delegitimate not only the form of realism but the content of nationalism, it will to that extent seem to us to be misleadingly to be postmodern. *Mis*leadingly, because what we have here is not postmodern*ism* but postmodern*ization*; not an aesthetics but a politics, in the most literal sense of the term. After colonialism, the modernizers said, comes rationality; that is the possibility the novel rules out ... Far from being a celebration of the nation, then, the novels of the second stage—the postcolonial stage—are novels of delegitimation: rejecting the Western imperium, it is true, but also rejecting the nationalist project of the postcolonial national bourgeoisie.

Unlike Pynchon and other postmodernist writers, therefore, 'Ouologuem is hardly likely to make common cause with a relativism that might allow that the new-old Africa of exploitation is to be understood—legitimated—in its own local terms'. Rather, in Appiah's humanist globalism, local (or African) terms are translatable—into universal terms. In keeping with the way intellectual responses to oppression in Africa have appealed to 'a certain simple respect for human suffering', Appiah concludes then that the basis of the creative project of nationalist delegitimation is very much not the relativist one of postmodernism. It makes better sense to see it as 'grounded in an appeal to an ethical universal' (p.152). The humanistic case for Ouologuem and others is summed up this way:

> Postrealist writing; postnativist politics; a *transnational* rather than a *national* solidarity. And pessimism: a kind of *post*optimism to balance the earlier enthusiasm for *The Suns of Independence*. Postcoloniality is *after* all this: and its *post*, like postmodernism's, is also a *post* that challenges them in the name of the suffering victims of 'more than thirty [African] republics.' But it challenges them in the name of the ethical universal; in the name of *humanism*, '*le gloire pour l'homme.*' And on that ground it is not an ally for Western postmodernism but an agonist, from which I believe postmodernism may have something to learn (p.155).

What Appiah sets out for us here is the mutual interrogation of the 'posts' and 'Africa'—as the name of an exclusive nationalism. He presents his humanist case for sympathetic translation based on the 'lesson' that in the transnational 'circulation of cultures ... we are all already contaminated by each other' (p.155). However, the universalism of a refurbished humanism cannot lose sight of the lessons of postmodernist relativism either: ethical rigour demands that the two cross over— translate—productively into each other in the following:

> For what I am calling humanism can be provisional, historically contingent, antiessentialist (in other words, postmodern), and still be demanding. We can surely maintain a powerful engagement with the concern to avoid cruelty and pain while nevertheless recognizing the contingency of that concern. Maybe, then, we can re-cover within postmodernism the postcolonial writers' humanism—the concern for human suffering, for the victims of the postcolonial state ... while still rejecting the master narratives of modernism. This human impulse [is] an impulse that tran-scends obligations to churches and to nations (p.155).

Ken Harrow, in an intervention in a debate on 'Postmodernism and African Studies', traces the evolutionary trajectory of the cognitive self-positioning of Carol Boyce Davies in order to provide, in miniature, a report on the career and the current state and disposition of Africanist knowledge. Harrow finds that the re-spected black and Afrocentric feminist critic has moved from the exclusionary 'Africanism' of her early co-edited book *Ngambika: Studies of Women in African Litera-ture* (1986) to a self-consciously *conjunctural* Africanism in her most recent book, *Black Women, Writing and Identity* (1997), which is subtitled 'Migrations of the Sub-ject'.

It would appear that the migrancy Davies alludes to—induced by the globalizing currents of an imperial and postimperial history—does not only capture the condi-tion of the black subjects she writes about but limns as well the condition of the intellectual subject doing the writing. Davies's 'intellectual migrancy' is evident, as Harrow assesses, in the way she 'employs a wide gambit [*sic*] of postcolonial and postmodern thinkers', "articulating multiple subjectivities and discursive positions and agency", all aspects we'd expect from a postmodernist' (Harrow 1997).

Yet while Davies's later scholarship, in saying 'yes' to the 'posts', owns up in that to a contemporary obligation it owes to a post-imperial 'migrant' world, nevertheless this scholarship also comes structured in a 'no'. For it is framed by Davies, as Harrow reminds us, as 'resistant postmodernism', which as such emerges 'in resist-ance to western hegemonies'. As well, its 'agenda ... negotiates between all manner of theory that is centered in western universities and life "on the ground" in Africa and the diaspora' (Harrow 1997).

Here, then, is a model Africanist scholarship that, as in Appiah's outlined above, is exemplary in its conjunctural navigation and negotiation betwixt and between. In it the accommodationist thesis of Africa-for-the-world does not preclude the national-ist thesis of Africa-for-itself; nor has Africa-for-itself forgotten to name its obligations to the world at large. In this mutual inscription, where Africa-for-itself and Africa-for-the-world find themselves in each other, we find the scholarly fruit of the lesson contained in Césaire's caveat: 'There are two ways to lose oneself: by segregation in the particular and by dilution in the "universal"' (quoted in Miller 1990: 24). Obligation to 'migrancy'—or the universal—and loyalty to 'home'—or the particular—need not be mutually exclusive. Hence it is that we find Harrow recommending to his interlocutors in the Africanist community of scholarship: 'Let's drop the idea of "being" a postmodernist, and simply move on with the same kinds of negotiations, eschewing a know-nothing attitude of rejectionism that refuses what it finds too much trouble to learn' (1997).

Sound counsel; yet, for all that, the recommendation contains an overly one-dimensional reading of rejectionism. For it is vital, also, that Africanist accommodationist negotiation in the 'posts' be vigilantly self-aware; that it come wearing the protective armour of a healthy rejectionism. I speak here of a 'know-something' rejectionism, the kind that, backed by and confident in its knowingness, will not hesitate to say a thunderous 'no' to wrongheaded postmodernist/post-Africanist propositions and prescriptions of the kind proffered by Ekpo and those who share his intellectual orientation and theoretical persuasion.

References

Achebe, C., 1989, *Hopes and Impediments: Selected Essays*, New York: Anchor-Doubleday.

Adesanmi, P., 2004, 'Africa, India, and the Postcolonial: Toward a Praxis of Infliction', *Arena Journal* 21: 173-196.

Ahmad, A., 1992, *In Theory: Classes, Nations, Literatures*, London: Verso.

Appiah, K.A., 1992, *In My Father's House: Africa in the Philosophy of Culture*, New York: Oxford University Press.

Ashcroft, B., G. Griffiths and H. Tiffin, 1989, *The Empire Writes Back: Theory and Practice in Post-Colonial Literatures*. London and New York: Routledge.

Chinweizu, O. Jemie and I. Madubuike, 1983, *Towards the Decolonization of African Literature*, Washington, DC: Howard University.

Davies, C.B., 1994, *Black Women, Writing and Identity: Migrations of the Subject*, London and New York: Routledge.

Davies, C.B. and A. A. Graves, eds., 1986, *Ngambika: Studies of Women in African Literature*, Trenton, NJ: Africa World Press.

Ekpo, D., 1995, 'Towards Post-Africanism: Contemporary African Thought and Postmodernism', *Textual Practice* 9 (1): 121-135.

Gikandi, S., 1992, 'The Politics and Poetics of the National Formation: Recent African Writing', in A. Rutherford, ed., *From Commonwealth to Post-Colonial*, Sydney: Dangaroo, 377-89.

Gikandi, S., 2001, 'Theory, Literature, and Moral Considerations', *Research in African Literatures* 32 (4): 1-18.

Hall, S., 1996, 'When was "the Post-Colonial"? Thinking at the Limit', in I. Chambers and L. Curti, eds., *The Post-Colonial Question: Common Skies, Divided Horizons*, London and New York: Routledge, 242-260.

Hall, S., D. Held, D. Hubert and K. Thompson, ed., 1996, *Modernity: An Introduction to Modern Societies.* Cambridge, MA and Oxford: Blackwell.

Harrow, K., 1997, 'Postmodernism and African Studies: Reply', 11 November 1997. *H-AFRICA@H-NET.MSU.EDUhttp://www.h-net.msu.edu/~africa/threads/pomothread.html>*

Irele, A., 1992, 'In Praise of Alienation', in V. Y. Mudimbe, ed., *Surreptitious Speech: Présence Africaine and the Politics of Otherness, 1947-1987,* Chicago and London: The University of Chicago Press, 201-224.

Jameson, F., 1991, *Postmodernism, Or the Cultural Logic of Late Capitalism,* Durham, N.C.: Duke University Press.

Janz, B., 1995, 'Reply: Postmodern and Modern Africa', 26 May. *H-AFRICA@H-NET.MSU.EDU http://www.h-net.msu.edu/~africa/threads/pomothread.html>*

Jeyifo, B., 1990, 'For Chinua Achebe: The Resilience and Predicament of Obierika,', in K. H. Petersen and A. Rutherford, eds., *Chinua Achebe: A Celebration,* Oxford and Portsmouth, NH: Heinemann; Sydney, Coventry, Aarhus: Dangaroo, 51-70.

Jeyifo, B., 1992, 'Literature in Africa: Repression, Resistance, and Reconfigurations', *Dissent*: 353-360.

Kanneh, K., 1998, *African Identities: Race, Nation and Culture in Ethnography, Pan-Africanism and Black Literatures,* London and New York: Routledge.

Korang, K.L., 2003, '"Africa and Australia" Revisited: Reading Kate Grenville's *Joan Makes History*', *Antipodes* 17 (1): 5-12.

Korang, K.L., 1992-1993, 'An Allegory of Re-Reading: Post-Colonialism, Resistance and J. M. Coetzee's *Foe*', *World Literature Written in English* 32 (2)/33 (1): 133-150.

Korang, K.L. and S. Slemon, 1997, 'Postcolonialism and Language', in M-H. Msiska and P. Hyland, eds., *Writing and Africa,* London: Longman, 246-263.

Lazarus, N., 1994, 'National Consciousness and the Specificity of (Post)colonial Intellectualism', in F. Barker, P. Hulme, and M. Iversen, eds., *Colonial Discourse/Postcolonial Theory.* Manchester and New York: Manchester Universtiy Press, 197-220.

Lazarus, N., 1999, *Nationalism and Cultural Practice in the Postcolonial World,* Cambridge: Cambridge University Press.

Lee, B., 1995, 'Critical Internationalism', *Public Culture* 7 (3): 559-592.

Limb, P., 1997, 'Postmodernism and African Studies: Reply', 12 November. *H-AFRICA@H-NET.MSU.EDU http://www.h-net.msu.edu/~africa/threads/pomothread.html>*

Loomba, A., 1998, *Colonialism/Postcolonialism,* London and New York: Routledge.

Lowe, C., 1995, 'Postmodernism and Modern Africa', 27 May. *H-AFRICA@H-NET.MSU.EDU http://www.h-net.msu.edu/~africa/threads/pomothread.html>*

Magubane, Z., ed., 2003, *Postmodernism, Postcoloniality, and African Studies.* Trenton, NJ and Asmara: Africa World Press.

Martin, W. G. and M.O. West, 1995, '"The Decline of the Africanists" Africa and the Rise of the New Africas', *ISSUE: A Quarterly Journal of Africanist Opinion* 23 (1): 24-26.

Martin W. G. and M. O. West, 1999, 'Introduction: The Rival Africas and Paradigms of Africanists and Africans at Home and Abroad', in W. G. Martin and M. O. West, eds., *Out of One, Many Africas: Reconstructing the Study and Meaning of Africa.* Urbana and Chicago: University of Illinois Press, 1-36.

Mbembe, A., 2000, 'African Modes of Self-Writing', *CODESRIA Bulletin* 1: 4-19.

Mbembe, A., 2001, *On the Postcolony,* Berkeley: University of California Press.

McClintock, A., 1994, 'The Angel of Progress: Pitfalls of the Term "Postcolonialism"', In F. Barker, P. Hulme, and M. Iversen, eds., *Colonial Discourse/Postcolonial Theory*, Manchester and New York: Manchester University Press, 253-266.

Miller, C., 1990, *Theories of Africans: Francophone Literature and Anthropology*, Chicago: University of Chicago Press.

Mkandawire, T., 1997, 'The Social Sciences in Africa: Breaking Local Barriers and Negotiating International Presence', *African Studies Review* 40 (2): 15-36.

Mudimbe, V. Y., 1994, *The Idea of Africa*, Bloomington and Indianapolis: Indiana University Press.

Mudimbe, V. Y., 1988, *The Invention of Africa: Gnosis, Philosophy and the Order of Knowledge*, Bloomington and Indianapolis: Indiana University Press.

Mukherjee, A.P., 1990, 'Whose Postcolonialism and Whose Postmodernism?' *World Literature Written in English* 30 (2): 1-9.

Ngate, J., 1988, *Francophone African Fiction: Reading a Literary Tradition*, Trenton, NJ: AWP.

Nkosi, L., 1998, 'Postmodernism and Black Writing in South Africa', in D. Attridge and R. Jolly, eds., *Writing South Africa: Literature, Apartheid, and Democracy, 1970-1995*, Cambridge: Cambridge University Press, 75-90.

Okeke, P.E., 1996, 'Postmodern Feminism and Knowledge Production: The African Context', *Africa Today* 43 (3): 223-233.

Owomoyela, O., 1994, 'With Friends Like These Who Needs Enemies: A Critique of Pervasive Anti-Africanisms in Current African Studies Epistemology and Methodology', *African Studies Review* 37 (3): 77-101.

Owomoyela, O., 1996, *The African Difference: Discourses on Africanity and the Relativity of Cultures*, New York: Peter Lang; Johannesburg: Witwatersrand University Press.

Paolini, A., 1996, 'The Place of Africa in Discourses about the Postcolonial, the Global and the Modern', *New Formations* 31: 83-118.

Parpart, J. L., 1995, 'Is Africa A Postmodern Invention?' *Issue: A Journal of Opinion* 23 (1): 16-18.

Parry, B., 1994, 'Resistance Theory/Theorising Resistance: Two Cheers for Nativism', in F. Barker, P. Hulme and M. Iversen, eds., *Colonial Discourse/Postcolonial Theory*, Manchester: Manchester University Press, 172-196.

Quayson, A., 2000, *Postcolonialism: Theory, Practice, Process*, Cambridge: Polity Press.

Robotham, D., 2000, 'Postcolonialities: The Challenge of New Modernities', *International Social Science Journal* 52: 357-371.

Said, E., 1993, *Culture and Imperialism*, New York: Knopf

Sangari, K.K., 1990, 'The Politics of the Possible', in A. R. JanMohamed and D. Lloyd, eds., *The Nature and Context of Minority Discourse*. Oxford: OUP: 216-245.

Shohat, E., 1991, 'Notes on the "Post-Colonial"', *Social Text* 31/32: 99-113.

Slobin, K., 2000, 'Tracking the Imaginary, Postcolonial Subject in West Africa', *Qualitative Inquiry* 6 (2): 188-211.

Spivak, G., 1991, 'Theory in the Margin: Coetzee's *Foe* Reading Defoe's *Crusoe/Roxana*', in J. Arac and B. Johnson, eds., *Consequences of Theory*. Baltimore: The Johns Hopkins University Press, 154-180.

Wylie, K., 1997, 'Postmodernism and Africa: Reply', 11 November. *H-AFRICA@H-NET.MSU.EDU http://www.h-net.msu.edu/~africa/threads/pomothread.html>*

Zeleza, P. T., 2003, *Rethinking Africa's Globalization, Vol. 1: The Intellectual Challenges*, Trenton, NJ and Asmara: Africa World Press.

Index

ABANTU for Development 302
Abdel-Malik, A. 399
Abiodun, Christianah 358
Achebe, Chinua 39, 72, 103, 109–10, 193,
    377–8, 382
'action networks' [Ng and Ng] 200
Adams, W.M. 257
*Addressing Misconceptions About Africa's
    Economic Development* [Adjibolosoo and
    Ofori-Amoah] 246
Ademuwagun, Z. et al. 255
Adesanmi, Pius 14, 115n
Adjibolosoo, S. and Ofori-Amoah, B. 246
Adjustment in Africa [World Bank] 222–3
Africa and the Disciplines [Bates, Mudimbe
    and O'Barr] 2
'Africa effect' (Africa dummy theory) 214,
    218
The Africa that Never Was [Jablow and
    Hammond] 102
African American Vernaculars (AAV) 118
African Arts [US] 322
African Association of the Study of
    Religions (AASR) 341, 364n
African Culture and the Christian Church
    [Shorter] 352
African Economic Community (AEC) 217
African Economic Development [Hance] 248
African Economic Development [Nnadozie]
    225
African Economic Review 226

African Finance and Economic Association
    (AFEA) 224, 226
African Gender Institute [UCT] 303, 304,
    306, 307–8, 311n
African Heritage Studies Association
    (AHSA) 146–7
African Initiated Churches (IAC) 350, 354–
    5, 353
African Intellectuals [Mkandawire] 389
African National Congress (ANC) 355
African Religions and Philosophy [Mbiti]
    423–4
African studies: architecture of knowledge
    3–12; decolonisation 16, 28; disciplinary
    encounters 12–21; enlargement 28; in
    Africa 136–8, 142, 143, 144, 150–4; in
    the UK 136–7, 138–40, 145–6, 155–6;
    in the US 140, 141, 146–9, 156;
    interdisciplinary challenges 21–8;
    'library' 22
African Studies Association (ASA) [US]
    146–7, 223, 331
African Studies Review 226
African Studies Since 1945 [Fyfe] 2
African Union 217
African Widows [Kirwen] 352
African Witchcraft and Otherness
    [Bongmba] 429–30
African Zionist Churches 354–5
Africana Studies [New York University]
    420
'Africanism' 39

Afuba, Chris 332
Against Race [Gilroy] 437n
AGENDA [Durban] 302
Aghion, Philippe and Howitt, Peter 211–12
Ahmadu Bello University 302, 334
Airhihenbuwa, Collins 26, 377
Ajayi, J.F. Ade 143, 172, 349, 397
Ake, Claude 187, 400
Akeh, Afam 113
Akpan, W. 54
Aladura churches 356, 357
Alice Lakwena church 356
Allen, J.A. and Kitch, S.L. 30n
All African Conference of Churches 349, 354
Althusser, Louis 419
Altvater, E. 195
Aluko, T.M. 193
Ama Nazaretha [church] 355
Amadiume, Ifi 319
American Academy of Religion (AAR) 341, 343
Amin, S. 245, 396
Amselle, J.-L. 53, 54
ancestors 424, 433, 437n
Anderson, Benedict 117, 125, 178
Anonymous [1986] 277, 278
Anozie, Sunday 104
anthropology: and African exceptionalism 40, 41, 47–55; and colonialism 13; and culture 41, 44–7, 56; and development 405–7, 409; and race 40–1, 42–3, 44, 51, 56; in African studies 13–16; methodologies 91–4; origins 12–13, 56; postcolonial 75–95
Anyamba, A.J. and Eastman, R. 257
apartheid: and Christianity 352–3; struggles in South Africa 419
Appadurai, Arjun 78, 81, 83, 106, 169
Appiah, Kwame Anthony 28, 70, 426, 427
Apter, Andrew 48, 51, 53, 57n
Aron, Janice 190

art: and European modernity 324–8; creativity in 326–7; in African studies 24–5, 321–36, 433–45; in US universities 336n
Art Journal [US] 329–30
Arts Council of the African Studies Association (ACASA) [US] 322
Aryeetey-Attoh, S. 249, 251, 257
Asante, S.K.B. 209
Ashcroft, Bill et al. 105
Association of African Women on Research and Development (AAWORD/AFARD) 301
Association of Evangelicals of Africa and Madagascar 349
Association of Kenyans Abroad (AKA) 224
Association of Nigerians Abroad (ANA) 224
Association of the Study of Religions in South Africa (ASRSA) 364n
An Atlas of African History [Fage] 237
Atmore, Antony 145
Auma, Alice 357
Awanyo, L. 237
Axelson, Eric 144–5
Ayandele, Emmanuel 349
Ayeni, B et al. 255

Babalola, Evangelist 356
Ballad of Rage [Kan] 113, 114
Bamba, Shaikh Amadu 359
Bandura, A. 390
Bannerman, R.H., Burton, J. and Wen-Chieh, C. 390
Bantu Philosophy [Tempels] 353
Bantu Prophets in South Africa [Sundkler] 354
Bantu-speaking societies 423
Baran, Paul 209
Barash, D.P. 12
Barkan, J.D., McNulty, M.L. and Ayeni, M.A.O. 239

Barnard, Alan 54

Barnett, T. and Blaikie, P.M. 253, 254

Baron, R.A. and Byrne, D. 281

Barrett, David 354, 356

Barro, Robert 214

Basch, B.F. 379

Bascom, J.B. 241, 243

Bassett, M.T. 242

Bassett, T.J. 244, 246, 257–8

Bassett, T.J. and Crummey, D. 237

Bates, R.H. 2, 191

Bauer, P.T. 245

Bay, Edna 319–20

Baye, Richard 334

Beetham, T.A. 365n

Being a Minor Writer [Gilliland] 109

Belkahia, Farid 323, 333

Bell, C. 343

Bencharifa, A. and Johnson, D.L. 241

Benson, Thomas 3–4; against interdisciplinary studies 4

Berg, Elliot 190

Bernstein, A. 250

Bertocchi, Graziella and Canova, Fabio 214

Better Health in Africa [World Bank] 252

Beyond the Horizon [Darko] 115

Bhabha, Homi 105, 113–14, 419

Biblical Hermeneutics [Mosala] 353

Biblical Hermeneutics of Liberation [West] 353

Biedelman, Thomas 339

Biko, Steve 419

Billig, M. 283

Black Consciousness [Biko] 419

Black Skin, White Masks [Fanon] 435n

Blackness in Latin America and the Caribbean [Torres and Whitten] 108

Blakely, T.D., van B. Walter, E.A. and Dennis, L.T. 341, 342

Blommaert, J. 123, 128–9

Bloom, D.E. and Sachi, J.D. 214

'blurring' [Geertz] 7, 30n

Blyden, Edward 351

Boahen, A.A. 142, 151

Boas, Franz 44–5, 46, 57n

Bond, P. 250

Bongmba, Elias Kifon 25–6, 340, 353, 429

Boserup, Ester 236, 237

Boston University 224

Botswana: HIV/AIDs in 382; urban and rural studies in 257

Bourdillon, Michael 342

Braithwaite, Kamau 420

Bretton Woods Institutions (BWI) 190, 191, 192, 195, 198, 217–18, 395, 396

Brewer, A. 228n

Brizuela-Garcia, Esparanza 16

Brookfield, H. 245

Bromfit, C. 118, 122

Burkina Faso: health services in 255

Busia, K.A. 340

Byerlee, D. 217

Cabral, Amikar 169, 176

Caliban's Reason [Henry] 433

Camara, Ery 321, 327

The Cambridge History of Africa 16

Cameroon: church/state relations in 353; health in 348, 365n; literacy in 405; missions in 348; witchcraft in 431–2

Camp, Sokari Douglas 332

Campbell, D. 241–2, 243

Can Africa Claim the 21st Century? [World Bank] 215

Capitalism and Underdevelopment in Latin America [Frank] 245

Carmody, P. 249

Carnegie Corporation 141

Carney, J.A. 238, 240, 244

Carter, Gwendolen 147–8, 156

Catholic University of Kinshasa 353

Centre of African Studies [UCT] 153–4

Centre of West African Studies [University of Birmingham] 146

Centre for Contemporary Cultural Studies [University of Birmingham] 419

Centre for Gender Studies and Advocacy [University of Ghana] 303

Centre for Research and Training in Women and Development (CERTWID) [Addis Ababa] 303

Centre for the Study of African Economies (CSAE) [Oxford] 226

Césaire, Aimé 68–9, 70

Chabal, P. and Daloz, J.-P. 189, 192–3, 194

Chenery, H.B. 209

Chenery, H.B. and Srinivasan, T.N. 205

Cherubim and Seraphim church 356, 357

Chilembwe, John 355, 357

Chinweizu 101, 104, 105, 107

Chirwa, Elliot Kamwana 355

Chodorow, Nancy 315, 317

Christ Apostolic Church 356

Christian Missions in Nigeria 1841–1891 [Ajayi] 349

Christianity in South Africa [Elphick and Davenport] 352

The Church in Africa [Hastings] 346

Church of Christ in Africa 356

Church of Jesus Christ on Earth 356

The Church Struggle in South Africa [de Gruchy] 352

Circle of Concerned African Women Theologians 353–4

civil society: in African political science 189, 197

Clark, John Pepper 103–4, 111

Clarke, Peter 350

College Art Association (CAA) [US] 321, 327, 329

Collier, Paul 214

Collier, Paul and Gunning, Jan William 214–15

Collins, A. 281

'colonial library' 169, 171

colonialism: critiques of 66–9; in history teaching 180; supremacism in 377

Comaroff, Jean 343, 355, 362

Comaroff, Jean and John 13, 52, 57n, 70, 71, 343, 346, 434, 438n

Commission for Africa 383

Communal Areas Management Programme for Indigenous Resources (CAMPFIRE) [Zimbabwe] 239–41

communication research: alternate models of 407–12; in African studies 26–7, 402–12; failure of 394–5

Conrad, Joseph 39, 375–6

The Conservation of Races [Du Bois] 171

Contemporary Art of Africa [Magnin and Soulillou] 335

Conversation with Ogotemmêli [Griuale] 339

Coon, Dennis 279

Cooper, B.M. 251

Corbridge, S. 246

Cornia, G.A. and Helleiner, G.K. 252

corruption 53, 54

Costello, A. 252

Côte d'Ivoire: traditional medicine in 256

Council for the Development of Social Science Research in Africa (CODESRIA) 300–1

Cox, James 342

Crummell, Alexander 427

Crummey, Donald 353

Crush, Jonathan 245, 246

cults, African 341, 364n

cultural relativism 46–7, 55

cultural studies: Africa in 420–1; in African studies 27, 28, 416–19

Cultural Universals and Particulars [Wiredu] 431–2

culture: and art 324; and Boas 44–5; and empowerment 384–5; and identity 386–7; and race 41, 42, 43, 47; Shona 319

Cummings-John, Constance 298

Curtin, Philip 141–2, 148–9, 157, 426

Dahomey 319–20

Daneel, M.L. 341, 357

Dangarembga, Tsitsi 319
Danquah, Mabel Dove 298
Dar es Salaam Declaration on Academic
    Freedom [1990] 298
Darko, Amma 114
data collection: difficulties in Africa 405–6
Davidson, Cathy 4
Davidson, C.N. and Goldberg, D.T. 31n
Davis, L.J. 11–12
Davis, S.F. and Palladino, J.J. 279
debt burden 219–21
decolonisation: levels of 102; teaching of
    180
Decolonizing the African Mind [Ngugi wa
    Thiong'o] 382
De Figueiredo, A. 54
De Gruchy, John 352
democracy: in Africa 171, 178, 197–8, 258,
    400–1
Department of Education [US] 2; *see also*
    Title VI
Department of Women and Gender
    Studies [University of Makerere] 304,
    310
Department of Women Studies [Univer-
    sity of Buea] 304
dependency theory 188, 209–10
Derrida, Jacques 436n
Desai, Gaurav 106
development: and globalisation 173–4;
    and the state 199–200; communication
    theories of 402–7; geographical
    critiques of 240–1, 245–6; in African
    studies 27, 224–5, 393–412; theories of
    204–5, 213
Development from Within [Taylor and
    Mackenzie] 240, 246
The Development Process [Mabogunje] 246
Development Studies: A Reader [Corbridge]
    246
diasporas, African: 71, 110–14, 171, 183,
    224, 329, 357, 418, 420
Diawara, Manthia 420

Diaz Bordenave, J.E. 402–3, 404
Dike, Ndidi 334
Diop, Cheikh Anta 327, 376, 390, 405
disciplines 3; boundaries 8; champions 7;
    in African studies 12–21
Discourse on Colonialism [Césaire] 68, 69
Dissent on Development [Bauer] 245
Djite, P. 129
Drakakis-Smith, D. 243
Dube, Musa 353
Du Bois, W.E.B. 57n, 159n, 171, 376, 426
Du Cille, Ann 114n
Dudley, Billy 187, 188
Dumont, R. 245
Durkheim, Emile 12, 62–4, 85, 343
Dussel, Enrique 421
Dyer, J.A. and Torrance, J.K. 257

Eboussi-Boulaga, Fabien 353
Economic Adjustment in Low-Income Countries
    [IMF] 223
Economic Community for West African
    States (ECOWAS) 217
Economic Development [Todaro] 225
Economic Development in the Tropics
    [Hodder] 248
economic history: in African studies 22
economics: debt theory 219–20; depend-
    ency theory 209–10, 228n; endogenous
    growth 211–13, 227; in African studies
    18–19, 28, 203–28; Marxist 206–7;
    neoclassical 205–6, 210–11, 219–20;
    neoliberal 217–20; of development
    204–5, 216–17, 227; organisations and
    curricula in 223–5; stages of growth
    theory 207–8; structuralist 208–9; trade
    219
Economics of Developing Countries [Nafziger]
    225
Economics of Development [Perkins] 225
Ecumenical Association of Third World
    Theologians 353
Eden Revival church 357

education, in Africa: tertiary 298–301; women's studies in 301–5
Ekpo, Dennis 28
Eliminating Hunger in Africa [Griffith et al.] 243
El Salahi, I. 323
Elphick, Richard and Davenport, Rodney 353
Emory University 224
The Empire Writes Back [Ashcroft et al.] 105
End of History [Fukuyama] 79
'end of poverty' [Sachs] 394
Englund, H. and Leach, J. 81–2, 96n, 97n
Enwonwu, B. 321, 322
Etherington, Norman 352
Ethiopia: food production in 257; regional disparities 247
'Ethiopian' churches 355
ethnography 62–3; and African cultural exceptionalism 47–55; and commodification 78; and method 79, 80; postcolonial 75–95
Eurocentricism 12, 16, 17, 22, 51, 63, 66, 72–3; and economics 203–4; and geography 244, 251; critiques of 65–70; in art scholarship 328–29; in knowledge production 313, 398–99
Euromodernity 102, 103; in African art 323–7, 330
Evangelical Association of Africa and Madagascar 354
Evans-Pritchard, E.E. 48–9, 340, 363
Existentia Africana [Gordon] 434
Exit, Voice and Loyalty [Hirschman] 188
'expectations of modernity' [Ferguson] 394
Eyoh, Dickson 18

Fabian, Johannes 108, 125
Facing Mount Kenya [Kenyatta] 340
Fage, John 136, 137, 139, 141, 155
failed states 258, 399
Fairhead, J. and Leach, M. 237, 239, 244

Falk, Richard 344
Falola, Toyin 16–17
family systems: Yoruba 317–18
Fanon, Frantz 71, 101, 114n, 376, 389, 424–5, 431, 435n, 437n
Fasholé-Luke, E. et al. 350
Fédération des Eglises et Mission Evangéliques du Cameroun (FEMEC) 365n
Fei, J.H.C. 208
Feierman, Steve 157, 158
Feminist Africa 307, 311n
Feminist Press 311n
Feminist Studies Network 307, 309
FEMNET 302
Ferguson, J. 393, 394
FESTAC '77 53–54
Financing Health Care in Sub-Saharan Africa [Vogel] 252
First World Festival of Negro Arts 324
Fishlow, Albert 212
food, politics of 242–4
Ford Foundation 2, 138, 140, 149
The Forest People [Turnbull] 48, 49, 50
Fortes, Meyer 364n
Foster, D. 277, 280
Foster, Robert 95
Foucault, Michel 251, 282, 383, 425, 426
Fowler, Raymond D. 280, 281
Freire, Paulo 404
Frank, André Gunder 209, 245
Frankenstein, or The Modern Prometheus [Shelley] 435n
Friedman, Susan 31n
Fukuyama, Francis 79
Fuller, Steve 12
fundamentalism 177–8
Fyfe, Christopher 2

Gaile, G.L. 243, 247
Gambia: commodification in 240; Jahely-Parchar project 238; land conservation in 239

Garber, Marjorie 8
Gardner, Katy and Lewis, David 405–7, 409
Gareau, F.H. 412
Garuba, Harry 112–13, 114
Gatu, Bishop John 351
Geertz, Clifford 7, 30n, 78, 129
Gender and Institutional Culture in African Universities project 311n
gender: African critiques 315–20; and religion 363; courses in African universities 303–9; future challenges 309–11; geographical critiques 240–1; in African studies 23–4, 72, 297–311, 312–20; in Yoruba society 429–30; women in higher education in Africa 298–9
Gender Studies Department [University of Zambia] 304
geography: GIS (geographic information systems) 234–6, 257; human 234–6, 236–57; in African studies 20, 233–59; physical 234–6, 256–7
Geography and Empire [Godlewska and Smith] 246
George, Olakunle 106
Gerschenkron, A. 208
Ghana: art in 336; cocoa in 238; development in 247; gender in 241; health care in 252; SAP in 249
Gifford, Paul 353, 362
Gilliland, Gail 109
Gilpin, R. 222
Gilroy, Paul 71, 175, 437n
globalisation 168–9, 170–5, 219; in economic thought 221–2; in geographic thought 238–9
Gluckman, Max 339
Golding, P. 402, 408
Godlewska, A. and Smith, N. 246
Goffman, Ervin 383
Goldberg, David 47, 55, 70
Goldman, A. 236, 258
Good, C.M. 254, 255, 256

Gordon, Lewis 28, 433
Gore, C.G. 255
Goulbourne, H. 400–1
Gould, P.R. 242, 253, 254
Graeber, D. 80, 82
Gramsci, Antonio 419
The Great Transformation [Polanyi] 195
Grey-Johnson, C. 196
Griffith, D.A. et al. 243
Griuale, Marcel 339
Guinea 244
Gunn, Giles 6–7
Guyer, Jane 48, 53
GWSAfrica.org 307, 309
Gyekye, A. 386, 426–7, 428, 432
Gyimah-Brempong, Kwabena 214

Haar, Gerrie ter 357
Hadjor, K.B. 409
Haggard, Sir Rider 102
Hall, Catherine 70
Hall, Stuart 71, 278, 326, 336n, 419, 420
Hallencreutz, Carl and Moyo, Ambrose 353
Hallett, Robin 152–3
Halloran, J.D. 404, 410, 411, 412
Hamelink, L.J. 408
Hance, W.A. 248, 249
Handbook of Development Economics [Fishlow] 212
Haraway, D. 316
Harney, Elizabeth 333
Harris, William Wade 354
Harrist church [Ivory Coast] 355, 356
Harrod, Roy and Domar, Evsey 207–8
Harries, R. 125, 126
Hart, G. 250
Hartmann, P. et al. 403–4, 410
Harvard University 420
Hassan, Salah 322, 326
Hastings, Adrian 346, 353, 365n
healers, traditional 255–6, 274, 377–79

Health and Culture: Beyond the Western Paradigm [Airhihenbuwa] 379

health care: and models of behaviour 380n, 381–89; and missions 348; and stigma 383, 384, 387–89; faith healing 357; geographical studies of 251–6; in African studies 26, 375–89; primary 252; public 377–80

Hearing and Knowing [Oduyoye] 354

Heart of Darkness [Conrad] 39, 376

Heasley, L. and Delehanty, J. 242

Heath, Shirley Brice 123

Hegel, G.W.F. 12, 62, 102, 422

Helleiner, Gerald K. 204–5

Hendry, Joy 54

Henry, Paget 433, 434

hermeneutics 365n, 418, 431

Herskovits, M.J. 141

Heryanto, A. 121

Hess, Janet 335

Higher Education Partnership [US] 311n

Hirschman, Albert 188, 217

history: crisis in institutions 135, 149–59; global 168–84; historiography in 135–65; in African studies 16–17, 22, 28, 56, 62; national 168–84

A History of African Christianity 1950–1975 [Hastings] 353

HIV/AIDS 253–4, 354, 357, 363, 377–8, 380, 381, 385, 387–89

HIV/AIDS in Africa [Kapileni et al.] 254

Hodder, B.W. 248

Hodgkin, Thomas L. 143

Hoggart, Richard 419

Home and Exile [Achebe] 109–10

Hook, D. 276–7, 280

Hopes and Impediments [Achebe] 382

Hopkins, Anthony 22

Horton, Robin 347–8, 365n

How Europe Underdeveloped Africa [Rodney] 101, 151, 245

Howard University 224

Hudson, N. 43

'human factor perspective' [Ofori-Amoah] 247–8

humanities 5, 7–8, 11, 31n, 81

Hume, David 422, 437n

Hunter, John 253

Hutcheon, L. 110

Hyndman, J. 245

The Idea of Africa [Mudimbe] 108

identity: and culture 375–89; politics 417–18, 421–2, 435n

Idowu, Bolaji 338, 339, 340, 350, 351

IDRISI [Clark University] 258

'imaginative sociology' [Comaroff and Comaroff] 91–4

Imagined Communities [Anderson] 117, 123

In the Castle of My Skin [Lamming] 418

In My Father's House [Appiah] 426

informal sector 196

Instability and Political Order [Dudley] 188

Institute of African Studies [University of Ghana] 143

Institute for African Development [Cornell] 224

Institute for Gender Studies [University of South Africa] 303

intellectuals, African 276, 285, 297–8, 302, 389, 418, 419, 422–3

Interdependent Development [Brookfield] 245

interdisciplinarity 3–12, 29n; and the disciplines 3–4; champions of 4, 6, 7; challenges of 21–8; definitions 9–10; metaphors of 6–7; newness of 5–6; origins of 8–9; subtypes 9

International Association for the History of Religions (IAHR) 341, 343, 364n

international financial institutions (IFI) 222–3

International Monetary Fund (IMF) 174, 179, 218, 223, 248

international non-governmental organisations (INGOs) 197, 198

International Society for African Philosophy and Studies 438n
An Introduction to the History of West Africa [Fage] 137
invented tradition/inventionism 425–29, 432, 434
The Invention of Africa [Mudimbe] 47, 108, 425, 428
The Invention of Women [Oyewumi] 319, 327–8
Irbouh, Hamid 323, 333
Irvine, J. and Gal, S. 119, 125
Isichei, Elizabeth 344, 346
Issues in Contemporary African Art [Nzegwu] 321, 327, 332, 333, 335
Ivey, G. 277
Iwuanyanwu, Obi (Obiwu) 104

Jablow, Alta and Hammond, Dorothy 102
James, Wendy 339
Jameson, Fredric 107
Jarosz, L. 239
Jegede, Dele 335
Johnson, Miriam 316
Johnston-Anumonwo, I. 241
Joseph, J. 129
Journal of African Business 226
Journal of African Economies (JAE) 226, 228n
Journal of African Finance and Economic Development (JAFED) 224, 228n
Journal of Africana Philosophy 437n
Journal of Modern African Studies 226
Journal of Theology in Southern Africa 352

The Kairos Document 352–3
Kalat, J.W. 275–6, 278
Kalipeni, E. 244
Kalipeni, E. et al. 254
Kampala Declaration on Intellectual Freedom [1991] 298
Kan, Toni 113-14
Kanneh, K. 47, 55

Kanogo, Tabitha 67–8
Kant, Immanuel 421, 437n
Kasente, D. 305, 310
Kasfir, N. 197
Kasongo, E. 394
Kates, R. 242
Katz, C. 244
Kaunda, Kenneth 297–8
Keita, Lansana 375
Kelley, R. 71
Kenya: agricultural innovation in 236; church/state relations in 353; food security in 243; gender studies in 241; Machakos District 237; pastoralism in 242; rural/urban development in 247
Kenyatta, Jomo 169, 341
Kerkam, Ruth 330, 334–5
Kesby, M. 254
Khan, Mushtaq 194, 198, 199
Kilby, Peter and Johnston, Bruce 217
Kimambo, I.N. 151
Kimbangu, Simon 356
Kirwen, Michael 352
Kivulu, Zakayo 356
Ki-Zerbo, Joseph 389
Klein, Julie 7, 8
Kochelmans, J.J. 9
Konadu-Agyemang, K. 257
Kopytoff, Igor 427
Korang, Kwaku 28, 106
Kull, C.A. 236
Kunczik, M. 410

Laburthe-Tolra, P. and Warnier, J.-P. 396, 409
Lahiri, Jhumpa 114
Lambo, Adeoye 26, 378
Lamming, George 418
Lancaster, M., Schaber, G.G. and Teller, J.T. 256
Land in African Agrarian Systems [Bassett and Crummey] 237–8
land tenure 237–8

'language elasticity' [Airhihenbuwa] 385–6
languages: and literacy 406; and applied
  linguistics 120–2, 130; bilingualism
  119–20; census ideology and 125–8;
  deconstruction of 15; devaluation of
  382; in African studies 14–15, 102–3,
  117–31; 'indigenous' 123–4; 'media-
  tion' in 130–1; multilingualism 117–18,
  127–8; 'problem' 117, 120; social
  construction of 118–20, 121, 123–4;
  structuralist tradition and 124–5
Lasker, J.N. 256
law: and interdisciplinarity 3, 30n
Leach, Edmund 82
Leinhardt, Godfrey 340
Lekganyane, Engena 354
Lerner, D. 396
Lévinas, Emmanuel 428–30
Levy, B. 190, 191
Lewis, Arthur 208
Lewis, D. 306
Lewis, I.M. 80
Liberia: church/state relations in 353
Liddicoat, Anthony J. 120
Lightfoot, D.R. and Miller, J.A. 251
lineage 318–20
Lipumba, Nguyuru, H.I. 223
literature: in African studies 14, 28, 30n, 72,
  101–15; postcolonial theory and 105–
  14
Little, P. 242, 258
Living Tradition in Africa & the Americas
  [PAS exhibition] 156–7
local, the 82–3
'local knowledge' [Geertz] 129, 171
Logan, B.I. 255
Logan, B.I. and Mengisteab, K. 249
Lumpa church 356

Mabogunje, A.L. 246, 247, 248
Macamo, Elisio 378
MacEwan, Arthur 222
Machakos District [Kenya] 237

Mackenzie, F. 238
Madagascar: peasant resistance in 239
Mafeje, Archie 12, 39–40, 48, 51, 52, 56, 82
Mafeking/Mafikeng [South Africa] 75–6,
  85–9, 90–1, 95n
Magnin, André and Soulillou, Jacques 330,
  331, 335
Magubane, Bernard 66–7
Magubane, Zine 70
Mali: desertification in 256
Malik, Sy 361
Mama, Amina 23, 299, 305, 306
Mamdani, Mahmood 150, 153–4, 189,
  197, 396, 403
Mandela, Nelson 170, 176
Manganyi, Noel Chabani 280, 433
Mannheim, Karl 314
Manning, Patrick 22, 68
Mapping African Sexualities programme
  308–9, 311n
Marais, George 80, 81, 83
Marais, J.S. 145
Maranke, Johane 356
marginality: in African studies 183, 203–4;
  in politics 417–18; of African visual
  culture 325
Mario Legio church 350
market, the: in African political science 189,
  195–7, 199
Marks, Shula 145
Marx, Karl 85, 206
Marxist approaches: in African studies 66–
  8, 206–7
Marxist Theories in Imperialism [Brewer]
  228n
Masowe, Johane 357
Mather, C. 238
Matzke, G.E. and Nabane, N. 239
Mauritania: and SAP 249
Mayer, J.D. 253
Mazrui, A.A. 401
Mbembe, Achille 183, 353
Mbiti, John 339–41, 349, 423–4, 436n

Mbon, Friday 342
McClintock, Anne 70, 72
McCracken, John 352
McDade, B.E. 250
McGeary, Johanna and Michaels, Marguerite 327
Mehretu, A. 246, 247, 248
Mehretu, A. and Mutambirwa, C. 249
Mehretu, A. and Sommers, L.M. 247
Mehretu, A., Wittrick, R.I. and Piggozi, B.W. 255
Melson, R. and Wolpe, H. 188
metadisciplines 5
metanarratives 13, 22, 81, 83, 406
method 79, 81–2, 424–5, 437n
Mid-America Alliance for African Studies (MAAAS) 224
Middleton, John 339
Mignolo, Walter 11
migration 183, 245, 250
Miller, Joseph 22
Miner, H. 65, 249
Mkandawire, Thandika 22–3, 190, 192, 196–7, 198, 199, 298, 389
Mkhize, N. 276, 280
The Modern World-System [Wallerstein] 245
Modernity and Its Malcontents [Comaroff and Comaroff] 52
modernisation: critique of 188; geographical critique of 247; in African studies 27, 65–6, 393, 396–402, 411–12
modernity 81–2, 169–70, 187, 313, 326, 331–3
Moll, T. 281–2
Moore, D.S. 238
Moore, Sally Falk 83
More People, Less Erosion [Tiffen, Mortimore and Gichuki] 237
Moroccan Association of Researchers and Scholars Abroad (MARS) 224
Morocco: artistic traditions 333; pastoralism; settlements 251
Morrison, Toni 39, 54, 55

Mosala, Itumeleng 353
Mousa, E. 359, 360, 361
Mudimbe, V.Y. 47–8, 70, 108–9, 122, 425–6, 427
Mulago gwa Cikala, M. (Mulago, V.) 353, 365n
Murton, J. 237
music: in African studies 176
Mustapha, Abdul Raufu 18
Muthwii, M.J. and Kioko, A.N. 122
Myers, G.A. 246, 251
Myth, Literature and the African World [Soyinka] 115n
The Myth of Population Control [Mamdani] 403

Nafziger, E. Wayne 225
Nagel, T. 118, 130
The Namesake [Lahiri] 114
Namibia: rivers in 256–7
naming, politics of 109–10, 114–15n; and language 128–9
Nast, H.J. 251
National Defense Education Act, Title VI [US] 140
National Education Act [US] 160n
National Endowment for the Humanities (NEH) [US] 2
nation-building 177
nation-state 123, 168, 184n, 394, 399
nationalism: and African historiography 144–5, 169, 171–2, 186; and African political science 189; and African studies 68–9
natural sciences 4–5, 7–8, 11
Nazareth Church 355, 356
Négritude 68–9, 70, 102, 107
Nellis, M.D. et al. 257
neoclassicism 205–6, 219–20
neoliberalism 174–5, 182, 190, 198, 217–20
Nervous Conditions [Dangarembga] 319
Neumann, R.P. 239

Newell, William 4, 10; proponent of
    interdisciplinary studies 4
New Language Bearings in Africa [Muthwii
    and Kioko] 122
New Left Review 419
Newman, James 245, 258
New York University 224
Ngugi wa Thiong'o 102, 382, 420
Niang, C.I. et al. 386–7
Nicholas, Lionel 279, 280
Nicholson, S.E. 256
Nickling, W.G. 256
Niger: gender in 251; resources in 242
Nigeria: and national history 172, 173; and
    the state 193–4; church/state relations
    in 353; environmental change in 240;
    famine in 242, 256; HIV/AIDS in 381;
    hometown associations in 239; Islam
    in 360–1; literature of 111–14; maize in
    236; oil wealth of 53, 239; settlements
    in 251
*Nigeria: Modernisation and the Politics of
    Communalism* [Melson and Wolpe] 188
Nigerian Association of the Study of
    Religions (NASR) 364n
Nisa [Shostak] 48, 49, 51
Nkrumah, Kwame 143, 177, 218–9, 335,
    401
Nnadozie, Emmanuel 19, 222, 225
non-governmental organisations (NGOs)
    178, 197
Noor, Shariff Ibrahim 333–4
Northwestern Univeristy 140, 141, 147
nuclear family 315–17
The Nuer [Evans-Pritchard] 48–9, 50–1
Nurske, Ragnar 208
Nwafor, John 353
Nyamnjoh, Francis 26–7, 382, 394, 395
Nyamweru, C. 244
Nyong'o Peter Anyang 401–2
Nzegwu, Nkiru 24–5, 321, 327, 331, 332,
    334, 433–4, 436n, 438n
Nzenza-Shand, Sekai 319

Obudho, R.A. and Taylor, D.R.F. 247
'occult economy, the' [Comaroff and
    Comaroff] 77, 78, 79–80, 83–5, 89, 90,
    91, 92, 94
O'Connor, A.M. 242
Odjo, Lassissi 325
Odutokun, Gani 334
Oduyoye, Mercy Amba 354
Of Revelation and Revolution [Comaroff and
    Comaroff] 438n
Ofori-Amoah, B. 246
Ogbu, Kalu 350–51
Ohio State University 224
Okoye, Ikem 323, 330, 332
Okullu, Henry 353
Oliver, Roland 139, 146, 155
Olivier de Sardan, J.-P. 194
Olodumare: God in Yoruba Belief [Idowu]
    340
Olupona, Jacob 340, 341, 357
Ominde, S.H. and Baker, G.J.K. 247
Onwudiwe, Ebere 48
Oppong, J.R. 254, 256
Oppong, J.R. and Hodgson, M.J. 255
Organisation of African Unity (OAU) 217
Orientalism [Said] 102, 105, 245, 420
Ortner, Sherry 80, 83
Osei, W.Y. 241
Oshitelu, Josiah O. 356
Osundare, Niyi 101, 107, 108, 115n
Other, the 39, 40, 41, 47, 49–55, 72, 107–8,
    152
Ould-Mey, M. 249
Our Common Interest [Commission for
    Africa] 383
Our Heritage [Serequeberhan] 431
Out of One, Many Africas [Martin and
    West] 2
Owusu, J.H. 249
Oxford History of South Africa
    [Thompson and Wilson] 145
Oyewumi, Oyeronke 24, 319, 427–29

Parker, Ian 282, 289
Parker, Richard and Aggleton, Peter 383
Parrinder, Geoffrey 339
pastoralism 241–2
p'Bitek, Okot 340, 341, 397
Pearson, Birger A. and Goehring, James 350
'pedagogy of the oppressed' [Freire] 404
Pedler, F.J. 242
Peel, John 354, 365n
Peet, R. 245
Pels, Peter 57n
PEN-3 health model [Airhihenbuwa] 384–90
The Peopling of Africa [Newman] 245
Pereira, C. 310, 311n
periphery, the 205, 209–10, 246
Perkins, Dwight 225
Phenomenology of the Social World [Schutz] 433
Philips, Cyril 139
Phillips, D.R. 259
philosophy: in African studies 15, 420–34
Pickles, J. 250
Pierre, Jemima 12–13
Piety and Power [Sanneh] 353
Platvoet, Jan 339, 340
Polanyi, K. 195
policy analysis: and modernisation theory 400–3; by geographers 246–9
The Political Economy of Growth [Baran] 209
political science: in African studies 17–18, 28, 187–200; nexus of civil society, market and state 198–200
Politics and Christianity in Malawi 1875–1940 [McCracken] 352
population growth 206, 236–7, 244–5, 258
Population Growth and Agricultural Change in Africa [Turner, Hyden and Kates] 236
'posts' 21–2, 28, 70, 101, 325

postcolonialism: in African studies 28, 70–2, 419–21; in anthropology 75–95; in literature 105–15
postcolonial state, the 181–3
postcolonial theory 13, 14, 17, 70–2
Power of Development [Crush] 246
Preachers, Peasants and Politics in Southern Africa [Etherington] 353
Premier Festival Mondial des Arts Nègres 324
Des Prêtes nous s'interrogent 354
Princeton University 420
Program of African Studies (PAS) [Northwestern] 141, 147–8, 156–7
Providence Industrial Mission 355, 357
Prozesky, Martin 342
Pruitt, Sharon 334
psychology: and the individual 280–5; as discipline 288; definitions 278–80; Fanon and 390; in African studies 20–1, 274–90; numbers of psychologists 286–7; topics in 285–8
public health: see health care

race/racism: concept 40–1, 171; history of 42–7, 55–7
Radcliffe-Brown, A.R. 339
Radical Geography [Peet] 245
Ralston, B. et al. 243, 247
Ranger, Terence 144, 352, 355
Ranis, Gustav 208
Ransome-Kuti, Funmilayo 298
Ratele, Kopano 20–1
rational choice theory 188, 191
Regional Disparity in Sub-Saharan Africa [Mehretu] 246
The Religion, Spirituality and Thought of Traditional Africa [Zahan] 339
religious studies: African traditional religions 25, 338–41; Christianity 25, 344–57; in colonial period 340–41; critical dialogical pluralism 342–4; in African studies 25–6, 68, 71, 338–66;

Islam 25, 358–61; regional Christianity 350–51
Relocating Agency [George] 106
Reno, William 194
rent-seeking behaviour 198
Ribot, J.C. and Oyono, P.R. 197
Ricardo, David 206
Riddell, J.B. 247
Rigby, P. 57, 58n
ritual 52–3, 54, 343, 365n
Rocheleau, D.E., Thomas-Slayter, B.P. and Wangari, F. 241
Rockefeller African Dissertation Awards [US] 258
Roder, W. 240
Rodney, Walter 101, 151, 245
Rodrick, D. 222
Rogers, E.M. 402
Rogerson, C.M. 250
Roitman, Janet 194
The Roots of Egyptian Christianity [Pearson and Goehring] 350
Rostow, W.W. 207, 245
Rousseau, Jean-Jacques 435n
Rowe, John 148
Rushton, J.P. and Bogaert, A.F. 253

Sachs, J.D. 168–9, 393
Sahel: and climate change 256; and drought 242
Said, Edward 72, 102, 123, 245, 419
Sala-i-Martín, Xavier 214
Samarin, W. 121, 129
Samatar, A.I. 249
Sanders, R. 251
Sanneh, Lamin 350, 353
Sartre, Jean-Paul 103, 107
'saturation hypothesis, the' [Ofori-Amoah] 246
Schiller, H.I. 412
Schism and Continuity in an African Society [Turner] 364n
Schoeffeleers, Matthew 342

School of Oriental and African Studies (SOAS) 138–40, 145–6, 155–6
Schramm, H. 402
Schroeder, R.A. 239, 240
Schumpeter, J.A. 205
Schutz, Alfred 434
Schweitzer, Albert 376
Scully, G.W. 214
Sen, A. 244
Senegal: contemporary art in 333; family relations in 386–7; Islam in 359; public health in 382, 388
Senghor, L.S. 68, 103, 115n, 176
Serequeberhan, Tsenay 431
Servaes, J. and Arnst, J. 407, 409
Seventh International African Seminar [University of Ghana] 350
Shannon, G.W., Pyle, G.F. and Bashshur, R. 254
Shelley, Mary 419, 435n
Shembe, Isaiah 355, 356, 357
Shepperson, George 354
Sherif, M. and Sherif, C.W. 281
Shibe, Simungu Bafazani 355
Shorter, Aylward 352
Shostak, Marjorie 48, 50
Shumway, David 5
Sierra Leone: health care in 255; modernisation in 247
Simon, D.D. 250
Simpson Grinberg, M. 408
Sindima, Harvey 344, 345
Singer, H. 216
Skocpol, Theda 72–3
slave: narratives 421; trade 171, 244, 423
Smith, Abdullahi 189
Smith, Adam 206
Smith, J. et al. 236
Snow, C.P. 12
sociology: Africanist 13, 62–73; historical 72–3; Marxist approaches 66–8; nationalist approaches 68–9;

postcolonial approaches 70–2; structural functional approaches 65–6
Soja, E.W. 247
Solow, R.M. 210, 211
Somalia: Islamisation of 358; SAP in 249
Song of Lawino [p'Bitek] 397
Songs from an African Sunset [Nzenza-Shand] 319
South Africa 28, 75–7, 80, 83–4, 85–9, 90; census language in 126–8; Christianity in 352–3; geographical studies 250; history/historiography 152–3; HIV/AIDS in 381, 385, 387–89; Islam in 358–60, 361; land reform in 238; psychology in 286–7; racism in 386
South African Network of Skills Abroad (SANSA) 224
South East Africanists Association (SERSAS) 224
Southern Africa Migration Project [Crush] 245
Soyinka, Wole 115n, 401
Spear, Thomas 350–51
Spear, Thomas and Kimambo, Isaria 351
Spears, Russel and Parker, Ian 282, 288
Spivak, Gayatri 419
The Stages of Economic Growth [Rostow] 207, 245
Stanley, W.R. 239
state, the: crisis of, in Africa 181, 182, 189; 'the cultural state' 192–5; in political science 188, 189–92; and religion 362
State and Church in Southern Rhodesia 1919–1939 [Ranger] 352
statism 181
Stern, N. 213, 214
Stiglitz, Joseph 218, 223
Stock, R. 251, 258
Stocking, George 42–3, 44, 45, 57n
Stolen Moments [Akeh] 114
Structural Adjustment Programmes (SAPs) 174, 175, 197, 216, 218, 243, 248; effects on health in Africa 252–3

structural functionalism 64, 65–6; in economics 208–9; modernisation theory 65–6; pluralist school 65, 66
Subject to Colonialism [Desai] 106
Sudan: food crisis 243; Islam in 360–61
Sudarkasa, Niara 317–18
Sufi orders 358–60
Summers, L.H. and Thomas, V. 390
Sundkler, Bengt 344, 346, 354, 355
Swahili 358
Swainson, Nicola 67
Swan, T.W. 210

Taaffee, E.J., Morrill, R.I. and Gould, P.R. 247
Tajfel, Henri 289
Tamrat, Tadesse 353
Tanzania: land resources in 239; modernisation in 217; socialism in 144, 151
Tanzania Gender Networking Programme (TGNP) 302
Tanzania Media Women's Association (TAMWA) 302
Tarhule, A. and Woo, M. 256
Tasie, G. and Gray, Richard 350
Taylor, D.R.F. and Mackenzie, F. 240, 246
Tayob, Abdulkader 361
Teller, J.T. 256
Tempels, Placide 348, 353
Theology and Violence [Villa-Vicencio] 352
Theory of Economic Development [Schumpeter] 205
Thompson, Leonard 138, 145
Thread in the Loom [Osundare] 115n
Tiffen, M., Mortimore, M. and Gichuki, F. 237
Tile, Nehemiah 355
Time and the Other [Fabian] 108
Title VI funding [US] 2, 140, 148, 156, 157, 160n
Todaro, Michael P. 225
Torres, Arlene and Whitten, Norman 108

Toward the Decolonization of African Literature [Chinweizu et al.] 104, 107
'transnational formation' [Gilroy] 175
Trevor-Roper, Hugh 102
tribalism: and art 332; and language 121
The Tropical World [Gourou] 245
Trouillot, Michel-Rolph 45, 46, 47, 53, 55, 56
Tufuoh, I. 142
Tunisian Scientific Consortium (TSC) 224
Tunolase, Moses Orimolade 356
Turnbull, Colin 48, 49, 50, 51, 58n
Turner, B.L., Hyden, G. and Kates, R.W. 236
Turner, Harold 353, 354
Turner, M. 242
Turner, Victor 343
Turshen, M. 253
Tutuola, Amos 111

Uganda: psychology in 286–7; public health in 381, 388
Ugarteche, Oscar 218
'Underdevelopment and Dependence in Black Africa' [Amin] 245
UNESCO General History of Africa 16
United Nations Children's (Emergency) Fund (UNICEF) 252
Universities of Venda and Pretoria Centres for Gender Studies 303
University College of the Gold Coast [Legon] 136, 142, 150–1
University of Birmingham 27
University of California, Berkeley 224
University of Cape Town (UCT) 137–8, 144, 152–4
University of Dar es Salaam 144, 151–2; 'New Dar School' 151, 152, 188
University of Ghana 136–7, 142–3, 150
University of Ibadan 143, 172
University of Illinois, Urbana Champaign 1, 2, 244
University of London 136–7

University of Wisconsin, Madison 140, 141, 148–9, 157–9
University of the Witwatersrand (Wits) 152, 153
University of Zambia 297
urbanisation 249–51
The Uses of Literacy [Hoggart] 420

Vail, Leroy and White, Landeg 67
Vansina, Jan 148, 149, 157, 158
Venn, Henry 348–50
Villa-Vinencio, Charles 352
Visweswaran, Kamala 47
Vogel, R.J. 252

Wahi, Obi 102, 125n
Wallerstein, Immanuel 65, 67, 245
Wasserstroom, Jeffrey 9
Watchtower movement 355
Watts, M. 238, 239, 242
Webb, Colin de B. 152
Weber, Max 64, 78, 85
Welbourn, F.B. 355
Welbourn, F.B. and Ogot, B.A. 354, 355
Weiner, D. and Levin, R. 250
Weiner, D. et al. 242
West, Cornel 110, 377
West, Gerald 353
The West and the Rest of Us [Chinweizu] 101
West Africa Review 226
White, Paul 184n
White, R.A. 409
Wilks, Ivor 148
Wimbum 432
Wiredu, Kwasi 431–2, 433
witchcraft 52–3, 54–5, 76–7, 92, 340, 364, 388–90, 429–31; *see also* 'occult economy'
Wittgenstein, Ludwig 433
Women in Nigeria [group] 302
Women's Research and Documentation Centre [University of Ibadan] 301–2

women's studies 8, 30n; in African studies
    23–4, 28; *see also* gender
Woo, M. and Tarhule, A. 256
Wood, W.P. 245
World Bank 174, 179, 190, 191, 196, 211,
    213, 215, 217, 222–3, 237, 248, 252–3,
    395, 396
World Development Report [annual] [World
    Bank] 215
World Health Organisation (WHO) 252,
    253
World Trade Organisation (WTO) 174,
    179, 219
Wortman, C. et al. 278
The Wretched of the Earth [Fanon] 101, 431
Writing Ghana, Writing Modernity [Korang]
    106
Wubneh, M. 247
Wundt, Willem 279–80, 285
Wynter, Sylvia 429

Yale University 421
Yankah, Kwesi 319
Yeboah, Ian E.A. 241
Yoruba: beliefs 341; society 317–18, 428–
    30
Young, Robert 70

Zahan, Dominique 340
Zambia: HIV/AIDS in 389
Zanzibar: Islam in 360, 361
Zeleza, P.T. 17, 21–2, 23, 331
'zero grazing' [Uganda] 383
Zimbabwe: church/state relations in 354;
    food production in 242, 243; HIV/
    AIDS in 358; land reform in 238; SAP
    in 249; wildlife management in 239–40,
    319
Zimbabwe Women's Resource Centre and
    Network 302
Zinyama, L.M., Matiza, T. and Campbell,
    D. 243
Zion Christian Church 356
Zulu Congregational Church 356

CPSIA information can be obtained at www.ICGtesting.com
Printed in the USA
LVOW061641300113

317929LV00006B/866/A